THE BUILDINGS OF ENGLAND

EDITOR: NIKOLAUS PEVSNER
ASSISTANT EDITOR: JUDY NAIRN

SURREY

IAN NAIRN,
NIKOLAUS PEVSNER,
AND BRIDGET CHERRY

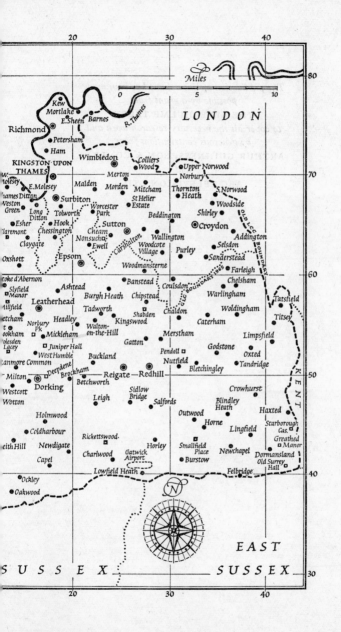

The publication of this volume has been made
possible by a grant from
THE LEVERHULME TRUST
to cover all the necessary research work and
by generous contributions from
ARTHUR GUINNESS, SON & CO. LTD
and
ABC TELEVISION LTD

THE BUILDINGS OF ENGLAND

Surrey

BY
IAN NAIRN
AND NIKOLAUS PEVSNER

★

REVISED BY
BRIDGET CHERRY

PENGUIN BOOKS

Penguin Books Ltd, Harmondsworth, Middlesex, England
Penguin Books Inc., 7110 Ambassador Road, Baltimore, Md 21207, U.S.A.
Penguin Books Australia Ltd, Ringwood, Victoria, Australia

—

First published 1962
Second edition 1971

SBN 14 071021 3

—

Printed in Great Britain
by William Clowes and Sons, Limited, London, Beccles and Colchester
Collogravure plates by Clarke and Sherwell, Limited
Set in Monotype Plantin

FOR JUDY
who assisted in more
ways than one

CONTENTS

*

Map References

*

The numbers printed in italic type in the margin against the place names in the gazetteer of the book indicate the position of the place in question on the index map (pages 2-3), which is divided into sections by the 10-kilometre reference lines of the National Grid. The reference given here omits the two initial letters (formerly numbers) which in a full grid reference refer to the 100-kilometre squares into which the country is divided. The first two numbers indicate the *western* boundary, and the last two the *southern* boundary, of the 10-kilometre square in which the place in question is situated. For example, Godalming (reference 9040) will be found in the 10-kilometre square bounded by grid lines 90 and 00 on the *west* and 40 and 50 on the *south*; Shirley (reference 3060) in the square bounded by grid lines 30 and 40 on the *west* and 60 and 70 on the *south*.

The map contains all those places, whether towns, villages, or isolated buildings, which are the subject of separate entries in the text.

FOREWORD TO THE FIRST EDITION

This is the first volume of The Buildings of England *which is the result of joint authorship. Mr Ian Nairn, who, as his text proves, is a born topographer, has written most of it. I visited and wrote about 25 or 30 per cent only. The boundary between his contribution and mine runs as follows. My territory, from E to W, includes Addington, Sanderstead, Kingswood, Tadworth, Epsom, Esher, Claremont, Whiteley Village (Burwood), Oatlands. All the places S and W of these are Mr Nairn's territory, except for Sutton Place which I wrote and about fifty to sixty medieval churches and a few houses which we wrote together. Conversely Mr Nairn is responsible for the descriptions of the new estates at Ham and the LCC estates at Wimbledon. The introduction is by Mr Nairn.*

Our thanks for help are due first to librarians: Miss M. D. Liggett of Guildford, Mr S. C. Dedman of Godalming, Mr Richard Parker of Farnham, Mr H. Cross, formerly of Kingston and Mr F. J. Owen, now there, Mr Gilbert Turner of Richmond, Mr William Myson of Wimbledon, and especially Mr T. E. Callander of Croydon, who dealt patiently with the added complication of having his town almost rebuilt about his ears between original journeys and page proofs. Secondly we are grateful to the Ministry of Housing and Local Government (abbreviated MHLG*) investigators who made the Surrey lists so complete and catholic. Two of them, Mr Arthur Oswald and Mr John Harvey (both of course authors of much more than the* MHLG *lists) looked over their parts of the county in proof and made a lot of most valuable suggestions. Mr H. Molesworth Roberts helped with Beddington, Carshalton, and Wallington, Mr John Harris with Kew, Mr E. Croft-Murray with Richmond, Mr Morris Snellgrove with Leatherhead, Dr Rolston with Haslemere, Mr John Brandon-Jones with houses by Voysey and Philip Webb, Mrs Grenside with Walton-on-Thames and Oatlands, Mr Bruce Money with Bletchingley church, and Mr F. D. Y. Faulkner of the British Railways, Southern Region, with railways. Mr M. W. Thompson of the Ministry of Works gave unpublished information on his research at Farnham Castle, and Mr Kenneth Gravett and Mr Francis Jekyll read the proofs at short notice.*

The preliminary extracting for the volume was done by Miss G. Bondi, and we both want to thank her. The archaeological sections of the introduction and gazetteer were revised in proof by Mr J. V. S. Megaw. In addition we are grateful as always to the National Buildings Record for their cooperation and to Sir Thomas Kendrick for allowing the use of his lists of Victorian glass (marked TK in the gazetteer). Finally we want to thank all the rectors and vicars who read the proofs of the entries on their churches and helped in other ways – those of Ewhurst, Stoke d'Abernon, and Christ Church Surbiton were the most informative, that of Nutfield the most unexpected – and also the owners of houses who allowed us to visit them. I would add as always that mention of a house in this volume does not necessarily mean that it is open to the public.

As usual, Mr Nairn or I saw everything ourselves, except the buildings included in brackets. Not listed are bells, chests, chairs, hatchments, altar tables, and plain fonts in churches, or movable furnishings in houses. Brasses of post-Reformation date are mentioned rarely, as is church plate of after 1830.

Once again, may I ask all readers to let me know of any errors and omissions that they may find?

N P

FOREWORD TO THE SECOND EDITION

For the second edition it was necessary to make two types of altera-
tions to the original text. The first involved the correction of factual
errors and the inclusion of some buildings and details that were over-
looked, or were unknown, when the first edition was written. The
second and larger task has been to put on record the architectural
developments which have taken place in Surrey over the last ten
years. This has involved both the inclusion of new buildings – for
these see *the Postscript to the Introduction – and the sadder duty of*
recording alterations and demolitions to buildings mentioned in the
first edition. Additions and alterations to the original text have been
made according to the following principles. As far as older buildings
are concerned, minor factual corrections, or details derived from
published sources, have usually been included without comment.
Details based on information from private individuals, or from un-
published sources, have been acknowledged. In the cases of both old
and new buildings, anything that I have not seen has been added in
round brackets (   ), following the practice of the first edition.
Buildings which I have seen are added in pointed brackets ⟨   ⟩.
Although I visited as many new buildings as possible, it was not
feasible to check personally every corner of the county, and there will
no doubt be omissions as a result. My criteria for including new
buildings were firstly architectural merit, and secondly whether build-
ings had made an appreciable change to the character of the locality
as described in the first edition. Mr Nairn's admirable brief town-
scape (and villagescape) introductions were indeed the trickiest parts
of the book to bring up to date. His general comments must stand as
the verdict of 1961. I have only added to them a few remarks on new
developments when the sense made it absolutely necessary. The
exceptions to the bracket rule are some of the alterations to the
perambulations, where it would have been too complicated to
bracket all the minor changes that were needed. To bring the
perambulations up to date I have checked as much as possible on
foot; otherwise I have relied on information kindly supplied by
librarians and other people with local knowledge. Croydon required
the most radical treatment, and was revisited and rewritten by
Sir Nikolaus Pevsner. The entries on prehistory have been
revised by Mr Derek Simpson, and those on Roman material by

Mr Nigel Sunter. For all the other changes I must bear the responsibility.

I have in general altered the original text as little as possible. All entries on important demolished buildings have been left in the book. It may be of interest to list the major losses here. The most scandalous case was the destruction of Pitt Place, Epsom, the most regrettable loss art-historically Thomas and Henry Hope's mansion at Deepdene. Other notable buildings which have gone are Bourne Hall, Ewell; Mount Felix, Walton-on-Thames; and Newark Mill, Pyrford. There have been many minor losses. But the recent establishment of conservation areas (following the Civic Amenities Act) is an encouraging step in the other direction.

The boundaries of the area covered in the second edition of Surrey *are illogical. In 1965 the new Greater London Council took over from Surrey the Boroughs of Croydon, Kingston, Merton, Richmond, and Sutton. In return, the Urban Districts of Staines and Sunbury in the county of Middlesex were added to Surrey. As work is not yet in hand for a new edition of the* Buildings of England *volume on outer London (which will include most of the rest of Middlesex), this volume still includes the parts of Surrey which are now in London, and also the places formerly in Middlesex which are now part of Surrey.**

In order to find out about all the changes necessary I relied in the first place on recent publications and my own observations, but especially on the many people who kindly wrote with comments and observations about the first edition. We are especially grateful to the following: Mr B. F. L. Clarke, Mr Alec Clifton-Taylor (who has also contributed a new introduction on Building Materials for the second edition), Miss E. M. Dance of Guildford Museum, the late Rupert Gunnis, Mr John Harris, Mr John Harvey, Mr Rodney Hubbuck, Mr David Lloyd, Mr D. M. Palliser, Mr B. F. J. Pardoe, Mr D. F. Renn, Mr Geoffrey Spain (GS), who provided references to buildings in Victorian architectural journals, Mr Nicholas Taylor (NT), who has generously contributed much to the entries on Lutyens from his research, as well as helping in many other ways, Mr D. J. Turner, Mr S. J. Totman, Mr T. E. C. Walker, Mr B. Watkin, Mr G. Wilson. Many people gave us the benefit of specialized knowledge of their own localities, in particular: Mr J. C. Batley of the Bourne Society, Mr J. C. M. Blatch (Pyrford and Old Woking), Mr R. C. W. Cox (Croydon and its suburbs), Mr R. C. Gill (Barnes, Mortlake, and East Sheen), Mr L. M. Montagu of Merton His-

---

* These are Ashford, Laleham, Littleton, Poyle, Shepperton, Staines, Stanwell, and Sunbury. The entries on these have been transferred from *The Buildings of England: Middlesex*, and brought up to date.

torical Society, Mr H. V. Molesworth Roberts (Beddington, Carshalton, and Wallington), Mr N. H. Nail (Cheam and Ewell), Mr Nigel Temple and Mrs W. O. Manning (Farnham), Mrs K. Percy (Limpsfield and Oxted). We are also grateful to Mr J. Brandon Jones for help on Voysey, to Mr Paul Thompson for information on Butterfield, to Mr Anthony Quiney for information on Pearson, and to Mr Denis Evinson (DE) for lists of Roman Catholic churches.

I also wrote to many people for information about recent developments and I am particularly grateful to the following local librarians who went to great trouble to check and collect information: Mr E. J. Adsett and Miss E. M. Jowett (London Borough of Merton), Mr C. F. Ball (Chertsey), Miss E. Booth (Haslemere), Mr W. P. J. Critcher and Miss E. M. Hosking (Staines and Sunbury), Miss H. G. Hathorn (Cranleigh), Miss S. Mather (Horley), Mr A. O. Meakin (London Borough of Croydon), Mrs K. McLeod (Dorking), Mr F. J. Owen (London Borough of Kingston), Mr R. Parker (Farnham), Miss M. D. Liggett and Mr D. Potter (Guildford), Mr R. Smith (London Borough of Sutton), Mr G. Turner (London Borough of Richmond), Mr V. White (New Haw), Mr J. C. Williams (Leatherhead). I must especially thank Mr Raymond Ash, the County Architect, who gave me much help and advice, answered numerous questions, and very helpfully arranged for me to see the recent work of his own department; the Planning Department of the Surrey County Council also helped me with information, and Mr K. Harvey of the Historic Buildings Department of the Surrey County Council kindly allowed me access to his department's unpublished material. Mr Hugh Lea, Borough Architect of Croydon, most helpfully supplied us with many details about developments in Croydon. We must also thank: Mr R. A. Bromley, Engineer and Surveyor of Walton and Weybridge, Mr O. Farrant, Clerk of Bagshot Rural District Council, Mr R. Ingle, Town Planning Officer of Frimley and Camberley, Mr D. N. Ward, Engineer and Surveyor of Woking, who all gave me details about their areas, and, finally, the many architects who answered letters about their recent buildings.

Without the help of all these people, it would have been impossible to revise this book, but they cannot be held responsible for any failures to take account of new changes and developments. We will once again welcome information on errors and omissions.

BC

Some three or four mile out of town,
(An hour's ride will bring you down,)
He fixes on his choice abode,
Not half a furlong from the road:
And so convenient does it lay,
The stages pass it every day:
And then so snug, so mightly pretty,
To have an house so near the city!

The Cit's Country Box,
by Robert Lloyd, 1757

INTRODUCTION

SURREY is one of those English counties that will not fit into the traditional pattern. It was so remote in the Middle Ages that it does not possess a large medieval parish church; yet today there is hardly anywhere in the county where one can feel free of London. It has been in the forefront of English architecture only once, in 1900, and has since seen the endless debased multiplication of the type of building it pioneered. A history of English medieval architecture could be written without once mentioning a surviving Surrey building; a history of the suburb or the folly could almost be written without going outside the county. All through the county there are these paradoxes and somehow Surrey always seems to get the worst of the bargain.

This may be too gloomy a picture, for there is plenty of architecture to see in Surrey, but it is very often the small, the picturesque, or the *recherché*. And Surrey landscape is exactly those things. It is a small county, with 462,000 acres the eighth smallest in England, and compact, as English counties go, 40 miles wide and just under 30 miles deep. What is more to the point, nowhere in the county is further than 50 miles from London, and its population of 1,600,000 is the eighth largest in England.* Within that space there is remarkable variety in both SCENERY and GEOLOGY. What is spoilt is utterly spoilt, what is left alone, or more often vigorously preserved, is enchanting. Certainly in one respect – for varied short-distance walks – it is difficult to match Surrey anywhere. Five miles will often take in as many different types of landscape. All the ridges in Surrey run from W to E, and hence the landscape, though intricate, is never tortuous and involved in the way that West Dorset is. The pattern is followed quite regularly through the county, though it sometimes takes a sharp eye to spot the transitions.

The N boundary is formed by various clays and sands which

* This was the situation before the most recent county boundary changes in 1965, following the London Government Act of 1963. Before 1888 Surrey included all London S of the Thames. In 1965 the London boundaries were once again pushed further S. For details of these see above, Foreword to the Second Edition. Surrey now comprises 418,300 acres, and has a population of 994,420 (1968). This volume still includes the parts of London which were in Surrey when the first edition was written.

run down to the Thames valley. Along the river and E of Kingston it is largely London Clay, the scenery flat like Middlesex or very gently rolling like southern Essex. It is easy to spoil and very largely spoilt.* w of Kingston the beds are mostly gravel and sand, sufficiently typical for the Bagshot Sands to have become a generic geological term – scrubby heathland with occasional hillocks, like the New Forest, but shorn of the New Forest's eerie remoteness, except by tricks of light or weather.

To the s of this comes the chalk of the North Downs, which over most of the county have the traditional pattern of a very gradual dip slope to the N – so gradual that it can be appreciated only on exposed sites, such as near Epsom racecourse – and a steep scarp on the s, averaging 800 ft at the top and about 350 ft at the bottom. The scenery here is half-way between the bareness of the South Downs and the thick woods of the Chilterns, effective only in parts (on the Kent border, for example, there is very little sense of height), and those parts usually in the valleys or close to the edge. In the centre of the county, the Mole cut a valley through the chalk which has become, thanks to the C18, a model of sophisticated parkland. Beside it Box Hill is a case of the well-known view being deservedly famous, for the slopes underneath are concave and the onlooker seems about to topple down on Dorking. Further w, the view s from Newlands Corner also more than justifies its reputation, with range after range of hills composing themselves as elegantly and harmoniously as a Claude landscape. A second valley was cut through the chalk by the Wey at Guildford, though a much narrower one. From here w to Farnham the chalk is only 400 yards wide and forms the famous Hog's Back, which carries the main London–Winchester road for the whole of its length and presents a continuous counter-point for 10 miles. To the N is an open sea-like view of heaths and clays leading, eventually, to the Chilterns on the horizon; to the s a confused foreground of little sandstone hills with Hindhead and Blackdown behind them – a geological textbook as well as a splendid bit of landscape.

To the s of the chalk different beds outcrop in a short space (there are fields near Wotton which are chalk at one end and sandstone at the other). At the foot of this scarp, chiefly E of Dorking, and almost unnoticed in the landscape, is the hard Upper Greensand, which forms the Reigate stone, the only

---

* The main exception, another Surrey paradox, is now almost entirely surrounded by buildings: Richmond Park. As an example of Tudor landscape which has never been enclosed, it is one of the best 'chases' in the country.

Surrey building stone to be used outside the county. S of this
is a valley of Gault Clay, which can be traced in a tenuous way
across the whole county, most clearly in the E, where it is called
Holmesdale. S of this again is the Lower Greensand, thick in the
W of the county and a thin ridge from Dorking eastwards, forming
an answering shape to all the views S from the chalk. This is
quintessential Surrey, the pinewood hills which so attracted the
Victorians: steep bracken-covered slopes, occasional patches of
arable land, especially S of the Hog's Back, low-toned farmhouses
hugging the valley contours, nearly always a splendid view S. Each
part has its own special blend. In the W are isolated hills like
Crooksbury and Hindhead; in the centre the mass of the Hurtwood, almost all wooded and still remote (Leith Hill, at 965 ft,
is the highest point in South-East England); in the E the commons
like the Kentish Charts with abrupt views over the Weald. It
has often been derided (by Bernard Shaw, for one) as being
pretty-pretty, small-scale, playing at mountains. If people are
always asking Surrey to be great and grand they will never
enjoy the county; but of its specialized and unabashedly
pretty kind this landscape is probably the best in the
country.

The Greensand hills continue to the W and SW boundaries and
over into Sussex to form the Midhurst country. The rest of the
county is all Weald, heavy clay and heavy countryside, best when
it is either in its semi-primitive state, as around Baynards Park,
where villages and hamlets still seem to be clearings in the surrounding forest,* or when it has been completely tamed and
emparked, like the countryside near Leigh. The middle state of
smallish farms and copses is flavourless compared with Sussex
and, especially E of Horley, has been over-built, resulting in a half
country that seems almost worse than continuous sprawl.
Occasionally there are a few ridges – at Outwood, e.g., a tiny bed
of limestone has formed a weatherproof cap a few inches thick on
top of the hill, and prevented erosion, and in the extreme SE
beyond Lingfield the land begins to rise to the Wealden sandstone
of East Sussex. From Dry Hill, a mile from any road on the
Kent and Sussex border, the view is of ridge after ridge of
Sussex's Ashdown Forest; the effect to a Surrey topographer
(and he often feels it in East Surrey) is of tantalizingly better
buildings, vernacular and otherwise, just over the county bound-

* In 1961 Surrey was second by proportion in the order of wooded counties.
12.3 per cent of its whole surface was trees, and that is neglecting hedgerow
timber.

ary. This variety has naturally produced a variety of BUILDING MATERIALS. For these *see* the separate note on pp. 78–83.

Before beginning the strictly chronological description of Surrey monuments, a few words on farmhouses, villages, and towns, and then on the growth of the whole of Surrey as one vast suburb. For FARMHOUSES and COTTAGES there is so much material, particularly in the Weald, that it is difficult to single out a few. The traveller will meet with them easily enough. What he will also meet with to a depressing degree, far more than in Sussex or Kent, is sweeping restoration, imitation, and cosification. Surrey, like Kent, has an enormous number of houses for yeomen who were half-way between serf and squire, often going back to the C15. Most of them keep their timber-framing and some simple kind of medieval roof, consisting of queen- or kingposts and several beams. But they are easily spoilt and overlaid, and in the gazetteer the pruning of these has been rigorous, the standard normally being genuineness of total appearance rather than whether one old beam in a welter of new ones happens to be noteworthy.

The worth-while Surrey VILLAGES are almost all s of the chalk, and in differing materials they express the same spirit – small-scale, pretty, villages of vignettes rather than a splendid overall plan. The vignettes are naturally well known, but are none the 4 worse for that. The best are at Witley and Alfold in W Surrey, in both cases tile-hung* cottages grouping with the church, and at Bletchingley, Godstone (partly C19), and Limpsfield in East Surrey. All five are extraordinarily similar, in spite of being 30 miles apart and separated by villages of a different sort. There are also one or two stone-built hamlets in the middle of the Surrey hills which have a delightful mixture of cosiness and a surprising sense of remoteness: Hascombe, Holmbury St Mary (largely Victorian), and, especially, Coldharbour. Quality Street at Merstham is also worth mention here, though its effect is very largely that of sophisticated conservation of *c*.1900. There are also a few village greens, which naturally give more scope for 3 village-making. Kew and Ham are very impressive and quite different from the others; big, formal greens surrounded by urban C18 houses, almost entirely a result of being on the Thames and near London. The other village greens are all near the Sussex 5 border. Brockham and Chiddingfold are small and dominated

---

* Recently tile-hanging has again become popular. The tiles used in a completely modern way on *Eric Lyons*'s terrace of houses at Sandpits Road, Ham, are an early example of this fashion.

by their churches. Tilford is an oddity where the village street leads off a green with hardly a house around it, Dunsfold a splendidly rough and shaggy big green, Sussex rather than Surrey. The best of all is Ockley, a big green with the whole of one side a blend of buildings and open fields. For individual cottages the best villages are Chiddingfold and Thursley.

In the rest of the county, Chobham, on the Bagshot Sands, has a small, coherent brick high street like a Buckinghamshire village, Thorpe, near the Thames, is pure Middlesex – big houses with stock-brick walls – Farleigh, near the Kent border, and Wisley, on the Wey, are the remote hamlets which occur all over the chalk or Weald, hardly enlarged since the original Norman settlement (both are astonishingly preserved so near London), East Clandon on the chalk is unremarkable but unspoilt, flint and brick, and Wanborough on the N side of the Hog's Back is a good-looking, compact hamlet like the groups on the chalk of northern Hampshire and, with its big silo, still more like the Pas de Calais.

The old Surrey TOWNS are either very good or quite spoilt by second-degree consequences of being near London: the latter category includes Leatherhead, Epsom, Reigate, and Chertsey. Dorking has a high street with an almost perfect shape and total effect but hardly an individual building worth a glance – a nice underlining of the difference between townscape and architecture. Guildford, the county town, is a classic example of the wide, jostling Home Counties high street on a steep hill down to the Wey. Farnham has two splendidly grave, formal streets, West Street mostly planned and Castle Street mostly unselfconscious accident, the overall impression of both being c18. Godalming and Haslemere have good parts to them, in a typically pretty Surrey way, and Richmond has a big, formal residential green due entirely to the nearness of London. Perhaps the most surprising town centre is Kingston upon Thames, where, in spite of heavy through traffic, the church, town hall, and a pair of interlocking triangular ₂ market places make up a delightfully compact city-in-miniature.

Kingston, the crowning place of several Saxon kings, is now choked with traffic that has nothing to do with it and joined to London by a nondescript flood of building. The GROWTH OF LONDON is the most important thing about modern Surrey; no other English county is so dominated by a neighbouring city.*

* London's other main contribution to Surrey, the traffic problem, was already thick enough on Derby Day to be drawn by Rowlandson in the early c19.

Throughout the C18 gentle, urbane ties to London were being woven. Before 1800 the results were all beneficial, the type of suburbanization that, with care, could still take place on a much larger scale: urban houses in Richmond, and Kew and Ham, riverside villages of big houses and later of bijou cottages (Petersham is a gem of this type when the traffic allows it to be; Thames Ditton is plainer but quieter; parts of Mortlake and Barnes are a less elegant echo of Chiswick Mall on the Surrey side). Hardly anything more happened until the railways came. Ribbons of early C19 houses can in fact just be traced now from London to Epsom and London to Croydon, but there was nothing on the scale of the colossal twenty-mile ribbon N of London as far as Hoddesdon. Railways came early; in fact the earliest public (horse) railway in the country ran from Wandsworth to Croydon in 1803 and on to Merstham in 1805. Steam lines followed quickly: via Kingston (now Surbiton) and Woking to the SW in 1838, via Redhill and Horley to the S coast in 1841. The four places named are significant, for in their present form they are due entirely to the railway. Surbiton, Woking, and Redhill were entirely new, Horley a wholesale enlargement. Were they conceived as dormitories from the beginning? (In 1860 Woking-to-London took 42 minutes; by fast trains it takes 27 today.) With the railways came the institutions: Brookwood Cemetery 1854, Brookwood Asylum 1867, then the Epsom asylums–one-fifth of the population of Epsom! But the line of continuous building did not spread over the County of London boundary until after the first World War, except between London and Croydon, where Thornton Heath has a desperate kind of mid-C19 artisan character, and in the upper-class suburbs of Kingston, Wimbledon, and Sheen. When it came, it came with a rush, spurred on by the Morden line extension of the Underground, which was opened in 1926. And then the sprawl exploded. The builders were in fact really no more greedy and heedless than they had been in the C19, but were now serving a metropolitan population of five or six millions, newly accustomed to better space standards, newly able to buy a house. Worcester Park is the perfect expression of this. It and its like finally sealed off the countryside from the real urban population of London. In 1938, just in time, the London Green Belt was set up. In spite of a few post-war nibblings by authorities who ought to know better, it has remained, and that the countryside S of Chipstead or around Box Hill or near Farleigh on the Kent border is still marvellously rural is due purely to this. Outside the green belt, except for the Surrey hills, which have been protected, a particularly mean kind of village expansion has gone on all over the county, throwing out the old pattern, maybe pickling a few old cottages for appearances' sake, and not putting anything worth-while in its place. Meanwhile, the older suburbs have become geared to this juggernaut of mass-produced housing, and the pattern of places like Wimbledon or Surbiton is first – if any – the remaining c18 houses, usually well preserved, then whole-sale demolition of the big houses of 1840-80, as the leases fall in (generally ninety-nine years). Those which survive are usually institutions which have been added to and hence represent a considerable investment. The grounds of the others are either grubbed up and houses jammed into them or, more happily and quite frequently, for this is one of the things that planning can see to, most of the trees are kept, fewer houses built, and something approaching a true suburb is created instead. Like Southern California, Surrey is entirely directed to serving urban man – in the Green Belt as much as anywhere else.

Turning from the overcrowding of today to the wastes of PREHISTORY there is not much which need be written here. For the earliest periods we may note the palaeolith-bearing Thames and Farnham gravels – the earliest implements include typical early Acheulian hand axes related in form to those of the Somme valley. In the Mesolithic period, Surrey has the earliest extant buildings in England, although 'man-made dwellings' is a better description of the shingle pits at Bourne Mill, Farnham, and Abinger.

In about 3000 B.C. the first Neolithic farming communities arrived from the continent; for a while they must have lived side by side with the Mesolithic settlers. This Windmill Hill group concentrated on the southern downlands, and although no settlement has yet been found on the chalk of the Farnham–Guildford area, there was a typical unchambered long barrow at Badshot Lea, Farnham, until 1936. Other signs of Neolithic activity are given by flint workings lesser in extent but similar in form to the famous Grimes Graves in Norfolk. They occur at East and West Horsley and Redhill, though the first of these may be partly medieval.

The single beaker from Titsey and another from Mortlake Road, Kew (now in Guildford Museum), are the last evidence the county has to offer for that culture which formed the bridge be-tween the last stages of the Neolithic and the first use of copper and bronze. For the rest of the Bronze Age the record is hardly any better. The unsystematic excavation of the county's round barrows dates from the time of Elizabeth I; Camden's report in 1586 of twenty-five on Thunderhill above Addington gives some idea of what once may have been. Still, there is the triple barrow at Crooksbury and other important groups at Chobham, Banstead, and Reigate, the latter including evidence of use in Late Bronze Age times with the coarse cremation-filled urns of that period.

The Iron Age shows the first major visible structures in hillforts such as those of the Greensand (Anstiebury, Holmbury) and St George's Hill with its strategic position above the Wey and Mole. The earliest signs of occupation show affinities with settlers from Northern France and the Low Countries. Sites along the Thames (St Ann's Hill Chertsey is the only hill-fort) may be due to later expansion (*c.*300 B.C.) from this point of entry. The Wealden culture of *c.*100 B.C., a distinctive mixture of continental Hallstatt and La Tène features, occupied the fortifications at Anstiebury, Hascombe Hill, Holmbury, and Dry Hill Lingfield. This was a long-lived group, some sites (Ewell, Ashtead, and Waddon) showing occupation well into the period of the Roman conquest. But at others (St George's Hill, Farnham, Wimbledon, and the now destroyed Carshalton) the evidence is of the ousted trans-Rhenish Celts, the Belgae, whose incursions in the South-East from *c.*100 B.C. onwards were the last major disturbances before the coming of the Romans.

In the ROMAN period Surrey can have been little more than one part of the southern supply area for London; the Belgae, whose tribal centres such as Wheathampstead and Colchester were taken over by the new overlords, had made little impression on the county; it never seems to have had a cantonal settlement and was never a *civitas* in its own right. Indeed it seems to have survived as a non-Belgic enclave. Although a major settlement may yet await discovery in the Farnham district, visible Roman antiquities are rare. The roads are, as usual, the best preserved record. Stane Street, starting at the old London crossing at Southwark (excavated in 1945–7), runs down to Chichester, leaving the county near Ockley on the Sussex border with Ewell as an important settlement *en route* and a second posting station at Merton. A good stretch of it has been preserved at Holmwood, while feeder roads join it from Ashtead with its large villa and brick and tile works and Farley Heath, site of a remarkable Romano-Celtic temple enclosure unparalleled outside the continent.* A branch leaves Stane Street at Kennington and passes Caterham with a good section of metalled terrace still visible. Another main route branches off from Watling Street to Peckham, forms the Kent border, then passes Titsey, another religious site with settlement and fulling works. Other important sites include the Farnham pottery works and bailiff's lodgings with aqueduct and the series of farms and their fields near the old North Downs trackway, especially at Farthing Down, Coulsdon.

After the departure of the legions early in the C5, the history of Surrey is obscure. The area was settled early by the Saxons (possibly the Middle Saxons from the Thames valley), as cemeteries at Croydon, Beddington, and Mitcham testify. Already in the C6 Surrey was disputed territory between the kingdoms of Wessex and Kent. During the C7 and early C8 it changed hands several times between Kent, Wessex, and Mercia until the decisive defeat of Beornwulf of Mercia by Egbert of Wessex in 825. After this Surrey remained part of Wessex, although peace was repeatedly disturbed later in the century by Danish raids. In 893 a large Danish army was defeated by Alfred's son Edward at Farnham.

Even in prosperous areas, battles tend to make short work of existing architecture and to leave little incentive for rebuilding: and ANGLO-SAXON building in Surrey makes a poor showing, by comparison for example with Sussex or Hants. There are walling and blocked openings at Stoke d'Abernon, double-splayed windows at Thursley and Witley, the altered central tower of St Mary at Guildford with its pilaster strips, and also just one hint at something more ambitious, in the shape of part of a nightmare capital at Betchworth consisting of several circular abaci, one above the other. The viewer is completely at a loss to visualize the original building which incorporated it. The very plain, regularly built W tower at Compton could also be Saxon.

With NORMAN ARCHITECTURE there is more to see, though none of it is on a large scale and very little is of more than local importance. The simplest type of Norman village church, standard over the whole country, consisted of a regular aisleless

---

*Dug rather than excavated c. 1848 by Martin Tupper, who wrote his excavation report in verse. To the archaeologist of today this expression of his methods causes nightmares; but he tried his best, though:

'Many a day have I whiled away
Upon hopeful Farley Heath,
In its antique soil digging for spoil
Of possible treasure beneath.'

nave and chancel. Several have survived more or less complete in Surrey: Farleigh, Pyrford, Wisley (these last two in adjacent parishes and very similar), the chancel of Addington, keeping its E end with three tiny windows, and most of Tatsfield. These churches were probably built soon after the Conquest, but there are also a few more tangible signs of Early Norman heaviness and massiveness, e.g. one narrow re-set arch at Betchworth, the central tower at Albury – built without transepts, as often happened in England – and a set of doorways with rough, thick mouldings at Witley, Old Woking, Mickleham, and Ewhurst. Of these the first three are crude, but Ewhurst is very impressive in its forceful simplicity, and the best piece of Norman architecture in the county. It is apparently dated c.1140, and this, if correct, is a sharp reminder that what looks early may not in fact be so. But the spirit is still pure Early Romanesque.

Sometimes these Norman churches proved too small in a couple of generations. Fetcham and Chobham both have Norman naves enlarged by aisles which cannot be later than the mid C12, the tell-tale proof being older windows left in the spandrels of the new arcade.* Surrey has several of these later Norman arcades, and they all follow one pattern, which is also typical of Hampshire and Sussex: round piers, scallop capitals, usually round arches – the pointed arch does not mean much. In Surrey they occur at Chobham, Fetcham, St Mary Guildford, Great Bookham, Laleham (formerly Middlesex), Little Bookham,‡ Mickleham, Puttenham, and Walton-on-Thames. Compton has exactly this type of piers and arches, but the capitals have begun to experiment with foliage and crockets.

The doorways that go with these arcades are unprepossessing and slapdash – Romanesque at the end of its tether, the style which is seen at its worst in the West of England, e.g. at Glastonbury. Compton, Cobham, and Pyrford have one order of zigzag, Shere and Merton both have doorways where a diamond shape is broken through ninety degrees around the edge of the order. The Shere doorway incidentally already has jamb shafts of black Sussex marble, anticipating the effect that C13 builders pursued so unremittingly.

Cobham also has the only Norman W tower, a poor one; and

---

* At Fetcham the splay is made up of Roman bricks; at Chobham the woodwork of the lean-to aisle roof is an extraordinary construction which may be medieval.

‡ Here the aisle was blocked later, probably before the end of the Middle Ages, a good pointer to show how remote the county was before the C18.

with two remarkable Late Norman chancels, Compton and Ripley, the story of Romanesque building in Surrey is over. The chancel at Ripley is small but very circumstantial: only two bays but with huge piers to support an intended vault, a heavy string course flowing over the piers in the oddest way (perhaps a sign of breaking up of the old strict articulation ?), window splays given nook-shafts, and so on. At Compton the details are plainer but the 11 idea is almost unique; a two-storeyed E end open to the church, the only remaining one in Britain, with the lower stage given a vault and an enriched arch, all built immediately inside the existing walls of an earlier Norman chancel. Nobody has been able to find out why this was done. The most likely explanation is the need for an extra chapel plus some circumstance which prevented lateral extensions.

The upper chapel of Compton preserves an elegant wooden guard rail at its open end, one of the earliest pieces of church woodwork in the country, and this is a good place to mention other Norman CHURCH FURNISHINGS. There are a few plain, crude, stone fonts (Thursley, which is early, and Alfold) and one at Thames Ditton shaped like a block capital; there is also one first-rate lead one, at Walton-on-the-Hill, with saints in relief 3 seated under arcading around the bowl, the best of its kind in the country. C12 WALL PAINTING is confined to one rare example at Witley, with figures under arches illustrating scenes from the life of the Virgin. A little later, but still stilted and Romanesque in spirit, is the astonishing Last Judgement that covers the w 16 wall of Chaldon church. The drawing is naïve and the colouring is now drab, but it is a successful attempt to make the whole of a wall into a picture book, rather like what was done in a much more sophisticated way 350 years later in sculpture with the w front of Bath Abbey.

Surrey ought to have had at least one large Late Romanesque church, for the Benedictine Abbey of Chertsey, originally founded in 666, was rebuilt from 1110 onwards, to a plan rather like Romsey in Hampshire. But Chertsey was completely pulled down to provide stone for Hampton Court, and similar fates overtook nearly all the county's MONASTIC BUILDINGS. At Merton (Austin Canons, founded 1114), only one doorway, already mentioned, remains; of the late and royally favoured foundations of Sheen (Carthusians) and Richmond (Observants, or reformed Franciscan friars) nothing remains at all. Only two other houses have fragments above ground – Newark and Waverley – and those fragments are all C13. But the first church at Waverley, whose plan has been recovered, belongs to the C12 and was complete by about 1160. One would give a lot to know what it looked like, for Waverley was the very first Cistercian house in England, founded in 1128, only thirty years after Cîteaux itself. The plan expressed perfectly the extreme austerity of the Cistercians in their early years: unaisled nave, short, square-ended presbytery, short transepts, each with one E chapel. The first church at Tintern, the second English Cistercian house, was similar. We cannot even guess at the elevations – did it for example have pointed tunnel-vaulting such as can still be seen at Fontenay in Burgundy ?

However, the first signs of the EARLY GOTHIC style in Surrey are of the late C12, and their provenance seems to have been derived in a roundabout way from Canterbury. Canterbury is connected in some way with the rich half-Gothic of New Shoreham in Sussex, and the design of one of the capitals at New Shoreham reappears at Reigate among a whole anthology of emerging Gothic designs. It has leaves in the stiffest of patterns just coming to life, in one case blown sideways round the capital, quite symmetrically, with a touching stilted formality. These early capitals are a worth-while study in Surrey. As well as at Reigate they occur at Banstead – a quite different type, with one large crocket at each corner – at Carshalton, with leaves mostly a little later and looser, and in just one capital at Leatherhead, the others being plain, as though the carvers were an independent body who were paid by the capital, as it were. Nothing else is as interesting. Piers can be round, octagonal, and, in one remarkable case at Reigate, quatrefoil – a continuous flowing shape, not four shafts put together. Arcade arches can be grooved but not chamfered (Reigate, s aisle), or double-chamfered (Leatherhead, Carshalton). Spatially, Leatherhead and Reigate are worth visiting, in spite of restoration, for the arcades set up a splendid dominating rhythm. Leatherhead particularly is an incredibly strong effect to come from such simple means. The pointed arch is much less of a trade mark of the style than a lightening and liberation of space and ornament: Ash has an unmistakably Early Gothic door with vibrant foliage capitals, but it still retains the round arch. Puttenham shows in several stages how the new style affected a typical village building in the Hants–Sussex style mentioned earlier. St Mary Guildford was given a vaulted triple-apsed E end c.1180, a remarkable thing to do to a parish church. Two of the apses remain, but the third was sliced off for road-widening – this has a familiar sound – in 1825.

After 1200 Surrey church architecture settled down into an undistinguished EARLY ENGLISH vernacular. Capitals are almost always plain with circular abaci, piers are round or octagonal. Cases are too numerous to mention separately (e.g. Worplesdon, Betchworth). The style suited a poor county, and suited the austere ideas of the Cistercians when they rebuilt Waverley Abbey from 1203 to 1278. None of the church survives, but the fragments of the monastic buildings – one wall of the monks' dorter and the vaulted cellarium – are exactly this style. Handled by an architect, it could be extremely effective, and Chipstead is very impressive both inside and out. Here, the 14 designer – and, unequivocally, he was a designer – had a very individual way with his lancets, recessing them outside and giving them triangle-headed splays inside. The w tower at Merstham has some of the same character. Several other E.E. idioms are evident, but rarely in units larger than a window or a door. There are two vaulted chancels – at St Mary Guildford and (very nicely proportioned and detailed) at Stoke d'Abernon. St Mary Guildford and Shere have doors and arches with multiple orders of marble shafts in the way of Salisbury.* Tatsfield had two and has one lancet window wrought about inside with complex mouldings and nook-shafts: Ockham has a magnificent window of seven lancets (the only other one in England is at Blakeney in Norfolk) with elegant foliage capitals. It may have come from Newark Priory, where two periods – late C12 and mid C13 – are represented by enigmatic flint walls from which all the dressed stones have been removed. Godalming has a large, impressive C13 lead spire. Farleigh and East Clandon have the minor peculiarity that, like some Sussex churches, their E ends have two lancets instead of the customary three. It all sounds like an auctioneer's catalogue, and in fact the architectural history of Surrey can concern itself with very few complete buildings until the C16.

One of these standard C13 arcades can be dated accurately at 1254 – an aisle to the chapel in Farnham Castle. Farnham is the most important medieval DOMESTIC BUILDING in Surrey. The county was never renowned for castles. The most primitive form is simply an earthen mound or motte, and several of these remain (e.g. Bletchingley, Abinger). They have always been supposed to have had only a timber stockade on top, and in fact excavations at Abinger have revealed fragments of wood in the post-holes. Of

* The C13 fragments of Chertsey Abbey that came to light in the excavations are in this style also.

the three bigger castles, Reigate has no remains worth notice, but Farnham and Guildford have. Both were originally big C11 mottes, but developed from this in very different ways. Guildford was a royal castle and had one of the grimmest of Henry II's keeps built on its motte in *c*.1170, in the style of Porchester. Eight hundred years have not mellowed it. Farnham Castle belonged to the bishops of Winchester, and hence in the early C12 to Henry of Blois, Stephen's brother. What he and his successors did with Farnham was rather odd. They completely enclosed the motte in a shell keep of twenty-three sides, levelling it at its base, and then built the living quarters around it in a triangular courtyard. Most other C12 castles had living quarters independent of the keep – Durham and Richmond, Yorkshire, for instance – but they were then part of some larger defensible complex: Farnham is like a forerunner of a C15 manor house. In spite of additions it keeps its C12 chapel, kitchens, and a remarkable fragment of the hall in the shape of a wooden pier, now completely encased in later panelling, with a scalloped capital just like the local masonry style. The plan has been recovered and shows a big aisled hall with wooden arcades, the type of the original Westminster Hall. Thereafter until the C15 there is only one more Surrey house worth mentioning here, the manor house at Walton-on-the-Hill, where a stone-built hall and chapel with a few good simple late C13 and C14 details are inextricably embedded in a C19 house.

Back to church architecture, and back as before largely to isolated details. The Late E.E., that is GEOMETRICAL, is best described in terms of windows – the slow, painstaking growth of bigger openings and tracery patterns inside them. In fact, just as with round and pointed arches, windows of very different shape were probably going up at the same time. The seven lancets at Ockham must date, from the details of their capitals, from about 1260, which is after the bar-tracery windows at Westminster. They must thus have been built at almost the same date as the earliest big Geometrical window in Surrey, at Godalming, where one can almost see the mason playing with his compasses: one big and two small circles above one slightly bigger and four slightly smaller lancets. This can be paralleled almost exactly in the forms of thirty years later by the restored S transept window at Albury Old Church, with one big and two small quatrefoils above five lancets. Other windows at Albury have a variant of Y-tracery where the two lights have heads of their own which have broken away from the side of the window. But complete

buildings in the style are few*: are two, in fact, Byfleet and
Dunsfold. They are both small, but there the resemblance ends.
Byfleet is what one would expect from a once remote village in a
remote county, towerless, aisleless, Y-tracery in the side windows,
three-light intersecting tracery in the E window – late C13 style
done on the cheap. Dunsfold has very nearly the same dimensions, 20
but is a perfectly worked out miniature of c.1270, perhaps by
royal masons, relying almost entirely on proportion and restrained detail. One can imagine how different a chapel put up by
the Bishops of Ely or Lincoln in the 1270s would have looked.
Capitals are plain, windows have two lights with a circle enclosing
a trefoil above, i.e. are just one stage later than Westminster
Abbey. Everything, down to the piscina and sedilia, is detailed
with care and restraint. Aisles were intended but not built,
although transepts were. It is a model church, designed just as
strictly as anything put up by the Camden Society.

Internal detail, where it occurs, is just as sober and free from
ornamental excess. The most elaborate is the plain but aesthetically admirable arcading of piscina and sedilia at Old Coulsdon, a 17
good example of a simple thing well done. Blind arcading round
the chancel walls is a Surrey quirk, though the other examples
have antiquarian, not architectural interest. They occur, more or
less preserved, at Chertsey, Bletchingley, and Merton.

Slowly, after 1300, this changed into the flowing lines and
relative luxuriance of the DECORATED STYLE in Surrey. There
is no consistent Dec in Surrey, and again it is largely a matter of
recording details. The style of Lincolnshire, or even the sparser
wiry Dec of Kent and East Anglia, is a long way away here. The
only building which may have possessed the encrusted character
we think of as 'Decorated' is the ruin of St Catherine's Chapel at
Guildford (before 1313), but no ornament remains. There is only
one complete Dec church, at Cranleigh, and the inside there can
give some idea of the comfortable spatial jogtrot of early C14
village architecture. Piers are octagonal, windows are generally
square-headed enclosing two ogee lights. Like some Sussex
churches, Cranleigh has a windowless clerestory. At Thorpe
there are odd single-light windows with trefoils and quatrefoils
in the heads; at Fetcham a very impressive two-bay arcade with
continuous mouldings, giving the impression of having strayed
from a much bigger church. Horley has windows with 'Kentish
tracery' in them, very renewed (i.e. tracery where the head
includes a quatrefoil giving the whole window a down-pointing,

* Merstham has a late C13 clerestory: alternate trefoils and quatrefoils.

off-balance look). Charlwood has a near variant of this, and there are a number of curvilinear windows, i.e. windows which are predominantly vertical but break out into twisty shapes at the very top. These are at Old Woking, Shere, Worplesdon, and Witley. The last two are identical. But the low architectural temperature can best be illustrated by the chancel of Great Bookham, rebuilt by Chertsey Abbey in 1341. They considered it important enough to be given a commemorative stone, yet the side windows have cusped Y-tracery, the E window has modest reticulations, and there is no ornamental detail inside.

Nor is there much more to mention in the PERPENDICULAR STYLE. In fact there is only one Perp church of even moderate 21 size (Lingfield),* which can hardly be said of any other English county. There are quite a number of details in aisles and porches, and in quite a variety of styles, perhaps because Surrey was midway between Winchester and Canterbury, London and Chichester, and was influenced by all of them. Winchester influence can be seen directly in the chancel of Effingham, repaired by order of William of Wykeham in 1388. The new windows there, with two lights under segmental heads, have in a very simple way the same character as the remodelling of Winchester nave. These windows also occur at Beddington, in the Carew Chapel. The more familiar Perp windows made up of panel tracery, three main lights splitting into six small lights in the head, as used by Yevele at Canterbury, occur also. But most of Surrey Perp work combines these with a type which has three lights under a segmental label, a racy, rather rough, but effective style. It seems to be chiefly C15, and this variant of it seems to come from Kent (e.g. Egerton, Woodchurch) or from London (St Helen Bishopsgate, St Olave Hart Street). The impression it gives is almost deliberately primitive and off-hand, unwilling to be courtly, and this would certainly fit Surrey history in the C14 and C15, for the county was prominent in the rebellions of 21 1381 and of 1450. The best example is at Lingfield, where a college was founded in 1431 by Sir Reginald Cobham. The college probably accounts for the odd plan of double nave and chancel and N chapel of exactly the same dimensions – a lucid, restrained interior which grows on repeated visits. The arcades

---

* Croydon was so until the fire of 1867. It was rebuilt by *Scott* 'on the old lines', but he subtly managed to change its character completely from being Kentish to looking like a more southerly counterpart of Herts or Bucks churches like Ware or Chesham. This, in its own awful way, was quite a technical achievement.

here are the familiar national pattern of four attached shafts with four hollows between, the end responds consisting of a single shaft and continuous mouldings. These also occur at Oxted, which had a Cobham connexion, and windows of the Lingfield type appear at Leigh (a late C15 rebuilding of a small aisleless chapel), at Burstow, and in the Slyfield Aisle at Great Bookham. The other Perp details worth mention follow no coherent pattern, but are good enough to make one wish that more C15 work survived in Surrey: four-light square-headed windows at Merstham and Burstow, and an unusual five-light window at Stoke-next-Guildford made up largely of five mullions running the whole height of the window (the same pattern occurs in the w window of nearby Worplesdon). Oxted and Merstham have good simple stone porches of the same type with the outside door given a hood-mould and spandrels. Egham has a good simple wooden porch now used as a lychgate, and there are other wooden porches at Bisley and Elstead. Walton-on-the-Hill, in spite of restoration, has various fragments of good quality. Chiddingfold has impressive big arcades in a church still without clerestory or large aisles.

The greatest Perp achievements in parish church building are normally the towers, and this brings home Surrey's extraordinary mixture of bad material and bad luck with a vengeance. There are barely a dozen Perp STONE TOWERS in the county, and they are mostly variations on surrounding types, e.g. the Middlesex type of two diagonal buttresses and a taller attached stair turret (Stoke-next-Guildford in flint, West Molesey in ragstone). Croydon, a replica of the original, has an amateurish composition with angle buttresses below and polygonal buttresses above. Farnham has the lower stages of what would have been an impressive big tower of Winchester provenance with polygonal buttresses, completed quite competently in the C19. But the only complete tower in the county to show any signs of individuality is Worplesdon, where the standard Middlesex type was carried out in the local heathstone to give it a distinctively soft and pretty effect which is as marked in reality as it is fugitive in either words or photographs.

However, with TIMBER TOWERS* there is more to look at. There are a lot of timber bell-turrets, usually depending on beams suspended from the top of the walls, sometimes using a mixture of timber uprights and beams bonded into the walls. As well as this there are a few complete timber belfries, as in Essex. These

* Frimley had until the C19 a complete timber church, of 1606, looking very like those still existing in Cheshire.

2—S.

are built up with four corner posts and various systems of diagonal bracing, usually in repeated St Andrew's crosses, the bottom stage having a lean-to around the framing. This is then clad *au choix*. Great Bookham has flint below and weatherboarding above, and could easily be in Essex. Tandridge* and 6 Newdigate are too restored to give much enjoyment, but Burstow and the upper parts of Horley make use of the Surrey trick of shingles, i.e. wood cut up and used like tiles instead of in boards. Both have great elegance and both are probably by the same person (who need not have been a c15 person; it is a comparatively easy job to alter the outside appearance whilst keeping the old framing, and both towers have an c18 look about them). Quite apart from these, and apart from any other timber tower in England, is the extraordinary performance that went on at 28 Thursley to support a very modest bell-turret half-way down the nave. Here a cage of four huge corner posts was put inside the much older existing masonry nave, and the cross-braces arranged so that the view eastwards was not obscured. It is both impressive and sophisticated and looks as though it could support a complete tower and spire: perhaps it was meant to.

Of late medieval monuments and CHURCH FURNISHINGS Surrey can provide reasonable measure, though the search is rather like a treasure hunt. To take furnishings first, the pews or 18 rather benches at Dunsfold are just as simple and elegant as the church itself and must be late c13. Lingfield has misericord stalls, Croydon a lectern, and the small museum that is Gatton's 50, church interior has a German medieval wall pulpit and very good 68 Flemish Late Gothic stall-backs, oddly like the North of England in spirit. There are only two screens worth mentioning: Gatton again has a good example from an unknown English church, probably in South-East England, with four-light bays and sturdy 26 carvings; Charlwood has a local screen, very prettily restored by *Burges*, with a repeated pattern of single-light bays. Littleton 19 (formerly Middlesex) has good late medieval pews, choir stalls, and screen. Not a single late medieval font or wall painting is worth notice, but there is a fair amount of glass, though not as much as one would expect considering that Chiddingfold was one of the centres of English glass-making. The best is a c14 window at Buckland. Other reasonable English work is at Compton (c13), Shere (c14), and Stoke d'Abernon (c15, brought from elsewhere).

* An odd form of framing here: the sides are given the customary diagonal bracing, and the E face has a vast scissors-truss almost independent of the corner posts.

There is a good deal of medieval foreign glass put in at various times, e.g. at Great Bookham and Stoke d'Abernon, none of it first-rate, and c17 glass in the chapel of Abbot's Hospital, Guildford.

For MONUMENTS there is hardly anything before 1350 – a priest at West Horsley and a knight at Horley – and not much afterwards. The best are at Lingfield: Reginald Lord Cobham † 1361 with a stiff effigy, but delightful babwineries at head and 24 foot, and another Reginald Cobham and his wife † 1446 with good 25 alabaster effigies and again delightful animals and angels at head and foot. Two late tomb recesses are worth notice, very similar, slick and crisp as Late Perp shopwork often is – at Mickleham † 1515, at Beddington †1520. But with BRASSES Surrey has something of unequivocally national importance. At Stoke d'Abernon is the earliest surviving brass in England, and one of the best, Sir John d'Abernon † 1277, a magnificent figure in chain-mail, 7 ft long. The brass of his son, † 1327, is also at Stoke, still very good but a little more wiry and a little less grand. The best later brasses are at Lingfield and are of the early c15. One, unnamed, is a splendidly elegant lady with a sideways sway to her, apparently c.1420.* Good small brasses are at Byfleet and Shere, and there are innumerable rough c15 and early c16 brasses, not all of which are mentioned in this book, for they are no more worth serious notice than mass-produced Victorian lecterns or pews.

Mass production of a more worthwhile kind is the staple product of late medieval DOMESTIC ARCHITECTURE in Surrey. The social pattern of the county, like that of Kent, tended to produce few big landlords but very many yeoman farmers, and from the c15 onwards they rebuilt, especially in the E half of the Weald, to a pattern of timber-framing as standard as any a speculative builder could provide today, though a good deal better-looking. The fully developed pattern is of a central hall going up through two floors – almost always horizontally split up subsequently – wings with single-storey rooms, the first floor given an overhang and the roof eaves carried between them usually on spandrels, giving the effect of a recessed centre. Surrey has nothing like so many of these houses as Kent, and very many of those that remain have been killed with kindness. The best-known example is at Brewer Street near Bletchingley. Other good 31 examples can be found at Limpsfield, Lingfield, and Oxted. Of

* At Lingfield there are also effigies incised on encaustic tile, not brass or stone.

larger buildings the most important in name is the Archbishop's
Palace at Croydon, built in two courtyards, mainly between 1380
and 1500; however the architecture there is very humble, and the
27 set of C15 halls is far more worth a visit. They are Old Surrey
Hall, Crowhurst Place (of the C15), and Beddington Place (of
c.1530), and in typical Surrey fashion each has been wrought
around, Beddington by C18 and then C19 total rebuilding, the
88 other two by incredible fairy-tale restorations of the early C20.
What remains in each case is only the hall roof, each a mixture of
hammerbeam and tie-beam, each quite different, each very
suave and sophisticated. Clearly, architectural ability was not
absent from the county, yet not a single church roof is worth
mentioning here.* The most typical mark of late medieval
display in house building is the gatehouse. In Surrey Bishop
Waynflete built two c.1475, both in brick: Esher Place was dis-
armingly remodelled by Kent in the early C18, but the wrongly
23 called Fox's Tower, dating from 1470–5, built on to the N side of
Farnham Castle, has been less altered and is one of the best of its
type in England. Its subtle asymmetry is in a way more typical of
a Renaissance intellect – just like the asymmetry of the best
French Flamboyant churches – than the formality which Henry
VIII imposed on his palaces in the name of the Renaissance.
This spirit must have been shown much more strongly in
Richmond Palace, named after the title of Henry VII, who rebuilt
it from 1499. Nothing is left of this, except outbuildings. Old
29 engravings show a forest of towers with bulbous tops like an
enlargement of the corner turrets of King's College Chapel, and
hints at elevations like Henry VII's Chapel or Thornbury
Castle, using mannered, exaggerated vertical strips of windows.
Two more royal palaces, at Woking and Weybridge, have all but
disappeared, and it is sad that Surrey's contribution to Wolsey's
Hampton Court should have been purely menial – stone from
Chertsey Abbey, mentioned earlier, and a set of conduit houses to
pump water from Coombe Springs, above Kingston. Several of
them are still there.‡

The RENAISSANCE in Surrey, when it came in fact as well as
in spirit, did so with a bang. Sutton Place and Nonsuch – the
latter completely destroyed, the former almost complete – were

---

* Westminster Hall roof was built and set out (i.e. framed up on the ground
and then dismantled for transport) at Farnham.

‡ *Talman* in the late C17 planned a Trianon on the Surrey side of the river,
at Thames Ditton, on the axis of the E front of Hampton Court, but nothing
came of it.

two of the most important houses of their time, and they show the
two stages of a process which would have produced full-blown
copies of true Italian Renaissance buildings by about 1560, if
religious and political differences had not steered us away from
France and Italy and in on ourselves, and then, later, towards
the Netherlands. Henry VIII, with his strange development from
a courtly elegant youth to an intolerant and syphilitic old man,
settled the course of English architecture as no monarch has
done before or since. The first stage was the piecemeal employ-
ment of Italian craftsmen for tombs and ornamental work, first
with the court, then with the up-to-date courtiers. Sir Richard
Weston, who built Sutton Place c.1520–30, knew France from
visits. He had conceived a liking for Italian arabesque and
grotesque ornament, and employed it throughout his new house, 35
to the extent of making the ornamental unit into the module
for the whole design. In the sense that the whole building is
built up of whole numbers of standard mass-produced ornamental panels, Sutton Place is prefabricated. The forms that
these units make up are generally basically Perp and generally
rather gauche – Sutton Place is not a great work of art – but
they are disposed with complete symmetry. The two-storeyed
entrance hall is entered centrally, and the rooms are arranged
symmetrically around it. This is apparently the earliest example
of the type in England, and apparently without parallel for fifty
years or more. Sutton Place is now an open-ended quadrangle; 33
until the late C18 this was closed by a gatehouse and screen, but
otherwise the house has survived almost unaltered. It does not,
incidentally, link up closely with any of the other courtiers' houses
of the 1520s. The nearest parallel in character is Layer Marney.

By the time Henry VIII came to build Nonsuch, what had 30
earlier been a proper artistic pride had become something very
like megalomania. He employed artists from all over northern
Europe as well as Italians, and heaped their products on to a vast
symmetrical pile with double courtyard: None-Such indeed,
the ancestor of the Elizabethan or Jacobean prodigy houses. The
outside was pargetted and slate-hung, the inside was presumably
a kind of museum collection of the works of whatever artists
Henry could get together. Coherence and integrity were the last
things to be expected: this was the bullfrog puffing and blowing.
Some contemporary pieces of royal interior decoration (probably
not from Nonsuch) survive at Loseley – panelling, painted
grottesche, probably one large fireplace. The most memorable
relic of this spirit (though it may actually date from 1550 or 60) is

36 the fireplace now in Reigate Priory. It probably did not come from
Nonsuch, as Evelyn mentions it at Reigate in the 1650s at a time
when Nonsuch was still in good condition. In point of artistic
achievement it is perhaps the best thing of its date in the country,
firm but not insensitive, splendidly large-scale – it dwarfs its
present surroundings – but not coarse. Pairs of columns enclose
niches with strapwork framing at the side, and the Royal Arms
are carried with a fine marauding swagger over the centre.

The ordinary style of the county had nothing to do with
this, but carried on Tudor and a simplified Late Gothic into
ELIZABETHAN and JACOBEAN architecture. In fact, in contrast to these imported splendours, the local style is more demure
than in most counties: gables and mullion-and-transom windows
in brick, stone, and half-timber. In brick there is Hobbs Farm at
Crowhurst and Lucas Green Manor House at Chobham. The
latter has inserted bands of terracotta, unornamented, as a tiny
sign that new techniques were abroad. Then came the big and
dull Pendell Court (1624) and the much prettier Great Fosters
near Egham (1598), where the stair-wells run up to square-ended
tops which make a lively complement to the familiar gables.
34 Inside, Great Fosters has the best of Surrey's Jacobean overmantels. In stone there is Loseley of 1561–9 – very plain, very
dignified, and in its severe yet serene way one of the most
impressive Tudor houses in England.* There is also Tudor
House at Haslemere, Smallfield Place of c.1600 – a rough, tough
house, looking more like County Durham than Surrey – and then
New Place at Lingfield (1617), almost indistinguishable from a
Cotswold manor house (it is part of the family of Sussex Tudor
buildings around East Grinstead).

Half-timbering for anything bigger than cottages occurs only
around Guildford, and the repertoire is entirely made up of
simple square framing, diagonal patterns, and curved braces
cutting into the corners of the squares and in repeat making a
pattern of circles.‡ The best example, worth putting in any
32 national list of half-timbered houses, is Great Tangley near
Shalford, of 1584. The best of the others are Lythe Hill Farm
near Haslemere and East Manor House at Bramley. Among
cottages the timbering gradually became more regular and the

* Baynards Park was built c.1590 by the same family and seems to have
been a brick and stone edition of Loseley, but it is now almost unrecognizable
under C19 additions.

‡ Just as in the West Midlands. Was there a connexion, and if so, why was
only one of the West Midland patterns made use of ?

type persisted well into the C17 (at Stoke-next-Guildford 1663, at Guildford 1672), and the best examples are worth a good look for their relaxed domesticity. Inevitably, some must have been left out of our journeys. Among the best are Boswells Farm at Oakwood (not now used as a house and hence completely unaltered), Norton Farm at Worplesdon, Bonnet's Farm at Capel, and Burningfold Farm at Dunsfold. It ought to be said that for each genuine example remaining, half a dozen have been made aesthetically and historically valueless by pretentious or over-cosy restoration. Many were altered – this time with advantage – in the C18 by applying tile-hanging to an earlier frame. In memory this seems the most typically Surrey material of all. The habit seems to have started in the late C17, and one of the best examples, quite untouched and beautifully mellow, is The College at Lingfield. Flint and half-timber occurs at Shere, and very rough pargetting, or patterns in plaster, at Hartswood Manor Reigate 1615, and in Quarry Street, Guildford.

In this same simple gabled Tudor style are a few almshouses, oddly pinched and unattractive, as they tend to be near the Thames Valley. The best is the Wyatt Almshouses at Farncombe, 1622; the biggest is the quadrangle of Whitgift's Hospital, 1596, still holding its own at the central crossroads of Croydon. In the same style are the Windsor Almshouses at Farnham, 1619, and – at last going classical – Cleave's Almshouses at Kingston of 1668. There is only one PUBLIC BUILDING worth mentioning, the Guildford Grammar School of 1557–86 – not so much for its rather limp architecture as for its completeness and the degree to which each small addition can be documented.

The continuity of this vernacular style has taken the story well into the C17 and has outrun chronology, as Tudor fashions died hard in Surrey – there is a gabled building at Hambledon dated 1710. But about 1590 a thicker, richer style came into use, what we loosely call JACOBEAN, employing shaped gables (the most common has a curved top, a step, then double-curved sides), strapwork, and doorways made into 'frontispieces', with compositions of up to three storeys (five in the Bodleian at Oxford). With them went a more extended plan, usually H-shaped. One of the earliest examples of this, now long demolished, was Wimbledon House of 1588. Ham House of 1610 has the same plan, still to be traced under later alterations, but most of its character is now mid and late C17. The pre-C18 Clandon was of this type, so is Eagle House at Wimbledon of 1613, so are the remaining fragments of Byfleet Manor House of 1617, made

up very successfully into a late C17 house and one of the best
hybrids in Surrey. But the outstanding example, and one of the
39, best in the whole country, is Abbot's Hospital at Guildford of
40 1619–22, a cathedral among almshouses. Its founder, George
Abbot, was a local boy who had made good – made best, in fact, for
he became Archbishop of Canterbury. His hospital is a superbly
coherent design in rose-red brick – definitely a *design*, in the sense
one would use of a building by Inigo Jones. It looks like a self-
conscious bit of commemoration, and in one respect it is certainly
self-conscious: Abbot or his architect gave the building a huge,
very successful, and quite unnecessary gatehouse, just as though
it were a semi-fortified house of the late C15. It probably represents in spirit the exact halfway point between Gothic Survival –
the gatehouse as a legitimate continuing expression of splendour,
equivalent to the four corner turrets of Wollaton – and Gothic
Revival – the gatehouse consciously recalling a more or less golden
past. Art history can happily be left to argue, here: the building
can be enjoyed in its own right as a final summing up of Elizabethan extrovert virtues, equivalent to Shakespeare's regal
swagger rather than Webster's glistening melancholia.

George Abbot's tomb, in Holy Trinity church across the road
from the hospital, is as bad of its kind as the hospital is good.
But in order to put it in place, the story of C16 and early C17
CHURCH ARCHITECTURE in Surrey must first be told. A few
words will do it, as in almost every county in England, because
church building came to a standstill after the Reformation and
Dissolution. What was built afterwards was humble repair work
and replacement in a minimum Gothic style. Again the question
for art historians is whether it is survival or revival, a question
which would probably have puzzled the village masons who put
these simple buildings up. There are the brick towers of Thorpe,
22 Barnes, and Littleton (formerly Middlesex), the central tower of
Chipstead (1631), and two small complete brick churches –
Malden of *c.*1627 and Morden of 1636. As late as 1699 a plain
Gothic W tower was added to Ockley, doubtless then a very
remote village in the Weald. Others in the area would still be with
us if the C19 had not regarded them as being 'debased'. Elizabethan detail was normally only employed on parts of buildings,
where the building could be treated as the extension of church
furnishings. The roof of the Lumley chapel at Cheam, of 1592, is
a particularly lovable example of this.

In tombs and CHURCH FURNISHINGS the county is not rich,
compared with its neighbours and considering that the spiritual

energy which was spread over both building and furnishings in the Middle Ages was channelled without much diminution – England was still a pious country – into a few modes of expression: pulpits, seats, and *memento mori* of all kinds. There are a few pulpits, usually badly mauled in c19 restoration, ranging from the simple cottage-furniture effect of Alfold to a type with rough geometrical patterns on the sides (Pyrford), and then to full-blown Jacobean detail at West Molesey, Compton (big but not good), and Stoke d'Abernon. The latter is not really good but it is very typical, even to keeping its hourglass. Mickleham has a Belgian pulpit of *c*.1600. The only Renaissance glass worth mentioning is foreign too: at Ashtead, good work from southern Holland, and at Gatton, average work from Germany and Antwerp. There are few Tudor MONUMENTS, or really only one, that to Sir Thomas Cawarden † 1559 at Bletchingley. It charts the change quite tellingly, being in the plain up-to-date style of the 1560s, a tomb-chest with restrained classical decoration around the sides. This quickly developed into a richer and jollier style, exactly paralleling the change in the design of whole buildings. It is perfectly expressed in the series of Lumley monuments at Cheam of 1580–1620, some with recumbent figures, and one with delightful architectural perspectives in low relief (Jane Lady Lumley † 1577 but designed in 1590), in imaginative range and quality of carving a good deal above the average. Then again after 1600 the monuments became curlier still, heavier, and, if one is lucky, more memorable, giving an effect as rich and indivisible as an image in Jacobean poetry. In Surrey one is not lucky until the very end of the style, in the 1630s. The earlier tombs are merely pompous and heavy, and to split them up into types (recumbent, semi-recumbent, kneeling, etc.) is not really worth while because the classifications do not correspond to any kind of artistic boundaries. The attitudes are noted under individual entries; the examples are at Croydon († 1604), Addington († 1612), Stoke d'Abernon († 1613), and East Horsley († 1626). There are also several at Holy Trinity Guildford, among them Archbishop Abbot (mentioned at the beginning of this section), erected as late as 1640 by the *Christmas Brothers*, the leading official sculptors of the old school – enormous and elaborate, twenty years behind the times, and quite lifeless.*

* Surrey being a yeoman county, there are in proportion many more small monuments – usually a kneeling pair of figures facing each other over a prayer desk. John Goodwine † 1618 at Horne is very typical and shows clearly the original colours in which such monuments were painted – surprisingly rich and subtle colours, incidentally, unlike most modern repaintings.

By the 1630s there are better things to see in Surrey than this, however: strange expressions of ideas on resurrection and mortality, exactly like the conceits of the latest Jacobean and Carolean writers. It is truly appropriate that John Donne's monument of 1631, showing himself clothed in a shroud, should have started a fashion. Surrey has no direct copies, but at Coulsdon, Grace Rowed † 1631 looks up to heaven whilst an elaborate allegory is acted out in both words and things – copious inscriptions, skulls, and picks and shovels. And at Egham, in a famous monument, Sir John Denham † 1638 starts up from his grave at the Judgement Day, his spirit remade physically whole while his erstwhile body is still hugger-mugger with the skeletons in the charnel house below. This is a sermon in stone of some richness and subtlety, and luckily here the carving can match the content. Sir John's two wives are also commemorated at Egham, in a monument of about the same date but completely different in character: from a circular opening in the familiar type of thick architectural surround the two faces appear, carved and painted, with expressions of what one can only call peasant cunning, a brilliant but quite instinctive realization of character. Finally, among the medley of C16 and C17 brasses those at Weybridge † 1586 and at Cobham (undated) have been given some genuine post-medieval life of their own, instead of further debasing an already debased tradition.

That brings us, in terms of national styles, to Inigo Jones and his belated importation of the Italian High Renaissance into England – sometimes done better than by the Italians themselves. There is none of this in Surrey (Inigo's work at Oatlands and Bagshot has disappeared), but there is instead a remarkable amount of work of about 1630 which is called throughout the book ARTISAN MANNERISM. This needs some explanation. At almost exactly the same time as the Court first employed Inigo Jones, the City of London took over a handsome, thick style of building in brick which was partly Jacobean, and rather more an importation of ideas which were then current in Holland – shaped and pedimented gables, and shouldered lintels to windows – and from Flanders, in simplification of the gross and jolly version of Italian architecture brought to Antwerp by Rubens. The easiest way to imagine it is as the architecture of the typical small monument of the time applied to whole buildings. Its centre was the City of London, and in particular the City Companies and their surveyors; but naturally enough, almost all of their work in London has gone. It spread throughout South-

East England and East Anglia,★ and Surrey has more of it within
a small radius than any other county – warm, rich, and humane,
at its best quite up to the best of the Court style. With their unaffected use of brick the designs often come full circle and
resemble the brick palaces that their Italian equivalents (not
people like Vignola and Tibaldi, but the ordinary local mason)
were putting up in the towns of Northern Italy.

The style as a whole is easy to recognize, but there were
obviously several hands working with different mannerisms, and
these have never been sorted out. The best known 'Artisan' house
in Surrey is Kew Palace of 1631, built by a merchant, which is 41
vigorously compartmented into three storeys, each with its own
order of pilasters, each window with its rusticated frame, each
pair of bays gathered under a Dutch gable. Yet nothing else in
Surrey has quite the same character, and the nearest equivalent
to Kew (possibly a copy) is Barnham Manor near Bognor Regis
in Sussex. The second big 'Artisan' house in Surrey, West Horsley 42
Place of c.1630, again uses single-storey pilasters, but uses them
with a grand swing across a long front flanked by shaped gables in
brought-forward wings. The gables at West Horsley may be c18
reconstructions, but it is still one of the most typical and attractive
early c17 houses in the country. It is connected with a number of
other local houses, probably by imitation: Old House at Mickleham, 1636, Old House at Shalford, and parts of Chilworth
Manor, then down to farms and cottages of which most Surrey
parishes have one. Of the third house, Slyfield Manor, large and 45
very puzzling fragments remain. They include one big shaped
gable above superimposed coupled pilasters, more or less in the
style of West Horsley, attached to a longer and slightly later
range, of 1650 or 1660. This has an eaves cornice and giant
pilasters, and looks as though it had a good deal to do with the
houses *Peter Mills* had built in Great Queen Street, London in
1637.

This work ought not to be dismissed as merely an interesting
byway. The designers at their best were using the style with a
marvellous facility and felicity, able to turn every gabled bay into
a different kind of happy composition.

Although Kew Palace and the Queen's House at Greenwich
are as clear an antithesis as Cromwell and Charles I, the situation
was not always so clear-cut. In Great Queen Street, Mills was

★ Occasionally mixed with what must surely be Dutch or Flemish designs
transplanted direct – Woodbridge Town Hall in Suffolk, for example, looks
purely Dutch.

probably inspired by Inigo Jones's Covent Garden Piazzas, and
43 in one other Surrey building, Pendell House of 1636, there seems
to be an even closer hybrid. It has a completely symmetrical
plan,* with pairs of rooms opening off a small central hall-
corridor running the depth of the house from the front door to a
staircase like one of those at Greenwich; yet this is clothed with
plain undemonstrative brick elevations whose few decorative
details are 'Artisan'. It really looks here as though one person
gave the plan and another worked up the elevations.

The interiors of these houses were mostly very plain, and only
Slyfield has anything worth a special visit‡: a big barrel-vault in
the gabled part, with delightful arabesque plasterwork which is
still purely Jacobean, then ceilings with rough editions of the
geometrical patterns introduced by Inigo Jones (they also occur
45 in a house in West Street Farnham), and a good staircase with
rusticated newel posts (also at Old House Shalford) and bizarre
doorcases with half-pilasters let into the jambs.

But the most ornate Surrey interiors of c.1640 belong to yet
another type of house – that put up in the style of Inigo Jones but
not strictly in imitation of him. At Ham House big alterations
were made in 1637–8, consisting of plaster ceilings of Inigo Jones
type – accurately carved, not rough copies – and a splendid
46 staircase and long gallery. The staircase has the whole of a flight
treated as one ornamental composition, an idea which was slowly
developed during the Commonwealth and which became almost
universal after 1660. Usually the composition was made up of
flowers and fruit, but here the panels are of military trophies
and the staircase consequently has an urgency and a braggadocio
which has gone from the smoother later examples. The long
gallery has a recurring motif of delicate yet crisp pilasters, and is
spatially one of the best rooms of its date in the country, the
realization in strictly architectural terms of what Jacobean long
galleries like Hardwick or Blickling did through sheer size and
through atmosphere.

These houses have been described at some length – but after
all, this is the first point at which Surrey makes a contribution to
the history of English architecture as a whole. What happened to
the style after 1640 is a perfect illustration of the hit-or-miss

---

* This may be an alteration of the more typical plan of a big hall entered
off-centre. But on the whole to assume this gets the architectural detective
into more difficulties than assuming symmetry.

‡ There was a complete panelled room at Poyle Park, Tongham. The
fireplace is now in the London Museum.

pattern that makes English provincial architecture such an exciting bran-tub. The driving force had gone, and the result was first a few modest but attractive farms and cottages (Brook Place Chobham 1656, Manor House Ripley 1650, Crossways Farm Abinger) using shaped gables and other mannerisms.* The style was particularly happy on this scale, but after the Restoration it declined into deplorably rough and overloaded brickwork, principally at Godalming, but also at Dorking and Farnham (the original parts of Bailiff's Hall). This is simply a style on its deathbed.

Yet this same style in the hands of an unknown architect or architects produced some superbly virile buildings at Guildford in the later C17. Here the repertoire of the City of London masons is enlivened by the gaiety that seemed inseparable from the 1670s and 1680s. The Guildhall, refronted in 1683, looks like a ship's superstructure more than anything else, with gables, cupola, pedimented windows and pilasters all jockeying for position on the Guildford skyline. Related to it are several houses in Guildford High Street with a predilection for big windows arranged in vertical strips with the minimum of wall between. The best of these is Child House.

Again style has outrun chronology, which is as it should be. In fact for part of the C17 representatives of three styles were being built simultaneously: belated Tudor, Artisan Mannerism, and post Restoration Wren-style. This story could be taken even further up to around 1700; for at Littlefield Manor Worplesdon the ornate brickwork of the Artisan style shook hands with the ornate brickwork of English Baroque. It is effectively a handsome Queen Anne house equipped with curly shaped gables.

To go back again, the new style of the early C17 in its purest form did not touch Surrey – or if it did, it has left no buildings.‡ The only way in which it can be traced is in a few CHURCH MONUMENTS, none of them great. The plainness and new-found gravity of Inigo Jones's Greenwich is echoed in the plainness of the Cecil monument at Wimbledon of 1638, a black marble tomb slab without figures. Sometimes the gravity simply froze out the emotional content to give correct lifeless effigies, like Sir John Evelyn † 1641 at Godstone; sometimes it took a Jacobean conceit

* Notably, at Ripley, shouldered lintels, i.e. flat lintels raised a few inches above the top of the window frame by curved brickwork, a very Dutch trick. At Crockford Bridge Farm, Addlestone, is an end gable of the type which ends in a projecting lug rather than a point, very common in Holland but almost unique in England.

‡ Except perhaps for some fragments at Byfleet Manor House.

and made it more elegant but less effective, like Mrs Mary
Andley † 1655 at Sanderstead, who is disposed in her shroud on a
marble slab with only her face visible. After the Restoration the
monuments reflect exactly the split in architectural style: on the
one hand fat and florid tablets like a fragment of an Artisan
building, often well done like Robert Foster † 1663 at Egham; on
the other hand grandiose compositions awkwardly or unskilfully
carved, waiting for the spirit of a new style to give them life.
The latter kind can be abstract, like Sir Edward Nicholas † 1669
at West Horsley, or with life-size figures, like Archbishop Sheldon
† 1677 at Croydon by *Jasper Latham*. The difference in style with
size is probably not an accident. Artisan Mannerism was a
middle-class style, and the middle class did not run to big
monuments.

Sculpture was, very properly, waiting for the Baroque, the
most sculptural of all styles. DOMESTIC ARCHITECTURE had
a simpler job, and one which in retrospect looks very like the
political job performed by the two bloodless revolutions of 1660
and 1688: to evolve a plain, simple, adaptable background in
which men could live amicably, without reflecting violent divisions of class or religion in its architecture. The style is associated
with Wren but in fact came into England a little earlier, primarily
with Hugh May and primarily from Holland and such buildings
as the Mauritshuis in The Hague. In Surrey it appears first in the
alterations made by Bishop Morley to Farnham Castle in 1677,
and in the additions to Ham House of 1673–5. The alterations to
Farnham consisted chiefly in refacing the Great Hall, which is an
angular, plain piece of work. The style may well have come from
the City of London, not the Court; for once accepted it was so
commonsense that it spread very quickly. The additions to Ham
House are mostly rich and sober interiors, very like Hugh May's
work, which make a fascinating comparison with the work done
at Ham in the 1630s. Then come houses like Waterloo House at
Epsom, Park Farm House at Ashtead, and Byfleet Manor House
of 1686, which incorporates earlier fragments very successfully
(and which has a tenuous *Wren* connexion). Again, not to stretch
the parallel too far, incorporating earlier fragments was something
which was typical of the C17 social and political climate. Wren
continued with this plainness to the end of his life, and the grand
and simple porticoed Trumpeters' House at Richmond, if not
actually by him, must have been built by a close disciple.★

★ Another *Wren* attribution is Wrencote at Croydon, but this is really a
heavily detailed and conservative later C17 type (still half-H shaped) with some

Fetcham Park by *Talman* is in the same style. It is now submerged under fearful terracotta alterations, but it was never much of a building. The interiors of these houses are unremarkable,* except that there is a set of staircases and painted stair-wells. These are of 1710 at The Grange Farnham, at Hoe Place Old Woking, of *c.*1720 by *Laguerre* at Fetcham Park, and a splendid one at Reigate Priory of *c.*1710, which in its coherence and sense of the well as a 48 spatial unit, not as so much convenient space for decoration, is one of the best in England.

In none of these houses was Surrey particularly up to date; yet, paradoxically, in the treatment of the surrounding landscape it led the whole country. This was largely due to *John Evelyn*, diarist, amateur architect, and gardener. At Wotton on his brother's estate he and a relation *George Evelyn* introduced between 1643 and 1652 what was really the first Italian garden into England, terracing a steep hillside and fitting a little temple into the bottom of it. The unexpected thing about it is that it is all sited very close to the house. Evelyn's work still exists at Albury, and a smaller layout at Chilworth Manor must have been inspired by it. Then, in the 1680s, *Sir William Temple* set out his garden at Moor Park in a formal Dutch style and then wrote about it. The layout here is overgrown but could have been recovered.

For late C17 church building there is nothing to mention here, for CHURCH FURNISHINGS very little, far less than one would expect so near London. What there is often comes from outside the county – an opulent font at Worplesdon from Eton College, the first-rate reredos from Wren's demolished City church of St Matthew Friday Street erected ingeniously if improperly as an overmantel at Polesden Lacey, and the handsome Baroque choir 50, stalls at Gatton, brought from Ghent. Littleton (formerly in 68 Middlesex) has elaborate Baroque altar rails, also perhaps from Flanders. The only noteworthy piece Surrey can claim as its own is the refitting of Farnham Castle chapel about 1680 with panelling in the best City of London style, with beautifully carved cherubs and swags of fruit.

All this woodwork has found itself, as it were; it is speaking in one full-blooded, unreflecting style which informs every part of it. There are no hesitations and no neuroses. The same attitude

---

misunderstood up-to-date details added – it has one of the thickest and most prodigious cornices in England. All this does not mean, however, that it is unattractive.

* Albury has one good overmantel carved in late C17 Dutch style that came from a Drummond house in Scotland.

came into all branches of architecture and decoration within about thirty years, the actual date varying for different types of building (much as the Modern Movement appeared as a coherent style earlier in furniture than in office blocks). The easiest thing to say about it is that it is all-overish: every object, whether monument or mansion, is to be seen all at once and as a whole. It is worth looking for especially, because it coincided almost exactly in Surrey with a definite building period and also with the first time that the county really lost its isolation and seemed to become part of the national pattern. This is odd, because one part of the county was very important in the national pattern, yet no signs of this are left in Surrey building. The whole southern strip was part of the Sussex Wealden industrial area, the biggest in Britain at that time, with the wood used both for shipbuilding and as fuel to smelt the local ironstone. The map of southern Surrey is full of tell-tale references – Furnace Farm and Hammer Bottom near Haslemere, for example; yet all that is left is a few ponds and just one or two unexpected uses of iron in everyday objects – iron tomb slabs at Crowhurst, an iron cartouche over the door at Moor Park. One could wish that C19 and C20 industry were so easily effaced. Again, Chilworth had one of the biggest C17 gunpowder mills in the country, but now all the buildings have gone, and there is no sign of industrialization in the sleepy cottages that remain.

Two other economic forces happily left many more visible signs on the county – agricultural prosperity and what can only be called the earliest wave of suburbanization.

The first is quickly dealt with. Farnham became at the end of the C17, quite suddenly, a very prosperous corn market. Defoe called it 'the greatest in England', something which it seems difficult to imagine in Farnham today, when almost all the agricultural land around it is pasture or hop-garden, and in a few years this was reflected in a crop of houses – first The Grange of 1710, then Willmer House of 1718, The Old House at Weybourne of 1724, and one or two smaller houses. The Grange is rich and plain – the two are not necessarily opposites – but Willmer House is an astonishing *tour de force* of gauged and cut brickwork, a perfect illustration of Baroque 'all-overishness' with no single element of the front more important than any other. In this case it has defeated its own ends, because the total composition does not say enough to make the effort worthwhile. Old House at Weybourne, which must be by the same designer, strives for less and achieves more, with only the central bay adorned and accentuated. There is nothing else as violent as these houses in South-East England, and the tradition died hard around Farnham; for Tilford House of *c*.1740 and Sandford House built next to Willmer House as late as 1757 still have Baroque intentions, although the detail slowly becomes more uniform and Palladian. Again, the bigger town house tries too hard and lacks feeling, while the smaller country house (Tilford) attempts just one effect – giving the central bay an uplift – and brings it off perfectly. Most of the other Surrey towns have one or two big early C18 houses, though not on the same scale or of the same quality. They mostly stick to the type of segment-headed windows, handsome big doorcases, and an elegant polychromy of grey and red bricks common to all of South-East England. Examples are at Haslemere (Town House), Godalming (as late as 1753), and Reigate (The Barons). In the same style Reigate provides the only Baroque PUBLIC BUILDING in the county, the Old Town Hall of 1728, indistinguishable from a town house were it not for the arcaded ground floor. It makes a jolly town incident but no more. In the country yeoman farmers rebuilt or refronted their houses in brick in just the same spirit as they had built their timber-framed hall-houses in the C15 or C16. Good examples are at Chobham, Pyrford, Limpsfield, Tandridge, and Gomshall.

But this cannot account for the remarkable number of houses that were built in the northern part of Surrey between 1690 and 1730. What produced them can only be described as suburbanization, and on a bigger scale than has so far been realized. The full story should include all London s of the Thames, which was part of Surrey until the County of London was formed in 1888. Thus, in dealing with the present curtailed county all the manifestations can be fairly ascribed to a true flight from London rather than straightforward expansion of its edges; in 1700 there were several miles of country between the present Surrey boundary and the edge of built-up London. The first positive confirmation we have of this is at Epsom, which became a fashionable spa about 1680. When Defoe was writing he could already speak of gentlemen driving themselves to town every day – the very first commuters in England. The gentlemen in the big houses around surely did the same, on occasion, a supposition strengthened by a look at the type of person who built or lived in them – city merchants (Tadworth) or financiers (Carshalton and Eagle House Mitcham, [52,] both connected, like Wanstead in Essex, with the directors of the [57] South Sea Company. The Bubble burst in 1719 and this coincides very nearly with the end of the building wave).

One other type of suburbanization needs mentioning, the enlargement of riverside villages, more familiar on the Middlesex side with the chain Hammersmith–Chiswick–Twickenham–Hampton–Sunbury. It took various forms. Sometimes, purely metropolitan uniform terraces of houses were set down almost in the fields, like Hammersmith Terrace and Montpellier Row Twickenham. On the s bank it happened at Wandsworth, now inside the County of London, and especially at Richmond. Here
54 Maids of Honour Row of 1724 is a *beau idéal* of this sort of building – sober, handsome, not trying to be an assertive individual design in itself, content to be an inflection in the larger pattern of the town as a whole. More often there were moderate-sized houses in moderate-sized grounds. There are several at Thames Ditton, at Ham (Ormeley Lodge of c.1720 is one of the nicest examples anywhere), and particularly at Petersham, which would be the most elegant village-suburb near London if only the traffic could be kept out of it. The two best houses, Montrose House and Rutland House,* are separated by an endless screen of lorries, cars, and London Transport buses. Epsom also, of course, has its quota of early c18 houses, though they are mostly maltreated and none of them are first-rate.

The bigger houses tended to belong to one homogeneous style, and only the two earliest stand apart from it. Eagle House at Mitcham is a very late and not very good example of a type which otherwise does not now exist in Surrey, the compact, four-square symmetrical block with tall hipped roof and top balustrade, and most of the interest and movement in the design taking place above the cornice. It was invented or adapted by Sir Roger Pratt decades earlier, in the 1650s and 1660s, and at Mitcham ultra-conservatism paid for its timidity with lifelessness. The other
52 early house, Tadworth Court of c.1700, is very different. The style is very like Talman's, which is to say Wren in his Hampton Court mood, and the centre of the s front is one of the most elegant in the whole country. (The wings are rougher, and though obviously built at the same time, they do not look as though they were built by the same person.) The designer is unknown, and so is the house, even though it is under twenty miles from London. Surrey makes a show of its second-rate buildings and hides away its really good ones.

All the other houses are in more or less a Vanbrugh–Hawks-

---

* Built in 1666, remodelled 1720. If part of the front survives from 1666 – it is just possible – it is a very early and very elegant example of the Hugh May style.

moor style, which is the very individual, powerful, and noble reshaping of classical design that happened in England at the beginning of the c18 almost independently of the rest of Europe. Hawksmoor was Wren's Clerk of Works, and Wren himself was mixed up in the movement, though we do not know how far. It certainly became a style adopted by the whole of the Office of Works, for example in dockyards and barracks. This is the explanation of the expression 'Office of Works Vanbrugh' sometimes used in the detailed descriptions. *Vanbrugh* built himself a house at Claremont after 1708 – again suburban – which has gone; outbuildings and particularly the Belvedere remain, however, and will be mentioned later. *Hawksmoor* remodelled Ockham Park *c.*1725, which has gone except for the stable block, and Addiscombe House. This has gone completely, but it must be mentioned here for its portico, typical in its extravagance, which Hawksmoor, being a genius, could so often bring off successfully. The portico was the full height of a three-storey house. It had only two columns supporting it and was 40 ft high and 25 ft wide. Nothing as splendidly absurd as this has survived, alas. The richest house is Carshalton built before 1714, whose elevations mix the new spirit with late Wren, although a Water House in the grounds is purely Vanbrughian (*Henry Joynes*, Vanbrugh's Clerk of Works at Blenheim, probably built it). The Water House has a central tower, thickly moulded brick arches, and peculiarly shaped 'battlements', which are really a Jacobean reminiscence and which must also be mentioned later. Sanderstead Court (now demolished) had a smaller front in the same style, and it occasionally appeared in town houses also (Curfew House Chertsey of 1725, built as a school). Probably the best looking of the houses is one which was not put up by a close follower of Vanbrugh at all, but by the young *James Gibbs*. It is Sudbrook Park at Petersham of 1726. Gibbs's style is the sort of blend of Wren and Vanbrugh that a country builder might use,* but much better done. It obviously came much more naturally to Gibbs than the heartless Palladian style he was forced into later. Sudbrook also has the best interiors, including a grand central saloon which is 55 decorated with a firework display of plaster carving. The other houses are oddly lacking in them and only Carshalton has some 57 rooms and corridors worth notice. The houses were not complete

---

* What this meant in Surrey is shown by Milford House of 1730, which has plenty of fine swaggering detail inadequately put together. It has an air of being connected with *John James*, one of the first of our bad architects whose name we know. Alas, he was not the last.

without the iron gates in front, something of a Surrey speciality
because of the local iron smelting. The best examples, as good as
any in the country, are at Beddington Place – the Baroque house
there was rebuilt in the C19 – Reigate Priory, Durdans at Epsom,
and Albury, where the very good and very odd design is
explained by their being an importation 'from a Hungarian
convent'.

Baroque CHURCH BUILDING in Surrey is negligible. There is
only the top of the tower at Kingston, built in a nice rough style
by *John Yeomans* in 1708, and the Newcastle Pew in Esher Old
Church, built in an incredibly pure and delicate classical style
by *Vanbrugh* c.1725. But in CHURCH MONUMENTS the Baroque
found one of its natural modes of expression, and the story of
these must be carried on from the 1680s, where it was left with a
number of individual sculptors looking for a style. The first
English sculptor to practise the full Baroque swagger was
Bushnell, who almost certainly did the Broderick monument of
49 c.1680 at Peper Harow with two splendid busts. Hard on his heels
came the City carvers, who took up the style amazingly quickly
and amazingly well. There are plenty of late C17 tablets in Surrey,
usually with a scrolly pedimented frame and often with beautifully
carved swags of fruit or flanking goddesses. One of the best is to
Elisabeth Evelyn † 1691 in Epsom church, another good one is at
Mortlake to Francis Coventry † 1699, by *William Kidwell*. Later
good tablets are, among many others, at Capel † 1720, at Leatherhead † 1723 by *Stanton & Horsnaile*, at Lingfield † 1695 and
† 1718, and at West Horsley † 1704. Bigger monuments had busts
as well as a frame, e.g. Robert Shiers † 1700 at Great Bookham.
The most important had full-size figures in various attitudes, like
Sir William Lewen † 1721 at Ewell (semi-reclining) and Sir
William Scawen † 1722 at Carshalton (reclining), the latter
staccato and abruptly composed, a kind of equivalent to Vanbrughian architecture which it is rare to meet in monuments. They
are good but not great: but that qualification does not apply to
51 Sir Robert Clayton † 1707 at Bletchingley, one of the grandest
monuments in England. Sir Robert and his wife are standing,
over life size, under an immense architectural frame. It is typical
that this should be the work of an ordinary City mason, *Richard
Crutcher*, and that it should be his only known monument. The
leading sculptors would doubtless have trimmed off the gaucheries
in the architectural background – but they would also have
smoothed out the superb personal carving in the figures and in the
child in embroidered clothes underneath. We still do not fully

realize that these big English monuments of 1700–30, taken all together, are one of the great things of European art.

In the long run Palladianism, Classicism, Academism would be the death of this kind of art: the two temperaments had no common ground except psychological insight into the sitter's character. But in fact the style did not so much die as have a local anaesthetic, with the big monuments becoming by slow steps first frigid and then ridiculous, and the small monuments going their own way into a delightful Rococo and then into an equally delightful equivalent of the late C18 novel of sensibility. The situation can be shown exactly in Surrey by four big monuments of 1730–50. At Reigate there is Richard Ladbroke † 1730 by *Joseph Rose the Elder*, where a good many of the new ideas, e.g. more correct architectural detail, Roman dress for the reclining figure, are still put together in a purely Baroque way, with a feeling for the all-over effect of the monument. Splendidly carved, it is a perfect foil to the Clayton monument – and again, Rose was a City mason and we only know of one other monument of his. At Ockham Lord King † 1734 is by *Rysbrack*, the best of the academic sculptors. Though the composition is conventional, with Lord King and his wife seated either side of an urn, Rysbrack's splendid carving of the figures* makes the monument memorable. When this is lacking the result is an anticipation of the official monument of yesterday – and today – like Colonel Moore † 1735 at Great Bookham, frigidly Roman amid his military trophies. And finally, the truly individual sculptor would go on with his individual style whatever was happening around him. The best of these in the mid C18 was *Roubiliac*, who continued his very personal variety of Baroque (perhaps Baroque combined with Jacobean imagery ?) to the end of his life – an exact equivalent to Handel's Baroque music. His monument to Richard Boyle † 1740 at Walton-on-Thames was not erected until 1755, but he still composed it in an entirely Baroque way which can only be seen and not described: figure, daughter, tent, gun, tree, flags. It is not quite up to the level of the Argyll or Nightingale monuments in Westminster Abbey, but it is not far off.

Smaller monuments show much less variation. The formal classicism of Rysbrack's style could not look really frigid on a small scale, and there are two delightful busts in architectural frames, one, unnamed, at Sanderstead, and Diana Fielding

---

* His reliefs at Clandon Park are also first rate academic sculpture in their own right, as well as being charming decoration.

† 1733 at Ashtead, probably by *Rysbrack* himself. Most masons preferred the freedom given by combinations of cartouches, cherubs, urns, and reliefs, and produced one of the few English manifestations of the Rococo. The best are at Seale † 1762 by *Nutcher* of Swaythling, and at West Horsley † 1750 by *Nicholas Read*, Roubiliac's pupil.* Then, gradually, sentiment replaced 'movement' and before sentiment became sentimentality or sheer mass-production it produced delightful vignettes in classical terms with an urn at Addington † 1769 by *Wilton*, or in semi-
65 romantic terms with an exquisite relief of a fight at Great Bookham † 1776. The only big late C18 monument is to Speaker Onslow † 1778 at Holy Trinity Guildford, unsigned and not bad. Here the big names begin to be more numerous than the worth-while monuments – an ominous sign. *Westmacott Senior* appears at Old Woking and Chipstead, *T. Hews* at Hascombe, *Van Gelder* at Compton. The *Bacons* and later *Flaxman*, *Chantrey*, and *Baily* appear everywhere. Hardly any need be noticed here, and not all of them are noticed in the individual descriptions, for the simple reason that they are just not good enough. Except for a crop at Egham (one *Flaxman*, three *Bailys*) they are all small, and the only one worth a look is an unusual *Flaxman* at Kingston, done before he became well-known. The elegant was much more likely to appear in an unknown sculptor like *William Pistell* (tablet at Effingham † 1844). But when the equally unknown *Legrew* commemorated his mother at Caterham Old Church in 1832 he could manage no more than the standard sentimental kneeling figure. Three odds and ends take the story up to the beards and pink marble of Victorian sculpture. One is that in Horsell church are two cases of late C18 anachronistic designs – one with kneelers, the other with figures striking purely Baroque rhetorical attitudes. The second is that the ubiquitous firm of *Coade* turned their capacity for mass production to a particularly odd use in supplying label-stops for the windows of Chertsey church and then stamping each with the company's name. And the third, on a purely vernacular and much fresher level, is that there are not many carved gravestones worth notice – the best are at Thursley – but that a few churchyards, notably Mickleham, still keep their wooden grave boards, with the inscription on a long plank between two posts.

To go back to DOMESTIC ARCHITECTURE, by 1730 the English Baroque was as good as dead. Two waves of conformism

---

* Also at Thorpe † 1754 by *Sir Robert Taylor* with one of his mongol cherubs, not very nice.

and a political swing had killed it – the first wave culminating in Wanstead and Volume I of *Vitruvius Britannicus* in 1715, the second being the buildings of Lord Burlington in the 1720s. This meant at best crisp copies of Palladio and Inigo Jones, and at worst a very serviceable vernacular which nourished English provincial architecture for nearly a century. Very little of this can be seen in Surrey. The earliest building in the style, White Lodge in Richmond Park of *c*.1727, by the *Earl of Pembroke* and *Roger Morris*, shows the style at its worst in a mechanical imitation of one of Palladio–Burlington's ideas. Clandon Park was begun earlier (after 1713, finished by *c*.1730), but Clandon, by the Venetian *Leoni*, is a puzzle. The inside is one of the gayest sequences of Palladian rooms in England, done whilst the newly found crispness and classicism was still fresh, with plasterwork probably by *Artari* and carving by *Rysbrack*. But the outside has 66 four unrelated, badly composed brick façades in a more or less Baroque style. Did Leoni change his style half-way through, or was he called in to decorate an existing building? (Or did the C19 confuse the evidence, as Mr Harris has suggested?)

But after the flood of early C18 houses there is remarkably little – isolated rooms in older houses (Carshalton, Wotton); Woodcote Park at Epsom, dull and reconstructed after a fire; then a few country builders' houses, usually of plain brickwork, usually with a pediment, such as Ham Manor at Cobham, Pyrcroft at Chertsey, and Ashley House at Epsom. The 'pattern-book' medium-size Georgian house, generally two and a half storeys with central pilasters and pediment so common almost everywhere in England, is represented only by one small mansion, Puttenham Priory of 1762, stone-built and handsome, with just enough ornament for its size, and one big farmhouse, Killinghurst near Chiddingfold. It is difficult to see why: perhaps C19 rebuilding in Surrey was more savage towards these Plain Janes than towards the curly brickwork of the C17 or the early C18.

After 1760 there is more to see, and in more than one style. Palladianism, set hard, continued its weary way until in the hands of architects like Capability Brown it became merely a rather despised necessary adjunct to the landscaped park. This is the exact effect of Claremont, built by *Brown* in 1770, an astringent porticoed lump (for the interior *see* p. 57), and of *Sir William Chambers*'s Peper Harow of 1763. Lesser-known architects often did better, for instance *Kenton Couse* with the handsome stone-built Botleys, 1765, and one may perhaps also include Juniper Hill Mickleham by *John Staff* (still, incidentally, a Baroque

composition), Norbury Park, 1783 by *Sandby*, Morden Park, and
Unstead Park. The best mid-c18 house in Surrey is also, very
67 loosely, Palladian: *Sir Robert Taylor*'s Asgill House at Richmond of 1760 is basically a Late Palladian villa, superbly executed
but with enormous plain eaves instead of the customary cornice
and balustrade, which give it an oddly Regency look. Either
Taylor or one of his assistants* deserves to be better known as a
first-rate artist as well as a successful business man.

The first reaction to this is represented by the Adam style,
primarily a matter of interior decoration using light and elegant
geometrical patterns. *Adam* himself is represented by his earliest
known decorative scheme, at Hatchlands, a plain, newly-built
brick house for Admiral Boscawen. It was done in 1756-9, just
after Adam's return from Italy, and it shows him still unsure of
himself, unwilling to let his pretty arabesques, based on Quattrocento *grottesche* and on remains from Etruscan tombs, fill the
56 whole space. Adam's other Surrey interiors, in The Oaks Carshalton, have now gone, and there is not much else in the style –
a very pretty single room at Juniper Hall, probably by an amateur,
Lady Templeton, and hence freshly designed, the lovely painted
room at Norbury Park of *c.* 1775, designed by *Sandby* to match
the outward views over the landscape, and the straightforward
handsome interior of Waverley, also of *c.*1775, where the planning
and relationships of rooms is of more interest than the decoration. The style did not transplant very well to the outsides of
buildings, whether done by Adam or his imitators, because in
effect it meant applying fancy dress where it stood least chance of
being effective. This is exactly the effect given by the queer,
rough exterior of Waverley, where the marks of the Adam style –
the plaster ovals and swags, and elegant string-courses – are
spread with evident impatience over a staccato, still Palladian
composition.

Better results were obtained by trying to revive Palladian
detail with a new delicacy and lightness of touch, the effect often
obtained by *Robert Mylne*. As it happens, Surrey has one of
Mylne's most handsome villas, The Wick at Richmond of 1775.
Wandle House at Mitcham is so similar that it is probably his
also.‡ The style was particularly happy in the hands of thoughtful
local masons, e.g. in Browne's Lodge of 1786 at Reigate and
especially in the set of late c18 houses at Farnham, brilliantly

* Perhaps the latter, because Taylor's other house in Surrey – Thorncroft,
at Leatherhead – is negligible.
‡ Addington Palace is also by *Mylne* but has been terribly altered.

combining delicacy and crispness. These houses are almost always brick, but occasionally quite circumstantial symmetrical designs were carried out in the homely weatherboarding, and hence look very like New England. There is one in West Street, Dorking, and another at Ashtead.

The style which eventually won the day was inspired first by Imperial Rome at its heaviest and then by Greece. It is called generally NEO-CLASSICAL. In Surrey there is very little of it, and that mostly in interiors – first of all in Claremont, where *Henry Holland* and possibly *Soane* provided an up-to-date interior for a conservative carcase. The effect there is grand and heartless, and smaller examples like the elegant stair-well at Moor Park are much more appealing. The only wholly Neo-Classical house in Surrey, and from the outside an extremely ugly one, is Ashtead Park, 1790 by *Bonomi*. Here the circular saloon has both scale and feeling. Pure Greek-Revival architecture of this date is, oddly enough, very hard to find in Surrey. The best examples are both by *James Wyatt*, the lodges at Ottershaw of *c*.1795, and the parts of the Military Academy at Camberley of 1810 that are on the Surrey side of the border.

By 1780, however, Roman-derived architecture had begun to be only one possibility among many. A diverse and seductive set of alternatives was available under the loose heading of GOTHICK or MEDIEVAL REVIVAL. And in this, Surrey is one of the most important of English counties, at least historically. The story can be taken back possibly even to Abbot's Hospital Guildford, and certainly to the Belvedere which *Vanbrugh* erected about 1720 in the grounds of his house at Claremont. This is a kind of miniature keep with four corner towers, and corresponds exactly to the intense masculinity which Vanbrugh admired in Gothic buildings, and which made all his classical houses tend to look like castles. The next stage in reviving a medieval style – or what was thought to be a medieval style – was put up within a mile of Claremont, and was invented by somebody apparently completely opposed to Vanbrugh's other architectural ideas. *William Kent* is known chiefly as Lord Burlington's faithful disciple, and was incidentally a decorator and landscaper of genius. In fact, in many ways he and Vanbrugh thought alike, although the results looked so different, and the medieval revival was part of this common ground. Kent invented C18 Gothic as we know it, an affair of incorrect ornament incorrectly applied. At worst this was jolly: at best it could be splendidly witty, and this is what Kent made it, mixing classical and Gothic details to a point which

makes the job of disentangling them from the design rather like
unravelling a skein of wool. In Surrey he had designed his
remodelling of the medieval palace Esher Place by 1733. The
58 wings have gone, but the gatehouse remains, surrounded by its
spiritual descendants, suburban villas. At Kew Gardens all his
work has gone* – it included a Gothick Merlin's Cave made up of
bark. At Woburn Park near Addlestone there was a complete set
of landscape ornaments and a primitive landscape park, all now
demolished or spoilt.

90   What Kent did as a *jeu d'esprit*, *Batty Langley* tried to translate
into rules and orders, in his many pattern books of the 1740s.
The temple at Painshill, a flimsy octagon of plaster and wood,
open on all sides, shows the influence of these. Painshill had one
of the best of all these landscaped gardens – really a very
sophisticated kind of joke. It survived intact until the war. At
Wimbledon there is a Gothic House of 1763, at Leith Hill a tower
of 1764 and 1788 with a rather more restrained approach to
medieval building, equivalent to what was being done by Sander-
son Miller in other parts of the country. And in The Oaks
Carshalton, now demolished, *Adam* (or somebody adapting his
designs) produced *c*.1775 a very gauche mixture of classical and
Gothic, a foretaste in quality and ineptness of the serious Gothic
houses of the C19.

The question then became: why stop at Gothick? The door
had been opened in fun to the labyrinth which the C19 and C20
explored so earnestly. Chinese architecture was introduced, most
improperly, by the strictest of academicians, *Sir William
Chambers*, and Surrey has the most famous Chinese building of
59 all, the Pagoda at Kew of 1761. This makes a foil to the classical
Orangery and Observatory, and was originally accompanied by
a Mosque and Alhambra.

All these buildings were designed more for ornament than for
use. They come under the heading of FOLLIES and follies
deserve a very special place in Surrey. As Barbara Jones has said,
it was a splendid folly county, with every kind of curious object
being put up in parks and gardens. There are enough of them to
suggest that they were put up not so much as a mark of eccentri-
city as because they were part of a fashion to be followed by
men-about-town, the sort of men who to be able to stay about
town would buy an estate close by: one more kind of suburbanization. Horace Walpole set up a house near Twickenham in

* But Kew Palace still has his mock-Jacobean work of the 1730s, similar to
that in Hampton Court.

Middlesex, and many of his imitators must have done the same in Surrey. Follies are flimsy things, and the pattern of Surrey has always been rootless and get-rich-quick – hence get-poor-quick also, hence a quick turnover of estates, so that a lot of them have gone. But a fine selection remains. As well as those noted there are mock ruins at Mitcham (early C19), a tower at Caterham, a complete set of small buildings at Busbridge, a cruciform Gothick dairy by *Wyatt* at Ottershaw (now demolished), a grandly crazy circular house of tree trunks at Hersham, and one of the best architectural jokes in England, the tiny temple of 1765 61 that did duty as Gatton Town Hall when elections were held there for the pocket borough. Until the war, Surrey had two of the best grottoes in England, at Painshill, now, sadly, fallen in, and at Oatlands, now, incredibly, blown up by the Ministry of Works.

Nor did construction stop in the C18. At Clandon the *Inwoods* built a pure classical temple in 1838, at Oxenford *Pugin* built or arranged a sham ruin in the early 1840s. The impulse has never died, whether it be in patchwork houses of salvaged fragments (Mortlake), half-timbered carillons (Windlesham), or a genuine Maori meeting house (Clandon again). Present-day controls are hardly the best climate for follies, but they will undoubtedly go on being built, and the very best of luck to them.

It may be only coincidence, but whilst follies were multiplying, CHURCH BUILDING in the C18 in Surrey had almost stopped. There is one big, dull Palladian town church (Holy Trinity Guildford, 1749 by *James Horne*), and one small and sweet late C18 village-church rebuilding (Pirbright, 1784), and there are parts of Kew (1710 and 1770) and Richmond (1750), and Shepperton (1710) and Sunbury (1752) – the last two formerly in Middlesex – much altered and added to. Mostly the old town and village churches became steadily more dilapidated, more of a patchwork, and more attractive, until the whole lot was tidied up and regularized in the C19 – nowhere more thoroughly than in Surrey. In the early C19 there was a little more activity. Egham church of 1817 by *Henry Rhodes* is a complete but very bad-tempered and not very competent interpretation of Neo-Classical ideas, a true counterpart to Ashtead Park. There are also one or two grisly stock-brick churches in the minimum Gothic style called Commissioners' Gothic, mostly connected with various small-scale new settlements all over the county. In some other counties the style had spirit and swagger, but not here. Virginia Water, 1831 by *Pocock*, and Mitcham, 1819 by *George Smith*, are the best. Others, sometimes very horrible, are at Frimley, Chertsey, Addlestone, and Epsom. However, Gatton, rebuilt in 68 the 1830s, is a *bijou*, perhaps the best example in the country of the tendency for the church to become an extension of the landlord's parlour or sculpture gallery. As well as all the imported woodwork there is at Gatton a pew with tables, chairs, padded benches, and fireplace, with a completely separate covered way linking it to the house. .

There is not much pre-Gothic-Revival NONCONFORMIST ARCHITECTURE worth notice: one grandiose chapel at Dorking of 1834, purely mid-C19 in spirit, the astonishingly unspoilt Providence Chapel at Charlwood, one of Surrey's nicest surprises, and the showy Perp-style Irvingite church of 1840 at Albury, which is good fun if not good architecture and which was designed by *McIntosh Brooks*, assisted by *Pugin*, which takes us into the next building period again.

C18 CHURCH FURNISHINGS are equally meagre: a reredos at 62 Carshalton, pulpits at Morden and Petersham (the latter unusual, in a delicate almost Chippendale style), fittings generally at Egham. The dearth here is astonishing, and not explained altogether by sweeping C19 restoration. None of the other Home Counties is so poor.

What again is odd – and as the reader will by now have realized, Surrey architectural history is a long series of paradoxes – is that there is quite a lot of C17 and C18 INDUSTRIAL ARCHITECTURE – not in the Shropshire or Yorkshire sense of grim early mills, but to do with the gently mechanized agriculture of South-East England. First, windmills. Surrey has one of the oldest in the country – incredibly it is still used as a windmill – at Outwood, dated 1665. It is a post mill, i.e. built up with a single central trunk around which the whole of the mill chamber revolves – which makes the survival even more unlikely. The usual later mills were tower mills, where only the cap revolved and the remainder was a solid structure, either of brick (Shirley and Wray Common, Reigate; the latter more circumstantial than most mills, with a classical doorcase) or weatherboarded (the twin mill at Outwood Common, which has now collapsed, and was built as late as *c*.1870). There are also several watermills, and these come in as many vernacular materials as were to hand: normally 8 weatherboarding (Haxted, Newark Mill at Pyrford – the best of the Surrey mills, now, alas, destroyed), but also tile-hanging (Shalford) and brick (Elstead – a delightful ensemble with millowner's house and rustic cupola perched on the mill shed).

Guildford has also a pre-c19 weatherboarded crane on the riverside. This kind of happy, humane, direct manner of industrial designing never really stopped, and it eventually became part of modern architecture; the impressive flour mills at Addlestone, of 1901 and 1906, could, except for a few details, be mistaken for early c19 buildings. Surrey has also several c18 bridges, including a rough set by *Gwilt*, the county surveyor (Cobham, Leatherhead), and two by *James Paine*, who had an estate in Surrey. They are at Chertsey (1780–5, altered), and Richmond (with *Kenton Couse*; 1774), one of the best c18 bridges in England, given full Palladian dress, with a splendid springing rhythm of increasing arches towards the centre.

DOMESTIC ARCHITECTURE has been taken up to 1800. At that time, and especially in Surrey, it offered a splendid variety of styles, but the total effect was mean, unhealthy, and unsatisfactory: the situation of the 1920s and 1930s, except that the early c19 architects were professionally much more competent and were at least working at the end of a genuine tradition, not at the end of an artificially warmed-up one. Straightforward classical design is almost absent. The nearest thing to it were some parts of Deepdene, Dorking, of *c*.1818, all now demolished. Here the 69 dilettante owner, *Thomas Hope*, built in a smooth, large-scale style nearer what was going on in contemporary Paris (and also contemporary Boston or New York, incidentally, in their 'Federal Style') than anything else. Stucco Gothick at its most gimcrack is represented by the present Nonesuch House (1802, *Wyatville*) and the slightly better Ewell Castle (1810, *Henry Kitchen*), Tudor by the first parts of East Horsley Towers (1829, *Barry* – it must have been almost his first Tudor building) and by a really despicable *Basevi* house, Fox Hills near Chertsey. The coming Italian style appeared first, appropriately enough, as dress for asymmetrically planned villas – Southborough House Surbiton, 1808 by *Nash*, is small and plain, but Mount Felix, Walton-on-Thames, 1837 by *Barry*, now demolished, was much bigger and grander. Some of the detail here was as fine and as sincere as his Pall Mall clubhouses. But the best achievements are in the comfortable yet gay style not usually associated with the big architectural names and for which there is no better word than REGENCY. It uses smooth stucco, often with balconies and trellis work, and always with complete freedom from pomposity. Godalming Market Hall of 1814 by a local man, *John Perry*, is a perfect example. Nearly as good are the riverside buildings at Barnes and Mortlake and the very Colonial-looking Bridge Hotel at Chertsey. These really belong to the same family as the many small stucco or weatherboarded boxes which began to appear on the main roads from London – the first sign inside the present county boundaries of urban population as a whole on the move outwards.

To this rather stale architectural climate the full-blown GOTHIC REVIVAL – Pugin's 'Gothic is Christian architecture' – can only have come as a relief. At least and at last architecture was going somewhere definite, even if the direction were dubious. *Pugin* cannot be kept out of the architectural history of any county, but he has already been mentioned as a folly builder, or at least a ruin-arranger, which is not what one would expect from the fiery denouncer of shallow Regency taste. For the same land-owner at the same time, at Peper Harow in 1844, he did more: he built simultaneously in exuberant Late Norman* and in rich Early Gothic to give the impression – a sophisticated, Regency impression – of a slow-growth medieval church. So here is the prophet not practising what he preaches. The enjoyment of this is a recherché pleasure and typical of Surrey.

Pugin's more serious style can be seen in the remodelled transept of 1839 at Albury; high, soaring, gilded and stencilled, very nearly successful. And at Oxenford, next to the sham ruins, he built a tithe barn and gatehouse which are a complete vindica-tion of his ideas and his ability. Here he was thinking in Gothic, as Morris and Philip Webb were to do, building angular pointed buildings for an angular pointed age, saying the same thing as the engineers: that form and function are indivisible. Surrey has no railway architecture to exemplify this, but it has got the Palm 70 House at Kew, the most daring of all the experiments with glass and iron, a splendid double-curved envelope, anticipating aircraft hangars by a century. The designer was nominally *Decimus Burton*, but in fact the idea is due to the engineer *Richard Turner*. This was and is a very typical situation, and probably explains the uneven quality of the other mid-c19 Burton buildings at Kew.

However, the immediate future belonged to Pugin the ardent churchman rather than Pugin the true if wayward exponent of real architecture. In Surrey his example let loose a flood of

---

* There are several other Neo-Norman churches in the county, typical of the 1830s and 40s. They start early with *P. F. Robinson*'s restoration at Mickleham (1824), then come an outstandingly good central tower at Ewhurst by *Ebbels* (1838), Claygate (1840 by *Kendall*), Albury Weston Street (1842 by *McIntosh Brooks*), and a wild church at Hale by the normally timid *Ferrey* (1844). There is also one Italian Romanesque church – a Catholic one – at Kingston, by *Charles Parker*, 1846-7.

churches, first by his pupil and biographer *Benjamin Ferrey* (Shalford 1846, spindly; Brockham 1846, solider and more sober; 5 Kingswood 1848, a disarming replica of medieval Shottesbrook in Berkshire; Esher 1853, too rich and too hard) and then by almost every other important architect. The architects, alas, are often more important than the churches, though they have created an image of the Victorian village church in their own right – the original Surrey vernacular made more spiky and excitable. *Scott* did this at Westcott in 1852, *Messrs Francis* did it at Lyne in 1849 – a Gilbert Scott church almost before Scott had thought of it himself – *Pearson* built an early and vapid church at Weybridge in 1848. But the most prolific church builder in Surrey was *Henry Woodyer*, who was a pupil of Butterfield and practised in the county from 1846 onwards. From Butterfield he took, not the hardness and integrity of thought, but rather the will (and some of the Butterfieldian means) to create an overall emotional effect. He used Butterfield's vocabulary to serve Pugin's ends. Surrey has most of his best churches: St Martha Chilworth of 1848, a rebuilding of a ruin, solid Romanesque; York Town Camberley of 1851, big and picturesque, splendidly sited amongst pine trees – the image of John Betjeman's Surrey; Buckland of 1860, a disarming and delightful village church; Hascombe of 1864, 73 another village church with one of the best High Victorian interiors in the country combined with an austere closely-reasoned exterior; and Dorking of 1868, his biggest church, 72 where sheer sincerity made a noble and convincing space out of a conventional 'Middle Pointed' interior. There are several more Woodyer churches and many more Woodyer restorations without these virtues, and of course the other side of the coin to all this activity is that the lightly restored churches of Surrey can be counted on the fingers and toes. As the C19 left Surrey richer in Gothic Revival churches than almost any other county, perhaps the result was worth it.

Butterfield himself built only two churches in Surrey. The See p. 595 Guards Chapel at Caterham of 1886 is late, hard, and unexpectedly good for its date. But most of his artistic invention had burnt out in the 1860s, and this is shown only too clearly in his St Michael Weybridge of 1874. The wave of harshly detailed, multicoloured churches which his first buildings inspired is reflected directly in Surrey only in *Sir Arthur Blomfield*'s honest St Andrew Surbiton of 1871, far better than anything he built later, and in a polychrome church by the adaptable *Scott* at Ottershaw (1864). But indirectly it operated in two ways. About

1860 most churches became harder and crisper, less insipid. If the architect had something to say, this was a good thing; if not, it simply showed up his faults more clearly. *Scott* did his usual competent job at St Matthias Richmond (1858) and a good deal better at Ranmore Common (1859) and at Shackleford (1865). Busbridge (1865) is a good church probably by *G. G. Scott Jun.* *Pearson* built Titsey (1861) in an ugly, chunky style typical of him in the 1860s, *Bodley* did a nice atmospheric village church at Valley End, Windlesham (1867), *Burges* was oddly subdued at Outwood (1869)* and completely irrepressible at Lowfield Heath 74 (1867), where his combination of a rose window and a lean-to W loggia would convert anyone to liking Victorian architecture. *Street* built and paid for Holmbury St Mary (1879), one of his last churches, which has all the right intentions but is stillborn for lack of feeling – a comment one could make of the Law Courts also. There were so many big names a-building that lesser-known people hardly got a look in: Seale of 1861 is a shaggily picturesque building by one *J. Croft*. The work of the extremists, who replaced Butterfield's originality in the name of emotional and decorative integrity by originality for its own sake, is represented in only two churches, both by *E. B. Lamb*: Englefield Green of 1859, where the oddities are semi-repressed and keep popping up inside a conventional framework, and Addiscombe of 1868, one of the wildest of all Gothic Revival churches, with a kind of Greek-cross plan and the walls subordinated to an enormously ornate timber roof. Lamb, had he been born later, would clearly have made a superb Art Nouveau architect – a case of the man and the style missing one another by a few years.

The later C19 has less to show. *Pearson* built two very good churches in his late style, impeccably detailed and beautifully proportioned, yet still full of feeling: a carefully circumscribed perfection if you like, but a perfectly legitimate one. Both are tall, apsed, and vaulted. St John Upper Norwood of 1878 is in stock 75 brick and stone. St Michael Croydon, designed in 1875–6, in red brick and stone, is one of his very best churches, with a tiny ambulatory around the E end, and a S chapel which is a complete, separately-vaulted church within a church, a spatial toy worthy of Soane. One of his last churches, St John Redhill of 1889–95, seems to show him impatient with this, trying to break through to a stronger, simpler way of expression, with colossal transverse stone bows barging across his customarily pious 'spatial vessel'.

* With an impressive tower almost without period detail, by *Manning*, 1876.

Nothing else comes up to this, and the lesser churches became smaller and genteel as they tried to capture a Surrey flavour consciously. West Byfleet, 1912 by *Caröe*, and St Christopher Haslemere, 1902 by *Spooner*, are about the best. In fact the very end of the Gothic Revival produced more than the late C19, principally the school chapel at Charterhouse, 1922 by *Sir Giles Gilbert Scott*, with a typical C20 eclectic's muddle outside but unexpectedly fine and coherent inside, soaring in the Liverpool Cathedral way. *Sir Herbert Baker* did a coy church at Woldingham (1933), *Sir Ninian Comper* did an alas rather tawdry refitting of Carshalton (1936–46), and *Sir Edward Maufe* designed the just completed cathedral at Guildford, begun in 1936, with again a rather mealy-mouthed exterior but a cool interior of real spatial imagination, something which shows in almost every interior Maufe has built. That he chooses to cover this in various stylistic fancy dresses cannot obscure this ability, evident also in his Romanesque church at Weston Green (1939), and his Neo-Georgian Runnymede memorial (1953).

We are still not finished with C19 churches – the C19 in Surrey has almost more of interest than all the other centuries put together. Odd buildings in odd styles need to be gathered up like a rag-bag: Islamic, in the Mosque at Woking by *W. I. Chambers*, 1889, sincere and dignified, not tawdry, as it could so easily have been; nightmare Romanesque, in the now disused church at Petersham by *Kelly*, 1907–8; Celtic crossed with Art Nouveau, in the Watts Memorial Chapel at Compton of 1896–1901, most of the design by *Mrs Watts*, a brave failure; what can only be compared to early Frank Lloyd Wright in St Thomas Chilworth, built as the Greshambury Institute by *Seth-Smith*, 1896; and, finally, the extraordinary church built by *Sidney Barnsley* in 1891 at Lower Kingswood – as extraordinary as its Byzantine contents – where the architect cut through the Gordian 9 knot of styles and simply produced style. This is a fresh, un-affected, and extremely religious-feeling building which cannot be pigeon-holed, only appreciated.

Along with this prodigious list of churches, there is a lot of CHURCH FURNITURE worth notice. The Victorian rebuildings usually have the rich, bulgy fonts and pulpits, often in marble, which in Surrey at least are underrated; they are as legitimate and often as original a contribution as the C18 box pews or the C15 screen. For pulpits, particularly, Betchworth; for fonts, Haslemere, Capel, Ranmore Common (very rich and splendid), Oakwood, and the startling font cover at St Nicholas Guildford.

William Morris's firm is usually associated with stained glass but
77 did decoration also, and the organ at Beddington of 1869 is one
of the best examples we have of this. Stained glass worth notice*
is, in the bright hard 1860s style, at Titsey (*Clayton & Bell*),
Hascombe (*Hardman*), and Lowfield Heath; in the softer, more
sinuous Pre-Raphaelite style at Cobham, at Stoke-next Guildford,
and by *Morris & Co.* at Nutfield and Busbridge. Busbridge has
the most striking late C19 church fitting, the metal rood screen
filling the chancel arch, designed by *Lutyens* and *Starkie Gardner*.
Magnificent at a distance, it is a little spoilt close to by being too
sugary. St Peter, Staines (formerly Middlesex), has impressive late
C19 fittings by *Fellowes Prynne*. And, finally, there are typical
Victorian monuments at Peper Harow (*Weekes* † 1836), Titsey
(*Matthew Noble* † 1872 and *Brock* † 1895), and Limpsfield (again
by *Matthew Noble* † 1860). The eerie Waterlow monument
76 † 1869 in Reigate churchyard makes a compelling composition
out of Victorian urns and angels which, taken separately, would
not be remarkable; and there are several good Art Nouveau
tombstones in the cemetery at Compton.

Public and domestic architecture had been left in the doldrums
of the 1830s. As far as quality is concerned they stayed there for
thirty years. But the quantity and variety multiplied. This is
particularly true of PUBLIC BUILDINGS, which in Surrey became the handmaiden of an expanding London with a newly
awakened civic and social conscience. Almost a dozen lunatic
asylums, a vast Necropolis (at Brookwood, 1854; it was well laid
out by *Sydney Smirke* and *Sir William Tite* and it now looks
like a garden suburb with all the houses become mausolea),
then later the removed Charterhouse School of 1872, Holloway
College of 1879, and the Holloway Sanatorium of 1884. The
80 lunatic asylums need no comment. Charterhouse was an extremely
good example by *P. C. Hardwick* of a fairly common type –
'Collegiate Gothic'; i.e. gothic details pulled and stretched to
form a fair working compromise with the C19. But there is
nothing common or routine about the two buildings erected for
Holloway, the patent-medicine millionaire and philanthropist.
78 The College (at Egham) is French Renaissance, the Sanatorium
79 (at Virginia Water) is Flemish Late Gothic. Both were designed
with tremendous success and gusto by *W. H. Crossland*, a North-
Country architect; both are nearer in spirit to continental

---

* The E window at Farnham was designed by *Pugin* for the 1851 Exhibition but is very poor.

Baroque palaces than anything else, The only other buildings worth notice here are a decent Italianate Town Hall put up at Chertsey in 1851 by *George Briand*, and a rather improper Italianate Town Hall, now Market House, at Kingston upon Thames, 1838 by *Charles Henman Senior*. Later in the century, in 1892–6, his son put up the big Jacobean group of Croydon Town Hall, mechanically detailed but excellently composed.

This leaves C19 DOMESTIC ARCHITECTURE, the most important part of the Surrey story. No history of the subject could be written without mentioning some of these buildings, and quite a coherent history could be written without mentioning anything else. The tale starts off quietly enough in the 1840s and 1850s, with Regency skittishness having settled down into a choice of two or three applied styles all treated with equal vapidity. The best was probably the straightforward ponderous continuation of Georgian ideas, e.g. at Silverlands near Chertsey, architect unknown. Until recently, more fancy Italianate was represented by the big additions to Deepdene, and by the house *Cubitt*, the famous builder, put up at Ranmore Common across the valley, in deliberate rivalry to Deepdene. The other alternative was Gothic-Jacobean-Tudor, which all tended to look the same. In Surrey this was begun very poorly by *Pugin* at Albury in 1846, and continued in the 1850s and 1860s in a sudden spurt of building which is very typical. Surrey heathland scenery, after years of unpopularity (Cobbett) or rather timid approval, suddenly became the ideal of the mid-Victorians, perhaps because of its convenient resemblance to the Scots Highlands. All at once a crop of houses sprang up – and sprang up largely on new sites, which is not at all typical of the pattern in the rest of England. A list will do for most of them: Pippbrook (now the Council Offices) at Dorking by *Scott*, 1856, Lythe Hill by *F. P. Cockerell*, Greathed Manor near Lingfield by *Kerr*, 1868, very See p. 595 wild, Foxwarren Park by *Frederick Barnes*, 1860, even wilder, with a Model Farm which is a true Struwelpeter mid-Victorian 71 nightmare. The style persisted into the 1870s and 1880s – e.g. in Nutfield Priory by *Gibson*, 1872, in Bagshot Park by *Ferrey*, 1877, Marden Park at Woldingham, and Cobham Park and Shabden by *E. M. Barry*. Even a progressive firm like *George & Peto*, when building Woolpit, Ewhurst, for a Doulton in 1888, produced a design so loaded with encaustic tiles that it must be mentioned in this section. Few of these are worth looking at, but they can no more be ignored even in this Introduction than they can be ignored on going about the county: no firry hill but has an elephantine pile on or near it. The activities of Lord Lovelace, tinkering with his country seat at East Horsley Towers from 1855 onwards in a wild goulash of Continental Gothic, come as a welcome relief. If for nothing else, East Horsley is worth a visit for the crazy melodrama of its entrance approach.

Better things were on the way. The first sign was a coltish house of 1860 by the young *Philip Webb* at Fairmile near Cobham (his second house; his first was the famous Red House for William Morris). This applied to domestic design the integrity and fitness-for-purpose which Butterfield was creating in his early churches. Nothing was facile or mechanical, everything was sincere, thought out, tailored to the individual building: the qualities which the functionalists of the 1920s and 30s preached so loudly and practised so little. The style Webb used was a simplified, spare Gothic, rather like the back and sides of an industrial church (he was in Street's office at the time), and the result is original, praiseworthy, and a historical landmark – but not architecture. It has got to be said that Webb often simply could not give his volumes and spaces body and conviction. His houses all seem to be brilliant two-dimensional sketches waiting to be realized. He built several more in Surrey – Coneyhurst near Ewhurst (1886), Willinghurst near Cranleigh (1887), Upwood Gorse at Caterham (1873 onwards), Hurlands at Puttenham (1898; his last house) – and they all share this lack of solidity.

What was much more important at the time, however, was the so-called QUEEN ANNE REVIVAL. It was another style revival, but it was done sincerely and without dogma, and, most important, it exactly suited the progressives of the generation after the 1851 Exhibition, who needed a reaction from ornateness, from ostentation, and from the pointed arch. It fitted the needs so well that, although it began with near-symmetrical designs bearing some relation to Queen Anne prototypes, tile-hanging and asymmetry ran away with it to make a style in its own right. (In America, wood shingles and asymmetry did the same in the same years. In genesis they seem to be almost independent.)

The style has always been associated with *Norman Shaw*, who certainly popularized it and broadcast it over most of the counties of England. But he probably did not invent it. The first appearance in Surrey is in a tiny and very circumstantial lodge at Kew – all roof and chimney, no walls – by *Eden Nesfield*, as early as 1866. Nesfield was Shaw's partner at this time, and designed other buildings in a rich, brick classical style (Kinmel Park in North

Wales, e.g.), whilst Shaw was designing bulky hulks of brick and half-timber until the 1870s. Surrey can show Shaw's complete development, from Hopedene (Holmbury St Mary) of 1873, one of his best early houses, built with an eye to the masses rather than to surface decoration, through Pierrepont of 1876 and Merrist Wood (Worplesdon) of 1877, each with some half-timber and some tile-hanging – the first too ostentatious, the second a very happy mixture* – and then to Alderbrook (Cranleigh) of 1881, now demolished, which was largely tile-hung but still gauche and rather unfeeling, Shaw's besetting fault. Later in the 1880s come the pretty tile-hung houses which are the mind's-eye image of the Norman-Shaw house. For adaptability and humanity without loss of scale, they have probably never been equalled. Surrey has two, and both are delightful: Banstead 81 Wood of 1884 and Burrows Cross (Shere) of 1886. The style could become a cliché, as Shaw's own houses on the Portsmouth Road at Guildford show; and in his last Surrey house, The Hallams (Wonersh) of 1894, he reverted oddly enough to his old hard, thick way of designing in the 1870s.

Nine Shaw houses have been mentioned – a startling indicator of how much building, and of what quality, was going on in this small county. The style, once created, was imitated times without number. One of the earliest and prettiest examples is the Onslow Almshouses at Guildford of 1879 by *George & Peto*. Sometimes the imitations were as good as the real thing. Pickhurst at Chiddingfold, by *Brydon*, whose buildings are always worth looking at, is a splendid house; Broomells (Capel) by *J. H. Wadling* is as good as Shaw, and so is Woodhambury (Woodham) by *W. F. Unsworth*.

Shaw was father to Lutyens and stepfather to Voysey, and both did their best work in Surrey in the 1890s. But first, odds and ends of other styles need to be tidied up. *J. F. Bentley* of Westminster Cathedral built St John's School Englefield Green in French Renaissance, and Derry's Hill Wonersh in an odd, stilted classical style that seems to be fumbling towards Art Nouveau. Neither of them are good buildings. *Robinson & Duchêne* built a vast château at Esher Place (1895) in a thoroughgoing but lifeless way reminiscent of the Rothschild houses. And last but certainly not least is the superb portico wrapped round

---

* Pickard's Rough (Guildford) was a very good house of 1878 in this mixed style, but it has been altered. Incidentally, *G. E. Street*'s own house of 1873 at Holmbury St Mary, though with more overt Gothic details, has the same feeling and is as good as Shaw.

82 Gatton Park in 1891. The detail is purest Corinthian, done with impeccable taste and with feeling and sensitivity too – no mechanical reproduction here. It is one of the very finest monuments of the Classical Revival in England, and it is, indisputably, sixty years out of context.

With *Lutyens* we return to being historically up-to-the-minute. He was brought up at Thursley, and most of his early jobs were in Surrey. In 1890, when he was only twenty-one, he built Crooksbury in a very accomplished tile-hung Norman Shaw style, softer and sweeter than Shaw himself ever built. The early nineties show several houses seeking out a style (e.g. Munstead Place of 1891, Chinthurst Hill Wonersh of 1893). Then suddenly, about 1895, the numbers on the combination lock clicked and he produced half a dozen masterpieces, free Tudor freely arranged, with utter mastery of volume and spatial effects and of surface textures (mixed with occasional extreme gaucheness, such as the materials used at Goddards Abinger of 1898. The genius and the charlatan were very close together in Lutyens). The houses immediately made their mark and have not been decried since, in all the critical hurly-burly of the last fifty years. In Surrey there is first Munstead Wood, 1896, for Gertrude Jekyll, the landscape gardener who acted as a patron, and who designed gardens which complement Lutyens's houses perfectly. Then comes the reconstruction of part of Crooksbury called Fig Tree Court, of 1898, a lovely job, Fulbrook near Elstead of 1896, an uneven house with 85 a marvellous lodge, and the best pair of all, Orchards, Munstead 86 of 1897, and Tigbourne Court near Witley, of 1899. They are tremendously personal houses. Although often imitated, the Lutyens *cachet* is unmistakable, once seen, and almost unique in architecture in being feminine but not effeminate, as personal as the series of houses Frank Lloyd Wright was building in the same years. The difference between them is that Wright was at the beginning of a living style, Lutyens near the end of a second-hand one. Style was a toy, to be changed at will, and unhappily Lutyens was enough of a child to want a frequent change of toys. At Crooksbury in 1898 he designed the first of his classical façades, straightforward Neo-Georgian, but he replaced it in 1914 by a pastiche of his Tudor style. After 1900 his buildings were almost all classical, first gay and pretty (Amesbury School Hindhead of 1903, Millmead at Bramley of 1904), then becoming progressively heavier and drearier. But Lutyens was not really to blame for the Neo-Georgian style, although his change of heart must have given it a tremendous fillip. In Surrey the responsibility falls more squarely on the shoulders of *Ernest Newton*,[*] whose Red Court at Haslemere of 1894 has all the succeeding decades of sterility implicit in its purse-mouthed exactness. Newton built several more houses in Surrey, but only Ardenrun Place Crowhurst is worth a look, and that for fortuitous reasons – that it was burnt and almost demolished, leaving only fragments as mysterious as a Vanbrugh ruin.

Meanwhile another architect had been producing houses in Surrey which the whole world was looking at. (This is no exaggeration. For a few years, around 1896–1900, Britain was leading the world in finding a way out of the impasse of style revivals, and Surrey was leading Britain.) *C. F. A. Voysey*, with much greater artistic integrity than Lutyens, but less talent, had evolved an equally personal architecture of long, low roofs, low-toned materials – slate and roughcast, usually – and ground-hugging outlines. It corresponded to the deliberately rustic and cottagey work of the Art and Crafts at that time, and could be summed up as the reaction of a generation becoming sick of unfeeling architectural expertise. Voysey houses are the same everywhere – this can be a serious failing – and his style did not alter much throughout his life, so that the Surrey buildings can be listed all together: Lowicks near Frensham (1894), Greyfriars at Puttenham (1896), New Place Haslemere and Norney Shackleford (both 1897), Prior's Field Puttenham (1900), and Vodin Pyrford (1902). 87 Undoubtedly the small, simple houses are best, e.g. Lowicks, Vodin, and especially Greyfriars, all designs which are really burying themselves in the landscape so that the result is an amalgam of man and nature. When Voysey tried more formal extended compositions (Norney) the results are very solid, very honest, but curiously unpleasant. In a way, all his life he was building out a shepherd's cottage in the Lake District.

Some of his co-builders did have Surrey in mind, however. *Alfred Powell* had built in local terms something as simple as Voysey at Long Copse Ewhurst in 1897. *H. Thackeray Turner*, the first secretary of the S.P.A.B., built his own house (Westbrook at Godalming, 1900) and Mead Cottage Guildford in a style very close to Voysey – using the same elegant type of iron gutter supports, for example – but softened and built in warm local Bargate stone, and hence more attractive. And in Wycliffe Buildings, a block of flats in Guildford of 1894, he produced 83

---

[*] And of course originally on Norman Shaw himself, building houses like Chesters and Bryanston in the 1890s.

something which is quite the best of its kind in the country, beautifully adapted to an awkward wedge-shaped sloping site, with all the subtle play of gables and eaves that the LCC used a little later. Its humanity and friendliness is a model to flat designers today.

Thackeray Turner's few later buildings were stale and dull, and this is true of almost all the good domestic architects of the 1890s. But for some years the ease and vitality of the style carried along lesser architects to produce buildings that were rarely ugly or empty and sometimes approached Lutyens or Voysey. Worth a note here are buildings by *Macartney* (Sandhills Bletchingley), two rare southern houses by *Sir Robert Lorimer* (Hascombe), and several houses at Guildford by *Baillie Scott*. They all combine varying proportions of Tudor and C17 details, and also varying proportions of Voysey and Lutyens details, into an agreeable and very humane new style.*

So, in 1900, Surrey led the world. By 1914 both it and England were nowhere. Lutyens's change in style has already been recorded: most of the profession followed like sheep and turned to a genteelly accurate Neo-Georgian, starting heavy and Early Georgian, as Lutyens did (Ottershaw Park, by *Niven & Wiggles-worth*, 1910), and becoming gradually Later Georgian, lighter and emptier. Meanwhile the free-Tudor style which so nearly grew naturally into modern architecture (and would have spared us the modernistic as well as the Neo-Georgian) lost heart, lay down and died. *Baillie Scott*'s Gate House at Limpsfield of 1924 is its last gasp.‡

What is worth looking at in the early C20 is a strange assortment in which chronology ceases to matter. It was the crack-up of architecture. In the 1900s a local man, *H. R. Poulter*, did some pretty Neo-Georgian buildings in Camberley. At the same time Polesden Lacey was superbly fitted out in the Edwardian style (a living style because related to some kind of emotional need). The alterations were carried out by one of the best practitioners in the business, *Poynter*. Strangely enough, apart from this, the Edwardian Baroque style passed Surrey by: bigger sites and bigger bank-balances were needed. The crazy fairy-tale restora-

---

* Two odd churches by *Caröe* ought to put in an appearance here because they look more like parts of Lutyens houses than anything else, with details imitated wholesale. They are St Paul Camberley of 1902 and St Mary Woking of 1907, and they are not good.

‡ *Falkner*'s houses at Dippenhall, near Farnham, the last still being built in 1963, are an eccentric postscript.

tions at Crowhurst and Old Surrey Hall by *George Crawley* 88
must find a place here, living proofs that any style, if taken far
enough and sincerely enough, will produce worth-while architecture. So must, at the other extreme, the painter and art-critic
Roger Fry's house at Guildford of 1913, self-designed, with
severely classical proportions but without any classical detail – a
kind of cubist house, appropriate to the man who introduced
cubism to England. Bright lights in a dreary welter of Neo-
Georgian after the Great War are Pyrford Court, very largely
designed by its owner, the *Earl of Iveagh*, and hence fresh and
alive, the American chapel at Brookwood Cemetery by *Egerton
Swartwout* (1929), and the clever series of buildings and restorations by *Falkner* at Farnham, culminating in 1930 in the decent
Town Hall there. The transition, still fundamentally Georgian
but with the details simplified and mixed with just a little of the
romanticism of Sweden and Holland in the 1920s, is represented,
surprisingly prettily and pleasantly, by Wallington Town Hall,
1935 by *Robert Atkinson*.

Poor Surrey was doubly unlucky. Not only did its architecture
wither away, but the type of house it had made world-famous
became in a debased form the ideal of speculative house-builders
of the 1920s and 1930s, was and is visited on the county by the
thousand, and has now made almost the whole of it into a suburb.
At its cheapest it does not bear looking at; when it was carried out
with more money, enough money to give each house a comfortable
woodland setting, it created a new type of landscape which is
worth a special note here, the HIGH-CLASS SUBURB.

This way of designing is at least as old as Nash with his Park
Villages, but was not taken up until the 1900s. It means winding
roads, trees everywhere, complete informality, houses appearing
piecemeal among the scenery. It may be a specialized pleasure,
but at its best it is completely delightful. The best examples in
Surrey are the Wentworth Estate (Virginia Water), St George's 1
Hill (Weybridge), large parts of Camberley and Hindhead,
Woodcote Village (Purley), Camilla Lacey (West Humble,
Dorking), and Dormans Park (Dormansland). Such a thing
could also be done accidentally with very little money if the house
units were very small – shacks, in fact – and there were insuffici-
ent funds to provide municipal trappings (Tatsfield). These
examples, high or low, were not the same as, and do not look like,
the Garden Suburbs. In those, a whole way of life was attempted,
with shops, churches, and community buildings. Here the aim
was frankly just a luxurious environment. The only communal

estate in Surrey was Whiteley Village, built in 1914–21 by a whole chapter of architects, compactly designed around a symmetrical plan. With a little more imagination it could have been brilliant.

Finally, and not before time, MODERN ARCHITECTURE. As England had wilfully turned away from its own native modern architecture, it had to come in as a continental importation, twice as shocking as it need have been – cubist houses, bright (at first) with concrete walls and stainless steel or chromium stair-wells, done in a deliberate and necessary spirit of *épater le bourgeois*. Surrey's first modern building is the second of the famous series of houses built by *Connell, Ward & Lucas* in the 1930s – Adling (formerly New Farm) at Grayswood of 1932. It looks very dated now, in design as well as materials, but their work matured later in the thirties. The house at Wentworth, Virginia Water, of 1937, and especially the daring additions of 1936 to a Regency house at Redhill, are architecture, not architectural pyrotechnics, with a scale and intellectual content which is hard to find today. They were followed less imaginatively by *Maxwell Fry* (Miramonte Coombe, 1937) and *Raymond McGrath* (St Ann's Hill Chertsey, 1938, a famous case of the successful placing of a modern house in matured C18 grounds). Just before 90 the war, one of the best of these houses was built for himself at Claremont by *Patrick Gwynne*, keeping all the vigour and sureness of the new-born style but without any of its gaucheness. Apart from houses before 1939 there is only Sutton Baptist Church to mention, 1934 by *Cachemaille Day*, a decent extension of Gothic, and perhaps Twickenham Bridge, Richmond, by *Maxwell Ayrton*, 1933, not for itself but for its strange anticipation of the much better Waterloo Bridge.

The war caused a break of nearly ten years. After it a newly set up planning organization, combined with misguided ideas on how a building ought to harmonize with the Surrey landscape – by exterior quirks of style rather than interior harmony of design – heaped a final indignity on the county, from which it is only now recovering. Modern architects still find it more difficult to put up modern buildings in Surrey than almost anywhere else, whilst misinterpretations and malformations of traditional Surrey vernacular multiply without hindrance. As a direct result, until the 1960s the County Architect's department did not produce a single building worth mentioning in this book – a big loss when local authority work in other Home Counties is remembered. Most of the modern buildings have been houses and flats, foremost those of *Eric Lyons* at Richmond and particularly at Parkleys, Ham Common, a delightful and delightfully landscaped 92 estate whose tile-hanging makes a genuinely c20 comment on the native Surrey style. Two simple, honest housing estates are worth mention – at Warlingham (*A. W. Kenyon*) and at Weston Green (*G. B. Imrie*), both of 1948. Flats with the same quiet kind of professional self-respect have been put up on several sites in Wallington by *Pite, Son & Fairweather*, old people's homes at East Horsley by *Clifford Culpin*, 1958, very good single houses at Oxshott by *Powell & Moya*, 1955* – and in the late 1950s many more modern houses. The equivalent in public and industrial buildings is a good factory at Camberley by *John Bickerdike* (1956), extensions to Southlands College Wimbledon, 1957 by *Yorke, Rosenberg & Mardall*, and Gatwick airport by the same 91 architects, 1958, an exciting bringing together of road, rail, and air travel which, when the tall office block is built on top, will be one of Britain's architectural landmarks.

All these buildings are in either a straightforward projection of traditional forms or a crisp industrial vernacular of glass and steel. That they are all 'quiet' buildings does not mean that they are dull, incidentally: the worth of all the examples mentioned here is unlikely to burn out as some of the pyrotechnics of the 1940s have burnt out. In reaction against this quietness a thick new style grew up after 1955, a style intent on jerky rhythms, often using exposed concrete framework, often apparently wishing for more 'expression' (a dangerous thing to pursue consciously). The only examples in Surrey before 1960 are the flats at Ham Common by *Stirling & Gowan*, 1958. By comparison 93 with nearby Parkleys they look like an ideological theorem imposed on the inhabitants, and we have had enough of that in the c20 already. But the style undoubtedly has guts and plenty of potential, especially if it is humanized: in spirit it is oddly like the bloody-mindedness of some of Vanbrugh's followers, and it would be nice to see a bloody-minded style in England again. The real tragedy is that styles follow each other so quickly that none of them can be fully explored, let alone exhausted. Whether we can convert our occasional flashes of brilliance into a homogeneous style depends on the architects of Britain. What they will do is anybody's guess: what is certain is that some Surrey buildings are bound to be in the middle of the process. It is no longer the inaccessible Wealden county, by-passed north and

---

* But some violently half-timbered flats at Weybridge date from 1957 – *not*, of course, by Powell & Moya.

south by architectural lines of force. It is a garden suburb, in places a very pretty one, and as long as the whole country does not come to look like Surrey, that is a very pleasant thing for it to be.

POSTSCRIPT TO THE INTRODUCTION (1970)

The most immediately remarkable aspect of building activity in Surrey during the last ten years has been the increase in size of buildings. When the first edition was published, outside Croydon, there was hardly a single tall building in Surrey. Now, with the move of offices out of London, there are numerous towers of thirteen storeys and more, and large office blocks, supermarkets, and multistorey car parks are becoming commonplace. The best of these, architecturally, are at Sutton, where there are, to use Mr Nairn's phrases, both 'quiet' buildings, and ones with more 98 'expression' – the work of *Robert J. Wood & Partners* and *Owen Luder* respectively – as well as a delightful minor shopfront by *Michael Manser Associates*. More often, the new commercial buildings are individually undistinguished or distressingly gimmicky, and appear to have been designed with little regard either for their older surroundings or for each other. This is especially true of Croydon. Here the General Accident building of *Biscoe & Stanton* of 1961–3 is a relatively early example of the desire to avoid the rectangular shape at all costs, which has been followed by others designed in the same spirit. Pembroke House by *Vincent & Wynn* is a good representative of the quieter tradition. But whatever their merits, it is physically impossible to 97 ignore such buildings. At Croydon they add up to one of the most ruthlessly new centres in the country; here, and on a smaller scale at, for example, New Malden and Sunbury-on-Thames, they emphasize with great visual force the shift from the old centres to the new ones around the railway stations. They often form landmarks in hitherto featureless areas, as at Tolworth on the Kingston bypass, where the tower by *R. Seifert & Partners* is so far the tallest in Surrey. Tolworth also has a very large piece of road engineering. The slicing up of Surrey by huge roads is another feature of the sixties, and will be one of the seventies – one which so far has done little to improve the uncivilized traffic conditions in town and village centres (although radical schemes for pedestrian areas now exist for Woking and Guildford). Recent factories, less prominent than shopping centres and office blocks, are less self-conscious, and often better. There are good examples

at Carshalton by *B. & N. Westwood & Partners* and at Leatherhead by *Clifford, Tee & Gale* and by *Michael Manser Associates*.

But the most interesting recent buildings are the educational
and community buildings – a very different situation from that
surveyed ten years ago. The University of Surrey, by the 96
Building Design Partnership, on the slopes below Guildford
Cathedral is the most important individual scheme. Here there
is no compromising with the past – a telling contrast with the
cathedral above – nor any dallying with contemporary motifs.
The architectural details are plain, even austere. The mood is
created entirely by the close-knit grouping of deliberately simple
shapes on a dramatic site. The greatest number of educational
buildings are by the County Architect, *Raymond Ash*. The change
of approach in the County Architect's Department is one of the
most encouraging developments of the last few years. Their
buildings are now in a completely modern idiom. (There is room
only for a selection in this book.) The most memorable is the
West Surrey College of Art and Design at Farnham, a bold 94
design in plain brick, steel, and glass, rational and free from
clichés. The many gay and crisp primary schools are in a gentler
vein. They succeed equally well as focal points in new housing
estates, and in more rural settings. Among the larger recent
buildings for the community, one may mention here three
theatres, by *Robert Atkinson & Partners* at Croydon, by *Scott,
Brownrigg & Turner* at Guildford, and by *Roderick Ham* at
Leatherhead, the last two making especially good use of their
very different sites; and two excellent swimming baths, by *Arup
Associates* at Walton-on-Thames, and by *Leslie Gooday* at Rich- 95
mond. The lesser buildings such as branch libraries, youth clubs,
and community centres required by an expanding population are
also now increasingly visual as well as social assets. Recent
churches too are nearly all resolutely, and sometimes too consciously, modern. Variations on a central plan are fashionable for
all denominations. Among more successful efforts one can list
the Roman Catholic church at Horley by *J. H. Alleyn*, the
Methodist church at Woking by *E. D. Mills*, and St Mark,
Wimbledon, by *Humphrys & Hurst*.

Most of the buildings mentioned above are simply the result
of more and more people living in Surrey (a development which
has received official encouragement) and this means an enormous
quantity of new housing. The areas which have expanded most
rapidly are those around Croydon, Woking, and Camberley – all
near the Green Belt but still within easy reach of London. Staines

and Sunbury (formerly Middlesex) are now largely suburban. Further S, Horley (near Gatwick airport) and Cranleigh are growing fast. Individual housing schemes which can be singled out here are *Eric Lyons*'s imaginatively laid-out small estates at Weybridge, and two much larger and quite different developments; the attractive and spacious Parkmead estate at Cranleigh, by *Highet & Phillips*, and the high-density concrete township of Roundshaw, Beddington, on the site of Croydon airport, by *Clifford Culpin & Partners* for the London Borough of Sutton and the G.L.C. Despite all this expansion, Surrey is still a haven for the discreetly sited private house. There are interesting recent examples, to mention only a few, by *Leslie Gooday* at Weybridge, by *Patrick Gwynne* at Witley, by *Derek Lovejoy* at Woldingham, by *Leonard Manasseh* at Petersham, by *Michael Manser* at Godalming and Leatherhead, and by *Peter Womersley* at Camberley.

BUILDING MATERIALS

BY ALEC CLIFTON-TAYLOR

SURREY is not as devoid of building stones as is sometimes supposed; although not of the first quality, stone in the southern half of the county is plentiful. The geological division is along a line running ENE from Hale, close to Farnham, past the northern fringes of Guildford, Leatherhead, Epsom, and Sutton to Croydon.

N of this line are the Tertiary and Pleistocene clays, sands and gravels of the so-called London Basin. In the whole of this area, only the Bagshot Beds, with their occasional bands of pebbles, have yielded usable stone. There, in the NW of the county, the choice was twofold: and a builder in, say, the Cotswolds would not have thought much of either. Much the commoner was pudding-stone, a conglomerate composed of small flint pebbles and lumps, sometimes very crumbly, of sandstone, held together with a natural cement of iron oxide. It is one of the least attractive of English stones and one of the least durable, but it was used fairly extensively, *faute de mieux*, for the churches of this part of Surrey. The other stone was sarsens, which are also sometimes called greywethers and (as in this book) heathstone. Sarsens are boulders of grey siliceous sandstone which vary greatly in size and shape, and are found scattered about on or just below the surface of some of the heaths and downs of southern

England: in Surrey they also occur well to the E of the Bagshot Beds. But the supply was never equal to the demand. Their siliceous character made them difficult to work, and too hard for ashlar. Nevertheless they are incomparably more pleasing than pudding-stone, as can be well seen at Chobham, where the tower of the church is of sarsens and the rest mainly an inedible-looking dark brown pudding.

The southern half of the county is Cretaceous, and the Chalk line of the North Downs, continued westwards by the Hog's Back, is one of the most striking features of the Surrey landscape. Geologically and scenically, with the Chalk, the Greensand, and the clays of the Weald, this is a much more interesting area, and one in which in former times stone was quarried extensively. Reigate stone, often called Firestone, was in great demand in the Middle Ages, and not only in Surrey. Even before the Conquest ox-carts were dragging it to Westminster for Edward the Confessor's church, and in 1176 it was used for London Bridge. In the C13 and C14 it went to the priory church of St Mary Overy (now Southwark Cathedral), to both the Palace and the present Abbey of Westminster, and to Windsor. It was used at Eton in 1443, at Hampton Court in 1520, and at the Palace of Nonsuch in 1538. The quarries and mines (for much of this stone was mined) were not only at Reigate; they were at Gatton, Merstham, and all along the narrow belt at the foot of the North Downs past Bletchingley to Godstone, also in the Farnham area, where it is known as Malmstone.

All this stone, from the Upper Greensand formation, is comparatively soft, particularly when first dug out, so lends itself both to an ashlar finish and to mouldings and carvings: this proved invaluable for internal work of all kinds. Externally, however, it was by no means as good. In particular, it will not endure a smoky atmosphere. When Wren, in 1713, wrote his *Memorial* on Westminster Abbey, he recorded that 'the whole Fabrick . . . is now disfigur'd in the highest Degree'. In the country, when it has not decayed it can be attractive, for this is a light-toned stone: a sandstone so calcareous that it could with almost equal accuracy be described as a sandy limestone.

Tougher, coarser, and decidedly more durable than Reigate stone is the calcareous sandstone, stained with iron to a light tawny-brown tinge, known as Bargate. Curiously enough there is no such place as Bargate in Surrey. Sometimes, in older books, and in the first edition of this book *passim*, it is called Burgate stone, and this, it has been suggested, might indicate a connexion with Burgate House, Hambledon, which is, however, over a mile distant from the nearest deposits of the stone. There were many small quarries in the Guildford–Godalming area. Chilworth Manor, for example, is largely built of a light buff-coloured stone, akin to Bargate, from a quarry (long abandoned) only two or three fields away. Like the Reigate group, Bargate sandstone has a very long history. In the C12 it was the main stone for Guildford Castle: it was still being used on a big scale over seven centuries later by *P. C. Hardwick* for Charterhouse and in the 1890s by *Lutyens* at Munstead Wood and Tigbourne Court.

The term Carstone is applied in Surrey to irregular veins of very hard ferruginous sandstone which occur in the Lower Greensand (Folkestone Sands). St Martha on the Hill, above Chilworth, is built of it, and it is to be seen at various places between Albury and Tilford, where it was used both for the bridges and, much later, the church. It can only be employed as coarse random rubble, but it is very resistant to the weather. Small pieces set on edge were used just outside the churchyard at Farnham as a substitute for cobble paving.

A local building practice very much in evidence in the Greensand region of Surrey is the insertion into the mortar courses, while they were still soft, of tiny pieces of Carstone or, less often, chips of flint, which look like little necklaces strung round each block of masonry. This curious practice, which goes back to the Middle Ages, is known as galleting. One of the pleasing features of Tigbourne Court is the respect which the architect paid to a long Surrey tradition by the introduction of gallets.

Sandstone, in heavy slabs, was also widely used for roofing in that part of the county lying between the North Downs and the Sussex border, and not only for stone-built houses; Brewer Street Farm at Bletchingley is a beautiful example of a C15 half-timbered house still mainly roofed in this fashion. Known generically as Horsham slates, these slabs, which turn dark brown after prolonged exposure, came also from beds of hard but fissile sandstone at several other places in the Weald Clay. It is a pity that in Surrey comparatively few roofs of this kind survive, for they have a splendid presence.

No more than a passing mention need be made of the shelly limestone formerly worked in small quantities in the Weald Clay at Ewhurst, Charlwood and Outwood. This stone would take a polish and was therefore called 'marble'. Geologically it belongs to the same group as the much better known Bethersden marble of Kent and Petworth marble of Sussex. Its value was purely internal.

The North Downs are scarred with many chalk quarries, some enormous as at Betchworth and at Sutton. But the chalk was usually needed for lime, not for masonry. Chalkstone was used internally at a number of old Surrey churches, such as Banstead, Carshalton, Fetcham, and Great Bookham, as the material of the arcades, and also at places away from the chalk outcrop, such as Stoke d'Abernon, Wisley, Pyrford, Compton, and Godalming. Externally it is seldom seen, but the base of the E face of Guildford Castle keep is chalkstone; it provided most of the dressings at Loseley, and here and there, as at Merstham, it furnished the infilling for timber-framed houses. In the context of building materials, however, the chief importance of Surrey's chalk is that it yielded vast quantities of flint.

The walls of at least two-thirds of Surrey's old churches are faced with flint: from the ridge of the North Downs northwards it was the obvious material to use. Sometimes it was mixed with chalk rubble. Technically the craftsmanship was somewhat rough-and-ready: Surrey has nothing to compare with the elegant flushwork of East Anglia, and the Wiltshire–Dorset taste for chequerwork and flint-and-stone bands is also rare here. (Some chequerwork can be found at Leatherhead church and on the Norbury Chapel at Mickleham.) It is partly because of the extensive use of flint, often unknapped, that so many of Surrey's churches lack graciousness.

Flint was also employed extensively for domestic building, but until superseded by brick the large majority of Surrey's houses were timber-framed, generally with lath-and-plaster infilling, for this county has always been abundantly wooded. In rural districts the half-timbered survivals are happily still considerable. They range from handsome yeoman farmers' houses like Brewer Street Farm and Great Tangley to humble cottages, mostly of the C16 and early C17, which are sometimes delightful. In recent years many of Surrey's half-timbered houses have, it is true, been subjected to a face-lift or more in what is known as the 'Stockbroker's Tudor' style, but in the hands of a sensitive architect even this can yield results which, surprisingly perhaps, are very enjoyable, as at Crowhurst Place.

Wood was also freely used in Surrey for country churches. No medieval timber arcades survive, but over forty churches still have their wooden towers, mostly of C15 origin: they are one of the most attractive features of Surrey's architectural landscape, especially when carrying a shingled spire, as was usual. For centuries the shingles were of cleft oak, but nowadays they are all of Canadian cedarwood. This, like oak, has the happy property of turning silver-grey within five years, as could be seen after the charming spire at Burstow had been re-shingled in 1961.

The lower part of the tower at Burstow is weatherboarded, as are many Surrey cottages, farm-buildings, barns, and a few larger houses such as Whitehall at Cheam. The farm-buildings, as elsewhere in the South-East, are often coated with black tar, which under a roof of mellow red tiles can look uncommonly well. On houses the weatherboarding was often applied in the late C18 or early C19 over a much earlier timber frame, for greater internal comfort. It is amusing to find, as one travels around Surrey, that weatherboarded cottages still survive in a number of places that have now become urban or suburban, like Mitcham or Epsom.

Suburban Surrey is nevertheless almost entirely a creation of brick and tile, or, for the older houses, Welsh slate. The utterly anonymous buildings, of which this county has perhaps more than its fair share, are almost always in these materials. The Victorian brickwork is mostly ugly. Today even buildings that are architecturally characterless often show quite pleasant bricks. There is plenty of clay in Surrey available for brickmaking, some of very high quality: the Thames valley, the Claygate Beds, the Reading Beds (Tertiary), the Gault belt, the Atherfield Clay along the s margin of the Lower Greensand, and the Weald Clay – all these formations were once dotted with little brickworks, a few of which are still in operation. Bricks were made here before the advent of the Tudors: Bishop Waynflete's gatehouse at Esher and tower at Farnham Castle both belong to the reign of Edward IV. The C16 saw the erection of fine brick houses like Sutton Place and Great Fosters, and at smaller half-timbered houses brick was employed for the chimneys and later also for nogging (infilling). Early in the C17 came the splendid Abbot's Hospital at Guildford; and the Artisan Mannerist houses of the sixteen-thirties and forties described in the General Introduction (pp. 42–4) are almost all of brick. By this time churches too (e.g. Malden and Morden) were usually brick-built. Beautiful Georgian brickwork can be seen at Farnham, Richmond, Reigate, Epsom, and elsewhere. By the middle of the C18, except in the s w of the county, it was unusual for a Surrey builder to use any other material than brick.

Tile-manufacture in Surrey goes back even further, for in the second half of the C13 Chertsey Abbey was producing the best floor tiles in England. Others, not so good, were made about the same time at Waverley Abbey near Farnham. Excellent plain roofing tiles have been made in Surrey for several centuries, so good, in fact, that, as in Kent, there has been little cause to resort to thatch, which is fairly rare in Surrey. Very common, on the other hand, in rural Surrey, as in Sussex and Kent, is vertical tile-hanging, a practice which would appear to have started in the last quarter of the C17. Intended, like weatherboarding, primarily to make houses drier and warmer, plain tile-hanging in Surrey, which is generally confined to the more exposed upper floors, is invariably a pleasure. The fancy designs are usually Victorian, and can be depressingly mechanical.

FURTHER READING

The nearest of the further reading must be the *Victoria County History* (VCH), complete in 4 vols and index (1902–14) under the editorship of H. E. Malden and, as regards architecture, under the supervision of Sir Charles Peers. The standard earlier county history is Manning and Bray (3 vols, 1804–14). The annual volumes of the *Surrey Archaeological Collections* (SAC) as always need to be read. The MHLG lists have been mentioned in the Foreword; in addition the Surrey County Council, which is very progressive in this way, publishes an annotated *Antiquities of Surrey* of its own (the 5th edition came out in 1965). This, the VCH, and the SAC are of course invaluable also for the archaeology of the county; another volume on archaeology is D. C. Whimster, *The Archaeology of Surrey* (1931) in the Methuen County Archaeologies. Stained glass is dealt with by A. V. Peatling, *The Ancient Stained and Painted Glass in the Churches of Surrey* (1930), brasses by Mill Stephenson, screens by Aymer Vallance, and alabaster monuments by Mr A. Gardner. Lutyens, Norman Shaw, and Voysey are covered in books or articles, other domestic architects of the time hardly at all: there is an important missing book here. The main sources for the places formerly in Middlesex, now in Surrey, are mentioned in *The Buildings of England: Middlesex*. To these must be added M. Robbins, *Middlesex* (1953) and the recently published volumes of the *Victoria County History*: I (1969) and III (1962). The latter covers Shepperton, Staines, Stanwell, and Sunbury.

SURREY

★

ABINGER

A scattered village around the 550 ft level, on the slopes of the Surrey Hills. There is a green near the church but no houses round it, and houses further s but no green. A little suburbanized, like Peaslake, further w.

ST JAMES. Bombed in the war and restored by *Frederick Etchells* in 1950 and again in 1964, after a fire. The reinstatement is well done outside, but the scraped interior is too hygienic and genteel. The outside is a very good example of Surrey vernacular; the nearest parallel is Essex, and the differences are worth noting – the bell-turret is shingled (although it was weatherboarded before the war) and there is a little more consequence about the body of the church. Big-scale Norman nave with three windows high up on each side (four only are original), the type of Portchester, Hants. E.E. chancel and N chapel as at Wotton, and just as at Wotton the chancel detail is ornate and false, the chapel detail is simple and genuine: triple lancets to the s and three lancets in the N wall. The arcade between them is renewed also. – SCULPTURE. Crucifixion (S porch); C15 alabaster, Nottingham work, given in 1945. – (STAINED GLASS. E window by *Lawrence Lee*, 1967. Much the best modern glass in the county, portraying the Living Cross in vivid abstract colouring. NT) – PLATE. Set 1736. – MONUMENT. Alastair Mackenzie † 1910 by *Albert Toft*. Bad, but interesting in that the flowers the dead boy is holding form Art Nouveau patterns almost against the sculptor's will. – (WAR MEMORIAL in the churchyard by *Lutyens*, 1921, re-erected 1949. NT)

MOTTE. NW of the church, in a garden, a small overgrown Norman earthwork of standard type. Excavations here have revealed wooden post-holes and a stout palisade, and have proved what had always been supposed – that many of the Norman mottes never supported anything more permanent than a timber house. Probably many were never used after the time of Henry II's demolition of adulterine castles.

CROSSWAYS FARM, 1 m. NW, beside the A25. A first-rate C17 vernacular farmhouse, the main front facing E with a central gabled two-storeyed porch and thick brick cornices and string courses in Artisan style. The main cornice is thickened above the keystones, as at West Horsley Place. Several of the windows have the Dutch mannerism of curved relieving arches above the windows with flat tops (cf. Ripley, Godalming, etc.) – here with the flat central section slightly dropped below the rest instead of raised above it. A good set of BARNS on the N side, in the familiar tile and tarred weatherboarding, here combined with Wealden stone.

To the S of the village is GODDARDS, a *Lutyens* house of 1898–9 in a promising asymmetrical style but ruined by slack elevations and a remarkably unhappy choice of materials – rough-cast walls with brick dressings under a tile roof with heavy dormers. In the hands of someone like Prior such materials would be intended as a deliberate shock, and be organized accordingly; in this case, in Wilde's words, it looks very like carelessness. (The house was built as a hostel where lady social workers could recuperate;* two large rooms with inglenooks were added by *Lutyens* to l. and r. when it was converted into a private house in 1909–10. Garden court laid out by *Miss Jekyll.* – To the l. of the front, a C17 cottage converted by *Lutyens* into a village post office in 1899 but now a cottage again. NT)

On the main road to the N is Abinger Hammer, perhaps the original village centre, with another small green and a typically pretty vignette of tile-hung cottages around a narrow stretch of road W of it, spoilt by heavy traffic. Typically also, the vignette is made up of both original and revival. The best of the former is OLD HATCH FARM and its barns, part brick, part half-timber, and the best of the latter the picturesque CLOCK HOUSE, by *W. O. Milne* and *J. C. Hall*, 1891. Further E, PADDINGTON FARM is undoubtedly C15, with a close-timbered oversailing gable at each end: all plastered, as it doubtless was originally.

ABINGER HALL. Formidable brick and terracotta Tudor by *Waterhouse*, 1872. Just plain ugly, not interesting. Now demolished.

W of the village, at Sutton, two more farms worth a look. SUTTON

---

* The present owner has restored to its original purpose the SKITTLE ALLEY, a delicious white-walled tunnel spanned by red-brick arches (NT).

PLACE FARM is a big three-storeyed house of *c*.1700, with
segment-headed windows and two good tarred-weatherboarded
barns. FULVENS FARM, though of the same type, was done
fifty years earlier. Long brick two-storey front with central
projecting two-storeyed gable and a brick pediment above the
first-floor window. One of the best farms in Surrey.

¾ m. E is FRIDAY STREET, a well-known group of Surrey cottages, none remarkable, in a superb setting at one end of a
pond in a steep wooded valley.

In a field near Abinger church and motte is a MESOLITHIC
SITE. A pit of 14 by 10 ft, dug 3 ft into the Greensand, remains,
and hearths and post-holes found within it suggest a simply
roofed temporary dwelling. Microlithic flint implements found
in the area show that it was inhabited by people of the
Horsham Culture *c*. 5000 B.C.

ADDINGTON

ST MARY. Norman chancel with original windows, especially a
stepped triplet at the E end of widely spaced windows. One
blocked window in the N wall looks older than the others.
C13 S arcade of three bays with alternatingly round and octagonal piers and double-chamfered arches. The aisle is
characteristically narrow. Lancet window at the E end. The N
arcade is of 1876 by *St Aubyn*. (The tower was partly rebuilt
in brick *c*.1773. B. F. L. Clarke) – STAINED GLASS by *Kempe*
in the S aisle, 1891 and 1898. – PLATE. Silver-gilt Cup, Paten,
and Almsdish 1725. – MONUMENTS. Brasses to John Leigh
† 1509 and wife, 2 ft 2 in. figures (chancel floor N). – Brass to
Thomas Hatteclyff † 1540, 2 ft 2 in. figure in armour (chancel
floor S). – Sir Olliphe Leigh † 1612, his wife, parents, and
grandparents. Stiffly semi-reclining effigies one on top of the
other, and above them the smaller figures of the older generation, each couple kneeling and facing one another across a
prayer desk. The pairs are flanked and separated by obelisks. –
Two more kneeling figures of about the same period are
preserved, taken out of their context. – Mrs Lovell and Mrs
Leigh, both † 1691. Attributed by Mrs Esdaile to *Nost*.
Hanging monument without figures. Unusually severely
framed inscription plate with, as its only ornament, two
hanging garlands of bunches of very boldly carved flowers. –
Mrs Grizzel Trecothick † 1769. Signed by *Wilton*. Tall and
broad curvy pedestal and low and broad urn on it of un-

commonly high quality. – Barlow Trecothick † 1775, Lord Mayor of London. Large plain urn of white and brown marble. Very restrained. – In the churchyard an ornate cross on a very ornate pedestal. This is the monument to Archbishop Tait † 1882 and five other archbishops as well.

ADDINGTON PALACE (Royal School of Church Music). Built by *Robert Mylne* in 1773–9 for Barlow Trecothick, and later a palace of the Archbishops of Canterbury. Of fine ashlar blocks of Portland stone. Originally a three-storeyed balustraded block of seven bays with wings and one-storeyed pedimented end pavilions. The centre of the house has a pediment towards the garden (with its splendid cedar trees). No columns or pilasters at all. Many additions in the same style. (The interior was reconstructed by *Norman Shaw* for F. A. English, a South African diamond merchant who bought the house in 1897. The hall has an elaborate classical marble and alabaster chimneypiece.) Two good brick and stone LODGES and stone gatepiers towards GRAVEL HILL.

⟨ROYAL RUSSELL SCHOOL, Coombe Lane. Completely hidden from the road. An extensive series of buildings, of 1924 and later by *Sir Aston Webb* and his son *Maurice Webb* and of *c.*1964 by *Robert Matthew, Johnson-Marshall & Partners* (in charge *P. A. Newnham*), an effective and uncompromising juxtaposition of formal neo-Baroque with an industrialized building system (Laingspan). The Aston Webb buildings form two and a half sides of a large quadrangle. They are of red brick with yellow stone dressings, with much brick rustication. The main wing has an exterior façade with a central pediment with paired Tuscan columns, and a cloister facing the quadrangle. At r. angles, two apsidal-ended halls flanking the chapel, with a tower standing forward with open belfry surmounted by a stumpy octagonal stone spire. Rich Baroque interior, typical of the High Church taste of the period; tunnel-vault on an enormous cornice and modillions, screen of four huge columns in front of the sanctuary. The new buildings, of two and three storeys, complete the quadrangle not entirely symmetrically with a cloister on thin steel supports opposite the brick one. There is a considerable variety of windows and cladding materials within the rectangular framework. The new buildings make no concessions, but neither do they try to dominate the scene, and the result is harmonious. Separate new JUNIOR SCHOOL to the s in the same style.⟩

On the Downs s of Addington a housing estate called NEW

ADDINGTON was started in the 1930s. This has been taken
over and enlarged by Croydon corporation as a kind of
unofficial new town and has become the extreme example of
'prairie planning', or the pointless over-provision of open
space, in the county. Everything is so far apart that it becomes
a joke. So far, no buildings worth a visit. ⟨Not much improvement recently. In CENTRAL PARADE there is now a LIBRARY
(opened in 1964), with a zigzagging roofline, between the
poorly detailed COMMUNITY CENTRE (1955) and SWIM-
MING BATH (1959–63), all by the *Croydon Borough Engineer's
Architect's Department*. No attempt to integrate the buildings
as a group. At the end of Central Parade, ST EDWARD'S
CHURCH, by *Caröe & Partners*, red brick, conservative and
uninspiring. At the N end of New Addington, however, some
much better new building. FIELDWAY leads around cheerful
tile-hung terraces and a twelve-storey block of flats (1965). In
DUNLEY DRIVE near by, CHURCH OF THE GOOD SHEP-
HERD (R.C.), 1962 by *Tomei & Maxwell*.⟩

FORESTDALE *see* Selsdon.

COLENTINA. Pretty house with butterfly roofs, by *A. C. Bayley*,
1954–5.

Of the twenty-five barrows reported in the C19 to be on Thunder
Hill only one, a large bowl-shaped mound *c*. 110 ft in diameter,
can now be traced. Most of this group may originally have been
a Saxon cemetery; reports of 'urns' cannot now be checked.

ADDISCOMBE *see* CROYDON, pp. 180, 181, 182

ADDLESTONE   *0060*
1 m. S of Chertsey

ST PAUL. 1836, a grim, lean exterior – stock-brick, lancet
windows, W tower – and a vile interior. The architect was not
a local builder, but *James Savage*, the architect of St Luke's
Chelsea, a man whose reputation is grossly overvalued.

Addlestone is a spiritless mixture of C19 and C20 suburbia. ⟨The
centre, between Station Road and Garfield Road, has recently
been completely rebuilt with an odd jumble of isolated buildings – a wasted opportunity. S of Station Road, CHERTSEY
COUNCIL OFFICES by *Jellicoe & Coleridge*, 1962–5. Two
ranges at r. angles, the one at the back partly on stilts, with
carefully landscaped gardens visible beyond. The entrance on
the r. is reached by a long covered way. The drum projecting

from the roof behind this is the top of a circular stairwell. On the l. pleasantly straightforward COMMUNITY CENTRE by *M. L. Fielding*, 1967. Dark brick, white boarding. The hall at the back has a slightly zigzagging wall with tall narrow windows between plain brick panels. The path between these buildings leads to Garfield Road. On the r. council flats (firmly fenced off from the Council Offices' gardens). On the l. POLICE DIVISIONAL HEADQUARTERS by the County Architect, *Raymond Ash*, 1966–8. Large, three storeys, buff brick. The best parts are the impressive glazed staircases at the sides. Opposite, one of the delightful recent PRIMARY SCHOOLS by the County Architect, *Raymond Ash*, 1966–7. Single-storey blocks on three sides of a small courtyard. These schools are built on a semi-industrialized system developed by the County Architect's Department, but each building differs in layout and details, and the colours and types of cladding materials are chosen sensitively. Here there are yellow and grey spandrel panels, tile-hanging, and a dark grey boiler chimney behind. The effect is gay and friendly, exactly the opposite of SURREY TOWERS, the seventeen-storey flats across the road, by the Chertsey U.D.C. Engineer and Surveyor, *N. C. Goldsmith*, 1962–5. (If there had to be a tower block in Addlestone, why not for the Council Offices?)⟩ From pre-suburban days there remains CROCKFORD BRIDGE FARM, s of the centre, on the way to Newhaw, a stuccoed, timber-framed farmhouse, with a shaped C17 gable at the E end (it originally had two) of unusual type, with straight sides and a small semicircular top on shoulders. It is common in Holland, but very rare in England.

WOBURN PARK (St George's College). A very incorrect Italianate house (and, especially, gate lodge), up to Greek Thomson's standard of aberration, plus agreeable Norman Shaw style dormitories and disagreeable Neo-Georgian additions of 1956. The architect of none of these seems to be known.* This is the site of Woburn Farm, a famous early experiment in landscape gardening, where Philip Southcote, inspired by Addison, built after 1735 a *ferme ornée*. There was a garden to match, laid out by *Kent* in a style which, from descriptions of its intricacy and rapid change of scene, was purely Picturesque, i.e. historically a long way ahead of Capability Brown's cool, opened-out views. The landscaping has all disappeared. One rusticated brick arch, presumably by *Kent*,

* The Norman Shaw bits perhaps by *Dunn & Hansom*, 1878.

remains beside the entrance drive. (There are remains of another NW of the house, and a GROTTO on the lawn. MHLG)
w of this is WOBURN HILL, 1815, a pleasant, double-bowed, stock-brick front, urbane and beautifully landscaped, facing w on top of a smoothly rising meadow. (N of Weybridge Road HAMM COURT FARM with a C16 brick dovecote. MHLG)
On the way to Weybridge, Hamm Moor Lane leads first to AMALGAMATED DENTAL PROSTHENIC PRODUCTS, with a straightforward curtain-walled, three-storey office block by *Russell Diplock Associates*, 1957 – incredibly gauche colours used under the windows – and finishes beside the Wey Navigation at the FLOUR MILLS, gaunt and impressive, one of the best pieces of industrial architecture in Surrey. Two mills at r. angles, both with a big top clerestory. The older is six-storeyed with steep gables, shallow buttresses low down, and a shallow but big-scale Gothic cornice. The windows are all at one end and the rest is sheer stock-brick walls, oddly like an enlargement of Vanbrugh Castle – the sort of staccato nobility that Philip Webb aimed at in his few industrial buildings and the London Board School designers did in their schools. It was built in 1901 by *Christy* of London. The other is of 1906, also by *Christy*, in a style which looks purely Late Georgian, five storeys with segmental windows and shouldered gables framing the long top clerestory. (Two concrete silos, 120 ft high, have been added recently.)

ALBURY

0040

In the gentle rolling scenery of the Tillingbourne valley, w of Shere. The village drifted from its old site in the park in the early C19 to a hamlet ½ m. w then called Weston Street. This is the present Albury, and its character is that of a heavily picturesque informal estate village of the 1850s.

ST PETER AND ST PAUL. The old church, in the park near the house. Disused since 1842, and consequently one of the few really attractive churches in Surrey. The nave N wall and the base of the central tower are assumed to be Saxon; the evidence for this is best seen on the N side of the tower, where there is an odd quoined projection which is meaningless unless the tower was built up on earlier foundations. The rest of the tower is Norman, built without transepts, and has a small N window and then two stages of two lights, the lower deeply recessed inside an arched surround (as at Cobham) and quite effective.

The tower arches have a little carving, including the so-called nutmeg motif.* The tower is finished with a bulbous shingled C17 cupola, making a picturesque composition from the house. The chancel now roofless, C13, with the surround for a big, late, four-centred E window. S transept c.1290, with an ambitious entrance arch and windows with ornate tracery, renewed but authentic. The two windows in the E wall have an early variety of Y-tracery – the two lights have heads of their own inside the larger heads, a gawky experimental effect. Also a show S window of five lights with one big quatrefoil and two smaller ones below, conceived more as a frame for an impressive glazing pattern than for its own sake. The tracery looks convincing, though the VCH calls it 'modern', which probably means *Pugin*, who redecorated the whole of this transept in a fervent glowing style in 1839 – an extreme contrast to the rough plastered walls of the rest of the church. The walls were covered with red, blue, and gold decoration by *T. Earley*, the window filled with vivid STAINED GLASS by *Wailes*, a genuine and nearly successful attempt to bowl the onlooker over by sheer force of decoration. S aisle of the C14, with a rough three-bay arcade. Wooden S porch, simple Late Perp, with elegant bargeboarding. Most of the windows are 'Churchwarden' and clear-glazed. – WALL PAINTING (S aisle). A big St Christopher, C14 or C15, nearly gone. – MONUMENTS. Brass to John Weston † 1440 (S aisle floor). Effigy in armour, 2 ft high, partly restored. Dumb, conventional C15 work, apparently identical with that to Richard Fox at Arkesden, Essex. – Several C17 tablets of low quality, and Sir Robert Godschall † 1742, bigger, with a sarcophagus, stock-Palladian.

IRVINGITE CHURCH, N of Albury Park. Henry Drummond, who bought Albury in 1819, was a supporter of Edward Irving, the founder of the Catholic Apostolic Church, a weird blend of ritual and Presbyterianism. Most of the original meetings were held at Albury, and Drummond provided this new church for the sect, designed in 1840 by *William McIntosh Brooks*, apparently assisted by *Pugin*. Dashing, incorrect Perp, Commissioners' Gothic style, with big W tower and an octagonal chapter house on the N side, in a mixture of sandstone and carstone. Good fun.

ST PETER AND ST PAUL, Weston Street. 1842, also by *McIntosh*

---

* The westernmost has a rough scallop pattern around the arch, approximating to the crimping in Compton church, but carried out in very low relief on the stone itself, not on the plaster surround.

Brooks, and an odd building for the 1840s: Romanesque, 'built in imitation of the church at Thaon in Normandy',* but of brick, so that the effect is half Italian. Aisleless nave and attached NW tower which would hardly be out of place on Lake Como. Apse and transepts 1868 by *Sir A. W. Blomfield* in the same style (the N transept rearranged as a Memorial Chapel by *Sir Edward Maufe* after the Second World War), awful institutional interior. – PLATE. Set, 1714.

ALBURY PARK. The original Albury was Tudor, half-timbered and something like Great Tangley Manor. *John and George Evelyn* almost rebuilt it for the Duke of Norfolk in the C17 at the same time as they altered the gardens. This house was again altered *c.*1700, then by *Soane* in 1800, by *Hakewill* a little later, and was finally completely and depressingly remodelled by *Pugin*, mostly in 1846–52. Architecturally it now has little to offer, but it keeps to a remarkable degree the crowded, jostling effect of an C18 or C19 collector's house, particularly in the central top-lit picture gallery. The outside elevations are some of the worst things Pugin ever did. He was presented with a rambling, additive house, partly classical, partly gothicized by Hakewill, and he gave the whole thing a completely unconvincing Tudor dress, with brick dressings to the windows; battlements and gables, and a set of sixty-three ornate brick chimneys culled from every imaginable Tudor source, each one different. The entrance (W) front is as dull and silly as any of the pasteboard Gothick castles that he lambasted. The N front,‡ facing the remains of the Evelyns' gardens, is better, because less symmetrical, though completely without conviction – a big gable balances a tower and a two-storey porch like a spindly fragment of Peterborough Cathedral. The NE corner is not bad, three little dormers facing E with a blackletter inscription below, something like the sort of house Pugin would have put up if left to himself. Inside, the Pugin interiors are all completely mechanical, and Soane is recognizable only in the very plain staircase, a typical example of *c.*1800, with one arm winding round a narrow oblong well, and in the even plainer Drawing Room, with a *Flaxman* fireplace with caryatids. The Dining Room has a fireplace and a pair of free-standing

* At Henry Drummond's request; he was abroad when the building was put up and was very disappointed to find it brick and not stone on his return.

‡ Impressive ironwork GATES form the garden entrance at this NW corner, Baroque of *c.*1700 and clearly not English, with thick curly patterns and multiple planes of ironwork. They were in fact brought from a 'convent in Hungary', and are said to be Flemish.

Ionic columns which came from Northumberland House near Charing Cross. Several more chimneypieces in the house: plain big late C17 in the Library, presumably by the *Evelyns*, an *Adam* fireplace from Syon in the Duchess's boudoir, and, in the entrance hall, the best thing in the house, a late C17 overmantel brought here by Drummond, consisting of spirited military trophies carved in very high relief, quite different from English work of the time. In fact it is probably Dutch, attributed to *J. van Santvoort*, *c*.1690, and was brought from Scotland. There is similar work in Holyrood House.

Historically the main interest of Albury is the GARDENS, laid out by *John and George Evelyn*, originally in 1655–8, chiefly in parallel terraces along the side of the hill 200 yards N of the house. A cavern excavated under the main terrace in imitation of a Roman Bath bears the date 1676. The intention, as at Wotton, was doubtless Italian. Evelyn built a tunnel right through the hill, which still exists, and said of it 'such a Pausilippe is nowhere in England besides' (i.e. the grotto at Posilippo near Naples). (Near the Roman Bath are some splendid *Coade* stone capitals from Soane's portico. J. Harris)

Pretty cottages are scattered throughout the village and hamlets, few worth special notice. In the park, ORANGE COTTAGES are timber-framed with Bargate stone infilling. Beside the Irvingite church is THE GRANGE, quite a big house, with altered half-timber work including ornamental curved braces as used at Great Tangley. In the village a lot of ornate estate building of *c*.1850, some of it perhaps by *Pugin*,* and one good C17 cottage on the way to the church, late half-timbering using big structural curved braces and brick infilling.

See p. 595

FARLEY HEATH. The heath was once the site of what was probably the largest Romano-British settlement in the county. At different times two kilns and many traces of houses have been found and recorded. The most important antiquity on the Heath, however, is the ROMANO-BRITISH TEMPLE AND ENCLOSURE, apparently placed in the SW corner of a rhomboidal double earthwork of some 9 acres. This is now cut through by the road from Cranleigh to Albury. The temple was enthusiastically excavated by Martin Tupper, the 'Proverbial Philosopher', in 1848–9, and there were subsequent, more scientific excavations in 1926 and 1939. The site lies on a branch road from Stane Street which probably ran on to Bagshot. It is now clear that the outer earthwork is probably medieval; the

* ALMSHOUSES by *E. W. Pugin & James Murray*, 1857 (GS).

inner enclosure with its small temple, *c.*25 yards square, an irregular ten-sided curtain wall round the holy *temenos*, follows the pattern of local Romano-Celtic religious centres. Its best parallel in this country is at Colchester, and abroad, even closer, Coblenz – also sited in open country by a trunk road. Pottery and coins indicate a date of use before the end of the C1 A.D.; an inner wall to the *temenos* across its NW corner may be a later rebuilding, and the site seems to have been destroyed, 'by fire' according to Tupper, in the first half of the C5 A.D. The general area of the temple shows much occupation perhaps connected with the nearby kiln sites of the C4 A.D. Roman coins within the *temenos* range from 25 B.C. to A.D. 382, while Celtic coins from the neighbourhood support the native background to the shrine. Later votive offerings were in the form of bronze and stone axes. Unfortunately much has been lost owing to the depredations of the intervening years. The most important discovery made by Tupper (whose significance he passed over) was a decorated bronze strip, probably for a priest's sceptre. Examination of the crude figures pricked out on it suggests an identification with the Celtic Taranis, interpreted variously as the equivalent of Dispater or Jupiter. The *cella* and surrounding portico of the temple have been marked out with stones taken from the robber trenches and set in concrete. Tupper's finds from Farley Heath were deposited by him in the British Museum.

E of Newlands Corner is a fine bowl BARROW, 60 ft in diameter and 4–5 ft high. It appears to have been opened, but with no recorded result.

ALDERBROOK *see* CRANLEIGH

ALFOLD

The village is made up of several straggling hamlets, partly Victorian, on the Sussex border S of Cranleigh. There is only one picturesque feature worth notice, but that is very picturesque indeed – the tiny *place* formed by two tile-hung cottages beside the footway to the church, another of the picturesque cameos in which Surrey excels. However accidentally or unconsciously arrived at, this group provides an experience on the same level as a good Lutyens house. It is worth while seeing how it is obtained – chiefly by the repeating small-scale rhythm of the scallop-edged tiles (plain tile-hanging would not have the same effect at all), but also by the contrast given by the plain white-painted ground floor, brick in one cottage, brick and half-timber in the other.

ST NICHOLAS. The outside impression is all of a heavy Wealden church of *c.*1300, with huge roof partly of Horsham slate, sweeping down over nave and aisles without clerestory or dormer windows. The exterior detail is all homely, mainly cusped lancets and twin lancets (the E window is C19). In fact however the S arcade is late C12 (round piers, round capitals, and unchamfered pointed arches, reasonable proof of a remote parish). N arcade and chancel arch are early C14, with complex arch mouldings (including sunk quadrants) of three orders dying into octagonal piers (or responds) – a thick, effective style not met with elsewhere in Surrey. Several contemporary windows. S porch good C14 woodwork, simple and heavy, in authentic condition. Small shingled bell-chamber supported by an impressive big C15 cage inside the W end. It is similar to Thursley in that it is built up in a rectilinear way, i.e. with four huge corner posts and small curved braces supporting horizontals, rather than with the complex of diagonal braces normally used for big timber belfries. – FONT. Norman; massive tub font of the same type as that formerly in Hambledon and now in St Martha at Chilworth. Heavy circular bowl roughly ornamented with blind arches, each with a kind of Maltese cross in it. No stem, just a thick cable moulding round the base. Probably early, before 1100, and quite impressive. – PULPIT. Simple Jacobean, with sounding board. Ornamental patterns abstract and low-relief, just as they would be on a rustic C17 sideboard.

Of the vernacular buildings ALFOLD HOUSE is worth a look, on the main road ½ m. NE of the church. L-shaped, half-timbered, mostly black and white, with a Horsham slate roof and a bewildering variety of functional timberwork, both close- and open-spaced; probably early C16.

ANNINGSLEY PARK *see* OTTERSHAW

ANSTIEBURY CAMP *see* COLDHARBOUR

ARDENRUN PLACE *see* CROWHURST

8050

ASH

An appendage of Aldershot, Hants, and a sad village, with its tiny green turned into an asphalted roundabout in the 1950s. The church with its heavy shingled broach-spire gives an illusory impression of West Kent.

ST PETER. Early medieval walls and fragments. C15 tower with C19 shingled spire. Ferocious restoration and N aisle (now the nave) of 1865. One tiny Norman window reset in the N aisle, one C13 lancet on the S side of the chancel. Very good S door, of *c*.1200, round-headed but purely Gothic in feeling, with stiff-leaf capitals, jamb-shafts with fillets, and deeply cut arch mouldings. Though badly weathered, very delicate indeed – one of the best Early Gothic details in Surrey, perhaps done by the Chertsey Abbey masons as Chertsey owned the advowson. Timber and brick C16 S porch and bulky Perp tower with primitive windows in heathstone. The tower arch inside has its plaster surround crimped and the reveal painted red, as at Worplesdon. – FONT. Wood, C17; octagonal bowl on eight octagonal columns and a circular central post. – ROYAL ARMS of George III, under the tower. In good condition. – PLATE. Cup 1575; Paten 1674; Flagon 1734. – MONUMENT. Tablet to John Harris, 1759 (E wall of chancel). Spirited provincial Palladian. The word 'memento' is carved below the inscription, and the mementos themselves are carved below that: skulls and bones, stylized as if they were carved on a tombstone, but not naïve.

ST MARK, Wyke. 1847 by *Woodyer*, his first church, but no hint of individuality.

NORMANDY. *See* p. 389.

ASHFORD*

0070

One of the least rewarding villages in this area N of the Thames. Now much built up.

ST MATTHEW. 1858–65 by *Butterfield*, but with little to disclose the power of the designer of All Saints, Margaret Street, London. The exterior might have been more eventful if the tower, standing S of the S aisle, virtually on its own, had been completed as originally intended by the architect. The bald interior has little to recommend it. – PLATE. Chalice by *E. Pearce*, 1711; Paten, 1715; large Chalice and Paten, 1812. – BRASS to W. Goode † 1522 and wife. – The site of the Norman chancel E of the present church is marked by a floor slab preserved in the churchyard.

* Formerly in Middlesex.

St Michael, Fordbridge Road. 1928 by *Sir Giles G. Scott*. Incomplete.

Clockhouse Farm, NE of the church in Clockhouse Road. A brick front behind two magnificent monkey-puzzle trees, the side front of the house half-timbered.

Welsh Charity School. 1857 by *Henry Clutton*. Gothic, not Clutton's French Renaissance. A long stone front with ten steep gabled dormer windows and three-light windows. The centre with a richer Gothic entrance; influence from Ruskin's favourite Venetian. In the entrance hall a niche with a life-size figure of Albert Edward Prince of Wales (later Edward VII) as a handsome boy in a kind of Veronese dress, surrounded by Gothic foliage.

(Abbotsford County Secondary School. Recent extensions by *R. & M. Finch* in association with the County Architect, *Raymond Ash*.)

1050   ASHTEAD

Main-road village between Epsom and Leatherhead, still with some character, because the irregular building line has remained though nearly all the old buildings have gone. The church and Ashtead Park are by themselves on the slopes of the Downs to the SE.

St Giles. Tower C16, in a typical Middlesex style (cf. Twickenham or Edmonton). Squat, with diagonal buttresses and big square stair-turret. Heavily restored. The rest completely renewed in 1862, when a N transept was built too. Vestry of 1891. Very frilly roofs inside, also of 1862, a preposterous job. – font. Octagonal, C15, with quatrefoils on the bowl. – stained glass, E window. Crucifixion, C16 work from Herck near Maastricht. Complete composition, very effective as an overall pattern (primarily of gold and light blue, with a few inflections of deeper colour), although the design is pedestrian and the colours lack sparkle. Comparison with the Kempe-ish stuff in some of the other windows brings out the point of pattern immediately. The best details are the elaborate Mannerist architectural backgrounds. – monuments. Sarah Bond † 1712, a very pretty London-style cartouche, two cherubs holding up the elaborately draped backcloth, the carving far more vigorous than the normal run (N side of chancel). – Several more tablets of *c*.1700 in the chancel. One to Thomas Howard † 1701 is a straightforward hack job by *William*

Stanton. Another to Henry Newdigate † 1629 is apparently by *Grinling Gibbons*, carved in 1693 (a contract exists for it). It is shockingly rough. The only charitable explanation is that it was made deliberately anachronistic. – Diana Fielding † 1733. Rysbrack's style and Rysbrack's quality. Assured bust in circular black marble surround with an impeccable Palladian surround; more verve than most monuments of this type.

A triangular EARTHWORK round the church which has Roman material incorporated in it may be connected with a villa. To the NW is a broad, shallow, ditched polygonal ENCLOSURE with occupation debris of the C2 A.D. This includes flint and tile masonry perhaps salvaged from the villa complex at Ashtead Common and re-quarried for the church.

ST GEORGE, Lower Ashtead. 1905 by *Sir A. W. Blomfield & Son.* Very simple brick with the beginnings of a good brick capital-less interior. The firm did good honest work in the 1900s after Blomfield senior had died.

⟨ST MICHAEL (R.C.). By *Peter French,* 1966–7. Octagonal, with clerestory lighting below a dark sloping fascia. Excessively woody inside. Good straightforward purple brick presbytery behind.⟩

ASHTEAD PARK. An ugly house but a very instructive one, showing how an insensitive late C18 architect could short-circuit the Regency altogether and produce a building that could pass for the mid C19. Designed by *Bonomi,* 1790, and executed by *Samuel Wyatt.* An uncompromising stock-brick house of seven by three bays with single-storey wings, altered in the C19, but the florid detail apparently original, and more Louis Quinze than anything else (like Wyatt's work at Trinity House, Tower Hill).* Heavy four-bay porch on the garden side. On the entrance side a Bonomi speciality, a heavy T-shaped Tuscan Doric loggia and porte-cochère, with a central four-bay projection giving enough room to drive a carriage underneath; one of the first in the country. Above on both fronts a strange tripartite window and surround with very deep lugs (as used e.g. in the interior of No. 1 Bedford Square), and above that a 'Laurenziana' pediment – i.e. open, with the ends scrolled and touching, an extraordinary motif for the 1790s. On the second floor a smaller plain tripartite window, with the centre light on the entrance front later blocked and filled with

* David Watkin suggests that these details are part of the later C19 remodelling.

William IV's arms. All this is very heavy and typical of Bonomi, revealing an utter impatience with Palladian architecture and at the same time an inability to invent an effective alternative.

The interiors are similarly eclectic and exasperated. The entrance hall is now sumptuous neo-Jacobean, leading on the r. to an Adam-style staircase with pretty balustrade and ceiling, sandwiched into a narrow well in the Adam way. Beyond that is the Old Library, with the original bookcases, and plasterwork in a subdued Chambers style. Straight ahead from the hall is a circular Saloon (*see* below). To the l. of this is the present Library, now neo-Jacobean, to the r. an elaborately decorated Drawing Room in straightforward Late Palladian style. So here are three C18 rooms in three different styles, all done without much feeling; in fact alone in the whole house the Saloon shows Bonomi's real inclinations (as do interiors such as Great Packington church in Warwickshire), towards centrally planned rooms and large-scale Late Roman decoration. A circular room with alternate niches and pairs of scagliola or brown marble Roman Doric columns *in antis*. Four niches, four pairs of columns – a noble design. Two pairs of columns frame doors, the third frames the hall entrance, the fourth the window on the garden side.

Plain Soane-style STABLES, which are free of the sourness that hangs over the rest of the house.

Only one house worth notice in THE STREET: No. 6, an attractive weatherboarded cottage of c.1800, three by two bays with classical doorcase (off-centre). This is about the best Surrey example of the Thames Estuary fashion of weatherboarding in the late C18 and early C19, and has more formal Georgian detail than most.

⟨In Epsom Road, FOREST LODGE, by *Michael Manser Associates*, completed in 1968, a single-storey house with all-glass walls.⟩

⟨In WOODFIELD LANE, running N from The Street, LIBRARY and CLINIC by the County Architect, *R. J. Ash*, 1967–8. Two blocks at r. angles with a lower common entrance. The walls have vertical panels of buff brick between the windows, forming a crenellated roof-line. Off Woodfield Lane on the other side, WESTFIELD, The Marld, an estate designed by *Eric Lyons & Partners* for Span, with terrace housing around a green. The houses have monopitch roofs, projecting canted porches, and upper floors with dark vertical boarding and windows pushed right to the edges of the dividing walls.⟩

(Further w, two old people's homes: BROOKER'S CLOSE, off Green Lane, by *Roger G. Simmons*, 1969, with bungalows in the centre, surrounded by two-storey flats, and MOLE VALLEY PLACE, off Ottways Lane, by *Michael Manser Associates*, 1966–8, with bungalows linked by covered walks.)

On the E side of Ashtead Park, in Farm Lane, is PARK FARM HOUSE, a nice example of the London masons' style before the Building Acts of 1707–9 banned eaves cornices and flush windows in London. Six bays and three storeys, with simple doorcase. Glowing orange brick. Eaves cornice, brick strings between the storeys, windows without reveals, the second floor still keeping its casements and small panes.

ROMAN VILLA. A fine Romano-British villa of corridor type was discovered on Ashtead Common and excavated in 1926–8. The villa, which was 135 by 70 ft square, contained, in addition to its impressive corridor and porch, twelve living rooms and a four-room bath annexe. 150 ft from the porch, along a carefully constructed approach road made of selected flints, stood another and much larger bath house, perhaps designed for communal use. It contained no less than six rooms, one of elaborate circular shape. Decorated tiles with a hunting scene were found, some of which have been incorporated in St Giles church. These and others indicate a local tile factory, while the coin and pottery finds revealed occupation from the early C1 to the mid C3 A.D. A strange pottery 'cake stand' suggests a portative altar, judging by parallels at Verulamium (St Albans) and on the Rhine and Danube. The road seems to have led into Stane Street; some earlier pottery points to settlement in the Late Iron Age by Belgic-influenced Wealden folk.

BAGSHOT

'Not only good for little but good for nothing' – Defoe, in the days when Bagshot Heath was vast, dangerous, and unenclosed. Today it is demure, almost a backwater – largely C19 workers' houses with a curiously urban air, in a landscape of rhododendrons and holly hedges.

ST ANNE. 1884 by *Alec Cheer*. Polychrome brick with attached s tower with octagonal belfry. Bad, purposeless ugliness.

BAGSHOT PARK. The sentence above applies, with more force. 1877 by *Ferrey* – his last building, according to the DNB – and scarifyingly ugly brick-and-stone Tudor like a Bournemouth hotel. Either mid-Victorian heartiness had a shattering effect on

the sensitive designer of buildings like St Stephen Rochester
Row, or – to be more charitable – he left most of the designing
to his son in old age. (The client was Queen Victoria's son, the
Duke of Connaught. NT)

PENNYHILL HOUSE. A gaunt, late C19 Tudor-style house,
built c.1873 on a hill. In splendidly landscaped grounds laid
out by *Colin Heywood*, the present owner.

Nothing in Bagshot is worth a close look. The centre is an open
space backed by a viaduct, trying to be a town square with
village buildings. QUEEN ANNE HOUSE is a big, plain, five-by-
three-bay early C18 house. James Butler's ALMSHOUSES
beyond the railway are almost featureless C17 brick, dim and
altered. The human touch is much more fun in RALPH'S
VILLAS, RALPH'S COTTAGES, and RALPH'S TERRACE,
three speculations of c.1840, side by side on the road to
Camberley.

I m. out on the Guildford Road a house by *Maxwell Fry*, 1937.
Thirties-modern, but dumb, in the exact sense of the word.

BANSTEAD

2050

ALL SAINTS. Flint and stone. Small. Essentially of the late C12
to early C13. Sturdy, broad tower with later shingled spire.
Externally the details are all renewed. The restoration was
done by *Street* in 1861. The interior, however, is very rewarding. Arcade of two bays, the piers octagonal, their capitals
with four big crockets. The arches completely unchamfered.
E of the two bays a small arch with two slight continuous
chamfers. The tower arch and chancel arch have slight chamfers too. Chancel chapels of two bays: that on the S has an
octagonal pier with the plainest capital and slightly chamfered
arches; that on the N has a very curious octagonal pier, its sides
alternately hollowed and sunk so as to leave narrow fillets at
the angles. Capitals with four leaf crockets, slightly chamfered
arches. – FONT. Octagonal, Perp, with panels with divers
tracery patterns. – (STAINED GLASS with *Webb* canopies. A. C.
Sewter) – PLATE. Silver-gilt Set 1788. – MONUMENTS. Paul
Tracey † 1618, a babe. Tablet, nave E wall, with the little
creature in a chrisom robe. – Mrs Elizabeth Till † 1748. Well
carved Rococo cartouche. – Nicholas Lambert † 1755. Hanging
monument, no figures, but good garland in the 'predella'. –
Wilmot Lambert † 1815. Grecian, with a rising female figure. –

(In the churchyard a good series of late C18 tombs by *James Colecom* of Merstham. F. Burgess)

About ¼ m. ENE is the WELL, circular with a big roof. WELL HOUSE, which was next to it, has been demolished and replaced by flats. It had a fine early C18 doorway with broken segmental pediment on carved brackets. A little further E WELL FARM HOUSE, also probably early C18, seven bays, two storeys, red brick. A little to the S of the Well is ROSE HILL SCHOOL, again early C18, but much added to. Giant angle pilasters with oversized pulvinated frieze. Segment-headed windows.

⟨At the E end of the High Street, around WALTON LODGE, a series of buildings illustrating the development towards the modern style in the County Architect's Department: LIBRARY (*J. Harrison*, 1963-4); CLINIC (*R. J. Ash*, 1965-6); JUNIOR SCHOOL (*J. Harrison*, 1963-4), and on the r. two OLD PEOPLE'S HOMES (*R. J. Ash*, 1966-9); AMBULANCE CONTROL HEADQUARTERS (*R. J. Ash*, 1967-9); also ADULT TRAINING CENTRE by *Berry Webber & Partners* and *R. J. Ash*, 1967-9.⟩

BANSTEAD WOOD. Now a hospital, and with very large additions, but the original house is clearly recognizable. It was built in 1884-90 by *Norman Shaw* for the Hon. Francis Baring. Brick, with the upper floor tile-hung and with many gables and star-shaped chimneystacks. An extremely attractive design, in Shaw's nicest home-counties manner. 81 *See p. 595*

SOLOM'S COURT, off the road to Chipstead. By *Sir Guy Dawber*. Published in 1906. L-shaped plan with the forecourt in the re-entrant angle. Grey brick with red brick dressings and roughcast for the upper floor. Free Tudor style with a variety of gables and dormers, but also a Venetian window on the S side.

Traces of NEOLITHIC HUTS have been reported on the Downs, and there is certainly considerable material of the period over the area. There are also several BARROWS on the Downs: four bowl barrows form the Galley Hills, but these are much disturbed by the golf course. One skeleton is all the reported finds.

BARNES

2070

The area to visit in Barnes lies just W of the S end of Castelnau – Church Road, with the church, and on to Barnes Green.

ST MARY. Of the medieval church the chief survival is the E wall of the S aisle. It was originally the chancel. This is evidently

C13, with three stepped lancets and a vesica window over. As for the rest, the brick tower at the w end of the s aisle is late C16 or C17, of a current Thames-Valley type; everything else except for some Perp windows is Victorian and after, the nave, chancel, and N aisle rebuilt in 1904–8 by *Charles Innes*. – PAINTING. Remains of C13 ornamental painting on the E wall of the s aisle above the lancet windows. – STAINED GLASS. Three figures in a s aisle window by *Wailes*, 1853. – MONUMENTS. Brass plate to two young girls of the Wylde family, 'which died virgyns' in 1508 (9 in. figures). – Sir Richard Hoare, of Barn Elms, † 1787. Seated mourning woman and child by an urn, by *J. Hickey* (R. Gunnis).

(ST MICHAEL, Westfields. By *Charles Innes*, 1891–3.

HOLY TRINITY, Castelnau. By *Thomas Allom*, 1868.)*

To the E of the church is THE HOMESTEAD, early C18, five bays, two storeys, yellow and red brick. Weatherboarded wing to the l. In front of the house a row of pollarded lime trees. To the w of the church STRAWBERRY HOUSE (formerly the Rectory). Early C18, with added second floor and parapet. A plain exterior, but a good staircase with three twisted balusters to each tread and carved tread-ends. Further w, facing BARNES COMMON, THE GRANGE, also early C18, and, to its l., the CONVENT OF THE SACRED HEART, partly C18 and partly Early Victorian Gothic. At the w end of STATION ROAD, also facing the Green, MILBOURNE HOUSE, with an irregular C18 front, but inside some earlier decoration, an Elizabethan or Jacobean fireplace in the entrance hall and the remains of a Jacobean staircase.

Two pleasant stretches of houses lie along the river in BARNES TERRACE: Nos. 3–14 and 28–31, all C18, and mostly with cheerful iron verandas or balconies. Especially handsome No. 3 with a Tuscan porch and a balcony with wooden trellis work over, and No. 7 with a very broad bow.

Other points of interest are as follows. In BARNES COMMON an island of houses including some weatherboarding. CASTELNAU has much friendly, remarkably standardized Early Victorian villa architecture, mostly semi-detached with typical arched windows with continuous mouldings. By *Henry Laxton*, 1842. (R. C. Gill). The same in THE BOILEAU, an inn which lies in a good position at the junction with Lonsdale Road. Tuscan porch.

* Information from Mr R. C. Gill.

(In Lonsdale Road ST PAUL'S SCHOOL by *Feilden & Mawson*
(in charge *B. Feilden* and *R. Thompson*), 1966–8. The structure
is Clasp Mark IV.)

(Off Willow Avenue is a small single-storey house by *Timothy
Rendle*, 1967–8. It is approached by a bridge over Beverley
Brook. The house is of brick and timber, with an emphatic
horizontal roof-line.)

BARN ELMS, the mansion of Sir Francis Walsingham, Secretary
of State of Queen Elizabeth from 1579 up to his death in 1590,
was rebuilt by Thomas Cartwright in 1694, then remodelled
by Richard Hoare in 1771. It was demolished in 1954. Nothing
remains, except the ornamental pond and the ICE HOUSE on an
artificial mound into which its pit extended. The area which
was famous as that of the Ranelagh Polo Club has been converted into an LCC Playing Area with CHANGING ACCOM-
MODATION, etc., in the excellent LCC style of the 1950s.

BAYNARDS PARK
2 m. SE of Cranleigh

0030

Baynards was built, in countryside which is still fairly remote, by
Sir George More of Loseley some time after 1587. The house
he built seems to have been very much like a brick and stone
edition of Loseley, but was so much altered in the C19 that
there is now no visual pleasure to be got from it. The original
details can be traced only on the entrance side (N), and then
simply by the type of brick and the colour of the stone dressings
(the C19 used Bath stone or some similar limestone throughout). This front seems to have had three storeys, two end
gables, and a projecting bay including the porch, which was
off-centre and balanced by the main bay window of the hall,
very much as at Loseley. Only the very top of the bay with the
porch looks trustworthy; all the windows are quite new. The
big, separately roofed block which projects on the garden side
also is an addition. These alterations are by *Rickman* (drawings
dated 1834).* The style throughout is brick and stone Tudor,
picturesque enough at a distance but unattractive close to.
Almost everything inside is C19 also, as are the elaborate mock-
castellated entrance courts, the lodges around the estate, and a
big block of COTTAGES to the s beside BAYNARDS STATION,
which retains a charming air of being private rather than
public property.

* *Ferrey*'s obituary mentions that he also did work at Baynards Park.

BEACON HILL *see* HINDHEAD

3060

BEDDINGTON

ST MARY. Quite a big church for what was a village when it was built. There are late C11–C13 masonry fragments. Nave arcade probably C13, aisles early C14, as shown by the N aisle window and the original S aisle one (now W window of the Carew Chapel) with curvilinear tracery. Tower and porch, and possibly chancel, probably of *c*.1390, when Sir Nicholas Carew left money for the rebuilding, the Carew Chapel S of the chancel a little later. Flint and stone, with a W tower, nave and aisles, chancel, and higher S chapel. An outer N aisle was added when the church was restored by *J. Clarke* in 1850 (GS). Interior with tall tower arch, arcades with very odd piers – octagonal with short fronts and long diagonals, which are however in the middle stop-grooved in a rather unlikely way. The S chapel is of two bays, and the arcade here has a pier of the familiar four-shafts-and-four-hollows section and complicatedly moulded arches. Nave roof, chancel arch, chancel roof with very big angels, and decoration probably date from the restoration of 1869 by *J. Clarke*, who certainly added the W vestries at this time. The dormer windows are by *H. P. Burke-Downing*, *c*. 1913.* – FONT. C13, square, on five supports, of Purbeck marble of a usual type: with shallow blank arcading. – REREDOS. Former reredos in nine painted parts (Last Judgement) now in the N aisle (W wall). By *Clayton & Bell*, given in 1869. – PULPIT. 1611, but still with linenfold panels, though separated by posts with arabesque decoration. –

77   ORGAN GALLERY. By *Morris & Co.*, 1869. A delightful piece. The player's space screened like a minstrel's gallery. Painted dado with floral ornament and a tier of small figures. – CHANCEL STALLS. Seven on the S side and two on the N have MISERICORDS with shields, foliage, and two heads. – PLATE. Chalice and Paten by *R.D.*, 1551; Flagon 1639; Paten on foot 1707. – MONUMENTS. Brasses, in the chancel, three hidden by the stalls. The other two are of Nicholas Carew † 1432 and his wife. The figures measure 4 ft 7 in. They lie under cusped round arches. – Also Katheryn Berecroft and her sister † 1507. The figures here are only 10 in. long. – Sir Richard Carew † 1520 and wife. Fine Perp recess in the Carew Chapel. Chest front with elaborate quatrefoils. On it brasses 20 in. long. Back

---

* These details were kindly supplied by Mr H. V. Molesworth-Roberts.

recess with coarse panelling up the jambs and along the depressed arch. Cresting. – Sir Francis Carew † 1611. Alabaster.
Recumbent effigy, the head on a rolled-up mat. Kneeling
family in relief against the front of the tomb-chest. Back wall
with two columns, but no arch. Obelisks and achievement at
the top.

(ALL SAINTS, North Beddington. 1931 by *H. P. Burke-Downing*.
R. Hubbuck)

(ST ELPHEGE (R.C.), Stafford Road, South Beddington. By
J. H. Beart-Foss and *Father Benedict Williamson*, 1908.
HVM-R)

(ST MICHAEL, Milton Road, South Beddington. By *W. D.
Caröe*, 1906. Later additions. HVM-R)

BEDDINGTON PLACE (Carew Manor School). In the buildings extending to the NE of the church, the Carew mansion
of Henry VIII's time survives. It was rebuilt by Sir Nicholas
Carew *c*.1530–40, and largely rebuilt again *c*.1740. The HALL
is over 60 ft long and over 32 ft wide. It is very tall, and has tall
two-light windows and a splendid hammerbeam and arch-
braced roof with tracery over the collar-beams and two tiers of
double-curved wind-braces.* In the garden outside the Hall
an early C18 ORANGERY WALL, nearly 200 ft long, with tall
blank arcading divided into pairs by simple pilasters. The iron
GATES at the W entrance are said to be replicas. The big red-
brick enlargement, later an orphanage, was built in 1837 and
after. (Later C19 alterations were carried out by *Joseph
Clarke*, who also designed a picturesque half-timbered lodge
in 1878. GS)

⟨ROUNDSHAW (entrance from Forester's Drive). Croydon Airport closed down in 1959. The new housing on part of the site
(377 acres) is planned for *c*.7,600 people, and was designed by
Clifford Culpin & Partners for the London Borough of Sutton
and the GLC. The plan was prepared in 1963. At the time of
writing some of the houses and flats, and one primary school,
are in use; shops, community buildings, and more schools are
to follow. The general plan is a grid, with buildings of varied
heights, mostly two-storey terrace houses and four-storey
maisonettes and flats, with, at the far end, one very large
eleven-storey block. The dominant feature of the plan is the
strict segregation of traffic and pedestrians, particularly carefully worked out for the larger blocks. These are built in pairs,

* This resembles the roof of Eltham Palace, *c*. 1470–80 (HVM-R).

linked by a wide deck or platform above garages (the plan allows for the garaging of c.2,000 cars, i.e. one car per dwelling). Both upper and lower maisonettes have doors opening on to this deck, from which one can reach bridges over the roads, play spaces, etc. – a much more humane system than the old-fashioned type of balconies. The colours are kept neutral. The larger blocks are of concrete slabs with a ribbed surface, the smaller houses of purple brick with grey, white, or black details. With little landscaping completed so far, no shops, and the flat, undeveloped parts of the airport stretching round about (with an impressive view of the Croydon skyscrapers on the horizon), the mood at the moment is somewhat stark and isolated, but this may change. At the SE corner of the site is a PRIMARY SCHOOL, a simple single-storey building in dark brick with white boarding, and next to it the exciting BOILER HOUSE (which provides heat and hot water for the whole site), with an enormous white chimney and the machinery visible through all-glass walls.⟩

A ROMAN BATH BUILDING and associated cobbled area overlie earlier occupation material of the C1, C2, and C3. Traces of building material to the S may suggest the whereabouts of the villa.

WOODCOTE. See p. 537.

BELMONT see SUTTON

BENHILTON see SUTTON

²⁰⁴⁰

BETCHWORTH

Half-way between Dorking and Reigate, facing the North Downs on the parallel sandstone ridge, here at its lowest and barely visible. Modest but satisfying Home Counties village with one long street, breaking up at the N end into isolated big houses and long walls. This end is rapidly changing (1961) into a pattern of carefully designed smaller houses, which need not necessarily be a bad thing.

ST MICHAEL. Bigger than the Surrey average. Most of the bones of the building are mid-C13, and it must have been a gloomy all-lancet church with a huge pitched roof, like so many in Sussex. The issue was confused inextricably by the C19, first by E. C. Hakewill in 1851, who removed a Norman crossing tower and built a new tower at the end of the S aisle, and then in another restoration in 1870, when most windows were renewed in yellow limestone instead of the grey firestone. The 1851 alterations, though more drastic, were far less visually destructive than this deadly self-righteous renewal.

The oldest parts of the church are in fact of the C11. One capital, re-set in the s window of the tower, is certainly pre-Conquest. It is one more puzzling fragment to add to our meagre knowledge of the Late Saxon style: simply eight circular roll-mouldings, one above the other. It is difficult even to guess at the detail of the building that could house such a bloody-minded fragment. Pre-Conquest architecture was certainly not dull. Also C11, but emphatically post-Conquest, is the arch between the s aisle and the tower. If it looks crazily narrow now, especially with the sturdy Norman shafts reconstructed, the reason is that it was re-set in 1851. It was originally the much wider arch from the Norman nave into the Norman crossing tower. It has one order of shafts on thumping big block capitals, with fragments of some form of leaf decoration on the outer order and a single-step arch. The E arch of the present tower is of the late C12, with a chamfered arch resting on square imposts. The s chancel arcade is of the very early part of the C13, with simple circular capitals, octagonal abaci, and arches with one step and one chamfer. The nave arcades are both C13, but differ in details. The N arcade has fat circular piers, circular abaci, and double-chamfered arches, the s arcade semi-octagonal responds and one octagonal and one circular pier. The arches here have smaller chamfers. The clerestory has irregular circular openings, very much renewed: they could be C13, C15, or even C17. The E windows of both chancel and s chapel were Perp and are now Dec. The total effect is quite soulless. – FONT. By *Eric Kennington*, 1951, Romanesque tub shape and detail which is really naturalism squashed flat: nothing like the quality of his theatrical effigy of T. E. Lawrence at Wareham. – CHEST. Massive and undatable dug-out, with seven iron staples. – PULPIT. Lush 1885; five kinds of marble and inlaid mosaic panels of Faith, Hope, and Love. This sort of furniture is undervalued. It is as full of life and as robust as a Jacobean pulpit, and in fact must reflect a similar standard of values. – (STAINED GLASS. N transept by *Clayton & Bell*; s choir aisle by *Belham & Co.* (*H. S. Murray del.*), 1881.) – PLATE. Two flagons, two cups 1639, one of the latter from St Bride Fleet Street. – BRASS (N side of chancel). Thomas Wardysworth, vicar, † 1533. Small figure holding a

chalice. Full face; a little naïve. – MONUMENTS. (Sir Benjamin
Brodie, bust of 1842. – Col. Edward Goulburn and wife † 1891.
Pink marble tablet: a very early example of Neo-Georgian.
NT) – Arthur Jaffray † 1864. Typically mid-Victorian, by *E. B.
Stephens*: a naturalistic bust under a Romanesque arch. –
(Elephantine LYCHGATE, 1864.)

BETCHWORTH HOUSE, at the S end of the village. A confused,
moderate-sized building, mostly dull stuccoed early C19 with
typical wide eaves, probably by *Cundy*, 1808. The E front,
however, is domestic Georgian: five by two bays with brick
quoins, a central Gibbs-rusticated door, and an octagonal
cupola above dated $\frac{1\ 6}{7\ 5}$ which is presumably to be read 1765.

At the N end of the main street is BROOME PARK, with a plain
early C19 ashlar front and a good, though neglected, TEMPLE
of *c.*1760 in the grounds NE of the house. The temple is
circular and domed, with Late Palladian plasterwork inside.
The outside has a lot of intermittent rustication, in low relief,
and a (later) crude Greek Doric portico.

S down the village street there are some unremarkable cottages,
until the road divides, one branch turning a corner and revealing an almost formal cul-de-sac approach to the church, which
appears sideways-on in a frame of tarred weatherboarded
barns on the W side and simple C17 brick cottages on the E
side: one of them keeps a C15 half-timbered gable. The main
road turns left past the OLD HOUSE, a formidably direct early
C18 building, as stark as a warehouse; simply ten bays and
three storeys of plain brickwork with no ornamental detail
except brick string-courses and the simplest kind of arched
doorcase. Beyond this the road goes between the E end of the
churchyard on one side and a wall on the other – i.e. an
agreeable and very English variety of scene in a short distance –
and then comes to another group near the E end of the church,
with THE DOLPHIN, a big, lumpish, mansard-roofed pub of
*c.*1700, and OLD MILL COTTAGE to the S, a genuine C16 or
C17 cottage in a county which has so many fakes and restorations. Note especially the gable and overhang at the W end,
with its covering of plaster and roughcast.

Another lane runs E from the Dolphin. On the S side of it first
of all MORE PLACE, restored C15 with a stone chimneystack
at the N end and exposed close-timbering on the W front.
Then WONHAM MANOR, demure and rather silly brick
Gothick with a few fancy stucco hoods and battlements,

possibly by *Lewis Wyatt*, who exhibited a design for Wonham in 1810. (The core of the house is probably older; inside are wainscoted rooms which look *c.*1700.*) Finally, beside the Mole is WONHAM MILL, an unpretentious C19 water mill, still used, and partly rebuilt (1957, by *E. W. Banfield & Son*) as an admirable if unconscious bit of modern industrial architecture: steel frame and steel cladding all exposed and painted grey.

BETCHWORTH CASTLE, nearer Dorking than Betchworth. There were two licences to crenellate – 1379 and 1448. The building was converted after partial demolition in 1690, and finally dismantled in 1860.‡ There survive a lot of masonry fragments on a knoll in the park, never excavated, and with very little architectural detail. They represent a C15 stone manor house (see the remains of two-storey Perp windows at the NE end, presumably the solar) with quoined additions of *c.*1600 to the entrance front to convert it into an E-shaped building. Later (C18?) brick porch. All very ruined. There is now no house in the park, but the stables remain, by *Soane*, 1799, now converted to cottages as Nos. 8–14 CASTLE GARDENS. They are half-H-shaped, single-storeyed except for the middle of the N side, and thickly patterned in Soane's 'primitive' style – flint and brick, single and paired pilasters, and alternative open and blind arches. As sophisticated an attitude to the countryside as Marie Antoinette's Hameau at Versailles, but done in terms of the Picturesque. Nature has become stern, not pretty. No attempt at spatial revelations such as those in the Chelsea Hospital stables.

(BETCHWORTH PARK GOLF CLUB, s of the A25. By *Clifford, Tee & Gale*, 1966.)

BISLEY

Partly heathland, on which are the N.R.A. rifle ranges where the famous annual competition is held; the rest, E of A322, is mainly carefully preserved farmland. KNAPHILL, nearer Woking, is Victorian working-class with BARRACKS and BROOKWOOD MENTAL HOSPITAL, both mid-C19 stock-brick agglomerations. ⟨Knaphill now has much recent housing, and more is planned. Housing for 14,000 people is to be built around an artificial lake, on a site between Knaphill and Horsell. In HERMITAGE ROAD, the WINSTON CHURCHILL

---

* Information kindly provided by Dr A. Gomme.
‡ Information kindly supplied by Mr D. F. Renn.

COUNTY SECONDARY SCHOOL by *Raymond Ash*, the County Architect, 1964–7. Very large, for 990 children. Two long ranges in front, with green and cream spandrels and shallow pitched roofs, linked by a lower range with assembly and dining halls to a neat four-storey classroom block behind.⟩

ST JOHN BAPTIST. By itself in fields, a pleasant ensemble which does not stand a close look at the details. Old work mostly carstone, probably C13, with new N aisle (1873) and early C19 stock-brick chancel (which replaced a timber-framed one). Shingled belfry on C14 timber framing standing inside the nave (but not structurally clear of it, like the Essex belfries – beams with complicated mouldings tie it into the walls) and good florid late C14 timber W porch with heavy bargeboarding. The inside has decent modern PEWS and a Jacobean PULPIT.

(HOLY TRINITY, Knaphill. 1907 by *J. H. Ball*. Red brick Romanesque. NT)

(In Church Lane, THE OLD COTTAGE, with C14 work.*)

BLACKDOWN
1 m. E of Frimley Green

9050

Entirely a military settlement. The Garrison Church (ST MICHAEL) is fun – clerestoried and aisled, corrugated iron, kept in tip-top condition. It used to be painted red and orange, and looked exactly like a toy church.

BLACKHEATH
1 m. NE of Wonersh

0040

A very trim, largely Victorian hamlet on the hills above Albury, still remote as places around Guildford go.

ST MARTIN. A queer little building of 1895 by *C. Harrison Townsend*, of the Whitechapel Art Gallery and the Horniman Museum, in a sort of Spanish-Mission style, with a low bell-cote. Very minor, with none of the impressive Art Nouveau details of his church at Great Warley in Essex. Inside a good deal of marbling and some rather bad frescoes by *Mrs Lea Merritt*.

GREYFRIARS. A Franciscan monastery. Simple Late-Gothic-Revival stone buildings of 1895, by *F. A. Walters*, soberly and honestly detailed. Church and dormitories under one roof.

* Information from Mrs R. F. Cooper and Mr K. Gravett.

BLETCHINGLEY

The best of the villages off the sandstone ridge E of Reigate, one long street running downhill from W to E. Probably originally a medium-size triangular market-place* now partly encroached on by a block of tile-hung buildings with a picturesque alley – Middle Row – between them and the original street-line. The church stands at the NE corner, with a small square open space in front of it. Simple, pretty, and very satisfying.

ST MARY. Superficially, as seen from the village street, an impressive Perp church of the type of Sevenoaks or Cranbrook in Kent. A closer look shows very much restoration and re-building. The big, unbuttressed W tower, 20 ft across inside, is Norman (see e.g. the two-light window on the W side). C17 top in the Perp style, entirely renewed in 1910 by *Baker-King*. The tower arch has big square responds, corner shafts, and very stilted carving of upright leaves and upright volute-like leaves. Norman also the chancel, see the reveals of a N window close to the E end. The rest of the chancel C13, with lancet windows W of the Norman reveals. The chamfers of their reveals stand curiously on short shafts which in their turn stand on wall seats, as if the plan had been changed mid-way up from wall arcading to the present lancet arrangement. The E lancets date from the restoration of 1870 by *J. L. Pearson* (the E window was formerly Perp).‡ Of the same time as the chancel the remarkably wide S chapel. Lancet windows on the S side, one low-side shafted lancet and a small circular opening below said to be connected with the cell of Roger the Hermit, mentioned in the C13. The rest of the S chapel is late C15, Lingfield style, three-light windows with segmental heads. The S doorway is renewed, but its richly moulded arch is C13 again. Chancel arch and S arcade mid-C15 Perp, the normal four-shafts-and-four-hollows type. N aisle 1856 by *Rhode Hawkins*. All the S windows 1856 in a sort of fancy Early Perp. At the E end of the aisle, a rood turret. Quite a rich two-storeyed Perp S porch. Also inside the church, now in the N aisle, is a Perp niche, an ogee arch under battlemented cresting. – FONT. C15, standard design, octagonal bowl with quatrefoils, octagonal stem with trefoil-headed niches. – REREDOS. By *Street*, 1870, with Bishop Wilberforce put among the apostles in his own

---

* Bletchingley was originally both a market town and – until 1832 – a borough.

‡ Information kindly supplied by Mr A. Quiney.

lifetime. Bad Butterfield-style. – PULPIT. Straightforward
Jacobean, given in 1630 by the son of the builder of Pendell
Court. – STAINED GLASS. Two S aisle windows by *Comper*
and *Kempe*, easy to distinguish; both bad. – PLATE. Chalice
1576; Paten 1707; Flagon 1733. – MONUMENTS. First, a set
of BRASSES, jogged around as much as the architectural details
have been. C15 Priest (N side of chancel). In the N transept some
sets of children, and some arms, all very small and all hugger-
mugger on one plate. Also a full-face C15 female figure about
18 in. high, and Thomas Warde† 1541 and his wife, in primitive
style, e.g. the violent hair, and with an unrelated and even more
crudely drawn Trinity above. The figures are actually probably
C15, pirated to make a memorial to Mr Warde. – Sir Thomas
Cawarden † 1559 (S chancel arcade), Anne of Cleves's Steward,
hence an up-to-date tomb, though of poor quality. A simple
chest, without effigy, ornamented only with pilasters and
panels containing strapwork, rosettes, and bows. On the chest a
small brass plate with exquisite Italic writing. The monument
is forward-looking in more senses than one; to quote from the
guide, 'Under King Edward VI Sir Thomas became an ardent
Reformer . . . under Queen Mary Sir Thomas became a
Roman Catholic'. W of the monument, the beginnings of an
unfinished canopy. – Sir Robert Clayton† 1707, Lord Mayor of
London (S chancel chapel), one of the most splendid early C18
monuments in the country. Signed by *Richard Crutcher*, and
his only known work. It is a huge composition, husband and
wife over-life-size under a towering aedicule filling the whole
of the E wall of the chapel. Sacheverell Sitwell's comment,
'in the Corinthian manner, that is, not yet Roman at all, and
still less Italian, but only English and of Queen Anne's reign',
is very true; his assessment 'one of the most entirely satisfying
works of art in the whole kingdom' is an over-statement.
While the figures are superb, with character expressed directly
through the moulding of faces and garments without any
expressionist tricks or distortions whatever, the architectural
frame is muddled; e.g. the awkward segmental arch inside the
broken and split pediment. As well as the figures, there are
sturdy cherubs on either side, and a pathetic baby in embroidered clothes below, still looking almost Jacobean.* This majestic
style came originally from Holland (Admiral Tromp † 1658 in

* There is a puzzle here. The baby died in 1669, and is in fact commemorated separately at Ickenham, Middlesex, with a similarly pathetic figure. Did
Crutcher copy this, or did he do both monuments?

the Nieuwe Kerk, Amsterdam, J. van Wassenaer † 1667 in St
James at The Hague) rather than France or Italy, and had a
sudden and glorious flowering in the City of London about
1700. – Lady Clayton † 1772 by *Tyler* (s chancel chapel).
Cherub with urn in big niche. Standard but attractive. – Sir
William Bensley † 1809 by *Bacon Jun.* (N transept). Equally
standard but with sentimentality added; a mourning figure,
ships (ex-R.N.), and elephants (ex-East India Company). –
Compare this with the simple polychrome tablet to William
Pellatt † 1801 (transept), where some local mason has thought
for himself – however minor the result – and not turned in a
stock design.

Surprisingly little architecture in the village, whose attractiveness
is an aggregate of tile-hung and brick gables, though none the
less effective for that, especially the N side, with its stepped and
irregular building line. Starting from the w there are fragments
of the C12 CASTLE to the s of the road, in the grounds of
Castle Hill. They are in the form of a wide, flat mound, not a
normal motte, on the very crest of the ridge, with the remains
of a rectangular keep and a lobed bailey. As it was demolished
in 1264 as part of the warfare between Simon de Montfort and
Henry III, the lack of evidence is not surprising. In the High
Street on the s side there is GLENFIELD, early C18 with a late
C18 joke for a porch: wood columns and Adam palm-leaf capitals set under Ionic capitals about twice as big as they should
be. Further E the WHYTE HART, with a plain stucco Tudor front
of *c.*1800 on a C16 frame. On the N side brick and tile-hanging
until MIDDLE ROW forks off to the church, with its w end
admirably punctuated by a large tree. In Middle Row a couple
of tile-hung overhangs, and SELMES, an effective mid-C19
butcher's shop. N from the crossroads, beyond the church, is
ORCHARD CROFT, formerly the Godstone Union Workhouse,
the oldest bits utilitarian brick by *John Whichcord Sen., c.*1840.
s from the crossroads is Outwood Lane, with THE GRANGE
on the E side, *c.*1700, with the upper storey tile-hung and
casements – apparently original – employing a weird variant
of the Venetian window with the head of the centre light
segmental instead of semicircular.

Quite a number of houses further out. To the N is Pendell (*see* p.
405) and Brewer Street, with several cottages, and particularly
the impressive C15 BREWER STREET FARMHOUSE. Close 31
timbering ('post and pan') throughout, all now exposed. High
central hall, now divided, with hipped Horsham slate roof,

two side gables with overhangs. Entrance under the southern-most gable, centre recessed in the Kentish way but without any curved braces forming spandrels (an early form, therefore ?). N again an intriguing fragment in PLACE FARM, formerly Bletchingley Place, Anne of Cleves's house. It is now plain early C18 brick with just one tantalizing four-centred brick arch, partly blocked, as the doorway: presumably this was the base of the gatehouse. Big and good BARN to the W, tarred weatherboarding on a stone base.

s of the ridge, on the way to Outwood, is SANDHILLS, a house of 1893 by *Mervyn Macartney*, L-shaped free Tudor, in an advanced style without being original. Perversely, the end wall facing S with a view over the Weald is nearly all blank brick-work. To the E the best cottage in the plain is RABY'S, formerly Coldharbour Farm, with wide, irregularly spaced half-timbering, unrestored. This is on a cul-de-sac lane to SOUTH PARK FARM, a handsome mock-C18 house, rebuilt in 1949 after bomb damage by *E. D. Jefferiss Mathews*. The stables are of *c.*1650 with brick mullions and hood-moulds, attractively converted into a chapel (ST MARK'S) in 1909. Very happy group with the surrounding cottages, partly due to the one-way access and the corresponding remoteness.

3040
BLINDLEY HEATH
2 m. NW of Lingfield

ST JOHN EVANGELIST. 1842 by *John Whichcord & Walker*. E.E. with W tower and broach-spire. The apsidal chancel and S aisle are of 1886 by *G. M. Hills*.

(ST THOMAS MORE (R.C.), High Street. 1959 by *R. C. Hosford*. – TRIPTYCH by *D. O'Connell*. DE)

(COMFORTS PLACE, Tandridge Lane. Timber-framed, brick and tile-hung. C15–17. D. M. Palliser)

(RED BARN, corner of Tandridge Lane. Originally a C15 hall house. Kingpost roof. Altered in 1689. Arthur Oswald)

BOOKHAM see GREAT BOOKHAM and LITTLE BOOKHAM

0060
BOTLEYS
Between Ottershaw and Lyne

Four-square Late Palladian, beautifully sited on a hill. Now the nurses' home to a mental asylum, whose wards fill the grounds.

Built in 1765 by *Kenton Couse*, who was a Flitcroft pupil and inherited Flitcroft's ability to assemble strict Palladian detail without any originality but with impeccable proportions. The result is better than the routine 1760s Palladian of Carr of York or Capability Brown (or even Sir William Chambers, cf. Peper Harow). Seven-bay N and s fronts with three-bay astylar pediments and rusticated basements. The E front with a little more detail – swags in the pediment and attached Composite columns supporting it. Big, fairly tactful C20 extension on the w side. Inside, a simple entrance hall with a screen of coupled Ionic columns opposite the door. Plain staircase and plain big rooms. A simple entrance arch at the Chertsey end of the park was demolished in 1956 to make a rounded-off corner with concrete posts and wire, a contemptible piece of 'improvement'.

BOURNE

1 m. s of Farnham

ST THOMAS. 1911, lancet Gothic by *H. Sidebotham*. Supervised by *Sir Charles Nicholson*, hence simple whitewashed interior, and simple wagon roof with kingposts. Indifferent quality; unfinished. Part of the former church, by *J. Colson*, 1862, survives as a Lady Chapel.

(The BOURNE SCHOOLS are by *Basil Champneys*, 1869. David Watkin)

BOWLHEAD GREEN *see* BROOK

BRAMLEY

A long, winding, nondescript street on the Guildford–Horsham road; part Victorian, part vernacular cottages, part walls and trees, but nothing kept up long enough to set a pattern, and no centre.

HOLY TRINITY. Minor C12 fragments in the shape of the head of a Norman arch equipped with new jambs and set up as the w doorway. Complete simple C13 chancel, of comfortable squat proportions. All the windows lancets with blunt-ended splays, hence probably early, c.1220: a triplet in the E end. The remainder all 1850, and 1876 by *Woodyer*. The chancel still has a little architectural character. – PLATE. Paten, c.1590. – MONUMENT (s aisle). Henry Ludlow † 1730. Big, well-carved urn and flambeau in Palladian architectural frame (with the proportions gone a little awry in the pediment). Typical of the then new anti-Baroque style of Kent and Rysbrack.

CEMETERY CHAPEL, s end of the village. 1881. Compact cruciform design with octagonal belfry broached from a square base. Well proportioned.

Starting at the N end of the village, Gosden Common has a few cottages and GOSDEN HOUSE, bulky stone-faced early C19. Further s is a crossroads. Along the road to the w is MILL-MEAD, built by *Lutyens* in 1904–7 for Gertrude Jekyll as a building speculation. Small, L-shaped, still with a piquant garden wall screening the house from the street, still with a piquant gabled entrance, but the main block away from the road is now classical, here quite agreeable and personable Early Georgian. (Traces of the *Jekyll* garden still survive. NT) Minor houses all down the village street. At the s end on the w side is EAST MANOR HOUSE, with half-timber work of two dates – *c.*1550 on the gabled front facing the street and *c.*1580 at the back with a little star-patterned timber-framing. Inside, late C16 mural paintings, chiefly floral patterns, done on linen stretched and nailed to the wall surface.

UNSTEAD MANOR HOUSE, ¾ m. NW. Impressive brick and timber house, T-shaped, mostly C16, but the s gable earlier with an overhang above close timbering. Unrestored.

(LITTLE TANGLEY, ½ m. N. A dim house of 1877 given a new porch and staircase hall by *Lutyens* in 1899, and also extended by him at the back with a steep roof slope and two giant chimneys. Amusing side entrance with three canopies of different heights hanging on iron hooks. Another extension at the opposite end, with a pretty inlaid-tile loggia, since filled in. – The STABLES, now a private house called Edgton, are one of *Lutyens*'s first works: 1890. Pretty half-timber and tile-hanging, with a dovecote. – GARDEN. Fragments of a *Jekyll* layout. NT)

sw along the Hascombe road, SNOWDENHAM HALL is a formidable house of 1868 with additions of 1887, by *Ralph Nevill.** The centre diapered brickwork with a huge bay window, and one big half-timbered extension at one end balanced by a longer tile-hung range at the other with two small half-timbered bays on its own account. Overpowering; the effect as wild as E. S. Prior in its apparently chaotic but in fact balanced discords of shapes and materials.

* Information obtained at the extreme stretch of 'living memory' from Mr J. Buckingham.

Beyond this NURSCOMBE FARM, a good, unrestored example
of the late C16 Surrey farm. Exposed timber on the N side *See*
(diagonal braces) and plastered gables on the S. p. 595

BREWER STREET *see* BLETCHINGLEY

BROADHAM GREEN *see* OXTED

BROCKHAM 1040
2 m. E of Dorking

A delightful village: a triangular green stopped at the S end by the 5
side elevation of the church, whose simple colour pattern is as
startling and effective as if John Piper had invented it for one
of his paintings. The N side comfortable and cottagey, transformed by having the tremendous slopes of Box Hill as a
backcloth. The E side mostly trees, the SW corner a little more
formal, with HOPE HOUSE, smooth Regency stucco. A model
of how a memorable group can be made without a single building that is noteworthy in itself.

CHRIST CHURCH. Far more important as a townscape object
than as architecture. By *Ferrey*, 1846, in cruciform C13 style,
with an effective polychrome of firestone walls and limestone
dressings. Simple honest interior, much more solid than
Ferrey's normal style. – STAINED GLASS (nave). By *Mayer* of
Munich (Faith, Hope, etc.). Mid-century, bad but typical.

A few buildings are worth a special note. E of the green is
BROCKHAM COURT, with a simple three-by-two-bay late C18
front. SE in Wheeler's Lane is WAY HOUSE, a long range of
tile-hung estate cottages of 1871; multiple gables with the
end house canted forward towards the street, making a very
picturesque group. To the SW FELTONS FARM has a good
set of tarred Surrey barns forming a quadrangle with the C17
farmhouse on one side as the smallest building in it.

BROCKHAM WARREN. Small Regency house right on the edge
of the Downs, E of Box Hill. Two storeys, central bow, big
ground-floor veranda. Very typical.

BROOK 9030
1 m. SE of Witley

Pleasant tile-hung cottages – the best is the village pub – and a
tiny green, but nothing special.

BOWLHEAD GREEN, ¾ m. w of this, is more remote but similar, an odd thing when both are between two villages – Witley and Thursley – with some of the most picturesque cottages in Surrey. s of Bowlhead Green, at EMLEY FARM, a good set of barns, including one brick and timber-framed.

9050

BROOKWOOD

CEMETERY. Founded in 1854 on 2,400 acres of heathland by the London Necropolis Company when dying Londoners became a serious numerical problem. Designed apparently by *Sir William Tite* and *Sydney Smirke*. Whoever did the landscaping made a magnificent job of it, planting Wellingtonias and big conifers that have matured splendidly to give a sombre complex landscape unlike anything anywhere else in the country. Originally a railway line served it, with two simple white painted wood station buildings by *Tite* (one survives). The chapels are not of interest, but some of the mausolea are, ranging from Gothic caskets like the Bent Mausoleum to the late C17 English style (Wood Mausoleum) as well as more obvious classical derivatives; there is even one like a miniature Einstein Tower.

In the sw corner is the Military Cemetery (largely 1914–18). Fairly weak neo-Baroque for the British and magnificent landscaping for the American: a long lawn bordered by evergreens with the Mausoleum at the end (McKim, Mead & White-style classical) and the Stars and Stripes flying in front of it, laid out and landscaped by *Egerton Swartwout* of New York, 1929. It is bursting with panache, which is an odd word to use of a cemetery: the quality that makes U.S. Neo-Colonial so much better than our own Neo-Georgian. (Canadian War Memorial Building 1945–6 by *Maufe*.)

(ST SAVIOUR. A neat church of 1909 with Lutyenesque details (e.g. the porch) by *J. H. Ball* (cf. St Agatha, Portsmouth). NT)

2050

BUCKLAND

w of Reigate. A small and very trim oblong green with the church and the main road at the s end and good views across to the North Downs. In fact, so trim that it looks suburban even though all the elements have stayed rural.

ST MARY. Effectively all 1860, by *Woodyer* (the four-post belfry framing is old), and a very pretty job indeed. Nave, chancel, and bellcote, all in dark Bargate stone. The style is Woodyer's own brand of Gothic, particularly effective at the w end with delicate windows in the belfry and a big window with solid curvilinear head below. This is Victorian village-church building at its best, completely appropriate to the size of the building, and early enough in Woodyer's work to be free of mannerism for its own sake. The inside, inevitably, is much weaker, but the fittings are generally pretty, e.g. the FONT COVER and the SPIRAL STAIRCASE to the belfry. – STAINED GLASS. Some by *Hardman*, on both sides of the chancel e.g., but shown up by one of the nave windows, C14, with figures of St Peter and St Paul under (partly renewed) canopies. Very good – about the best in the county – with beautifully fired dark blues and reds. – REREDOS. Gilded and very thistly, 1851–Exhibition style. Said to be German.

(SCHOOL on the N side of the green with tile-hung gable also by *Woodyer*, 1862. NT)

The best cottage at Buckland is STREET'S FARM, on the w side of the green. C17, now plastered, with a tarred weatherboarded barn alongside it. S of the church is BUCKLAND COURT, now with rambling stucco-classical elevations of *c.*1835. It has two simple roughcast octagonal late C18 lodges on the main road, and the remains of peculiar STABLES, much decayed since the war. They were originally a gimcrack late C18 stucco composition on a shallow curve with one round castellated tower in the centre and one at either end. Now only the southernmost is left, with very elaborately panelled carved entrance doors, Jacobean style.

(CHINERY HOUSE, by *Michael Manser Associates*, 1966. Simple single-storey steel-framed and glass house.)

BURGH HEATH
I m. SE of Epsom

2050

(ST MARY, Brighton Road. 1909, flint chequerwork exterior.
GREAT BURGH. 1912 by *Ernest Newton*. Large and plain Neo-Georgian.
At LITTLE BURGH, a former RIDING SCHOOL, octagonal.*)

* Information kindly supplied by Mr S. J. Totman.

BURPHAM
1½ m. NE of Guildford

St Luke, By *Woodyer*, 1859, a decent job. Simple, aisleless, lancet chapel-of-ease with a well-proportioned coherent interior. Five-light E window and weird SEDILIA.

BURROWS CROSS
Between Shere and Peaslake

Burrows Cross House. Small, demure house by *Norman Shaw*, 1886–9, in his very best tile-hung style. Long, low garden front, and delightful entrance courtyard with a most complex arrangement of masses – U-shaped, with differing wings, the centre itself in two parts, with a gabled section brought forward. All the first floor tile-hung. Without any pretensions at all, or any of Shaw's insensitiveness. It is difficult to imagine that the same man did both this (or Banstead Wood) and The Hallams, near Wonersh. Was it built by one of his assistants with a surer touch than Shaw himself? (Further extensions by *Shaw* c.1895 for B. W. Leader. NT)

(HAZELHATCH. A small tile-hung house by *Lutyens* of 1896–7 for the Hon. Emily Lawless, an Anglo-Irish lady novelist. Exterior with gables derived from Webb's Joldwynds. Staircase window deeply recessed internally to provide room for Miss Lawless's built-in writing desk. Originally a *Jekyll* garden. NT)

BURSTOW

In the Weald plain near the Sussex border, E of Horley. Much of it is timidly suburbanized, but the group by the church keeps its big trees and seclusion, like an East Berkshire village.

6 St Bartholomew. The notable thing about Burstow church is the timber tower at the W end, like an Essex belfry (in Surrey cf. also Newdigate and formerly Horne). Built up with four corner posts on a stone base, diagonal bracing, and aisles on three sides (W, N, and S) with lean-to roofs concealing extra buttressing for the upper stages. It has weatherboarding below and superbly detailed shingles above – the best in the county (and hence probably in the country) – giving the tower a flavour all of its own. This upper stage is battered, rising to a delicate broach-spire and four corner pinnacles, also shingled.

This is exactly the same style as Horley (*see* p. 318) and from its subtlety and deftness looks C18, though the framing is, of course, medieval, and probably C16, judging by the detail of the w door. The belfry is clearly a separate construction, for the church has a w wall of stone.* The body of the church is effectively Perp, though one Norman nave window (N) and one Norman chancel window (N; now into the vestry) remain. Perp s aisle (with oddly rough piers, quatrefoils set diagonally). Big square-headed Perp windows of four lights (cf. Merstham). Weald stone with firestone dressings, an unusual combination. Pretty Victorian bargeboarding to both nave and aisle. The inside not heavily restored, with honest details like the PISCINA and pair of niches on either side of the stilted chancel arch, all Perp. (The restoration was by *Ferrey*, 1884–95.) – FONT. Perp, octagonal. Quatrefoils on the bowl and leaves on the cove between bowl and stem, i.e. one stage more elaborate than most Surrey fonts. – CHEST. Formidably Wealden. Big, with semi-circular top, entirely iron-bound in thin vertical strips. Presumably of *c*.1600. – PLATE. Cup 1667.

Not much in the parish. By the church, OLD COURT is simple C18 brick rebuilt in 1786. To the N BROADBRIDGE FARM is a prim house of *c*.1780, three-by-two-bay, with the top storey tile-hung; an odd effect, probably a C19 addition. 1 m. N again is BURSTOW LODGE, with simple tile-hanging and stucco concealing a C15 hall house. (Inside, kingpost roof and original doors and fireplaces. MHLG)

BURWOOD
1½ m. S of Walton-on-Thames

BURWOOD PARK SCHOOL. Early C19 (before 1809). Of three wide bays, rendered. Porch of four Tuscan columns. One-storeyed one-bay wings. The grounds originally extended over 400 acres.

FOX OAK, Seven Hills Road. By *Halsey Ricardo*, 1886–7 and 1892. A picturesque composition. With gabled timber-framed upper floor. The garden side made L-shaped by the addition of 1892.

MENTAL HOSPITAL, Queen's Road. Built as the Metropolitan Convalescent Institution in 1840, enlarged in 1862 and 1868. Architect *J. Clarke*. Large, Late Classical, symmetrical and very plain.

* The tower arch is recent, according to the VCH.

BUSBRIDGE

¾ m. SE of Godalming

No old village; originally there was only Busbridge Park and scattered cottages. The church is N of the house and nearer Munstead.

JOHN THE BAPTIST. By *Scott*, probably *G. G. Jun.*, 1865–7, as it is a good example of the masculine style and the response to the *genius loci* of this rare architect. Bargate stone, very pretty shingled central tower, gabled transept ends (an architectural composition of lancets) without the transepts to go with them, i.e. simply in the line of the nave walls, giving some odd cross-lighting effects inside. The inside space firm but flavourless, and hence not a bad vehicle for the late C19 additions done under the influence of Gertrude Jekyll. First the STAINED GLASS in E and W windows by *Burne-Jones* made by *Morris & Co.*,* 1899, with familiar blues and greens. The W window is especially effective with its cinquefoil roundel above filled with a delightful pattern of foliage. (The chancel s windows have *Morris & Co.* glass of 1905. R. Hubbuck) Far more remarkable the mysterious and moving ROOD and CHANCEL SCREEN combined, made in iron by *J. Starkie Gardner* from designs by *Lutyens* of 1897, installed in 1899. It fills the upper parts of the knobbly Middle Pointed chancel arch, a system of slender uprights ending in mid air in a complex set of loops and scrolls and supporting, clear of the frame, Christ with outstretched arms above two kneeling angels face to face – the latter the favourite Art Nouveau composition acting as the roots of a tree-like composition which leads to the figure of Christ above. With exquisite calculation Lutyens arranged that the composition is always seen against the dark chancel roof, to increase the sense of mysterious transparency, and then adjusted the forward projection of the figure of Christ so that it always dominates whilst still remaining part of the composition. In the end perhaps the calculation is too exquisite; a pretty religious fairy-tale, remote from reality. Perhaps there was some blockage in Lutyens which always prevented him making the leap from wit to true feeling. The quality of carving is hard to see from ground level but is probably fairly sweet. Luxurious marble slabs set into a small stone screen below, increasing the sense of contrast. They must also be by *Lutyens*.

In the churchyard a WAR MEMORIAL by *Lutyens*, 1920–2,

* Who also made the altar frontal, designed by *William Morris c.*1870.

slim and elegant, with the same over-developed sense of volumetric relations as his Cenotaph in Whitehall. Also by *Lutyens* tombs to Gertrude Jekyll † 1932 and Sir Herbert Jekyll † 1932 and his wife † 1937: three tomb slabs in front and an intricate composition of an urn and stone balustrade behind, oddly like Soane translated into the blunt obtuse forms of the 1930s. (Also a gravestone to their mother, Mrs Julia Jekyll † 1895, by *Lutyens*. NT)

BUSBRIDGE HALL. Built or remodelled in 1775 by *John Crunden* to be a bulky standard Late Palladian house. This was demolished in 1906 and a big new house by *George & Yates* built on the ridge to the s, the Cadogan Square style in the country: Dutch gables alternating with bow windows, not inspired. The old stables were given Dutch trim and made into a separate house, BUSBRIDGE LAKES. The late c18 landscape gardening goes with this, a chain of four lakes, thick romantic planting – more romantic and overgrown now than its creators ever intended – and a complete set of garden ornaments, none of them remarkable. They include a HERMIT'S CAVE, two BRIDGES, GROTTO, RUSTIC PAVILION, and RUINS, all rock-work, a later stuccoed BOATHOUSE, and a sweet DORIC TEMPLE which consists simply of a wall in the middle with a door in it and a portico *in antis* at either end, a sort of mirror building.

MUNSTEAD. *See*. p. 376.

BYFLEET

0060

A shattered village s of Weybridge. A few old houses remain. Much of this century's contribution is beneath contempt. ⟨Most of the recent housing, however, is of the unexceptionable tile-hung variety now common all over Surrey. WEYMEDE, off Parvis Road, by the river, is an estate by *Eric Lyons* in his new manner (1963–6). Yellow brick terraces with sharp split-pitched roofs, as at Castle Green, Weybridge.⟩ Until the late 1940s the church was in a green oasis; the manor house still is, an unexpected and charming ensemble among trees by the Wey.

ST MARY. An exception for Surrey: bellcote, nave, and chancel all rebuilt *c*.1290 in very simple Late E.E. Flint and pudding-stone rubble, all the windows two-light except for the three-light window which has intersecting tracery. There is no elaboration at all. Inside is a very simple belfry frame – two posts only, supporting beams tied into the outer walls on three sides – and an odd chancel arch, without capitals but with a thick inner order which is abruptly corbelled off at the springing line of the arch.* This queer mannerism has been aped to disastrous effect in the Victorian s transept (1864, by *Woodyer*). There is also a big Victorian s aisle of 1841, so that all the simple village effect has gone. – PAINTINGS. Fragmentary consecration cross and a seated King over the N door; very faint. – PULPIT. Cut-down Jacobean, like Pyrford. – ROYAL ARMS. 1843, carved wood, attractively stylized. – STAINED GLASS. Fragments, including one complete Saint (N side of chancel). – BRASS. Thomas Teylar, rector of Byfleet, *c*.1480 (the exact year of death was never filled in). An elegant figure with scroll, 20 in. high. – PLATE. Cup 1570.

ST JOHN BAPTIST, West Byfleet. By *Caröe*, 1910–12, in an attempt to evoke Surrey style. The oblong shingled crossing steeple is not bad, but the rest is Caröe's timid quarter-Art-Nouveau, and the inside, particularly, is a complete specimen of the fussily-detailed, genteelly-roofed type of design which has been the bane of English church architecture for nearly fifty years. (Good diamond-shaped FONT. NT)

⟨WEST BYFLEET is around the station, 1 m. W. In STATION APPROACH, a large new SHOPPING CENTRE by *Scott, Brownrigg & Turner*. Dull five-storey office block on top of the shops. In front, standing forlornly in a car park, a trim little circular LIBRARY by the same architects, 1964. Dark brick panels between tall windows, nicely poised on a recessed base.⟩ For NEWHAW, 1 m. N, *see* p. 383.

Very little in the village of Byfleet itself. The CLOCK HOUSE (now surrounded by recent housing) is a big, rambling house, all stuccoed, the centre late C18. Opposite another plain C18 house. ⟨At the junction of High Road and Royston Avenue is a good new LIBRARY by the County Architect, *Raymond Ash*, 1967–9, and in HART ROAD, the continuation of Church Road, a JUNIOR SCHOOL also by *Raymond Ash*, 1966–7. The usual components (*see* e.g. Addlestone) but here with the dark blue boiler chimney prominent near the entrance – a good forceful interruption in a dreary road.⟩ The lane beside the Clock House leads to Byfleet Manor House and also to the MILL (small, weatherboarded, C18, rather battered) and to the MILL HOUSE, a big, lumpish Georgian house, probably of *c*.1750, five by three bays with a bracketed doorcase.

---

* This detail is certainly pre-C19; see early sketches hanging in the church.

MANOR HOUSE. A great surprise, with its small-scale formality
and mellow bricks; in fact one of the most attractive late C17
houses in the county. As so often in England, this effect is a
hybrid, the house of 1686 incorporating a few details – very
puzzling ones – from the earlier house. Byfleet Manor was a
royal hunting lodge and was given by James I to Prince Henry
and then – in 1616, according to Aubrey – to Queen Anne. An
elevation has survived, long and symmetrical with a crowded
roof-line of shaped gables, on an E-plan with two additional
turrets in the internal angles and a central three-bay arcaded
porch flanked by tall windows. It is a design very like Aston
Hall Birmingham, and in no way out of the run of big Jacobean
houses. Yet Anne of Denmark was Inigo Jones's patron, and the
Queen's House at Greenwich was started in 1616; it is very
odd that she should simultaneously commission a completely
conservative house and a revolutionary one. (The explanation
may be that she was responsible only for the classical porch,
added to an earlier house. J. Harris) What remains of this
house is one huge chimney with careful stone mouldings at the
W end of the present house; two Doric and two Ionic pilasters
from the porch skilfully re-used to frame the central bay of the
later building; and impressive tall GATEPIERS in front called
by Aubrey 'Ditterling' piers (i.e. Wendel Dietterlin, the
German pattern-book designer of the late C16. Normally this
was just a generic attribution: in fact the piers are reasonably
like plate 70 of his *Architettura*). These are very typical of
Jacobean Mannerism, capped with spiky urns and with two
grotesque faces on the side facing into the courtyard. Inside
there are a couple of fireplaces in the same style, a re-arranged
plain STAIRCASE with flat balusters, and also a couple of
overmantels consisting of a well carved band of foliage. These
could equally be of *c*.1680.

In 1686 the tenant made a smaller house, using the existing
materials (the string courses are re-used window sills and
jambs end to end, e.g.), and made a very sober, elegant job of it.
Five by two bays; the re-used Jacobean pilasters give the elevation just the right amount of fantasy. *Wren* had to sign the
authorization to rebuild, and while there is no reason to connect
him with the design it does happen that it is just the sort of
elegant plainness on a smaller scale that is evident in a Wren
house such as Winslow, Buckinghamshire. The garden (s)
front is plain simple late C17 work. *E. P. Warren* added tactful
asymmetrical wings in 1905, when the house was restored.

CAMBERLEY

The first part, York Town (after Frederick, the Duke of York of
the rhyme and the steps), grew up as a simple grid when the
Royal Military College was moved to Sandhurst in 1809. The
rest followed when the Staff College was added in the 1860s and
the town gradually attracted retired military men. In its own way
this later C19 development was classic: unselfconscious shops and
artisan housing to a very humane scale N of the railway line, and
an Augustan landscape of big conifers, rhododendrons, curved
gravel roads, and big Norman-Shaw-style houses S of it. It is an
almost exact equivalent, in 1880 terms and by accident, of Nash's
designed layout for Regent's Park and the workers' housing E of
it. The pattern is now being spoilt because extra houses are being
crammed in without keeping enough of the trees. It is typical of
the attitude that tries to make all England look like a bad suburb
that it cannot recognize a good suburb when it sees one. But there
is, at last, one good modern house; FENWYCKS, Tekels
Avenue, by *Kenneth Wood*, 1960. ⟨The pattern is likely to
change further. Camberley lies just beyond the Metropolitan
Green Belt, and has therefore been able to absorb people
moving out of London.* Most of the new housing lies to the
E, and is unremarkable (but *see* Frimley, p. 249). The centre
also is changing. Houses N of the station have been demolished
for redevelopment, and the gravel roads are disappearing.
The M3 MOTORWAY will run between Camberley and
Frimley.⟩

ST MICHAEL, York Town. 1849–51 by *Woodyer*,‡ well landscaped in character. Freestone, with a bold Bargate stone
tower and broach-spire, added in 1891, towering up above the
main road on a knoll surrounded by enormous evergreens.
Woodyer's training in Butterfield's office shows to advantage
in the firm proportions and decided details (e.g. the flèche
and the dormers), but the inside is just gauche, despite typical
Woodyer details such as the medallions in the spandrels
added in 1864. The religious sincerity has not been translated
into artistic terms.

ST PAUL, Church Hill. 1902 by *Caröe*. Half-timbered, with a
prodigious build-up of forms around the crossing, the vestry

* The population figures for the Urban District of Frimley and Camberley
for 1951–68 show the largest increase in the whole of Surrey: 1951: 20,386;
1961: 29,750; 1968 (estimate): 42,260; an increase of 107·2% for the whole
period, and of 42·1% for 1961–8 alone.

‡ Arcades and aisles added in 1858–9.

chimney lifted straight from a Lutyens house (cf. St Mary, Woking). The inside never given a thought.

ROYAL MILITARY ACADEMY. The parts in Surrey are the huge detached staff houses at York Town, THE TERRACE, or Tea Caddy Row, 1808, four by three bays, stock-brick, presumably by *John Sanders*, and *Wyatt*'s lodges, 1807–12, at the E end of the grounds, in Camberley itself (they are so much part of Camberley, as is the effect of London Road, 1½ m. long with shops on one side and the RMA grounds on the other, that they are included here: for the main building *see* the Berkshire volume). The lodges are over-suave Doric: two side pavilions *in antis* and central block wrapped around with a Greek Doric colonnade. This is polished neo-classicism taken to the limit where it slips away from the beholder altogether, and even the effect of painting the recessed surfaces buff cannot bring it back. ⟨Also in Surrey is the third college, EAST BUILDING, 1966–9, by *Gollins, Melvin, Ward & Partners*. In DAWNAY ROAD, N of Barossa Common, MARRIED QUARTERS by *Bicknell & Hamilton*. Well planned white brick terraces.⟩

STAFF COLLEGE. 1862 by *Pennethorne*. Prince Albert caught his fatal chill watching it being built. Enormous Louis-Quatorze hôtel in stone and stock brick. The centre has good florid detail with carved trophies: attached to something less indigestible – say Office-of-Works-Vanbrugh, which Pennethorne would no doubt have much rather built – it would look magnificent. His frustrated career was one of the minor tragedies of the C19. Grand Roman entrance hall encircled by a gallery. (N of the College the ALANBROOKE LECTURE HALL by *A. M. Gear & Associates*, 1960–1. It is designed both as a conventional theatre and for lectures on military tactics. Yellow brick outside, grey inside, without mannerisms. A model of its kind. NT)

(W.R.A.C. SCHOOL OF INSTRUCTION, Portsmouth Road. By *Gollins, Melvin, Ward & Partners*, 1962–5. Single-storey buildings of white-painted brick and timber, taller buildings of dark brick with the concrete structure exposed and used to articulate the exterior. The beam ends and floor slabs above them project beyond the wall face. The OFFICERS' MESS has a framework of free-standing mullions in front of the windows.)

MUNICIPAL BUILDINGS, London Road. 1906, dashing curly Edwardian Baroque, the style at its gayest and best, by *H. R.*

& B. A. Poulter of Camberley. Five by two bays, pedimented and columned centre; plenty of spirit, and unmistakably 1900 spirit at that. These architects built in a very happy neo-Wren style, e.g. the former showrooms of R. P. OVER, London Road, 1908, and DENNISTOUN, Upper Park Road, further E, S of the station.* ⟨In PARK STREET is a small but interesting house by *Lutyens*, WITWOOD, 1897–8. Formal front with concave centre flanked by arches to the garden; the back asymmetrical and tile-hung.⟩

See p. 595

⟨E of the centre, several good new buildings by the County Architect, *R. J. Ash*, including the FIRE STATION, London Road, of 1965–7 and N of this, in Kingston Road, FRIMLEY AND CAMBERLEY COUNTY SECONDARY SCHOOL, 1965–7, for 570 children. The school has buildings of different heights, with a three-storey curtain-walled block at the back, and a sober, quite monumental single-storey entrance, with the doorway between plain walls of dark brick with raked joints.⟩

⟨HEATHERIDGE COUNTY PRIMARY SCHOOL. 1966–7. Hidden away in woodland E of the A325. A pleasant building with details in muted colours (pale green, dark grey), much more in sympathy with its surroundings than the new housing near by. In PRIOR ROAD, another PRIMARY SCHOOL, 1965–6, less well sited, but interesting because it was one of the first buildings to break with the traditional building style hitherto used by the County Architect's Department, and to make use of a semi-industrialized system (cf. Addlestone, p. 90).⟩

⟨S of Portsmouth Road, off a drive to Collingwood Hall, COLLINGWOOD, an excellent single-storey house by *Peter Womersley*, 1961–2, with rooms arranged on an H-plan, the living area in the centre between covered terraces.⟩

On the S side of A30, at York Town, an industrial estate with two modern factories. LINATEX, by *E. H. Eames*, 1955, makes reasonable use of standard clichés with a big metal-clad shed. SHARPLES, by *John Bickerdike*, 1955–7, with an admirably detailed curtain-walled office block, is a good example of the patterns that can be obtained so easily from curtain-walling – here in the rhythm of blank glass windows, yellow venetian blinds open or closed, and structural columns sometimes exposed (at the ends) and sometimes hidden behind the curtain-wall (along the side).

* More than twenty Poulter designs are kept at the Camberley Museum. Other *Poulter* buildings are Nos. 24–26 HIGH STREET and OLDFIELD LODGE, York Road (NT).

CAMILLA LACEY *see* WEST HUMBLE

CAPEL

1040

One long and rather nondescript street along the Worthing Road, a mixture of Weald cottages and the cheerful C19 brick of hamlets like Holmwood to the N.

ST JOHN THE BAPTIST. Originally early C13, cf. the lancets on the S side of the chancel. Effectively all rebuilt in 1865 by *Woodyer*, and what interest the church has is in these C19 details. Pretty shingled bell-turret and spire carried on a composite (old) frame made up of two big posts and the W wall. The N aisle is very much Woodyer: ornate square-headed windows with deep reveals and a separate set of columns inside. – SPIRAL STAIRCASE to the belfry, *c.*1860, gawky and effective, the same design as at Buckland. – FONT. 1865 and very handsome: octagonal bowl on circular stem, all polished brown marble, with gilt incised ornament on the bowl. Quite free of any period reminiscences, purely rich and C19. Designed by Woodyer? The other fittings not up to this standard. – MONUMENTS. John Cowper † 1590 and wife. Small naïve kneelers, prettily painted. – Robert Cowper † 1720, handsome tablet in the City-baroque style. Corinthian frame with side volutes enclosing drapes. Good: could well be a minor job of someone like Green of Camberwell. – PLATE. Two-handled Cup dated 1655.

Nothing much in the village street: the most striking building is in fact the stone-built, gabled WEBB ALMSHOUSES of 1871, on the E side. But there are a lot of good Weald farms, less restored than in most Surrey parishes. To the E MISBROOKS and ALDHURST FARM are both attractive half-timbered buildings, originally of *c.*1500. Beyond them, in a remote cul-de-sac, TEMPLE ELFOLD is the L-shaped remainder of a large C16 timber-framed building, now tile-hung. To the SE TAYLORS FARM contains a two-storeyed C14 hall (VCH), and to the S along A24 are two neatly complementary timber-framed houses, Osbrooks and Bonnet's Farm. OSBROOKS has regular timbering with herringbone infilling, probably of the early C17. Originally E-shaped with two extra gabled wings added by *Detmar Blow* which are now quite indistinguishable from the old work: comfortable and suave. BONNET'S FARM (said to be early C17 but looks a good deal earlier) has a gaunt N front with regular-spaced timbers but irregular infilling (part normal brick, part herringbone brick, part plaster), a two-storeyed gabled porch, a subsidiary gable, and a Horsham slate roof. It is one of the most impressive of Surrey farms.

To the NE of the village is BROOMELLS, by *J. H. Wadling*, 1892. Tile-hung gabled Norman Shaw imitation, very common in Surrey, but much better done than most, the style applied symmetrically with surprising success. Enormous tile-hung lateral end gables with typical corbelled out white casement windows balanced by two symmetrically placed tile-hung cross gables. Symmetrical multiple chimneystacks also.

STANE STREET. There is a fine stretch of Roman Stane Street on the line from Buckinghall Farm Ockley to Hollow Way Dorking.

CARSHALTON

The centre of Carshalton is still a delightful spot. There is plenty of water, of which good use is made, and there are plenty of enjoyable buildings large and small. The only aesthetically major one is of course Carshalton House.

ALL SAINTS.* The church lies in a slightly elevated position, above the High Street and the pond. From here it is entirely the work of the *Blomfields*, uncle and nephew, in 1893–1914. It is big, and, with the little polygonal turret by the vestry in addition to the old tower with its C18 spike, it makes quite a lively composition. But behind, to the S, the medieval church appears, externally only in the former chancel, with blocked lancet windows‡ and a C15 E window of three lights, and the lower part of the former S aisle wall. The upper parts are an alteration of the early C18 – cf. the arched windows and their surrounds. (The S aisle was raised in 1723 and the church 'beautified'. B. F. L. Clarke) Medieval also the lower parts of the tower, which was an axial tower. Inside, the church of 1893 has at the W end a half-octagonal baptistery, and wide nave and aisles. The medieval N aisle, which was Norman, was destroyed, but some capitals from it survive in store. The present S aisle was the nave of the medieval church; its S aisle is now an outer S aisle. The arcade survives here, with its octagonal piers and leaf-crocket capitals and its double-chamfered pointed arches, a good and typical work of the late

* For further details on the church see the excellent guidebook by H. V. Molesworth-Roberts, revised edition 1966.
‡ Now obliterated.

C12. The tower arches are also pointed, possibly inserted in earlier walls. The w arch rests on moulded capitals. In the old chancel, now Lady Chapel, rounded-trefoil PISCINA. Late medieval kingpost roof. – REREDOS designed by *Bodley* c.1900 and painted in panels by *Comper* in 1931–2. – REREDOS in the Lady Chapel. Good early C18 work with pilasters and a segmental pediment, gilded and painted by *Comper* in 1936. – SCREEN with ROOD also designed by *Bodley*, c.1914, and also decorated by *Comper* (1931). – ORGAN PROSPECT with an amazingly lavish organ (w end), by *Comper*, 1931–8. – PULPIT. Georgian, with *Comper* additions (1946). – Fine wrought-iron COMMUNION RAIL (Lady Chapel); early C18. – STAINED GLASS. In the Lady Chapel by *Kempe*, 1895 and 1900. Also other windows by him. – PLATE. Cup and Cover 1569; Cup and Cover 1634; Flagon 1640; Almsdish 1681; Dish 1710; whole Set 1727; large ALTAR CROSS by *Reginald Blomfield*, illustrated in 1892, still entirely in the Arts and Crafts style, with heart-shapes and thorn-trails. – MONUMENTS. Tomb-chest to Nicholas Gaynesford † 1497 (s chapel, N wall). Above it kneeling brass figures. The brasses were originally enamelled. The work was done before his death. – Brass to Thomas Ellingbridge and wife. She died in 1497 (s chapel, floor). Mutilated; large figures under canopies and between shafts. – Brass to a Cleric, late C15, fragmentary (s chapel floor). – Brass to Joanna Burton † 1524 (nave floor). – Tablet to Dorothy Burrish † 1685. With cherubs and drapery (s chapel, s wall). – Henry Herringman † 1703, by *W. Kidwell* (s chapel, s wall). Lively scrolly tablet with putti and putti heads. The putti keep a curtain open. No effigy. – Sir John Fellowes † 1724. Tall standing wall-monument without figures. Big, heavily fluted sarcophagus. On it two vases and a tall obelisk on a pedestal. – Sir William Scawen † 1722 (outer s aisle, E end). Reclining effigy. Above it sarcophagus with a weeping cherub standing on it. Big Corinthian columns l. and r. carrying urns. A disjointed composition. – John Braddyll, by *Rysbrack*, 1753. Tablet with pediment and Rococo cartouche at the foot (s aisle E end). – Sir George Amyand † 1766. Fine plain urn in a fine plain niche. – Michael Shepley † 1837, by *E. J. Physick* (chancel N wall). With a woman kneeling by the dead man. The group is placed under a baldacchino niche.

GOOD SHEPHERD, Carshalton-on-the-Hill. 1930 by *Martin Travers & T. F. W. Grant*. Stock brick; a Spanish Mission gable, a copper clerestory, and a Baroque interior.

(HOLY CROSS (R.C.), North Street. 1933 by *W. C. Mangan.*
DE)

(METHODIST CHURCH, Ruskin Road. 1926 by *Andrew Mather.*
Round-arched Georgian; porch with antefixes. H. V. Molesworth-Roberts)

CARSHALTON HOUSE. Built between 1696 and 1713 and lived
in by Edward Carleton. It was sold in 1714 to Dr Radcliffe and
in 1716 to Sir John Fellowes, of the South Sea Company.
After 1730 the house passed to Philip Yorke, later Earl of
Hardwicke. A large, solid block of nine by seven bays, built of
yellow and red brick, with two storeys and an attic storey above
the cornice. Hipped roof. To the s the first and last bays and
the three centre bays project a little. All accents are marked
by pilaster strips of rubbed red brick. The original entrance
was on the w side, where there are now large extensions of the
school to which the house belongs. The only decoration outside
is to the s, a porch with Corinthian columns and pediment,
added probably about 1750, and to the E a richly carved doorway with a segmental pediment on brackets. Wrought-iron
rails flank the steps up to s as well as E doorways. Inside by
far the finest rooms are the Entrance Hall and the sw corner
room to its s. The former is of *c*.1750, the latter probably of
c.1720, in a very personal taste.* The entrance hall has a low
groin-vaulted centre resting on four attached columns and continued to the w and E by short tunnel-vaults. The staircase to
its N is unaccountably small (all balusters twisted). The corner
57 room has glorious arcading against the wall, with the arches
alternating with coupled fluted Ionic pilasters carrying a short
stretch of straight entablature. But to the w two small square
corner cabinets are divided off the room, and the space between
is made into a lower groin-vaulted alcove screened from the
room by two fluted Ionic columns, which here take the place of
the pilasters, and an arch. What was the purpose of this room ?
The alcove has a w window and so would not be suitable for a
bed, and there is no evidence from the Carleton inventory that
the room was a bedroom. The other rooms are less noteworthy,
except for a painted room (NE) with landscapes by *Robert
Robinson* on the tall main panels of the panelling as well as the
dado. The Hall in the middle of the s side has panelling and a
fine doorcase with columns and pediment, the centre room on
the E side a light and pretty Rococo ceiling and a Rococo

---

* John Harris suggests that the work of *c*.1750 may be attributed to *Sir
Robert Taylor.*

fireplace. But above this is an overmantel with excellent carving in the Gibbons tradition. (CHAPEL. 1899–1900 by *E. Ingress Bell*. DE)

The GARDENS were probably laid out by *Charles Bridgeman* about 1719–20 and seem to survive partly in that form. If that is so they are amongst the earliest remaining gardens in the new picturesque style of the C18. To the E of the house is a spacious lake (now frequently dry), and at its S end a fine GROTTO with chambers and passages (now mostly blocked up) behind a stone façade of five bays. The outer bays have small segment-headed windows, the slightly projecting centre rusticated arches and pilasters. Beyond the lake on the E boundary rises the curious and impressive WATER HOUSE, a tower the design of which might well be due to *Vanbrugh* himself.* Red and yellow brick, five by five bays with a tower rising above the centre on the far (E) side. Arched windows, broad pilasters, with free capitals with a kind of fluting or gadrooning. The ground floor has coved rooms, the middle one with an oval centre, the l. (NW) one a marble bath with a sunk basin. The tower contains a pumping engine to lift the water from the river to a cistern which supplied the house. Externally the upper storey of the tower has large open arches, buttresses with bases rising to the level of the sills of these arched openings, and a top with typically Vanbrughian fancy battlements and pinnacles. The GATEPIERS of the main entrance to the grounds are fine too, with lions' heads as supporters.

Carshalton reveals itself most dramatically to the traveller arriving from Sutton. The road skirts the S wall of the grounds, turns sharp l., meets the gates, sharp r., and arrives at the wide and varied ponds and their bridges which form the centre of the village. Meanwhile, to the l., WEST STREET, with first the Water House looking doubly forbidding from here, and then a few nice weatherboarded houses (Nos. 2–12). The river See p. 595 Wandle meanders along just N of the ponds and, as one follows its course along FESTIVAL WALK, one arrives soon by the OLD RECTORY, a red brick house of the early C18 with blue brick chequering. Doorway with segmental pediment on carved brackets. The rear (W) part of the house is earlier. Festival Walk ends in NORTH STREET, where are a few more nice

* It seems to have been built in 1719–20, and a payment to *Henry Joynes*, who was from 1705 to 1715 Comptroller of Works at Blenheim under Vanbrugh, points in that direction. After 1715 Joynes was Surveyor of Kensington Palace.

houses. To the E of North Street THE GROVE, a public garden, once the grounds of a private house, with a fine, if small, stone BRIDGE of one segmental arch, called for no good reason the Leoni Bridge. Leoni did however design a house for Carshalton (*see* below). ⟨North Street leads back to the church and the beginning of the High Street. W of the church, pleasant OLD PEOPLE'S HOMES, in a friendly vernacular style. Brick and weatherboarding, with overhanging gables. The architects are *Thompson & Gardner*, for the London Borough of Sutton, 1967. On the N side of the High Street, new SHOPPING CENTRE and flats, running back to The Grove, by *Robert J. Wood & Partners*, 1967–8. At the N end of The Grove, in Mill Lane, offices and laboratories of VINYL PRODUCTS, a neat two-storey curtain-wall block with royal blue spandrels, 1964. Behind, a larger, fussier building now under construction, by *Norman Bailey, Samuels & Partners*.⟩ S of the High Street was *Leoni*'s house, designed in 1722 for Thomas Scawen, which was never completed.* This was called CARSHALTON PARK. A later house, CARSHALTON PLACE, probably of the early C19, was demolished in the 1920s. All that remains is a former TEMPLE now used by the Electricity Board. It is in THE SQUARE – a nine-bay stuccoed structure with a central four-column portico of Tuscan columns. Also in Carshalton Park a GROTTO at the end of a long canal-like sheet of water. Centre of three arches and four broad piers, the central arch taller and wider than the others. To the l. and r. of the centre bays with segment-headed alcoves. Inside a Vestibule with niches at the ends, and an Octagon Room behind with coved ceiling.

⟨BRITISH INDUSTRIAL BIOLOGICAL RESEARCH ASSO-CIATION, 1 m. S, on the hill, E of Woodmansterne Road. Good buildings by *B. & N. Westwood, Piet & Partners*, 1962–4.⟩

1½ m. S was THE OAKS, demolished in 1957–60. It was built about 1770 for Lord Derby, the one for whose wedding *Robert Adam* designed the magnificent Supper Pavilion illustrated in his *Works in Architecture*. It was put up at The Oaks. The house also supplied the name for the Epsom race. The house was a large, irregular, very red castellated affair, with turrets and even machicolations. It was a simpler adaptation of part of Adam's very ornate designs which survive in the Soane Museum. The SE end had a raised centre flanked by circular turrets and the rooms inside decoration of the highest quality.

---

* The design appeared in his translation of Alberti's *De re aedificatoria*.

The principal room was a rectangle with apsed projections in 56
the short sides. The apses were segmental. The wall with the
fireplace had sumptuous arcading with arches in the Venetian
rhythm on fluted Corinthian columns and coupled columns.*

CASTELNAU see BARNES

CATERHAM   3050

Until 1856 Caterham was a simple Downs village. Then the
railway terminus came to the valley – the first building was an
ornate station hotel quite by itself in the countryside – and the
present town sprang up round it. The railway has never been
extended, so that the town plan is still the same; like so much of
C19 Surrey, a period piece of its own. Much later, in the 1930s,
housing seeped s from Coulsdon to alter the remnants of the
original village on the hills to the standard outer-London
pattern.

St Lawrence, Caterham-on-the-Hill. The original small
downland church, disused from 1866 but refitted for occasional
use in 1927, and so an invaluable example of what most Surrey
churches were like before the C19. Not as attractive as it might
be, because of the Churchwarden-Gothic alterations outside
and messy fittings inside. Originally it was an apsed Norman
church. Part of one window on the s side remains, and also an
indication of the beginning of the apse on the outside of the
s wall of the chancel. To this was added a s chancel chapel at
the end of the C12 (one bay, stiff-leaf capital to the E respond),
a N chapel at about the same time (carved foliage frieze to the
imposts of hard plaster in a most curious style, quite possibly
not made at the same time as the imposts, equally reminiscent
of Breedon-on-the-Hill, i.e. Anglo-Saxon work, and of Art
Nouveau), a s arcade (two bays with plain imposts separated by
a chunk of walling, the whole now blocked), and then a N
arcade (circular piers, circular abaci, double-chamfered arches.
The arches of the other parts just enumerated have only slight
chamfers.). Chancel arch, perhaps mid-C13, dying into the
imposts. The E end of the chancel was rebuilt c.1790 in clunch
and brick. The ROOFS are a rough lot, but varied – kingpost in
the nave, wagon roof in the chancel, queenpost in the aisle. –
MONUMENT. Elizabeth Legrew † 1825, a sentimental kneeling

* Mr Marcus Binney considers that this room was almost certainly by
Taylor.

figure in an ogee niche. '*Legrew* sculpt, 1832': she was his mother.

St Mary, opposite the old church. 1866–88 by *W. & C. A. Bassett Smith*. Routine Middle-Pointed at its worst.

St John, Caterham Valley. 1881, also by *W. Bassett Smith*. Of Bargate stone, with a big Somerset-style w tower and a big joyless interior. N aisle chapel by *T. G. Jackson*. – font. c13, from the old church. Circular bowl on a circular stem and four attached shafts which all share the same base and abacus. Quite neat. – stained glass. E window of 1885. A lot of flowing angels, especially up in the curvilinear tracery lights; Art Nouveau forms without any Art Nouveau expression (without any expression at all, in fact). Whom by?

(Sacred Heart of Jesus (R.C.), Whyteleafe Road. 1881 by *E. Ingress Bell*. DE)

(St Thomas (R.C.), Station Road, Whyteleafe. 1961 by *F. G. Broadbent*, with NW tower with aluminium spire. – stained glass. W window by *P. Fourmaintreaux*. DE)

Caterham Valley has not much of interest. The pretty weatherboarded late c19 Wesleyan Chapel of 1883 by Mr *Ranger*, N of the station, was demolished in 1969. Opposite the E end of the church is a small Telephone Exchange on a curved, sloping site. This was built in 1953 by the Ministry of Works (architect in charge *W. S. Frost*), and it is unexpectedly subtle and sensitive, with a great deal of trouble taken to see that the forms compose up- and down-hill. Brick, plus one long rubble stone panel on the ground floor with a pergola and good close Swiss-style planting. ⟨Little of note has been built since. In Stafford Road, rather pretentious Clinic and Library by the former County Architect, *J. Harrison*, 1961–4. Two red-brick buildings linked by a screen wall and approached by fussy flights of steps. Further down the hill in Croydon Road, a long block of shops and flats by *Roy Chamberlain*, 1966.⟩

The old village on the downs is NW of the station, producing the odd result of a narrow, curving, ex-village High Street, duplicating the suburban shops below in the Valley.

⟨St Lawrence's Hospital, Coulsdon Road, Caterham-on-the-Hill. School for sub-normal children by *Richard Mellor* of the *South-West Metropolitan Region Hospital Board* (*M. Burrows* and *Ernest Howes*, job architects), 1963–4. The best recent building in Caterham. One and two storeys, stepped downhill away from the gaunt c19 hospital buildings, with a splendid view. Dark grey brick, thick white window frames, cedar fascia. The classrooms are arranged around a small court, and have their own outdoor play areas.⟩

GUARDS DEPOT. Begun in 1877, with stock-brick blocks by the *Board of Works*, surprisingly spread-out and leafy, plus an admirable chapel by *Butterfield*, 1881, one of the best of his later buildings. Astringent but subtle polychrome – stock bricks with patterns of black brick and chequered flint in gable ends and tops of aisles. Tiny windowless clerestory, and a typically ugly detail in the stubbed-off bellcote. The E end is a masterpiece, with big buttresses flanking the E window, gabled above and bigger and smoothly rounded below. Here, for once in late Butterfield, is power and not simply ill-temper. The inside is something of a disappointment, partly because the polychrome brick has been whitewashed. Only the polychrome piers remain (alternate limestone and red sandstone), and a few Butterfieldian details, like the crucifix and quatrefoils pierced in the roof truss separating nave and chancel, and particularly in the W buttress, which dies out at the level of the top of the windows to reappear *outside* at the same level as the corbelling for the bellcote.

⟨RANK ORGANISATION, Godstone Road, Whyteleafe. Neat three-storey offices on stilts, by *Andrews, Emmerson & Sherlock*, 1964–5.⟩

S W of the Caterham Valley centre there are steep wooded valleys and leafy suburbia. At Arthur's Seat on top of the downs is a folly TOWER, demure and overgrown, like a disused church in Norfolk. Flint with brick dressings; *c.*1800. ½ m. further E, and much more prominent, is the same thing in mid-C19 terms, in the battlemented WATER TOWER of the waterworks, 1862. 'Architectural features of the building by *R. W. Drew* of Pall Mall', as the *Illustrated London News* said. N of this, in Tupwood Lane, is UPWOOD GORSE, built by *Philip Webb* for Queen Victoria's dentist in 1873, and twice added to by Webb, presumably as the practice enlarged. The early parts are more pointed and angular, the later ones smoother and tile-hung; the result, inevitably, is like one of the rambling vaguely Norman Shaw houses of which there are so many in Surrey. Yet for Webb this was clearly a discipline and not a pretty style, and this shows in the details, such as the tunnel-like entrance and the boldly massed chimneys.

WAR COPPICE or CARDINAL'S CAP. An Iron Age HILL-FORT once considered incomplete. Excavations in 1950 showed that the circular double-ditched bank measures $\frac{1}{3}$ m. across from E to W. 3 m. away, on Farthing Down, Coulsdon, is a considerable concentration of Iron Age fields.

CHALDON
3050

ST PETER AND ST PAUL. A small Early Norman window in the W wall. Otherwise late C12 and early C13. The handsome little SW stone tower with a shingled broach-spire dates only from 1843. The church is small, of flint. Nave arcades of circular piers. The capital of the S pier is clearly earlier than that of the N pier. The arches on the S side have one slight chamfer, on the N side they are simply double-chamfered. Former N chapel with blocked arch from the chancel; C13 responds. S chapel with C14 arch without capitals and Dec E window. The entrance from the S aisle is by a low arch. – EASTER SEPULCHRE. In the chancel N wall, Perp, with a frieze of enriched quatrefoils and shields. – PULPIT. Dated 1657, a rare date for a pulpit. Still the Jacobean type, but the panels are framed by guilloche bands. – STAINED GLASS. E window by *Powell*, 1869. – WALL PAINTING. Of *c*.1200, and one of the most important English wall paintings of that date – important rather than beautiful. It is of a rare subject midway between the Ladder of Salvation and the Last Judgement, sharing its position with that usual for the latter, but the prominent ladder with the former. Professors Tristram and Constable call it the Purgatorial Ladder, and this iconographical rarity in itself makes it highly interesting. The figures are silhouetted against a background of dark red ochre, much repainted, and the treatment is hard and matter-of-fact. There is little of emotion to be extracted from it, as soon as one does not believe literally in what is represented. Hard also is the composition – two horizontal tiers and two vertical halves, divided by the ladder up which naked little bodies are scrambling. Their goal is the wavily outlined Heaven with a demi-figure of Christ in a medallion. The lower tier represents Hell, the upper tier Purgatory. On the l. is a huge cauldron attended to by two big devils, on the r. are again two big devils. They hold up a saw on which some are trying to carry on the trades which were theirs when they were in the body. A potter holds a pot, a woman wool, two blacksmiths a horseshoe. But the potter has no wheel, the woman no distaff, the blacksmiths no anvil. Around these two principal scenes appear the Seven Deadly

Sins inserted wherever there was space. They are from l. to r. Sloth (three souls trying to walk while a beast is below them instead of the firm ground), Gluttony (a pilgrim throwing away his coat and bourdon and grasping the bottle instead), Pride (a woman raising her arm which a beast is clutching), Anger (two struggling figures), Luxury (a couple embracing with a devil ready to interfere), Avarice (a figure with money-bags tied round his waist and neck), Envy (one figure attracting another, while a devil tries to prevent him). At the extreme r. of the bottom tier is the Tree of Good and Evil with the Serpent and many fig-like fruits. In the purgatorial zone the scene of Christ in Limbo (the Harrowing of Hell) is painted immediately above this. To this scene corresponds on the l. the weighing of Souls by the Archangel Michael. A devil is trying in vain to weigh down one pan. – TABLET. In the chancel on the N side, dated 1562, with an inscription with admonition and prayers. The inscription is flanked by elaborately decorated tapering pilasters and crowned by a steep pediment with modillions.

CHALDON COURT. Behind the church. In spite of the unpromising exterior, the house contains the remains of a pre-Reformation house with tie-beams, kingposts, and arched braces (MHLG).

(WILLEY FARM, Pilgrim's Lane. C17 timber-framed house; granary and cylindrical water tower both of flint and brick, C19.)

(Also in Pilgrim's Lane, TOLLSWORTH MANOR, C16 and earlier. SCC Historic Buildings Department)

CHARLTON see SUNBURY

CHARLWOOD

2040

A Weald village on the Sussex border, near Crawley New Town (and now even nearer to the Gatwick runway extension). Plenty of old cottages remain, both tile-hung and timber-framed, but the remoteness and sense of place have gone.

ST NICHOLAS. A Norman framework, altered piecemeal and given a C13 S aisle which was enlarged out of all recognition in the C15 to form the present nave and chancel. Norman details remain in one window on the N side of the nave and in the crossing tower, with much altered small lights above and two* arches below, the W with a rough double order, the E arch apparently completely re-detailed in the Georgian century. To this Norman church a S aisle was added in the C13. It has two bays with an octagonal pier and arches differing slightly in detail. The doorway, the lancet windows, and the two-light window with plate tracery are contemporary. Inside, a string course ending in a knobbly leaf boss of later date (re-cut from a C13 boss?). This is connected with the lengthening of the aisle and the building of the S chapel in the C15. At the same time the chancel (now vestry) was given its form. The arcade between chancel and chapel is clumsy Late Perp. Concave-sided octagonal pier, four-centred arches. The details of the arch from the crossing into the S transept may well be yet later. The most handsome window in the church is the N window of the nave: two cusped lights support an ogee quatrefoil set diagonally, an effect of contrived elaboration very near the spirit of Kentish tracery (and one which recurs in the next parish at Horley). The S porch is C15, with a pretty sundial dated 1791. Kingpost roofs and a pleasant impression. The restoration which preserved it was by *William Burges*, 1858. – PAINTINGS. A lot on the S side of the nave, including the story of St Margaret (E) in three tiers, *c.*1350, and the Three Living and the Three Dead – three kings on horseback meeting three skeletons (W) – of the late C14. Almost gone now, as has so often happened with medieval paintings uncovered in the C19. The restoration showed that the painting had originally been ruled out in foot squares, presumably for ease of enlargement from small drawings. – SCREEN. Almost the only piece of sizeable medieval woodwork in Surrey. Straightforward Late Perp with narrow bays and trefoiled heads and no attempt to collect the bays into traceried groups as in a Devon screen. Above this, wiry and decorative cresting (prettily painted by *Burges*) with the usual vine-trail below a repeated motif of winged dragons holding the initials R S (Richard Sander, † 1480) and, in the centre, angels holding I H S and a crowned M. Everything very small-scale and pretty, obviously a distinct school whose productions have all but disappeared. – FONT. Octagonal, looks C17. – BRASS. Nicholas Sander † 1553 and wife, kneeling figures with sons and daughters behind. About 10 in. high and all done with folk art naïveté (S chancel wall).

* Not four: i.e. the church never had transepts, a fairly common Norman arrangement in village churches, cf. South Lopham, Norfolk, or, in Surrey, Albury Old Church.

Several old cottages around the church, but nothing special. ¾ m. N, on a cul-de-sac from the road to Horley, is PROVIDENCE CHAPEL, a startling building to find in Surrey, or even in England. A simple, completely untouched weather-boarded chapel of *c*.1800 with a big veranda in front, still with its original casements, and still preserving the communal atmosphere of pre-Wesleyan Nonconformity – the notice board says 'ministers various'. Surrey has so few completely spontaneous vernacular monuments of any date that this is doubly worth a visit. It would not be out of place in the remotest part of East Kentucky.

Charlwood follows the Wealden pattern of many isolated medieval or Tudor house sites. To the SE is CHARLWOOD HOUSE, a big, close-timbered C15 house, of almost Cheshire size, with two cross gables but without any Cheshire-style ornament; only the hypnotic rhythm of the vertical timbers, probably originally covered, but now all exposed except on one half of the E elevation. N of the village is CHARLWOOD PLACE, a simple, C17 yeoman's house, U-shaped, with regular timbers and brick infilling. ½ m. N again NORWOOD HILL, with two pleasant farms opposite one another: BRITTLESWARE FARM, big and tile-hung with a complex pattern of gables; and MORGANS, an example of the other type of Surrey Weald vernacular, unaffected half-timbering, here fairly regular and wide-spaced, of *c*.1600.

Finally, to the W of Norwood Hill are RICKETTSWOOD (*see* p. 443) and HIGHWORTH FARM, another timber-framed cottage of *c*.1600 with a simple and very good set of tarred weatherboarded and tile barns. Plain gables, not hipped, and no cross gables over the barn doors (cf. Somerset Farm Elstead for the more sophisticated type).

CHARTERHOUSE SCHOOL

9040

Moved from Finsbury in 1872 into a complete set of new build-*80* ings by *P. C. Hardwick*. They consist chiefly of one big open-ended quad facing SW. All in Bargate stone, the style a standard C19 commercial Gothic, but all the same a brilliant study in asymmetry, far above Hardwick's usual level. Big central tower; both wings also have smaller unequal towers attached.*

---

* The S wing contains the former chapel, and in the passage at its E end there is C18 stonework from the old buildings containing beautifully lettered schoolboy carving of the 1780s and 1790s.

Within this framework there is scarcely a matching detail in the whole elevation – see especially the way in which the end towers are quite different, yet in perfect balance. This is probably the most picturesque of the C19 public schools. In the quad STATUE of Thomas Sutton, the founder, by *Goscombe John*, 1911. Also a cloistered quad at the back by *Hardwick*, the commercial Gothic detail a distinct advantage here in that there is no suggestion of being mock-Oxford or Cambridge. Everything is worked out in picturesque vinegary C19 terms. Great Hall 1885 by *Sir A. W. Blomfield*, Horologium 1911. Then came the Chapel (*see* below). The latest addition, and a much more hopeful one, is the crisp, twostoreyed Art School, 1958 by *James Dartford* of *G. A. Jellicoe & Partners*.

See p. 595

CHAPEL. Built in 1922–7 as a war memorial. A look at the number of those killed from the classes of 1911 and 1912 brings home the effect of the Great War in a fearful way: the public schools probably had the worst mortality rate of all. Designed by *Sir Giles Gilbert Scott*. A confused eclectic exterior, more or less Early Gothic, tall and aisleless with very tall lancet windows, widely spaced, pushing up above the eaves with separate gables. The inside, however, is very impressive. The tall lancets are enclosed between thick stone piers and vaulting ribs so that only the rhythm of splays is visible from the W end. Fine proportions, and especially fine apse, preceded by an arch of four orders with a typical Scott reredos combined very well with the E windows (again windows which look ugly and pointless from outside). All the fittings designed by *Scott* and all in the same Flamboyant Gothic style as Liverpool Cathedral. There is a good deal of the overpowering semi-mystical spatial effect of Liverpool, too.

CHATLEY HEATH *see* HATCHFORD

2060

CHEAM

ST DUNSTAN. 1862–4 by *Pownall*. Large and dull, with NW tower with broach-spire, and apse. Lancet windows, quatrefoil windows in the clerestory. Arcade with crocket capitals. – PLATE. Set 1755.

In the churchyard is the remaining part of the medieval parish church, the LUMLEY CHAPEL. It was originally the chancel. Of flint, with round-arched, blocked windows. Renewed Perp

E window. To the S blocked C13 arch to a former S chapel. Octagonal pier and double-chamfered arch. The roof inside is a delightful remodelling of 1592 (date on one of the pendants). Along the top of the walls plaster frieze, the tie-beams also plastered with a fruit trail. Ceiling above tunnel-vaulted, with the typical pattern of thin ribs. – PLATE. Set 1755. – BRASSES. Civilian, *c.*1390, *c.*3 ft 6 in. (a piece in the middle missing). – Civilian, *c.*1390, demi-figure, *c.*12 in. – John Yarde † 1449 and wife, made *c.*1475, less than 7 in. figures. – John Compton and wife, 1458, demi-figures, 9½ in. – William Woodward † 1459, demi-figure, *c.*7 in. – Thomas Fromonde † 1542 and wife. Palimpsest of kneeling figures and St John Evangelist of *c.*1420 and a scroll, heart, etc., dated 1500. – MONUMENTS. Jane Lady Lumley † 1577, designed in 1590. Incomplete. Three alabaster panels with kneeling figures. Quaint architectural backgrounds. Two of the panels are placed on the front of a tomb-chest, the third above, against the back wall. – Elizabeth Lady Lumley † 1603. Alabaster of good quality. Recumbent effigy, well carved clothes. The monument was made in 1592, before her death. – John Lord Lumley † 1609. Large inscription plate flanked by two black columns. Strapwork and arms at the top. No figures. – Philip Antrobus † 1816. By *Henry Westmacott*. Grecian with two flanking Greek Doric columns.

37

See p. 595

ST PHILIP, Cheam Common Road. 1873–4 by *Carpenter*. Red brick, lancet windows, no tower. Bellcote on E end of nave. Dull interior.

(ST CECILIA (R.C.), Stonecot Road, North Cheam. 1957 by *H. S. Goodhart-Rendel*. DE)

ST ANDREW PRESBYTERIAN CHURCH, Northey Avenue and The Avenue. The older part (red brick and terracotta with a flèche) is the Church Hall. It is by *Matley, Brotherton & Mills*, 1924–7. The larger new part, 'moderne' in style, without a tower, is by *Maxwell Ayrton*, 1931–3. An addition of 1956.

S of the church, in MALDEN ROAD, just a little survives of the old village, especially WHITEHALL, a very good timber-framed house of *c.*1500, with a centrally placed projecting porch and attics added in the mid C16. The house was weatherboarded in the C18. The W part, with the drawing room, seems a C17 addition. N of Whitehall, Nos. 89–91, weatherboarded cottages. Some more of these also in PARK LANE. In PARK ROAD, CHEAM COTTAGE, C17, and Nos. 3–5, Early Georgian. In MALDEN ROAD, nearer the church, the RECTORY, an c18 brick house of five bays. A little s of Whitehall, in BROADWAY, OLD COTTAGE, a c15 timber-framed house moved from a site near by in 1922, and Nos. 43–55, more weatherboarded cottages. It is a great pity that this bit of survival is deprived of its effect by the adjoining shopping parades and by a Baptist church of 1907 right opposite Whitehall.* Near the church is a good new BRANCH LIBRARY.

The village of Cheam lay on the E side of the Little Park of NONSUCH. For Nonsuch Palace *see* p. 383. For Cheam Hare Warren *see* Sutton, p. 476.

CHELSHAM

3050

A North Downs village SE of Croydon, just clear of London sprawl. One rough green but no village centre: scattered cottages in a flint and brick vernacular that is even more hard-bitten than the Chiltern style.

ST LEONARD. By itself in a lovely position, but does not live up to it. Of medieval flint, made almost unrecognizable in 1870–1 (the culprit was one *Spencer*). Aisleless. The herringbone courses on the s side of the chancel may indicate an early phase. The next phase is demonstrated by an elegant shaft in the SE corner. The capital with upright lancet leaves looks *c*.1190. It may have belonged to a wall-arcading of the chancel. A very similar shaft was set in the NE corner, probably at a restoration. This has an early c13 stiff-leaf capital and may have carried an image. To the SE shaft belong the chancel lancet windows, to the NE shaft the odd PISCINA with a triangular top instead of an arch. The top has stiff-leaf decoration. Later windows. Authentic are one Geometrical window on the N side in something like original condition, two-light, Reigate stone‡ with an encircled quatrefoil in the head of the arch, and the easternmost Perp window in the s wall, two-light square-headed, interesting in that the hood-mould has diamond-shaped stops at either end, a Cotswold trick uncommon in the Home Counties. New chancel arch, new E window, new tower top, new roofs, but the base of the tower is c15, and inside the c15 tower arch remains, unrestored. – FONT. c13, square bowl on central stem and four corner shafts, standard pattern.

* Extension 1938. Hall 1920.
‡ Even here, pieces of limestone have been rammed in where 'restoration' required them. After a hundred years they have not softened at all.

– SCREEN, originally a parclose screen on the S side of the nave, cut down to half-size in the restoration and re-used as a chancel screen; *c.*1530. Very interesting combination of thick Gothic tracery and turned columns with crude Renaissance detail. Originally it was topped by a frieze with heads on roundels. Similar to Lullingstone, Kent. – ROYAL ARMS of Elizabeth II. 1953 by *Marjorie Wratten*; a pleasant surprise. – PLATE. Silver Cup 1733.

ST CHRISTOPHER, nearer Warlingham. Pretty, weatherboarded mission church. 1907 by *J. C. King*, with no stylistic ties at all. E extension 1967 in the same style.

WARLINGHAM PARK MENTAL HOSPITAL. The *Little Guide* says 'In this parish the Corporation of Croydon built a large lunatic asylum in 1902': large indeed, by *G. H. Oatley* (later *Sir George*) and *W. S. Skinner* of Bristol. Polychrome brick tower.

The big houses in Chelsham (Fairchildes, *Devey*'s Ledgers Park) have gone. The only old building worth notice is the early C18 FICKLESHOLE FARM, five by two bays, flint with red brick dressings, segment-headed windows.

(BEDDLESTEAD, I m. SE. Flint with brick dressings, early C19 outside. This conceals a late medieval hall house with king-post roof. Arthur Oswald.)

CHERTSEY

Thames-side town on the edge of the continuous built-up area of Outer London. A simple plan, with the three main roads meeting in a T by the church. A fourth arm is formed by a footpath leading N to the site of the abbey and to the most attractive part of Chertsey.

ST PETER. Right on the road, at the centre of the town. Tower medieval, rubble freestone and puddingstone patched with brick – an attractive mixture. All the outside detail Church-warden Gothic but a C15 tower arch inside. Chancel medieval, all renewed outside, but two odd two-bay wall arcades inside (cf. Chipstead and Merton). The arches die into almost square piers with shallow cinquefoiled niches above them.* The chancel arch is also original, good, complex C15 work, two orders of shafts with foliage capitals and intricate continuous mouldings around them. The rest is all in freestone, of 1806–8, begun by

* Could they be a remodelling of C13 arcading?

Richard Elsam but completed by *Thomas Chawner* after trouble over the estimates. It is a repellent bit of Gothick, a hall-church with square piers and four tiny attached shafts, one at each corner, supporting gauche vaults. It is rather like a humourless parody of the nave of St Mary Warwick. The big aisle windows have sickeningly fawning figures as label stops which look mid-C19 but in fact belong to the 1806 rebuilding and are by *Coade & Sealy*. The firm stamped each window splay as though it was a monument. – (REREDOS. 1869 by *T. Blashill*. NT) – TILES. A few in the chancel from Chertsey Abbey, whose pavements were famous all over the country; poor stuff compared with the specimens which went to the British Museum and the Guildford Museum. – MONUMENTS. A lot of late C18 tablets, none remarkable. Pratt Mawbey † 1770, N side of chancel, adequate late C18 by *John Walsh*. – (Sir Joseph Mawbey † 1798 by *H. Westmacott*. NT) – Emily Mawbey † 1819, aged twenty, is by *Flaxman*, with a relief of the raising of Jairus's daughter, but is if anything rather worse than the other Grecian tablets. Sentimental group. Christ is raising her from a couch. Her parents on the l., Christ's disciples on the r.

CHERTSEY ABBEY. To all intents and purposes the abbey has disappeared completely, a great loss. The ground plan has been excavated but is now underground again, and ABBEY LODGE on the site is small, plain early C19. There is one simple stone arch, probably C13, in the wall of Colonel's Lane, now blocked and with a later brick top; there is the ABBEY BARN opposite with the s side and w wall original rubble stonework and the rest Tudor brick (it could be pre- or post-Dissolution), now only in fair condition, with corrugated asbestos roof; and there is another Tudor brick barn, now THE ABBEY BARN YOUTH CLUB, formerly Manor Farm Barn, to the s. Nothing of architectural importance, and no evocative fragments either, to commemorate one of the most famous of English abbeys. There is a typically Tudor reason for this – the abbey was too conveniently near Hampton Court, and the mason John Nedeham is known to have been in charge of removing materials for Henry VIII's new work there in 1538.

The abbey was Benedictine. It was founded by Erkenwald in 666, recolonized after the Danes *c*,950, and a new abbey begun by Hugh of Winchester in 1110 and completed by the mid C13. The ground plan of this as recovered in the C19 showed a strange variation on the perpetual English theme of the square E end. Most Early Romanesque churches had an apse either with flanking apses at the end of chancel aisles (St Albans, Durham) or with an ambulatory with apsidal or polygonal chapels opening off it, and usually three of them (Norwich, Gloucester). At Southwell the E end was squared and the side chapels made into apsidal ends to the aisles. Chertsey took this one stage further by keeping the ambulatory around the square E end and making the apsidal chapels open off it, the side chapels small, the central chapel longer. It may have looked rather like Romsey, Hants, also a Benedictine church, begun in 1120 with an E end to almost the same plan.

Architectural fragments unearthed at the same time included Purbeck marble shafts and voussoirs with dog-tooth and nailhead mouldings.

OLD TOWN HALL, London Street. An Italianate building of 1851 by *George Briand*. Not a brilliant design, but a good sort of building to have in the townscape chest. Five bays, an open arcaded ground floor and a pilastered upper floor with heavily balustraded three-bay balcony. Brick with stone dressings. Really a Palladian town hall in different dress, not a C19 building at all. It is now the MUSEUM. Inside are some tiles from the abbey.

⟨PUBLIC LIBRARY, Guildford Street. By *Larkin & Turner*, 1962–3. Handsome single-storey building around a courtyard, near the car park, in a pleasant setting by a stream.⟩

⟨ST PETER'S HOSPITAL. Operating theatre and maternity unit by *R. Mellor* and *B. W. East* of the *South-West Metropolitan Region Hospital Board*, 1964–9.⟩

CHERTSEY BRIDGE, ¾ m. E of the centre. 1780–5 by *James Paine*, who lived near Chertsey. Severe ashlar stonework, five arches over the water with one more on each side brought forward slightly and spanning the bridge approach. The rhythm of the arches is very noble, but the bridge as a whole is ineffective, because of the conflict between the round arches and the triangular shape of the parapet. The apex of this touches the keystone of the central arch, and the line allows only a few inches of plain ashlar above the other arches, which is far too close for visual comfort. At Richmond Bridge Paine had the apex much higher, and though the result looks artificial, it does solve the problem. Weak parapet details – are they part of the alterations made in 1894?

Of Chertsey's three main roads two have little to offer. LONDON STREET runs E towards the bridge, starting with the Town

Hall on the N side. The rest of this side is cottagey, except Nos. 11–13, a group of late classical houses of c.1830, partly in Bath stone and partly stucco. No. 41, further E, has a pedimented shaped, i.e. Dutch, gable to the street, roughcast; presumably late C17. On the S side No. 34 is a typical bit of Victorian town building – polychrome Jacobean with elaborate grinding compositions of gables very close together on a flat front. 1858, the right half 1897 with commemorative Diamond Jubilee terracotta medallion. Beyond, Nos. 44–48 need mention, a weird and ruthless C18 pulling together of a range of C16 timber cottages, forced into one long squat pedimented composition, whilst still keeping its overhang with bow windows built in underneath. No. 60, DOVER HOUSE, is C18, with an early C19 yellow brick façade; two storeys, three bays. In Bridge Road there are two more buildings much nearer the bridge. BELSIZE GRANGE is a big, plain, dumb, early C18 brick house. Then, beside the bridge, BRIDGE HOTEL, an extraordinarily objective early C19 building. Stock brick, now whitewashed, with enormous eaves supported by two-storey cast-iron verandas and sheltering a first-floor gallery: perfect riverside architecture with a very modern look, because all the detail is severe and industrial, not pretty in the Nash-Regency way.

GUILDFORD STREET runs S from the church. On the E side only No. 124, the upper half of a delicate, two-bay, very early C19 design, the type which Sir John Summerson called 'unmistakably stamped with the careful elegance of the war period', and Nos. 118–120, stuccoed and probably of c.1835, retaining the care and the taste but not the elegance, with contemporary ironwork balcony and contemporary shop-front with Corinthian columns below. Then the WESTMINSTER BANK, Nos. 114–116, early C19, three bays, three storeys, yellow brick, and Nos. 94–108, a row of generally C18 cottagey shops. On the W side, stranger bedfellows. Starting at the S end, the GEORGE INN, though altered, is basically a C15 timber-framed building, No. 69 is completely plain Late Georgian of three by three bays, No. 83 still has a Georgian bow shop-front, Nos. 111–113 is a lumpish front of c.1750 above the inevitable later shop. Messrs LONGS near by is the beau idéal of commercial Victorianism: violent polychrome, with plate-glass windows between huge Jacobethan piers below and arcading above. Finally BARCLAYS BANK is in an expert Wren style, of 1905 by C. G. Miller, with a handsome swag in the pediment, and, alas, complete inability to match this to the bank front underneath.

The third street, WINDSOR STREET, runs W from the church and retains some of the authentic Home Counties C18 urbanity of big trees and smooth brickwork, mainly because there are few shops. On the S side No. 25, now PEARL ASSURANCE, is unaltered C18. It has a pattern-book doorcase of *c.*1770 in a big plain brick front of perhaps 1730: mere 'plain Georgian', however big. No. 33, THE CEDARS, has almost the same proportions and plainness, with big Italianate eaves. On the N side is a group of C18 houses. Nos. 8–16 have plain C18 fronts framing No. 12, CURFEW HOUSE, the only domestic building in Chertsey worth a real look. A queer design of five by three bays with arcaded ground-floor window surrounds and a thumping centrepiece, a round arch with a big keystone above the entrance, and a heavy surround and broken pediment to the first-floor window. The style is clearly 'Ordnance-Vanbrugh', and most of the motifs can be found on the buildings at Woolwich, though here they are toned down and handled insensitively. The date is 1725, and oddly enough it was apparently all built as a school (by Sir William Perkins). No. 12 was the master's house, and the houses on either side were for boys and girls.* This is an inexplicable performance, unless Nos. 10 and 14 were later rebuilt: they look late C18. Perhaps it was a late effort of one of Hawksmoor's assistants. The attic storey is a clumsy match and might be later. (No. 24, the SUN INN, is early C18 with pedimented centre doorway and wooden cornice. In ALWYN'S LANE, off Windsor Street, THOMAS WILLAT'S ALMSHOUSES, two Gothic cottages, yellow brick, of 1837. N of Windsor Street in STAINES LANE, BURLEY ORCHARD, 1874–5 by *W. H. Herring*, the Chertsey iron-founder. Brick, asymmetrical Gothic, two and a half storeys, with gables and carved bargeboards. Original iron fireplaces, a conservatory, and in the grounds, lamp posts and an iron bridge. MHLG)

½ m. W, on the road to Lyne, is PYRCROFT, with a good mid-C18 front. Five by two bays with cornice and panelled parapet above, the central first-floor window (on the landing) round-headed and breaking through the cornice. The house must be of *c.*1750. The impression is still mildly Vanbrughian, a characteristic of the mid C18 in Surrey.

Beyond this is ST ANN'S HILL, another Surrey viewpoint

* Information kindly provided by Mr E. N. Medd.

famous from C18 literature, with St Paul's plainly visible on a clear day. On the s slopes in 1938 *Raymond McGrath* put an International-Style house into matured C18 grounds with big cedars (improved at the time by *Christopher Tunnard*), another of the extreme juxtapositions of old and new which England pioneered immediately before the war (cf. The Firs at Redhill). A very successful landscape effect, but rather a cold-hearted house. Circular E end balanced by a long living wing with horizontal bands of windows. The estate belonged to Charles James Fox. The grounds are now a public park. (Some of the C18 garden buildings still survive, including FOX'S TEA HOUSE of 1794. It has Gothic arches, a lower grotto-like room with imitation stalactites and windows portraying Fox and the Prince Regent, and a chinoiserie staircase leading to the upper floor. Now in bad condition (B. Jones). There is also an C18 TEMPLE OF FRIENDSHIP, with entrance flanked by Ionic columns. Inside, an apse with niches with busts, and inscriptions in praise of friendship in English and Italian. In the garden of SOUTHWOOD, originally part of the ST ANN'S HILL grounds, is an octagonal gazebo dated 1794. By St Ann's Hill Road, C19 MAUSOLEUM CHAPEL, red brick, with marble sarcophagus of Lady Holland † 1899. MHLG)

(At ANCHOR GREEN, ANCHOR HOUSE, early C18, two and a half storeys, wooden eaves cornice. Good staircase with close string and heavy turned balusters. THATCHED COTTAGE, timber-framed, C17. MHLG)

₁₀₆₀ # CHESSINGTON

ST MARY. A kind, small old village church in a new housing estate. Flint with a straight w bell-turret with shingled broach-spire. The spire restored by *Hesketh*, 1854 (GS), the s aisle by *Jackson*, 1870. In nave as well as chancel early C13 slit lancets with rere-arches still round inside. Two-light E window, probably C17. In the chancel s wall SEDILIA, no more than two blank arches. In the back wall they have small windows of uneven sizes. – SCULPTURE. Annunciation, C15 Nottingham alabaster (s wall). – PLATE. Cup 1568.

BURNT STUB (Chessington Zoo). Partly early C19 castellated, but mostly Later Victorian in a neo-Jacobean style.

₉₀₃₀ # CHIDDINGFOLD

A large, pretty village in the Weald near the Sussex border.

From the s it starts in an almost urban way with a terrace of
C17 and C19 tile-hanging, then sweeps up around a sharp bend
to a triangular green with the church on one side of it. It is a
village of vignettes, especially on the NE side of the green, away
from the main road, with bulky, irregular tile-hung cottages
almost disappearing in foliage – particularly CHANTRY HOUSE
and the houses on either side of it. Chiddingfold was one of the
centres of medieval glass-making, forges being worked until
1615.

ST MARY. The antiquarian interest almost removed by a
sweeping restoration in 1869 (by *Woodyer*, who should have
known better; his outré detail is not at all a fair exchange).
The parts that remain are still striking enough. The s side of
the chancel is an impressive composition of lancets quite
unlike other C13 work in Surrey. The lancets are very long and
deep, three together towards the E end, one slightly shorter and
one 'low-side' at the W end, obviously put together with a
good deal of care. Also old and also striking are the four-bay
nave arcades. They are an odd composite job. Their shafts
belong to the C13 but were lengthened (and perhaps reduced
from a circular to their present slim octagonal form) in the
C15. The arches are of the C15, but the complex mouldings of
the N arches towards the aisle are again of the C13. The present
height of the arcades is impressive, giving a quite unexpected
scale to the interior. The odd thing is that before the restoration
they went with lean-to aisles and a tiny clerestory, an effect
similar to the church at Wokingham, Berks. The chancel arch
is also of the C13 and was also heightened, but only fairly
recently. It has semicircular responds and roll-mouldings in
the arch. A little later, but C13 too, the rough N chapel arcade
of two bays. The big W tower, with its clasping buttresses,
lancet windows, and twin bell-openings with plate tracery,
looks convincing C13, but is ascribed by the VCH to the C17.
It was heightened by 12 ft in 1869–70. – CHANDELIER (nave).
Dated 1786. It makes a good contrast in vitality with the many
mock-C18 chandeliers in Surrey. – STAINED GLASS. In the
W window of the s aisle multiple fragments of simple coloured
glass made into a pattern. Of no aesthetic value, but interesting
in that all the fragments were found on the sites of the glass-
working furnaces in the parish. – E window, brightly coloured
Victorian, by *Warrington*, the centre panel a Crucifixion set
against an effectively stormy slate-blue sky. – MONUMENTS.
Several small late C18 tablets in the s aisle with elegant

inscriptions in gold on black marble. All obviously by the same local hand.

⟨ST TERESA OF AVILA (R.C.). Yellow stone. Neo-Norman apse, the nave in a weak sub-Tudor. Amazingly conservative: the date is *c.*1961.⟩

Apart from the pretty tile-hung cottages to be seen everywhere, one or two houses in the village need mentioning. Opposite the church is the CROWN INN, certainly C15 and possibly older, as a house consisting of hall and solar was let as an inn in 1383. It is a big, half-timbered building with recessed centre in the usual way, the curved wooden spandrels ornamented with a tracery pattern in low relief. Good kingpost roof inside. It was all tile-hung until the 1940s. Further E, on the green, the OLD MANOR HOUSE has an elegant but expressionless front of 1762, five bays and two storeys with a Tuscan Doric doorcase.

W of the village, first COMBE FARM, a very pretty vernacular house with the centre C17 tile-hanging on a C16 timber frame and C18 brick additions at either end. Unrestored, and worth a dozen over-restored examples. Beyond, COMBE COURT is bad Victorian Tudor, but the farm in the park to the W has very good FARM BUILDINGS, complex and picturesque, with multiple gables and a circular tile-hung corner turret, done without affectation in a Philip Webb style.

To the S of this, HAWLANDS is a good C16 timber-framed cottage with first-floor overhang.

(In Sydenhurst Lane, BLACKHAMS, a good timber-framed house, with some brick and tile-hanging. C17 or earlier. MHLG)

SE and S of Chiddingfold are Highstreet Green and Ramsnest Common, two unaffected hamlets with unaffected cottages at last far enough from London to be free of over-building and over-restoration. Nothing worth special notice.

PICKHURST, I m. SE. A house of 1883, by *Brydon*, in the usual tile-hung Norman Shaw style, and better than most of Norman Shaw's own buildings. Medium size, and using almost exactly the same ideas and motifs as Shaw but using them with a good deal more spirit and a good deal more sensitivity than Shaw normally employed. One big two-storey bow window balancing a big gable nearly in the centre of the front, and a smaller gable at one end. The gables are mostly half-timbered with a little pargetting right at the top, an effective and unexpected touch. To the E of this is OLD PICKHURST, a bulky late C17 sandstone farm with ornamental brickwork patterns, a simpler, later cousin of the houses in Godalming High Street.

At High Ridings is the site of a group of ROMAN BUILDINGS excavated in 1883. They were occupied in the C4 A.D. There was much *terra sigillata*, coins, and a bronze head.

CHILWORTH

A C19 and C20 working-class hamlet between Shalford and Albury. It was formerly a great place for gunpowder, both in the C17 (gunpowder mills) and the 1914–18 war (ordnance factory). Very little can now be seen of either.

ST THOMAS, Shalford Hamlet. An extraordinary little building, built as the Greshambury Institute by *W. H. Seth-Smith* in 1896. Square plan with tower annexe to the w. Battered corner buttresses, continuous clerestory under big overhanging eaves, pyramid roof with central cupola, itself with battered supports. All brick, the detail possibly taken from Voysey but the impression quite different: assured, crisp, spatial rather than picturesque. It looks more like a fragment of an early Frank Lloyd Wright house than anything else. Seth-Smith is all but unknown, part of the sudden and underrated flowering England had in the nineties. He went on, as so many of the others did, to do bad work in the early C20. (The interior is also remarkable: four curved beams, probably laminated, rise from the corners to create a centralized space astonishingly like churches of the 1960s. NT)

ST MARTHA ON THE HILL. Although by itself high up above the valley, this has always been, rather inconveniently, the parish church of Chilworth. It was in ruins by 1845 and was almost rebuilt by *Woodyer* in 1848–50, using the old materials where possible. The result is a very impressive job in the Norman style, making no attempt to be a copy, but at the same time expressing the spirit of the lonely exposed site perfectly. Dark Bargate stone with sandstone dressings. Cruciform, with a low, authentic-looking central tower, and a minimum of carved detail. The inside similarly solid and responsible. In fact some fragments were taken over or were reproduced, e.g. the four pointed crossing arches, *c.*1170, of square section with simple chamfers at the corners, and the archway into which the w door is placed, a big, bare early C12 design. This was the tower arch of a w tower. The original church had no tower over the crossing. – FONT. C12 tub font, brought from Hambledon.

Much of the carving on it was done in 1850, but to an authentic pattern.

CHILWORTH MANOR. The present entrance front is probably very rustic C18, like an enlarged cottage. It incorporates C17 fragments in the Artisan style – certainly the big brick doorcase and its smaller stone doorcase inside, big enough to have fitted one of the pre-Fire City Halls, and possibly the Dutch gable above. The bricks in the gable are C18 or C19 but the design looks authentic. It may have been a reconstruction or adaptation, as at West Horsley Place. At the back more circumstantial Georgian detail. Plain brickwork on the W side and a frantic composition of stucco pilasters to the N, perhaps c.1825 in a wild attempt to emulate Nash. Four bays, with one pilaster at either end and three between each window, with uneven spacing between them, an unnerving effect. This faces the walled GARDEN, the best thing at Chilworth, a complete late C17 design laid out in terraces up the side of the hill. It is possibly a copy of Evelyn's layout at Albury, though here placed much nearer the house.

On the hill S of St Martha some five circular banks with external ditches have been interpreted as Early Bronze Age HENGE MONUMENTS and connected with the Pirbright structures. These are about 100 ft in diameter. There is also a tradition associating the St Martha's rings with local C7 martyrs.

CHIPSTEAD

(Partly suburban, partly a Victorian model village, with pretty cottages about a crossroads, and an ornamental pond. D. Lloyd)

ST MARGARET. A large and impressive C13 church with transepts and crossing tower, keeping a blocked late C12 N door (now reset in the N aisle). The crossing tower has a date 1631; the S transept and N aisle are C19; the S transept was rebuilt in 1855 by the Rev. *P. Aubertin*, the N aisle in 1883 by *Norman Shaw*. The extremely pretty Perp W doorway and window above are also Shaw's. The doorway was originally C12. Chancel with lancet windows – a noble row of five in the N wall. N transept with E lancets, a N front with three tall lancets and a quatrefoiled oculus, and a W doorway which now leads into the N aisle. This also has a quatrefoiled oculus over. The priest's doorway (copied from the N transept W doorway) dates from 1857. The crossing tower rests on arches with two slight chamfers. Rib-vault with broad, plain, slightly chamfered ribs.

Nave with four-bay s arcade. Circular piers, double-chamfered 14
arches. Clerestory with small quatrefoil windows with rere-
arches. They are now visible only inside the church. A very
curious feature of the chancel and transepts is that the lancets
are to the inside finished with triangular heads. The same applies to the w doorway in the n transept.* – STONE SEATS along
part of the chancel N and S walls. Their ends are treated as
arms in a curiously Grecian manner, with a kind of stylized
leaf or palmette arranged down the face of the curved arms. –
FONT. Big, octagonal, Dec, with divers tracery patterns. The
base dates from 1827. – PULPIT. Jacobean. – ROOD SCREEN.
Plain, Perp, with one-light divisions. – STAINED GLASS. The E
window incorporates C15 fragments, but most of the work was
done by the Rev. *P. Aubertin* in 1851. (The s transept circular
window has early C14 fragments with a panel of C13 pieces
below.) – PLATE. Cup 1664; Paten on foot 1714. – MONU-
MENTS. Rev. James Tattershall † 1784. By *R. Westmacott Sen.*
Good, with a big urn in front of an obelisk. – Sir Edward Banks
† 1835. He started as a labourer and by 'self-educated talent'
rose to become a distinguished 'contractor for public works'.
Among the many buildings he was responsible for, Waterloo
and Southwark Bridges are represented on his monument. The
centre is a bust in a niche. By *Thomas Smith* of London. –
Archibald Little † 1844, by *R. Brown* of London. Grecian,
with a seated mourning female figure by a pedestal with an urn.

(FAIR DENE SCHOOL, Hogscross Lane. With some exposed
    timber-framing and an oversailing gable. Many more recent
    additions. MHLG)

SHABDEN, ½ m. SW. *See* p. 451.

CHOBHAM   9060

The N end is heath, partly taken over as a military vehicle-
testing station – an appalling thing on a big open space so near
London. The s end is Woking Suburban. In between, old and
cared-for farms and one of the few village centres in West Surrey.

ST LAURENCE. A typical Surrey story of interesting fragments
    all but ruined by restoration.‡ Original church C11, cut through
    *c.*1170 by the present s arcade (splays of the earlier Norman

---

* It has been pointed out that this feature also occurs in Lambeth Palace
crypt (*c.* 1190–1210).
‡ By *Ferrey*, 1866 (GS).

windows in the spandrels). Enormous roof covering nave and s aisle in one sweep down to 8 ft above the ground. The s aisle walling is a rough chequerboard of puddingstone and heathstone with c15 windows. Tower c15, all heathstone with a lead spike: an offhand design, with crude stone dressing and a tower arch without capitals. The w porch is of timber, late c15 or c16, and probably re-set. Inside, there is no overall effect because of rebuilding, but the c12 s arcade is handsome: four bays: the w bay has very heavy square pillars, the other bays have circular piers carrying square multi-scalloped capitals as at Great Bookham. The arches are all identical, pointed with a slight chamfer. This looks as if the arches are a later, though not much later, replacement. Why does the w bay differ? Does it imply a former tower? Of the same date as the arches, i.e. late c12, the s chapel of one bay with the same arches. The chancel arch belonging to this building has been renewed. Chancel and s transept of 1898 and N aisle of 1866, externally all of the deep brown of consistently used puddingstone. The s aisle externally c15. Of the same date probably the very curious s aisle roof, a makeshift affair looking decidedly Heath Robinson. Corbels stick out of the arcade wall. They carry detached posts. Arches from the posts to the rafters of the lean-to roof. Wind-braces between wall-plate and purlin. – FONT. Wooden octagonal bowl. Could be c15, could as easily be c17 survival work. – CHEST. c13 with triple locks. – PLATE. Cup 1562; several c18 pieces. – MONUMENTS. Sir William Abdy † 1803. Polychrome marble tablet, still taut and not sentimental, and probably therefore by a local man, not a Bacon or a Westmacott. – Mrs Bainbridge † 1827. Tablet with a mourning woman. By *Willson*. – Thomas Bainbridge † 1853. Without figures. By *H. Hopper*.

CHOBHAM PLACE, ½ m. N. Seven-by-three-bay stuccoed front, late c18 (e.g. the 'palm-leaf' porch), vamped up by c.1850 with extra detail round most of the windows. Unattractive, but in a remarkable little park like a fragment of Epping Forest.

WESTCROFT PARK, 1 m. NW. Plain early c19 house with, in the grounds, an odd half-timbered tower of c.1910 containing a carillon of twenty-five bells. Built by Mr H. O. Serpell, who had always wanted to own his own peal.

BROOK PLACE, 1 m. W. A charming small c17 manor house, built in 1656, with shaped gables and a complex plan which gives plenty of chance for them to compose. As a result it looks even more commonsense and comfortable than a Cotswold manor. Four bays with two end gables, the elevation split, with the E half brought forward and given its own gable at 90 degrees to the others. Well restored by *J. D. Coleridge*, 1927.

GORDON BOYS' HOME, West End. Crushingly utilitarian, polychrome brick. 1885 by *Butterfield*. Harshness and protest gone to seed. The feeling is absent (as it so often is in late Butterfield), but the grinding vocabulary is unaltered.

There are old cottages and farms all over Chobham; the MHLG lists fifty-three. Chobham is as much a repository of yeoman building as some of the Kent Weald villages. Many of the cottages and farms are in the HIGH STREET, where there is nothing outstanding – mainly brick and stucco C18 – but a pleasant townscape effect because the street is on a curve and a slight hill with the building line broken halfway by the church tower, set back, and flanked by two trees in the church-yard. This is the inverse of the effect of the tree in the High at Oxford: where that punctuates the concave side of the curve, these two carry the eye across the gap in the convex side formed by the churchyard.

The rest can only be described topographically. Starting at the N and travelling clockwise, CHOBHAM PARK FARM has a brick front of *c*.1700, five by two bays with an eaves cornice. Further E is STANNERS HILL FARM, C17 timber-framing and brick. S of the Weybridge road, BROOKLANDS HOUSE is another early C18 front, five by two bays, grey and red brick, a nice group with a small timber-framed two-storeyed C17 barn. S of the village CASTLE GROVE HOUSE is rough brick classical, dated 1643, with a double order of pilasters at the corners. Beyond West End is LUCAS GREEN MANOR HOUSE, a long front, partly modernized but with an impressive C16 W end. W gable above a three-sided bay, and another big gable on the main S elevation, both using cornices of unornamented terracotta to make decorative patterns. Mullion-and-transom windows with hood-moulds. Timber-framed dovecote in front. STRAWCOCK FIELD, on the Bagshot road, is a neat conclusion to the list. 1947 by *Henry Braddock*, a simple pitched-roof brick house, well detailed, with plain modern windows, a perfect counterpart to the C18 brick farms. (CEDAR HOUSE, Philpott Lane. 1934 by *Lutyens*, as a proto-type for Messrs Colt. NT)

VALLEY END. *See* Windlesham.

WEST END COMMON. Here there are four ditched bowl

BARROWS in line, the central two overlapping and the end two having a diameter of c.100 ft. There are no recorded finds.

CHURCH COBHAM see COBHAM

8030
CHURT
2 m. NW of Hindhead

On the N slopes of Hindhead. Vernacular cottages displaying tile-hanging and brick and stone walls, mostly very pretty. Small triangular green, which is convex and highest in the middle, so that all the buildings round it are seen over the brow – an odd effect.

ST JOHN. 1868 by *Ewan Christian*. Small Surrey-style Dec chapel, acceptable because nicely sited.

BRON-Y-DE or CHURT PLACE, I m. E. A gauche, almost styleless house by *Philip Tilden* for Lloyd George, 1921. Mansard roof and big graceless loggia all over the garden front.

CLANDON PARK see WEST CLANDON

1060
CLAREMONT

Sir John Vanbrugh in 1708 bought the site of the present house and built a house for himself. He liked the site, which he called 'romantick' and consequently crenellated his house and his walled garden. Before 1715, however, he sold the estate to Thomas Pelham, Earl of Clare and later Duke of Newcastle. Pelham asked Vanbrugh to enlarge the house considerably, and renamed it Claremont. Vanbrugh began work c.1715, replacing the battlements with a pediment, and adding side wings on arcaded basements. A two-storey room 100 ft long was added in 1719–20. Vanbrugh also added to the outbuildings and garden furnishings. For the gardens themselves Pelham called in *Kent*, who provided a lake with an island, a temple on the island (*see below*), and a grotto. The estate was sold again in 1768. Lord Clive, who bought it, pulled down Vanbrugh's house and replaced it by a more manageable and aesthetically more acceptable building by *Lancelot Brown* and his partner *Henry Holland*. Brown, better known as Capability Brown, was, it seems, responsible not only for the remodelling of the gardens, but for at least some of the work on the house.* The carcase of the house cost £15,584. Holland's young pupil *John Soane* was employed on the house from 1772. (He was then nineteen.) He later claimed that he was responsible for the design of the Entrance Hall.

The house is a block of white brick, nine by seven bays in size and detached on all sides. The kitchens are reached by a tunnel in order not to interfere with this all-round dignity. The house consists of an elevated basement, a principal storey, and a half-storey crowned with a balustrade. The front has a giant portico of four detached Corinthian columns, reached by a staircase of twenty-two steps with a simply elegant iron balustrade. The back has giant pilasters instead. The sides are quite plain. Of the interiors the finest is the Entrance Hall with its red scagliola columns, its oval ceiling, and its discreet square, oblong, and oval panels in relief on the walls. The Great Drawing Room (now Assembly Hall) has an equally fine and equally restrained plaster ceiling. The walls were re-done *c.*1930, but the fireplace with two female termini caryatids is original. Wide open-well staircase with restrained balustrade and glazed circular opening in the ceiling. On the top landing a pair of attenuated columns. Other good interiors, and especially plaster ceilings of great finesse. In the basement one fireplace remains of *Vanbrugh*'s time (re-set). It is in what is now the Secretary's room. Also in the basement a sunk marble bath in a vaulted room.

More of *Vanbrugh*'s work survives in the gardens, first and foremost the astonishing BELVEDERE on a hillock to the w. It is one of Vanbrugh's most characteristic designs and historically of great significance as an early example of medievalism. It was built of brick in 1717 and is a narrow oblong with four square angle towers. The building is of two storeys, the towers are of three. All windows are arched with the heavy unmoulded horizontal bands along the walls at the height of the springing of their arches which are so typical of Vanbrugh. The towers have open arches in their top storey and are embattled. Between the towers the building projects on two sides and recedes on the other two. The ground-floor room has a shallow vault.

Also by Vanbrugh are, near the house, the amazingly heavy WALLS of the walled gardens, 600 ft long, and the WHITE

* Designs were commissioned already in 1769, and Clive and Brown signed a contract in 1771. Holland did not join Brown until 1772.

6—S.

COTTAGE, formerly the Gardener's Cottage. This is of an irregularly cruciform shape, again with the typically heavy, unmoulded details. Its façade has three bays with an arched entrance, windows in blank arches l. and r., a lower upper storey, and a steep pediment. The base of the pediment is broken by a blank arch, which also surrounds the recessed upper middle window. The STABLES close to the White Cottage, with their clock turret, date from *Brown*'s time. *Vanbrugh* did more work away from the house and close to the present main entrance from Esher. But here the description should perhaps be topographical rather than historical.

The GATE LODGES and GATE are by *Holland* (altered by *J. W. Hiort*; Colvin). They are ample and reticent. Inside the gates the N, W, and S fringe of the estate has been broken up and given over to villas in their gardens – a typical Surrey development (cf. e.g. Esher Place). Among these is WHITE WALLS in ALBANY CLOSE, on the S fringe, by *Sir Hugh Casson*, *c.*1935. On the W fringe close to the gates is the HOME FARM HOUSE, which must be by *Vanbrugh*. White brick, with a pediment above a round-arched corbel-frieze and blank arches below. S of this and E of the NE side of the walled garden is a C19 OBELISK erected in memory of Lord Clive, Leopold Prince of Saxe-Coburg, and his wife Princess Charlotte. The latter two lived at Claremont. Further SW, beyond the house and NW of the belvedere, the CAMELIA HOUSE of *c.*1820, with curved ends. In the lake on the ISLAND the ruins of a handsome domed TEMPLE by *Kent*, astylar with heavy rusticated ground floor and a broken pediment above the arched entrance.

In the S fringe of villas, due S of the belvedere, a MILESTONE on which it says 'XVIII miles to Cornhill'. There was a seventeen-mile-stone at Milbourne Lane, Esher.

SW of Black Hill Road, off the PORTSMOUTH ROAD on its W side, about 200 yards from the road, is THE HOMEWOOD, built by *Patrick Gwynne* in 1938–9. One of the best private houses in the modern style built in England between the two wars. Ground floor with garage, boiler house, etc., all the principal rooms on the upper floor. L-shaped main block and, connected with its E end by a hall with circular staircase, the bedroom block, whose W wall cants forward from its N and S corners towards the connecting link. Large living room with dining part and balcony in the long arm of the L, facing S. In the short arm staff bedrooms. The ground floor is brick, the upper floor concrete. The entrance drive runs under half the See p. 595 bedroom wing.

CLAYGATE

1060

1½ m. SE of Esher

HOLY TRINITY. 1840 by *H. E. Kendall*. Grey brick, Norman style. Towards the street the apse with two small flanking towers, turning octagonal in their upper parts and provided with spires. This façade is of 1860, but may correspond to Kendall's original design (Colvin).

(HOLY NAME (R.C.), Arbrook Lane. 1961 by *F. G. Broadbent & Partners*. DE)

RUXLEY TOWERS. Among later additions one very tall and very bad stucco Gothic tower of *c*.1830 with a frightening silhouette of gargoyles.

SEMAPHORE HOUSE, Telegraph Lane, Hinchley Wood. 1821–2. Simple three-storey tower with flat roof. One of the series in the line from Portsmouth to Whitehall. (*See* also Pewley Hill Guildford, p. 289, and Chatley Heath Hatchford, p. 308.)

COBHAM

1060

A large village, S of Esher, in two parts, both in unhappy transition: Street Cobham through traffic along the Portsmouth Road, Church Cobham to the E through suburban expansion from London. Fragments of old street compositions remain, but nothing more, and as yet nothing positive has replaced them.

ST ANDREW. Norman W tower, carstone and flint, with simple renewed two-light bell-openings and an unmoulded arch towards the nave on unmoulded imposts with a dainty many-scalloped frieze. Norman S doorway of standard type, with jamb shafts, three-scallop capitals, and a main order of zigzag, an inner roll moulding, and an outer hood-mould of billets. Of indifferent quality. The church was originally aisleless, with one humble two-bay arcade between chancel and N chapel (circular pier, circular abacus, slightly chamfered arch). One blocked lancet in the chancel N wall, late C12, and a few three-light C15 windows in the S aisle also survive from the medieval church. All the rest a farrago of restoration and enlargement (two new aisles and s chapel – 1853, 1872, 1886, 1902). – STAINED GLASS. A pair of windows at the W end of the S aisle; violent colours and Pre-Raphaelite drawing. The w aisle window in particular is a riot of bright reds and blues. – BRASSES. Nativity, c.1500. A tiny scene, approx. 6 in. by 4 in., like a manuscript illustration (s wall of chancel). – Delightful palimpsest attached to the N jamb of the arch between the s aisle and the s chancel chapel. The original figure of a priest is of c.1500, the palimpsest an inimitable bearded figure in armour of the late C16. Approximately 18 in. high.

In the churchyard a big MAUSOLEUM to Harvey Combe † 1818 and family, with sarcophagus under a big canopy: Soane's funerary style done with a bit more ostentation.

COBHAM PARK, s of the village. Very ugly French Renaissance by *E. M. Barry*, 1870, keeping late C18 STABLES.

BRIDGE over the Mole on the A3. Simple brick, by *George Gwilt Sen.*, 1782–3, widened on the N side in 1914.

Street Cobham is a bottleneck on the Portsmouth road. The only notable building is the WHITE LION, a long, mid-C18 brick front, nine bays, with a pedimented centre. The road from here to Church Cobham – BETWEEN STREET – contains first Nos. 59–61, another example of Surrey waywardness. 1938 by *Bert Heffer*, with pantiles, quoins, half-timber, brick-nogging, patterned brick, and ornamented plaster frieze (much of it was pre-cast). Nearly opposite, No. 38 is straightforward modern by *F. Tischler*, 1954. CHURCH STREET to the s keeps its scale but little else – perhaps worth a look are LIME HOUSE, four by two bays of typical brickwork of c.1740, and CHURCH STILE HOUSE beside the churchyard, with regular timbering and a double overhang, a rare thing in surviving Surrey timber work. Said to be C15 but looks later.* Brickwork of c.1700 at the back. Beyond the churchyard CHURCHGATE HOUSE is tile-hung, of c.1700, near a pretty ogee-windowed LODGE, which seems to be C18 Gothick altered in the C19.

The main road to Leatherhead, now MILL ROAD, ends with a well-known group on the N side of the river, impaired now that the MILL itself is mostly demolished. Most of its effect is through the curve of the river counterpointed by two sober C18 houses, Cedar House and Ham Manor. CEDAR HOUSE has six bays of plain brickwork of c.1750 with a change in height half-way along, a disarming effect. The gatepiers and ironwork in front are much more circumstantial than the house. (The gate has Sheridan's monogram, and comes from his house at

* Miss E. M. Dance tells us that the work is probably associated with a lease of 1624.

Eltham. At the back a medieval part, with a large traceried window brought from another place.) HAM MANOR is slightly earlier C18, five bays of pattern-book design with mansard roof and Tuscan Doric doorcase. (Further s, in Tilt Road, ASHFORD FARM HOUSE, two storeys, three bays, the l. side with brick cornice and Ionic pilasters (cf. Slyfield Manor). Timber-framed part at the back, and some C16 wall painting with foliage inside. MHLG)

s of the village first COBHAM LODGE, a styleless small stuccoed box, c.1810 by *J. B. Papworth*. Very poor, a reminder that he designed much better at Cheltenham than anywhere else. Then DOWNSIDE, an attractive hamlet with a big rough green largely surrounded by C19 model cottages. Pretty asymmetrical tile-hung SCHOOLS of 1867.

To the W PAINSHILL PARK (*see* p. 404); FOXWARREN PARK (*see* p. 246); CHATLEY HEATH (*see* Hatchford).

COLDHARBOUR

A hamlet 700 ft up on the Surrey Hills, sw of Dorking, unlike anywhere else in the county. Stone-built, scattered along the hill top above rough grassland with a broad view s over the Weald. As remote as south-west Shropshire, and quite unaffected by the mild suburbanization that has affected Peaslake and Abinger further w.

CHRIST CHURCH. 1848 by *Ferrey*, a simple, sensible stone chapel in the style of c.1280. Much bigger in scale than Ferrey usually is – e.g. the s porch and chancel arch. (Restoration by *Caröe*, 1904: roof, fittings. D. Lloyd)

ANSTIEBURY CAMP, 1 m. NE of Leith Hill. An Iron Age fort, oval in plan, enclosing $11\frac{1}{2}$ acres. To the NE and NW the defences are triple banks with double ditches, and there are signs of a third ditch to the NE. An entrance at the NNE is probably original. A date of construction between the C2 and the C1 B.C. may be guessed – the site awaits proper excavation. Holmbury Camp is near by (*see* Holmbury St Mary).

COLLIERS WOOD

NE of Merton, E of South Wimbledon

LONDON TRANSPORT UNDERGROUND STATION. By *Charles Holden*, 1926. One of a standard type of stations on the

Northern line, the first to depart from a Neo-Georgian tradition. The character is decidedly that of concrete, the forms heavy and cubic. Emphasis on the corner. All these stations are placed at corners. The principal window subdivided not by columns but by square piers carrying balls.

⟨APEX TOWER, opposite the station. 1966 by *Bader & Miller*. Well proportioned, with strongly projecting mullions, but all in a grim dark grey. Small car park behind, with spiral ramp.⟩

METHODIST HALL, High Street. By *E. D. Mills*, 1936. In the modern style.

COLNBROOK END *see* POYLE

9040

COMPTON

1½ m. SW of Guildford

Under the Hog's Back, but already on sandstone and in an intricate landscape of small hills. A well-preserved place with a curious character, that of a street of separate cared-for cottages which never becomes a village: the church and the bigger houses are hidden away behind trees, and there is no central space. The effect is due largely to the large number of careful and cosy C19 and early C20 cottages.

ST NICHOLAS. The oldest parts are of the C11. The tower is impressively plain, unbuttressed, with simple rectangular openings for the bell chamber. Very good rubble masonry (see quoins), and entirely of Bargate stone; hence perhaps pre-Conquest, from the negative point of view that if the Normans had put up such a carefully-built tower they would have provided representational detail in the bell chamber also. Shingled broach-spire above. C11 also the part of the W wall just S of the tower, in the same careful stonework, and the chancel walls – a very long chancel – with two blocked windows with a simple hollow moulding outside, one on the N side and one on the S. The fame of Compton is in the extraordinary Romanesque additions made to the chancel in the later C12, which have given it a two-storeyed sanctuary, a vaulted chamber below and a separate chapel above, open to the chancel and separated from it by a Romanesque guard rail, one of the earliest pieces of church woodwork in the country (*see* below). The ribbing in the lower chamber is quadripartite, the ribs heavy and single-chamfered. There is a good keystone but no boss. This two-storey arrangement is something extremely rare. It existed however also at Melbourne in Derbyshire. No-one has as yet been able to explain it. Was it connected with a manor house, on the pattern of the familiar double-chapels of palaces (Bishop's Palace Hereford, the Sainte Chapelle in Paris, St Stephen's Chapel in the Palace of Westminster, etc.), or was it something like the two-storeyed transepts of Jumièges or the balconies in the transepts of Winchester, or ought it to be compared with the raised chancels above half-sunk crypts in so many Italian Romanesque churches, or can there have been other liturgical requirements? The construction can be followed fairly closely, for one of the blocked CII windows, if opened, would cut across the springing of the vault. So the C12 chamber was built *inside* the existing chancel – the walls are thicker in the sanctuary than in the chancel itself* – to take the upper chapel. Were it not for this evidence, some sort of conversion of a three-part church such as Elkstone in Gloucestershire would have been an easier explanation. The work is of *c*.1160. The arch leading to the lower chapel has two orders, a deeply cut inner roll-moulding and an outer moulding of saw-tooth ornament like formalized beak-heads, supported on small nook-shafts. Outside this is a label made up of dog-tooth ornament (a remarkably early use of the motif). The chamber above has an altered and re-set PISCINA which seems to have been moved in the C12 alterations. The pillar is incomplete, and the head has the same two-order detail as the blocked CII windows, and hence may have been re-used. Of the same period as this remodelling of the chancel the small chamber to its S, which holds a wooden staircase to the upper chamber. It has a Norman S window and is supposed to have been a cell or oratory.

A little later, perhaps *c*.1180, came a big enlargement of the nave, which was given new aisles with three-bay arcades, new chancel and tower arches, and a new S doorway. All the work has the same general spirit, coarser than that of the sanctuary. Very small windows, unchamfered arcade arches very slightly pointed, the chancel arch with nook-shafts and an order of zigzag ornament above, in high relief and badly restored, the other arches with a plain label.‡ Some of the capitals are scalloped and some have stylized foliage. In the two E capitals

* And were simply butted up inside the existing walls; the restoration of 1906 revealed that the original plaster still remained on the inside of the CII walls.

‡ The plaster itself is crimped to produce an extra band of ornament, the best example of this local habit. *See also* Worplesdon and Puttenham.

on the s side the foliage has become much more crowded and
curly and is midway between pure Romanesque and the style
of the Reigate capitals. The s doorway has one order of zigzag,
the N doorway is simpler and blocked. Dormer clerestory, low
aisle walls and sweeping lean-to roofs, as at Chobham; the N
side remains, the s side was raised in the C15. There are few
other additions. In the late C13 the w bay of the chancel
received lancet windows, two 'low', two normal. The Saxon
tower has a shingled broach-spire of uncertain date. Also a
C19 window in the E wall of the sanctuary, now blocked up
again, a Dec window at the E end of the s aisle, and several
C13 lancets. The church was well restored by *Woodyer*. – FONT.
Early Norman, like the capital of a big arcade. Square bowl
above big circular stem and ring. – WOODWORK. Guard rail in
the sanctuary. Late C12, and thus a very precious survival.
Simple round arches on elegant thin stems, just like a C17 rail,
but the capitals, although worn, clearly have crockets. – ALTAR
RAILS, PULPIT (with sounding board), and TOWER SCREEN,
formerly chancel screen. All Jacobean, of *c.*1620, ornate but
lifeless. – RECESSES. In the N aisle, pair of subtly shaped C14
heads to vanished tombs. – STAINED GLASS. Small trefoil
roundel in the E wall of the lower chapel, of the Virgin and
Child, probably C13. (Also some C17 glass similar to that at
Abbot's Hospital, Guildford. Miss E. M. Dance) – MONU-
MENT (inside porch). Edward Fulham † 1694 and family,
erected 1778. Simple, handsome Late Palladian tablet with
urn above, by *Van Gelder*.

CEMETERY CHAPEL. The Late Victorian painter *G. F. Watts*
lived at Compton. He had a big, half-timbered house (LIM-
NERSLEASE) designed by *Sir Ernest George* in 1891, and his
wife designed this burial chapel in 1896. The house is in the
Norman Shaw style, big and dull. (COTTAGE by *Clough
Williams-Ellis*. NT) The outside of the chapel is a mixture of
Italian Romanesque motifs, ornament derived from Celtic
manuscripts, and the heavy symbolism so dear to Late Victorian England: 'the ground plan symbolic of Eternity (a
circle) through which runs the Cross of Faith'. So the plan
outside is a Greek cross with four curved walls between the
arms, with many bands of terracotta ornament delicately and
crisply cut, all with an elaborate symbolic intention (described
in detail in a guide leaflet inside the church). The obvious
natural style for this would have been Art Nouveau, and had
the artistic climate been homogeneous Mrs Watts would

Compton, Watts Chapel, by Mrs Watts, 1896 (*Reproduced by courtesy of the Architectural Review*)

naturally have used it.* But in England each small advanced group was working separately, and so the chapel desperately attempts Art Nouveau effects from the outlandish standpoint of the Celtic Revival.

The inside was designed in 1901, and this *is* Art Nouveau. It is a very startling and effective room, though not a pleasant one because of the intolerable torpor and weariness of the motifs. There is nothing like Mackintosh here – it is one of the most soporific rooms in England. It is not architecturally great either, because ornament and structure are not really related to one another. The plan has become a circle with four deep embrasures representing the arms of the cross, oddly vaulted by pairs of thick parallel ribs, like the Monks' Kitchen at Durham. This vigorous structure is completely covered by writhing decoration carried out entirely in gesso, i.e. fibre soaked in plaster of Paris. Elongated angels hold cameos in ornate frames looped downwards and linked to form a chain; more angels above, cherubs' heads on the vaulting ribs, any bare space filled with Art Nouveau curves. Heavy colours – dull gold, dark reds and greens – and again a completely symbolic interpretation almost impossible to describe and certainly impossible to infer from the room itself. Above the altar, a version by *Watts* of his painting 'The All-Rewarding'.

The WATTS GALLERY to the E of Limnerslease was opened in 1904. It is in a weak blend of Voysey and Lutyens (by *C. Turnor*). Watts died in the same year and is buried in the churchyard in a CLOISTER designed by *Mrs Watts* in a semi-Moorish Monreale way, one more attempt at finding a style.

Several good Art Nouveau TOMBSTONES in the burial ground, the best to Julian Sturgis † 1904, the owner of Voysey's Greyfriars.

EASTBURY MANOR, immediately W of the church. By *Ewan Christian*, 1874. Atrocious brick and stone.

The things to notice in the village street are CYPRESS FARM at the N end, a pretty tile-hung C17 cottage, the clever picturesque mixture of original and C19 cottages near the church, especially pretty looking N, and the double overhang of a cottage further S, with wide-spaced regular framing.

(BRIDGE, N of the Watts Chapel, carrying the Guildford bypass over the alleged route of the Pilgrims' Way, designed by *Lutyens*, 1931. NT)

---

* And had Watts been able to use it in his paintings he might have been a minor master instead of a brave but baffling failure.

ROMAN VILLA. A small Romano-British villa, containing seven rooms in addition to a bath building, has been excavated here. It was of corridor type, and in fact contained two corridors, running along the N and S sides, both paved with coloured tesserae. There were signs of crude painted plaster in one room; pottery including *terra sigillata* and coins give a date in the C2–3 A.D. The site is N of Limnerslease, near Donne Lane.

CONEYHURST see EWHURST

COOMBE see KINGSTON UPON THAMES, pp. 333, 335

COOPERS HILL see ENGLEFIELD GREEN

COULSDON

3050

ST JOHN EVANGELIST. Nicely placed at the E corner of the large green. At its W corner a farm with a C16 BARN, flint and brick and timber framing. The church is essentially of the later C13. C15 W tower of irregular stone and flint with a later shingled spire consisting of a truncated pyramid roof with a spike put on. Of C13 features note the W lancets of the N and S aisles and, internally, the beautiful blank N and S arcading in the chancel, which rests on circular shafts. The W bay has the shafts very short and growing corbel-like out of the wall, as if taking stalls or a screen into consideration. Excellent SEDILIA 17 with detached circular piers and richly moulded pointed-trefoiled arches. The PISCINA, though small, continues the same composition. Double-chamfered tower arch. C15 arcades of two bays, with tall octagonal piers and double-chamfered arches. Big, very dominant extension on the S side, 1958 by *J. S. Comper*. This is, alas, imitation Dec. – STAINED GLASS, N aisle, by *Kempe, c.*1899. – MONUMENT. Grace Rowed † 1631. A small but very remarkable tablet, in the S aisle, comparable with some Evelyn monuments at Wotton. Diptych with segmental pediment. Between the two black inscription plates the small figure of a woman stands on a skull, which lies on a pedestal with pick and shovel. She looks up to heaven, which is represented by a sun and clouds in the pediment. Out of her mouth comes a scroll with writing, and there are plenty of other emblematical inscriptions. The upper half of the black inscription plate appears to be hidden by a brown cloth, also made of stone, which again is covered with inscriptions.

(ST AIDAN (R.C.), Chipstead Valley Road. Begun in 1931 by
A. Scott, the nave completed in 1966 by *Burles, Newton &
Partners*. – SCULPTURE. Crucifix by *D. Prudens;* Virgin and
Child and furnishings by *X. Ruckstuhl*. – STAINED GLASS by
P. Fourmaintreaux. DE)

(TAUNTON FARMHOUSE, Taunton Lane. Irregular flint, brick,
and tile-hung exterior of various dates, but inside the remains
of a timber-framed C15 hall-house with its original roof above
the first floor inserted in the C17. MHLG)

⟨COULSDON WOODS, N of Old Coulsdon, is a large estate begun
in 1967 by Messrs Wates. The most original parts are the
terraces of houses running up the hill, with garages tucked
away beneath gardens and footpaths, designed by *K. Bland*
of *Wates*, with elevations by *Frederick MacManus &
Partners*.⟩

FARTHING DOWN. On the chalk ridge a fine series of ROMANO-
BRITISH OR 'CELTIC' FIELDS associated with the N–S ridgeway. A scatter of C1–2 A.D. native pottery suggests a settlement
centred on Woodplace Farm near the hospital; a second site
must lie at Horley.

A group of about fourteen BARROWS on the line of the
ridgeway is the survival, now to be seen in three clusters, of an
original cemetery of some thirty mounds. In 1760 a skeleton
was found, and in 1871 a number of Saxon inhumations, iron
knives, a sword, a shield boss, etc., giving a date for the whole
in the late C6–7 A.D.

⁰⁰³⁰

CRANLEIGH

A haphazard, accidental small town rather than a village; in fact
an old centre of the iron industry. Big triangular green at the
NW end becoming very long and narrow to the S, with formal
French-looking tree planting as it becomes the main street.
Most of the buildings are C19 and C20, though attractively
cheerful and wayward, and few of any date need special notice.
The best old groups are the attractive brick houses N of the
church and the very pretty, very small-scale tile-hung shops
and cottages around the ONSLOW ARMS. Opposite this is, of
all things, a monopitch-roofed shop of the CO-OP, built in
1939 under *L. G. Ekins* and now looking very dated indeed.
Further S a nice new POST OFFICE, 1959 by *G. A. H. Pearce*
of the Ministry of Works. ⟨Cranleigh is expanding rapidly.
Recent buildings in the centre include STOCKLUND SQUARE

s of the High Street, a shopping centre with fussy maisonnettes above, by *Covell, Matthews & Partners*, 1966–8; and a large SWIMMING POOL now building s of the church. Much indifferent new housing s and w of the town, but one outstanding estate, PARKMEAD (to the E, s of Ewhurst Road), by *Highet & Phillips*, 1963–7. At the entrance from Ewhurst Road is a long four-storey crescent sweeping around a large green. Beyond the green are two schools by *Barber, Bundy & Greenfield* and the County Architect, *R. J. Ash* (Infants 1966–7, Junior 1967–8); on the r. are shops and bungalows. The houses scattered among trees around the perimeter of the estate form nicely varied compact groups, with crisp roof-lines and much painted weatherboarding.⟩

ST NICHOLAS. Effectively all Dec, a rarity for Surrey, and with the heavy solid Wealden character common in Sussex (e.g. Horsham or Bury). Nave and aisles, unaisled chancel, clerestory without windows, and lumpish w tower with big clasping NW stair-turret* built in carstone (compare the gravelly texture with Bargate stone of the same colour). Harsh restoration done in 1864–6, when the N and s transepts were lengthened and the s porch added. The interior is very spacious. The aisles open to the nave in two very wide and high bays. The tower arch and chancel arch are very wide and high too. w of the chancel arch clearly the beginnings of yet another wide and tall transverse arch, which was not continued and is now capped by two early C20 statues. It looks as if it had been the w arch of a former crossing. Moreover the responds and intermediate piers and the w crossing arch as well as part of the tower-arch responds are of buff stone, different from the rest. The most likely explanation is that the arcade responds and the circular intermediate piers are remains of an earlier, late C12, arcade with narrower arcade bays and lower arches, and that the church then had a crossing. The tower-arch responds may come from the former E arch of that crossing or be *in situ*. In any case they were heightened when the arcades were also rebuilt, reduced to two bays, and given taller arches. All this was probably done *c.*1330, the approximate date of the s aisle w window (reticulated tracery). Of about the same time the squat w tower. Of the arches of the former crossing that to the E may again be *c.*1330, but the s arch (triple shafts and moulded

* The whole tower keeps its unfilled put-logs or scaffold holes, so familiar in the brick buildings of northern Italy.

capitals) is evidently C13.* In the chancel triple SEDILIA, big-scale C14; heavily restored. – SCREEN. In the S transept. Very simple C14, made up of single panels with cusped tracery in the heads. More ornate fragments worked up into the pulpit. – LECTERN. Attractive, late C16, a gross twisted column for a stem and a strapwork base. It looks German or Dutch. – BRASSES. Fragments collected on the N side of the chancel and a bad half-effigy of a Priest, of c.1500, in the chancel floor. – ⟨MONUMENT. Rosa Chadwyck Healey † 1880. Large, elaborate brass with angel under a Gothic arch; wall paintings of St Rosa and St Tabitha above.⟩

Very good, honest stone LYCHGATE of 1880, Philip Webb's style. Stone bows underneath as well as a timber roof; said to be by *Street*.

CRANLEIGH SCHOOL, ½ m. N. Built in 1865 by *Woodyer*. A quadrangle, with the chapel in one corner. Clever but un-sympathetic asymmetrical Tudor, more or less in Butterfield's style. The chapel apsed and clerestoried. Additions to the W of 1929 by *Sir Edwin Cooper*; a three-storey Neo-Georgian block, a Memorial Hall with a silly portico *in antis*, and a detached headmaster's house beyond. The high standard of finish is more American than English.

To the NW, beyond Cranleigh School, is Smithwood Common, with SMITHWOOD FARM on the W side, a perfect example of the extremely complex geometrical result that can happen quite accidentally by repeated additions. Brick and tile-hanging, C16 to C18, multiple gables and chimneys. NE of this is PITTANCE FARM, not remarkable architecturally but a nice complete example, now quite rare in Surrey, of the unspoilt C17 farm-house forming a quadrangle with its barns. Brick, sandstone, weatherboarding, and tile-hanging. W again, on the Guildford–Horsham road, is SMITHBROOK MANOR, a half-H-shaped half-timbered C16 house (a hall-house originally?), bigger than the usual run of half-timbered farms.

WYPHURST, I m. NE. Strung-out house of 1871 and later. The earlier parts a Norman Shaw composition with tile-hanging and half-timbering, the additions by *Sir Reginald Blomfield*, c.1910, in red brick with stone dressings, in a flaccid half-Tudor.

WILLINGHURST, 2 m. N. Built as Lapscombe, by *Philip Webb*, 1887, now very much altered and partly demolished. Stone

* The VCH prefers to regard the incomplete W crossing arches as a begin-ning for a chancel arch, which was not continued because almost at once a larger chancel with a chancel arch further E was provided.

below and tile-hung above, with Webb's typical Queen-Anne-derived segment-headed windows. Honest but very arid – the same effect as late Butterfield and perhaps for the same reason, that the capacity for protest was exhausted. The long, low stables, now themselves made into a house, seem more attractive to mid-C20 eyes.

ALDERBROOK, E of Willinghurst, now demolished, was one of *Norman Shaw*'s early tile-hung houses (1881). He was here just escaping from his indigestibly rich half-timber and Gothic detail, which still showed in the entrance door, the crow-stepped chimneybreast, and the bow windows on both entrance and garden sides. Entrance side with typically complicated arrangement of tile-hung recessions and gables. Not really attractive.

RYDINGHURST, 1 m. W of the village. With a simple early C17 brick N front and three Dutch gables, the outer ones with triangular pediments, the centre with a segmental pediment. The exactly matching S front is C19.

BAYNARDS PARK. *See* p. 105.

CROOKSBURY COMMON *see* ELSTEAD

CROOKSBURY HOUSE 8040
1 m. NNE of Tilford

By *Lutyens*, who in later life would not re-visit it, because 'it had too many memories'. It has indeed, and one of them is the ghost of Lutyens's artistic integrity. The house is his potted biography. The original building is of 1890–2, his first country house. It consists of one half-timbered wing at the W end, in style leaning heavily on Norman Shaw (the chimney could have come directly from Pierrepont, e.g.), and the tile-hung service wing to the l. of the forecourt. The garden side (s) is also tile-hung. This is one of the best things he ever did, informal, with strong horizontals formed by the eaves and by curving out the foot of the tile-hanging, a local trick he was fond of (cf. Fulbrook). The effect here of space flowing uniformly in all directions is a true equivalent to Frank Lloyd Wright. The inside of this part, with intimate space floating from room to passage to staircase, all on different levels, is as experimental and fresh as anything Wright was doing in 1890. Then in 1898–9 an E wing was added to create Fig Tree Court. The wing is Tudor (plus a very little mild Art Nouveau ironwork) on the w and s, and had Lutyens's first classical exterior on the e side, segment-headed and quoined Queen Anne style. The house changed hands, the new owner wanted Tudor – and Lutyens provided it. In 1914 he fitted up a big-scale, soulless, symmetrical roughcast front in place of the Queen Anne work of 1898, and added another chimney to Fig Tree Court in the style of Tigbourne, which in the circumstances was a sort of self-abuse. It is all a very sad commentary, particularly as the first work is so good. (The 1914 work also included large tile-hung service wings. N of these are the STABLES, partly of 1890, but mainly of 1901–2, one of Lutyens's earliest 'Wrenaissance' designs, with a lively cupola and a subtle splaying of the wings. Garden by *Gertrude Jekyll* mainly of 1892 and 1902, with high gabled walls and brick revetted terraces. Down the drive is a COTTAGE of 1889, Lutyens's first complete building. L-shaped, roughcast, with a single splendid chimney. NT)

See p. 596

CROSSWAYS FARM *see* ABINGER

3040

CROWHURST

An unspoilt Weald parish near the Kent border; rolling, ordinary farmland, no centre to speak of, no railway station, and hence no suburbanization.

ST GEORGE. Simple chapel of Weald stone, unrestored by Surrey standards.* Nave and chancel, plus bell turret on simple timber framing carried by side walls (rebuilt in 1947 after a fire), and a single-bay aisle, the crude slightly chamfered pointed arch of *c*.1190. (The e window of the s aisle is Dec, but has an earlier semicircular moulded rere-arch on nook-shafts.) The other windows are either c13 lancets (chancel) or Dec (the segment-headed two-light windows in nave and s aisle) or Perp (the three-light e and w windows). (The e part of the chancel was rebuilt in the c15; cf. the changes in plinth and masonry.) – FONT. Ungainly c13 work, consisting of an octagonal bowl which is broached from a larger square base, on a central stem and with four shafts at the corners. – PLATE. Chalice and Paten 1638; Paten 1722; Flagon 1736. – STAINED GLASS. Amongst other fragments, most of the tracery lights of the e window contain c15 glass: angels and seraphim under canopies. – MONUMENTS. Three medieval tomb-chests in the

* It was 'made plain and repaired' in 1652.

chancel, two with canopies, all with brasses, all routine work. On the N side John Gaynesford the elder † 1450, without canopy; on the S side John Gaynesford the younger † 1460, under an elaborate battlemented canopy with faces, beasts, monsters, and foliage in the spandrels and the cusps, and a spirited brass.* Also an unnamed tomb-chest under a simple four-centred arch. – Two standard late C17 tablets facing each other in the chancel: Thomasina Maryott † 1675 and Justinian Angell † 1680. – Also a cast-iron slab on the chancel floor, to Anne Forster † 1591, a reminder of the Wealden iron works. The figure is bundled up in a shroud. The design is said to have been re-used as a fireback, a grisly bit of furniture for the living room.

The churchyard contains a famous and enormous hollow yew tree, 33 ft round. There used to be (from the early C19) a circular bench inside it.

CROWHURST PLACE, ½ m. SW. Early C15 wealthy yeoman's hall house, built for the Gaynesford family about 1425 and restored ('realized', as musicians would say) out of all recognition by *George Crawley* after 1918. As at Old Surrey Hall (*see* p.396), the result is something remarkable in its own right. The original house, as it survived, was simply a moated, timber-framed hall with a withdrawing room at the S end and a screens passage to the N with three doors now opening into one big room with late (*c.*1600?) linenfold panelling. Crawley added a N wing, a S extension, and whimsies in the grounds such as a circular stone dovecot and a gatehouse down the drive. He also altered the elevations to a degree – new gables, new Tudor chimneys, new porch, new oriel. Looking at pre-restoration photographs, one can hardly believe that it is the same building. The only really trustworthy original details are in the hall roof, an astonishingly assured piece of woodwork, though of only two bays. It is almost impossible to describe accurately. It is in two stages, both provided with coving; but in addition both stages have tie-beams, the upper stage very close to the ridge, the lower with a massive moulded beam resting on the walls. C15 panelling in the SW bedroom, and very pretty Crawley decoration on the ceiling. It was his own house: an extreme example of the English flight from reality around the 1914–18 war. In the grounds is a big timber-framed C16 BARN with brick infilling, Horsham slate roof, and four-centred entrance arches that look like Mr Crawley.

* Is not the arch at least fifty years later than the brass?

ARDENRUN PLACE. Eerie. 1906 by *Ernest Newton*, for Woolf Barnato, the racing motorist. The house in which Neo-Georgianism assumed its final impeccable sterility. Originally a central block and two pavilions, formal gardens, all the details correct Late Wren. Lutyens is often blamed for this style: Newton may well have been the real culprit. It was burnt in 1933, and all that is left is one of the pavilions, and that is now derelict. The gardens are a wilderness, and the effect is perhaps how one of the short-lived Baroque houses must have appeared to the mid C18. Meanwhile MOAT FARM, near by, is in tip-top condition, a beautifully suave building of *c.*1800, five by two bays, of the finest Wealden ashlar, the only ornament a segmental fanlight over the door.

Two farms in Crowhurst deserve notice. One is MANSION HOUSE FARM opposite the church, a late medieval house given a brick front to the street in the late C17, with stilted segmental windows. It is picturesque and rather Dutch-looking. The other is HOBBS FARM, 1 m. w of the church in Tandridge Lane, a grim, late C16 brick front, with Horsham slate roof and a set of grouped diagonal chimneys at each end. Quite different from the typical Weald vernacular of timber-framing and tile-hanging; possibly a stray in brick from the near-Cotswold type of stone house built around Ashdown Forest in Sussex (cf. Smallfield Place and New Place at Lingfield).

CROYDON

Coombe Hill House	*see p.* 190
Norbury	*see p.* 387
Shirley	*see p.* 458
South Norwood	*see p.* 461
Thornton Heath	*see p.* 482
Upper Norwood	*see p.* 492
Woodside	*see p.* 538

INTRODUCTION

Croydon is now visually part of London, as the built-up area never comes to an end between Piccadilly Circus and the s end of Croydon. But up to the C19 Croydon was very much a town in its own right, though already Defoe says that it was 'full of citizens from London'. Its chief architectural importance in the Middle Ages, and even after, was connected with the fact that the Archbishops of Canterbury had a palace here and that some of them did much for Croydon. Its importance for today, however, lies in the fact that during the last ten years the area around and NW of East Croydon Station has suddenly become the most consistently modern-looking area in the whole of England. This development is due to a number of causes: closeness to, yet independence of, London – only 18 minutes by fast trains, and a train every ten minutes – closeness to the vast southern residential suburbs of London, a borough council (since 1965 that of the borough of Croydon within Greater London) eager to receive commercial newcomers, and of course lower rents than in Inner London. Up to the time of writing 5,131,775 sq. ft of office space has been provided.

CHURCHES

ST JOHN THE BAPTIST, Church Street. The largest parish church in Surrey. Burnt in 1867 and rebuilt, essentially to the same design, by *Sir G. G. Scott* in 1870. Medieval the two-storeyed s porch and the tower, except for the overdone pinnacles, which are Scott's. The size and ambition of the old church were due to its being built at the expense of archbishops. Six bays (originally five). Tall piers of the usual moulding with four shafts and four hollows. Moulded arches. Three-light clerestory windows. Big three-light aisle windows with transom. Vaulted tower hall. s porch, two-storeyed. The lower floor vaulted. Of the old church many fragments remain, notably a late C15 tomb recess in the N aisle and two big C14 corbels (one with a head) at the w end of the s aisle. – LECTERN. A fine, big pre-Reformation brass lectern with a sturdy stem, a foot on three small lions, and an eagle top. The same type as at St Mary Redcliffe Bristol, St Martin Salisbury, etc. – WALL PAINTING (chancel N wall). Fresco of the Feeding of the Five Thousand, 1885. – PLATE. Silver-gilt Chalice 1621; silver-gilt Flagon 1641; silver-gilt Paten 1681; silver-gilt Almsdish 1706; Almsdish 1740; silver-gilt Chalice 1830. – MONUMENTS. Brasses to Gabriel Silvester † 1512, a 3 ft. 4 in. figure, and to William Heron † 1562 and wife, the figure being only 1 ft 9 in. long (chancel arch r. and l.). – Hugh Warham, c.1536–8 (?). Tomb-chest in the s chapel with elaborately enriched quatrefoils. Canted recess with three ogee-headed niches. Coarsely panelled vault. – Archbishop Whitgift † 1604. Alabaster; recumbent effigy in prayer. Background with an arch, with two allegorical figures in the spandrels and against the back wall under the arch two putti by the inscription plate. Top with obelisks and achievement. – Archbishop Sheldon † 1677. By *Jasper Latham*. Damaged and inadequately put together. Semi-reclining figure. The pillow lies on a rolled-up mat – a standard Elizabethan and Jacobean motif. Of the background the cartouche remains, but the two putti who held it have disappeared. – (J. S. Copley R.A. † 1815, signed by *Morton Edwards*. Good Grecian tablet with portrait medallion. NT)

ST ANDREW, Southbridge Road. 1857 by *Ferrey*, with many additions. Odd bell-turret with spirelet on a detached shaft which sprouts out of a buttress bisecting the w front.

ST AUGUSTINE, St Augustine's Avenue, South Croydon. 1881–4 by *J. Oldrid Scott* (GR). Flint and yellow stone, with a crossing tower. Competent and restful interior with broad crossing arches. The detail is Dec.

CHRIST CHURCH, Sumner Road. By *Teulon*, 1851–2 (GR). A Commissioners' church. Several odd features, such as the w 'transept' immediately w of the s porch, and the crazy turret with spire on the E end of the nave. The tracery patterns are peculiar too. The chancel is later.

EMANUEL, Normanton Road. 1899 by *T. Roger Smith* (GR). *See p. 596* The late H. S. Goodhart-Rendel, in an unguarded moment, called this the ugliest elevation he knew.

ST JAMES, St James's Road. A Commissioners' church. 1827–9 by *Robert Wallace*. Yellow brick with thin lancets and a lean tower. In the tower odd triplet openings. The chancel is of 1881 by *Charles Henman*.

ST MARY MAGDALENE, Canning Road, Addiscombe. By *E. Buckton Lamb*, 1868–70, except for the tower, which was completed only in 1928–30. The tower stands at the NE corner, next to Lamb's apse. But this E front, with the main entrance through the tower, odd as it is, cannot be sufficient preparation for the nightmarish interior, a debauch of High Victorian inventiveness comparable only to Lamb's other churches at West Hartlepool and Gospel Oak, Hampstead. The plan is roughly central, the transepts being identical and the two-bay nave corresponding to the single-bay chancel. The church is covered with the most ingenious and unexpected timberwork, big beams in all directions, resting on marble columns which in their turn stand on brackets. It all works up to a small timber lantern over the centre of the crossing. In the aisles also timbers reach up towards the nave: the whole impression is that the walls are only there on sufferance, as a necessary podium to this enormous roof. Lamb was obsessed with roofs. In this purposefully composed cacophony such anomalies will hardly be noticed as the detached columns which reach up in front of the transept ends and connect with them at the top by stone work that cuts vertically right across the oculus windows. The church certainly deserves study, chiefly as a reminder of how far some Victorian church architects were from a mechanical imitation of the medieval past. This ruthless individualism is the necessary counterpart of Pearson's noble correctness. – (The VICARAGE is also typically *Lamb*, 1870. NT)

(ST MATTHEW, George Street. 1866 by *A. W. Blomfield*; chancel 1877. Parallel with it the PARISH HALL, 1960–1 by *E. F. Starling*, with the fashionable steep-pitched roof, cross-gables, and restless glazing-bars. NT)

ST MICHAEL, Poplar Walk. By *J. L. Pearson*. It was designed in 1875–6 and built in 1880–3.* Big, with an incomplete s porch tower, transepts, an apse with ambulatory, two turrets with spires on the E ends of the chancel aisles, and a flèche over the crossing. Lancets and plate tracery. The interior is one of the most satisfying of its date anywhere. It is brick-vaulted throughout, and a tiny ambulatory runs right round the E end giving exciting cross-views. The most interesting part is the s chapel. This opens from the chancel aisle and has itself a nave and aisles. They are of equal height and are separated by the slimmest shafts. – The FONT with canopy, the PULPIT with canopy, and the surprisingly splendid, almost Baroque-Gothic, richly gilded ORGAN CASE are all by *Bodley*. – (ROOD by *C. G. Hare*. H. V. Molesworth Roberts) – STAINED GLASS. Some (N chapel E, and W end) by *Kempe*, 1895 and after. – Next door the VICARAGE. Competent neo-Wren by *H. B. Walters*, 1904.

(ST MILDRED, Addiscombe. By *C. G. Hare*, 1931–2. H. V. Molesworth Roberts)

ST PETER, St Peter's Road. A Commissioners' church. 1849–51 by *Sir G. G. Scott*. In a very prominent position. With w tower and spire. Rather dull, though competent, as Scott so often is.

(ST DOMINIC (R.C.), Violet Lane, Waddon. 1961 by *Tomei & Maxwell*. DE)

(ST GERTRUDE (R.C.), Purley Road. 1903 by *F. A. Walters*. DE)

---

* Information from Mr A. Quiney.

(OUR LADY OF THE ANNUNCIATION (R.C.), Bingham Road,
Addiscombe. 1964 by *Denny & Brian*. – SCULPTURE.
Crucifix and Lady Chapel Reredos by *M. Clark*. DE)

(OUR LADY OF REPARATION (R.C.), Wellesley Road. 1883 by
F. A. Walters, incorporating parts of *E. W. Pugin*'s church of
1864. DE)

⟨ST PAUL (Presbyterian), Croham Road, South Croydon. 1905
by *Charles Henman Jun.*, the architect of the Town Hall. Brick
with stone dressings, pretty Flamboyant details, spirelet over
the crossing.⟩

⟨BAPTIST CHURCH, Tamworth Road. 1866. Dignified classical
façade.⟩

WEST CROYDON CONGREGATIONAL CHURCH, London
Road and Campbell Road. By *Church*, 1886. Gothic, E.E.,
with Croydon's most ambitious spire.

FRIENDS MEETING HOUSE, Park Lane. The meeting house
proper, tall and with a big roof, is by *Hubert Lidbetter*, 1956.
It is connected by a colonnade with the adult school hall, by
W. Curtis Green, 1908.

PROVIDENCE BAPTIST CHURCH, West Street. 1847. Three
bays, with three-bay pediment. Stock brick.

PUBLIC BUILDINGS

TOWN HALL AND LIBRARY, Katharine Street. 1892–6 by
Charles Henman Jun. Not a bad design, though of course
debased in most details. The grouping is good, with the tall
tower at the r. angle of the Town Hall and at its foot the
diagonally placed porch to the Library, which lies a little
recessed, forming a quiet close off the road, and quiet also in
its façade, with the range of tall Dutch or North German
pedimented windows with two transoms. Behind the Town
Hall, on both sides of Fell Road and fronting on Park Lane, is
TABERNER HOUSE, 1964–7, by *H. Thornley*, architect to the
Borough Engineer, a high slab on a podium, the slab narrow-
ing towards both ends (like the Pirelli Building in Milan). A
bridge is provided between the blocks E and W of Fell
Road.

FAIRFIELD HALLS with ASHCROFT THEATRE and ARNHEM
GALLERY. By *Robert Atkinson & Partners*. Built in 1960–2.
Large, with a symmetrical façade to Park Lane. Infinitely more
acceptable than the same architects' Technical College – *see*
below. What a change of heart between 1953 and 1960.

LAW COURTS, Barclay Road. By *Robert Atkinson & Partners*, 1968–9. To its N, i.e. S of the E end of the Technical College, is a MULTISTOREY CAR PARK, 1961–2 by *D. H. Beaty-Pownall*.

ARCHBISHOP'S PALACE (Palace School), Old Palace Yard. The earliest evidence of a manor of the Archbishops of Canterbury at Croydon is of 1215, but there is architectural evidence of a house about fifty years earlier.* The house at Croydon became a favourite summer residence of the archbishops and was in addition something like the administrative centre for the estates in Surrey, Middlesex, and Hertfordshire. The main buildings date from the late C14 to the late C15. Only later alterations were made, and in 1780 the whole palace was sold.

The palace is an irregular group of buildings with two small enclosed courtyards. The buildings consist of basement and main floor with in some parts a second floor. Only the GREAT HALL, among the principal apartments, is on the ground floor. The hall is 56 by 38 ft in size and projects to the E from the main group. It was built by Archbishop Courtenay c.1381–96 and rebuilt by Stafford c.1443–52. It is of flint rubble with stone dressings. Of Courtenay's time is the two-storeyed porch and some adjoining walling. The ground floor of the porch is vaulted with diagonal and ridge-ribs. The kitchens etc. originally lay further E still, but were pulled down after the E end of the hall collapsed in 1830. The hall has a noble roof with big arched braces, collar-beams, and wind-braces. Splendidly moulded beams. Three-light windows high up with stepped lights under four-centred arches. At the W end of the S wall was originally a big bay window. In the LOBBY to the W of the hall an early C17 STAIRCASE with open well and turned balusters. It leads to the GREAT PARLOUR, or Guardroom, or Arundel's Hall, built by Archbishop Arundel c.1397–1414. This is 51 by 21 ft and has in the centre of its S wall a later large, wholly renewed oriel window giving on to the S courtyard. In the W wall a blocked gallery with turned balusters. C18 fireplace. S of the Lobby is the LIBRARY, with the so-called Queen Elizabeth Room over. This part was perhaps built by Archbishop Bourchier in the C15. It joins up at its S end with the C16 LONG GALLERY. This is of timber-framed construction but has C18 brick facing and windows in its S wall,

---

* This is one small round-headed basement window NW of the NW corner of the S court, and also some fragments of chevron ornament re-used in the undercroft below Arundel's Guardroom.

the wall which is one of the main approaches to the palace. The W wall towards the churchyard is also of brick, but in this case late C15 brick. Towards this W wall runs between the two inner courts, in continuation of the Parlour, the DINING ROOM, with a good moulded ceiling of Morton's time, and further N along the N side of the N court the CHAPEL. The chapel was built probably by Archbishop Bourchier, i.e. c.1460–80, but lengthened to the W by Morton so as to line up with the new W wall. The chapel is 70 by 24 ft, of brick, with straight-headed five-light windows. The E window is of seven lights, under a four-centred arch. The ceiling is C17. – FONT. Of a type easily recognizable as belonging to the 1660s. – SCREEN. Original, heavy, with plain, one-light divisions. – STALLS. Partly of the C15 (especially the carved ends), partly of the time of Archbishop Laud. – ALTAR RAILS. Early C17. – WEST GALLERY. Not *in situ*. Of the time of Archbishop Laud. Simple geometrical ornament. – STAINED GLASS. E window by *Clayton & Bell*.

TRINITY SCHOOL OF JOHN WHITGIFT. Now at Shirley (*see* p. 458). The old buildings, demolished in 1965, were on the site of the Whitgift Centre in North End: 1869–71 by *Sir Arthur Blomfield*. Red brick and stone dressings. Symmetrical one-storeyed composition in the Tudor style with a central tower.

WHITGIFT SCHOOL, Nottingham Road, Haling Park. 1931 by *Leathart & Granger*. Light red brick, neo-Tudor. (New MUSIC SCHOOL, 1966–7, with a hall to seat 300.)

RUSSELL HILL SCHOOLS of the Warehousemen, Clerks, and Drapers.* 1864 by *John G. Bland*. Red brick, a long, symmetrical composition, with steep roofs, gables, and dormers. Gothic with plate tracery. Raised centre with a spike. Many additions.

TECHNICAL COLLEGE AND COLLEGE OF ART, Park Lane. By *Robert Atkinson & Partners* (*A.F.B. Anderson*), 1953–9. The largest Technical College in the S of England when it was built. Brick and Portland stone over steel framing. Large, and depressingly conventional at a time when so many technical colleges went up which were fresh, light, and up-to-date. Symmetrical façade to Park Lane. Extensions 1969–71.

FREEMASONS ASYLUM, Freemasons Road. A cheerful symmetrical composition by *Dawkes*, 1852. Red brick and much

* Administratively at Purley.

stone trim. The centre is a big Dutch gable, the ends have two smaller such gables each. In between three gabled porches and three small straight gables on each side.

SALVATION ARMY CITADEL, Ellis David Road. In a glaring red brick, with central pediment and castellated cornice.

POST OFFICE, Cherry Orchard Road. Large and modern in style. By *E. T. Sargent* of the *Ministry of Public Building and Works*, 1962–7.

FIRE STATION, Old Town. 1960–1. By *Riches & Blythin*. Partly three-, partly four-storeyed, an attractive composition.

WADDON MARSH POWER STATION, Beddington Farm Lane. By *Robert Atkinson*, 1950 etc. Large, red, and imposing, though decidedly heavy in the details. The type is that created by Sir Giles G. Scott at Battersea, but it has been handled by others with more crispness and elegance than it is here.

S of the Power Station, in COMMERCE WAY, a factory for Messrs PHILLIPS. Designed by *Wallis, Gilbert & Partners* and built in 1955–7.

WATERWORKS, Surrey Street. The polygonal chimney at the back of the bargeboarded building with the date 1851 is part of the engine house of the atmospheric railway which went from Forest Hill Station to West Croydon and operated from 1845 to 1847. The distance was five miles and the trains reached a speed of nearly 45 m.p.h.* The castellated tower-like building did not belong to the atmospheric railway. Additions and alterations in 1865 and 1912.

WATER TOWER, Park Hill Recreation Ground. Brick, in the Norman style, 100 ft high and very prominent.

SWIMMING POOL, Purley Way. Good concrete Diving Board by *C. E. Boast*, the Borough Engineer, 1935.

WADDON CAVES, Alton Road. A long, flat-bottomed, V-shaped trench, *c.* 8–16 ft deep, led down to the stream now in the municipal park. Off this were a number of underground HOUSES with doors and rough-worked lintels cut in the chalk. Excavation in 1902 produced a scatter of Neolithic material, but a larger amount of Iron Age and particularly Belgic pottery. Occupation continued to the C3–4 A.D. This odd group of structures recalls the native *fogous* of the South-West.

---

* The Surrey Iron Railway from Wandsworth to Croydon has nothing to do with this. It worked from 1803 to 1846 and was dismantled in 1848. I owe all this information to Mr T. E. Callander, Chief Librarian, Croydon.

PERAMBULATIONS

Croydon, with over 250,000 inhabitants, is by far the largest
town in Surrey. Until a few years ago it was an independent
town, looking in its centre smaller than its size, i.e. smaller than,
say, Leicester or Portsmouth. Now Croydon is within the Greater
London Council, and its commercial centre has radically
changed, in site as well as appearance. The vast majority of the
buildings to be mentioned belong to the last ten years. The
Perambulation therefore falls into two parts, and The New
Croydon precedes The Old Croydon.

(A) The New Croydon

The impact of the new hits the arriving traveller at once, whether
coming in a car from the N by way of Wellesley Road or in a
train by way of East Croydon Station. What also hits him after
the first ten minutes is the lack of any major planning. Secure
a site and evidently you could build – four- or twelve-storeyed
– pretty well as you wished and could afford. The result looks
thrilling from a distance and from the air, rather like a chunk
of inner Johannesburg, but breaks up from near by into
separate buildings, very few of individual architectural merit.
Turn E from the station for a moment and you have the two
principal ones which cannot be denied individuality, though
they may well be denied architectural merit. The first is
LOWNDES HOUSE by *R. Seifert & Partners*, 1968–70, octagonal and twenty-three storeys high, i.e. the highest building in
Croydon so far. It has a curious rhythm of canted bays projecting in alternating positions. So in fact no floor plan is
strictly octagonal. They are square with splayed corners, the
splay of one always placed above the middle of a side of the
next lower. Behind is the building of GENERAL ACCIDENT,
FIRE AND LIFE INSURANCE, 1961–3 by *Biscoe & Stanton*,
eight-storeyed, oblong, with precast concrete elements, designed unfortunately so that the whole looks rather like folded
paper, canting forward and backward. Even the angles do this,
so that one feels like stretching the shape straight or squashing
it. The window mullions also cant inward and outward, contra-
dicting the plain oblong glazing. N of this, at the corner of
Cherry Orchard Road, is the large COMMERCIAL UNION
HOUSE, one of the best of New Croydon. By the *Austin-Smith/
Lord Partnership*, 1965–8. Partly twelve-storey and partly
nine-storey, it has a projecting frame clad in white mosaic, with

a crisp rhythm of paired uprights and strong horizontals. Recessed walling is in black mosaic, with black-painted window frames. An almost detached three-storey block forms a porte-cochère.

(To the E of the new centre is PARK HILL VILLAGE, a Church Commissioners' estate of mid-Victorian villas now being replaced by *Wates* housing. Much of it is pleasantly brick or tile-hung, in the Eric Lyons tradition: HILL RISE, Park Hill Rise, 1962–3 by *K. W. Bland*, Wates's chief architect, and HILLMERE, Brownlow Road, by *Bland* and *Austin Vernon & Partners* (opposite is ARCHBISHOP TENISON'S GRAMMAR SCHOOL, curtain-walled, by *George Lowe & Partners*). MARESFIELD and COTELANDS in Park Hill Road are groups of flats by *Austin Vernon & Partners*, 1968–70; opposite is TURNPIKE HILL, by *F. G. McManus & Partners*, 1966–8, three-storey terrace houses, austerely detailed in pale brown brick with slate-grey panels and grouped excellently round landscaped courtyards (the plum-coloured tower block is by *Bland*). Further S in Park Hill Road is ST BERNARDS, twenty-one houses in three terraces of 1968–70 by the Swiss architects *Atelier 5* (partner-in-charge *Anatole du Fresne*). It is a group with few equals in Britain: the architects have sensitively adapted the stepped terrace system of their Siedlung Halen at Bern (itself derived from Le Corbusier's 'Roq et Rob' project of 1949) to the gentler suburban slopes of Surrey, replacing rough concrete with brown stock brick and timber stained or painted white. Each house is approached through an enclosed garden (with an outdoor eating room under a pergola) at an upper level, the living room having a panorama to distant hills. The bedrooms open on to a second, lower garden. Car parking is underground. Less demanding terraces next door by *John Bridges* of Wates, 1969–71. NT). See p. 596

Turning w from East Croydon Station one looks down GEORGE STREET with two neutral jobs on the l.: ESSEX HOUSE, a slab on a podium, and SUFFOLK HOUSE, four-storeyed throughout. Both are by *Raglan Squire & Partners*, 1960–1, i.e. among the earliest of the New Croydon. Between the two sits snugly the rockfaced St Matthew's church, enjoying a considerably increased visual value by contrast with its neighbours. Opposite Essex House, at the corner of DINGWALL ROAD, the new AUSTRALIAN MUTUAL PROVIDENT SOCIETY, 1968–70 by *Fuller, Hall & Foulsham*. The broad fascia above the shops has concrete decoration not of the fashionable wild kind.

High slab above. In Dingwall Road on the E side WETTERN HOUSE, by *Ian Fraser & Associates*, 1962–3. Opposite lower building, also recent. Then at the S corner of Lansdowne Road CAROLYN HOUSE, 1961–3 by *D. Rowswell & Partners*, and at the opposite corner No. 17 LANSDOWNE ROAD, by *R. Seifert & Partners*, 1964–5, the ground floor open, with pairs of raking concrete posts. Opposite this, on the E side of Dingwall Road a MULTISTOREY CAR PARK. After that a few mid-C19 villas still survive. CHURCHILL HOUSE, at the corner of Sydenham Road, is one of the most attractive designs, with rounded corners and facing of vertically set black tiles. It is of 1965–7 by *D. Rowswell & Partners*.

Now through Bedford Park, which still has some Early Victorian houses, to WELLESLEY ROAD. This is becoming part of a fast-traffic system, with an underpass under George Street and a flyover above the High Street (*see* below) and then N again along Old Town and Church Street.

In Wellesley Road at the time of writing the northernmost recent building is RANDOLPH HOUSE, by *William J. Harvey*, 1963–9, with wild concrete reliefs l. and r. of the entrance. PEMBROKE HOUSE by *Vincent & Wynn*, 1963–7, is one of the best, a nearly square tower of nineteen floors, the top excrescences hidden by vertical concrete slabs. In BEDFORD PARK on the S side SUNLEY HOUSE, 1965–8 by *Fitzroy Robinson & Partners*, large and utilitarian, and at the corner of Wellesley Road, yet larger, of four wings in the four main directions, LUNA HOUSE by *Denis Crump & Partners*, 1967–70. On the other (S) side of SYDENHAM ROAD this job continues as APOLLO HOUSE. The entrance motifs N and S of Sydenham Road are identical. In Sydenham Road itself CANTERBURY HOUSE by *T. P. Bennett & Sons*, 1963–5.

Back into Wellesley Road and on its W side the very large WHITGIFT CENTRE, 1965–70, covering eleven acres.* The planner was *Anthony Minoprio*, the architects *Fitzroy Robinson & Partners*. One high tower (ROTHSCHILD HOUSE), two tall slabs, and some lower offices flank a N–S pedestrian shopping precinct on two levels, made possible by the fall of the land. To the S an open square with the polygonal FORUM restaurant in the middle; to the N a very successful smaller square, roofed over by a light glass canopy open at the sides. Most of the

* The buildings are on the site of the Trinity School of John Whitgift (*see* p. 184 and p. 458).

architectural details are banal, but the centre functions unusually well as a shopping precinct. The upper level has direct
entrance from Wellesley Road, the lower direct entrance from
North End. Underneath is a service road for servicing the shops
and offices. Access to the offices is by a special service road from
Wellesley Road. Further N in London Road, the continuation
of North End, is ZODIAC HOUSE, a very large development
with shops, offices, and flats, by *William H. Robbins*, 1964–7.
In LANSDOWNE ROAD opposite the Whitgift Centre first the
Y.M.C.A. by *E. F. Starling*, then on the S side at the corner
of the tucked-away Walpole Road, the ROYAL AUTOMOBILE
CLUB offices, 1960–1 by *R. Seifert & Partners*. Opposite, on
the N side, RONEO VICKERS and SPILLERS, a complex by
Newman, Levinson & Partners, 1962–4, and then on to the
corner buildings of Dingwall Road – *see* above.

S of Lansdowne Road along the E side of Wellesley Road the
PRUDENTIAL by *E. Roy Moore Associates* (*Sydney Clough,
Son & Partners*, consultants), 1962–3, and BLACK-CLAWSON
HOUSE by *Newman, Levinson & Partners*, also 1962–3. Then
NORFOLK HOUSE by *Howell & Brooks* (*T. P. Bennett & Son*,
consultants), 1958–9, the start of the New Croydon, a tall slab at
r. angles to the street set on the usual podium. The S front of this
is in George Street and faces Suffolk House (*see* above).
Behind Norfolk House to the N, i.e. in WALPOLE ROAD, is
SOUTHERN HOUSE, by *G. & D. Crump*, 1963–7.

S of George Street Wellesley Road becomes PARK LANE. On the
W side a vast development, ST GEORGE'S HOUSE with
KATHARINE HOUSE towards the town hall, St George's Walk
inside, and the W front to the High Street. It has a shopping
precinct, but what an opportunity for a consistently planned
whole is wasted. So close to the centre this could have made a
determining architectural contribution. As it is, it doesn't. It
is all by *Ronald Ward & Partners*, 1962–4.

(B) *The Old Croydon*

St George's House lies, as has just been said, N of the Town Hall.
It also lies S of the corner of George Street. At that corner, i.e.
really the corner of George Street and NORTH END, is
WHITGIFT'S HOSPITAL, founded by Archbishop Whitgift
and built in 1596–9. Red brick, symmetrical street front with
three gables, the middle one taller and wider. Small two-light
windows with hood-moulds. Flat doorway with flat open pedi-

ment. The quadrangle inside with the two-storeyed dwellings.
The CHAPEL is in the SE corner and has a pretty Perp E window. The style is altogether as conservative as e.g. contemporary collegiate work in the universities (Second Court, St
John's College, Cambridge).* (Further up North End, next to
the entrance to the Whitgift Centre (*see* above), a remarkable
building of 1910, now HORNE'S, in a style similar to early
Charles Holden. Sheer brick tower-like masses at the corners
relieved by chunks of Art Nouveau foliage. An identical Art
Nouveau tower was built in 1926 on the other side of the then
Trinity School entrance as an adjunct to BURTON'S. NT)

S along the HIGH STREET the impact of the New Croydon still
continues. DAVIS HOUSE by *G. & D. Crump*, 1960–1, then
the BRIDGE which is part of the FLYOVER and cuts the High
Street in two. Just past that visual obstacle WRENCOTE, the
finest house in Croydon, totally deprived of any visual impact
by its present surroundings, dwarfed and buffeted. It dates
from the earliest years of the C18 and is of red and rubbed
brick with wings and a recessed tripartite centre, a later C17
rather than C18 type. Angle pilasters, an extremely richly
carved frieze, and a hipped roof. Modest doorway with
brackets carved as beasts' heads. Staircase with twisted balusters. The adjoining Nos. 119–121 has a very similar doorway
with brackets of human heads. The immediate neighbour of
Wrencote to the S is GROSVENOR HOUSE, 1960–1 by *H.
Hubbard Ford*, eleven-storeyed. S of this one of the best recent
arrivals, LEON HOUSE, 1968–9 by *Tribich, Liefer & Starkin*.
This consists of a slab of two staggered parts and a low, well-
set shopping plaza to its N. S of Leon House is LENNIG
HOUSE, by the same architects, only ten storeys high, the sill
bands of the windows of reeded concrete.

Off the High Street to the E up Coombe Road, where on the l.
very soon COOMBE HILL HOUSE (now Ruskin House), again
early C18 and very satisfying to look at. Yellow and red brick.
Five bays and two and a half storeys. Giant angle pilasters and
parapet. Segment-headed windows. Pedimented doorway on
Tuscan columns. Staircase with three slender balusters to each
step: two twisted differently, the third columnar. Carved
tread-ends. (A good wrought iron GATE in the garden. MHLG)

In SOUTH END, the continuation of High Street, Nos. 17–19 are

---

* The building was restored by *Butterfield* in 1860. He added the flint
plinths, porches, and spirelet, and rebuilt the chimneys (D. Lloyd).

c18. Near by, EBBUTT's furniture depository, built as a steam boot factory in the 1860s (at that time the biggest industrial premises in the town).* Three storeys, with a convex castellated centrepiece, and one curved corner, with finely detailed neo-Romanesque brick arcading and heavy cornices. Further s, cleverly angled on a corner site, the SWAN AND SUGAR LOAF, with pretty stucco decoration, dated 1896. s again, in BRIGHTON ROAD, ADVERTISER HOUSE, the former water company premises, altered by *Haines, Macintosh & Kennedy* for the Croydon Advertiser. Long, neat two-storey range, with curtain walling above the older brick wall. Opposite, on an island site, VOLKSWAGEN offices, an oval building of five storeys on stilts, with two central staircases, one cased in, one in an open well. It is by *Raglan Squire & Partners*, 1964–7. Back to the High Street. On the w side the former buildings of the Croydon Advertiser (now a pub), 1894–5, quite a good Jacobean front with four storeys of pilasters and a polychrome treatment of purple and buff terracotta. Beside it an arcade leading to a steep drop, the best townscape effect in Croydon, then to Surrey Street.‡ A little further away FLATS in DUPPAS HILL TERRACE, on rising ground, a three-ray plan, the ray to the E of ten storeys. By *Riches & Blythin*, completed in 1954. Further w, in PURLEY WAY, Waddon, WAYLANDS TRAINING CENTRE, by *H. Thornley* of the Borough of Croydon Architect's Department, 1964–6. (Nos. 335–345 Purley Way are a Regency pair, with pedimented side annexes, ruined by shops in front.)

CUDDINGTON see WORCESTER PARK

DEEPDENE
1040

½ m. E of Dorking

c18 England abounded in amateur architects, but nearly all of them were noblemen, and perhaps especially the younger sons of noblemen, like Horace Walpole. *Thomas Hope* was an exception, or the harbinger of the c19 millionaire collector. Born in Amsterdam in 1769, the son of a rich merchant of Scottish extraction, he collected on the grand scale for both his town house and Deepdene, his country seat. His collections

* Information from Mr R. C. W. Cox.
‡ The Arcade is by *Alfred Broad*, 1893–7 (R. C. W. Cox).

have been dispersed; some of the furniture he designed is now in the Victoria and Albert Museum and in the Royal Pavilion at Brighton. He was a propagandist for the Greek Revival in its most severe form, in the spirit of the French late c18 neo-classicists who were trying to interpret the grammar underlying Greek design. It was he who got Wyatt's designs for Downing College Cambridge replaced by Wilkins's more correct Grecian. His work at Deepdene, however, shows that he was by no means exclusively interested in the Greek style.

Deepdene was originally an estate belonging to the Howard family. The grounds were already famous in the c17. Mr Charles Howard's 'Amphitheater garden' – a long valley, terraced and planted, with grottoes and a subterranean passage – was visited by Evelyn and Aubrey. The house was built by the tenth Duke of Norfolk between 1777 and 1786. It was Late Palladian in style, with a w front of thirteen bays and two and a half storeys, a big three-bay canted centre, and elaborate ramped stairs, something like a late Robert Taylor house. It survived, stuccoed over, with the detail vamped up, and the end bays heightened, as the centre of the w front until the demolition of the house in 1969. Fortunately, before this happened, the complicated story of Hope's alterations to the house was studied in detail by Dr Watkin.*

Hope acquired the house in 1807. He made his own designs for the alterations, with *William Atkinson* as executive architect. By 1818–19 the old house had been redecorated, two side wings added, one with a tall tower, and there was a new entrance wing extending at r. angles from the E side, with a semicircular porch flanked by obelisks. This wing was linked to the old house by a hemicycle of pilasters carrying a balustrade decorated with antique masks. To the E was a separate block with kitchen and dairy. The asymmetrical effect was carried still further by the addition in 1823 of a long s wing extending diagonally from the house, containing orangeries, conservatories, and sculpture galleries, in an eclectic mixture of styles: the sw corner of the main house was given Gothic details, the roof of the conservatory was decorated with pediments and acroteria, while one of the sculpture galleries, which was in the form of a covered amphitheatre, had a façade with triangular-headed openings. The key to Hope's approach, as

* D. Watkin, *Thomas Hope and the Neo-Classical Idea* (1968). Most of the following paragraphs are based on the detailed account of Deepdene in this book.

has been pointed out by Dr Watkin, can be found in the sub-title of John Britton's unpublished History of Deepdene: 'The Union of the Picturesque in Scenery and Architecture with Domestic Beauties.' Hope's originality lay in the creation of deliberately picturesque effects through the free grouping of details in different styles, but especially classical and Italianate details. Italianate features also appeared in the grounds, thereby creating the picturesque unity between house and setting which Hope advocated in his essay of 1808: *On the Art of Gardening*. In their use of classical detail, Hope and Atkinson, oddly enough, reached just the same conclusion that Percier & Fontaine did in France at the same time – that using the obvious trappings of Greek architecture only where they were functionally necessary was a liberation, not a restriction. Plain walls could then have astylar treatment which was freed from all classical discipline.

The later alterations to the house developed the Italianate interest at the expense of the picturesque. Surviving drawings, probably dating from before Hope's death in 1831, show various schemes for a new entrance front with a grand staircase hall in an Italianate style. The new E side eventually built by Thomas Hope's son Henry in the 1840s consisted of an eleven-bay front with the whole of the first floor arcaded, the centre five bays two-storeyed (with higher work behind, including two small square open towers or loggias), the end three bays each of three storeys with a big balcony. The detail was good, the material ashlar. At the same time the W front was refaced, the end bays of the original house heightened, and a central dome was projected, but not built. Thomas Hope's conservatory wing was later replaced by a more regular one, but the main part of the house survived in mutilated condition, until the demolition. The inside in its final state was tragic – fragments of Hope detail lost in a warren of partitions and corridors. Most of the rooms on the W side contained fragments of ceilings and wall decorations, some of which may have dated from the later building period. Thomas Hope's small dining room, or boudoir, with its green marble chimneypiece, survived almost complete. In addition, Henry Hope's large two-storeyed hall remained, though without its statues. This, following Thomas Hope's and Atkinson's suggestions, had an arcaded ground floor and a first floor with a gallery behind Corinthian columns. There was a spacious square lantern with columns. A two-arm staircase with heavy Grecian cast-iron

7—S.

details started, but did not continue, monumentally. Running off the hall was a big vestibule with impressive astylar doorcases with continuous mouldings. This may be a case where the French copied Soane at the Bank of England and were themselves recopied: honeysuckle motifs were painted everywhere. Adjoining the vestibule was Thomas Hope's staircase, with bronze banisters in the shape of palmettes. The landing was originally supported by a stucco caryatid. The effect of all this decoration was rich, unemotional but impressive. It could still have made an impressive house with sumptuous decoration in the modern style, by someone like Sir Hugh Casson, making the most of all these fragments. This was not to be. The house was sold by its owners, British Rail, to a development company, who demolished it in 1969. A large office block by *Scherrer & Hicks* is to be built on the site. It is a disgraceful and depressing story.

DIPPENHALL see FARNHAM

DOCKENFIELD
4 m. s of Farnham

8040

No centre, all the houses small, the appearance of a squatting settlement next to Alice Holt forest on the Hampshire border.

GOOD SHEPHERD. Small chapel by *W. Curtis Green*, 1910, very domestic and carefully textured. Bargate stone, galletted, with brick dressings. Blank E end, simple interior – clearly another architect who was happier in the Voysey tradition than in the neo-Baroque to which he usually turned later.

THE OLD HOUSE, ½ m. E. A late C17 brick refacing of an earlier E-shaped house with walled garden to the E and converted oasts at the end of it, all carefully restored so that the effect is that of a good Lutyens house. Restoration 1924 by *Palmer-Jones*.

(GREAT HOLT, I m. S (now St Teresa's Convent). Farmhouse of 1749 with a large half-timbered house of 1904 tacked on, by *Chuter*, Shaw's builder at Pierrepont, and for the same family. The bedroom fireplaces may be by *Lutyens*, whose designs of 1904 were otherwise abortive. NT)

DORKING

1040

Absurdly little architecture for a Home Counties town which has never been industrialized, and old prints show that it never has

had a lot – part of the same paradox that has made Reigate and
Leatherhead into some of the dullest towns near London. However, Dorking High Street is worth a special look. Although it
has no notable buildings, it is a beautiful shape as townscape,
serpentine and irregular – but not formless – with the s side
higher than the N. The network of residential streets and footpaths to N and S of it has unexpectedly happy scale, particularly N
of the church and in Cotmandene to the SE and Rose Hill to the
SW. Thanks to Woodyer, Dorking is the only Surrey town to be
dominated by its church.

ST MARTIN. Entirely of 1868–77 by *Woodyer*, and his most
important church (s chancel chapel 1912). Most Woodyer
churches have weak overall design and intriguing detail; this
one has splendid proportions and oddly underplayed detail,
very like late Butterfield (Woodyer was a Butterfield pupil).
Clerestory, lean-to aisles, tall W tower and spire, dominating 72
the whole town. Close to, just as in some Butterfield churches,
the mock-Dec detail nags and grinds, working out what may
well have been a C19 psychological problem, because a lot of
Woodyer's work is neurotic. Here, some of it, like the thistly
clock faces on the tower and the triplets of clerestory windows,
achieves a perverse nobility of its own. The inside is just as
well proportioned, a rare thing, and although the details are
thin the result is not simply a bit of fake-medieval space without the conviction of detail to back it up; as in Pugin's churches
the whole space is thin and fervent. Very acutely pointed
arches and complex arch sections, and a multi-shafted chancel
arch, hence a net of upward-reaching verticals. That the means
to this purely C19 effect are not at all C19 is undeniable but
relatively unimportant. The fittings nearly all High Victorian.
They are poor, but all help the rich, soothing effect. – ⟨PULPIT.
Said to have been brought from Holland *c.*1837 for the former
church. It incorporates a panel with St Martin and the beggar,
probably C17, and figures of apostles and busts of angels,
which appear to be late Gothic.⟩ – STAINED GLASS by almost
everyone, including *Powell* (s transept) and *Hudson* (E window).
– MOSAIC of Crucifixion over the chancel arch by *Powell*,
*c.*1890. – ALTAR FITTINGS. Very dignified, two huge candle-
sticks and formerly a corona of seven suspended oil lamps (now
only one is left). – MONUMENTS. Miscellaneous tablets from
the old church, skied and almost invisible in the tower. They
include one good Rococo design.

(ST JOSEPH (R.C.), Falkland Grove 1895 by *F. A. Walters*. DE)

(ST MARTIN, Pixham. An attractive village church by *Lutyens*, 1903. Exterior with echoes of Philip Webb (the twin gables on the N side) and H. H. Richardson (massive round-headed entrance door with a radiating pattern in tiles). The interior was dual-purpose, with a curtain to screen off the sanctuary when the nave was in use as a clubroom. Totally different treatment of the two parts: the nave has a big plain tunnel-vault in white plaster looking almost like concrete; the sanctuary, in Lutyens's sweeter version of Bentley's Westminster Cathedral style, has a beautifully proportioned dome on a square base, patterned with chalk, tiles, and sandstone. NT)

(ST PAUL. By *Ferrey*, 1857, N aisle 1860, S aisle 1869. R. Hubbuck)

CONGREGATIONAL CHURCH, West Street. Quite a handsome Italianate front dated 1834. Brick with stone dressings, stylistically ahead of its time; it looks mid-C19.

FIRE STATION, West Street. Built as the Public Hall. 1871 by *C. K. Driver* and *C. H. Pew*. Big bad Italianate.

COUNCIL OFFICES, London Road. Built as PIPPBROOK by *Sir George Gilbert Scott*, 1856. Very ugly: the ugliness of carelessness and insensitivity, not of protest. Harsh Gothic with a big Geometrical billiard room at the back.

COUNTY HOSPITAL, South Terrace. Built as the WORKHOUSE by *William Shearburn* in 1841. The main building faces W above Horsham Road. It is faintly unusual in that it is humane Grecian rather than utilitarian. Pedimented centre and wings.

⟨So far Dorking has surprisingly few notable recent buildings. Good new TELEPHONE EXCHANGE at the corner of London Road and Reigate Road by *K. W. Judd* of the *Ministry of Public Building and Works*, 1966. Nicely detailed, the upper walls with dark spandrel panels and tiles with a raised pattern. There are also some pleasant new schools: POWELL CORDEROY COUNTY PRIMARY SCHOOL (by *E. Tory & Associates* and the County Architect *R. J. Ash*, 1967–8) and additions to the BOYS' SECONDARY SCHOOL (by *Howard V. Lobb & Partners* and *R. J. Ash*, 1967–9) both in Longfield Road, and prominent to the S of the A25, and ST MARTIN'S CHURCH OF ENGLAND SCHOOL (by *R. J. Ash*, 1968–9), an attractive small primary school tucked away N of the station. But a comparison with the first edition of this book will show how many worthwhile older buildings have disappeared lately; the projected widening of North Street will not improve matters.⟩

HIGH STREET runs from E to W and has very little in it. Starting at the E end, Nos. 150–6 (s side), houses of *c.*1840 with nice iron balconies, then the WHITE HORSE HOTEL, with a long irregular frontage looking mostly C18 and early C19, but with earlier timber-framed parts behind. Then, towards the E end, Nos. 44–46, an early C19 shop-front, now a wine-merchant's. It was formerly the 'Medical Hall', a chemist's shop. Finally Nos. 20–22, now ROBERT DYAS, has a sweeping C18 double-bowed shop-front, as ostentatious as any present-day Oxford Street gimmick. The fascia is one continuous curve, convex–concave–convex. Above it a pilastered upper storey in local brick, C17 Artisan. More of this work round the corner in CHEQUERS YARD, where the lower windows, unblocked when the building was gutted and renovated in 1968–9, have brick mullions and transoms. Plain brick pilasters between the windows on both storeys. During the alterations considerable remains of WALL PAINTINGS were found, Jacobean in style, and apparently contemporary with the internal timber-framed walls of the building (suggesting that the exterior brickwork may have been a later casing to an earlier house). Fragments are exhibited in the shop; the most elaborate has panels of stylized flowers and foliage divided by guilloche borders. There is also part of a royal coat of arms.

From the W end of the High Street streets radiate N, S, and W. NORTH STREET is short. No. 3 (formerly the KING'S HEAD INN) has an interesting pilastered front of similar Artisan character to Nos. 20–22 High Street.* Seven bays (truncated at the S end) with the last-but-one bay at either end narrower than the others. Mullion-and-transom windows. The date is perhaps *c.*1635–50. The other side of the building, much altered, visible from a yard N of the High Street, has two dormer windows with brick mullions, and one surviving Ionic pilaster. (The details of this differ slightly from those on the front of No. 20 High Street.) Adjoining at the N end is an older, lower, timber-framed building. On the other side of North Street, Nos. 1–2, a good jettied house with moulded beam. The house next to it has at the back an upper window supported by carved brackets, perhaps C16. At the end of the street, the honest Victorian CORN STORE of J. W. Attlee is of *c.*1860, polychrome. Beyond, S of CHURCH STREET, LESLIE HOUSE, a quite elaborate Gothic house of stone, dated 1838, similar to some of those on Rose Hill. WEST STREET starts with one

---

* Threatened with demolition for road-widening.

more Artisan fragment in Nos. 58–61, which keeps a thick den-tilled brick cornice of *c.*1660 (like the houses at Godalming, *see* p. 258), then WEST STREET HOUSE, mid-C18 with two big two-storey bows – the whole building weatherboarded and nautical-looking and unexpected, in the small-scale street. Further w, at the corner of Vincents Lane, is THE VICARAGE, a much altered house which seems to have been half-H-shaped Tudor originally, with a pair of tall gables and stacks towering above the street at the end of each wing.

SOUTH STREET is almost a blank. At the top of the hill, P.D.S.A. HOUSE, by *David Landaw & Partners,* 1966, has re-placed BELGRAVE, 1907 by *Draper & Walters,* which had a strange, narrow front in free Classical, with a convex bow window recessed into the front. Off South Street is ROSE HILL, starting via a convincing mock-Tudor arch beside an indifferent pair of big late C18 houses (ROSE HILL HOUSE and BUTTER HILL HOUSE). Beyond is an unusual and attractive estate of 1840–60, with Italian and Tudor villas arranged around an irregular central space on a steep hill, exactly in the Picturesque manner of Nash's Blaise Hamlet. Naturally enough, the houses have less charm than Nash's *cottages ornés,* but the landscaping is still big-scale and admirable. S of this is another romantic mid-century estate, around Tower Hill. The earliest house, TOWER HILL COT-TAGE, is built around what looks like a small folly tower in flint and brick dated 1828. Here also GOODWYNS PLACE, a big house of *c.*1900 by *H. Thackeray Turner,* in free Tudor without any of the individuality of his buildings at Guildford. ⟨s of this at North Holmwood, GOODWYNS, an unusually good estate by *William Ryder & Associates* for the Dorking U.D.C. Nicely sited on a slope, with plenty of open space. The earlier parts at the bottom with red brick houses in closes, then three- and four-storey flats climbing up the hill, and two tall blocks (1965), more elegant than average because of the way each side projects and recedes. The terrace housing in Rough Rew to the s, though by the same firm, is disagreeably gim-micky by comparison.⟩ To the E COTMANDENE has some pleasant cottages and a very nice scale, and w of the Horsham Road HOWARD ROAD etc. forms another *c.*1840 development, possibly laid out by *Shearburn,* with a good stuccoed pub, the ARUNDEL ARMS.

NE of the town, at Pixham, is the FRIENDS PROVIDENT AND CENTURY ASSURANCE, 1957 by *Easton & Robertson.* Terribly harsh semi-modern. Mostly two-storeyed, mostly pitched-roof. Gable ends in copper.

MILE HOUSE, I m. SW, on the Coldharbour road. An endearing though very minor example of the local C17 rustic classicism. Tiny two-gabled front, stone-built with brick dressings, the first floor with shouldered heads to the windows, and the second-floor windows with very thin brick scrolled volutes on either side. Only a circumstantial cottage, probably of *c.*1670.

For Deepdene, E of the by-pass, *see* p. 191. For Milton and West-cott, w of Dorking on the A25, *see* p. 368 and p. 510.

DORMANSLAND

I m. SE of Lingfield

An odd, one-class community like some of the hamlets in NW Surrey, all tiny cottages, the oldest C17 and C18, but the majority Victorian. There was presumably a good reason for this; was it originally squatting on common land?

ST JOHN. 1883 by *Sir Arthur Blomfield*. Bad.

BAPTIST CHAPEL. 1817, completely plain gabled two-storey brick box, still keeping to the C17 habit of a string course between the storeys.

The cottages are all minor, and the most noteworthy are in fact C20: the FORD ESTATE COTTAGES in Hollow Lane, by *F. C. Eden*, 1920. This is a sober roughcast stepped terrace, the type of housing that the Voysey style should have led to. The spirit – of a simple job simply and comfortably done – is something that we are slowly working back to.

The other buildings are scattered about. LULLENDEN, 1½ m. SE, near Old Surrey Hall (*see* p. 396) and the Sussex border, has a C15 hall range, very much restored. MOOR HAWES, I m. due S on the East Grinstead road, is a picturesque and unspoilt C17 Weald cottage with two typical features – one end-gable slightly hipped, and a tile-hung lean-to addition at the other. Finally, just S of the village is THE BEACON, *c.*1825, an odd, small Grecian house with idiosyncratic detail – a Soanic attitude but not Soane's style. Three-by-two-bay centre with central cupola behind, very wide pilasters with key ornament incised on them, and rough Corinthian capitals. Together with the opened window shutters, they make a complete all-over pattern of the façade; a bloody-minded way of overcoming Grecian plain-ness.

(MOOR FARM, Moor Lane. Good Wealden farm of *c*.1600. Arthur Oswald)

DORMANS PARK. Laid out after 1884, when the railway came (came incidentally with good workmanlike station fittings: wood and iron platforms in a cutting with long covered ways down from the road, roofed with corrugated iron. The station building itself is dull polychrome brick). It was first called Bellagio and then rather ironically became Dormans Park. Pleasant examples of late C19 housing, the best houses by *R. A. Briggs*, all set in a typical true Surrey suburb – gravel roads, trees everywhere, houses hardly visible.

DRY HILL CAMP. On the highest point of the Hastings Beds is an Iron Age FORT of some 24 acres. To the SE and N there is now only a single line of defences, but on the E and SW is a triple bank with double ditch. The entrance on the N may be original. Sandstone blocks were used to support the ramparts.

DOVER'S GREEN *see* REIGATE

DOWNSIDE *see* COBHAM

1050   DUNLEY HILL
2 m. W of Ranmore Common

Small, comfortable-looking house in the Norman Shaw style by *George & Peto*, 1887. Two gables to the front (s) and a small tower behind. Pretty, but done without conviction.

0030   DUNSFOLD

An attractive, genuine village in the Weald, well S of Godalming, mostly built along the W side of an enormous long common. This is narrow at the N end and widens out into something of the size and wildness of a heath at the S, with scattered houses round the edge completely lost in the scrub. Mostly brick and tile-hanging. More a Sussex than a Surrey village, not least in its lack of gentility; the continuous houses at the NW corner and the rough grass in front make attractive partners. Before the war it was the most remote village in Surrey: now, well hidden, an airfield tests jet fighters.

20 ST MARY AND ALL SAINTS. A complete village church of *c*.1270, quite a rarity in any county. The advowson was then held by the Crown, and all the visual evidence points to its

having been built by royal masons, so that it is possibly a complete example of what the generation after Westminster Abbey thought suitable for a small and fairly remote village church. The answer is as functional and commonsense as that of any present-day architect designing for the Liturgical Movement. Everything is provided for and worked into the fabric, and there is no surplus ornament or display – an architect's building. The C19 alterations and renewals had better be mentioned first: chancel arch heightened and widened and now without capitals, new NE vestry, and the E window raised and its tracery renewed. The W window is three-light, intersected, cusped, of c.1300–20, the shingled bell-turret is C15 by the looks of the big four-post cage supporting it. The rest is original. Aisleless nave, N and S transepts, aisleless chancel. The S transept has a free-standing NW pier and the beginnings of an arch to the W, which shows clearly that the builders intended a S aisle, but this never seems to have been continued. The windows, all Late Geometrical, are of a stage later than Westminster Abbey. Bar tracery; the circle in the tracery is not foiled but encloses a pointed trefoil, carefully moulded. Deep splays inside, hence an elaborately broken-up wall surface. The quality of the design shows particularly in the arrangement of a door and windows of different heights on the S side of the chancel, and the more complicated arrangements needed to accommodate piscina and sedilia. The doorways have delicate jamb-shafts, circular abaci, and careful multiple mouldings; the transept arches have octagonal responds and capitals and seem rougher than the rest of the work. Are they possibly later? (*see* e.g. the inconsistencies in the string course in nave and transept where it meets the columns). PISCINA and SEDILIA have simple circular shafts and capitals and trefoil heads under thick mouldings, as direct as a piece of engineering. – PEWS. C13 too, [18] quite a rarity, and in their elegant simplicity as much above the over-complicated detail of C15 woodwork as other C13 church furnishings often are. The bench ends plain, carried up into two knobs with a deep down-pointing cusp between. – ROYAL ARMS of George IV, 1828. In good condition.

Of the farms and cottages, the RECTORY, E of the church, has a C15 timber frame under its tile-hanging; FIELD PLACE to the NW is a good example of the big isolated Weald farm, tile-hung with tarred weatherboarded barns; HOOKHOUSE FARM to the N is as good an example of a smaller farm in the same style. S of the village green BURNINGFOLD FARM is yet one more example of this style of big yeoman buildings. Two gabled tile-hung wings and a quite ornate timbered centre, a diagonal pattern above and close-set posts below. C15 and C16 with contemporary features inside.* (BOWBRICKS on the w side of the green, a villa of *c.*1840, was the home of *Thomas Underwood*, the builder of Lutyens's Munstead Wood and Orchards. The inglenook in the living room, of 1902, shows Underwood's own creative ability in Lutyens style. NT)

9040

EASHING
1 m. w of Godalming

A small, pretty hamlet with a short street running down from the Guildford by-pass to the medieval BRIDGE, one of the Wey Valley series (cf. Tilford and Elstead), picturesque and not yet duplicated. Segmental rubble arches and cutwaters pointed upstream and rounded downstream, as at Tilford. E of the bridge THE MEADS, one half C16 timber-framing and an original Tudor doorcase, the other half now C18 brick and stone, galletted (i.e. with small dark chips of stone set in the mortar).

Beyond this a utilitarian modern two-storey MILL, an unexpectedly ruthless contrast for Surrey, and then, uphill, STYLES COTTAGES, a good unrestored example of C16 timber-framed Surrey building with completely random infilling of stone and brick and tile-hanging. Opposite a tiny derelict CHAPEL built like an ornamental Victorian potting shed, i.e. with fancy rustic patterns. It was probably done from Peper Harow, as there is similar work there.

EASHING HOUSE. Mostly demolished in 1957. It was a heavy pedimented and stuccoed house built in 1729–36. The STABLES, of the same date, remain, dour and pedimented, with stock-brick dressings and Bargate stone accurately cut to resemble brick (cf. Peper Harow). The former BREWHOUSE also remains, now a cottage. Restored close-timbered C16 work, quite impressive.

0050

EAST CLANDON

On the suburban chain between Guildford and Leatherhead, but far better than the neighbouring villages. Unaffected agricul-

* Much enlarged in 1922 by *H. Chalton Bradshaw*, with a *Jekyll* garden (NT).

tural group, no plan, simply one zigzag road winding between
brick and half-timber cottages with the small church as one extra
incident. The effect is almost entirely due to the little things
which keep continuity between one house and the next – hedges,
walls, footpaths. Modern suburbanization could easily be fitted
in on these terms – as has a simple COUNCIL ESTATE by *H. S.
Goodhart-Rendel*, 1949, with its informal grouping and gravel
road. None of the old cottages is worth special notice, but it is a *See
p.
596*
very pleasant village to walk through.

ST THOMAS. Small and genuine. Nave and chancel, modern
lean-to aisle, and bulky shingled bell-turret. The nave walls
are probably C12 but all the detail is Perp. The chancel is early
E.E., rough but in authentic condition as few Surrey medieval
buildings are. Simple single-chamfered chancel arch, wide
splayed lancets in the chancel, the E window having two and
not three (cf. Farleigh), an unusual detail possibly carried over
from Norman practice. Authentic late C13 doorway on the N
side, with shouldered lintel – a detail often re-used by the
Victorians. A single arch between nave and aisle of standard
mid-C13 Surrey type. The intention was however to continue
to the W – see the pier instead of a respond. Circular, with circular capital. Double-chamfered arch. The aisle itself and the
bell-tower are of 1900 and by *Sir T. G. Jackson*, a good match
for the rest of the building. Part of the framing for the bell-turret
is old – simply four big posts without cross bracing, the beams
above tied in to the top of the nave walls in addition. – FONT.
Plain C18, elegant bulgy shape. – COMMUNION RAIL. Simple
village-late-C17, the balusters like chair-legs. – PLATE. Cups
1569, 1661; Patens 1675, 1776. – MONUMENT. Stuart Lord
Rendel † 1913. Tomb-chest with incised cross under a neo-
Gothic surround, designed by *H. S. Goodhart-Rendel*. Above,
a pretty mock-Jacobean plaster ceiling, also by him.

EAST HORSLEY

A suburbanized village between Leatherhead and Guildford;
very little character and no village centre.

ST MARTIN. Tower originally Norman (cf. the window above
the W door) with inserted C13 detail and C18 roughcast top,
all very plain. The rest effectively all 1869, renewed by *Woodyer*
in the original C13 lancet style, except for the chancel arch,
which is well proportioned mid-C13, and the two westernmost

bays of the nave arcade, which are lumpish and probably C15
(octagonal piers, arches with hollow chamfer). Internal proportions surprisingly good. – BRASSES. Several, all small.
Robert de Brantingham, c.1400. Half effigy of a civilian, 13 in.
high. – John Bouthe, Bishop of Exeter, † 1478 (chancel floor).
An unusual design, a kneeling figure in profile carrying a
crozier, with shield and inscription. – John Snelling † 1498
and his wife and family, just rough hack work. – PLATE. Cup
and Paten 1634; Set 1649. – MONUMENTS. Thomas Corn-
wallis † 1626, Groom-Porter to Queen Elizabeth, and his wife,
plus two small kneeling figures of children. Recumbent
alabaster effigies on chest, achievement on the wall behind.
Standard work, though well done: competent stiff effigies
without any imaginative qualities at all. – James ffox † 1753.
Good Rococo cartouche.

EAST HORSLEY TOWERS. Towers indeed; the entry up the
main drive must be one of the most sensational in England,
utterly unexpected in the placid Surrey countryside. Neo-
Norman entrance lodge, then an arch and a long curved tunnel
leading straight to a horseshoe-shaped cloister in polychrome
brick, finally beyond through a horseshoe arch and beside a
big round tower to the main entrance. The original house is
plain Tudor by *Barry*, 1820–9, a sober, dull design in flint
with stock-brick dressings and the same complete lack of
enthusiasm that taints many of Barry's non-Classical buildings.
The gabled third storey is later.

The first Earl of Lovelace, Byron's son-in-law, succeeded
soon after and set about improving the property. His first
addition was the Perp-style tower at the W end, which is flint
and more sober than the rest. Inside, the hall is dated 1847,
and one truss has a later inscription to say that it was bent by
steam in 1847. Lovelace read a paper to the Royal Society
about it. But about 1855 – inevitably, after travels on the Continent – he branched into an extraordinary Gothic style of flint
and polychrome brick, apparently without an architect. He
built a tall Rhenish tower at the E end in 1858 with a steep
pointed roof, huge horseshoe cloisters at the back of the original
house in 1859 with the cloister work at first-floor level, and a
chapel next to it (also at first-floor level) in 1860. There are
polychrome brick vaulting-ribs everywhere: the ribs are built
up with iron rods on the ridge; under one of the entrance
arches they are most ingeniously used to vault a parallelogram.
The chapel is over-detailed, with spandrel paintings of fancy

vaulting and cherubs, still in the Horace Walpole tradition. The style is more or less Italian Gothic. Some of the details are fantastic – e.g. in the cloister he simply used drainpipes as shafts. The overall judgement on all this is rather a sad one, sad in that such an inventive engineering talent thought of architecture in the typical C19 way as something to be added on to structure, not to grow inevitably out of it.

What character the village has is the outcome of a piecemeal rebuilding of c.1860 in the same manner as the additions to the Towers. There is one particularly violent two-towered lodge at a bend in the A246. Literally dozens of cottages, lodges, village schools, pub, etc., all with slight variations on the same unmistakable style: usually flint with bands of brick quatre-foils, often with machicolations and polychrome round-headed windows. They extend on to the Downs to the S and into Ockham to the N; they first intrigue, and then exasperate because they are not particularly well done. Their span is given approximately by three cottages close together near the church: 1856, 1862, 1867. The C20 contribution to East Horsley is indicated by the imitation half-timbered BISHOPS-MEAD PARADE N of the church (1934, designed in the office of *Frank Chown*, estate agent), and much more hopefully by FRENCHLANDS HATCH, ½ m. further N, old people's homes for the Architects' Benevolent Society, begun in 1958 by *Clifford Culpin*, landscape architect *Brian Robson*. An L-shaped group of single-storey cottages, plus a community hall at one end with a low-pitched copper pyramid roof. Very humane and beautifully detailed, the decoration limited to a little tile-hanging. No attempt to be aggressively modern, and no need to be. See p. 596

EAST MOLESEY

1060

ST MARY. 1864–7 by *Talbot Bury*. Short tower with spire. Plate tracery. Cross-gabled aisles. The S aisle is of 1883 by *Charles Barry Jun.* (MONUMENTS and BRASSES from the old church.)

ST PAUL. 1854 by *Salter & Laforest* (GR). Tower of 1888. – STAINED GLASS. By *Kempe* the window in the baptistery (1891) and the N aisle window with the Crucifixion (1899).

BRIDGE, linking East Molesey and Hampton Court. By *W. P. Robinson* (engineer) and *Lutyens*, 1930–3. Three arches, inevitably in Hampton Court Wrenaissance style. Also by *Lutyens* the smaller bridge over the river Ember, 300 yds S.

HAMPTON COURT STATION. 1848–9. Red brick, Jacobean.

In BELL ROAD, just S of the church, is THE BELL, basically
C16, timber-framed and rendered, with a picturesque symmetrical front and gabled porch. On the r. side a cottage
attached to it, on the l. weatherboarded stables. (Also in Bell
Road, OLD MANOR HOUSE, and QUILLETS ROYAL, C17
with C18 additions, and GREEN ARDEN, two storeys, five
bays, early C18. In ST MARY'S ROAD, PARK HOUSE, C17,
much altered in the C19, but with part of the original staircase
and a carved wooden overmantel of the late C17. In MATHAM
ROAD, MATHAM MANOR, originally C14, much altered later.
Good staircase with twisted balusters. In WALTON ROAD,
RADNOR HOUSE, an early C18 house of three bays with steep
double-curved gables and Doric doorway, has been demolished
recently. Some C18 and C19 cottages survive. MHLG) Further
W, at the corner of SCHOOL ROAD, some odd stone-faced
shops of c.1870, Italian Gothic in style. In BRIDGE STREET,
which runs from Walton Street to the bridge, KINGFISHER
COURT, 1933 by *Guy Morgan*. Quite interesting as an early
essay in the modern style, i.e. early as England goes. Two
small blocks of flats, three-storeyed, with, on the roofs, sun-
roofs of concrete designed like station platforms.

1070

EAST SHEEN

CHRIST CHURCH, Christ Church Road. 1862–4 by *Sir Arthur
Blomfield*. Stone, SE tower with pyramid roof, which collapsed
the day after it was completed, and had to be rebuilt. Cross-
gabled S aisle. Plate tracery. The N aisle was added in 1887.

ALL SAINTS, East Sheen Avenue. 1929 by *Newberry & Fowler*
(R. C. Gill). Red brick, with lancet windows and a flèche.
(Rebuilt after destruction by fire, 1965.)

What is worth looking at is mainly along Christ Church Road.
See
p.
596 Of the pre-Victorian East Sheen the chief survival is PERCY
LODGE, mid-Georgian, of three bays, with Venetian windows
(wooden mullions). Big bow window to the garden. In the
principal living room a good mid-Georgian fireplace. Good
gatepiers and wrought-iron gates. To the r. of Percy Lodge
WEST LODGE, the former stables of Percy Lodge. Opposite
MERTON COTTAGE, brick, with a double gable and segment-
headed windows, early C18. A little further NW the early C19
iron GATES, perhaps brought from elsewhere, to the former
Sheen Wood. In the Late Victorian decades a number of big

houses were built at East Sheen by architects such as Collcutt, Aston Webb, and Ingress Bell. They have now nearly all been replaced by more modest C20 detached villas. (Survivors are OAKDENE, No. 105 Christ Church Road, by *T. E. Collcutt*, illustrated in 1884; and LONGFIELD, off Christ Church Road, by *Ingress Bell*, illustrated in 1879. In Fife Road is THE HAL-STEADS by *A. W. Blomfield*, 1868. It was one of the first houses in England to be built of concrete. The contractor was *Joseph Tall*, the inventor of standardized concrete shuttering.*)

EATON PARK see FAIRMILE

EFFINGHAM

1050

Between the Bookhams and the Horsleys, a battered village of small old cottages, suburbanized since 1930 and largely since 1950. Sadly little character now, least of all suburban character.

ST LAURENCE. Aesthetically almost valueless through restoration. Fragments remain: big barn-like S transept of *c.*1250 with kingpost roof and two modern S lancets replacing an original single lancet. This must have looked very severe, and is now the only part of the church with any character. Perhaps built by Merton Priory. Chancel E window early C14 and genuine,‡ though hardened; chancel NW window of the same date, chancel N and S windows two-light late C14 under segmental labels. The chancel was repaired in 1388 by order of William of Wykeham because the priory had neglected the church, and these windows are, in a very minor way, the style of Winchester nave. S arcade, nave windows, and very ugly W tower all by *W. J. Shearburn*, 1888. – PLATE. Cup 1569; Set 1828. – MONUMENT. Maria Parratt † 1844, high up under the tower. Reclining effigy and mourning figure. Good: crisply done without sentimentality. By *William Pistell*.

ROMAN CATHOLIC CHURCH. 1913 by *Edward Bonner*. Thin flint, E.E. style, with a small tower. It now looks more medieval than the parish church. – Rough Perp FONT from a church in Oxfordshire.

(Next to the R.C. church is the RED HOUSE (now Corpus Domini convent), designed by *Lutyens* in 1893 for Gertrude Jekyll's

* Information from Mr R. C. Gill.
‡ The VCH says modern; but it was there in 1823, cf. an old drawing in the church.

close friend Susan Muir-Mackenzie. One of his most important early houses, in which can be seen the origin of that Tudor
mode of his which eventually culminated in Castle Drogo.
Bargate stone with red brick dressings; the tympana of patterned tiles above the windows are specially characteristic. The
skyline was severely simplified in 1955, but the tower-like
wing to the r. of the entrance, with its recessed gable, survives
intact, as does the huge chimney which anchors the hipped-
roofed service rooms to the l. The red paint inside the house,
which gave it its name, has disappeared. Originally a *Jekyll*
garden. NT)

The old centre is a crossroads N of A246, badly broken into by
new housing. To the s is the HOME COUNTIES DAIRY, by
Cow & Gate Architectural Department, 1957 (*R. V. Chellis* in
charge). An interesting idea, simply one huge hangar-shaped
shed with all the office accommodation fitted in at one end
and expressed in a random way on the end elevation: partly
curtain walling, partly solid wall, with a fancy pattern of
windows, etc. It solves effectively the problem of the split
between domestic-looking offices in front and ramshackle
factory buildings behind. However, as done here, it is more
attractively mad than impressive. w from the crossroads is
Orestan Lane, a cul-de-sac, and a few yards down it OLD
WESTMOOR COTTAGE, with quite a spectacular brick frontispiece of *c*.1630, a shaped gable above two orders of pilasters.
Roughly done, the style approximately that of West Horsley
Place. Finally, s of A246 is EFFINGHAM HOUSE, now the
Golf Club, also stuccoed early C19, with a heavy three-bay
entrance colonnade and a plaster relief over.

EGHAM

A characterless village on the Thames opposite Staines, and very
like a smaller-scale Staines, keeping a winding main street without any worth-while buildings it it. The most attractive part is
the collection of riverside cottages around the Swan Hotel by
Staines Bridge.

ST JOHN THE BAPTIST. From the old church the porch, now
used as a LYCHGATE; wood, C15, good work (cf. e.g. the
simple and effective spandrels), equivalent to the stone porches
at Oxted and Merstham. Also, in the SE corner of the nave,
re-set inscription saying that the old chancel was rebuilt by
Abbot Rutherwyke of Chertsey in 1327.

The new church was built in 1817–20 by *Henry Rhodes*, an architect in the Board of Works. It is a very ugly building, showing the strange effect of following Soane's ideas on proportion and detail without Soane's spatial imagination. A squat box, with short chancel and pilastered nave with rounded corners, and a squat w tower above – belfry, then an oval stage, then a pyramidal cap, and then a tiny *tempietto* for good measure. Especially Soanic the detail at the E end and the recessed orders of stock brick; the w end is in a way a sullen paraphrase of the motif of Soane's Dulwich Mausoleum. Interior plainer though ferociously ham-handed. Segmental chancel arch with beam beyond and indirect top lighting beyond that (with very queer clumsy detail close up), very effective as a separate unit but awkwardly joined to the big boxy nave. No columns, just a sweeping gallery. – Above this, on the w side only, a narrower and more elegant gallery to the l. and r. of the organ. – The original ALTAR PAINTING by *R. Westall* was almost destroyed by arson in 1949 (part remains under the N gallery) and was replaced with a Virgin and Child by *Hans Feibusch*, 1951. – ROYAL ARMS, N side, 1660 and good. Quick off the mark at the Restoration, as befits the church of Sir John Denham, the poet, Surveyor General, and predecessor of Wren. – PULPIT. Plain C18, from Little Livermere, Suffolk. – MONUMENTS. In the body of the church the following: Robert Foster † 1663, frontal marble demi-figure in circular frame, a standard City mason's type, but the face very well and powerfully modelled. – Also many minor Grecian tablets. – In the chancel: four Grecian tablets running the whole range of high-class early C19 sentiment. George Gostling † 1820 by *Flaxman*, and George Gostling, Hannah Gostling, and Lydia Gostling † 1828, all by *Baily*. All poor, though Lydia Gostling has a certain amount of Wedgwood crispness. – The most famous monuments are in the vestibules: Lady Cecile Denham † 1612 and Lady Eleanor Denham, Sir John's first and second wives, both on one monument in a City of London Mannerist architectural frame with a few odd details (quarter columns *in antis*, e.g.). Startlingly naturalistically painted relief of the two wives, the second holding her eldest son, the future poet. The shape is what the Italians call a *tondo*, and the composition of mother and child is indeed clearly derived from Florence about 1500, and especially early Raphael. The English contribution is the excellently rendered textures and sharp planes, just the opposite of the typical lifeless early C17 bust. – In the other

38 vestibule is Sir John Denham himself † 1638, the father of the poet. Another architectural frame, which in this case encloses metaphysics, not homely reality. Sir John rises from the grave in his winding-sheet on Judgement Day above a charnel house of skeletons, one of which is Lady Denham still recumbent and in her shroud, another above her head Denham himself, a dead face in contrast to the re-awakened face above. The inscription says 'made whole again', the same terrific faith in the resurrection of the body that flows through Handel's Messiah and perhaps subconsciously through all English Baroque monumental sculpture. The carver here is suggested as *Maximilian Colt* (Mrs Esdaile); the carving is certainly very good, the charnel house splendid with skeletons and bodies gruesomely huggermugger, the rising figure a little posed and theatrical against the simple background. The Latin inscription reads as follows:

Resurrectio mea est per Jesum Christum
ad aeternam beatitudinem

———

surge a somnis   surge a somnis

———

Quamdiu Domine Jesu, Quamdiu veni O Domine
Jesu veni.

———

Futura spero
ut a peccatis in vita sic a morte post vitam
ut secunda reddat primam et ultimam in
Christo resurrectionem ex omniparte perfectam.

Praeternita sperno
ex ossibus   armati.

PLATE. Two fine German silver Dishes made by *Theodore de Bry* at Frankfurt, 1604 (one now on loan to the Victoria and Albert Museum); silver Paten and Chalice 1618; Tankard 1749; Chalice by *Robert Hennell* 1793.

ST PAUL, Egham Hythe. Fag end of the Gothic revival, 1931–6 by *John Coleridge*. Neo-Perp with big crossing tower and spire. Promising mass but very weak detail.

(ST JOHN (R.C.). 1962 by *Archard & Partners*. DE)

U.D.C. OFFICES. Next to Strode School playing fields, set back from the High Street. Good, modern design by *Denis Clarke Hall & H. S. Scorer*, 1962–3.

GAS WORKS, London Road. By the river. One of the magnificent eighteen-sided gas-holders with external spiral access stairs familiar in the Home Counties (cf. Southall and Kensal Green). Built in 1928, engineer *Thomas Hardie*.

ROYAL HOLLOWAY COLLEGE, ½ m. w, *see* p. 444; MILTON PARK, 1 m. s, *see* p. 368; GREAT FOSTERS, 1 m. s, *see* p. 265.

Extraordinarily little in the village. In the High Street only parts of the RED LION, C17 Artisan brickwork, much altered, and The Old Bank, now BARCLAYS, rebuilt in 1896, quite a witty three-gabled Jacobean front, probably by *Ralph Low* of Staines. To the w at the foot of West Hill the DENHAM ALMSHOUSES, a very simple single-storey terrace of brick cottages dated 1624. At the extreme E end of High Street is MAGNA CARTA, an attractively mad house with a lot of pretty and very inaccurate stucco Gothic detail (e.g. the cornice) still purely in the spirit of a mid-C18 garden ornament. It looks *c.*1830, but the house was apparently built in 1745. Appropriately enough it faces Runnymede, and two sadly over-designed pyramid-roofed LODGES by *Lutyens*, 1930–2. Another bigger pair at the Windsor end, 1½ m. NW.

ELLEN'S GREEN

0030

3 m. SE of Cranleigh

A hamlet on the Sussex border in genuinely unspoilt Weald country – thick woods, small fields, and no bungalows, almost the last fragment of the true Weald left in Surrey. Cottages waywardly thrown around a green. One of them further N – POLINGFOLD – is picturesque, big, late half-timber with tile-hung end walls.

ELSTEAD

9040

Between Farnham and Godalming. A scrappy village, but only the details faulty; fundamentally an attractive plan with a road leading up from the medieval bridge to a small triangular green, and a cul-de-sac lane running s from this to the church.

ST JAMES. Fragments left over from the restoration of 1871 by *Garling*: C13 lancet, C14 and C15 two-light windows on the N side, and a well detailed and straightforward three-light C15 E window,* the best part of the church. Picturesque w end with

* Elstead was a chapelry of Farnham and hence the window was possibly put in by the Bishop of Winchester's masons.

bellcote ruined by a shocking C19 W window in plate tracery. Humble C15 timber N porch including a wooden doorcase for the N door, a rarity. Inside no fittings worth notice and no village atmosphere because of the C19 aisle. Rather a sad building. The nave has a kingpost roof and the bellcote is carried on four posts which form an independent frame but are bonded into the outer walls (unlike the 'mixed' framing of e.g. Bisley). – PLATE. Chalice and Paten 1668.

Few worthwhile cottages in the village. APPLE TREE COTTAGE, between church and green, is attractive unrestored Surrey vernacular, with the upper floor tile-hung above a rubble Bargate stone base and a big central chimneystack. All the visible parts are probably late C17. Between the green and the bridge is THE OLD FARM HOUSE, on the N side of the road, a big C16 timber-framed building, the framing completely irregular, with roughly square panels and brick infill.

The BRIDGE itself is attractive rough medieval stonework and of the same type as Tilford (see p. 488), five-arched with rounded cutwaters downstream. Brick parapet and, inevitably, a modern bridge doubling it on the N side. Beyond it, towards Farnham, is ELSTEAD MILL, a big four-storeyed mid-C18 brick building with hipped gables and an admirable rustic Palladian cupola of six Doric columns supporting a small lead dome. The MILL HOUSE, attached, is two-storey C18 brick. This is the best brick mill in Surrey, an admirable illustration of the honest and common-sense virtues of industrial vernacular – what the *Architectural Review* would call the functional tradition.

½ m. E of the village there is another medieval bridge over the Wey, SOMERSET BRIDGE, of similar type but smaller (four arches). Not doubled by a modern bridge, and hence much more attractive. Beyond it is SOMERSET FARM, a fairly regularly framed half-timbered house of *c.*1600, the S end lean-to, the N end new. It makes a very picturesque group with its BARNS of the typical Surrey type, with tile roofs and black tarred weatherboard walls. The biggest has a hipped tile roof and low eaves, except for the haywain entrance, which has a hipped gable of its own. Less pretty than Kent barns, less solid than the flint or clunch buildings of Hampshire, the best of these Surrey barns are impressively stark.

CROOKSBURY COMMON. The finest of the Surrey barrows, a round Bronze Age BARROW, in a triple group on Turner's Hill, N of Charles Hill, orientated N–S, with a surrounding oval ditch and outer bank measuring *c.*84 by 41 yards. The indi-

vidual finds increase in size from N to S. The group has had no
recorded investigation, although the central mound has a
pronounced dip in its centre.

FULBROOK. See p. 249.

ENGLEFIELD GREEN

9070

1 m. NW of Egham

ST SIMON AND ST JUDE. 1859 by *E. B. Lamb*, and not one of
his most memorable buildings – nothing like Addiscombe (*see*
Croydon). The plan is a fine example of ambiguity from outside. It is cruciform with a tower over the S transept but with
a longer nave away from the road, so that the chancel looks
like the N transept, and the tower looks as though it were over
the E end (which one could well believe from Lamb's work).
Tower top as though normal Gothic mouldings had melted
together, the E window clearly trying to be Art Nouveau – cf.
e.g. the blind panels beneath. The polychrome of the inside
walls is unforgettable, alternate bands of ornamented brick,
limestone, and Kentish rag, though oddly enough all the figure
carving quite conventional. Lamb was clearly thirty years
ahead of his time – and also alas of his style, so that the strictly
architectural value is fairly small. (In the churchyard, two very
curious little brick Gothic gabled MAUSOLEA to the Fitzroy
Somerset family – also obviously by *Lamb*. NT)

(ASSUMPTION OF OUR LADY (R.C.). 1931 by *J. Goldie*. DE)

The Green itself is big and attractive. In the NE corner THE
OLD HOUSE, built *c.*1715. Six by two bays of plain brickwork
later filled up with weak Tudor hood-moulds and a three-sided
porch. Palladian stables. Next to it ENGLEFIELD HOUSE, an
odd late C18 house (or possibly an altered early C18 house?),
pilastered, the centre having a blind segmental lunette filled
with radiating fan-like fluting and a squashed Venetian window
below.

The NW corner is admirable rhododendron-and-beech high-
class suburban landscape. Among the houses here PARK See p. 596
CLOSE by *Huntly Gordon*, 1900, has a free-Gothic gatehouse.
RIDGEMEAD HOUSE is a typical piece of better quality Neo-
Georgian by *Robert Lutyens*, 1937, and right on the Berkshire
border is ST JOHN'S (formerly Beaumont College Preparatory
School) by *J. F. Bentley*, 1888, in an unattractive C17 French
style, not helped by the architect's own contributions – wiry
Late Gothic detail and quadrant wings, one including a

chapel. For Beaumont College, *see The Buildings of England*: *Berkshire*.

(s of the London Road, in Roberts Way, is FOREST COURT, a house by *H. S. Goodhart-Rendel*, *c*.1911–12 (now divided into flats).* Symmetrical garden front of eight bays and two storeys. The middle six bays are raised by a recessed attic storey. Mansard roofs pantiled. The centre of the first floor is a narrow veranda of six bays, with square pillars. The whole is quite characteristic of Goodhart-Rendel's discreet C18 style with Continental rather than English motifs.)

(KINGSWOOD (Shoreditch Training College), Coopers Hill Lane. C18 and 1887. For the main buildings, *see* p. 596.)

COOPERS HILL MEMORIAL. Above Runnymede, at the top of an escarpment, on a superb belvedere site flanked by trees. A quadrangle with a tower on the edge of the scarp, containing the names of 20,000 aircrew killed in the allied air forces in 1939–45. Built in 1953 by *Sir Edward Maufe*. A tricky problem in judgement, especially to viewers committed to the Modern Movement; for while the style is at best delicate mock-Italian (e.g. the Tuscan cloister arches) and at worst like a bad R.A.F. Officers' Mess (e.g. the entrance side), the architectural control of the magnificent view and the sequence by which the visitor gets to the top of the tower is faultless. Maufe is the rare case of a man with genuine spatial gifts but out of sympathy with the style of his time. (Frank Lloyd Wright was another, to some extent.) The belvedere view is first glimpsed on the approach through the bronze entrance gates and the glass in the shrine underneath the tower, and then amplified in a tall room under the tower itself (with incised glass by *John Hutton*). Typically, the westward end just manages to include Windsor Castle. This front has quadrant arms with rooms in the end – East and West Lookouts – from which the view is explored diagonally. Then the visitor goes up a spiral staircase at the back of the tower, first to a gallery high up under the roof of the central space and hence looking down on the view, then to a low-ceilinged room with five small windows on each side making vignettes of the view. From the centre of this rises a spiral staircase, which the visitor then realizes‡ must finish on

---

* Mr J. C. M. Blatch kindly located this for us.

‡ Realizes because he has taken in from outside the position of these little windows relative to the tower roof-line. The whole sequence is worked out in architectural terms – i.e. is functional in a deeper sense than expression of purpose.

the roof in the open air with airliners continually overhead – a very appropriate thing in an Air Memorial – in a view which is now a full 360-degree sweep above treetop level.

(KENNEDY MEMORIAL, Runnymede. Memorial stone ten feet wide and five feet high. Landscaping by *Jellicoe & Coleridge*, 1965.)

EPSOM

2060

ST MARTIN, Church Street. An oddly composite building. Façade of 1824, flint and stucco, in the so-called Commissioners' Gothic. By *Charles Hatchard*. Above and behind the l. aisle rises the original Perp tower with a higher stair-turret. The interior of the nave is also Hatchard's, with thin Perp piers and aisles nearly the height of the nave. But the E end with crossing and transepts is quite different. It was begun in 1907 by *Sir Charles Nicholson & Corlette*, with cathedral ambitions. The style is a completely free Dec (cf. the tracery) but with round-arched motifs used where suitable. The stone here is of a brown brick colour, but there is also flint chequer. These E parts are vaulted. – FONT. Simple, octagonal, Perp, with quatrefoil panels. – (STAINED GLASS, N transept, by *Karl Parsons*. R. Hubbuck) – MONUMENTS. Several late C17 tablets, the best to Elisabeth Evelyn † 1691. Aedicule frame with barley-sugar Corinthian columns; a standard type but superbly carved (e.g. the cherubs' heads in the 'predella'). The columns rest on inward-turning consoles, a neat way of tidying up the composition. – John Brathwaite † 1800, by *Flaxman*. Standing Grecian woman by an urn on a pedestal. – J. H. Warre † 1801, also by *Flaxman*. Standing woman weeping over an urn on a pedestal. – Jane Rowe † 1810, by *John Bacon Jun.*, very much in the style of his father, with two amply draped women l. and r. of an urn on a pedestal. – Susan Warre, by *Chantrey*, 1821. Kneeling figure holding a baby.

CHRIST CHURCH, Epsom Common. 1876 by *Sir A. Blomfield*. Flint and stone with square NW tower. The windows lancet and late C13 types. – STAINED GLASS. E window recent, by *Powell's*, one S aisle window (Cana) 1883 by *Holliday*.

(ST JOSEPH (R.C.), Heathcote Road. E end 1930, nave and aisles 1961 by *F. G. Broadbent & Partners* replacing the original church of 1866 by *G. R. Blount*. DE)

⟨CONGREGATIONAL CHURCH, Church Street. Slightly bow-fronted upper room cantilevered out above the entrance. By *Charity, Thirtle & Duke*, 1963.⟩

TOWN HALL, The Parade. By *Pite Son & Fairweather*, 1934.
Simple Neo-Georgian.

EPSOM WELL, Well Way. A plain square flint pedestal. The
Epsom well was discovered in 1618 (cf. below).

EPSOM COLLEGE. Started as the Royal Medical Benevolent
College in 1853. The original brick buildings, Gothic and
rather grim, are by *T. H. Clifton*. (Domestic offices by *G.
Elkington*, 1862. GS) Later additions.

⟨SCHOOL OF ART, Ashley Road. By *R. J. Ash*, the County
Architect. Now building (1969).⟩

⟨EPSOM HOSPITAL, Dorking Road. Promising-looking new
buildings begun in 1968; low ranges with white ceramic cladding surrounding a taller block. The architects are *Mayorcas &
Guest*.

⟨WHITE HOUSE, Alexandra Road. Nurses' flats, by the County
Architect, *R. J. Ash*, 1967–9. A strong building of purple brick.
Six plus two bays, linked by glass to a plain staircase tower. At
the back, two tiers of glass corridors ingeniously cantilevered
out, providing access to studio flats. Split-pitched tiled
roof.⟩

MENTAL HOSPITALS (GLC). The LCC bought the Horton
Estate in the 1890s and built gradually five mental hospitals
and a colony for epileptics. The latter is of 1902 (by *W. C.
Clifford Smith*). The Manor was built in 1899, Horton Hospital
in 1901. Horton is nearly a replica of the hospital at Bexley,
Kent. It was followed by St Ebba's in 1903, by Long Grove in
1903–7, and by West Park in 1915–24. Their total population
is over 10 per cent of that of the borough.

GRANDSTANDS for the Epsom Races. All of after 1926, except
for the luncheon etc. building, which is of 1914.

Epsom is richer perhaps in Late Stuart, Queen Anne, and Georgian houses than any other place in Surrey. This is due to two
causes: Epsom Salts and Epsom Races. The well was discovered in 1618. When Pepys visited it in 1667, there was
'much Company'. These were exactly the years of its rising
fashionableness, which culminated about 1690–1710. In 1684
a daily post was inaugurated from London to run during the
season. About 1710 decay set in, but by then London merchants and their families had become used to settle at Epsom
for the summer. Defoe, writing *c.*1725, tells us that, and adds
that they themselves drove up to Town every morning and that
the town was deserted in the winter. And when a further fillip
was perhaps needed, the twelfth Earl of Derby, living at The

Oaks (*see* Carshalton), created the Oaks in 1779 and the Derby in 1780.*

The HIGH STREET is not one of the most rewarding streets in Epsom. Too much of the earlier buildings has been destroyed, and the E half especially has little to attract. In the W half any effort to regain the atmosphere of Epsom's C18 is thwarted by the grotesque CLOCK TOWER with the lavatories at its base (1847–8 by *Butler & Hodge*). On the S side HARSANT & LEE, with a good late C18 shop-front, double bow window, and largely original chemist's fittings. The best individual house is at the W end, WATERLOO HOUSE (now the NATIONAL POST OFFICE BUILDING SOCIETY), said to date from 1690. This was formerly the New Inn and had on its first floor an Assembly Room, one of the earliest in England. The building is of eleven bays, with a three-bay pediment. Unfortunately the ground floor is now all shop-windows. Off the High Street to the S first Church Street, then Ashley Road, then South Street. They must be taken in succession.

First CHURCH STREET, originally one of the finest streets in Epsom. It becomes clear here that Epsom in the C18 was, like the villages nearer London, a place for wealthy Londoners to keep a summer house or an estate. Coming from the High Street one ought to watch for the following. First the FIRE STATION by *Pite Son & Fairweather*, 1937, nice modern front and square practising-tower at the back. Then THE CEDARS, an impressive Early Georgian house in the Archer or maybe Vanbrugh style. Nine bays, yellow and red brick. Raised centre with a tripartite semicircular window. The windows in the l. and r. range have broad bands of projecting brick over. Top parapet raised at the corners. Fine doorcase with a carved coat of arms and carved brackets. In the room to the l. of the entrance Rococo plaster ceiling and good Rococo fireplace. Two splendid cedar trees outside the front garden. Then No. 18 of the late C17 (Victorian porch), No. 20 of the early C19 with a pedimented centre with giant pilasters, and No. 24, set back at an angle, early C18, of red brick, three bays, three and a half storeys. On the same side, EBBISHAM HOUSE, early C18, of white brick. Opposite, that is to the S of the church, was PITT PLACE, the principal house of Epsom proper. It was scandalously demolished in July 1967.‡ The house started as a Geor-

* The St Leger had been created at Doncaster in 1776.

‡ It is perhaps worth quoting the account of this deliberate and unprincipled act of vandalism, given in the *Report* of the Council for British Archaeology,

gian farmhouse and was made into a mansion by Thomas Lord Lyttelton *c*.1770. The farm part was on the N side, refaced with Late Georgian brick. It had one projecting wing; the other (with the kitchens) was an addition. Attached to the S side a room made up of a number of cast-iron columns supporting a pediment. The columns came from the colonnade of Nash's Regent Street Quadrant, removed in the mid C19. Inside, a stately late C18 Drawing Room and an upper room with Chinese decoration. As part of a fireplace in another upper room a pair of Tudor caryatids credibly said to come from Nonsuch Palace. The same provenance is assigned to the two lions on the stable gatepiers, to a head worked into the stable walls, and to several terracotta chimneys with fleur-de-lys ornament. (The present location of all these important pieces is unknown, which is deplorable. Mr J. Dent, Ewell and Epsom Librarian, kindly tells us that in the cellars of Pitt Place there were blocks of carved stone very similar to the Merton Priory stone seen in the foundations of Nonsuch (*see* p. 384). This stone may have gone from Nonsuch to Durdans, in Epsom, and from there to Pitt Place). In the grounds an Ice House, a Well House, and a flint-built Badger House. ⟨At the time of writing (1969) the site is still undeveloped, and the garden walls survive, a sad memorial. The N and E walls, very tall, by the church, are worth preserving.⟩

Now the second S tributary to the High Street: ASHLEY ROAD. Here the only house worth recording is ASHLEY HOUSE, a very fine house, dated 1769. White brick, five bays and two and a half storeys with a three-bay pediment and a good Adamish doorcase. The door leads to a corridor that goes across the house and has as its centre a little square separated by Ionic columns. Off this to the r. is the staircase. In the l. front room excellent fireplace and stucco panels.

After that SOUTH STREET, which gives access to the Woodcote parts of Epsom, where the majority of the noteworthy houses lie. In South Street THE SHRUBBERY, early C18 with a pretty doorcase with Corinthian pilasters, and then at the S end on the E side WOODCOTE HALL, large, of red brick, mid-Georgian,

1968. 'The Company which owned this building, one of the finest eighteenth century houses in the locality, was quite evidently intent on destroying it, despite two Building Preservation Orders made by the Ministry. Many features of architectural interest were systematically stripped, and demolition took place swiftly and unheralded one weekend when the [Civic Amenities] Bill was in its final stages.'

much pulled about. Seven bays, two storeys. Attic storey above the cornice. Centre with tripartite semicircular window and pediment over. One-storey pavilions form an entrance court.

From here Dorking Road turns SW, Woodcote Road SE. In DORKING ROAD the following: CLOCK HOUSE, big, early C19 façade, with a four-column Tuscan porch.* On the l. further on, THE HYLANDS, early C18, with a fine seven-bay front. Two storeys and parapet. Doorcase with rusticated Doric pilasters and a broken pediment. Inside a delightful staircase with a gallery. Contemporary wrought-iron GATES. (Additions in progress, 1969.) Next door HYLANDS HOUSE, bigger and a little forbidding. Early Georgian, of yellow and red brick. Brick quoins. The outer windows very narrow. The centre window on the first floor arched. Seven bays and three storeys with two-storeyed canted bays. Doorway with Corinthian pilasters and a carved frieze. WHITMORES, which was Early Georgian, has been replaced by terrible speculators'-Georgian-style of the sixties.

In WOODCOTE ROAD, WOODCOTE END HOUSE, partly c.1700, partly mid-C18. Interior of c. 1770, with oval entrance hall projecting as a shallow bow to the outside, and, to its r., a beautiful octagonal room with a discreet plaster ceiling. The staircase, if somewhat irregular, is charming too. It must date from the early C18. Nice small STABLES to the r.

At the end of Woodcote Road another junction, marked by the former WOODCOTE HOTEL, now called WESTGATE HOUSE. The house was damaged by fire in 1966, and is now being converted into offices. It looks early C19 from the outside, with its Tuscan porch, but the coved ceiling of the staircase was dated 1684. The ceiling, and the staircase itself, which may have been early C18 (it had turned balusters and carved tread-ends), have now gone. At the back, the staircase was lit by a Venetian window. From the corner where the house stands a footpath runs N. In this the C18 gatepiers and wrought-iron gates of a former house (Chandlers).

Opposite CHALK LANE HOTEL, an excellent late C17 house, WOODCOTE GROVE. Five bays and two storeys, with a three-bay pediment. Entrance hall with a screen of columns carrying segmental arches, and behind it a stone staircase with wrought-iron balustrade, rising straight for a few steps and then turning

* The house may be older. The Epsom Reference Librarian suggests that the back elevation has similarities to 'Mr Rooth's house in New Inn Lane', which is mentioned in 1711, and is illustrated in Vitruvius Britannicus.

r. at r. angles, a curious anomaly, as there is on the l. no symmetrical feature. Now offices, admirably restored. (Good interior details.) In Worple Road an entrance with wrought-iron
gates and an avenue towards the house. Opposite the house, in
Chalk Lane, MAIDSTONE HOUSE, mid-Georgian, of three
bays with Venetian windows l. and r. of the doorways.

Off Heath Lane, in WOODCOTE ROAD, lies DURDANS, built
in 1764–8 by *W. Newton*, seven bays with wide central canted
bay window. Much added to in the C19.* Fine wrought-iron
gates with cast-iron piers in Chalk Lane. These come from
Canons in Middlesex, the seat of the Duke of Chandos.

In WOODCOTE GREEN ROAD first GREEN HOUSE, late C17
with a doorcase exhibiting attached Tuscan columns against
rustication at their back. Pretty Chinese Chippendale staircase
inside. Then, lying back a good deal, WOODCOTE HOUSE,
early C19, stuccoed, of five bays with one-storeyed pedimented
end pavilions. Recessed centre with a two-column entrance. At
the far end of Woodcote Green Road, from Wilmerhatch Lane
the drive to WOODCOTE PARK, which, before the fire of 1934,
was the grandest house in Epsom. Even in its present state
it is still spectacular. The present brick parts of the façade are
a copy of what then had been in stone. They stand on a substructure which remains from Lord Baltimore's house. Centre
block with arched rusticated ground floor, quadrant arcades,
also arched and rusticated, end pavilions of four by four bays,
two-storeyed, with pyramid roofs, the ground floor again
arched and rusticated. A splendid curved staircase leads up
to the main floor of the house. This is of five bays and two and
a half storeys. The design of the house has been attributed to
Isaac Ware (J. Harris). A room in a pure French Rococo style
is now in the Museum of Fine Arts, Boston.

Large STABLES to the N, mid-C18. Also, nearer the exit, a
C17 brick BARN and a circular brick DOVECOTE.

BURGH HEATH. *See* p. 121.

1060

ESHER

ST GEORGE. A delightful, most endearing little church, tucked
away from the busy High Street, just behind the Bear Hotel.
Built of stone about 1540. Wooden bell-turret with pyramid
roof. Brick s chapel as the family pew of the Duke of Newcastle
(*see* Claremont), built in 1725–6, probably by *Vanbrugh*. At the

---

* Work by *G. Devey* recorded for 1878.

same time alterations to the chancel. The c18 windows are arched. N aisle added in 1812. Also brick, with a castellated E end. Nicely crowded interior. Open roof with tie-beams and collar-beams. The N arcade has tall round oak piers. – WEST GALLERY of 1840–2. – REREDOS of 1722 with nice carving. – c18 three-decker PULPIT. – The box pews were removed only in 1908. – NEWCASTLE PEW. Simple interior with a ceiling very sparingly decorated, but an extremely fine front towards the church like that of a garden temple or a summer house: two angle pillars and two columns, all Corinthian, carry a pediment. – PAINTING. Apotheosis of Princess Charlotte († 1817), by *A. W. Devis*. The painting is the pattern for the sculptural monuments in St George's Chapel at Windsor of 1824 and at Belvoir Castle of 1820–4, both by M.C. Wyatt. – MONUMENTS. Lady Lynch, 1702. Painting of a hanging wall-monument with kneeling figure like a Magdalen between columns. Rather a rarity. – Lady Fowler † 1738, signed by *Henry Cheere*. Frame in the Kent style, three cherubs' heads at the foot. – Mrs Ellis † 1804. Plain big Grecian tablet. – Princess Charlotte, by *F. J. Williamson* of Esher, formerly on the staircase at Claremont. Triptych. The centre shows Prince Leopold and the Princess tending the poor, the l. panel her death, the r. panel his acceptance of the Crown of Belgium with the approval of Britannia.

CHRIST CHURCH, Esher Green. 1853–4 by *Benjamin Ferrey*. A prosperous church. Buff stone with stone broach-spire. Transepts, clerestory. c13 details. – REREDOS in the Lady Chapel. By *R. Spencer Stanhope*, a copy of that in the English church in Florence. – STAINED GLASS. E window by *Sir Ninian Comper*, 1909. – PLATE. Chalice and Paten by *Omar Ramsden*, 1936. – MONUMENTS. Richard Drake † 1603, with kneeling figure. – Prince Leopold, Duke of Albany, † 1884, by *F. J. Williamson*. Marble bust in alabaster surround. – Leopold, King of the Belgians, 1867, by *Susan D. Durant*. Recumbent marble effigy, transferred from St George's Chapel Windsor (in the choir vestry).

FRIENDS' MEETING HOUSE, Claremont Lane. 1797. Grey brick. Very simple front of four arched windows with a small doorway in the middle. Pyramid roof.

Although the HIGH STREET is pleasant to walk along (traffic permitting*), it has hardly any house of special interest. At the NE end the URBAN DISTRICT OFFICES, probably of the late

* A new by-pass is planned.

C 17, with a big symmetrical stuccoed Early Victorian façade of thirteen bays and a very pretty early C 18 staircase with slender twisted balusters and carved tread-ends. Opposite the TRAVELLERS' REST, a pretty grotto-like 'Sedilia', erected by Henry Pelham (*see below*) about 1730–40. Up CLAREMONT LANE, past the Quaker Meeting House, ALSTONFIELD, a Neo-Georgian house by *Oswald Milne*, 1909, and then WILLOW GREEN, a modern one-storeyed house by *R. G. Simmons*, 1954. Opposite the gate lodges to Claremont MILBOURNE LANE turns E. On the l. a good new PRIMARY SCHOOL. Then Nos. 48–50, the sole survivor (1969) of a group of semi-detached weatherboarded early C 19 houses. (More of them in DAWES COURT off the High Street.) Further along another pair survives (Nos. 76–78 and 80). N of these, in Littleworth Road, CLAYGATE HOUSE, offices of Brown & Polson. Then in New Road, to the W, a pleasantly composed CRICKET PAVILION by *Emberton, Tardrew & Partners*, 1968, of pale brick with cedar boarding.

From the S end of the High Street PORTSMOUTH ROAD continues. Here the big polygonal stone LODGE (by *Sir Ernest George & Yates*, c.1905) to the former MOOR PLACE. (Moor Place itself is C 18 and has externally been altered, but contains good internal features. MHLG)

Architecturally the most interesting part of Esher is ESHER GREEN and the Esher Place estate. The green is pretty, with cottages on one side, Christ Church and the Church Schools of 1852 on the second, and the brick GATE LODGES to the estate on the third, which look early C 18.* ESHER PLACE was a house of Bishop Waynflete of Winchester. It was probably oblong or square with a spacious inner courtyard. Of this building, erected about 1475–80, all that remains is the gatehouse, the mason for which was probably *John Cowper*. It is
58 of red brick with blue brick diapering, three-storeyed with four-storeyed polygonal angle turrets, and was much altered when Henry Pelham, younger brother of the Duke of Newcastle (cf. Claremont) and famous statesman, bought the estate in 1729 and asked *William Kent* to incorporate it in a country house. Kent's work was Gothick – and what survives of it belongs to the earliest examples of that Rococo-Gothic which found its crowning achievement twenty years later at Strawberry Hill. Kent added the two three-bay ranges of three

* The R.I.B.A. has a drawing by *Kent* for park piers for Esher Place. In front of the gate lodges was a *ferme ornée* and stables, also by *Kent* (J. Harris).

storeys l. and r. Much of the gatehouse as it now is also belongs to Kent's alterations. He put a one-storeyed porch between the turrets and gave it an ogee-arched doorway.* Above this a typically Kentian triple window with ogee-headed lights. Also equally typical quatrefoil windows. The entrance hall was the gateway in Waynflete's time. It is rib-vaulted, and the ribs were stuccoed over by Kent. He also put small and pretty niches along the walls. Waynflete's staircase is in the NW corner. Kent built a new one in the NE corner. This has not survived, except for some window and ceiling decoration. The ceiling has a curious and highly characteristic mixture of fan-vaulting with acanthus detail. Kent's work in the gardens has all perished. It was famous in its day, and Thomson in *The Seasons* refers to 'Esher's peaceful grove, Where Kent and Nature vie for Pelham's love'.

In 1805 the estate changed hands, and the new owner built a new house, by *Lapidge*, on the hill to the SE. What remains of this is now the SW wing of a yet newer ESHER PLACE, a very large Frenchy mansion. It was built for the first Viscount d'Abernon in 1895–8 by *G. T. Robinson* and *Duchêne*.‡ Broad centre with a raised middle pavilion with French pavilion roof. Splayed wings. Inside a splendid imitation Dixhuitième stone staircase and much imitation Dixhuitième decoration. The SUNK GARDEN is by *Lutyens*, 1905.§ The grounds are divided up, and there are streets here of detached houses of between the wars, mostly in genteel or a little funnily-picturesque style. An exception is KINRARA by *Christian Barman*, 1935, an uncompromisingly cubist red brick house, stepped up from one to three storeys.

EWELL

2060

ST MARY. 1848 by *Henry Clutton*. – FONT. Simple, Perp, with quatrefoil panels. – SCREEN. Perp, with one-light divisions, much renewed. – PLATE. Paten of 1765. – MONUMENTS. Brasses to Lady Iwarby † 1519 (kneeling) and Margerina Treglistan † 1521 (standing), both in the S aisle at the W end. – Also brass of an Elizabethan couple. – Sir William Lewen

---

* A design by Kent for the porch is, according to Mr John Harris, dated 1733.

‡ Information received from Mr A. Woodcock of the Electrical Trades Union.

§ This is now attached to THE GARDENS, off Pelhams Walk. Well preserved topiary, and canal decorated with tiles-on-edge (NT).

† 1721. An exceptionally good standing wall-monument. Semi-reclining figure with wig. Background with Corinthian pilasters and an open segmental pediment. Below this cloth with cherubs' heads above the inscription. – Mrs Hallifax † 1795. By *Thomas Banks*. Female figure kneeling over a big urn (s aisle, E end, high up). For the old church, *see* below.

(ST CLEMENT (R.C.), Kingston Road. 1962 by *J. H. Alleyn*. DE) Ewell has preserved its centre in a very happy way (or had, until recently). The HIGH STREET, it is true, has only a few minor timber-framed and other cottages, but several of the larger houses survive and give Ewell intricacy and variety, though not one of them is of the same value as at least a dozen in neighbouring Epsom.

The centre is BOURNE HALL in the High Street, where London Road and Kingston Road meet it. The old Bourne Hall was disgracefully demolished in 1962. It has been replaced by a very large circular building with a shallow domed roof, completed in 1970, which contains a library, museum, exhibition gallery, halls, etc., by *A. G. Sheppard Fidler & Associates*. The old house dated from about 1775, five bays wide, two storeys high, with a three-bay pediment and stuccoed. Attached on the l. and r. were somewhat later pedimented conservatories. Doorway with Ionic columns. (Staircase with iron scroll balusters. MHLG) The grounds are not large, but were generously scattered about with furnishings. The entrance gateway, surmounted by a lion, has been restored, but the semicircular Ionic temple in the lake between the hall and the street has disappeared. There survive a flint and shell bridge and archway with pointed arch from the lake towards the pond outside the wall. Beneath an iron mill-wheel. On the same side another archway for water to be conducted to the DAIRY. This too has gone. It lay outside, at the start of Chessington Road, castellated, turreted, symmetrical, and stuccoed.

At the junction of LONDON ROAD and Kingston Road the SPRING HOTEL, the older parts nicely weatherboarded. In KINGSTON ROAD the MILL HOUSE, early c18 brick, has been demolished, but the attached mill buildings survive. These are four storeys high, gabled and weatherboarded. Then, winding round the gardens of Bourne Hall, CHESSINGTON ROAD, with FITZNELLS, a modest house with an iron veranda towards another little lake. Altogether Ewell succeeds in making a great deal out of its humble Hogsmill River. At the corner, CHICHESTER COURT, good new flats, 1968. Then in

Spring Street a three-bay house of the early C18 (Ches-sington House) and the larger Spring House, both with walls covered in mathematical tiles, with a canted bay window and a doorway with Tuscan columns and pediment.

After that, instead of turning back to Bourne Hall, having circled round its grounds, straight on into Church Street. Nice group on the r., starting with the tiny Watch House, a little cube with two narrow doorways under a blank segmental arch. It has recently been restored to its original state. After that an C18 brick house with a pediment-like gable and the fine Well House of *c*.1700, of six bays with a double porch to shelter two doorways. Three Tuscan columns, rusticated back wall. Opposite, in its grounds, Glyn House, with a short tower. This is by *Henry Duesbury*, 1839. Adjoining this the old churchyard, and opposite Ewell Castle, the largest house in Ewell, stuccoed and castellated, by *H. Kitchen*, 1810–14. It is a pity that it lies so close to the road. The composition has a gatehouse motif in the middle and the parts to the l. and r. of equal weight but treated deliberately without symmetry in the fenestration etc. Tall vaulted Entrance Hall with a staircase with iron balustrade. Opposite the house, in the churchyard the Perp Tower of the medieval parish church, to the s of the new church. This is of flint and stone and has a higher stair-turret. The flint is treated in part to form a rough chequerwork with the stone. Early C19 brick parapet curving up at the corners with staddle-stones on top. Wind vane of 1786–9.

(Packhorse Bridge. In a plantation in the riverside open space, just outside the grounds of Ewell Court House. J. D. U. Ward)

⟨Ewell Technical College, Reigate Road. Large, and more additions to come. The most recent buildings are the five-storey block with a lower tiered theatre in front, by the County Architect, *R. J. Ash*, 1965–7.⟩

Nonsuch Palace. *See* p. 383.

EWHURST

0040

A straggling roadside village running N–S under the s slopes of the Hurtwood E of Cranleigh. Three separate picturesque groups, but nothing to bind them together: a small square at the N end of the village, a few cottages beside the church, and Ewhurst Green ½ m. further s. The village is slowly being over-built in the wrong way – i.e. the new houses are trying too hard to be picturesque.

St Peter and St Paul. Picturesque, heavy-lidded, aisleless cruciform building of Weald sandstone with a lot of character. Much of this is due to the central tower, which fell in 1838 and was rebuilt by *Robert Ebbels* in the Norman style – not a copy of what was there before – which would be outstandingly authentic and effective for any architect at any time in the C19, let alone an almost unknown provincial practitioner whose main output was spiky lancet-Gothic chapels.* Simple two-light bell-openings, heavy corbel-table, heavy, stumpy, shingled broach-spire above. The chancel was largely rebuilt in 1838 also, but the rest is original and was lightly handled in the C19 restoration. Nave probably Norman, re-windowed. Impressive s doorway, the best piece of Norman decoration in Surrey: a massive early C12 design, plain but to a large scale, with big jamb-shafts, big single-scallop capitals, the arch with one thick rough order, and a big double roll-moulding under a hood, which runs into the imposts – the inevitability of Early Romanesque here taking over what was originally a Late Saxon decorative idea. Mr W. McG. Eager suggests that the doorway may have been altered in the restoration. Tower arches (rough, with continuous double chamfers) and transepts C13, with compositions of three widely spaced single lancets and a trefoil above in both transept ends. Segment-headed Perp windows in nave and s transept and big three-light C15 window above the simple wooden C15 w porch. Simple, satisfying interior with plain barn-type roofs. – FONT. Partly old, a tapering bowl of square section with St Andrew's crosses and chevrons on the sides. What date? The cover is partly pretty C18 work. – PULPIT. Standard Jacobean. – ALTAR RAILS. Handsome late C17, three-sided with recessed curved corners and twisted balusters, about the best in the county. Originally at Baynards Park.

The best cottage is undoubtedly DEBLINS GREEN, at the N end of the village, opposite the Bull's Head, a very nice example of the late, regularly built half-timbered house. Perhaps as late as *c.*1700. The bottom storey brick and half-timber, the upper tile-hung, using both scalloped and straight-edged tiles, with symmetrical small windows. The roof half-hipped and

---

* He designed the RECTORY here, E of the church, in a very spiky style. Most of this character has now disappeared.

tiled. Also at this end of the village the back of TUDOR HOUSE has quite a big array of close-set half-timbering with herring-bone brick infilling, perhaps C15 or early C16.

LUKYNS, 1 m. NE. One of *Ernest Newton*'s correct, symmetrical, uninspired Wren-style houses. The S front with three bow windows. Date, 1911. *Jekyll* garden.

1 m. NW of the village, on the slopes of the Hurtwood, some interesting country houses, hard to find and harder to see properly. They start with LONG COPSE, an extreme example of the primitive wing of the Arts and Crafts movement that was represented by Morris and the S.P.A.B. Low, unobtrusive, T-shaped stone house, partly roofed with Horsham slate and partly thatched, with exactly the same urge to dissolve into the landscape as that expressed so much more intricately by Voysey and Lutyens. Here, revealingly, the effect is of a Picturesque cottage of the most rustic sort, as though the Gothic Revival had never existed. By *Alfred Powell* of the Art Workers' Guild, 1897, with woodwork by *Gimson* inside. Built primitively, i.e. without mechanization, but, typically, the craftsmen employed by Powell were 'university men who worked with him'. Very early, and impressive in its undemonstrative way. G. F. Watts thought it the most beautiful house in Surrey. Opposite, CONEYHURST, by *Philip Webb*, 1886, a brick and tile-hung house in the usual Surrey manner, but with an extra sureness and security in volumes and detail visible on a close look. However, it has to be a really close look – it is not apparent straightaway and it might never be apparent if the viewer did not know the house to be Webb's. Whether this is a legitimate way of looking at buildings is a nice point. Further W is HURTWOOD, built as Hurtwood Edge by *A. T. Bolton*, 1910, a design like a Tuscan villa with taller corner tower but the materials and detail those of an early Lutyens house, a queer hybrid. (MARYLAND, also at Hurtwood, is a large Lutyens-style house of 1929 by *Oliver Hill*. NT) ½ m. N again is WOOLPIT, by *George & Peto*, 1885. Built for a Doulton, hence a lot of buff terracotta dressings, and hence much more reactionary and less sympathetic than George & Peto's usual work in the 1880s. Free Tudor with a small tower at one end.

ROMAN ROAD. There are fine stretches of Roman branch road from Rowhook to Farley Heath.

At Rapsley Farm is a ROMAN COURTYARD VILLA of the C2. A bath house, possibly entered from a timber hall to the N, formed the E side; on the W was an aisled hall, and to the S stood a timber building which had an apsidal end and which may have been a shrine. In the c 3 the bath however was converted into a dwelling and the other buildings were replaced.

FAIRMILE
¾ m. NE of Cobham

BENFLEET HALL SCHOOL. *Philip Webb*'s second house, built as Sandroyd in 1860 for the artist Spencer Stanhope, the year after his famous Red House, and in the same style. Dour, asymmetrical red brick. A splendid composition, but the detail almost thrown away. It needed Norman Shaw to exploit the style's decorative possibilities. The entrance side (N) has the only stylistic concession, a half-timbered gable balancing a stack of chimneys which could be by Lutyens; all the rest is deliberately utilitarian and graceless, with big segmental windows under pointed arches, etc. The w front typically take-it-or-leave-it, of two gabled bays with one- and two-light windows diagonally opposed: one- above-two-light versus two- above-one-light. Inside one *de Morgan* fireplace* and an unexpected outcrop of exposed brick arches on the first-floor landing. A true equivalent of Butterfield, and in fact in some respects a deliberate imitation of Butterfield (cf. Great Bookham).

Around Fairmile is now an estate called EATON PARK, of high-income houses in well landscaped grounds. One of them, BOSSINEY, is a good, crisp house by *Leonard Manasseh*, 1958.

FARLEIGH

Tiny hamlet on the North Downs, quite unspoilt – almost the most rural in Surrey. Flint and brick farms and barns. This extraordinary place is four miles from the centre of Croydon, eleven from the Isle of Dogs, and almost within sight of some of the worst sprawl in the country, at New Addington.‡

ST MARY. As surprising a survival for Surrey as the village: simple village-Norman, fairly gently restored, with new chancel arch and simple new bell-turret. All stuccoed, and not a window later than 1250. Nave and chancel c.1100, the chancel

* The de Morgan tiles have recently been stolen. The house has now been divided into flats.

‡ Paradoxically, it was included within the new GLC in 1965, but after local protest was restored to Surrey.

extended by 10 ft *c*.1250 and fitted up with lancet windows.*
The E end has two lancets instead of three (cf. East Clandon).
All nave windows Norman, w doorway Norman also, with one
order of shafts carrying block capitals, and no other ornament.
Simple village interior. – BRASS. John Brock † 1495 with his
wife and children (s wall of chancel). Main figures 15 in. high.

FARLEY HEATH *see* ALBURY

FARNCOMBE
1 m. NE of Godalming

9040

Largely a C19 annexe to Godalming, with its own railway
station. A few reminders of the pre-C19 hamlet, e.g. Nos. 44–56
FARNCOMBE STREET, C16 and C18 cottages.

ST JOHN THE EVANGELIST. Dull lancet chapel of 1847, 1860,
and 1875, all apparently by *Sir George Gilbert Scott* or his firm.
(Additions by *C. F. Hayward*, 1881. GS)

WYATT ALMSHOUSES, Guildford Road, Built in 1622 by
Richard Wyatt of London, ten dwellings and a central gabled
chapel in one long brick terrace. Subdued Tudor with a minimum of detail, the effect rather pinched, as so many C17 Home
Counties almshouses are. The back is more impressive, a
sequence of big coupled chimneys with lean-to porches
between (and above them a little weatherboarding – an odd
mixture). Behind, a new quadrangle of cottages, still in much
the same style, by *B. W. Ridley*, 1957–8.

FARNHAM

8040

A fine town, generally ranked as one of the best Georgian towns
in England. This is over-praise; it has two superb Georgian
set-pieces in Castle Street and West Street, but not the perpetual
surprise of Georgian buildings throughout the fabric of the town
of places such as Lancaster or Blandford. The rest is nicely
scaled old cottages, a fair bit of breezy C19 building, and a
depressing amount of Neo-Georgian. Farnham was largely preserved by the deliberate policy of one landowner, Mr Borelli,
and his architect *Harold Falkner*, starting in 1910 and culminating
in the replacement of the truly alien Victorian Town Hall in the
1930s. That was the high-water mark: today preservation has
become stultification, so that there are now streets, as in

* The quoins of the original E end can just be made out under the stucco.

Chichester, where there are more Neo-Georgian houses than true Georgian ones.*

St Andrew.‡ Big, mostly C15, but the exterior so violently restored in 1855 by *Ferrey* that little but the medieval proportions remains. The best part is the impressive w tower with polygonal buttresses, always a sign of consequence. Probably C15 and left unfinished at the Reformation. Upper windows, battlements, and pinnacles all 1865 by *Ewan Christian*, reasonably done. The tower arch remains unrestored; big-scale, with a single attached shaft and moulding inside two orders of continuous mouldings. This must be Winchester work. A similar tower with polygonal buttresses is at Newbury, Berks, and this has the same type of tower arch also. The body has nave and aisles of equal height like a Kent church, without clerestory (though this is said to have been destroyed in the Civil War). Inside there are three long parallel tunnels, with until recently the typical, depressing, over-restored impression of an English town church, but now much more cheerful since the restoration by *David Nye* in 1959, when the walls were whitewashed and much clear glass put in the windows. The Norman church must have had a crossing (evidence of a former crossing is still easily seen) and transepts. (Excavations in 1959 revealed foundations and crossing piers, indicating a N as well as a S transept.) There was also a vaulted chancel. The w vaulting shafts, or corbels, remain. The capitals are concave, one with palmette leaves, one with simple volutes – i.e. they look late C12. The C12 chancel was at least two bays long, as the exterior buttresses between the first and second bay can be seen in the N and S chapels. These chapels date from the later C12, but the semicircular responds with many-scalloped capitals of the arch from the S transept into the S chapel may be older.§ The arch, however, is pointed, with two slight chamfers. The chancel arcades have moulded capitals as well as many-scalloped ones. The chancel arch was heightened and its capitals renewed in 1841, and the chancel restored in 1848.

* For more detailed information on Farnham buildings, the reader is referred to the excellent book by Nigel Temple: *Farnham Buildings and People* (1963).

‡ The article on the church by A. R. Dufty, SAC vol. 61 (1964), has been used in revising this entry.

§ Mr Dufty suggests that the responds from a smaller transeptal chapel were re-used, with new abaci, bases, and arch, when the chapel was remodelled.

The three E lancets in the N chapel replaced a Perp window. In 1959 the altar was moved further W, creating a kind of ambulatory behind, and an E chapel – an effective alteration but spoilt by the feeble Neo-Georgian furnishings. The nave arcades are of five bays with octagonal piers and double-hollow-chamfered arches. They may date from a partial re-building of the church in the C15 after a fire. The arches between aisles and transepts and the widening of the N and S crossing arches probably date from the same time. The aisle windows now have reticulated tracery, but only that in the S aisle has been restored correctly. So the C14 nave may have had only one aisle. The tower, which, as we have seen, is later than the nave arcades, cuts with its E buttresses into them. Finally a Perp lengthening of the chancel, perhaps connected with a dedication in 1399. On the N side is a blocked arch from the N aisle into what was probably a chantry chapel of the late C15. The SEDILIA and PISCINA are the best detail in the church, perhaps made for the dedication of 1399. Four bays, ogee arches under square hoods, quatrefoils in the spandrels; complex and delicate without being fussy. – FONT. Good routine C15 work. Octagonal bowl carved with shields and figures. – SCULPTURE. St Andrew by *Eric Gill*, S chancel chapel. – ALTAR RAILS. Late C17, the sides with Doric columns, the centre with complex floral panels. As good as the woodwork in Farnham Castle chapel. – STAINED GLASS. E window designed by *Pugin*, and shown in the 1851 Exhibition. Oddly watery compared with the rich glass he used in his own interiors. – HATCHMENTS. C18 and C19. Now used to decorate the aisle walls. – PLATE. Two Cups 1797, Patens 1623, Paten C17, Paten 1676, Paten 1712, Flagon 1712, Cross 1956. – MONUMENTS. Very many C18 and C19 tablets, but hardly any worth notice. One or two Baroque cartouches high up at the W end of the N chancel chapel. – In the S chapel, Sir Nicholas Rycroft † 1827, showing a pilgrim resting on his journey, by *Sir Richard Westmacott*. – In the tower, a medallion bust to Cobbett under a simple pointed canopy. – At the W end of the nave, on the SE tower buttress, George Sturt, author of *The Wheelwright's Shop*, † 1926, by *Eric Gill*. Worth a look. Simple lettering, but as far from the vernacular they both sought as could be imagined; all Fine Art and inhibitions.

ST JAMES, East Street. 1876 by *Woodyer*, but a late and weary routine job. Dark Bargate stone. Scalloped soffit to the chancel arch. SCHOOL also by *Woodyer*.

ST JOAN OF ARC (R.C.), on the Elstead road. 1931 by *Nicholas &* *Dixon-Spain*. Acceptable to everyone at the time for the worst of reasons – by being sufficiently flavourless to avoid hurting anyone's feelings. Neo-Georgian with a barrel-vaulted interior looking as though it was concrete. Sculpture by *Vernon Hill*.

CASTLE. Originally, a palace of the Bishops of Winchester. Dominates the town in a comfortable domestic way, closing the view up Castle Street. What looks at first sight to be a picturesque ramble is in essence a complete C12 rebuilding. Successive additions have altered the elevations but retained the plan – a lucky accident, for Farnham is one of the best examples in the country of the first cautious departures made by the C12 from the purely military living quarters of the C11. Even taking account of the comfortable later additions, few other English C12 castles are so domestic. The earliest part of Farnham was a square tower which, to a height of about 50 ft, was surrounded by earth dug out of the ditch to form a motte. It was probably built in 1138, under Henry of Blois, King Stephen's brother, and was repaced later in the C12 by the shell-keep which still stands and which encloses the motte (cf. Berkeley Glos. and Carmarthen). Thus the keep had an earthen core,* and, whereas the normal C12 rebuilding would have had the main apartments in a tower keep, usually on top of the original motte, at Farnham they were arranged boldly around a triangular courtyard beneath it. As far as can be seen, the top of the keep originally never contained more than rudimentary chambers, to be used in an emergency.‡ Thus, when the keep was slighted after being defended by Denham in the Civil War, the apartments were largely undamaged. Later additions merely augmented the pattern: C13 chapel enlargement, outer walls and ditch, big brick tower 1470–5 on the SE side,§ new elevation to the hall and new chapel *c.*1670, new stables in the outer bailey *c.*1700, and a few – mercifully few – mild late C19 alterations in the W–E range.

The KEEP is an irregular polygon – twenty-three-sided, simply following the shape of the motte as closely as possible; without windows, and now without anything above motte level

---

* Which must incidentally have been almost impervious to sapping.

‡ Though a suite of rooms was built there in the C14 – a chapel in 1339, a hall in 1351–2, etc.

§ The dating, in opposition to the late date hitherto accepted, follows the research of Mr M. W. Thompson, published in SAC LVII. Most of the text has been revised in accordance with his suggestions.

except on the entrance side, which has the remains of a gateway-tower patched up with C16 diapered brickwork. The masonry is clunch with repairs all round the base in freestone. There is a splendid view into the courtyard from the stairs immediately under the gatehouse, which emphasizes the domesticity which is the memorable thing about Farnham.

The C12 apartments consisted of a hall in the S range, a chapel in the SW corner of the courtyard, and kitchens beyond. The E must have contained the main living quarters, but due to the alterations nothing can now be said with certainty. The HALL must have been a splendid room – and an extraordinary one; for it had wooden arcades and presumably a huge lean-to roof covering both 'nave' and 'aisles'. The N arcade disappeared in the C17 alterations, the S arcade was embedded in later walling where one square pier and its capital can still be seen inside a cupboard, a pier with a plain many-scalloped capital, just like the local masonry style. Two more were discovered in C19 alterations. At the W end a doorway leads to the kitchens, another odd C12 piece – this time of *c.*1190 – with jamb shafts and shaft-rings, and capitals with leaf-crockets supporting a segmental arch, clearly not a later alteration. To the l. and r. of this lavish doorway are small doorways – the arrangement which became standard in English halls in the C14, when the side doors led into buttery and pantry and the middle door into the kitchen. The middle doorway here is however so sumptuous that such a purpose would be surprising. Did the same doorway also give access to the chapel? The Kitchen (with five lancet windows to the S) lies in fact to the WSW of the Hall and the Old Chapel to the WNW.

The OLD CHAPEL has C12 windows (round-headed lancets) in the S side. A N aisle was added in the C13 (two bays, fat circular piers, circular abaci, double-hollow-chamfered arches) and later removed, so that the blocked arcade can be seen from the courtyard as well. It can be accurately dated – 1254 – and is a useful guide to similar work in Surrey. Round piers, round capitals with simple roll-mouldings and no other carving, and complex roll-moulded arcades, convex–concave–double convex.

The outer walls were built or rebuilt in freestone in 1340–2, the masons being *Robert Goseden* and *Robert le Hone*, with a small gatehouse, now altered and bearing a pretty Gothick cupola. Then in 1470–5 Bishop Waynflete built a TOWER on 23 to the S side of the castle, the most striking feature in a distant

view (where the proportions are altered through the upper
half only being visible above trees).* It is a splendid piece of
brick design, now with C18 segment-headed windows which
alter the patterning but make the sense of the brickwork even
stronger. Several of the original windows remain, bricked up.
It is extraordinarily sophisticated architecture – it makes
Hampton Court, in the same idiom, look like *nouveau-riche*
ostentation. Bishop Waynflete was evidently building a false
keep, though the idea may never have been conscious, with
false machicolations, and even shallower mouldings below the
parapet of the semi-octagonal turrets at each end (again turrets
too shallow to have served their original military purpose of
enfilade). The four-centred entrance arch is self-consciously
off centre, dovetailed into the base of one of the turrets with
alarming suavity: something which no other English building
now extant attempted. The design has no close equivalent;‡
comparison with other brick gatehouses shows how subtly
and suavely detailed it is. There is a sense in which it is more
Renaissance than the gauche ornamental system of a gatehouse
like that of Layer Marney.

Much repair was necessary after the Civil War. £10,000
were spent before 1684 to provide a new front to the Great
Hall. This is dated 1677. Slightly later, judging by its style, a
new staircase was built E of the hall and a sumptuous refurnish-
ing of the chapel undertaken.

The refronting of the GREAT HALL is a startlingly brusque
and plain piece of brickwork with segment-headed windows
in simple brick surrounds without other ornament, the kind of
effect that the Office of Works obtained more ostentatiously in
the 1720s. The brick surrounds are basically an Artisan motif,
and the designer for all this may possibly be a City of London
mason of the calibre of the designers of the post-Fire City
Halls. The one detail on this front which remains a mystery is
the remains of stone arcading at the Hall level. Was it a gallery
of the late C17 ? It cannot be, because the l. arch is cut into by
the late medieval brick tower. Can it have been C12 ? Hardly,
as the wooden arcading inside would make an open gallery in
this position (as at Durham Castle at the same time) rather
draughty.

The STAIRCASE is up-to-date, big-boned work of about

---

* The tower has until recently been erroneously attributed to Bishop Fox.
‡ The obvious place to look at is Esher (*see* p. 222), but the character of this
is quite different.

1680, with bowls of fruit on the newel posts. The CHAPEL is a superb refitting with Wren-style woodwork, not well enough known, and now without its reredos. Bold panelling, each bay separated from the next by the same design of a cherub with folded wings above a long vertical swag of fruit: for once the inevitable attribution to *Grinling Gibbons* might not be far from the truth. The work is as up-to-date as that of the staircase, technically superb but mass-produced. Each panel is identical.

In the grounds NE of the castle, the C17 RANGER'S HOUSE, brick, of five by two bays with hipped roof and eaves cornice, but ogee-headed windows with stucco surrounds on the first floor.* Recently restored.

TOWN HALL, corner of The Borough and Castle Street. Built in 1930–4 by *Harold Falkner*, to replace a brash Victorian building, in the interests of the unity of Castle Street. Neo-Georgian, inevitably, and rather pedestrian, but hard to criticize when it was done from such good motives at a time when all public buildings were Neo-Georgian anyway. Attached to it on the E side is the BAILIFFS HALL, built in 1674 in a violent last fling of Artisan brickwork, using the same jerky patterns as the houses in Godalming High Street. Only the side is original (there is an easily recognized change of brickwork); the front is a 'creative reconstruction' of 1934 by *Falkner*, a brilliant bit of expertise, far better than his Neo-Georgian, giving a delightful composition of niches and shaped gables. Before the 1930s, the site also included a half-timbered BANK of 1868 by *Norman Shaw*, and one characteristic brick chimney remains from this, sailing serenely above the Bailiffs Hall and making a very good match.

⟨WEST SURREY COLLEGE OF ART AND DESIGN, Borelli 94 Gardens. By the County Architect, *R. J. Ash*, 1967–9. A consciously functional, carefully thought out, and excellently detailed building, which creates a serious mood all its own. The first impression is austere: the building looks inward, and from the road all that is visible is long brick walls of a rich red with deeply raked joints, and a glimpse of the sharply angled workshop roofs behind. Effective entrance, with the porch roof neatly tucked between a two-storey block on the r., and an impressive round-ended staircase and water tower of plain brick on the l. Inside, a broad, light spine corridor leads l., connecting the workshops, between which there are small

* Nigel Temple considers that these windows are not later C18 alterations, but original, and thus 'pre-Gothick'.

courtyards. To the r. of the entrance, behind the two-storey block, is a spacious oblong court or cloister, with a covered walk on thin black supports. Behind this on the l. rises the sharp black zigzag of the workshop roofs, made of triangular steel trusses which provide a series of northern skylights. The court has been landscaped, with a sunken area and trees in the centre. The red brick was chosen to be in keeping with Farnham traditions, but the dark colours, together with the sharp angles and plain expanses of wall, add up to a style that is completely one of the sixties, and whose sources have of course nothing to do with Georgian Farnham but much with C19 industrial buildings – an interesting example of the change of spirit that has occurred in local authority architecture in the county within the last ten years.

This older approach is still illustrated by the POLICE STATION in Longbridge, by the former County Architect, *J. Harrison*, completed in 1963. Opposite the School of Art, OLD PEOPLE'S HOMES by the County Architect, *R. J. Ash*, 1967–9; two storeys, dark red brick relieved by some white boarding. S of East Street, tucked away behind the cinema, is a new HEALTH CENTRE, also by *R. J. Ash*, 1967–8. Three storeys, with attractively textured surfaces of curved tiles between windows with dark mullions. It groups surprisingly successfully around a lawn with a cedar tree with BRIGHTWELLS, an early C19 house with two canted bays and hipped roof.⟩

⟨FARNHAM GRAMMAR SCHOOL, Morley Road. In a stout Queen Anne style. 1906 by *Jarvis & Richards*. David Watkin⟩

HOSPITAL (former WORKHOUSE), on the Aldershot road. Very plain red brick classical, built *c.*1770, nine-bay centre and two-bay wings with mansard roof and dormers. Looks like a big C18 Surrey mill. New buildings in progress (1969) by *Derek Walker & Partners* and *B. W. East*.

Farnham's plan is very simple. The basis is one long street running E–W, and the narrow core or neck of this is a short piece called The Borough. West and East Streets are its continuation, Downing Street runs off S to the churchyard at its W end, South Street runs off similarly at its E end, and Castle Street, the former market place, runs N from its middle up to the castle. The impressive bits are N and W, and the humble bits were S and E. (Much of East Street has now been rebuilt.) The built-up area is in fact a landscape sandwich between the castle park on the N and the Wey on the S, a contrast which is still waiting to be exploited. To start with THE BOROUGH

itself, at the w end Nos. 4–6 on the N side are typically Farnham: partly original Georgian and partly *Horace Field*, e.g.
the careful front of No. 5 and the bow window shop-fronts of
No. 6 (the serpentine cornices are original). Opposite on the
s side the SPINNING WHEEL, a half-timbered front of *c.*1600
with a complex pattern of quatrefoils and three oriels. The
eye can recognize that the design corresponds to most of what
was there originally and it can recognize that it is not a bad
design, but the restored texture is so repellent that the building
as a whole seems valueless. Better by far the WESTMINSTER
BANK'S Italianate front slap on the axis of Castle Street and
the tallest building in the view s from the castle. Five bays
and three huge storeys under a huge cornice. The E part is
1865, but altered when the w part was added in 1904 by *Cheston
& Perkin*. E of this BORELLI'S, with a good early C19
shop-front and a very pretty yard beside it, tile-hung and
creeper-grown, the best of the Farnham yards. Then the BUSH
HOTEL of *c.*1840 or later, still Georgian, stock-brick with big
eaves. Beyond, EAST STREET continues for nearly a mile with
some old houses but nothing of real interest. ⟨The N side,
from Bear Lane onwards, has been completely rebuilt by *W. H.
Robbins & Associates*, 1966–9, as shops, offices, and flats. Some
attempt has been made to avoid a monolithic block by setting
back some of the frontages and using varied colours and surfaces, but the details are distressingly fussy, and the total effect
is still heavy and out of scale with the centre of the town.⟩ The
SEVEN STARS is an over-restored half-timber house, and No.
29, opposite this, is a plain front which still uses segment-
headed windows (though probably dating from soon after
1839: N. Temple). At the far end of East Street is ZINGARI
TERRACE, which looks early C19, but is in fact of 1861 by the
local builder *W. Birch*.

SOUTH STREET starts beside the Bush Hotel. (It was originally
New Road, connecting the town centre to the railway.) The
only building worth notice is the LIBERAL CLUB, and that
only for the name of its architect: *Lutyens*. It has a skittish
front, with alternating triangular and segmental first-floor
pediments, a careless slapdash design, but interesting, because
Nigel Temple has discovered that it was designed in 1894, and
so is an early case of Lutyens using a 'Queen Anne' effect.
(Behind it, public SWIMMING POOL with a remarkable entrance of 1897 in Lutyens's style, in fact by the twenty-two-
year-old *Harold Falkner*. Big round arch in a wall of hand-

made mottled brick. NT) The rest of South Street is just keeping-in-keeping Neo-Georgian, apart from the RURAL DISTRICT COUNCIL OFFICES by *H. Paxton Watson*, *c.* 1905, which has lively brick chimneys and stone carving.

CASTLE STREET runs N from the centre of The Borough, a perfect example of English unity-in-diversity, sweeping up to the S side of the castle, which is seen above trees, and then side-stepping at the last moment. Its effect is far more a matter of glowing vernacular bricks and repeated white reveals than of formal architectural design. On the W side first No. 5, big, early C19, still in the Farnham brick tradition, three storeys with big eaves, then No. 8 of 1869–70, with the tradition broken at last, Italianate and stuccoed, built by a local man, *Goddard.* Next to it No. 9 has an C18 brick façade in front of earlier timber-framing. No. 10 is an altered early C18 house, set back and detached. Then the whole of the rest of this side – Nos. 12–42 – is at what might be called a level of inspired ordinariness rare even in England: quite unselfconsciously, houses of 1750–1850 combine into something far more impressive than any individual building and at least as impressive as many of the much more consequential formal C18 effects on the Continent. The points to notice are the taut rise and fall of the roof-line, the colour pattern given by the occasional inflections of stucco in the predominant brick, and the fact that street angles and heights are never quite the same. A few individual details augment but do not dominate this anonymous masterpiece. No. 20 is delicate late C18 with a Doric doorcase, Nos. 32–33 are just pre-Victorian (the MHLG date is 1840) with mouldings that are thick but still severe. More than half of the upper end of this group is in fact Victorian. The sequence ends with No. 42, which looks like a converted Non-conformist chapel, five by two bays with a timid central pediment.

Crossing over from here to the E side there is more architecture but less charm. At the N end is CASTLE HILL HOUSE, probably of *c.*1760, with some additions. Five by two bays, no ornament apart from the doorcase and two string-courses – the pattern for London houses of the period but not usually for provincial ones: at York or Bristol there would be much more ornamental detail. Then comes No. 44, GUILDFORD HOUSE, a similar shape but stuccoed. With an ogee-roofed gazebo-like projection on the first floor, with Gothick glazing bars, probably early C19. Another one on the garden side. No. 45 is

another plain house with Doric doorcase. Further down No.
49 is reproduction work, a trap for the unwary: a very good
imitation by *A. J. & L. R. Stedman, c.*1929. After that comes
the NELSON ARMS, a humble roughcast pub, and the
WINDSOR ALMSHOUSES of 1619, for 'eight poor, honest, old
and impotent persons'. The homely gables of the almshouses
come as a shock among the Georgian urbanity: the town has
outgrown it (it was in scale in mid-c18 views). Tudor Gothic
of one and a half storeys (i.e. attic rooms in the gables) with
four plain gables above pairs of windows tied together by
hood-moulds, and a central stepped gable. This is the standard
Home Counties style for almshouses, not a very attractive
brand compared with the Cotswolds or Yorkshire, and not a
particularly good example of it. The back is a pattern of chimneys and lean-tos. Three plane trees have been planted in front
– the only trees in the street – as though to carry the street-line
through. Back to urbanity with No. 61, a good late c18 front
with a lot of individuality. Three bays on the ground floor and
five bays above. The central first-floor window has a semicircular head; below, a Doric doorcase and segmental arcading
framing the ground-floor bays. Perhaps the same designer as
No. 90 West Street. No. 62 next door is slightly earlier, and
the doorcases are an instructive comparison, the latter an
honest pattern-book design, the former full of delicacy and
inventiveness. Thereafter a sober minor run. The CASTLE
CAFÉ is c17 and tile-hung like a Weald cottage, No. 70 is
severest Palladian, and the street ends on the corner of The
Borough with Town Hall Buildings.

WEST STREET starts from the w end of The Borough. The s
side starts with the FARNHAM DAIRY, No. 12, Late Georgian
with an original shop-front, then ELPHICK'S, a more circumstantial design, almost certainly of 1776 (N. Temple), three
storeys with two lunettes on the top floor, ruined by its shop-
front. No. 20 is late c18. The ground-floor shop has a ceiling
of *c.*1670 like a miniature saloon – a central oval inscribed in
an oblong, i.e. a debased version of Inigo Jones ceilings of the
1630s. There are still a few strapwork flourishes in the oval,
but the detail otherwise is mostly vegetable. The character
very similar to the later ceilings at Slyfield House. Nos. 23–24
are dated 1790, delicately done with a distinctive frieze of
rosettes and fluting, near enough to No. 90 to be by the same
mason. Then comes VERNON HOUSE, originally a c16 half-
H-shaped house, completely redone in the c18 or later with

sash windows and cement-stucco (perhaps in 1727, the date on the drainpipe heads). The courtyard is closed by late C18 iron gates. Beyond again, after a demure stretch, are the show houses of Farnham, side by side: Willmer House of 1718 and Sandford House of 1757, both showing exactly the same sort of social and architectural provenance but done in two different styles. WILLMER HOUSE is towering all-over Baroque, the windows and wall decoration almost indivisible. Five by three bays with giant rusticated Doric pilasters at the ends, thick surrounds to the windows, segmental on the first floor (just as at Old House Weybourne, which was probably built by the same mason), straight-headed on the other floors. Doorcase with pilasters and the favourite London masons' motif of a central upward cusp in the architrave. This is one of the finest cut brick façades in the country considered as craftsmanship, but it remains an exasperating design: with everything emphasized the total effect stays as it would be if the façade was quite plain. The intention seems to have been to turn the whole front into one indivisible unit,* but it has not succeeded and remains a bewildering and rather forbidding *tour de force*. The vocabulary could just have come from London buildings like the newly laid-out terraces near Hanover Square, but is even so remarkable. ⟨The house is now FARNHAM MUSEUM. The interior has splendidly carved original panelling: in the hall an elaborate archway with Ionic pilasters and entablature with flowers and strapwork, and another archway between front and back rooms with Corinthian pilasters and carved spandrels. Fine oak staircase with turned balusters, decorated string, and ogee mouldings beneath the steps.⟩ Next door, SANDFORD HOUSE shows the very end of provincial Baroque (and by 1757 Strawberry Hill was half-built and Kent was dead), with most of the details taken from Gibbsian pattern books, but the effect still not Palladian. Also five-bay and three-storey. Correct Doric doorcase enclosing a segmental rusticated lintel, the cornice a frieze with rosette pattern, and a central single-bay split pediment. Again not quite successful; impressive but cold-hearted. The garden front has a good Regency veranda. Beyond on this side No. 40 is another indis-

---

* i.e. the Continental way of designing Baroque façades, attempted also in buildings like Stoneleigh Abbey, Chatsworth, and Moor Park; something quite different both from Wren's basically Palladian house-designs of carefully related solid and void and Vanbrugh's more deeply Baroque compositions in space.

tinguishable reproduction front by *Falkner*, and No. 41, a very
delicately detailed house of *c*.1780-5, five-bay and two-storey,
the ground floor arcaded, with a delicate frieze with roundels.
Like No. 90, and very like Mylne at his best. The inside is
mid-C19.

Opposite here the N side is cosy two- and three-storey cottagey
Georgian. Then, going back towards the centre, Nos. 88-94,
the best formal group in Farnham, all plain houses of 1760-84
(except No. 94, typically clever Farnham keeping-in-keeping*),
plain except for doorcases and thin cornices but with splendidly urbane smooth brickwork. This is English C18 town housing
at its very best – not a regimented best either, be it noted, as a
list of the main characteristics will show: No. 88 is of five by
three bays, Doric doorcase; No. 89 three by three bays; No.
90 five by two bays, very delicate, of *c*.1780, with central semi-
circular-headed window, the same hand as No. 61 Castle
Street; Nos. 91-92 a symmetrical three-storey pair; and No.
93 five bays and two storeys with eaves cornice and simple
bracketed doorcase. There is nothing so good as this further E.
The SURREY & HANTS NEWS office is a malthouse of *c*.1840,
with two-storey brick arcading, originally blind, converted by
Falkner to incorporate a superb tall shop-front with a complex
history. It is apparently a C19 copy of an C18 front in Cornhill,
now in the Victoria and Albert Museum, and came from Old
Broad Street, London. It has both Adam details and a Gothick
cornice. A door at each side, the l. hand one a replica made
when the front was inserted, two windows in the centre.
Further along the former LION AND LAMB, close-timbered
with brick infilling, dated 1537 on a brick panel under the
entry, but hopelessly restored. First-floor gallery facing the
inn yard. Finally No. 118 is a stucco front of *c*.1840, of no
value, said to be by *Harding*, a local surveyor. If so, a good
many more Farnham houses are also his: WOOLWORTHS' in
The Borough, for example.

DOWNING STREET starts with a pretty oblique view towards the
church down Upper Church Lane. Opposite a lane leading to
IVY HOUSE, still with something like its old gardens.‡ Half-H-
shaped, late C17, much altered. From here the street is mainly
Georgian. On the E side Nos. 46-47 is a five-bay pair of late
C18 houses, front doors flanked by Doric columns under an
extraordinarily stretched segmental fanlight with Adam detail.

* Actually as early as 1895 and by *H. Paxton Watson* (NT).
‡ The gardens have now been turned into a car park.

No. 49, probably of the same date, is much duller, with a Late Palladian doorcase. On the other side nothing until the road turns the corner and No. 4 closes the view from The Borough; huge early C19, five by three bays, big Doric porch, red brick. The street then runs E. No. 3 on the s side is another Farnham-Baroque house, of five by two bays with a lot of rubbed brick, cornice, and a central frontispiece with a bracketed doorcase, simple surround to the window above, and small pediment above that carrying the date 1717. Characteristic but not very nice because of the lumpish proportions. Next to this, set back, No. 2 has a very mannered stock-brick front of c.1860, possibly by *W. Birch*, recessed at the corners to give two big lugs below each end of the cornice. Recessed centre for the doorcase also, with rusticated splays, a weird effect. Big windows on the ground floor, and a central segment-headed window above the entrance, a throwback to a Baroque idea.

s of the Wey is another nucleus of battered old houses, surprisingly grim to those who think that Surrey Georgian was always urbane and smooth; these could come from any Midland town. Facing N at the end of Firgrove Hill is the WILLIAM COBBETT, Cobbett's birthplace, and much more attractive than most birthplaces. Simple late C17 brick range of four bays with a C16 half-timbered gable at the w end, not over-restored. Firgrove Hill also contains the other thing in FIRGROVE COTTAGE, a C16 cottage with quite an elaborate central gable – decorated not with complex framing but with carved bargeboards and beams, terribly restored. Between road and river is a good brewery, THE MALTINGS, with simple industrial buildings in glowing vermilion brick. The river frontage is of c.1902, the sw wing is earlier, and was formerly a tannery. It was threatened with demolition, but instead it is now to be converted into a concert hall and community centre – an excellent scheme. Near by in BRIDGE SQUARE No. 12 has been found to incorporate a late C15 hall.*

w of Downing Street is CHURCH LANE, making a loop into the churchyard and back. LOWER and MIDDLE CHURCH LANES are the best in Farnham to see unrestored cottage architecture of the C17 to the mid C19. Middle Church Lane faces the churchyard. The only house worth individual mention is the RECTORY, with a plain five-bay brick front of c.1740 with C19 porch and dormers. On the s side of the churchyard the demure tile-hung elevations of the OLD VICARAGE conceal a

* Mrs W. O. Manning kindly supplied this information.

good deal of a medieval house provided as a guest-house for pilgrims. Medieval bargeboard to the gable outside, and collar-beam roof inside.

THE GRANGE, NW of Farnham Castle. A very handsome and sober medium-size brick house dated 1710. Five by two bays and two storeys with bracketed cornice and very intricate cut brickwork mouldings on the first-floor centre window on the garden side. No real correspondence with any of the other Farnham Baroque houses. Inside, a tiny staircase treated on a huge scale with painted walls and ceiling, attributed to *Thornhill.*

MOOR PARK, 1½ m. E, *see* p. 372; CROOKSBURY HOUSE, 2 m. E, *see* p. 175.

(At DIPPENHALL, 1 m. NW on the Hants border, *Harold Falkner* built, with his own hands and the help of two labourers, nine houses, mostly in a whimsical free Tudor vernacular. Several incorporate genuine timber-framed buildings brought from elsewhere. The first was begun in 1921, the last was incomplete at his death in 1963. In chronological order they are: The Barn, Deans, Overdeans Court, Meads, Halfway House, Burles, Burles Lodge, Grovers Farm, and Black Barn. Burles, completed in 1937, consists of two barns from Gloucestershire placed end to end, making, according to Falkner, the longest overhang in England.*)

MESOLITHIC SETTLEMENT. Near Bourne Mill is the site of an important Mesolithic settlement of the Horsham Culture, excavated in 1929–47. The pit dwellings cut in the gravel overlying Upper Greensand are of similar type to those at Abinger.

CHARLESHILL. The Burrows are five much overgrown BARROWS, including one bowl.

CAESAR'S CAMP. A large Iron Age HILL-FORT, mainly in Hampshire. To the SE the defences are single, while on the level ground to the W they are double. Recent military activity has obliterated much of what was once a fine monument.

ROMAN WAY HOUSING ESTATE. An extensive POTTERY WORKS was in operation here from the C2 to the early C5 A.D. An aqueduct or open ditch was dug from the upper waters of the Bourne to the kilns. About 250–300 a bath house was constructed for the workers; at the end of the period this needed buttressing, and an apsidal plunge bath was also added. In the early C4 a manager's house with its own bath and an

---

* These details are all from Nicholas Taylor's article in the *Architectural Review*, February 1968.

upper storey was built, and the remains of this have been
preserved in the estate. The site seems to have been abandoned
in the C5.

For Hale and Heath End, now more or less northern suburbs of
Farnham, *see* p. 294.

FELBRIDGE
1 m. NW of East Grinstead, Sussex

ST JOHN. 1865 by *William White*, rubble Wealden stone in the
Dec style. Hard going outside, but the inside well proportioned, well detailed, and, unexpectedly, well carved.

FELBRIDGE PLACE. Mostly stock-brick of 1860, and that very
much altered, but inside an C18 staircase and Early Victorian
dining room (MHLG). *Soane*'s memorial COLUMN of 1785 was
moved from here to Lemington, Northumberland, in the
1930s.

FETCHAM
1 m. SW of Leatherhead

Dispirited fag-end of Leatherhead, the start of the characterless
chain of suburbanization that follows road and railway all the
way to Guildford. The ghost of countryside still visible.

ST MARY. A slow-growth medieval church, moderately restored.
The earliest parts are the W quoins of the formerly aisleless
nave and the wall above the S arcade with one deeply splayed
window with Roman brick dressings. They are probably C11
and probably pre-Conquest. The arcade itself, although rebuilt in the mid C19, is straightforward late Norman of *c.*1150,
with circular piers, square, large-scale, many-scalloped capitals, square abaci, and slightly chamfered round arches (cf.
Great and Little Bookham): a simple job well done. Perhaps of
the same date the base of the tower (at the E end of the S aisle),
with two round-headed windows to the S and a partly filled
in C13 arch opening into the chancel on the N. Chancel and N
transepts are C13. In the N transept very fine E wall with two
lancets flanking a lower and broader recess for an altar. This is
distinguished by dog-tooth enrichment. Simple S arch from the
N transept with two slight chamfers. To the l. of the chancel
arch a C13 recess, also for an altar. A little later, say *c.*1320–30,
the tall two-light N window of the N transept. The N arcade of
two bays is Dec, with octagonal piers and arches and con-

tinuous mouldings. A great surprise, the arch shapes beautifully smooth and subtle, the appearance of having been designed for a church four times the size. E window Perp. Tower top mid-C18 in simple builder's flint and brick without any recognizable classical detail. – MONUMENTS. Antony Rous † 1631. Standard pretty frame, well carved corpse with hourglass underneath. – Henry Vincent † 1631. Frontal praying bust, stock surround. – Tablet to John Bolland † 1829, by *Sievier*. Early C19 Grecian, richly done without sentimentality, a welcome change. – Robert Sherson † 1821, by *Rouw*, a similar effect, much more meaty than the 1820 average. Enfiladed urns in low relief above the inscription.

FETCHAM PARK. The outside looks all very ugly *c.*1870-classical by *I'Anson Jun.*, but is in fact a voracious remodelling of a plain brick and stone eleven-bay house built by *William Talman*, 1705–10, for Arthur Moore, M.P., a director of the South Sea Company. This has been treated in the most extraordinary way; terracotta inserts of swags and keystones, a pavilion-roofed French-looking porch in the middle of the E front, and a semicircular pedimented attic added to the centre of the W front. Also additions to N and S, the former incorporating competent C18-style plasterwork (now the school chapel). The main feature is the painted STAIRCASE, a handsome example of a standard early C18 type – three sides of a rectangle with the landing on the fourth side, as at Hampton Court. For each step one twisted, one fluted, one twisted baluster. The tread-ends and the undersides of the steps are carved. The whole of walls and ceiling painted by *Laguerre*, competent but not much more – not nearly as good as the Reigate Priory staircase. A lot of grisaille work in the hall, and one more ornamented ceiling in the present dining room (in the centre of the W front) with a circular painted centre and dashing coved plasterwork surround, rather Dutch. None of this first rate.

Nothing old remains in the village worth notice (except perhaps that the rambling OLD RISING SUN has for a nucleus a C15 stone hall with kingpost roof). The C20 has contributed only two decent 1930s pubs, the BELL (in the village) and the RISING SUN (on the road to Leatherhead), both concave-fronted, by *Joseph Hill*, 1937, and one modern house with a good representative collection of 1950 clichés, HIGHFIELD on the main A246 road, by *J. Harley*, 1955. The best part is the two-storey garage.

FLEXFORD see WANBOROUGH

FORD MANOR see GREATHED MANOR

FORT BELVEDERE see *The Buildings of England: Berkshire*

0060

FOX HILLS
¾ m. NW of Ottershaw

Originally Fox's Hills, i.e. Charles James Fox's, who planted them. House by *Basevi*, c.1840, in loveless and mean stock brick. Tudor without a single redeeming feature. Basevi, like Decimus Burton, must have been completely indifferent to Gothic architecture. Interiors mainly gutted and replaced in 1923 by clever imitation C18 work, hard to distinguish even at a close look.

0050

FOXWARREN PARK
1 m. W of Cobham

See p. 596 The house was built by *Frederick Barnes* of Ipswich – better known for his East Anglian Jacobean railway stations – in 1860. It is big and violent, with crow-stepped gables and glowing diaper polychrome brickwork throughout. Barnes must also have done the LODGES, the WATCH TOWER in the grounds, FOXHOLM to the N, and in particular the nightmare 71 MODEL FARM beside the Redhill Road. This is three-sided with multiple bargeboarded gables, a cottage in one corner, and brick slits for windows, grouped five or six at a time under crow-stepped gables. This is possibly the extreme example in the country, and is certainly worth seeing. The sinister and neurotic atmosphere comes off all too successfully – usually these Victorian excesses are just a joke – and rivals Soane at his most eerie. The emotional and intellectual level is nowhere near Soane, however.

8040

FRENSHAM

No group. A few estate cottages by the church, and a few more at Millbridge ½ m. NE and at Spreakley ½ m. NW, all on the edge of heathlands between Farnham and Hindhead.

ST MARY. Good, massive W tower, Perp, probably late C14, restored by *Caröe* in 1929. Rubble stone, with huge diagonal

buttresses. The rest was renewed in imitation Dec from one
end to the other in 1868 by *Hähn*. (At this time the N aisle of
1826 was given an E.E. arcade with opulently naturalistic
capitals. R. Hubbuck) The chancel has one lancet on the w
side and the nave has a kingpost roof, but there is nothing else
old: a shocking job. – BOWL. Enormous copper cauldron in
the N aisle, known as Mother Ludlam's; 3 ft wide, on iron
legs. It looks C17. – PLATE. Set, London, 1716. – MONUMENT
(N side of chancel). Puzzling, badly defaced pair of crocketed
pinnacles of *c*.1300. Lush, good quality carving. Presumably
part of a vanished tomb. – VICARAGE. 1896 by *Newton*.

FRENSHAM BEALE MANOR HOUSE, ½ m. SW of the church.
Mainly a big C16 timber-framed house, with C20 additions at
the S end, but the N end is stone-built and was originally the
chapel.

FRENSHAM HEIGHTS SCHOOL, Rowledge, ¾ m. NW of
Spreakley. Brick and stone neo-Tudor, big gables at the w end
balancing a tower at the E. Insensitive, but no less picturesque,
when seen in its setting, than Pierrepont. The architect was a
Mr *Waller*, a 'builder of institutions', who in 1900 remodelled
an earlier neo-Tudor building for Charrington, the London
brewer. (Sumptuous interiors: ballroom with rich plaster
decoration and a 'Jacobethan' hall with huge heavy baronial
fireplace. R. Hubbuck)

(FRENSHAM PLACE (now Edgborough School), 1¼ m. N, is a big
stone mansion with shaped gables of *c*. 1880. The two
COTTAGES by the walled garden are of 1891 by *Lutyens*. NT)

(SHORTFIELD HOUSE, 1 m. N. Of *c*.1885 by *Chuter*, Shaw's
builder at Pierrepont, and in the same style. NT)

¼ m. W of Spreakley is HALL'S PLACE, a restored C17 house
with impressive GATEWAY in the wall facing the road. It was
brought here in 1910 from 'an old manor house near Reading'
and is of *c*.1620, a gauche semicircular pediment between two
Doric pilasters crowned by obelisks and balls. A characteristic
piece of Jacobean display and the sort of fragment that is much
commoner on the Continent than in England.

BARROWS. Four barrows, some of the best in the county, lie on
Frensham Common, between the Great and Little Ponds.
They are of the bowl type.

LOWICKS, 1 m. SE, *see* p. 357; PIERREPONT, ½ m. NE, *see*
p. 413.

FRIDAY STREET *see* ABINGER

FRIMLEY

Small old village on the Hants border, now caught up with light industry, and, like Camberley, with a rapidly expanding population.* The main street had a faint coaching flavour, finally removed completely in 1959–60.

ST PETER. 1825 by *J. T. Parkinson*, the architect of Bryanston and Montagu Squares, London. (Altered in 1881 by *T. Goodchild*. GS) Hard-bitten Perp with a small W tower, and originally a mock pediment, now taken down. All in freestone. Awful institutional interior with later galleries. It replaced a completely half-timbered chapel of 1606. This part of England must have had almost as many timber churches as Cheshire before the C19.

ST ANDREW, Frimley Green. By *H. R. & B. A. Poulter*, 1911. Chubby brick and stone Perp: 'looks as though it was bought at Liberty's' (GR).

FRIMLEY PARK. The present entrance front (W) is early C20, with deep bow windows and a deep porch, attractive in an atmospheric way. The old entrance front (S), which was kept, is of *c*.1780, thin and rather cold-blooded, with a central blind arch enclosing a swag above a blunt Doric doorcase. One by three bays, all stuccoed. *Latrobe* is known to have worked here, and the front might be his; though it is not experimental like his houses at Hammerwood and Ashdown in Sussex, it shows an impatience with (and hence insensitivity in the handling of) Palladian elements typical of a whole group of designers in the 1780s – notably Bonomi and Henry Holland. The inside has late C18 fragments, a late C17 staircase apparently kept from the previous house, and startling Jacobean panelling to the dining room. Part of it screens off an alcove (one of the bays of the W front) with huge barley-sugar columns carrying carved vines.

See p. 598

Few old houses, and most of those killed with kindness. The best is CROSS COTTAGES, Cross Lane, Frimley Green, an L-shaped block with the projecting wing grey and red brick, dated 1713. The rest is a delightful C18 patch-up of materials on a timber frame, vermilion bricks below and slate-hanging above. ⟨E of this, CROSS FARMHOUSE, a long range, timber-framing and brick, C15 and C16. Further S, in THE HATCHES, BEDFORDS FARM, C15, and THE BARN, C17, much altered.⟩

* For recent population figures *see* Camberley, p. 128.

⟨There are few remarkable recent buildings in Frimley. The strangest are those of the MANOR HOUSE development, by *Derek Sharp Associates* (job architect *Laurence Abbott*), 1966–9, on a prominent site at the corner of Frimley Green Road and Church Road. This seems to be an eccentric reaction against standard speculator's vernacular (tile-hung and weatherboarded terraces etc.). Seven white brick blocks, each containing four dwellings. Each block has overhanging upper storeys, half-cylindrical projections, and round-headed and U-shaped windows of different sizes, the explanation for which is difficult to understand. At MYTCHETT, s of Frimley, is an attractive single-storey PRIMARY SCHOOL by the County Architect, *R. J. Ash*. It was built in 1965–6, and like the school at Prior Road, Camberley, was one of the first schools of this type by the County Architect's Department.⟩

YOCKLEY, 1 m. E. Sober classical house by *Sir Reginald Blomfield*, 1901–2, for Charles Furse, A.R.A. Long one-and-a-half storey ranges, brick and roughcast, nicely done. *See* p. 598

BLACKDOWN. *See* p. 112.

FULBROOK   *9040*

½ m. E of Elstead

Compact, medium-size house by *Lutyens*, 1896–9, making the best of its site on a knoll above the river Wey. An uneven building with genius and banality side by side. Mostly in the Tudor style. Competent symmetrical gabled stone entrance front on the W side, pedestrian half-timbered garden front to the S. At the same time, the tile-hung turret which jolts the W front out of balance,* and the (later) pergola attached to it,‡ are masterpieces of sensuous elegance, and the E front is a superb composition in the Norman Shaw style but without Shaw's long-windedness: two tile-hung gables balancing a big square chimneystack, the horizontal rhythms maintained by the outward sweep at the foot of each stretch of tile-hanging. (To the N, an enclosed kitchen court is flanked by two magnificent sweeps of roof. NT) How one architect could put all these things together on one building is almost beyond belief. To cap it all, the interiors are weakly classical, Lutyens's first

---

* It was in fact an afterthought, containing an extra lavatory (NT).

‡ This has been demolished, as part of a general dilution of the gardens (NT).

excursion into a fatal genre.* The planting is original and very good both in the gardens and around the walls and is by the wife of the first owner, *Mrs Gerard Streatfeild*, in collaboration with *Gertrude Jekyll*. There is also a LODGE, designed in 1897, another stroke of genius on a tiny scale. One gable and a very tall bold chimneystack, and delicate arches with typical intermittent voussoirs of tiles, Roman fashion, a miniature Tigbourne (*see* p. 486).

GATTON

2050

House and church only, under the downs N of Reigate, but formerly a borough with an odd and very English history. It was created in 1450 and conferred on Henry VI's steward in order to persuade him to vote Henry's marriage with Margaret of Anjou. It returned two members to parliament until 1832, when, with twenty-three houses, it was the most rotten borough but three in the country. What makes it unique is the urbane irony of the C18 owners, who solemnly erected the Town Hall (*see* p. 252) and set up an inscription deploring the death of the borough in mockromantic style.

68 ST ANDREW. Most counties have one church which has become an involuntary museum from the attentions of someone who went on the Grand Tour with an acquisitive eye. This is Surrey's example. The collector was Lord Monson, the date of his tour the early 1830s. The church itself was originally mostly Perp, and the E window may be original, but it was entirely made over into a picturesque Gothick composition in 1834, probably by *E. Webb*. He must have inserted fragments from other churches, e.g. the tall N window of the N transept (Y-tracery and a transom). There is a covered way from this transept (the private pew, *see* below) to the house, though in very bad condition; it ought to be kept as a rarity. Gothick details, simple outside, altogether lost in the plethora of woodwork inside – plaster wagon roof, seats facing inward as in a college chapel (the only way they would fit). The N transept is an untouched family pew, the perfect example of the English nobleman's wish to worship in comfort. It has a fireplace, panelled overmantel, padded benches, and comfortable chairs.

* (Yet the spatial dynamics of the long hall on the garden front are interesting: the room is divided up by deep moulded beams linking the bay windows to apsidal and straight-ended recesses in the opposite wall. Good fireplaces in dining and drawing rooms. NT)

With its atmosphere of being a sumptuous private chapel that has somehow got detached from the house, it is among the best in the country. – FONT. C13, and presumably *in situ*. Plain octagonal bowl on a central pillar and four attached shafts, all sharing one big foliage capital. – STAINED GLASS. W window with Henry VII's arms; deep rich glazing, but probably dating from *c*.1830. – S nave window probably German, *c*.1600. Saints in a gross scrolly frame. – S transept window with simple armorial glass, but a fancy wood surround to the top of the arch. – S chancel window by *Kempe*, 1879. Everyone praying, as well they might, to a pious Victorian, in these surroundings. – E window rather jumbled, mainly saints under a scrolled canopy; probably late C16. Antwerp Mannerist style. – E window of N transept with Virgin, Child, and donors, Flemish Late Gothic. None of this Continental glass is particularly good of its kind. – WOODWORK. A museum catalogue. W gallery supported by a good thick ROOD SCREEN, C15, thrown out from an English church in the early C19 (which one?). Four-light heads between buttresses, and the usual vine-trail brattishing above, very sturdily carved; more like the screen at Shoreham in Kent than Devon or East Anglia. So perhaps it is local. – NAVE STALLS. Flemish Baroque. Simple carvings ₅₀ under the seats, each arm-rest ending in a cherub's head *à la* Gibbons. Mass-produced and repetitive work; pretty, but designed to be one component in a bigger architectural ensemble. They are from Ghent. – NAVE PANELLING and coving above from Aarschot Cathedral in Brabant, dated 1515, the perfect illustration of the general similarities and detailed differences between the last phase of Gothic in Flanders and England. Here is the same basically Perp motif of ogee heads set against vertical panelling, and the same sobriety, but the carving is much more thistly and wiry, and the tracery heads are filled with Rayonnant motifs such as oculi. Good quality, and especially suited to being a panelled background, as here. – PULPIT, suspended at first-floor level as part of the S transept gallery-front. The carved scenes of *c*.1530 formed part of the same composition as the carvings now made up into the ALTAR TABLE. They are all inevitably attributed to Dürer, but are not German and seem to be Flemish. There is a Descent from the Cross and there was a Crucifixus with assistant figures. – CHANCEL PANELLING, completely surrounding a demure C13 trefoil PISCINA from the original church. From Burgundy. Linenfold below and round matchstick patterns above. – ALTAR RAILS from Tongres in Eastern Belgium. Very thickly detailed, clustered shafts leading to ogee heads under quatrefoils. Probably late C16, in what we would call Gothic Survival. – DOORS from Rouen, in the S transept, carved in linenfold pattern. – CHAIR, in the chancel, Late Gothic, possibly Flemish. – The LECTERN also looks medieval. Where is it from?

GATTON PARK. Originally a confused and indigestible early C19 house of several dates, in the overripe classical style of Belgravia. This was gutted in 1934 and entirely rebuilt by *Sir Edwin Cooper* in 1936 in poor quality Classical Revival, like an Officers' Mess, except for the three-bay centre of the S front, which is quite an expert stirring of the stylistic pudding. Luckily Cooper kept the extraordinary portico with its extraordinary date – 1891 – which forms the N front.* This consists of ten Corinthian columns wrapped round a projecting wing in temple fashion with a pediment above; the blank walls behind retain sober classical detail. The proportions are superb and the execution exquisite – in fact this is the best example in the country, though seventy years late, of what might be called Canova architecture, strictly classical forms handled with humanitarian C19 sensibility. The effect is completed by the delicate polychrome, for the columns are marble and the entablature and pediment are yellow limestone. And undoubtedly – for it is carved into the base of one of the columns – it was 'laid by Jeremiah Colman Junr. 1891'. The architect's name was *Sextus Dyball*, who died in 1888 and is buried in the churchyard.

Behind this there was, before the fire, a Marble Hall of *c*.1830 on the model of the Corsini Chapel in St John Lateran, Rome. Now there is a crashing anticlimax, a mean corridor leading to a small oval entrance hall, all by Sir Edwin Cooper.

TOWN HALL. A very English political joke. Built in 1765. An open Doric temple on a knoll in the park, six columns (of iron incidentally) and a pedimented roof, under which 'elections' (nominations, more accurately) for the rotten borough were solemnly held. In front an urn inscribed 'Stat ductis Sortibus Urna / Salus populi Suprema Lex Esto / Comitium Gattoniense MDCCLXV / H M Dolus Malus Abesto' – that is, 'When the lots have been drawn, the urn remains / Let the well-being of the people be the supreme law / The place of

---

* It was originally far more encumbered than it is now; from the N the rebuilding has done nothing but good.

assembly of Gatton 1746 / Let evil deception be absent.'
Political cynicism could hardly go further, but there may at
the same time have been an element of genuine if hyper-
sensitive melancholy behind it, the exact spirit which pervades
Gray's famous 'Elegy' (written 1751) and Goldsmith's
'Deserted Village'.

The park is now the Royal Alexandra and Albert School. The s
half is untouched, but the N is a travesty of a landscape park
with insensitive modern dormitories, by *Adams, Gray &
Adamson*, 1954, crowding right up to the Town Hall. The
school CHAPEL, 1956 by the same architects, is just a little
better. (Further buildings under construction in 1969.) The N
lodge is Picturesque and thatched, of *c*.1830, the s lodge is
fighting Italianate.

GATWICK AIRPORT 2040
1 m. s of Horley

Old CONTROL TOWER near the railway, 1936 by *Hoar, Marlow
& Lovett*. Circular (hence its name of Martello Airport) and
in the International Style – a neat idea, done quite without
finesse or feeling.

Superseded by the big new buildings by *Yorke, Rosenberg &
Mardall*, 1958, with *T. R. Evans* and *David Allford* in charge.
The main buildings are at the E end of the airfield, where the
new Brighton road and the Brighton railway run next to one
another. This conjunction has been imaginatively used to make
one of the few cases in post-war Britain of expressive function–
i.e. planning that can be seen to be good as well as being good.
The main block is long, three storeys running E–W and 91
spanning both road and railway (a six-storey block of offices
will be added on top of part of it later as part of stage three).
The station tracks are at the E end, and then comes the
Brighton road, with an elegant curved ramp above it leading
to the main entrance and concourse on the first floor. This runs
the whole length of the building and leads to the passenger
exits and a long open roof terrace above offices, jutting out into
the airfield itself. The style used is simple and industrial – a
curtain wall with exposed steel stanchions outside, exposed
concrete columns inside – but done without being either deliberately brutal or artfully over-contrived. The glass panels
under the windows have a pattern of burnt chemical oxides on
them. They were designed by *Peggy Angus* and are very

effective. The inside is less consistent, and internal colours are low-toned – white, black, dark brown – leaving bright colours to the transient things such as advertisements, book displays, passengers' clothes. With all this forethought, the stairs up from the car park are unnecessarily mean.

⟨By 1963 it was found that air traffic at Gatwick was expanding much faster than anticipated, so stage two, completed in 1965, involved some alterations to the original development plan. The main block has been more than doubled in area, and completely replanned internally. The projecting pier is now flanked, as was planned, by N and S piers, which are longer than originally intended. Subsidiary buildings have appeared to the S.⟩

Out in the airfield, to the W, a small CONTROL TOWER, concrete frame and brick infilling, also by *Yorke, Rosenberg & Mardall*; to the S TRANSAIR hangars and offices, straightforward modern, 1957 by *Clive Pascall & Peter Watson*.

GIGGSHILL GREEN *see* THAMES DITTON

GODALMING

Godalming is a rarity among English country towns in that it has no central open space of any sort. There are simply three narrow curving streets meeting at the Market Hall. Perhaps the explanation is that Guildford is only four miles away and that Godalming had been an industrial town (cloth-making) rather than a rural centre. This does not sound an inspired town plan; in fact it is transformed by the quality of the Market Hall, a shapely, smooth early C19 stucco building with an open arcaded ground floor subtly placed so that the curving views are always led through the 'outdoor room' under the market hall and tantalizingly around the corner. The perspectives change continuously as one walks on: the only point of rest, and a delightful one, is under the Market Hall itself. The ground floor was actually only re-opened in 1955 after a long period of use as a Victorian lumber room and public convenience. Godalming deserves full marks for this.

ST PETER AND ST PAUL. Slow-growth medieval church plus C19 restoration, which has taken away much of the character but not the historical interest. External views are impressive because of the huge and handsome lead spire, a rarity in this part of England. It has a complex section of a number of shallow V-shapes formed out of pairs of lead plates. The date is probably c13 (cf. Long Sutton, Lincs.).

The earliest parts of the church were in fact pre-Conquest, though nothing can be seen *in situ* now, except for two blocked double-splayed circular windows in the w wall of the tower, visible from the ringers' chamber. These must have been in the E wall of the nave, above the roof of the pre-Conquest chancel, which was on the site of the present central tower. The former chancel arch remained as the w tower arch until 1879, when it was removed by *R. Nevill.** The Normans built the central tower with simple rectangular slits to the bell chamber, now partly untrustworthy, and also the chancel, cf. the three blocked windows surviving on either side, some with painted decoration on the splays. The E tower arch is also Norman (single-stepped, no chamfers, no ornament), but was raised about 4 ft in 1879. At the w end of the s wall of this Norman chancel one jamb-shaft has been exposed. It is supposed to have belonged to a priest's doorway. Transepts followed in the late c12, together with roughly pointed N and s tower arches, a blocked window at the E end of the s aisle, and a small blocked N doorway (re-set). Of the c13 first the arch between s aisle and transept, still with roll-mouldings not chamfers, then the N and s chancel aisles (short circular piers with circular abaci and two slight chamfers to the arches) and the two E bays of the s arcade (tall circular piers with circular capitals and abaci‡ and double-chamfered arches). The s chancel chapel has traces of blocked wall arcading, the N chapel was rebuilt in 1840. The s chapel was lengthened a little about 1260 and then received its SE window of three equal lancet lights with detached inner shafting of Sussex marble and its interesting E window with Geometrical tracery. It is particularly instructive in that the idea can almost be followed out in the mason's mind: starting with five lancets, the centre one taller than the other four, he put a circle above the outer pairs of lancets, and then a slightly bigger circle on top, resting on the sides of these and the top of the central lancet. This is the best example in Surrey, though admittedly there is not much competition. The Perp doorway below it came from the w end of the nave. c14 work includes the N arcade and a third bay to the nave. The fourth bay is of 1840. The thickness of the two w walls consecutively pulled down is clearly visible. New w

* The designs had been made by *Sir G. G. Scott* before his death in 1878.
‡ The capital of the sw respond has upright leaves standing singly.

end and aisles 1879. – SEDILIA (chancel), Dec with ornamented hoods, and PISCINA (s chancel chapel), c13 and very objective as such pieces often are: a cross-shape like a mullion and transom supported by an octagonal colonnette. Two piscinas below, two aumbries above. – PULPIT. Cut-down Jacobean, similar type to Compton. Poor. – SCULPTURE. Ornamented pre-Conquest stone fragments, very worn, on a tomb-chest in the s chancel chapel. One of them (perhaps c12) is ring-shaped. What was it? – MONUMENTS. Tomb-chest in the s chancel chapel. Probably c14 – see the intricate detail of the roundels on the sides. – Brass to Thomas Purvoche † 1509 and wife. Thoroughly nasty early c16 work. The figures are 12 in. high. – (Brass to John Barlow † 1595, in armour.) – CHANDELIER. In the chancel, made in 1722. Central globe and sixteen candleholders.

On the n side of the churchyard is the PHILLIPS MEMORIAL CLOISTER by *Thackeray Turner*, 1913, to the heroic wireless operator who went down with the Titanic. U-shaped cloister with the end closed by a wall. Very much as Philip Webb might have done it, with all the brickwork and joinery simple. An impressive job. Planting by *G. Jekyll*.

ST EDMUND (R.C.), Croft Road. Low-voltage late Gothic Revival. By *F. A. Walters*, 1906.

CONGREGATIONAL CHURCH, Bridge Street. 1868, with Institute buildings of 1910. Yellow stone, with Gothic turret off centre at the e end. Picturesque from a distance.

MARKET HALL. 1814 by *John Perry*, a local man, and an admirable public building for a small town. As has been said, it plays a fine role in the townscape in the way that it gathers up all the street views, but it is also commendable in itself: polished, never trying to rise above its station, fitting its job exactly. An unequal octagon – three bays on the two long sides, one bay each on the other six. Open arcaded ground floor, plain upper floor, broad eaves cupola above, all smooth stucco. Very much the vocabulary of a Nash villa. Staircase cantilevered out on the n side, presenting an inexplicable backside view to travellers coming up Church Street.

BOROUGH HALL, Bridge Street. Dull Neo-Georgian by *J. H. Norris*, the Borough Surveyor, 1906.

⟨SUB-DIVISIONAL POLICE STATION. By *R. J. Ash*, the County Architect, 1966–8. Ingenious use has been made of the sloping site. A good simple block at the top of the hill, then, behind attractive tall purple brick walls which step down

Wharf Street towards the river, two storeys of flats set up high
on stilts. At either end, prominent concrete staircases, very
Corbusian.⟩

PERAMBULATION. All roads start from the Market Hall, and it
seems easiest to describe them in order from there. To the W
is OCKFORD ROAD, beginning with the POST OFFICE (N
side), big blank C18. Then, after a nondescript stretch of
cinemas, garages, and a Christian Science church, there is first
pleasant tile-hanging and half-timber (No. 14, etc.) and then
came the endearing Nos. 36–52 of c.1830, which from the
road were just four feet of blank brickwork, then roofs and
chimneys. Down a flight of steps and the mystery was explained: a change of level made possible complete two-storey
houses, built into the ground below road level. It is difficult
to imagine a more humane solution, or a less byelaw-minded
one. The houses faced the sun, with pedestrian access and with
gardens falling away further in a gentle curve to the river and
wooded banks beyond. ⟨Alas, they have all been swept away,
except for No. 54 at the end, and replaced by a clumsily
terraced-out garage.⟩ Further W on the same side C16 half-
timber cottages, No. 120 etc., and then FORD'S BUILDINGS,
dated 1801, very happy and unpretentious brick and weatherboarding, the whole group unrestored.

To the N of the market hall runs CHURCH STREET, mostly
cottagey and mostly over-restored. After No. 1, an impressive
but restored C16 timber front with overhang and complete
pattern of panels with curved diagonal braces, the best house
is in fact No. 24, with a dashing mid-C19 classical stucco front.
⟨At the bend, nearer the church, No. 33, THE PRIORY, an
C18 brick façade of two storeys, with a good doorway and a
Venetian window. Earlier timber-framed wing behind.
Opposite, CHURCH HOUSE, timber-framed, C16 with later
alterations including pretty carved bargeboards. In the small
streets to the W – MINT STREET and MILL LANE – more
very minor but genuine C16 and C17 cottages. Also in Mill
Lane, the FRIENDS MEETING HOUSE, a simple C18 brick
building with two windows, central door, and hipped roof.
The whole of this attractive, quiet area is threatened (1969) by
a so-called ring road which would run NE from Ockford Road
across Church Street, cutting the church off from the centre
of the town (despite the fact that Church Street is included
with the High Street in the County Council's list of conservation areas). May a better route be found. Although the High

Street is at present ruined by traffic, it is a poor solution to ruin Church Street instead.⟩

Godalming's main street is HIGH STREET, running E from the Market Hall and starting very typically with the impressive but restored Nos. 99–103, of three storeys, C16, timber-framed with two overhangs, the timberwork almost on a South German scale; no attempt to give an ornamental pattern to the framing. Then on the N side come BOOTS' shop (No. 80) and Nos. 74–76, obviously by the same hand, coming right at the end of the C17 Artisan tradition of brickwork in Surrey, and a deplorable end too. Thick rough cornices, feverish patterns – a flickering polychrome – in brick and stone. All sense of proportion, and even of picturesque outline, is gone. Boots' has two pedimented gables and jostling blind arcades between flat-headed first-floor windows; Nos. 74–76, dated 1663, has an altered top storey but an even more feverish first-floor pattern of ovals and rectangles, accentuated by the ornate C18 glazing bars in the Batty Langley style. The ground floors of both are shops, and they have similar patterning at the back. Both are good fun to have in a town, but nobody could pretend that they are good architecture. No. 59, almost opposite, as it happens teaches a small lesson in patterned façades – the first floor remains of a half-timbered front of *c.*1600 without windows but with curved diagonal braces in the local way. Back on the N side Nos. 58–64 must have been quite an impressive, if gouty, mid-C18 building before four separate and unrelated shop-fronts filled up the ground floor. Giant pilasters and a lunette remain. On the S side Nos. 25–45 is long, simple, early C19 brick 'Improvement', seventeen bays altogether, dated 1836 and keeping some original shop-fronts. Towards the E end of this is a mid-C20 improvement by which a dilapidated court (CROWN COURT) has been ingeniously made into a car park by removing the street house and keeping the half-timbered buildings in the court behind, utilizing the rearward one as an archway. The effect is arty-crafty, but the intention is admirable. Most towns would simply have blasted a hole in the main street. Up Pound Street on the S side yet another improvement in a more hopeful style: simple modern terrace houses built on the sort of restricted site which is normally left derelict. Stock brick and panels of tile-hanging. By *J. M. Ramsay* of Haslemere, 1958. Further along on the S side of the High Street, THE SQUARE, a long, timber-framed, tile-hung and brick house of *c.*1500, set back from the street. On its r., at the side of No. 13, is a minor shaped-gabled front of Artisan brickwork at its most Dutch, with shouldered window surrounds (as at Ripley) to ground floor and attic. Opposite is the KING'S ARMS, a grand mid-c18 coaching inn, more Berkshire than Surrey, with its grizzle bricks, central split pediment, and segmental windows. The date is 1753, the intention still Baroque. The street continues with some dreadful new shops, and then in a nondescript cottagey way as BRIDGE STREET. The BRIDGE itself is of 1783, the same heavy type as Cobham and also by the County Surveyor, *Gwilt*.

To the N, around Charterhouse School (*see* p. 143), medium-size mid and late Victorian houses, with RED HOUSE in Frith Hill Road by *Lutyens*, 1897–9, an irregular keep-like mass on a steep hill in simplified Tudor, a little like Edgar Wood's pioneer house at Stafford. It was built for an invalid, and hence has a very wide top-lit ramp-like staircase. It is a lot better than many of Lutyens's more famous houses. (The drawing-room and dining-room fireplaces are a significant contrast: the former a dynamic baroque composition of niches, miniaturized, the latter among the first of Lutyens's routine Neo-Georgian. The garden was by *Miss Jekyll*. NT) At the S end of Frith Hill Road a brick and stone WATER TOWER with, appropriately, the materials patterned as subtly as Lutyens would have done. ⟨CLIFFHANGER, Frith Hill, by *Michael Manser Associates*, 1963. Aptly named. A single-storey, steel-framed house which looks as if it is floating in the trees.⟩

NW beyond the station is MEATH HOME, formerly Westbrook Place, of seven bays and three storeys, the end bays brought forward and embellished. The embellishments are now largely of *c*.1850, but were carried out on a c18 framework – see the top-storey lunettes, e.g. (The c18 house was built *c*.1770 for the Gotbold family. The interior is mostly c19, but the staircase is of *c*.1770, with original plaster ceiling. Near by is LITTLE FORT, a small two-storey castellated tower, later enlarged, built in the early c18 by the Jacobite Oglethorpe family who lived at Westbrook Place. MHLG) To the N again is WESTBROOK, built by *H. Thackeray Turner* for himself in 1900. It is a house as comfortable and free from period allusion as anything Lutyens or Voysey were building at the time, with in addition a distinctive masculine rough-hewn overtone which makes Lutyens seem a little fussy. All Bargate stone. Entrance front L-shaped, with a heavy rustic Doric porch and, incidentally, the Voysey trade-mark of elegant scrolled

brackets as drainpipe supports. The garden front is quite
asymmetrical.

(NORTHBROOK, Hurtmore Road. A sizeable villa of *c.*1830.
Pediment and giant pilasters. Extensions of *c.*1880. Elaborate
little DAIRY of *c.*1893 by *Lutyens*, half-timbered with big
dormers. Further on, in Hurtmore, MONKSWOOD, 1912 by
Forsyth & Maule, with a *Jekyll* garden. NT)

FARNCOMBE. *See* p. 229.

FARNCOMBE. *See* p. 229.

3050

GODSTONE

Godstone village stretches along the main Eastbourne road, with
a first-rate square village green, spoilt neither by the main road
traffic nor by being only nineteen miles from London. The
church lies ½ m. off, up in the hills amid trees, with a picturesque
cluster of houses around.

ST NICHOLAS. Mostly C19, but with bits of a Norman window
set into the w wall next to the doorway. The N aisle is of *c.*1845,
the s aisle dates from the great and fanciful restoration undertaken in 1872–3 by *Sir G. G. Scott*, who lived at Rooknest (*see*
Ouborough, below). He added the s aisle, heightened the spire
on the picturesque SE tower with its shingled clock stage and
bell-openings stage, opened the nave roof, and refitted the
interior. – FONT. Octagonal, Perp, with pointed quatrefoil
panels. – STAINED GLASS. E window by *Ward & Hughes*,
*c.*1865. – PLATE. Chalice and Paten 1748; Flagon 1794; Spoon
assigned to the C17. – MONUMENTS. Sir John Evelyn † 1641.
White and black marble with recumbent effigies. – James
Evelyn † 1793, by *John Bingley* of London. With the usual
standing mourning woman. – Mrs Smith † 1794. Urn with
garland; pretty (chancel s side). – Barbara St Clair Macleay
† 1869. By *S. Summers*. Reclining effigy.

Immediately s of the church ST MARY'S HOMES, 1872 by
Sir G. G. Scott. A very picturesque timber-framed job, one-
and two-storeyed, with unequally projecting wings, including
a chapel with a flèche. Scott was at his best in such relaxed
work. (The chapel has a delightful un-Scottish interior: half-
timbered domestic nave with fireplace; neo-Norman chancel
and arch. D. Lloyd)

Opposite the almshouses a nice group of houses, including one
of the C18 with chequerboard brickwork and one timber-
framed cottage. On the way down to the village the OLD
PACK HOUSE – an exceedingly pretty timber-framed gabled

house with projecting wings, one of them with oversailing upper floor.

In the village the CLAYTON ARMS, opposite the village pond. Well preserved timber-framed building with courtyard. The structure C16, but much C18 alteration. Noteworthy also the BELL HOTEL, early C18 with an earlier wing at the back.

OUBOROUGH (formerly Rooksnest). Seven-bay Georgian house with portico of four Ionic columns carrying a balcony. The house was the home of Sir G. G. Scott in the early seventies.

(OLD RECTORY, SE of the church. Stuccoed, c.1800. Three-storey centre with pointed windows. Arthur Oswald)

GOMSHALL
1 m. E of Shere

Largely a collection of Victorian cottages along A25. The two buildings of interest lie to the S and are separated from the village by a railway embankment. To the W is MALTHOUSE COTTAGES with a big half-timbered gable, the detail unattractive and restored but authentic, made up of diagonal curved braces of the local type of Great Tangley Manor. To the E is the MANOR HOUSE, with an elegant plain five-bay brick front of c.1720 and an off-centre Doric porch. Red and grey bricks, the type standard anywhere near the chalk areas of England.

On the main road at the W end an odd early C19 LODGE with a big pediment and portico. The front wall behind has heavily rusticated surrounds, the pediment is filled with logs in patterns – a mild Picturesque aberration.

GRAFHAM
2 m. NW of Cranleigh

ST ANDREW. Apsed chapel of 1861–4, designed and paid for by *Woodyer*.* He lived in and designed GRAFHAM GRANGE near by, which was built from 1854, but the house was altered by *A. B. Burrell* in 1893 and 1906, when much of the Dec Gothic character was removed. The result is dull. Woodyer's NW turret survives.

* The then Bishop of Winchester was opposed to screens, and Woodyer wanted one. He circumvented the bishop by providing a wooden screen integral with the building. (The screen is painted, and there is also an excellent *Woodyer* REREDOS. R. Hubbuck)

9030

GRAYSWOOD
1½ m. NE of Haslemere

A trim triangular green, largely Victorian, in picturesque hilly
country near the Sussex border. ALL SAINTS fits happily
enough into the distant view, with its cosy timbered bell-turret
facing the green, but is bad close-to. By *Axel Haig*, 1900–2, in
local style.

ADLING (formerly New Farm). By *Amyas Connell* of Connell &
Ward, 1932, the second of the firm's small but startling houses
in which the Modern Movement in the full Corbusian sense
of the word was introduced to an alarmed and largely antago-
nistic England (the first was High and Over, Amersham, 1929;
Lucas joined the partnership in 1933). To English public
opinion, the sober brick of Dudok and the Stratford Memorial
Theatre of the very same year was one thing; this bizarre
juggling with concrete walls and random windows was quite
another. The house is roughly L-shaped with a tall glass staircase in the angle of the L, concrete walls, and windows in
horizontal strips. The construction is in fact entirely cantilever,
with free-standing columns occurring throughout the house.
Plenty of thirties details outside and in – e.g. the staircase
handrail and the cantilevered concrete entrance porch. It now
looks very dated, which is not true of all Connell, Ward &
Lucas houses. The truth seems to be that Connell's houses
were original and flashy, Ward's sound and sometimes very
good (The Firs, Redhill), and Lucas's often minor masterpieces (in Surrey, the house at Wentworth; also 66 Frognal,
Hampstead).

GRAYSWOOD MANOR HOUSE, ½ m. S. Symmetrical gabled
brick front, probably late C17.

1050

GREAT BOOKHAM

The spring-line N of the chalk produced the original settlement,
and the Leatherhead–Guildford railway line augmented it. The
population increased by 50 per cent between 1945 and 1961,
when the village was in unhappy transition. ⟨However, the
High Street still (1969) has plenty of village character.⟩

ST NICHOLAS. Picturesque at one end and completely restored
at the other, an odd effect.* The picturesqueness comes from
the weatherboarded W tower, in a most attractive Home

* The restorations by *Butterfield*, 1858 and 1885 (P. Thompson).

Counties vernacular style. The construction is similar to such a timber tower as Burstow, except that the bottom stage is flint. The framing inside has four big posts but diamond- and cross-bracing instead of the simpler diagonal bracing at Burstow. The effect is quite different, however, similar to the Essex family of steeples rather than to Burstow's sophisticated shingling. The rest of the building history is rather like Fetcham, the next village. Norman the two blocked windows above the N arcade, and the S arcade of four bays with fat circular piers, square scalloped capitals, and round arches, identical with Fetcham except that the arches are moulded. A little later, perhaps to be called Transitional, the N arcade, still with scallops but under octagonal abaci on octagonal piers and with single-chamfered pointed arches. Chancel datable 1341,* with a reticulated E window, all renewed, and two-light side windows with Y-tracery cusped, but built on earlier, perhaps C11, foundations. After this the S aisle deserves attention. Its W part is still narrow, i.e. of Norman dimensions. The first bay of the widened part was originally a porch, cf. its S entrance, the masonry to the r. of this, and the evidence for an upper storey. The rest, to the E of this, was the Slyfield Aisle. Big-scale work of c.1440 with three-light windows as at Lingfield. The N aisle was rebuilt (after having been blocked) in 1844-5 by *R. C. Carpenter*. – STAINED GLASS. A lot in the E window; six scenes from the life of Christ. From Costessey Hall in Norfolk, said to be C15 Flemish but looks German. The colouring is unremarkable, but the faces are startlingly vivid, Cranach or Grünewald faces. – PLATE. C17–18 pieces. – MONUMENTS. Small brass effigy to Elisabeth Slyfield † 1443 (beside pulpit). – Brass to Henry Slyfield † 1598 and his wife (S chancel arch respond). Shrewd Tudor carving of shrewd Tudor faces. Little feeling. Figures 2 ft high. – Brass to Robert Shiers † 1668 (floor of S aisle), dressed as a bencher of the Inner Temple. The figure is 2 ft 6 in. long, and as diagrammatic as the carving on an C18 tombstone. – Another monument to Robert Shiers † 1668, his wife † 1700, and his son † 1685. Three busts in a big ornate architectural surround which is too disjointed to be a moving composition but has some well-carved details, e.g. the winged skulls at the sides. Up-to-date busts with Baroque hair and

* By Chertsey Abbey masons. An inscribed stone survives which reads 'Hec domus abbate fuerat constructa Johanne de Rutherwyka decus ob Sancti Nicholai Anno milleno triceno bisque viceno primo Xpc. ei paret hinc sedem requiei.'

expression. Unsigned, but not a mason's job. – Arthur Moore
† 1735 by *Thomas Carter Sen*. An early example of the St
Paul's type of military monument – he was Overseas Pay-
master. Semi-reclining Roman figure in martial attitude;
obelisk with trophies behind. The carving bold but frigid,
clearly containing all the seeds of c19 academic portraiture and
blindness to character. – William Moore, his son, † 1746. Two
cherubs and an indifferent medallion; sentiment instead of
ardour. – In the s aisle Cornet Geary † 1776 (at Flemington
N.J. in the War of American Independence). First-rate; here
there is just the right combination of sentiment and ardour.
Britannia mourning over a base with portrait medallion, above
a splendid delicate relief showing his death in ambush. Often
these two parts of a monument do not fit together: here they
are combined in a composition as elegant and as tender as an
early Mozart symphony, a very rare combination indeed.
Unsigned, and it would be difficult to suggest a sculptor:
perhaps *Van Gelder*. – In the chancel Elizabeth Andrewes
† 1816 and several relations, probably erected c.1830. Dull
small Gothic tablet, but with a startling background – a weeping willow in low relief using the whole height of the chancel
and taking a surprised lancet window in its stride. This idea is
familiar from the N transept of Westminster Abbey in the late
c18 (lately and sadly removed) but is surprising in the c19. A
choir stall has to fit round the base and does so with a miniature
iron railing, just as though it were a real tree.

The village street runs N–S between railway and main road, with
the main crossroads and churchyard half-way between.
Immediately w of the church are CHURCH COTTAGES, c16
timber-framing. Worth a look to the s is No. 6 HIGH STREET,
nicely detailed stock brick of c.1825 with a dentilled cornice as
they sometimes occur in South London, and perhaps also
VICTORIA COTTAGES, irregular c16 timber-framing, small-
scale but unaltered. Its builder would doubtless be very
surprised at all the notice now taken of it. Beyond the A246
is BOOKHAM GROVE, mid-c18 with a jumbled N front – the
doorcase is to a bigger scale than anything else. The unequally-
spaced windows with broken pediments above look c19. To
the w of the central crossroads is the SCHOOL, a gloomy flint
design by *Butterfield*, 1856, now very much altered. Done without feeling, and unimportant in itself, yet interesting because
it was drawn by the young Philip Webb and suggested some of
the features in the Red House. (At the corner of the A246

(Leatherhead Road) and Eastwick Lane, a pair of cottages and terrace, also by *Butterfield*. P. Thompson) ⟨E of the central crossroads, in LOWER ROAD, at the corner of the playing field, attractive YOUTH CENTRE by *Raymond Ash*, the County Architect, 1967–8, a low square building of dark brick with white fascia boarding. Recessed entrance with bright orange doors.⟩

GREAT FOSTERS

0060

1 m. S of Egham

A good example of the simply detailed brick C16 house which is so common in the Home Counties and, in other materials, all over the country. Changes in the brickwork show that there was probably an earlier C16 house here, but all the visible detail outside is Late Elizabethan – the date over the porch is 1598.* The only thing out of the ordinary is that the staircases are housed in square-topped brick towers, which are as tall as the gables and add solidity and variety to the skyline and to the elevations. The main staircase projects in the middle of the garden front, the subsidiary staircase is at the S end of the main block among later additions. Square-topped staircases such as this occur e.g. at Eastbury Manor House in Essex, but are there used to complicate the internal corners of a half-H-shaped plan, not asymmetrically. The entrance front is five-gabled, almost symmetrical, with a central entrance and a simple, thinly detailed architectural surround. The garden front is a much subtler and more picturesque piece of near-symmetry, with pairs of gables at either end and the bold projection of the main staircase tower balanced by the strong horizontals of the six-light windows.‡ The windows throughout are of simple mullion-and-transom type with plain hood-moulds, the only ornamental detail being a balustrade pierced in a geometrical pattern. With the staircases extruded in this way a compact and convenient plan results: hall below, entered centrally with a big main room opening off at either end; the main bedroom directly above with an irregular long gallery behind facing the garden. Internal details are unrelated ornamental fragments. In the hall two big beams with Gothic mouldings which are

* On the grounds of the size of the bricks, the earlier part consists of the central hall, without either the wings or the staircase tower.

‡ It has turned out that the six-light windows are C20, and therefore so is the subtle and picturesque piece of near-symmetry.

probably part of the earlier house, pilastered panelling which looks C17, and a good overmantel (originally in the Tapestry Room), worth a special look to appreciate how attractive full-blown Jacobean work can be as long as it is looked at in its own terms – of richness and vitality – and not according to the degree of deviation from a Renaissance ideal. The staircase is cramped inside its brick tower, with a tiny well and simply ornamented newel-posts and pendants, the lowest newel-post actually touching the first-floor pendant above it. Odd panelling on the staircase walls, including pilasters with linenfold panelling on the bases. On the first floor the Tapestry Room has an overmantel (the pilasters flanking the fireplace are new) with figures of Ratio, Veritas, and Victoria and two splendidly carved cartouches. The work is very good, the figures especially elegant. Beneath it a folk-art C17 stone relief of Adam and Eve which is probably *in situ*. Renovated Jacobean ceiling similar to that in the Hall. The Italian Room has Quattrocento doors with delicate plasterwork inside and painted panels outside, imported in 1918 by *Romaine-Walker & Jenkins*, who also laid out the good formal gardens.

The STABLES are very simple Artisan brickwork – one rusticated doorway, e.g. – and are datable after 1631 by the owner's carved initials.

⁴⁰⁴⁰ GREATHED MANOR
1½ m. SE of Lingfield

Formerly Ford Manor. Formidable. A rock-hard stone pile by *Robert Kerr*, the author of the famous book on the English Gentleman's House. Built in 1868. An extreme example of a justly neglected type; over-confident to a fault, making no concessions to the landscape or anything else, and without any of the artistic sincerity that might make the style palatable in a house by Teulon or Waterhouse. Long front which seems to contain one of everything, starting with a tower at one end, ending with a French pavilion roof at the other, and with Dutch and English gables in between.

⁰⁰⁴⁰ GREAT TANGLEY
1 m. SE of Shalford

32 The most impressive of Surrey's moderate collection of half-timbered houses. It is dated 1584. It uses the simple but

effective repertoire of late C16 half-timbering in the Guildford
area: approximately square panels each with four curved
diagonal braces inside them forming a star-shape. This pattern
also recurs in the local ornate timberwork of North-East
Sussex and Kent (Middle House Mayfield 1575), and of
course, together with many other patterns, in Shropshire and
Herefordshire. It would be interesting to know how far these
parallels were coincidental, and if there were interchanges of
ideas between carpenters. Three-gabled S front, with subtle
variations in size and outline, probably quite consciously
designed. Small central gable above the porch tied in to the
bigger l. hand gable; r. hand gable bigger still and recessed,
all with double overhang. Ornamental timber-work with
curved diagonal braces throughout, making either a star-shaped
pattern or, when four ornamented panels are joined together, a
pattern of circles intersecting rectangles. There was originally
more of the house (another gable ?) at the W end. The back is a
ramble of half-timber offices, the interiors are simple panelled
rooms with some simple crude Late Elizabethan overmantels.

The late C19 additions are of interest too: sober rooms at
the W and E ends by *Philip Webb*, 1886, altered first in the early
C20 and then since 1945 – one of the first C19 additions to an
existing house to attempt to reproduce the spirit and deliberately avoid reproducing the letter of the old work. Webb's
best work remains unaltered: the long covered way across the
moat from the entrance drive, with exactly the same urge to
melt into the landscape, to make buildings and foliage indistinguishable, as Voysey or Lutyens – or indeed as Berlage in
Holland, or Eliel Saarinen in Finland, or Stanford White in
the U.S.A. In many ways this is a more compelling basic motif
of the late C19 than Art Nouveau decoration.

GREYFRIARS
½ m. NE of Puttenham

One of *Voysey*'s best houses, built in 1896 for Julian Sturgis.
Superb position facing s just under the brow of the Hog's Back.
The long, low, roughcast house ties itself self-effacingly into
the landscape, and the pleasure to be got in walking around it is
that of a continuous interchange between building and landscape without any single view that can be analysed in detail.
The garden side is a terrace with a magnificent view s, a long

range balanced by a gable at the w end. The door is off-centre
and flanked by two square projecting bays, partly covered with
creeper and facing a short strip of lawn as an intermediary
between house and view. The entrance side is more broken up,
with flat-topped and pointed gables, slight projections, again
creeper-covered, facing a thick semicircular hedge with steps
leading off to a flower garden on the w side. The horticultural
details are mentioned because, to say it again, the gardens are as
important as the house, or rather the two are indivisible. None
of Voysey's personal mannerisms have been allowed to obtrude. The w extension and present staircase are later additions of 1913 by *Herbert Baker*, who also did the garden.
Arched entrance and stables from the Hog's Back also probably later, but by *Voysey* himself.

Oddly enough, MONKSHATCH, the next house along the ridge,
was by Voysey's master, *Devey*, 1885–6. It was demolished,
except for the stables, in 1956.

₉₀₄₀

GUILDFORD

INTRODUCTION

Few towns in the South of England are as topographically blunt
as Guildford. Here the great E–W road along the chalk ridge
crossed the Wey. The ridge is both narrow and steep, and the road
dropped down steeply from the w, forded the river, and climbed
up almost as steeply on the E side. The E approach became the
town's High Street, the w approach remained a cottagey suburb.
Everything else followed from this. A royal castle was built s
of the High Street, parallel lanes developed N and s, clearly
subservient, as can be seen from their old names of Upper and
Lower Back Side (later prosaically North and South Streets*),
houses ribbon-developed s along the roads to Godalming and
Horsham, N along the road to Windsor. There was no market
place, no single focus, only the whole length of the High Street.
What gives Guildford its character is that the High Street is
steep, convex, and immediately answered by The Mount on the
other side of the river. The viewer is always in a cat's-cradle,
always like a swimmer in mid-stream, aware of both banks
simultaneously. A linear town is thus given a genuinely linear
fulfilment, unlike so many High Streets, which simply fade out at

---

* The earlier names were North and South Ditch, corresponding to rough-
and-ready medieval defence works. South Street is now Sydenham Road
and Castle Street.

either end, and the way in which this is heightened by the buildings makes it one of the best old towns near London.

CHURCHES

CATHEDRAL, Stag Hill, ½ m. NW of the town centre. Guildford was nominated as a suffragan bishopric to Winchester by Henry VIII in 1534, but his scheme never came into effect. Increased population finally forced an independent See in 1927, using Holy Trinity church as the pro-cathedral. The job of designing the cathedral was won in open competition by *Sir Edward Maufe* in 1932; it was begun in 1936, chancel and crossing were opened in 1954, the nave in 1961. The porches at the W end were completed in 1965–6. Maufe's style was sweet-tempered, undramatic Curvilinear Gothic, very much like Temple Moore's. The result is a cruciform church with bulky central tower, tripartite W front and two low side wings enclosing garths to N and S of it, all in brick with a minimum of stone dressings. At the E end is a Lady Chapel, lower than the chancel, flanked by sacristy and chapter house. Long narrow windows with mildly fancy tracery heads. It was conservative when it was designed – even by English standards – and without any of the genuine fervour of Liverpool. The outside looks as though it will never be more than a well-mannered postscript to the Gothic Revival. But Maufe's ability to create interior spaces (*see* also the Cooper's Hill Memorial, p. 214) expresses itself in spite of the style. The result is a very impressive and sober free-Gothic central 'vessel' treated with white plaster rendering and a minimum of Doulting limestone dressings, with deep, narrow window splays (so deep that no direct light is visible looking E from the crossing) between piers without capitals running up into transverse 'bows' or arches crossing the vault. Beyond, a stumpy ambulatory with a lot of spatial play with knife-thin pointed arches. This leads to vestries at the sides and to the Lady Chapel at the E end, an austere enclosed room (contrasting with the long vistas of the rest of the building), with plain walls below high, broad, five-light clerestory windows with angular arch-heads. Five-sided apse, low pitched roof. W of the choir, on either side, transverse barrel-vaulted transepts and hence a complex roof shape at the crossing. The nave has tall arcades, tall narrow aisles, and tiny clerestory windows high up. The result is noble and subtle, and has a queer power of compelling, not reverence, but contemplation. Best of all probably are the views down the aisles from the crossing. It is a great loss to the development of English architecture that Maufe felt impelled to harness this spatial imagination to a period style. The nobility is partly dispelled by the architect's own fittings in a sub-Comper style, e.g. the gilded tester high up over the altar and the strangely domestic (temporary) lamp-shades. Most of the other fittings also show the depressingly low standard of 1950s religious ornament.* The exceptions are perhaps ENGRAVED GLASS by *John Hutton* in the s transept and w doors, and a large CARPET (designed by *Maufe*) in the sanctuary. – For the rest, there is some *Eric Gill* STATUARY, but of very poor quality: St John Baptist over the s transept doors, and a Christ in Majesty on the E wall (executed after Gill's death by *Anthony Forster*). – On the s exterior of the Lady Chapel, Archangel Gabriel by *Alan Collins*, and on the Lady Chapel buttresses, St Martha and St Catherine by *Alan Collins*, St Cecilia and Lady Margaret Beaufort by *Dennis Huntley*. – Virgin and Child, of wood, in the Lady Chapel, by *Douglas Stephen*. – IRON GATES (N transept) and BRONZE DOORS (s transept), both designed by *Maufe*, the bronze doors made by *Vernon Hill*. – STAINED GLASS roundel at the E end by *Moira Forsyth*.

ST CATHERINE'S CHAPEL. Beside the Godalming Road, ¾ m. s of the centre, a beautiful site above the Wey water meadows. Built before 1308, a simple rectangle of rubble sandstone with grey ashlar dressings (not clunch). Now roofless and with all its decoration gone. It seems to have been unusually circumstantial and casket-like (e.g. the big buttresses dividing each bay and obviously originally bearing big pinnacles). Taller attached NW corner turret. Windows fairly small, subtly shaped, but with no indication of the type of tracery.

CHRIST CHURCH. *See* p. 290.

HOLY TRINITY, High Street. The Weston Chantry at the w end on the s side is C16 (founded 1540): two dispirited bays of flint and freestone chequerwork with three-light windows. All the rest was rebuilt in 1749–63, after the old tower fell, by *James Horne* of London, in a similar style to his now demolished church of St Catherine Coleman in the City of London. This is Surrey's only big C18 church, handsome and pedestrian at the same time: handsome in the smooth brickwork and the proportions, pedestrian in the details, such as the brick quoins and the doors, which are all under-scale for such a big building

* As bad as the style of the 1851 Exhibition, and with much less character.

on such an important site. Nothing deviates in the least from
the correct Palladian canon. Plain, round-headed windows,
intermittently rusticated door surrounds, five-bay nave* with
pedimented w end, and handsome battlemented w tower
(carrying an ornate wrought-iron flagpole, an unexpected
finial). Chancel and apse 1888 by *Sir A. W. Blomfield*, several
degrees thicker than the original. The interior was then
completely gutted, keeping only the w gallery, and is just one
enormous room with tripartite openings at the E end. – PULPIT.
Handsome and heavy. Thick bowl, canopy on two enormous
Composite columns. Of 1770, but still purely in the Wren
tradition. – PLATE. Cup and Paten *c.*1570, Norwich made;
Silver Alms Basin 1675; Silver-gilt Paten 1691; several C18
pieces. – MONUMENTS. Arranged topographically. Sir Robert
Parkhurst † 1637 (under the tower). Stiff figure lying on its
side, under a canopy. Still purely Jacobean; poor work. –
Similar tomb, without inscription, opposite. Recumbent
female figure on a table tomb, by the same mason (compare the
architectural detail), slightly better, with vivid scenes of
jumbled skulls viewed through the side of the chest (copied
from the Abbot monument; *see* below). Both these monuments
were mixed up in the rebuilding; the female figure e.g. may
be Elizabethan and from another monument. – In the nave:
Arthur Onslow † 1778, Speaker of the House of Commons for
thirty-three years. A semi-reclining figure on a plain inscribed
base; quite a noble effigy, in Roman dress, half-way between
pomposity and sentiment. The emotional content better than
the technique, an unusual state of affairs for a late C18 monument. Unsigned. – James Smyth † 1711, a foursquare dull
obelisk and sarcophagus. – In the s transept: Archbishop
Abbot † 1633, erected 1640. Buried across the road from his
foundation (*see* Abbot's Hospital), and evidently as conservative in his sculptural taste as in his architecture. The monument
was apparently designed by *Gerard Christmas* and certainly
carved by his sons *Matthew* and *John*, who sign it. They were
the leading conservative official sculptors of the day, i.e. pre-
Nicholas Stone with his new standards of expression and
technique. T-shaped, the long arm being a six-column canopy
above the expressionless figure, the short arms against the wall
containing niches with allegorical figures. Polychrome marble,
the six columns resting on pedestals built up of books, a
vivid scene of skulls in relief against the base below Abbot's

* Windows ingeniously altered from two rows to one in 1869, by *Woodyer*.

head, and an incredibly crowded skyline on top of the canopy
with scrolly pediments and small figures. The whole thing is a
vast allegory, but not an 'image' in the mid-c20 sense of the
term: that is, the allegory does not come alive imaginatively,
and there are no technical qualities to excite admiration once
the imaginative effect has failed. – Brass to Maurice Abbot and
wife, both † 1606, George Abbot's parents. Small, pretty plate
with kneeling figures, six sons below and an inscription below
that, the whole thing only 20 in. high. In spite of the naïve
technique, a better understanding of linear pattern than the
lifeless virtuosity of most c15 brasses. – IRON GATES to the
churchyard. The central gate 1712, the others 1813.

ST JOHN THE EVANGELIST, Stoke. The effect is Victorian,*
but one or two older details were allowed to remain. s chancel
arcade with round abaci, carrying complex many-moulded
arches, probably c14. N chancel arcade also with round abaci
but double-chamfered arches. The windows of the chapel have
simple c17 mullions and transoms, an unexpected survival.
The w tower is original too, though much restored. It is of the
standard Thames valley c15 type with taller attached stair-
turret, carried out in a rough chequerboard pattern of flint and
freestone. Finally the best feature, the vigorous E window, an
unusual design – five lights with the mullions running up
uninterrupted into the head of the arch, and deep concave
splays inside and out.‡ – FONT. Plain, c18, black marble bowl
and base, bulgy white marble stem. – STAINED GLASS. E
window of the N chapel filled with fragments, largely English
and largely armorial. – N window of the N chapel in memory of
R. S. Budgett † 1888. Two sets of four lights, sentimental
figures and mostly fairly weak colours, except for the greens,
but the designs pure Rossetti, especially the two centre lights
of the bottom set. It was designed by *F. J. Shields*, a friend of
Rossetti.§ Very pretty overall pattern. – PLATE. Flagon 1631;
Flagon and Chalice 1702. – MONUMENTS. Quite a lot of early
c19 tablets. Elizabeth Creuzé † 1804, the usual mourning
woman but very prettily carved, by *Bacon Jun.* – A similar one
by *Flaxman* to William Aldersey † 1800 (N aisle). – Henry and

* Restoration 1858 by *T. Goodchild* (GS).

‡ The Stoke advowson was owned by the Priory of St Pancras at Lewes,
the source for so many innovations in English medieval architecture.

§ ⟨This information comes from the excellent study of Guildford made
by the Guildford School of Art in 1968, called *Microcosm of Guildford*. We
are grateful to Mr Godfrey Rubens for letting us see this.⟩

William Parson † 1799. Almost contemporary, but locally done, and looks a century earlier. Thick marble surround to the inscriptions, Baroque cherub-heads above and below.

ST MARY, Quarry Street. Restored ouside,* but almost the only attractive town-church interior in Surrey, helped by the big rise in floor level from W to E: five steps to the crossing, three more to the chancel, another to the sanctuary. Unbuttressed central tower of flint, probably C11 and pre-Conquest. Bell-stage plain, with random slit-like windows and Roman tile quoins. The best evidence of this early work is inside, above the N and S crossing arches, where double-splayed windows and crude pilaster-strips appear, the latter also visible outside above the roof-line. After this come the N and S crossing arches, rough Early Norman, and also some blocked windows in the chancel which go with them.‡ Most of the rest of the church is an unusual rebuilding of c.1180 – nave arcades, W tower arch, apsidal N and S chapels (the chancel also originally had an apse, removed in 1825 for road widening) – very unexpected in a parish church of this date. The style is Transitional in the exact sense of that word: round piers, square multi-scallop capitals, pointed arches of square section with hollow chamfer (N side) or a keeled roll-moulding (S side); simple, large-scale work, midway between buildings like Fetcham and the Early Gothic of Leatherhead. One pier on the N side was altered later in the C13. The apsed chapels have some simple lancet windows (one original and one enlarged in the S apse) and a heavy vault with two big single-chamfered ribs running against the entrance arch. Against the curved E wall they rest on tiny shafts. About 1220 the chancel received its much more elegant rib-vault, two bays, the ribs in the first bay with two bands of dog-tooth between roll-mouldings, the piers made up of three clustered shafts gathered together into a thick capital. The group of shafts in the E corner shows the previous existence of an apse. A widening of the aisles followed c.1240 – cf. a typical arch between S aisle and S chapel, some lancet windows, and especially the N doorway, of two main orders on Sussex marble jamb-shafts with a forest of bold subsidiary roll-mouldings. This is the national Gothic style of the mid C13, rarely found in Surrey. Various late medieval windows, badly renewed: one

* Also by *Goodchild*, 1862 (GS).
‡ Excavations have shown that originally the nave was aisleless, and that earlier still, there was a timber building. The Early Norman church therefore was probably cruciform, incorporating the earlier tower in its centre.

Dec example in St John's (N) Chapel. Arch between N aisle and N chapel Perp, arch between chancel and N chapel *c*.1170, arch between chancel and S chapel probably C14. The whole of the E end is a very attractive maze of squints and diagonal passages. – WOODWORK. Part of a C15 reredos from the S chapel made up into the organ case. – WALL PAINTINGS. All over the N apse. Recorded in the C19, but now to all intents and purposes gone. They were probably contemporary with the chapel. – STAINED GLASS. The W window of the N aisle by the '*Royal Bavarian Art Institute for Stained Glass*' (TK) – i.e. Munich work of *c*.1850, with typical Cambridge-blue backgrounds to the heads. – BRASS. Two small C15 figures, N chapel. Bad work.

ST NICHOLAS, High Street. The Loseley Chapel on the S side survives from the medieval church. It is humble C15. All the rest 1870–5 by *S. S. Teulon*, executed by *Ewan Christian*, replacing a Commissioners'-Gothic church of 1837 by *Ebbels*. Rough-and-tumble C13 style, with an apse and a central tower. Ugly, but good and urban. 'Beastliness' confined to one transverse barrel-vaulted aisle inside. – FONT under a towering canopy of pure High Victorian design, painted and gilded. Ugly but genuine, like the church. – (STAINED GLASS by *Clayton & Bell*. R. Hubbuck) – MONUMENTS. In the S aisle John Knowles † 1741, a Rococo cartouche, late enough to have a naval relief below the inscription. – In the Loseley Chapel: Arnold Brocas, rector in 1395. Defaced recumbent effigy under three-arched canopy. Standard work. – Sir William More † 1600, also standard, and similar to the Parkhurst tombs in Holy Trinity. Husband and wife lying side by side, full-size. Stiff figures, gross surround. – Two more small kneeler monuments in the same style, one on either side, and also several small C17 and C18 tablets. – PLATE. Cup 1601; Paten 1791.

ST SAVIOUR, Woodbridge Road. By *H. S. Legg & Sons*, 1895. Prominent but poor and incredibly conservative. Spindly enclosure of a big wagon-roofed space. Big attached NW tower.

(ST JOSEPH (R.C.), Chertsey Street. 1881 by *E. Ingress Bell*. DE)

⟨METHODIST CHURCH, Woodbridge Road. By *A. Saunders*, 1966, with a very thin fibre-glass spire.⟩

⟨CONGREGATIONAL CHURCH, Portsmouth Road. By *D. Bundy* of *Barber, Bundy & Greenfield*, 1965. Octagonal, with clerestory lighting and folded roof.⟩

PUBLIC BUILDINGS

CASTLE. The oldest part is the huge C11 motte, added to in the usual way in the early C12 with a masonry shell keep around the top, now visible chiefly on the SW side. This was in turn replaced *c*.1170 by the impressive TOWER KEEP, built on the E side of the top of the motte, sheer and impregnable, a complete contrast to Surrey's other surviving castle, at Farnham. Guildford was a royal castle (work was recorded in progress in 1173–4), and the building represents the grim official architecture of Henry II, built in memory of the recent civil war and before the new ideas of castle building were brought back from the Crusades. It is 47 ft square externally and 63 ft high, of Bargate stone rubble and ashlar quoins, the only enrichment being the thick heavy buttresses at the rounded sides and at the angles. The main entrance was at first-floor level on the W side (the ground floor would have been cellars and storage, and the present entrance is modern). Now roofless and floorless, with nearly all the dressed stone details gone (one or two simple Romanesque windows remain, e.g. on the N and W sides), except for a little ornament in the CHAPEL, on the SW corner of the first floor.

The relevant extracts from the Pipe and Liberate Rolls were fully set out by L. F. Salzman in the *Victoria County History*, and contain points worth remembering in the study of medieval castles – e.g. that much of the outside was whitewashed and that the rooms were often painted inside. In 1256 Henry III gave instructions for marbling the hall pillars and arches, and for whitewashing the great chamber and marking it out in squares, with its ceiling painted green spangled with gold and silver. It is now rather difficult for us to visualize what all this looked like. Several windows have been enlarged and repaired in Tudor brickwork, and a faintly bizarre air provided by the ornate Late Victorian landscaping given to the motte by *Henry Peak*, Borough Surveyor, when it became public property in 1886. The other buildings are very fragmentary. To the SW, in what would have been the outer bailey, there is a square building with one C12 window. Beyond this, in Quarry Street (*see* p. 287), is a simple two-order arch from the outer gateway, part of extended C13 concentric fortifications. The king's master mason *John of Gloucester* gave advice on its erection in 1256.

GUILDHALL, High Street. Superb, the epitome of Restoration [47] panache, refronted in 1683 in a completely original version of what were originally mid-c17 Artisan motifs. The effect is more like the carved poop of a c17 ship than anything else. It is placed at the critical point in the High Street, one-third of the way down, where it is on the skyline from both sides, and rarely can a building have justified its position so well. Three bays, projecting pilastered first floor with big windows between under alternating segmental and triangular pediments – what is, effectively, an all glass front – with much narrower windows on the returned sides with their own squashed pediments. In front an iron balcony, the whole thing oversailing the ground floor on caryatid brackets; above, a trapezoidal pediment with an octagonal cupola balanced on the very edge – completely wrong by academic standards, completely right in the particular circumstances. From the centre of the pediment projects the magnificent clock, dated 1683 and possibly made by *John Aylward*, supported on one gilded beam and five splendidly ornamented iron ties. The clock is pedimented and has thick floral decoration at the sides – i.e. it is in pure City of London style, similar to the clock at St Mary at Hill. The inside is comparatively tame after this; simple staircase with handsome iron gate at the foot, leading to the panelled Council Chamber containing an early c17 fireplace (brought from Stoughton House) and overmantel, with handsome Royal Arms of 1686 above. The only detail out of the ordinary is the delicately executed plaster frieze in the mantelpiece, representing the four human temperaments, labelled, in a very c17 way, as Sanguineus, Cholericus, Phlegmaticus, and Melancholicus.*

⟨CIVIC HALL, London Road. By *Peter Shepheard*, 1957–62.⟩
⟨UNIVERSITY OF SURREY, Stag Hill. The Battersea College of Technology was designated the University of Surrey in 1966. The development plan of the *Building Design Partnership* was accepted in the same year, and phase one was completed late in 1968. Phase two is now in progress. The university is being designed for five thousand students. It is estimated that a third of these will study engineering and a third science. One thousand students were in residence by the end of 1969.

The basic layout is simple and compact. The academic buildings are at the bottom of the hill, the residential blocks are at the top, and the communal buildings – lecture theatres, library, restaurants – are in the middle. The laboratories form

* It has been pointed out that these are based on engravings by *Raphael Sadeler* after allegorical paintings by *Marten de Vos* (*Microcosm of Guildford*).

a tight, almost fortress-like enceinte around the N W part of the site. They have four storeys of ribbon windows with white spandrel panels, which are divided by concrete bands with a thin continuous horizontal projection at each floor level. The blocks are punctuated by plain yellow brick staircase towers. E of the laboratories, set back, is the Senate House, with the same details, but of seven storeys. Common rooms and the students' union are on the upper floors. E of the Senate House more academic buildings are under construction. To its W, and higher up, divided from the laboratories by a paved walk planted with trees, are two low buildings with restaurants, with 96 the lecture theatres between them, and the library at the far end. It is a pity that the noisy ventilating grilles of the laboratories face this walk. The theatres, of different sizes and heights, are linked by light, airy halls and corridors with glazed roofs. Both interior and exterior walls are of yellow brick. From the upper level of this building one can reach a roof garden above one of the restaurants, from which there is access to the library, a six-storey block with bold towers. There are also bridges from the roof garden to the laboratories. The sloping site has been exploited well to provide these various means of access, and when the planting is mature, the well composed vistas from different levels should be even more attractive. Although the details are uniform, the grouping and sizes of blocks and towers are not, so the effect is not dull. The residential buildings at the top of the hill are stark yellow brick cubes, five storeys high, with simple exterior staircases and regular fenestration flush with the wall surface: an effect reminiscent of the thirties. Beyond them rises disconcertingly the red brick Gothic tower of the cathedral. The restrained mood of the design of the university as a whole and the unobtrusive detailing of the parts are indeed entirely in the International Modern tradition, and there are none of the overworked stylistic gimmicks popular today. To the N, and very prominent from a distance, further students' residences with steeply pitched roofs are being built by *Maguire & Murray*. They appear to be in a quite different style and mood.⟩

⟨TECHNICAL COLLEGE, Stoke Park. Large, and further expansion to come. Neo-Georgian core by *Jarvis & Richards*, 1939, with new blocks at either end, six storeys at the top of the hill, two storeys at the bottom, both with rough ribbed concrete panels, by the County Architect, *R. J. Ash*, 1967–9.⟩

GRAMMAR SCHOOL, High Street. Founded in 1509, and given a charter by Edward VI in 1553. Routine Tudor architecture, but a good street building and a particularly good example of the tightly-planned town grammar school. One quad, opening directly off the street. The first block (s), opposite the entrance, 1557; W wing with master's lodging 1569; E wing with ushers' lodging 1571; street front completed about 1586. No discernible difference between the parts, all two- and three-light minimum Tudor (no hood-moulds, e.g.), all stone, except for the inner side of the N wing, which has an overhanging first floor of plaster and half-timber carried on wooden posts. The outer elevation to the street has three storeys and three bays, each topped by a gable with a ball finial. Arms of Edward VI in the centre above a small doorway with C16 door. More gables in the quad, which has a nice scale, although much of the detail was altered in 1889. Inside, big schoolroom on the top floor of the s side under a queenpost roof and with original fireplaces. Chained library on the N side. ⟨Opposite, new school buildings of 1958–63 by *J. Harrison*, the former County Architect, with advice from *Sir Edward Maufe*. Uninspiring Neo-Georgian, with a pediment at one end, set back from the street.⟩

⟨YVONNE ARNAUD THEATRE. By *Scott, Brownrigg & Turner*, 1963–5. Attractively sited by the C19 waterworks buildings on an island on the E side of the river. The plan is a blunt-ended ellipse, partly curtain-walled, with a *brise-soleil* of concrete mullions around the curved end.⟩

39 ABBOT'S HOSPITAL. At the top of the hilly part of High Street. Built in 1619–22 by George Abbot, Archbishop of Canterbury, originally for twelve men and eight women, a visible proof of the fairy-tale story of a local family that made good. He and his brothers were born of modest parents in Guildford; one became Bishop of Salisbury, another Lord Mayor of London. Abbot's Hospital is one of those buildings which carry out a standard style extremely well, in this case the standard official Jacobean style of Holland House and Blickling and John Thorpe's sketchbook. There is no hint here of Inigo Jones, and in fact the main feature, the huge gatehouse, is a deliberate anachronism looking back at least to Hampton Court and possibly to the semi-military gatehouses of the C15. Outside the universities, this is the last great gatehouse in the country and very nearly the best. Three storeys, with four big corner turrets and ogee caps, the street front made into a half-H with two wings with

shaped gables,* the other side forming a closed three-storey brick quadrangle. In itself this is not a remarkable recipe, and Abbot's Hospital succeeds on its purely architectural qualities, something very rare indeed in Jacobean architecture. The effect is chiefly the meticulous relation of gatehouse to wings and gatehouse to quad which combine with the tall proportions and intensely red brick to give an extraordinary effect of homogeneity. The outside is not centre and wings, but one single unit; the inside is less a four-sided quad than one large open-air brick room – by comparison even the most impressive of the Oxford quads or Cambridge courts is strung out and disjointed. The rear front to the garden is simply a formal functional arrangement of windows in a large brick wall. All the detail is fairly unsympathetic, which makes the artistic achievement even more striking. Simple three-, four-, and five-light mullioned windows, mostly without hood-moulds, and occasional Jacobean set-pieces such as the entrance door in the gatehouse (the arms above date from 1825) with a full-scale entablature carried on paired pilasters carrying diamond rustication. In the quad itself there is one small stepped gable and an archway which actually has chevron ornament; if original it must surely be some wild sort of Romanesque copy.

The other notable thing about Abbot's Hospital is the completeness of its original furnishings: superb original Jacobean doors, especially in the gatehouse, some of the best in the country, original bell in the quad, original chairs and tables inside. The interiors have plain panelling and a few ornamental details in no way out of the normal run of Jacobean ornament. On the first floor of the gatehouse is the boardroom with Doric pilasters and an elaborate fireplace. The Duke of Monmouth was kept here on his way to London after Sedgemoor. In the SE corner is the Master's Staircase, straightforward Jacobean in a narrow well. On the other side of the quad are the main public rooms, dining room underneath and banqueting hall above, with a standard type of Jacobean overmantel, linked by a simple staircase of c.1700. Finally in the NE corner the chapel, with simple woodwork, a wooden Jacobean alms box shaped like a mace, and two windows and their glass, said to come from the Dominican friary, finally demolished c.1620

* Not the shaped gables of the later C17 Artisan houses of Surrey, but an adaptation of standard Elizabethan–Jacobean gables such as those on Wimbledon or Holland House. They may well in their turn have influenced houses like Brook House, Chobham.

(it stood near Friary Street). The E window has a simple five-light intersecting pattern, the N window is of four lights under a four-centred head (i.e. both authentic, so that they are more likely to be truly medieval than an attempt at medieval revival). They are also over-scale for the chapel, which would be natural enough if they were transplanted. The stained glass is complete, showing Esau and Jacob, in crowded compositions. The best colour and design is in the golden pinnacles of the tracery heads. One window is dated 1621.

Finally, in the garden beyond the quad a simple early C17 SUMMER HOUSE with an ogee-shaped lead roof.

ROYAL SURREY COUNTY HOSPITAL, Farnham Road. By *E. W. Lowers*, 1862–6. A big, plain front facing S. In a dignified style, with classical proportions but without any period motifs at all, more usual in breweries or factories than in a hospital. The rhythm 3-2-5-1-3-1-5-2-3 bays, the centre taller and with a cupola. Very effective – the silly later Neo-Georgian porch shows the normal idea of such building.

HILLIER or ONSLOW ALMSHOUSES, Farnham Road – next to the hospital. Moved from Shoreditch in 1879. The new buildings are by *George & Peto*, and a delightful example of the fresh Norman Shaw style before it became cumbersome. They were in fact done concurrently with Shaw, not in imitation. Single-storey, half-H-shaped. Not quite symmetrical, and stepped downhill to increase the informal effect – stepped near one end of the long side, with a double gable at the join of the downhill wing, a disarming and very subtle effect. The details very pretty: caryatid porches, and big windows with tiny frames.*

STOUGHTON BARRACKS, Stoughton Road. A formidable design of 1876, architect unknown. Very harsh polychrome brick with one enormous multi-storey *donjon* and a curiously naïve – and hence attractive – polychrome stepped entrance.

GUILDOWN CEMETERY. Guildown Saxon cemetery was discovered in 1929 beside the Old Road to Farnham (itself a continuation of the ancient Harroway), between Old Road and Guildown Avenue. It contained more than 220 skeletons, of which 35 belonged to the pagan Saxon occupation of the C6 A.D. and the remainder to the celebrated 'Guildown Massacre' which took place five centuries later, in A.D. 1036. The massacre was carried out by Count Godwin, Earl of Wessex, on behalf of Harold Harefoot, whose claim to be the successor of King Cnut

* Threatened with demolition (1970).

the Count supported. The victims were the followers of
Queen Emma's son, the atheling Alfred. Alfred's men were
treacherously taken and summarily butchered by Godwin, and
Alfred himself despatched as a prisoner to Ely, where, after
being blinded, he was quickly executed. The dig confirmed at
almost every point the story told in the old chronicles; most of
the graves were shallow and usually contained three skeletons
thrown hugger-mugger into the trench. At least fifteen of them
had their hands tied behind their backs, and one had clearly
been beheaded.

PERAMBULATIONS

Everything in Guildford depends on the High Street; the
simplest way is to describe this from end to end, starting at the
bridge, going uphill looking at the N (l.) side, then coming back
looking at the S side. The rest of the town falls fairly simply into
the areas N and S of the High Street and the part W of the river.

(A) High Street

The character of Guildford HIGH STREET has been sketched in
already (see p. 268). One might add that it is an almost perfect
example of a bright and cheerful Home Counties street, whose
effect is that of unity-in-diversity. Its chief enemy until recently has been the genteel platitude put up through misunder-
standing the meaning of tradition, which dilutes the original
bold and adventurous character. What gives the High Street
its special visual character is the complex contours. High Street
is a convex hill, answered beyond the river by The Mount, a
concave hill, and there are other minor changes of level and
slope around the bridge and half-way up. To this must be
added the effect of the Town Hall clock, exactly placed so that
it defines the skyline of the views uphill and nets the background of the Hog's Back in the downhill views.

The N side starts near the bridge with Nos. 25–29, a typical local
Baroque house, though the ground floor has been completely
replaced by a shop-front. Lumpish, three-storeyed, giant
corner pilasters and unusually carefully detailed cornice. Nos.
43–45 is the same thing in early C19 terms, pedimented, with
an arcaded first floor and careful brick detail built in an unusually coloured stock brick which is deep yellow with a pink
tinge. Then came the LION HOTEL, long and stuccoed, demolished in 1957 for WOOLWORTHS, far better than the
standard product. The front was designed by *Thomas Sharp*,

a sober white plastered block of four bays and three storeys
with two single bays of brick stepped uphill from it. The old
lion is included in the shop-front. Beyond this, a cheerful
jumble, already taking as much fake and 'restoration' work as
it can stand, as far as the ANGEL, which begins the best stretch
of the High Street, dominated by the Town Hall. Early C19
stucco coaching-hotel front, cap-à-pie in grey and white with
good lettering. The back contains both half-timbering and
fragments of C17 work, hard to decipher (there is one violent
wooden window of c.1620 in the yard entry, with diamond-
rusticated jambs, the same style as the Abbot's Hospital door).
Underground is a C13 vaulted basement, probably a wine store:
thick chamfered ribs springing from round piers without capitals, a completely functional job. (Beneath No. 115 is a similar
vault, also late C13, but with moulded capitals and corbels
with carved figures.)

Then another jumble. No. 103 was of c.1700 with some of the
same character as the Guildhall but has been entirely rebuilt.
No. 117 is similar and may be by the same mason. The style is
like the now vanished post-Fire houses in the City of London,
perhaps reflecting in a minor way the same desire for big
windows and simple repeating patterns as produced the
Grand' Place at Brussels. Between these two HARVEY'S, a
four-storey early C19 design similar to Nos. 43–45, with the
same small pediment above, containing a squashed lunette.
Behind this running towards North Street is also HARVEY'S,
a five-storey shop by *G. A. Jellicoe and Partners*, 1957, with
straightforward modern elevations, using an exposed reinforced concrete frame and glass and wood-board infilling. This
is almost the biggest building in the town centre – conspicuous
in the view from the Hog's Back to the W for example – yet it is
quite invisible from the High Street and only partly visible
from North Street, appearing intermittently in the alleys
between them. This game of hide and seek with the viewer,
played by what he knows to be a very big building, is a delightful effect in itself, apart from maintaining the scale of the High
Street. On the fifth floor a ROOF GARDEN with elaborate
Swedish-style garden design.

Beyond the Town Hall is LLOYDS BANK, which was originally
the Guildford Old Bank, established in 1765. C18 brickwork
(the two downhill bays are facsimile of 1899). It still keeps its
original ground-floor front of Composite pilasters and columns
framing a central arch, with the most elegant Rococo plaster-

work in the spandrels, as though it were the doorcase to a drawing room; frilly sprays of leaves and flowers, more or less in the Bristol style. Then comes No. 155, CHILD (now GUILD-FORD) HOUSE of 1660, the best of the very individual late C17 Guildford houses. Three bays and three storeys, the upper storeys with pilasters and big windows filling almost the whole wall area between them. Ground-floor doorcase contemporary (with an C18 bow-fronted shop-window added on each side), and very typical of City of London carpenters' work of a few years either side of 1660. Central doorcase with scrolled volutes at the sides (cf. Cromwell House, Highgate, done in brick), shop-windows with carved panels of luxuriant whorled foliage and flowers underneath. The rear elevation is just as original and clear-headed, a two-bay wing of three storeys and base-ment under a gable. Plain casements, except on the ground floor, which has a very pretty bow window with curly orna-ment under, of the type of Sparrowe's House at Ipswich.* Inside, one plaster ceiling in the room at the back of the ground floor, in a simple geometrical pattern derived from Inigo Jones, roughly done (the type of 20 West Street Farnham). Bigger and richer ceiling in the same style in the main room on the first floor, a circle inscribed in a square itself inscribed in a larger square. The panels between the squares are given circu-lar and oval motifs and cherubs' heads, the central circle is richly vegetable. The ornamented ribs use the same motifs as are on the panels of the staircase, the best feature of the house. It is the familiar newel-post staircase round a narrow well, but treated with unexpected care. Ornate openwork floral panels beneath the banister rail, of the type initiated in Surrey, with different details, at Ham House. Newel posts carved above with bowls of fruit and below ending in floral pendants so that each pendant answers the bowl on the floor below, a familiar late C17 type. Small arcaded vestibule on the first floor, prob-ably early C18, with a well-moulded Victorian eagle on the first-floor landing. Largely original casements throughout, with many original elegant‡ wrought-iron fasteners. All this is datable about 1670, reflecting Inigo Jones at second hand. The architectural quality depends almost entirely on the individual

* No. 26 incidentally also has an apparently original rear elevation of the same Guildford type, i.e. exaggeratedly long windows made up into vertical strips.

‡ Really elegant, and worth a special look in view of the horribly fussy work that wrought iron means today.

craftsman's ability; here the woodwork is very good, the
plasterwork rather poor.

The High Street finally levels off at Abbot's Hospital (*see* p. 278)
and thereafter becomes less remarkable. NORFOLK HOUSE,
1959–60 by *Scott, Brownrigg & Turner*, is a much better match
for the street than such buildings usually are. An attempt to
create the irregular effects of buildings of different dates by
varying roof-lines and façades. It does not quite succeed but is
a brave try. Then, set back from the street, the new buildings
of the Grammar School (*see* above) which replaced ALLEN
HOUSE. (This was C17, remodelled *c.*1770, a five-by-three-bay
house with an Ionic porch in front and a Doric loggia between
two shallow wings at the back.) After this is a long range of
shops, then more Neo-Georgian buildings (including the
MUNICIPAL OFFICES by *T. R. Clemence*, 1931). ⟨Beyond
this, a large new block, rather fussy, with white mosaic panels
and brick dividing walls, by *Scott, Brownrigg & Turner*, 1962–4.
Further up the hill, the same architects have added an extension at the back of the C19 WHITE HORSE HOTEL (1962–4).
The extension has the saw-tooth windows so popular with
hotels in the sixties. Opposite is HENRIETTA HOUSE, a large,
straightforward four-storey block by *D. B. & J. S. Coombe*,
1966–8.⟩ The s side starts gradually at the top of the hill with
C19, then C18 buildings of domestic scale gradually disappearing piecemeal before Neo-Georgianism, then SOMERSET
HOUSE, a big house of *c.*1700 in the current Wren fashion.
Seven bays, the centre treated as a frontispiece with a Dutch
gable that looks mostly C20 improvisation, though possibly
with original materials. Heavy handsome ironwork and flight
of stone steps to the front door, undoubtedly original. Then
the Grammar School (*see* p. 278), and next door to it HIGH-
GATE HOUSE, big early C19 with a doorway 12 ft tall. From
there nothing to notice until Holy Trinity church, sideways to
the street and a fine companion to Abbot's Hospital opposite
with TRINITY CHURCHYARD behind it, an immediate contrast with the bustle of the High Street. It forms a tiny domestic square with brick and plaster buildings, especially effective
because the long brick sides of the church shut off the High
Street completely. ⟨Behind the w end of the churchyard, and
well concealed when one is in the High Street, is a large
MULTISTOREY CAR PARK (by *Courtaulds Technical Services*,
1962–3), with bold concrete ramps on the N side, but the rest
with feeble and over-fussy detailing.⟩ Beyond Holy Trinity,

back in the High Street is SAINSBURY'S. This was a wild
piece of polychrome brick and tile in Jacobean style – it fitted
in better than some of the post-war timidities of Guildford –
by *P. H. Adams*, 1905. It has been replaced (1961–3) by a tall
all-brown façade with large, aggressive, irregular boxed-out
windows. Timidity is no longer the danger at Guildford. The
architects once again are *Scott, Brownrigg & Turner*.⟩ No. 144
is earlier than most of the Guildford houses, an early C17 front
with two plastered bow windows stubbed off short at the
inevitable shop-front. No. 134 has pretty mid-C18 details (doorcase, first-floor bow window) in an altered front, and then
comes TUNSGATE, a massive, deep portico of two pairs of
Tuscan columns and pediment. Built as the Corn Exchange by
Henry Garling, 1818, and in 1935 shorn of the building behind
and made into a car park entrance* – both a successful case of
sympathetic re-use instead of demolition (cf. Godalming) and
the source of a queer, unintended Osterley-like effect in its own
right. As so often happens with early C19 public buildings, the
style is much more vigorous than if it had been done by one of
the big names. The portico is Tuscan, not Greek Doric. Next
to Tunsgate is Nos. 122–6, altered Tudor or early C17, three
gables, three bow windows, roughcast, and then a long nondescript stretch. Then comes the former W. H. SMITH'S on
the corner of Quarry Street, the front largely imitation, the
side keeping its C17 plastered gables.

(B) N of the High Street

Parallel to High Street runs NORTH STREET, with remarkably
little in it (it was originally the back lane of the single-street
town, and was not fully built up until *c.*1800). ⟨Since 1960 it
has been almost entirely rebuilt. There is still little worth individual mention.⟩ The best thing is the set of parallel pedestrian
alleys running between it and High Street. Near the river it is
joined to High Street by FRIARY STREET, with a few cottages
and a rare pre-C19 industrial survival in the CRANE on the
riverside, reached down an alley beside No. 15. A small
weatherboarded and tile building, half open for wagons to
drive in, half enclosed and containing an enormous tread-
wheel, 15 ft in diameter, geared to a crane on the waterfront.
Probably C18, and in fairly good condition. To the N of this, at

---

* The uneven spacing of the columns dates from these alterations (*Microcosm of Guildford*). The area behind is no longer a car park and is being
redeveloped (1970).

the end of North Street, was a neo-Norman range of varying height and degree of projection, two to three storeys, probably of c.1840. An archway inscribed SALVAM DOMINE FAC VICTORIAM led to an eight-house terrace of completely plain Late Georgian three-storey brick, now demolished. ⟨The E side of Friary Street is now under reconstruction (architects *Shepherd Fowler & Marshall*). The street has become pedestrian, an excellent development. The whole of the area N and NE of this is scheduled for redevelopment. The Brewery (*see* below) is to be demolished, and there will be a high-level link from North Street to the University, with offices and flats on a podium. Eventually traffic is to be excluded from both North Street and High Street. At the time of writing (1969) the only visible signs of all this are many empty, desolate areas, and a new indoor SPORTS CENTRE now building N of Onslow Street. By the time this new edition is in print, no doubt still more of the perambulation below will be past history.⟩

Friary Street continues N in Onslow Street and then in WOOD-BRIDGE ROAD, with some ambitious mid-C19 speculation on its W side. First WELLINGTON PLACE, 1852, a formidable set of semi-detached Tudor blocks, and then detached villas, Tudor and various shades of Italianate (some stuccoed, some brick and stone), probably all by the same builder. Indifferent quality. (Now partly derelict.)

N of North Street the layout becomes immediately intricate, piecemeal Early Victorian speculation, much of it grey stock brick and as hard-bitten as it would be in Suffolk or Norfolk. FRIARY BREWERY in Commercial Road is a completely informal industrial jumble of c.1860 with a big brick tower. Further E there was until recently another industrial survival in the angle between Lea Pale Road and Woodbridge Road, a weatherboarded workshop with long horizontal strip windows; a small but effective piece of early C19 architecture. E again in Martyr Road is the SURREY ADVERTISER office, with a modernistic glazed tile front and rounded corners, by *Hiscock & Duncan Scott*, 1936. Ward Street leads back from here to the E end of North Street, where there is a little more. On the S side two buildings once connected with Abbot's Hospital, whose rear elevation is clearly visible at the end of the garden. The first is ABBOT'S SCHOOL (now offices), with a C19 tower towards the street but a long, grim, three-storey range running back from it in exactly the same style as the Hospital (plain mullioned windows etc.). Built in 1619, but of no visual importance. Behind this, and numbered as No. 77 North Street, was a tiny Artisan brick building of *c.*1630, once an outbuilding of some sort to the hospital, with one curly shaped gable at the s end and three bays of pilasters above rusticated blind arches along the side. ⟨It was demolished in 1960. There is now a new PUBLIC LIBRARY, by *Highet & Phillips*, 1959–62, yellow brick, with a weak convex façade with a large window. Between the C19 tower and the library, JEFFRIES PASSAGE runs up to the High Street. It has been rebuilt quite attractively with shops with uniform boxed-out tile-hung upper floors (by *Central & Provincial Properties*, 1967–9). At the top of North Street is a very large new building (partly MAPLES STORE) by *Scott, Brownrigg & Turner*, 1963–4. Two and three storeys, the upper floors projecting, with thin black mullions and black spandrels. The building follows the curve of the street uphill and ends with a sleek, brash, rounded end at the corner of Chertsey Street.⟩ CHERTSEY STREET leads N, cottagey at first and then entirely early C19 when it becomes STOKE ROAD, with No. 2, a skittish flint and stock-brick front with all the windows ogee-headed. Beyond this is PARSON'S HOSPITAL, 1796, as conservative as the Parson tablet in Stoke church (*see* p. 272). Memorial inscription on a woolsack (the founder was a mercer), with pointed windows, the only concession to late C18 ideas. Otherwise a seven-bay handsome pedimented centre with a pretty octagonal classical cupola above, still the type of 1720. Almost opposite is STOKE HOTEL, an early C19 house with ogee windows and a frilly cast-iron porch.

N again is what is left of the old village of Stoke, in JOSEPH'S ROAD, W of the church. Only Nos. 7–11 remain, an attractive mixed half-timbered building with one close-timbered gable to the street with herringbone brick infilling, probably C16, and the remainder lower and with wider spacing, dated 1663. Beyond the by-pass is a forthright inelegant Victorian CORN MILL. Polychrome brick, five storeys under segmental blind arcades with a hoist at one end. By *H. Moon*, 1879 (GS). Beyond again is Slyfield Green, very depressed now, with SLYFIELD FARM, in Old Farm Road, a big, two-gabled brick and timber house of *c.*1600, now disused and threatened with demolition.

(c) s of the High Street

This walk starts one-third of the way up the hill, where QUARRY STREET runs s towards Horsham. First pleasant mixed buildings answering the curve of St Mary's churchyard. Then,

starting in architectural earnest, Nos. 5–6 on the W side, late
C17 with crude pargetting on No. 6 – no figures, only geometrical patterns: a rarity in Surrey, but probably mainly
through destruction of most of the other local examples.
Beside No. 6, ROSEMARY ALLEY runs down to the riverside
in a series of steps, giving first-rate picturesque views of the
backs of the Quarry Street houses – far more picturesque than
the street itself. It leads to the new THEATRE (see above) and
the WATERWORKS, part of which is an impressive big water
mill of c.1760 with Victorian additions. Brick, seven bays and
three storeys plus a bulky hipped roof, the style of Elstead
Mill.

Beyond this, interest moves to the E side, with No. 49, CASTLE
HOUSE, a big, very plain Palladian house of c.1740, five by
three bays with a hefty doorcase, and then the GUILDFORD
MUSEUM, part single-storey of 1911 by Ralph Nevill, with
unhappy mock-Jacobean gables, but mainly a very picturesque
enlarged cottage partly built into the outbuildings of the castle
(see p. 275) and next to the castle entrance. The front to Quarry
Street has a tile-hung gable above stone-built bow windows,
and another half-timbered gable, dated 1672, appears behind.
The front inside the archway has two gabled and tile-hung
wings. Altogether, this is the prettiest cottage ensemble in
Guildford. The W side then goes Tudor with MILLBROOK
HOUSE, and No. 21 next to it, both with plastered front and
gables to the road, No. 21 with a Dutch end gable (fake?) as
well.

Uphill from here to the SE is an odd area that was laid out with
expensive houses c.1900 and still has open country immediately
beyond. In WARWICK'S BENCH are no less than three houses
by Baillie Scott: MONKS PATH on the E side, demure Neo-
Georgian, GARDEN COURT* and UNDERSHAW on the S
side, the last built in 1910 in the Tudor style with a very
sophisticated entry from the street via a pergola running between low-roofed wings in the Lutyens way. All three are
fundamentally timid, which could not be said of the hard-
headed amateur design of DURBINS in Chantry View Road,
the house Roger Fry built for himself in 1913. Roger Fry was
the English discoverer of Cézanne, Picasso, and Matisse, the
leader of the English avant-garde of 1910 (which was at that
time ten years behind Paris or Munich), and the inventor of the
phrase 'significant form', the 1910 equivalent of art for art's

* With a Jekyll garden.

2. (above left) Kingston upon Thames, Market Place
3. (left) Kew Green, north side
4. (above) Alfold, church and cottages

5. (above left) Brockham, green
6. (left) Burstow church, west tower
7. (above top) Peper Harow Farm, granary
8. (bottom) Pyrford, Newark Mill (burnt down 1966)

9. (above) Lower Kingswood church, Byzantine capital
10. (right) Ewhurst church, south doorway, c. 1140

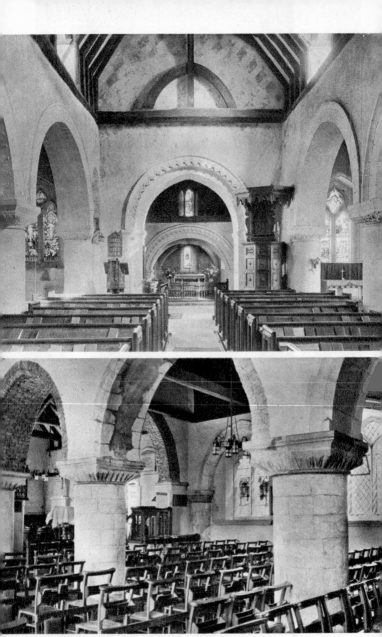

11. (above left) Compton church, *c.* 1180
12. (left) Laleham church, arcade, twelfth century
13. (above) Walton-on-the-Hill church, lead font, *c.* 1150-60

14. (above left) Chipstead church, thirteenth century
15. (below left) Reigate, St Mary, capital, *c.* 1200
16. (above) Chaldon church, wall painting of the Purgatorial Ladder,
c. 1200

17. (above) Coulsdon church, sedilia, thirteenth century
18. (above right) Dunsfold church, pews, thirteenth century
19. (below right) Littleton church, chancel stalls, fifteenth century

20. (above left) Dunsfold church, *c.* 1270
21. (left) Lingfield church, *c.* 1431
22. (above) Littleton church, chancel thirteenth century, tower
sixteenth and eighteenth centuries

23. Farnham Castle, Fox's (really Waynflete's) Tower, 1470-5

24. (above top) Lingfield church, monument to Reginald Lord Cobham
†1361
25. (bottom) Lingfield church, monument to Sir Reginald Cobham
†1446

26. (above left) Charlwood church, screen, *c.* 1480
27. (left) Old Surrey Hall, great hall, *c.* 1450 *(Copyright Country Life)*
28. (above) Thursley church, belfry late fifteenth century

29. Richmond Palace, *c.* 1500

30. Nonsuch, begun 1538

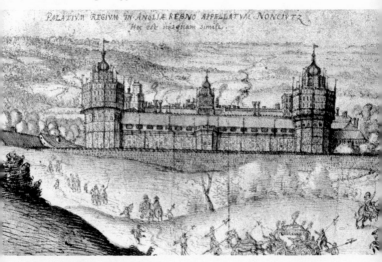

PALATIVM REGIVM IN ANGLIÆ REGNO APPELLATVM NONCIVTZ
Hoc est nequam simile.

31. (above top) Bletchingley, Brewer Street Farmhouse, fifteenth century
32. (bottom) Great Tangley, 1584

33. (above top) Sutton Place, courtyard, *c.* 1530
34. (bottom) Loseley, 1561-9, north front

35. (left) Sutton Place, terracotta panels over the entrance, c. 1530 (*Copyright Country Life*)

36. (below left) Reigate Priory, 'Holbein' fireplace, c. 1540-50 (*Copyright Country Life*)

37. (right) Cheam church, monument to Jane Lady Lumley †1577, designed in 1590

38. (below right) Egham church, monument to Sir John Denham †1638

39. (above) Guildford, Abbot's Hospital, 1619-22
40. (right) Guildford, Abbot's Hospital, doorway

41. (above left) Kew Palace, 1631
42. (below left) West Horsley Place, *c.* 1630 *(Copyright Country Life)*
43. (above top) Pendell House, 1636
44. (bottom) Slyfield Manor, *c.* 1625-40

45. (left) Slyfield
Manor, *c.* 1625-
40, staircase
(*Copyright
Country Life*)

46. (below) Ham
House, staircase,
c. 1637-8

47. (left) Guildford,
Guildhall,
refronted 1683

48. (below) Reigate
Priory, staircase,
c. 1710
(Copyright
Country Life)

49. (above left) Peper Harow church, monument to Sir Thomas
Broderick, by John Bushnell(?), *c.* 1680
50. (left) Gatton church, nave stalls, Flemish, late seventeenth century
51. (above) Bletchingley church, monument to Sir Robert Clayton
†1707, by Richard Crutcher

52. (above) Tadworth Court, *c.* 1700
53. (above right) Shepperton Rectory, façade, *c.* 1700
54. (right) Richmond, Maids of Honour Row, 1724

55. (above left) Petersham, Sudbrook Park, by James Gibbs, 1726, cube
room *(Copyright Country Life)*
56. (left) Carshalton, The Oaks (demolished), *c.* 1770, ballroom
57. (above) Carshalton House, room in the south-west corner, *c.* 1720
(Copyright Country Life)

58. (above) Esher Place, gatehouse, *c.* 1475-80, altered by William Kent
c. 1730
59. (right) Kew, the Pagoda, by Sir William Chambers, 1761

60. (above left) Painshill Park, Gothic Temple, *c.* 1740
61. (left) Gatton Town Hall, 1765
62. (above) Petersham, St Peter, eighteenth-century fittings

63. (left) Ockham
church,
monument to
Peter, first Lord
King, †1734, by
J. M. Rysbrack

64. (below) Walton-
on-Thames,
monument to
Richard Boyle,
by J. F.
Roubiliac, 1755

65. (left) Great
Bookham,
monument to
Cornet Geary
†1776

66. (below) West
Clandon,
Clandon Park,
relief in the
entrance hall, by
J. M. Rysbrack,
c. 1730

67. (left) Richmond, Asgill House, by Sir Robert Taylor, 1760-70
68. (above) Gatton church, gothicized in 1834

69. (above) Deepdene, entrance front, by Thomas Hope and William Atkinson, *c.* 1818

70. (above right) Kew, Palm House, by Richard Turner and Decimus Burton, 1844-8

71. (right) Foxwarren Park, model farm, probably by Frederick Barnes, 1860

72. (above) Dorking, St Martin, by Henry Woodyer, 1868-77
73. (above right) Hascombe church, by Henry Woodyer, 1864
74. (right) Lowfield Heath church, by William Burges, 1867

75. (left) Croydon, St Michael, by J. L. Pearson, designed in 1875-6, built in 1880-3

76. (above top) Reigate, St Mary, monument to Rebecca Waterlow †1869, by Samuel Ruddock

77. (bottom) Beddington church, detail of organ, by Morris & Co., 1869

78. (above left) Royal Holloway College, by W. H. Crossland, 1879-87
79. (left) Holloway Sanatorium, by W. H. Crossland, 1884
80. (above) Charterhouse School, by P. C. Hardwick, 1872

81. (above) Banstead Wood, by R. Norman Shaw, 1884-90

82. (left) Gatton Park, portico, 1891

83. (right) Guildford, Wycliffe Buildings, by H. Thackeray Turner, 1894

84. (below) Shere, well head, 1886

85. (above left) Munstead, Orchards, by Sir Edwin Lutyens, 1897-1900
86. (left) Tigbourne Court, by Sir Edwin Lutyens, 1899-1901
(Copyright Country Life)
87. (above) Pyrford, Vodin, by C. F. A. Voysey, 1902

88. (above left) Crowhurst Place, *c.* 1425, restored by George Crawley *c.* 1920
89. (left) Lower Kingswood church, by Sidney Barnsley, 1891
90. (above) Claremont, The Homewood, by Patrick Gwynne, 1938-9

91. (above left) Gatwick Airport, main block (incomplete), by Yorke, Rosenberg & Mardall, 1958
92. (left) Ham Common, Parkleys Estate, by Eric Lyons, 1954-6
93. (above) Ham Common, Langham House Close, by Stirling & Gowan, 1958

94. (above top) Farnham, West Surrey College of Art and Design, by
Raymond Ash, 1967-9
95. (bottom) Walton-on-Thames, Swimming Pool, by Arup Associates,
1962-5
96. (right) Guildford, University of Surrey, Academic Buildings and
Lecture Theatres, by the Building Design Partnership, 1966-8

97. (above)
Croydon, air
view

98. (left) Sutton,
Civic Offices, by
Owen Luder,
1961-4

sake. In England, unlike Vienna or Weimar, there was no community of spirit between architects and other artists, and the Glasgow school was almost dead. Fry was thrown back on his own critical instincts, and he did what Englishmen have so often done in time of artistic upheaval: he went severely classical. The result is a blunt, four-square block, two storeys plus a big slate mansard roof, containing all the bedrooms. Most of the space below is taken up by an enormous two-storey living hall. The ground rises by half a storey from front to back so that the main (rear) entrance leads on to a neat bit of split-level planning – down a half-storey to the hall and the ground-floor rooms, up the same amount to the first-floor rooms and the hall balcony. This is not merely the careless layout of a Mereworth, with one enormous room for show and the rest filled in anyhow, but a clear-headed attempt to plan simultaneously very large and very small rooms for different moods, something which gives one a good deal of respect for Fry. Clearly he was no woolly-minded art fancier. The outside elevation expressing the hall gives the same feeling of control – brick pilasters, roughcast between, the proportions of the big but small-paned windows worked out exactly,* and just one bit of chequer ornament over the door. No decoration inside except two painted panels facing the main entrance, Matisse-style, and not good; woman by *Vanessa Bell*, nudes by *Duncan Grant*.

Back in the centre, the area E of Quarry Street is a mixture of old cottages and car parks, a familiar story. (Redevelopment is in progress.) CHAPEL STREET has a little to see. Nos. 18–20 are plastered Tudor with an overhang. Opposite is the rustic neo-Baroque front of MILLS, a printery, by *T. J. Capp* of Guildford, 1908. Finally, up Pewley Hill on the Downs is SEMAPHORE HOUSE. It was built in 1821–2 as part of a telegraph line from Portsmouth to Whitehall (*see also* Chatley Heath near Hatchford, p. 308, and Hinchley Wood, Claygate, p. 163). An unpretentious stuccoed house, with an octagonal cupola.

NE of the High Street there is remarkably little. Pre-Victorian building finishes abruptly, with a big dull estate of *c*.1850 beyond. It has houses both Classical and Tudor (e.g.

---

* As exactly as Loos did with his Viennese houses. The underlying *Zeitgeist* was clearly the same: anti-Art-Nouveau, interested in form, not expression, hard, not flowing. Fry may have been copying Mackmurdo's famous Chelsea house here (25 Cadogan Gardens).

CARLTON HOTEL in London Road), and a dull estate church to go with them (CHRIST CHURCH by *Ewan Christian*, 1868). ⟨At the corner of London Road and Cross Lane, IMPERIAL LIFE HOUSE. This consists of an excellently composed and well detailed series of blocks adjoining at r. angles. They form an irregular U around the entrance court, building up from three storeys on the l. to six on the r. The architects are *P. L. Howells* (of Cow & Gate, the former owners) and *Fitzroy Robinson & Partners*, 1963–5. Further N, beyond the by-pass, modern flats by *Katz & Vaughan*, 1959. Since then, much new building, especially around Boxgrove. In Boxgrove Lane two crisp new SCHOOLS in effective contrasting colours: a Primary School by the County Architect, *R. J. Ash*, 1966–7, and a school for sub-normal children by *Leonard Multon & Partners*, 1967–9. The latter has a gay zigzagging gymnasium roof forming a pattern of white lozenges in elevation.⟩
MERROW, see p. 359; BURPHAM, see p. 122.

(D) W of the river

Immediately over the bridge, opposite St Nicholas church, is an untidy tangle of bus station and traffic islands: Guildford has kept its set-pieces intact but at a heavy cost to the ordinary urban fabric. Millmead goes S along the river bank from here, with pleasant industrial buildings and a fine view of the Quarry Street backs, now, alas, at first masked by the self-important bulk of PLUMMERS (by *G. Baines & Syborn*, 1963–7) which stretches from the bridge along the E side of the river. The building is out of scale with its surroundings, and the prim, lifeless river-walk beside it is no compensation. Millmead continues past a tiny cottagey riverside square to MILLMEAD HOUSE (Guildford R.D.C. offices), a house of *c.*1700, terribly altered and added to. The original part is four bays wide, the central first-floor window with an architectural surround. Later C18 attic and porch, multiple C20 alterations and additions. The back is less altered. It has one window with a delightful scrolled and broken pediment above it (not attached to any aedicule frame, just floating), in between the scrolls an urn, and under it a tiny inset of grey brick, a very individual touch, unlike any of the other Guildford houses.*

---

* The other masons to use grey brick as a panel inset instead of as part of an overall chequer or zigzag pattern were the Bastards of Blandford: cf. Coupar House there. But there is no other resemblance.

Parallel with Millmead on the other side of St Nicholas is Bury Street, starting with the CALEB LOVEJOY ALMSHOUSES, spiky-enough and pretty-enough Tudor of 1840. The road bends w to rejoin Portsmouth Road; at the bend is WESTBURY HOUSE, of *c.*1790, plain, of four bays and three storeys (or rather five bays on the ground floor and four on the others) with a big Tuscan Doric porch. Opposite, the big T-shaped offices of the C.E.G.B., by *Braddock & Martin-Smith*, 1960. Terribly bulky. The short uphill arm of Bury Street is superbly closed by one wing of Wycliffe Buildings (*see* below, Portsmouth Road). The s continuation of Bury Street is BURY-FIELDS. More cottages; on the E side a three-bay three-storey early C18 house, then on the w side THE COURT, a big half-H courtyard of houses (fifteen) by *H. Thackeray Turner*, *c.* 1902. Interesting plan, very advanced for the date, but timid Baillie Scott-like detail – a great comedown from Wycliffe Buildings. It looks like a slice of Hampstead Garden Suburb transplanted. Opposite this Nos. 39–41, pretty early C19 Classical, semi-detached, then the HAMBLEDON R.D.C. OFFICES, a sharp slap from the C20 at its worst (by *Coussmaker & Armstrong*, 1938). Beyond again MEAD COTTAGE, by *H. Thackeray Turner*, 1895, only tiny, but a far better building than The Court. It is a deceptively simple L-shaped cottage in Bargate stone, in the style of Wycliffe Buildings.

Straight up the steep hill from the w end of High Street is MOUNT STREET, starting with No. 4 on the E side, of the late C17, with simple recessed patterns in the brickwork, then MOUNT HOUSE, bulky and of *c.*1730. More pre-Victorian cottages further up on the other side (No. 33 etc. working-class early C19), but the total effect spoilt by piecemeal slum clearance without rebuilding. The most notable thing in Mount Street is the superb view of the whole length of High Street and of the town centre. Harvey's store and the car park on Pewley Hill look enormous, and Holy Trinity tower takes its place as the finial to the upward view, which it never does in the High Street itself.

PARK STREET runs N to the station, now with nothing of interest; a fine group of C16 cottages with multiple overhangs and completely authentic plastered fronts was demolished in 1957. They were the best of their type in the county and ought to have been preserved. Beyond, in the station yard, BRIDGE HOUSE, 1959 by *Scott, Brownrigg & Turner*, a seven-storey modern office block, admirably unaffected. Alternate bands of glass and pink granite chippings, no decoration except for 'BRIDGE HOUSE' in bold letters. A very good example of knowing when to stop.

PORTSMOUTH ROAD runs S towards Godalming from the extreme W end of the High Street. The beginning has now lost its earlier character completely. On the E side is the front of the C.E.G.B. offices, on the W a blank, with two plain eleven-storey blocks of flats higher up, by *Scott, Brownrigg & Turner*, 1963–4. Then on the E side WYCLIFFE BUILDINGS, by *H. Thackeray Turner*, 1894, a remarkable set of stone-built flats. Three storeys, on a wedge-shaped site with a steep slope down from the apex at the S end. This has a tower: the sides form splendid compositions of gables and functionally placed windows, without any period detail, but using Voysey's trick of elegant scrolled drainpipe supports. This is the style of the LCC's housing of *c*.1900, but better done and earlier than the famous Millbank Estate. It is up to the best English (hence, at this time, European) work of the nineties. Some of the interior detail just as remarkable – e.g. the stair handrail to Nos. 7–9, with the writhing Art Nouveau spirit applied functionally, not merely as a decorative trick. In horrid contrast, CONDOR COURT next door is contemptible thirties Neo-Georgian.

Opposite this is No. 22, called SWISS COTTAGE, and in fact a pretty Swiss chalet (tile-hung!) of *c*.1840, with curved brackets, ingeniously adapted to a steep site high above the road. Next to this a pair of bulky mid-Georgian houses with bow windows, Nos. 2–4 MOUNT PLEASANT. On the W side several early C19 pairs of speculative Grecian villas, Nos. 61–71, each pair sharing a four-column colonnade. Nos. 73–75 is another villa with battlemented recessed one-bay wings and Gothick windows. No. 79 is plain, three bays with an Ionic porch, but on the garden side four giant pilasters with bold Ionic capitals. Further S there are several levels of C19 speculation, mostly pleasant, including two identical pairs of *c*.1880 by *Norman Shaw*, Nos. 1–4 RECTORY PLACE. They are of his 'middle period', to use a cliché – i.e. in his pretty informal tile-hung style. Three storeys, with the two upper floors overhanging and tile-hung, two single-bay gables on the l. balancing a double bay on the r. Seen together in their carefully arranged prettiness, they seem to be just a gimmick for domestic design, compared with Wycliffe Buildings with its carefully thought-out use of the site. On the same side No. 97, HITHERBURY HOUSE, in exactly the same style, but bigger and more freely

composed; it still looks like what Gordon Cullen has called
an alibi for design.* Then, set back, recent three-storey,
weatherboarded terraces, less fussy than average, by *Scott,
Brownrigg & Turner*, 1965–7. More C19 tile-hung houses
hidden away behind. Another group further s must also be by
Shaw: a tile-hung arched entrance dated 1881 leading to two
asymmetrical cottage ranges perpendicular to the road. Not a
stock solution at all, and hence better. The continuously built-
up area ends with pleasant C18 cottages on the N side of the
mound containing St Catherine's Chapel. Opposite it
BRABOEUF, from outside asymmetrical Victorian Tudor in
Bargate stone, a restrained, competent design. This however
is simply an encasing of a smaller half-timbered manor house
of c.1590, and panelling, moulded ceilings, and fireplaces from
this remain, along with a cramped, plain late C17 staircase.
⟨The house has recently been renovated for the COLLEGE OF
LAW, and a new teaching block added to the s by *Scott, Brownrigg & Turner*, 1965–6. This is a civilized, reticent building
which does not try to compete with the older house. It has a
recessed ground floor in dark brick, and two upper floors with
pale grey spandrels and fascia. Further up the hill the POLICE
DIVISIONAL HEADQUARTERS; with extensive additions by
the County Architect, *R. J. Ash*, now building.⟩ Beyond, s of
the chapel, is OLD FRIARS, of c.1600, half-timbered, with a
complete gable of curved braces making quatrefoils, in the
fashion of Great Tangley Manor. This sort of pattern was
undoubtedly exposed originally.

w of the Portsmouth Road is GUILDOWN, built up c.1900 with
fashionable houses by fashionable architects. THE GRANGE,
Guildown Road, is by *Belcher*, 1902, classical details but
asymmetrical composition; adequate. LITTLE CROFT, near it,
is by *Lutyens*, 1899, small and not inspired, the garden front
pointlessly symmetrical with tiny oriels on the corners, the
entrance side better, with a big doorway of careful brickwork.
Above this LITTLEHOLME, Upper Guildown Road, by
Voysey, 1907, for G. Muntzer, the builder and interior
decorator, a familiar roughcast block with limestone dressings, rather arid, as a lot of his Surrey work is. The cottage
at the back, built in 1911, is simpler and better.

The next road s is Sandy Lane with PICKARDS MANOR on the
N side, a C17 farm with stone s front and two flanking stone

* It was disgracefully remodelled in 1965–6, hardly a detail surviving
unmauled.

barns. It lies on sandstone (although Guildown, a few yards away, is chalk), and this is straightaway reflected in the building material. Beyond, facing south, is PICKARDS ROUGH, 1878 by *Norman Shaw*, and a complete change in materials and quality from his weary tile-hanging near by in the Portsmouth Road. Asymmetrical, in stone and yellow plaster with a big gabled stone projection off-centre. All free Tudor. Great care has been taken to see that masses and details balance without any attempt at imposed design (or any of the elephantine massing common in Shaw's earlier houses). It was converted in 1958 into two houses by the startling expedient of demolishing two bays in the centre, which are linked by a terrace. Extreme care was taken with the surroundings also – enclosed walls on the entrance side, as subtle as a Lutyens forecourt, terraced gardens facing s, including a garden seat with a first-rate tiled panel above of peacocks in rich blue and green. One of Shaw's happiest houses.

GUILDOWN *see* GUILDFORD, pp. 280, 293

HALE

Between Farnham and Aldershot, a queer nest of lanes and C19 brick boxes on a sandy hill with a good view s to Hindhead. ⟨Hale, and Heath End to the N, have expanded rapidly during the sixties. There are two new schools by the County Architect, *Raymond Ash*. UPPER HALE PRIMARY SCHOOL, of 1967–8, is on the hill, with a good view s. Yellow and white details set off by dark brick, an effective contrast with the old village school beside it. HEATH END SECONDARY SCHOOL, E of Farnborough Road, of 1966–8, was planned for 850 children. Long low ranges in dark brick with white fascia, a taller hall behind, one four-storey classroom block; similar components to the school at Knaphill (p. 111) but here better composed on a more spacious site.⟩

ST MARK. 1844 by *Benjamin Ferrey*. Wild neo-Romanesque – the E end with a rose window e.g. and an attached round s tower. With an outside like this one expects fireworks inside, but the Romanesque is sadly only plaster-deep. Buildings like this one and Ferrey's earlier church at Morpeth, Northumberland, may be a shock to those who only know his essays in Gothic. – (STAINED GLASS. E window by *Clayton & Bell*, vivid medallions. – MONUMENT. Beautiful inscription to

Bishop Sumner † 1874, the church's founder, by his grandson *Heywood Sumner*, c.1895. NT)

THE HALLAMS

0040

1½ m. E of Wonersh

Hard, prickly house by *Norman Shaw*, 1894–5, and oddly enough a reversion to the mixed style of Pierrepont and Merrist Wood, midway between half-timbering and tile-hung picturesque-ness. Compact, medium-size, the entrance front with a two-storeyed half-timbered porch balancing one of Shaw's favourite immense bay windows and a big chimneystack rising up flush with the front wall. The garden side, with a good view s, is a simpler affair of half-timbered gables of different sizes at either end of a long tile-hung front with first-floor over-hang. All the detail unsympathetic. Hard, punchy planning inside too, the best thing about the house, commanding respect rather than affection – plenty of ideas but an almost complete lack of feeling in clothing them. The medieval idea of a two-storeyed hall and a screens passage with gallery over is given a new twist here. There is an immense hall with a kingpost roof, but the gallery is extended backwards and the main staircase fitted into the space obtained next to the 'screens passage', which remains as a corridor to the back of the house. The gallery thus extended through becomes the main landing for the upper floor of the house.

HALLIFORD *see* SHEPPERTON

HAM

1070

ST ANDREW, Church Road. 1830–1 by *E. Lapidge*, with a dull s aisle of 1860 by *R. Brandon* and a chancel by *Bodley & Garner*, 1900–1. Lapidge's work is of grey brick, Bodley's of red. Lapidge's front has two polygonal turrets, incorrectly detailed, and lancet-shaped Perp two-light windows. The s aisle has a rose window in its façade.

HAM HOUSE. Ham House is the largest house of its period in Surrey. Externally it is perhaps not as attractive as some in other counties, but internally it has high architectural and decorative interest. The present approach is not right. The original approach was from Ham Common by means of LODGES with Dutch gables which still exist and will be mentioned later, together with the other houses along the common. The C19 approach was from Petersham Road by a spectacular GATEHOUSE which, in its bulk as well as its display of Jacobean forms, makes nonsense of the house, to which it should be no more than an introduction. It is a typical Victorian attitude to try and outdo the historic building in terms of historicism. The gatehouse is said to date from as late as *c.*1900. Its architect seems unrecorded.

The entrance to the house is from the N. It has here a forecourt with side walls decorated with niches for busts and gatepiers to the river Thames across which, at Twickenham, Marble Hill is, and Orleans House was, visible. In the middle of the forecourt stands a *Coade* stone figure of Father Thames by *John Bacon.**

The plan of the house is roughly an oblong, with two wings projecting not quite at the end, to the N. But this is not the original plan. The house was first built by Sir Thomas Vavasour in 1610. It had then, as we know from one of John Smithson's drawings, an H-plan of the usual Elizabethan and Jacobean type. This plan can still be traced now; for all that was done later is to fill in the space between the S arm of the H and lengthen the S façade a little at both ends. This work belongs to the years 1673–5, but substantial and historically very remarkable alterations had been made before. About 1630 the house came into the hands of William Murray, first Earl of Dysart. Of the work undertaken for him, chiefly in 1637–8, as well as of that executed for his daughter and her husband, the Duke of Lauderdale, we are uncommonly well informed by bills, etc., happily preserved.

Externally the carcase of the building is Vavasour's, but with alterations of 1673–5 and the C18. It is of brick with stone dressings, three storeys high, and has a hipped roof. The N front has a five-bay centre twice recessed. The first step is of two bays depth and one bay width, open on the ground floor in arches. Originally there were turrets here, ending in ogee caps. The second, outer step has at its front a canted bay window. The principal doorway is in the middle. It has attached Tuscan columns and a metope frieze and is not a specially impressive piece. Originally this doorway was the entrance to a square porch continued above by a two-storeyed bay. The windows are of the cross type, except for the canted bays, where they have been given C18 shapes. They were here in the C17

* For another cast *see* Terrace Gardens Richmond, p. 440.

mullioned and transomed. Between ground floor and first floor
oval niches were made c.1673–5 and filled with busts, the same
motif as we have found in the forecourt walls. The s front is
entirely of 1673–5, except for the canted bay windows of the
H-wings of 1610 and the Venetian windows above them which,
like the sashing of all other windows, belong to the c18.

For the interior we can follow more or less the route pre-
scribed in the excellent guidebook.* The GREAT HALL is, in
accordance with its date, 1610, in the asymmetrical position
which was the English Gothic and Tudor tradition. All its
motifs, however, are later. The s windows of 1610 were
blocked when the s rooms were added. The room above, which
was the Dining Room, was thrown into one with it in the early
c18, when the gallery with its pretty balusters was made. The
plaster ceiling however is the first instance of the remarkably
progressive style adopted by William Murray in his alterations.
It dates from 1637 or 1638 and was made by *Joseph Kinsman*.
It is entirely in the new Inigo Jones style of e.g. the Queen's
House at Greenwich, with panels, oblong, oval, and otherwise,
framed by wreaths, guilloche, etc.

Adjacent on the E is the STAIRCASE, also rebuilt about 46
1637–8. It is of wood and rises through two storeys with a
spacious open well. It is as progressive as the hall ceiling; for
instead of the usual balusters and the usual strapwork decoration it has a balustrade with oblong openwork panels decorated
with rich trophies. The newel-posts are so decorated too, and
carry very handsome baskets of fruit. All this clearly heralds
the type of staircase which became popular for greater houses
about 1660. The plaster ceiling (again by *Kinsman*) is in the
most restrained style of Inigo. The doorcases on the other
hand, and this is specially noteworthy, are in the curious
mannered style which was current among some architects and
craftsmen about 1630–60 and has been called 'Artisan Mannerism' (cf. e.g. Thorpe Hall Soke of Peterborough, Wisbech
Castle Cambridgeshire, Tyttenhanger Hertfordshire, all of the
1650s). Their somewhat fantastic ears and broken pediments
are unmistakable. These doorcases are by *Thomas Carter*, a
joiner, and it seems a little doubtful whether he should be
regarded as the designer of the stair balustrade as well.

In the South Apartments the most interesting detail is the
paintings in the WHITE CLOSET, which have been attributed

* Victoria and Albert Museum, 1950 and later. By R. Edwards and P. Ward
Jackson.

convincingly to *Antonio Verrio*, who came to England from Paris about the year 1672.

One of the most important lessons to be learnt at Ham House is the difference between plasterwork of the 1630s at its most progressive and plasterwork of the 1670s in the then accepted style. To make these comparisons one ought to study the rooms on the first floor. Of William Murray's time are the NORTH DRAWING ROOM, immediately W of the hall gallery, and the LONG GALLERY which runs through the whole W arm of the H of 1610. In the latter the most remarkable motif is the extremely refined Ionic pilasters (by *Carter*), decorated between the volutes of the capitals with dainty garlands. The North Drawing Room has another Jonesian plaster ceiling by *Kinsman*, doorcases even more crazily elaborate than those of the staircase (by *Carter*), and a boldly Baroque fireplace surround with twisted and spiral-fluted columns of stucco, *à la* Bernini's recent baldacchino at St Peter's, or rather *à la* Raphael's Cartoon with the Healing of the Lame Man. Inorganically above these columns big, fat scrolls. In addition playful putti, nearly full-round, clambering about the frame of the picture over the mantelshelf – a surprisingly merry *tour de force*. Of the same date also is the small MINIATURE ROOM next to the North Drawing Room. Here the coving and ceiling are painted by *Francis Cleyn*. Cleyn also painted the inset pictures in the North Drawing Room.

The South Apartments on the first floor have plaster ceilings of *c*.1675. It is evident that they are still essentially dependent on Inigo Jones's innovations of 1620–30, but that these are now treated much more lightly. The detail is busier and finer than in the work of 1638. There are also big acanthus scrolls in some places, a motif which is not to be found in the earlier work. The examples to be studied are in the Blue Drawing Room, the Queen's Bedchamber, and the Queen's Closet. In the Queen's Closet the fireplace is of scagliola, that is stucco treated to look like marble. It constitutes one of the earliest uses of scagliola in England. The technique had been introduced in Italy early in the C17, and John Evelyn says in 1664 that it was still unknown in England.[*] In the same rooms excellent woodwork, too, notably the overmantel in the Blue Drawing Room.

FURNITURE. The house contains much of its original furniture. It is of high quality and high interest but can here,

* See R. B. Wragg, *Country Life*, vol. 122, p. 718.

according to the programme of *The Buildings of England*, find no place.

STABLES. To the w of the house, dated 1787 inside, but built with the use of some old materials.

GARDENS. These were landscaped by *Repton*, as he says in his 'Fragments' of 1816.

HAM COMMON. Ham Common and the adjacent streets have a variety of interesting and enjoyable buildings, old and new. First the N side. To the E of Petersham Road SUDBROOK LODGE, late C17, of five bays and two and a half storeys with hipped roof, and then ORMELEY LODGE, an exquisite early C18 house of five bays and two and a half storeys, the five-bay width composed in a nice rhythm. Slender segment-headed windows. At the angles giant pilasters. Beautiful doorway with Corinthian pilasters and a frieze carved with cherubs' heads and palm leaves. The windows above the doorway singled out by brick ears and an apron. Lower wings. Outstandingly fine wrought-iron gatepiers, gates, and railings. Through the doorway one enters at once the staircase hall, which cuts through the house to the garden entrance. The staircase has delicate balusters, for each step two twisted and one ornamentally turned, and carved tread-ends. Continuing to the E along Park Road towards the Ham Gate of Richmond Park (*see* p. 442), the last house on the r. is PARK GATE HOUSE, of yellow brick, 1768.

Then to the w of Petersham Road, all facing the common. First SOUTH LODGE, built in 1862–72 as the National Orphan Home for Girls. Yellow brick, Late Classical, with a central turret in the Italianate style. Tall centre and lower wings. Then ORFORD HALL, early C18, and after that the two LODGES to Ham House, three bays, with the middle one projecting and crowned by a Dutch gable. Then SELBY HOUSE, of five bays and two and a half storeys, red and rubbed brick. Arched ground-floor windows, parapet.

Turn r. to the N up HAM STREET. On the l. Nos. 57 and 59, two excellent one-storeyed flat-roofed houses of 1952–4, by *Stefan Buzas*. The position is not conducive to appreciation, but the design is crisp and impressive. In SANDPITS ROAD a terrace of five houses by *Eric Lyons*, yellow brick and tile-hung, as precisely and attractively drawn as his Parkleys Estate (*see* below), and in SANDY LANE a modern house by *M. Howard-Radley*, 1957, rather *outré*, with an overhanging weatherboarded upper storey of trapezoidal section.

Then back into the past with a farm on the l., then BEAUFORT HOUSE, and opposite first GREY COURT, late C18, and then the MANOR HOUSE, yellow and red brick of c.1780 with three-bay pediment. After that the grounds of Ham House.

Now the w side of Ham Common. Five houses ought to be noticed. From N to S: ENSLEIGH LODGE, a cottage with lower wings with a double-curved top to reach the walls of the cottage and two solid wood fanlights. Then GORDON HOUSE, C18, of five bays, grey brick, with canted bays in the two end elevations. Then some cottages, and after that FORBES HOUSE, by *Oswald P. Milne*, 1936, an unusually good piece of Neo-Georgian design. LANGHAM HOUSE is again C18, simply, of grey brick, with Tuscan porch; below it LANGHAM
93 HOUSE CLOSE, by *Stirling & Gowan*, 1958, a landmark in the emerging style of the late 1950s in England, in reaction against all-glass façades and thin, precise detailing: two- and three-storey with exposed concrete floors, a lot of yellow brick, and thick white-painted trim to the windows. There is probably more protest than is needed for the simple provision of a few flats. This is of course natural in an early commission, but for all that the attitude is far too common amongst this generation of designers. Finally, the CASSEL HOSPITAL is early C19 and especially good. Five bays and broad one-bay wings with tripartite windows with fan-lunettes. Roman Doric porch. Arched ground-floor windows. Nice entrance hall with at its back the staircase curving up in a bow. Thin iron balustrade.
92 The end is the PARKLEYS ESTATE, the most refreshing housing of the fifties in Surrey. By *Eric Lyons*, 1954–6. A total of 168 flats, built by private enterprise – a tenants' association. Two- and three-storeyed blocks, all crisply and quite light-heartedly treated. Shopping terrace in UPPER HAM ROAD. The first floor projecting and with a band of balconies. The second floor recedes again. Behind, two-storeyed terraces and small H-shaped three-storeyed blocks all of the same plan. Centre with glazed front reached by a long narrow canopied passage. Lobby and staircase behind the glass wall. In each wing two flats on each floor. All the houses are flat-roofed and nicely coloured. Yellow brick. Tile-hanging and odd coloured surfaces. Opposite, and far from refreshing, the huge, reactionary brick and stone front to HAWKER AIRCRAFT COMPANY, by *Sir Hubert Worthington* and *Norman & Dawbarn*, 1958. The style was an odd choice to house the manufacture of the most modern jet aircraft. Close to Parkleys, in HAM FARM ROAD

a good house by *L. Gooday*, with a low-pitched gable and one side of the roof much larger and lower than the other. Built in 1956. ⟨Further E, by the river, is RIVERSIDE, a large Wates estate of 1961–8. In the centre well-detailed shops and flats by *M. McQuisten* of *Wates*; church and school by *Covell, Matthews & Partners*. The rest, and especially the planning of the roads, less satisfactory.⟩

FOOTBRIDGE to Teddington. Iron, of lattice girder type to the island, of suspension type across the river. By *G. Pooley*, 1888.

HAMBLEDON
3 m. s of Godalming

9030

A scattered village, five or six fragments and no real centre; church and farmhouse by themselves, small village green further s, and another group to the N. The group of church, tile-hung Court Farm, and tile-hung granary is very picturesque, spoilt only by over-obtrusive Victorianisms which would be easy to soften.

ST PETER. All rebuilt in 1846 and not an attractive job, though using local stone and in local style. Shingled w bellcote, clean, empty interior. – PLATE. Paten 1691, London work.
w of the village the nucleus of the former UNION WORKHOUSE is of 1786, in the thick mansard-roofed brick style which seems to be typical of Surrey C18 industrial buildings. Several other minor buildings scattered about the parish. 1 m. SE is LOWER VANN, a mixture of C16, C17, and C20 (N end) all melted together with creeper to form a perfect prototype for Lutyens's houses. To the NE is MAREPOND FARM, with good stone and weather-boarded barns. To the N is HYDESTILE, with a few more pretty cottages and stone barns. Between Hambledon and Hydestile are *Ernest Newton*'s dull Neo-Georgian FEATHERCOMBE of 1910, and THE GLEBE HOUSE, a big gabled stone house of five bays with brick dressings. Plain and not very interesting except that it is dated – 1710 – and shows the transition in ordinary building between the gabled basically Tudor house and the pattern-book C18 house.

HAMPTON LODGE
1 m. SE of Seale

9040

The house was by *Porden*, 1798, a small Picturesque villa. It was altered out of all recognition *c*.1860 with mansard roofs, the original ground floor just legible, with Doric porch and simple arched windows. The park however is quite untouched, a superb bit of Repton-style gardening, probably the best in Surrey. It is not spectacular, but everything is mature and beautifully composed. Typically, the house faces a romantic wooded bluff.

HAMSEY GREEN *see* WARLINGHAM

HARTSWOOD MANOR *see* REIGATE

0030   ## HASCOMBE

A sequestered village in a fold of the sandstone hills SE of Godalming. Houses mainly stone and tile-hung. No memorable group, but a strong sense of locality and remoteness rare in the county. There are actually many biggish country houses of *c*.1900 around – the parish is next to Munstead – but they do not obtrude.

73 ST PETER. By *Woodyer*, 1864, and worth a very special look to see how good and how free from period associations a Victorian country church could be when the architect took pains over it.* Woodyer himself was an uneven architect, but this is one of his best buildings. Bargate stone, aisleless and apsed, with shingled bellcote and an independently roofed S chapel, of just the right proportion. The style is simplified late C13. All the details are worth notice, e.g. the way in which a string course ties together all the lancets in the S chapel (a Woodyer mannerism), so that it is effectively differentiated from the rest of the building. Some roguish details also – e.g. the E lancet in the apse appearing in the middle of a buttress. Impressive inside too, a rarer thing, with a complete mid-Victorian scheme of decoration which is worth careful preservation: high and dark, with sombre gilding round the deep apse and an ornamental effect as rich as anything that Art Nouveau produced. All the roof rafters in the apse are cusped and gilded, so that there is a continuous interplay of highlights. Deep E lancet made up into a rich composition, with the wall surface around it used as the reredos; stencilling and carved angel candle-holders: Butterfield's style done with

---

* This is a big qualification, and it would be silly to pretend that more than a very few Victorian country churches are worth looking at in this way.

more humanity. The nave was only decorated in 1890, so the original scheme was a plain nave with an elaborate chancel (D. Lloyd). – FONT. A queer square bowl of 1690 on a crude square stem. – ROOD SCREEN. Originally Perp, now all 1864. Covered with pretty decoration applied with a very sure hand by *Hardman & Powell* – the painting of the uprights e.g. – although the figures in the lower panels are sickly and sentimental. Rich colour pattern – scarlet, grass-green, brown, and gold. – STAINED GLASS. In the apse, bright and fitting the general effect. Also by *Hardman & Powell*. – MONUMENT. William Middlefield † 1785, by *T. Hews*. Attractive big tablet, halfway between Palladian strictness and sentimentality. Female and urn above, inscription in elegant script below, relief of angels below that. A lot of its charm is that the carving is slightly rough, almost that of a local mason, not polished and mechanical.

Of the vernacular houses, the unbelievably picturesque quad of WINKWORTH FARM is worth a look – it is beside the main road ½ m. N of the church – for the complete fusion of nature and landscape. (The centre of the farmhouse is C16 half-timber, and the sides of the quad were originally barns. Many alterations, however, have heightened the effect: remodelling of the barn on the r. by *Lutyens*, 1895 (planting by *G. Jekyll*); additions to the back of the main house by Lutyens's pupil *J. D. Coleridge*, c.1908; internal remodelling and the pretty spiral steps down from the road by *F. W. Troup*, 1914. Weatherboarding removed from the barn on the l. and brick-nogging added, 1962. The garden was enhanced by the post-1918 owner, *Dr Fox*, the creator of the Winkworth Arboretum (National Trust) up the hill. NT)

Some of *Lutyens*'s earliest work was done at Hascombe. His pair of lodges of 1890 at PARK HATCH, ¾ m. S, reflects the influence of his master Ernest George's Onslow Almshouses (*see* p. 280). HOE FARM, W of the church, is a good C15 farmhouse remodelled in the C17; *Lutyens* added the dining-room wing, c.1892, and the delightfully intricate staircase, with two arms which meet at a half-landing and then separate again. On the ridge, above Winkworth Farm, is a whole neighbourhood of wealthy houses on private roads. SULLING-STEAD, now High Hascombe, is of 1896–7 by *Lutyens* (long, low, and tile-hung) with a clever Neo-Georgian ballroom added in 1903; good *Jekyll* garden. WHINFOLD of 1897–8 is also tile-hung, but by *Sir Robert Lorimer*, Lutyens's Scots

equivalent, with a similar Neo-Georgian drawing room added
in 1903, this time by *Sir Walter Tapper*. Traces of a *Jekyll*
garden. HIGH BARN is also by *Lorimer*, 1901–3, and is
interesting as a whole-hearted attempt to imitate Lutyens's
style at Orchards (*see* p. 378). Lorimer's detailing is excellent,
but the composition is stiff and lacks Lutyens's sense of pene-
tration: for example, the pretty loggia on the garden side has
only a flat plaster ceiling where Lutyens would have vaulted it.
HASCOMBE COURT is by Lutyens's pupil *J. D. Coleridge*,
1906–7, with a fine Bargate stone entrance front in his
master's manner, but a sloppy garden front of half-timber;
another splendid *Jekyll* garden. HIGHLEYBOURNE and
WINKWORTH HANGER are competent tile-hung houses by
Lutyens's builder *Thomas Underwood*.*

s of the village is LOXHILL, with a good typical stone farm,
MARWICK FARM, completely asymmetrical in elevation and
roof-line.

1½ m. N is THORNCOMBE STREET, charmingly remote in a
steep sandstone valley, but with little of strictly architectural
interest: several C16–C17 cottages, THORNCOMBE PARK
with a five-bay stucco front of *c*.1830, and SLADE'S FARM
with a four-bay brick front of *c*.1720.

HASCOMBE HILL CAMP. An Iron Age hill camp, occupying
approximately 5¾ acres, on a high steep hill commanding the
heathy terrain of s Godalming. Associated with the larger forts
of Holmbury and Anstiebury (*see* Coldharbour), it is of
similar promontory type. The three sides of the hill on which it
is situated supplied a natural barrier to enemy access and
required only to be provided with a single additional ditch.
The exposed N face was fortified by means of a single rampart
and fosse, 120 yards in length. An entrance on the NE side may
be original. The site was probably constructed by members of
the non-Belgic Wealden Culture.

9030

HASLEMERE

A small town on the Sussex border, remote until the late C19,
when it became an Arts and Crafts centre (with the Dolmetsch
workshops, e.g.). Inevitably now a little arty-and-crafty. T-
shaped centre with the Town Hall in the middle. Little townscape. The impressive thing around Haslemere is the extreme

* This paragraph is greatly indebted to further information from N T.

subtlety with which late C19 houses are fitted in to the hilly, romantic landscape.

St Bartholomew. Tower probably C13, with a post-Reformation Gothic top (simple two-light lancet windows) under a pyramidal cap. The rest a hopeless Victorian rebuilding of 1871 in the E.E. style, by *J. W. Penfold*. – FONT. 1870 and looks it. Circular bowl on four columns and a central pillar, all with fat capitals, the whole thing in polished black and red marble. The richness of the materials and unselfconscious handling is what takes it out of the ruck of Victorian church furnishings. – STAINED GLASS. Two Flemish C17 panels in the W window. – Tennyson memorial window, N aisle, designed by *Burne-Jones*. – (TAPESTRY in front of the organ. Choir of angels. By *Morris & Co*.) – MONUMENTS. Capt. Charles Lydiard† 1807. Mourning female, urn, naval trophies. Very long and thin, a fraction above average. – (James Stuart Hodgson. A very large and ugly wall-monument with three angels, signed *P. Cockerell* and *A. Fabrucci*, 1899.)

St Christopher, St Christopher's Road, between Haslemere and Shottermill. 1902 by *Charles Spooner*. The outside is worth a look. Free Late-Gothic, as so many Surrey churches are, but done carefully, not as a matter of routine – compare e.g. the church at Hindhead two miles away. This shows in the proportions with low attached S tower and long nave roof without clerestory, and in the materials – galletted Bargate stone, with occasional chequerboard patterns. What was missing was any form of religious conviction, and hence the interior is pathetic, a single white-painted wagon-roofed space, faintly pretty in the manner of Sir Charles Nicholson. N chapel 1935.

St Stephen, Shottermill. Lancet Gothic of 1838, with a dumpy tower. In local Weald stone and mercifully still in some sort of vernacular. Enlarged in 1876 by *J. W. Penfold* (GS).

⟨Our Lady of Lourdes (R.C.), Weydown Road. 1924 by *F. A. Walters*. Tall chancel with effective clerestory lighting, lower nave and N aisle. E.E. in style.⟩

Town Hall. Rebuilt in 1814. The date is barely credible, because this looks like a perfect example of the late C17 vernacular public building – two storeys with the ground floor originally open, homely brick elevations under a tiny homely brick pediment, a big coved cornice with pretty ironwork brackets. This is a remarkable reminder of just how remote parts of Surrey remained until the railways came.

From the Town Hall three streets lead out: High Street to the N, Lower Street to the W, Petworth Road to the E. Very little in HIGH STREET. Near the Town Hall the WHITE HORSE HOTEL, a simple five-bay Palladian front of c.1740. Further N on the E side there is a very pretty group of cottages, Nos. 72-74, which looks unselfconscious and is in fact the result of very careful calculation by the architect (whom?) of part of No. 72, now the NATIONAL PROVINCIAL BANK, a late C19 tile-hung front, partly recessed, worthy of Norman Shaw himself. On the W side there are two big Georgian houses, both five bays and three storeys: the GEORGIAN HOTEL, perhaps of c.1740, with a very naïve front and stuck-on joinery details including a central broken pediment, and TOWN HOUSE, two very handsome storeys of c.1725, with segmental windows and a noble Doric doorcase, the third storey added c.1800 without much feeling for proportion.

The other streets of Haslemere are very much alike, with cosy tile-hung buildings. PETWORTH ROAD has Nos. 31-35 on the S side, one big L-shaped mid-C17 block, brick and stone below and tile-hung above. LOWER STREET has one pretty terrace of tile-hung houses (Nos. 29-35 on the S side) and a C17 tile-hung cottage on the N side in authentic condition (No. 56, YEW TREE COTTAGE). Further W, near the station, an ashlar stone cottage, a rarity for the county (TUDOR HOUSE). Simple, early C17, with hood-moulds over the first-floor windows. Running S from Lower Street is SHEPHERDS HILL, with the best bit of domestic building in the town, Nos. 9-29, terraced high above the road in the Surrey way. Here, each period expresses itself quite naturally – late C17 tile-hanging, late C18 brick, early C19 stucco, and Victorian brick and stone – and achieves harmony by respecting the street line. The terrace runs up a steep hill and is curved as well, a noble and complex effect.

Finally, next to the church, ½ m. NW of the town centre, is CHURCH HILL HOUSE, a simple, five-by-two-bay early C18 brick front with stone gatepiers. The porch is later, probably of c.1910.

Haslemere has dozens of late C19 country houses, nearly all of them hidden from view by their thick natural landscaping. A list of the worthwhile ones must be very incomplete. To the

E of the Hindhead road beyond Shottermill are HONEY-HANGER and HILDERS, now BRANKSOME HILDERS, both by *E. J. May c.*1900, both with elevations designed to fit the sunlight and the view SW from their ridge, both tile-hung and half-timbered, very hard to dislike. Further up the same slopes towards Hindhead is *Voysey's* NEW PLACE, built in 1897, a good and very typical Voysey house. Long and low, roughcast and slate-roofed, not small enough to look over-designed, not so big that Voysey felt bound to complicate the severe lines with extra details, as he did at Norney; very successful. There used to be a similarly direct GARDEN SEAT, now destroyed, and the same feeling is evident in the GARAGE at the entrance – one segmental arch under a big steep gable. *Gertrude Jekyll* collaborated on the garden. Also by *Voysey* a LODGE next to the garage, and a pair of COTTAGES in Polecat Lane, W of the house. The latter, of 1903, look a good deal altered.

N of the church, in Weydown Road, is BALLINDUNE, another house by *E. J. May*, this time of 1905. In the interval the model has become Lutyens rather than Norman Shaw: complex plan with several blocks of varying heights, in very free Georgian. S of the town, in Hill Road, off Midhurst Road, BROAD DENE of *c.*1900 by *Unsworth, Son & Triggs* is tile-hung on a Weald stone base, with a front right on the road, an unusual thing in Haslemere. Not bad, though a little contrived – e.g. the stone semicircular stair-turret. Beyond this, in Scotland Lane, is RED COURT, by *Ernest Newton*, 1894, an ominous house with sterile Neo-Georgianism just round the corner. Here the lodge is entirely classical and the house has segmental windows combined with gables in an acid way. The fundamental and fatal pettiness of scale and detail is already evident – the opposite of Voysey's ability to give scale to any size of building. It is historically important (*see* also Ardenrun near Crowhurst) because it was built four years before Lutyens's first classical elevation at Crooksbury.

Finally, ¾ m. SE of the centre, on the N slopes of Blackdown, is LYTHE HILL, a big, formidably ugly neo-Tudor house in very red brick with all the mouldings flattened out. It was the work of *F. P. Cockerell*, 1868, a sad building for any son of C. R. Cockerell to put up. Good late C19 landscaped grounds. See p. 598 E again is LYTHE HILL HOTEL, quite an impressive half-timbered house. Two-storeyed block, C15 or early C16, the centre slightly recessed in the Kentish way. At the E end has been added a bigger and more ornate wing of the late C16, the whole of the first floor and gable end ornamented with the local style of curved diagonal braces inside square framing so that the overall pattern is a grid of circles superimposed on a grid of squares. Some ornamental diagonal framing on the ground floor also.

HATCHFORD

0050

2 m. SW of Cobham

ST MATTHEW. Built by the Earls of Ellesmere, who lived at Hatchford Park. Nave 1850, chancel 1859 by *Francis & Sons* and bad. Similar work, though much more of it, was put by Lord Ellesmere into Worsley church near Manchester.

(HATCHFORD MAUSOLEUM, Wisley Common. Domed temple with Doric columns between rusticated arches, erected for Sir Bernhard Samuelson in 1906. His large copper table tomb signed by *Sir G. Frampton* was stolen from it in 1961 (SAC vol 59, 1962).)

(Off Pointers Road, N of Hatchford Park, CHATLEY HEATH SEMAPHORE HOUSE, the most interesting survivor of the line of semaphore houses from Portsmouth to Whitehall, built in 1821–2 to replace the wooden stations erected during the Napoleonic Wars. It is a five-storey octagonal tower, cement-rendered, with one-storey wings on each side. (*See also* Pewley Hill Guildford, p. 289, and Hinchley Wood near Claygate, p. 163.) Also off Pointers Road, CHATLEY FARM, a C16 timber-framed house with an C18 brick façade. G. Wilson; MHLG)

ROMAN BATH HOUSE. At Chatley Farm, on the E side of Ockham Common, is the site of a Late Roman bath house, excavated in 1942. A third of the building has been destroyed by the Mole, but it is clear that, as at Ashtead, it was isolated from any other structure, though there may be a nearby villa as yet undiscovered. The bath house had the usual cold (*frigidarium*), warm (*tepidarium*), hot (*caldarium*), and sweating (*sudatorium*) rooms. The *sudatorium* was converted somewhat crudely, at a late stage, into a boiler house. The occupation material included local pottery, perhaps from the Farnham hills, and tiles, perhaps salvaged from Ashtead (destroyed in the C3 A.D.). The bath house was in use mainly in the C4 A.D.; it ceased to be used *c.*360, perhaps because of the first Saxon incursions.

HATCHLANDS
Between East Clandon and West Horsley

Built in 1756-7 by Admiral Boscawen with prize money obtained
from his victories over the French, and decorated by *Robert
Adam* as his first commission after coming back from Italy and
Dalmatia. It is somewhat difficult to imagine a service chief
of the nineteen-fifties giving the job to Powell & Moya.
Boscawen built a Palladian house almost without ornamental
detail – only a pinched pediment on the w front and plain bow
windows on the s and e – in beautiful vermilion brick,* possibly to his own designs. His planning was quite ingenious,
with constant changes of floor level, and this provides the only
remarkable feature of the exterior – that the w front has three
storeys and the s front has two. So reasonable are the elevations
that the eye accepts this juxtaposition at the s w corner without any uneasiness. Some of the minor woodwork and plasterwork inside is possibly pre-Adam – perhaps the original parts
of the staircase panelling e.g. – for the carcase was finished by
the time Adam came on the scene; his designs, preserved in
the Soane Museum, are dated 1759. Adam was then thirty and
had been in Italy for four years, exploring Spalato and
designing vast compositions full of the 'movement' he so
much admired in the Neo-Classic style then being worked out
in France and in Rome. He was prevented from putting up
such vast compositions until very late in life, in Edinburgh.
His reputation was based on his interiors and particularly on
his ability to translate 'movement' from exterior composition
to interior space, to the composition of a room and to the
spatial sequence of a suite of rooms. This idea, and the light
decorative style of plasterwork which he invented to express
it, formed gradually in Adam's mind. It was fully developed
by the mid 1760s (Osterley and Syon), and it was already
clear in Harewood of 1760–1. But here at Hatchlands there
are only hints of the future Adam. The style is a mixture of
Palladian geometry and a quite new prettiness of detail.

Later alterations must be mentioned first. About 1790
Bonomi was called in and made recommendations described
by Goodhart-Rendel in his admirable guide as 'extraordinarily gauche and disagreeable, even for Bonomi'. Most of them
were not carried out, and all that now remains is an oversize

---

* Repton urgently recommended in a Red Book that the house should be
painted white; it must have seemed horrifyingly raw to the late c18.

pilastered doorway to the w front, niches in the entrance hall behind it, and a colossal and incredibly insensitive window to light the stair-well, replacing the familiar Venetian type. In 1889 the main entrance was moved to the E front and a good restrained neo-Wren porch was built here by *Halsey Ricardo*. Shortly afterwards the staircase was given a face-lift, and in 1903 a single-storey Music Room was added to the N side by *Sir Reginald Blomfield*. The outside is a beautifully detailed essay in Wren's Hampton Court style, with swags and niches; the inside has a heavy circle of columns and a dome inscribed in it and is overdone. Mr *Goodhart-Rendel* succeeded to the house in 1913 and gave it to the National Trust in 1945. Besides removing some Bonomi details that he could no longer bear to live with, he built a pair of pyramid-roofed LODGES to the E in West Horsley village.

To go back to the Adam interiors, the visitor enters through a small entrance hall of 1889. On his r. is the DINING ROOM, with a C20 ceiling adapting the design of the destroyed Alcove Bedroom on the first floor and a good original fireplace bearing a first-rate relief of a dog. On his l. is the LIBRARY, with both ceiling and fireplace undoubtedly by Adam. The fireplace has rams'-heads and key ornament alternating, and uses the same delicate buff and white polychrome marble as the others in the house. The ceiling has a Maltese cross pattern with very pretty reliefs of Justice, Time, etc. It is the nearest approach in the house to the typical Adam style, particularly in the window bay, which has one of the fan-shapes that became an Adam trademark, plus urns and a figure of Britannia in low relief. Incidentally the colouring throughout the house – largely in pastel pinks and greens – is of 1889 and conjectural. Beyond is the STAIRCASE, rising up three sides of a big square well. The railing is metal, to an ugly, half-Chinese pattern. It is certainly C18 but more likely to be due to Bonomi than Adam. Behind is Bonomi's vast window: above is a ceiling which is still purely Palladian in design and may be pre-Adam. The walls here carry pretty and convincing plasterwork of *c.*1900 (whom by?), but the plain mouldings of the main panels are original. On the l. is the DRAWING ROOM, the biggest room in the house. It has what must be an Adam ceiling, although no designs for it now exist, with a characteristic oval central ornament in an irregular octagon. In the old style are the trails of foliage making formal patterns between octagon and outer walls; in the new, the honeysuckle pattern in the octagon, another fan motif in the bay window, and the elegant reliefs of sea-horses and dolphins.* Adam designed plasterwork for the wall panels but this was never executed, although some rough setting-out still exists under the present silk coverings. The fireplace is much grander and less successful than the others in the house. It is all of white marble with big caryatid figures of Night and Morning at the sides. Beyond the stair-well is the old entrance hall, with a simple original ceiling and side niches by Bonomi. On the l. is the MORNING ROOM, with another pretty polychrome fireplace. The ceiling was never decorated. On the first floor a few more simple ceilings and fireplaces.

By strict standards the Hatchlands interiors must inevitably seem unsatisfactory. Adam was merely embroidering a suite of rooms, and his decorative manner is very uncertain; his next commission, at Shardeloes in Buckinghamshire, showed a great advance in technique and originality. Perhaps the most interesting thing is how he came to get the job.‡

HAXTED

4040

A hamlet on the Kent border, w of Edenbridge. OLD EAST HAXTED is a very restored C15 hall-house with a five-bay early C19 stock-brick house (WEST HAXTED HOUSE) added on the w side.§ DWELLY FARM is L-shaped, the rear wing of the C16, timber-framed and tile-hung, the front early C18, brick and tile-hung. HAXTED (Water-) MILL is late C18 industrial architecture, uncommon in Surrey. It is weather-boarded with a two-gabled mansard roof and tile-hung mill house next door – a charming group.

HEADLEY

2050

High up on the North Downs at the back of Box Hill, with Epsom grandstand prominently in the view N. Not yet really

---

* Dolphins like those on the Admiralty Screen in Whitehall, another very early Adam work and presumably one obtained via Boscawen. *Spang*, who carved the screen, may therefore have worked at Hatchlands also.

‡ John Newman suggests that the answer may be that Adam was introduced to Boscawen by his friend Gilbert Elliot of Minto, a Scotsman who *c.*1758 was an Admiralty official in London.

§ Mr Arthur Oswald gives the following traditional explanation, which is so odd that it must be true: it was originally one house, which was left to two brothers who were on bad terms and divided it up. One went to the Napoleonic Wars and could not afford improvements; the other prospered and refronted his part, which is dated 1805.

suburbanized: still a lot of the old quiet flint-hamlet character, though some has gone recently, notably from the village pub.

ST MARY. A harsh conjunction: nave and chancel 1855 by *Salvin* and appalling; tower 1859 by *Street* and not bad, if hard – awkward Early Gothic with a shingled broach-spire, obviously sincere. – (MONUMENTS. Two painted C17 tablets in the vestry, to Elizabeth Leate † 1680 and Margaret Warren † 1675. VCH)

HEADLEY COURT to the N is a big neo-Jacobean house by *E. P. Warren*, *c*.1910. It has the same mechanical approach as in big Victorian country houses, but the detailing is more deft. Inside, a lot of genuine imported C17 woodwork, e.g. the ceiling in the Billiard Room and the bedroom panelling from a house in St Ives, Hunts.

See p. 598 To the S, near the edge of the Downs, HEADLEY GROVE is long, low, stuccoed late C18 with a loggia.

HEATH END *see* HALE

1060

HERSHAM
1½ m. W of Esher

ST PETER. 1887 by *J. L. Pearson*. Buff stone, rockfaced. N tower at the W end with broach-spire. Lancet windows and windows with plate tracery. Straight-ended chancel with a group of three stepped lancets. Transepts only slightly marked inside. The aisle arcades run through to the chancel. – PAINTING (S transept). Large Annunciation, probably English, of *c*.1800.

(ALL SAINTS (R.C.), Queens Road. 1959–60 by *Tomei & Maxwell*. DE)

At the junction of MOLESEY ROAD and ESHER ROAD a former Nonconformist Chapel of 1844, remodelled in 1858, circular, of yellow brick, with lancet windows and a lantern. Close by, the former Minister's Manse with a simple porch. Next to this ROOKWOOD, a C19 folly, a circular cottage built of the trunks of gnarled trees with an equally gnarled central chimney.
See p. 598 (It cost over £600. Barbara Jones dates it *c*.1830.)

SOUTH WAYLANDS (Wayland's Farm), Esher Road, only ¼ m. W of Waynflete's Tower, but across the river Mole. Brick house of *c*.1600 with gables, nicely placed.

HIGHSTREET GREEN *see* CHIDDINGFOLD

HINCHLEY WOOD *see* CLAYGATE

HINDHEAD

High heathland, 850 ft up: highwaymen and invective from Cobbett in 1800, appreciation of the conifer-and-ravine landscape later in the C19. Now a breezy collection of shops and cafés along the Portsmouth Road, all of them derived from one or other of Norman Shaw's styles. Surrounding them big comfortable 1890s houses in grounds of rhododendrons and firs, the traditional image of Surrey.

St Alban, Beacon Hill. 1907–10 by *J. D. Coleridge*. Free-Perp, tiny aisles, mostly clear glazing. Derived from Temple Moore's style. Big but not good. Nave completed in 1930–1. Vicarage also by *Coleridge*, 1910–11.

The typical Hindhead house is perfectly exemplified by Thirlestane on the Farnham road. It is big, and it has tile-hanging and roughcast taken over from Norman Shaw's middle period. Two suntrap wings make a V-shaped house, facing sw, with complete asymmetry of gables and windows to suit the plan. It is more 'modern' than most of the modernistic villas of the thirties. Beyond this – near the fork of the roads to Tilford and Frensham – is Highcombe Edge, 1899 by *W. A. Pite*, combining Voysey proportions with neurotic free classicism, in details such as an attenuated cupola resting on lunettes. Stables tile-hung and asymmetrical, with a half-timber tower. Personal, but not very attractive because of the mechanical detailing: far better as Academy drawings than in the flesh. s of the Portsmouth road is Amesbury School, built as The Mount by *Lutyens* in 1903. One long, low Neo-Georgian range, the front using the fussy and heavy style all too familiar from later Lutyens, with a very characteristic doorcase with an immense block of undressed stone in the pediment.* However, the back facing w is extremely pretty. Central pediment, small windows, big roof, and an unexpected ability to let well alone and to allow the proportions and materials to make their effect unaided. (The upstairs passage has at the top of the stairs Lutyens's classical equivalent of inverted strainer arches. NT)

Off the road leading to the school is The Cottage, apparently by *H. H. Stannus*. It is typical of the smaller houses – bright and tile-hung on a very steep slope. All these houses appear in the landscape as red smudges on steep wooded hillsides. The total effect – as at Haslemere, almost entirely independent of

---

* This was, of course, intended to be carved.

See
p.
598 the individual quality of the designs – is as subtle a landscape
effect as any of Repton's.

HOLLOWAY COLLEGE *see* ROYAL HOLLOWAY COLLEGE

HOLLOWAY SANATORIUM

79 The building was opened in 1884. It is a companion building
to Holloway College (*see* p. 444), and also designed by *W. H.
Crossland*,* this time in a sort of Franco-Flemish brick-and-
stone Gothic carried through with a verve that is entirely
his own. A prodigious, very well proportioned front – nineteen
bays on each side of the central hall, punctuated with crow-
stepped gables, in a Bruges style. In the centre a big tower (an
almost literal transcription from the Ypres Cloth Hall)
appearing behind the independently roofed hall, which 'sells
the dummy' by hiding the join of wings and tower with
superb self-confidence. Justified self-confidence, as it happens; these two Holloway buildings are the summit of High
Victorian design produced long after the style had begun to
ebb – possibly because Crossland was a Northcountryman and
hence out of the London fashions. The interior has the same
self-assurance. A low vestibule leads to the stair-well through
a triple arch. The staircase has one arm splitting into two
(with a velvet-trimmed mirror at the half-landing!) and returning to the entrance of the hall on the first floor – an enormous room with a hammerbeam roof. All the decoration is
flat, gilding and rich reds and greens forming a shimmering,
restless pattern over the whole wall surface. Some of the portraits in the Great Hall are by students of the (then) South
Kensington School of Art, the present Royal College: an
oddly enterprising thing to do. The result is a blend of Burges's
decorative sense with the vitality Waterhouse showed inside
the Manchester Town Hall, and, needless to say, not a hint of
the existence of either Whistler or Morris. There is a chapel
in the grounds, quite sober after this riot of exuberance, with
a three-sided apse and a low vault (again borrowing Continental ideas, as also in the intersecting ribs in the stair-well
and even perhaps in the way arches are stretched Neumann-
fashion under the upper arms of the staircase). Crossland was

* But the original competition design was done, in partnership with
Crossland, by *J. Philpot Jones*, who died before work started (NT).

obviously an unashamed eclectic to a degree which makes the Streets and Scotts seem single-minded.

HOLMBURY ST MARY

4 m. SW of Dorking

1040

A small village in the middle of the Hurtwood, on the low-lying road (500 ft) across the hills between Shere and Ockley. It is largely Victorian, but, unlike Peaslake, it makes a virtue of it: picturesque cottages on a steep wooded site with a small triangular green near the church.

ST MARY. One of *G. E. Street*'s last churches, built at his own expense in 1879, two years before his death. It sums up very well the enigma of Street's later architecture, presented at such enormous length by the Law Courts: simultaneously extreme care over detail and extreme professional competence in composition and massing, and complete lack of anything to say, the perfect example of form without content. Mid-Dec style, on a hilly site, with joyless Surrey reminiscences such as the wooden bellcote, and lean-to aisles with E.E. arcades, four polished marble shafts to each pier. Clever adjustment of floor levels between nave, chancel, and raised N chapel; clever planning also in putting the vestries underneath this chapel. – STAINED GLASS in E and W windows and N chapel, all by *Clayton & Bell* from *Street*'s designs. – PAINTINGS. Italian triptych of *c*.1400, attributed to *Spinello Aretino*, given by Street. – (In the N chapel a late C15 Italian Madonna given in 1954.) – MEDALLION. *Della Robbia* roundel set into the W wall, given by J. R. Clayton (of Clayton & Bell). – (ALTAR CROSS, given by Street. Limoges enamel. – MONUMENT. In the outside S wall of the chapel the canopied tomb of Street's second wife † 1876. NT)

Holmbury has the familiar chain of late C19 houses on the S of the hills facing S over the Weald. Near the village, HOPEDENE (now six dwellings), by *Norman Shaw*, 1873, an interesting design, built up by hollowing out one single bulky mass instead of adding part to part. The entrance side mostly half-timbered, the garden side – almost as gawky and bulky as if it were by Prior – mostly tile-hung, making it look later than 1873.

Running SW from the village is a line of similar houses. First and best HOLMDALE, *G. E. Street*'s own house, 1873, much subtler and softer than one would expect Street to be. Tile-hung and half-timbered living rooms forming an L-shape with a taller stone tower on the angle. Very impressive. Gladstone liked it. Then MOXLEY by *Basil Champneys*, 1888, in Norman Shaw's tile-hung style but indifferent. Further W JOLD-WYNDS, originally one of *Philip Webb*'s biggest houses. Re-built by *Oliver Hill* in 1934, rather surprisingly in the International Modern style, with one long low wing and horizontal strip windows. Pink-washed and also indifferent. Webb's house was a good one. Finally HOLMBURY, a medium-size stuccoed classical house of *c*.1860.

(PASTURE WOOD, ½ m. E (now Beatrice Webb House). Large half-timbered house by *William Flockhart*, 1893, for Sir Frederick Mirrielees, Lutyens's client for Goddards (*see* p. 86). For him *Lutyens* added in 1906 a pyramid-roofed extension to the service wing, and, curling round it and ascending a whole storey, an exceedingly pretty outside staircase in a timbered cloister. Pergola of 1897 and formal garden next to it. Down the slope a fine ROCK GARDEN by *Gertrude Jekyll*, now being restored. STAINED GLASS in one of Flockhart's inglenooks designed by *George Bernard Shaw* and made by *Caroline Townshend*, showing Shaw, Sidney Webb, and E. R. Pease (secretary of the Fabian Society) in medieval dress, helping to build a new world. Other Fabians below, including H. G. Wells cocking a snook. Pair of COTTAGES also by *Lutyens*. THE OLD BARN, nearer the road, converted into a convalescent home in 1911 by *Voysey*. Now a private house. NT)

HOLMBURY CAMP. On Holmbury Hill, SW of the village, a more or less square Iron Age HILL-FORT overlooking the Weald. It measures 8 acres, and has a double bank and ditch on the N and W sides. To the S and E, where the defences are no longer clear, the slope of the hill would have acted as a natural defence. Excavations in 1930 were limited to the defences. Pottery recovered suggests but does not confirm a connexion with the SE Wealden Culture, and a date just prior to the Roman conquest.

HOLMWOOD
1–3 m. S of Dorking

A two-mile long common beside the Worthing road, with agreeably unpretentious C19 cottages all round. It probably started as a squatting hamlet without organized settlement.

St John, North Holmwood. By *Rhode Hawkins*, 1875, a hard, competent flint job with NW tower. Awful inside. – STAINED GLASS. E window by *Powell & Sons*, 1875; W window by *Kempe*, 1892.

St Mary Magdalene, South Holmwood. Wealden stone, assorted C19 dates: chancel 1838 by *J. B. Watson*, nave 1842 by *J. Wild*, aisles and tower mostly 1863, surprisingly sober and authentic-looking (arcades and tower arch e.g.). Whose?

(The Dutch House, South Holmwood (on the main road), is a somewhat outré Y-shaped house by *Lutyens*, 1901 (cf. E. S. Prior for the plan). Whitewashed walls, and a semicircular classical porch. Mansard roofs. Nice loggia at the back on red tile piers. Originally called The Mascot. Oak Tree House next door was formerly attached to it as the billiard room, added by *Lutyens* in 1904 for F. W. Pethick-Lawrence, but much altered in 1967, with new dormers in what was a gargantuan roof of plain tiling. NT)

Two more things to note. First, in Deepdene Avenue, North Holmwood, a post-war Surrey County Council school, in their then familiar timid half-modern style, but much better detailed than the average. All the elements are well related and strung out W–E at the top of a grass slope. The other thing is at South Holmwood, where an estate was laid out *c.*1870 with about six Victorian houses in big grounds (cf. Whiteknights at Reading, Berks), all in a thick gabled and tile-hung style, apparently by *J. P. St Aubyn*.

Goodwyns. *See* Dorking, p. 198.

Stane Street. A section of Roman Stane Street, with its raised metalling and *agger*, has been preserved by the Surrey Archaeological Society in Redlands Wood.

HOOK

St Paul. By *Carpenter & Ingelow*, 1881–3. Very red. No tower. Nave and chancel in one. N aisle. Details in the style of *c.*1310. – STAINED GLASS. E window designed by *Seddon* and executed by *S. Belham & Co.* – Chancel S window by *Kempe*, 1900.

HORLEY

Near the Sussex border. Fragments of an old village, but nearly all an unaffected mid-C19 gridiron that followed the buildings of the Brighton railway. Pleasant scale but no worthwhile buildings.

ST BARTHOLOMEW. One more case of C19 obliteration, this time by *A. W. Blomfield*. Until 1881 the church had a striking if ugly set of early C14 windows with 'Kentish tracery' (i.e. with downward-pointing cusps running against the upward pattern of the window, giving a strange and mannered *non sequitur* which stops the eye sharply at each window). The design still remains in the N aisle, completely renewed and with the old corbels cut off. This was presumably done by Chertsey Abbey, who appropriated the church in 1313; there is nothing else like it in Surrey. S aisle 1901. All the rest more or less C19, apart from the C14 N arcade and the very delicate and quite unrestored N doorway, which has two tiny shafts with joined capitals. This is also early C14, and gives some indication of what has been lost in restoration. Probably early C14 too the arch for a monument between chancel and N chapel. For the monument, *see* below. The most impressive part of the church is now the tower, set into the W bay of the N aisle. It has an elegant, thin shingled spire and, most unusually, a shingled bell-chamber, a *tour de force* in what is normally not a tractable material. It stands on four big, rough posts inside, and looks more like a northern French slate-hung belfry than the Essex weatherboarded bell-towers. It has C14 framing and probably post-Reformation shingling (the simple belfry courses look C18). Probably done by the person who shingled Burstow steeple. – PLATE. Cup, Paten, and Flagon 1714. – BRASSES. Two, both unnamed. On the N side of the chancel, an elegant and big (three-quarters-life-size) female figure of *c.*1400. The figure is full face, and oddly enough is much less intricate than the beautifully detailed ogee canopy flanked by thin shafts. – On the S side of the chancel, a homely, moving little figure of a Civilian, late C14. – MONUMENT. To a Salaman. Assigned to the early C14. Life-size knight with shield, the legs not crossed, the head on a cushion, the feet on a lion – a standard pattern and standard quality of carving too, though the type is unusual in Surrey.

⟨CHURCH OF THE ENGLISH MARTYRS (R.C.), Vicarage Lane. By *J. H. Alleyn*, 1961–2. One of the first R.C. churches in the county in the modern style. Octagonal, with a low ambulatory between four shallow wings, making a cruciform plan. Bell-tower consisting of two yellow brick slabs, linked by a covered walk to the porch. – STAINED GLASS by *P. Fourmaintreaux*.⟩

Very little in the town. Next to the church is the OLDE SIX
BELLS, both old and olde, with a C15 core and diamond-
shaped tile-hanging and Horsham slate roof. Where the lane
to the church meets the Brighton Road is just one very pretty
tile-hung C17 cottage, overawed by the traffic and mid-C20
suburbia all around. The town centre is ½ m. NE, by the railway. The best building is the simple weatherboarded pub, the
FORESTERS' ARMS, in Victoria Road, probably put up after
the railway came, and showing how long the traditional vernacular persisted. ⟨Also in Victoria Road, two good straightforward recent buildings: TELEPHONE EXCHANGE by
G. A. H. Pearce of the *Ministry of Public Building and Works*,
1960–2, and opposite, a LIBRARY by *Howard V. Lobb &
Partners* and the County Architect, *R. J. Ash*. The library
has an internal courtyard. Victoria Road leads NE to COURT
LODGE, a large estate by the Dorking and Horley R.D.C.,
1964–9. Average housing, but in the middle a quite exceptionally ugly eleven-storey block of flats. A neat PRIMARY
SCHOOL by the County Architect, *R. J. Ash*, 1968–9, yellow
brick with black boarding.⟩

HORNE

3040

No village: church and farm group plus a lot of hamlets, in the
least attractive part of the Weald plain. Too much modern
housing and not enough architecture.

ST MARY. The same old story: pitiful renewal and restoration,
this time by *Gordon M. Hills*, 1880. In this case he seems to
have shuffled the fragments like a pack of cards. What remains is one C14 window on the S side of the nave and two
square-headed C15 Perp windows with distinguished details
– deep reveals and bold mouldings. One is in the W wall, one
in the N aisle. The rest is all either new or the worst sort of
replica. The inside is completely characterless. Originally it
had a complete timber bell-tower, like Burstow: now there is
only a spiky 1880 bell-cote and spirelet, admittedly picturesque. New porch now propped up by two columns left over
from the demolished W gallery. – FONT. Octagonal; C15. –
SCREEN. Now at the W end, the simplest Perp type, narrow
bays with trefoiled heads. – PLATE. Set 1821. – MONUMENT.
John Goodwine † 1618 and his wife. Small kneeling effigies of
the usual type, but a lot of original colouring remains, dark red
and green, the figures black: not gaudy, at least not in its

present state. Even when new the effect must have been rich
rather than shrill, something worth remembering when the
C20 tries to reinstate Elizabethan colouring.

The other buildings are scattered around the parish. 1 m. to the
s is CHITHURST FARM, bulky brick and tile-hanging, everything now visible of c.1700. N of the church the barns of
HORNECOURT MANOR are a deliberate design (of c.1800) –
a half-H in cold utilitarian classical style, like part of a workhouse; the type rare in Surrey. ½ m. E of this is Whitewood
hamlet with JARVES, a simple Weald farm, tile-hanging above
brick, no overhang. It is in fact a refronting of c.1700 of a
C16 house (cf. the Tudor chimneystack) in which the overhang probably disappeared to gain extra space. E again is
HAYS BRIDGE REFORMATORY SCHOOL (formerly Court
Lees), by itself and utterly incongruous in the simple rural
landscape. Big and Neo-Georgian, by *J. Douglass Mathews
& Partners*, 1938. 1 m. s of this is HORNE PARK FARM, a
good example of a comparatively rare thing, the thoroughgoing picturesque mid-C19 farmhouse with farm buildings to
match. This example is formidable symmetrical Tudor. Three
dormers, overbearing slate roofs, two sets of coupled chimneystacks, very red brick and stone dressings. The same style as
many of the second-generation railway stations: vinegary
and ferociously ugly, 'good of its kind', and hence worth a
sympathetic look.

HORSELL

NW of, and swamped by, Woking. A few battered cottages remain from the old village.

ST MARY. A sorry mess of restoration and enlargement, partly
by *W. F. Unsworth*. C15 s aisle, mainly carstone, and s arcade.
C15 tower in flint, clunch, and heathstone, with diagonal
buttresses, like a smaller edition of Worplesdon, and fake Dec
belfry windows. The rest all new or renewed to extinction.
– MONUMENTS. Two worth notice, and oddly enough both
anachronisms: Sir John Rose † 1803 and wife (w wall), two
figures leaning on an urn but in contemporary dress and striking Baroque attitudes by the younger *Bacon* (Gunnis), and
James Fenn † 1787, in customary polychrome marble but a
unique design for the late C18 – a 'kneeler', husband and wife
facing one another (significantly, across a table piled untidily
with books, not the sedate reading-desk of its prototypes).

The two figures are striking free and rather gauche attitudes under a pointed arch. Unsigned, and with no clue as to the reason for this extraordinary Jacobean revival. R. Gunnis suggested that the sculptor may have been the elder *Bacon*. ⟨HORSELL CHURCH OF ENGLAND PRIMARY SCHOOL, Meadway Drive. By *F. Reginald Steele & Partners*, 1969. Crisp building in purple brick with white and grey details.⟩

HORSLEY *see* EAST HORSLEY *and* WEST HORSLEY

HURST GREEN *see* OXTED

HURST PARK *see* WEST MOLESEY

HURTWOOD *see* EWHURST

HYDESTILE *see* HAMBLEDON

JUNIPER HALL   1050
¾ m. s of Mickleham

All effectively *c.*1870 from the outside, with an enormous porte-cochère like a fragment of Marylebone Station. But the house incorporates some details of *c.*1770: outside, rusticated windows more like a C17 French design than an C18 English one, and inside one delightful room, the SCULPTURED DRAWING ROOM, attributed to *Lady Templeton*. Generally Adam style – low relief, pretty mouldings, oval ceiling patterns – with a few unexpected details such as the heavy swag over the door and the luxuriant foliage (luxuriant for the 1770s, that is) on the walls. The remarkable feature is the repeated use of Wedgwood plaques imitated in plaster, a big square panel as an overmantel and big oval panels on the walls, but also tiny scenes throughout the room, even on the door jambs. A very attractive design, with more personality than the average Adam room. The house has famous *émigré* associations from the Napoleonic Wars. Talleyrand and Madame de Staël both lived here – and so did the Chevalier d'Arblay, which is why Fanny Burney was married in Mickleham church.

II—S.

KEW

St Anne. Built in 1710–14. Nave and chancel only. Yellow
brick with arched red brick windows. Lengthened by *J. J.
Kirby*, Gainsborough's friend, in 1770. He also added the N
aisle. The s aisle dates from 1884. At the same time the church
received its E end with the odd octagonal cupola, and the odd
Venetian tracery of the windows. It is to this that the church
owes its peculiar character. Before then the W façade had been
given its present form. This was due to *Sir Jeffry Wyatville*,
and the date was 1836. Portico and polygonal timber bell-
turret. In 1850–1 a MAUSOLEUM was added E of the E end for
the Duke and Duchess of Cambridge (*B. Ferrey*). This
appears externally with a lead-covered half dome. The walls
have Italian Renaissance niches. The interior of the church
was altered in 1884 by *Henry Stock*. Five-bay arcades with
Tuscan columns of timber, vaulted ceiling. The crossing has
pink scagliola columns, the apse white and gold columns.
The dome, on squinches, has gold stars on a blue ground.
– WEST GALLERY. 1805. On cast-iron columns. – STAINED
GLASS. E window by *Kempe*, 1893, with figures between
Renaissance candelabra. – s chapel E window by *Mayer & Co.*
of Munich, in a sentimental German Renaissance style. –
PLATE. Set 1713. – MONUMENTS. Many, but none of major
importance. The following deserve mention. Lady Capel
† 1721. Urn between pilasters under a baldacchino. Weeping
putti l. and r. – Francis Bauer, the botanical draughtsman,
† 1840. By *Westmacott Jun*. Portrait medallion at the top,
pretty palette arrangement at the foot. The inscription plate is
framed by thick garlands of flowers. – Sir W. J. Hooker,
director of the Botanic Gardens, and author of the standard
work on ferns, † 1865, with *Wedgwood* medallion and panels of
ferns. By *Woolner & Palgrave*. – Sir J. D. Hooker, the son of
the former and also a director of the Gardens, † 1911, also with
ceramic panels of plants. – In the churchyard monument to
Clementina Jacobi Sobieski Schell † 1842 or 1843, called after
Clementina Sobieski, wife of James III, the Old Pretender.
The design in imitation of the Stuart Monument by *Canova* in
St Peter's in Rome.

(Our Lady of Loreto and St Winifride (R.C.), Ley-
bourne Park. 1906 by *A. J. C. Scoles* and *G. Raymond*. DE)

Kew Green. The parish church lies on the green, asymmetrically and very effectively placed. The green is triangular, as

greens so often are. Two of the three sides are lined with worth-while houses, mostly Georgian, and the entrance to the Botanic Gardens lies in the angle between them. Along the SW side from the E, first a nice group, Nos. 17–25, two- and three-storeyed, then No. 37 with a deep porte-cochère of 1838–40, then Nos. 39–41. The Gables is remodelled, but the shape of the gables is genuine C17. Then lesser things, until the Royal Cottage and the Herbarium House are reached, and with this the main gates. On the N side first the HERBARIUM, a big building with an eight-bay centre with giant pilasters, attached to a good seven-bay Georgian house of three storeys with projecting corner bays, a doorway with Ionic columns and a pediment, and an original staircase. The additions for use as a herbarium date from 1877 (at the back), 1902 (s), and 1932 (parallel to the original building). Then, starting with HANOVER HOUSE, a long group of square C18 houses, of different heights, with canted bays and iron balconies. The best is No. 71, late C18, of five bays with the middle three a little projecting and on the ground floor blank-arched. The group ends with No. 73. Other houses of note are No. 83, then WATERLOO PLACE, dated 1816, on the N side, E of Kew Road, and No. 20 on the E side.

CROWN BUILDING, Ruskin Avenue. By *J. C. Clavering*, superintendent architect under *W. S. Bryant* of the *Whitehall Development Group* of the *Ministry of Public Building and Works*, 1967–9. Square single-storey block on stilts, overlooking the Thames. This is the first purpose-built open-plan office in this country (following the German practice of *Bürolandschaft*), an experimental design intended as a possible prototype for future government offices.

ROYAL BOTANIC GARDENS

INTRODUCTION. The Royal Botanic Gardens at Kew have three sources: the Royal Palace, also known as the Dutch House, the gardens planted with rare trees and shrubs by Sir Henry Capel († 1696) and Lady Capel and praised e.g. by John Evelyn, and the park of Richmond Palace, stretching to the N.

For the DUTCH HOUSE, *see* p. 325 below.

As regards the PARK OF RICHMOND PALACE, a lodge on its outskirts was altered for William III, added to as RICHMOND LODGE by Lord Ormonde in 1704, and granted by George I to the Prince of Wales in 1722. It became the favourite residence of the future George II and Queen Caroline. She did much for the gardens, which stretched out to the w and parallel to Kew Gardens proper. The dividing line ran roughly along the present Holly Walk. Her gardener was *Charles Bridgeman*, the leading gardener of the transition from formal to informal, her architect was *William Kent*, and he built in the gardens a Hermitage with busts of philosophers and that celebrated folly Merlin's Cave, which was a tripartite structure with thatched beehive roofs and a Gothick ogee-arched entrance. Inside were wax figures of Merlin and his secretary, of Queen Elizabeth and her nurse, of Elizabeth Tudor, the Queen of Henry VII, and of the Goddess Minerva. It was built in 1735 and hence was very early Gothick, like Esher. When *Capability Brown* remodelled the gardens about 1770 etc. he swept this delicious toy away.

Meanwhile the eldest son of George II, Frederick Prince of Wales, and Princess Augusta had settled at Kew, asking *William Kent* to remodel or rather rebuild for them Sir Henry Capel's house. The result was the WHITE HOUSE, built in 1730–5. It stood to the SE of the Dutch House, separated from it by the road to Brentford Ferry, and the centre of its site is now marked by a SUNDIAL put up in 1832. The White House was a plain classical structure with a pedimented five-bay centre of two and a half storeys, pedimented two-bay and two-storey wings, and one-storeyed outer wings. All that remains is the KITCHENS, for which *see* below, p. 397.

The Prince of Wales died in 1751. His widow took a special interest in the gardens and in 1759 laid the foundation of the present Botanic Gardens by dedicating about nine acres of the gardens to botanical purposes. She was advised by William Aston. After her death, Sir Joseph Banks, trusted by George III, her son, worked on their development. The White House remained the country residence of George III and Queen Charlotte, until in 1801 they decided to build, just w of the Dutch House, a more ambitious and showy, if no more comfortable palace. This was designed by *James Wyatt* and was a generously crenellated and turreted castle with a central keep of four storeys. It had cast-iron beams, and its interior was never completed. George IV had it pulled down in 1827–8. The White House had been pulled down in 1822. So all that remained was the Dutch House and a number of garden temples etc. erected for Augusta, Dowager Princess of

Wales. The Botanic Gardens became a national institution in 1841.

KEW PALACE. Kew Palace, or the Dutch House, was built in 41 1631 by Samuel Fortrey, a London merchant of Dutch descent. It was built as a country house close to the river and is of the moderate size of 70 ft length and 50 ft depth. In its stead there had been a c16 house of which part of the basement, a fireplace on the second floor, and some re-used linenfold panelling (Library Anteroom) remain. It is built of brick, laid in Flemish not English bond, which was something of an innovation at the time, and treated with supreme skill and artistry. It is three storeys high and has to the main fronts three gables with double-curved sides and crowning pediments alternately triangular and segmental – also still an innovation in 1630. The windows originally had brick crosses of a mullion and a transom, and that was a relatively novel motif too. The style of the Dutch House is one which seems to have appealed to only a limited stratum of civilization: the connoisseurs and virtuosi appreciated the classicity of Inigo Jones, but the wealth of the provinces still went into buildings in the Tudor tradition, of stone in the North, timber-framed in the West. But in and around London there was a class, chiefly merchants, who scorned the Tudor tradition as old-fashioned, but could not make themselves accept the restraint of the Palladian style. For them such gabled brick houses were built, with their gables demonstrating by their crowning pediments their awareness of the Renaissance. Apart from Kew Palace the following houses belong to this group: Cromwell House, Highgate, London of c.1637–40, Swakeleys in Middlesex of c.1630–5, Broome Park in Kent of 1635–8, Raynham Hall in Norfolk of c.1635, and a few more. Kew Palace is wholly characteristic of the group and is its earliest dated representative (although Sir John Summerson has drawn attention to the pedimented gable of Lady Cooke's house in Holborn, drawn by John Smythson in 1619). One of the most characteristic features of the house is the evident delight in play with brickwork, such as the rustication round all windows. The centre bay is enriched by superimposed pilasters and, on the top floor, by columns – the pilasters on the ground floor have been removed – and by arched windows. The interior is very simply arranged, with a cross passage through from the present doorway to the river doorway and two main rooms to its l., and two to its r., on each floor. The details are mostly of the mid and later c18, see e.g. the staircase with three turned balusters to the tread and carved tread-ends. Specially interesting are the ceiling of one room on the first floor (Queen's Boudoir) with an original plaster ceiling of *c.*1631 – still in the Jacobean tradition – and the over-doors of a room on the ground floor (King's Dining Room) which are an c18 imitation of this Jacobean style, due in all probability to *Kent*, who was working at the White House *c.*1730 and was doing similar bits of Jacobean Revival at Hampton Court in 1732.*

THE GARDENS. Kew Gardens is nearly 300 acres in size. It cannot be compared with any of the other older botanic gardens in the world. Its combination of botanical interest and beauty of landscape is unmatched. The gardens are the consecutive work of two ages, the mid c18 and the mid c19. In the mid c18 Princess Augusta's gardens at Kew assumed their shape under *Chambers*, Queen Charlotte's gardens at Richmond Lodge (*c.*1764) under *Capability Brown*. Of Chambers's work it is mostly the small buildings which still exist. The principal alterations in the layout, after the Gardens had been passed on to the State – of the buildings the Perambulation will treat – are due to Sir William and Sir Joseph Hooker (*see* Kew Church, above), directors in 1841–65 and 1865–85. When Sir William was appointed in 1841, the Garden was 11 acres in size. He increased it to 76 in five years. The picturesque lake was excavated in 1845 and later enlarged; the pond in front of the Palm House dates from 1847 and is designed by *W. A. Nesfield*; and the four main vistas, Broad Walk, Holly Walk, Pagoda Vista, and Cedar Vista, are also by Nesfield.

PERAMBULATION. The main ENTRANCE GATES were put up in 1848. They were designed by *Decimus Burton*. The thick, scrolly iron gates were made by *Walker* of Rotherham, the equally thick garlands on the stone piers by *J. Heming Jun.* In one of the two outer niches is a statue of a child by *John Bell*, 1863. On entering one has at once on the r. the small house called AROID HOUSE NO. 1. This is by *John Nash* and was originally one of two pavilions flanking the garden façade of Buckingham Palace. Its companion is still *in situ*. It has glass walls with Tuscan pilasters along the sides and six Ionic columns *in antis* along the fronts. Even the pediments are

* In the house there is now *Kent*'s model for a palace at Richmond of *c.*1735 (J. Harris).

mostly glazed. To its w 'The Sower', a STATUE by *Sir Hamo Thornycroft*, 1886, on a later base by *Lutyens*. S of this is the ORANGERY, now Museum No. III, built by *Sir William Chambers* and dated 1761. It was for a long time England's largest hothouse. Chambers, then thirty-eight years old, was Princess Augusta's favourite architect and taught her son, the future George III, the art of drawing. The Orangery stood to the SE of her house, the White House. It is seven bays long with rusticated walls and arched openings. The first and last bays are pedimented. (It is of brick, still stuccoed with Chambers's secret form of stucco. J. Harris)

One should now take the BROAD WALK straight to the POND. The Pond lies between the Palm House and Museum No. I, two buildings equally characteristic of the sound and enterprising spirit of the gardens in the forties and fifties. The PALM HOUSE is one of the boldest pieces of C19 functional- 70 ism in existence – much bolder indeed, and hence aesthetically much more satisfying, than the Crystal Palace ever was. It was designed by the engineer *Richard Turner* of Dublin, with *Decimus Burton*, the architect of Hyde Park Corner, as the architect. The building took from 1844 to 1848. The Palm House is 362 ft long and in its centre 62 ft, in its wings 33 ft high. It consists entirely of iron and glass and has curved roofs throughout. The rise of the roofs up the wings and then up the centre is unforgettable. The vertical walls and the vertical strip at the foot of the centre roof are too low to interfere with the strong rhythm of the identical curves.* A short distance to the N of the Palm House is the Water Lily House, built in 1852 to house the recently introduced Victoria Regia. Opposite the Palm House across the pond is MUSEUM NUMBER ONE, built as such in 1856–7. This was designed by *Burton* and is as straightforward a job as the Palm House – stock brick, eleven bays long, and the detail in a utilitarian minimum-Classical. Also connected with this mid-C19 moment in the history of Kew Gardens is the CAMPANILE, S of the Pond. This must date from *c.*1850 too, is also of stock brick, and also in all possibility a design of *Burton*'s.‡ It was built as a chimney for the furnaces beneath the Palm House. Near the Pond also begins the chain of little temples etc.

* In front and facing the Pond the set of QUEEN'S BEASTS, stone replicas of the plaster originals carved by *James Woodford* for the Coronation of Queen Elizabeth II and displayed outside the w annexe to Westminster Abbey.

‡ He could be Italianate – cf. his Grimston Park Yorkshire of 1840.

with which *Chambers* and others embellished Princess Augusta's gardens. Chambers's temples all date from *c*.1760–3. They were published by him in a book in 1763. The first of these, the TEMPLE OF AEOLUS, is to the NE. It is a domed rotunda with Tuscan columns. It was rebuilt by *Burton* in 1845. The second is the TEMPLE OF ARETHUSA, SE of the Pond and N of the Campanile. This is of 1758* and has a front with two Ionic columns between two pillars and a pediment. S of the Campanile and the Victoria Gate is the TEMPLE OF BELLONA (1760). The façade of this has a portico of two pairs of Tuscan columns with a metope frieze and a shallow dome on a drum behind. Inside is a room with an oval-domed centre. On the walls garlands and medallions with the names and numbers of British and Hanoverian regiments connected with the Seven Years' War.

Some 800 ft W of the Temple of Bellona is KING WILLIAM'S TEMPLE or the Pantheon, built in 1837 to the design of *Sir Jeffry Wyatville*. This has four Tuscan columns with a metope frieze at the front as well as at the back. On the long sides the metopes are replaced by windows. Inside a number of finely shaped and finely lettered cast-iron tablets commemorating British victories from Minden to Waterloo.

S of King William's Temple the bulky and unmistakably clumsy shape of the TEMPERATE HOUSE, known originally as the Winter Garden. This is 628 ft long and was designed by *Burton* as late as 1860. It was not completed until 1899. After the Palm House it is an almost incredible anticlimax. So rapidly then did the pride in engineering pure and simple collapse which had blazed the victories of the Early Victorians. The naked beauty of the Palm House could no longer be tolerated, and fussy stone piers and roofs had to be introduced to make the buildings look like architecture.

Opposite the N end of the Temperate House to the E is the FLAGSTAFF, the trunk of a Douglas fir, 225 ft long, and erected on a mound in 1959. S of this and immediately S of the building called the NORTH GALLERY‡ (which houses – by hook or by crook – 848 flower paintings by *Marianne North*, painted in 1872–85) is a LODGE designed by *Eden Nesfield* and built in 1866. This is historically speaking an ex-

* This and the following dates follow Dr H. M. Martienssen's thesis on Chambers, London University 1951; unpublished.

‡ By the architectural historian *James Fergusson* to illustrate his theory of lighting temples (David Watkin).

tremely important work, as it is in a style supposed to have been created by Nesfield's former partner Norman Shaw about six years later. Red brick, walls with short pilasters, tall truncated pyramid roof with central chimneystack. Dormer windows with segmental pediments. The style was later wrongly called Queen Anne. Its sources are in the English brick architecture of *c.*1630–60 which itself was influenced by Holland. The Dutch House no doubt had inspired Nesfield.

s of this, *Chambers*'s RUINED ARCH (1759–60), picturesquely overgrown at the time of writing, and to its SW the REFRESHMENT PAVILION, a nice straightforward piece of building, light, generously glazed and with a raised centre. This was built in 1920 by the Ministry of Works (*R. D. Allison*) after its predecessor had been burnt in 1913 by Suffragettes. Here one joins the avenue called Pagoda Vista and can walk straight to the PAGODA. This supreme example of chinoiserie was built 59 of stock brick in 1761. It is 163 ft high and has ten storeys. On each of the upper storeys is a balcony with a pretty Chippendale railing all round, and on the top there were originally eighty enamelled dragons. Wooden spiral staircase inside. Although *Chambers* is best known as an academic Palladian and co-founder of the Royal Academy, there was a strain of fantasy in him which comes out very occasionally in details of his Palladian buildings – the Piranesian arches of Somerset House, the plan of the Casino at Marino – but to which he could give free rein only at Kew. Chambers had seen China as a young man, had written about Chinese architecture in 1757, and later published some wild theories on Chinese landscape gardening and the role of terror in it. Of the necessity of the latter he does not seem to have been able to convince Princess Augusta, but his desire to design exotic buildings was not satisfied with the Pagoda. He also built a Chinese Temple (1760), and in addition – remarkably early examples of a somewhat indiscriminate historicism – a Turkish Mosque (1761) and a Moorish Alhambra. They do not survive. Chambers was incidentally also responsible for some more classical furnishings at Kew, namely the Temples of Pan (1758), Victory (1759), Solitude (1760), the Sun (1761), and Peace (1763), and the Theateum Augustae (1760).*

* There was also a Gothic Cathedral, very gimcrack and very pretty. This was designed by *Muntz*. (A Chinese Temple of Confucius was almost certainly designed by *Chambers* in 1749 for Frederick Prince of Wales. J. Harris)

To the SE of the Pagoda, in the SE corner of the Gardens, is the LION GATE.

To the W of the Pagoda only two more buildings need attention. One is the CHOKUSHI MON or Gate of the Imperial Messenger. This is a replica of the famous gateway made for an exhibition in London in 1910 and presented to the Gardens. A little over ¼ m. W of this, in an area not at the moment open to the public, is the QUEEN'S COTTAGE, built and, it is said, designed by *Queen Charlotte*. It dates from *c.*1772 and belongs to the part of Kew Gardens which was the grounds of Richmond Lodge. These, as has been said before, were at that time rearranged by *Capability Brown*. This dear little cottage is of timber framing and brick with a thatched roof. It is oblong and has across the middle on both sides a gabled projection flanked by lower porches. The centre room on the upper floor is painted in the guise of a floral arbour. The work is attributed for good reasons by Mr Croft Murray to the *Princess Elizabeth* (cf. Frogmore, Windsor Great Park, Berkshire).

⟨In the NE corner of the gardens, by Kew Road, JODRELL LABORATORY AND LECTURE THEATRE, by *C. G. Pinfold* of the *Ministry of Public Building and Works*, 1965.⟩

9030
KILLINGHURST
2 m. SW of Chiddingfold

Big farmhouse in one of the few remote parts of the Surrey Weald. Rebuilt in 1760, and hence an unusual type for Surrey, though the formal Palladian farmhouse is common enough in counties like Shropshire or Yorkshire. Brick, of three storeys and three bays. Pinched central pediment, brick quoins, plain doorcase. Still with string courses – a conservative style, in fact that of William Halfpenny's many pattern-books of farmhouses. Set off perfectly by the thick informal landscape. A good quad of BARNS to the NE, stone and tarred weatherboarding.

1060
KINGSTON UPON THAMES

Kingston derives its name from the fact that some under-kings of Surrey had their residence here, *c.*675 or earlier. Later seven West Saxon Kings, including Aethelstan (925) and Edward the Martyr (975), were crowned here. Kingston received its first recorded charter in 1200. The new London Borough of Kingston upon Thames (total population 145,000) now includes Malden (*see* p. 358) and Surbiton (*see* p. 472). The town of Kingston itself suffers terribly from traffic congestion. What little there is of serious interest in the centre can rarely be seen for buses, cars, and lorries.

ALL SAINTS. The restorations of 1862–6 (*R. Brandon*) and 1883 (*Pearson*) have made the church visually Victorian. It is a large town church, nicely hidden behind the Market Place but now entirely open to the N towards Clarence Street and Wood Street. Flint with stone dressings. Of a large Norman church the W portal was found *c*.1865 but destroyed. The cores of the crossing piers are probably Norman too, and one piece of C13 moulding in the E respond of the N chancel chapel betrays enlargements of the Norman church. The crossing as it is now, with the N and S arches with continuous double-chamfered mouldings, looks *c*.1300. The crossing tower is crowned by a pretty brick top of 1708. The mason was *John Yeomans*. Wide nave of four bays. The nave arcades with simple octagonal piers are assigned to *c*.1400; the piers on the N side are a little slenderer. Perp N and S chancel chapels, that on the S of three bays with piers with the familiar four-shafts-four-hollows section. This work is connected with the creation of a chantry in 1459. – FONT. Of the late C17. The pillar does not belong. – ALTAR. 1951 by *Comper*. – SCULPTURE. Fragment of an Anglo-Saxon cross shaft with interlace. – PAINT-ING. Demi-figure of St Blaise on a pier of the S transept. – (STAINED GLASS. Remarkable W window, *c*.1865 by *Lavers & Barraud*, in rich colours: God the Father in glory with apostles and prophets. The oddly oversize heads portray local personalities. NT) – MONUMENTS. Brasses to Robert Skerne † 1437 and wife, 3 ft 3 in. figures (between chancel and S chapel). – Brasses to John Hertcombe † 1488 and wife, 9 in. figures kneeling (S transept). – Niche (Easter Sepulchre?) of the C15 in the S chapel, quatrefoil chest front, low four-centred arch. – Sir Anthony Benn, recorder of Kingston and London, † 1618. Recumbent effigy (next to the former). – Philip Meadows. By *Flaxman*, 1795. With a cherub on a cloud below an urn. The cherub is boldly carved and almost detached. Good. – Louisa Theodosia Countess of Liverpool, 1825 by *Chantrey*, detached figure of the Countess, seated. (Both this and the Flaxman by the N door.) – Henry Davidson † 1781 by *Regnart*. Standing mourning female figure by an urn. – Henry Davidson † 1827 by *Ternouth*. Seated figure in Grecian chair (both s transept).

LOVEKYN CHAPEL, *see* Perambulation.

(OUR LADY IMMACULATE (R.C.), Ewell Road, Tolworth. 1956–8 by *W. C. Mangan*. DE)

(ST AGATHA (R.C.), King's Road, Norbiton. 1899 by *J. Kelly*. DE)

ST ANDREW, Maple Road, *see* Surbiton.

(ST ANNE (R.C.), Kingston Hill. 1960 by *F. G. Broadbent*. DE)

ST PETER, Norbiton, London Road and Cambridge Road. A Commissioners' church. 1841 by *Scott & Moffatt*. Yellow and white brick, in the Norman style, with NW tower. Interior with Norman columns and still three galleries. One of Scott's first seven churches, which he afterwards called 'ignoble'; the censure not deserved in this case.

ST RAPHAEL (R.C.), Portsmouth Road. 1846–7 by *Charles Parker*. Facing the Thames. What should one call this style? It is certainly Italian, and may be anything from Early Christian to Early Renaissance, i.e. a w tower with typically Early-Victorian-Italianate top, aisle fronts recessed behind the tower with sloping roofs, windows all round-arched with so-called Venetian tracery. The façade composition is given added prominence by further recessed N and s wings with subsidiary domestic accommodation. Interior Renaissance with Ionic arcade columns. Tall and narrow nave with clerestory. The design repeated at St Albans Herts.

GUILDHALL, High Street. By *Maurice E. Webb*, 1935, extended 1968. Brick with stone dressings, strongly forward-curving front with a centrally placed tower. Big classical aedicule motif in its middle. Not a balanced or a well composed front. Inside a room with C16 linenfold panelling from the former town hall. Next to the Guildhall the CORONATION STONE, a shapeless block of grey sandstone on which the Saxon Kings are believed to have been crowned.

SURREY COUNTY HALL, Penrhyn Road. 1892–3 by *C. H. Howell*. Additions of 1930 and 1938 by *E. Vincent Harris*. Stone-faced. The older part livelier with a boldly placed tower and irregular gables. The newer ranges progressively chaster and more conventional.

MARKET HOUSE (former TOWN HALL), Market Place. 1838–40 by *Charles Henman Sen*. A rather funny Italianate building of yellow brick (now painted grey) with four short corner towers. On the first floor facing the Market Place STATUE of Queen Anne of 1706 by *Francis Bird*, who was paid £48 for it.

⟨COUNTY COURT, St James Road. By *C. G. Pinfold*, completed 1961.⟩

⟨KINGSTON COLLEGE OF FURTHER EDUCATION, Kingston Hall Road. Additions in progress (1969) by the Borough Architect, *J. H. Lomas*.⟩

⟨GYPSY HILL TRAINING COLLEGE, Kingston Hill. Hostel, communal block, and arts building by the County Architect, *R. J. Ash*, completed 1966–7.⟩

⟨KINGSTON HOSPITAL, Galsworthy Road. Good restaurant and stores by *W. E. Tatton-Brown* of the *Ministry of Health* and *Richard Mellor* of the *South-West Metropolitan Region Hospital Board*, 1964–6.⟩

CENTRAL LIBRARY, Fairfield Road. By *A. Cox*, 1903. Quite pretty, brick, Neo-Georgian, nine bays wide, with a big portal. In front a PIER, said to come from King John's Palace. It is a respond with a concave centre and triple shafts at the angles. The style looks *c.* 1300.

TELEPHONE EXCHANGE, Birkenhead Avenue. By *J. H. Markham*, 1937. With long window bands, but high, not low windows. Broad mullions between, faced with black glazed tiles.

(YOUTH CLUB, Parkfields Road. By *Kenneth Wood*, 1967–9.)

DR BARNARDO'S HOME, Gloucester Road. Built as the Princess Louise Home or Metropolitan Convalescent Home for Young Girls in 1875. By *Saxon Snell*. Yellow brick, symmetrical, with pointed windows but a central Italianate tower.

POWER STATION. By *Preece, Cardew & Rider*, engineers. Opened in 1948.

KINGSTON BRIDGE. 1825–8 by *Lapidge*, widened in 1914. There had been a bridge at Kingston ever since the early C13, if not earlier.

CONDUIT HOUSES. Cardinal Wolsey built a conduit stretching some three and a half miles from Kingston Hill and Coombe Hill to Hampton Court, passing under Kingston and under the Thames. Three of the Conduit Houses stand, and one of the intermediate inspection points. They are in the garden of the Convent of the Holy Family, George Road (Ivy Conduit), in the garden immediately to the W (Gallows Conduit – which has only one of the original twin buildings surviving, about 14 ft square, of Tudor brick with a pitched roof), and in the grounds of Coombe Springs, Coombe Lane (Combe Conduit

– this has both its original buildings, linked by an underground passage). The inspection point is Tamkins, overrestored, N of Wolsey Close in the Coombe Wood Golf Course.

PERAMBULATION. The church lies just N of the MARKET PLACE and away from it. In the Market Place the SHRUBSOLE MEMORIAL, 1882 by *F. J. Williamson*. High pedestal with a maiden with an urn on her shoulder and a child by her side. The Market Place is dominated by the Market House. To the W of this the showy four-storeyed building of Messrs Boots, with half-timbering and plenty of stone figures, and, attached to it, a humble but genuine C15 timber-framed house with an C18 alteration to the uprights, which are converted into pilasters. (In Hide's shop on the W side, a fine C17 staircase from Castle Inn. K. Gravett) At the SW corner of the Market Place the GRIFFIN HOTEL, with a friendly Early Victorian façade.

From here to the E, off Eden Street, the busy APPLE MARKET, not with any noteworthy houses, but of a nice funnel shape. ⟨In Eden Street is a large new SHOPPING CENTRE by *Ronald Ward & Partners*, with shops pleasantly staggered along EDEN WALK, but the whole dominated by the ramp to the car park on the roof. There is a tall glazed staircase tower which competes unfortunately with the church tower in the view from the bridge.⟩ From the S end of the Market Place starts the HIGH STREET. It runs along the river, which is however hidden by houses and industrial establishments. Then the CLATTERN BRIDGE over the Hogsmill River, a bridge of the late C12 with three semicircular slightly chamfered arches, much widened. No breakwaters. Further S No. 17, a pretty C18 house, low, with two canted bays. In the centre Venetian window and pediment. Tuscan porch. Nos. 37–41 are of the C15, with overhanging upper storeys. The original appearance comes out in EAST LANE. Another C18 house off Portsmouth Road, a little further S: No. 3 SURBITON ROAD, with two canted bays.

N of the church, in WOOD STREET and CLARENCE STREET, is BENTALL'S store, large, in a Hampton Court Wrenaissance, by *Maurice Webb*, 1931–5. By the same architect and equally prominent, BENTALL'S GARAGE and the stuccoed Italianate BENTALL'S REMOVALS STORE. From the E end of Clarence Street London Road starts. Here first CLEAVE'S ALMSHOUSES, 1668. Range of brick with six houses on each side of a gabled centre. This has a flat door surround of rusticated blocks of alternating size and three horizontal oval windows over. *Joshua Marshall* made the coat of arms in 1670. Then the former LOVEKYN CHAPEL or Chapel of St Mary Magdalene, a chantry chapel founded in 1309, partly rebuilt in 1352, and much renewed in 1886. E end flanked by turrets. Perp tracery. Inside two shallow recesses facing one another. Their purpose is unknown. After that a few Georgian houses, first TIFFIN'S SCHOOL, partly early C19, of yellow brick, then No. 143 (formerly VINE HOUSE) of five bays with lower two-bay wings (early C18), and Nos. 155–157 of three bays, late C17 (cf. the side doorways with straight hoods on carved brackets) but with an early C19 stuccoed Tudor-Gothic façade. Off London Road, down Albert Road, one gets to VILLIERS ROAD, with the OLD MILL HOUSE, a late C18 house of five bays with an Adamish porch.

Quite on its own, to the E of Kingston, is the district round COOMBE. This and KINGSTON HILL to its N were built over ^{See p. 598} with big houses in the later Victorian decades.* Few of these houses survive. As a rule only the gate lodges bear witness to them (e.g. COOMBE WARREN LODGE, Coombe Lane, which belonged to a big Jacobean house built by *Devey* in 1881). The estates have been broken up and smaller houses cover parts of them. Among such in WARREN RISE is MIRAMONTE by *Maxwell Fry*, 1937, typical of the most advanced style of that moment. By the entrance, garage with open spiral staircase to the upper floor. The house lies further back and is reached by a covered way. It is L-shaped with a s front which has long window-bands on two floors and a half-covered roof terrace. At the l. end of the front, projecting wing with a sun-room and a covered balcony over – a typical Fry motif. ROBIN HILL in COOMBE HILL ROAD by *Tayler & Green* is equally typical of the 1950s, beautifully landscaped. Also in Coombe Hill Road CEDAR COURT, a pre-Reformation timber-framed house from Colchester in Essex. This was re-erected here by Mr Walter Thornton-Smith, an antiquarian builder, in 1911–12.‡ Then a group of four houses (FAIR OAKS, etc.) by *Patrick Gwynne*, 1959, beautifully detailed as his work always is. Flat roofs, three houses almost level, one a little downhill, linked by undulating brick screen walls. Further E, COOMBE PINES

* Kingston Hill was developed by the National Freehold Land Society from 1853.

‡ Information from Mrs J. M. Robson.

in Warren Cutting is one of the best of the earlier houses, freely grouped and very dignified. By *Harold Bailey & Douglas Wood*, 1912. At the N end of Warren Road, VINCENT HOUSE is a good big house (big for post-war England, that is) by *Kenneth Wood*, 1958. Timber upper floor with a long balcony and a split pitched roof. Everything decorative comes out of the needs of the house, and is not put on as a cliché. (NUMBER ONE, Warren Park, is also by *Kenneth Wood*, 1965–8.)

KINGSTON HILL *see* KINGSTON UPON THAMES

2050

KINGSWOOD

ST ANDREW. 1848–52 by *Ferrey*, an almost literal copy of the C14 church of Shottesbrook in Berkshire. It looks very well, translated into leafy suburban surroundings. – PLATE. Chalice 1675.

ST SOPHIA, Lower Kingswood. 1891 by *Sidney Barnsley*. A most remarkable church, more even for its contents than its architecture. Built by Dr Edwin Freshfield and Sir Cosmo Bonsor. Red brick and stone with much variety of effect. Divers herringbone brick friezes. In a free Byzantine style. Nave and chancel in one, and apse. No tower, but a separate weatherboarded bell-steeple with a Byzantine folded dome.

89 Inside, the E end is entirely marble-lined, and so is the small square baptistery of 1935 at the W end. The church itself has a nave of only two bays with narrow aisle passages. Prettily decorated wooden wagon roof painted by *Barnsley* himself.*

9 – SCULPTURE. In the church are nine Byzantine capitals, brought back by Dr Freshfield. The two big ones in the nave arcades (S and N) are of the C4 and come from St John at Ephesus. Against the W wall smaller C6 capital from the same church (W wall, S end top), two capitals of *c*.400 from St John Studion at Constantinople (W wall above the doorway), two capitals from the Blachernae Palace also at Constantinople (W wall, N end, top and bottom), and an C11 fragment of a frieze from the church of the Pantocrator again at Constantinople (W wall, N end). At the E end of the nave Comnene capitals from the Bogdan Serail (N) and a site near the Blachernae Palace (s), both at Constantinople. The capital on

* Information from the Rev. F. Vere Hodge.

the w wall, at the s end, bottom, is also from the Bogdan Serail.

WOODWORK. *Barnsley*'s woodwork is more enjoyable than his architecture. Pulpit and lectern on the stone screen wall, ebony and holly inlay. – Two priests' seats with canopies. The inlay here includes mother of pearl. – Two prayer desks. – Stalls against the w wall. – Octagonal almsbox. – The style is similar to Gimson's.

KINGSWOOD WARREN. Castellated mansion of 1835–7, by *T. R. Knowles*, much altered by *William Smith* in 1873 (GS). The tower with stair-turret and the wall to its r. are still the original.

(WHEATCROFT, Forest Drive. By *Leslie Gooday & Associates*, 1958. A timber house ingeniously built into the side of a hill, with shingled monopitch roof and brick and boarded walls.)

KNAPHILL see BISLEY

LALEHAM*

oo60

The village makes no use of the Thames, in contrast to most Middlesex villages in similar positions. From the river Laleham is no more than 'enormous willows and queer suggestions of old houses on the banks' (William Morris).

ALL SAINTS. Outside the building appears C19 with the exception of the w tower and the N chancel (Lucan) chapel. The chapel is Early Tudor brick, diapered, and with four moulded brick three-light windows. The tower is an odd specimen of heavy-handed Early Georgian, all brick, with very broad quoins ending in capitals and a stone-dressed Venetian window on the w front. There is a heavy parapet on top. The tower is dated 1732. Inside, the church has Norman arcades 12 on the N as well as the s side of the nave. Laleham has demi-columns against the w wall and then three columns on each side (but the nave was originally longer towards the E). The s arcade is now blocked, as the s aisle was pulled down at an unknown date. The capitals are scalloped, the arches are single-chamfered, except in the NE arches where early C16 brick replaces them. In the s wall higher up are some reset bits from a former Norman doorway. Against the w wall of the N aisle a large PAINTING of Christ on the sea with Peter, by

* Formerly in Middlesex.

G. H. Harlow, probably *c*.1810. It was presented in 1811. In the W window, STAINED GLASS signed *W. M. Geddes*, 1926, an effective Expressionist design in rich colours. Against the S wall of the chancel wall-monuments to George Perrot † 1780 and his wife † 1784, by *W. Tyler*, and to Henrietta Hartwell † 1818 by *Chantrey*, both minor.

Close to the church, CHURCH FARM, a late C17 cottage; S of the church, DIAL HOUSE, C18, of three storeys, with a sundial dated 1730. (To the NE, in the BROADWAY, MANOR FARM, an early C18 brick house, with weatherboarded outbuildings, and THE LIMES and HIGH ELMS, both C18, altered later. MHLG)

FERRY LANE leads S to a triangular green nearer the river. In Ferry Lane, a single-storey modern house with internal courtyard, by *Peter Howard*, *c*.1965. On the E side of the green, MUNCASTER HOUSE, *c*.1700 with a large Victorian addition, then THE COVERTS, *c*.1700, of three bays and two storeys, and THE THATCHED COTTAGE, a sweet little affair of Blaise Hamlet type with a thatched veranda with rude treetrunks, probably early C19. The drive to the S leads to LALEHAM HOUSE, now The Abbey, by *J. B. Papworth*, 1803–6, compact, with a Greek Doric porch, and altogether very progressive for its date.

1050   LEATHERHEAD

Perhaps the most pitiful of Surrey small towns, because the old pattern here was smaller and humbler than most and hence was pushed aside more easily. Apart from the church, none of the older buildings is worth a visit, and the townscape has gone along with the old buildings.

ST MARY AND ST NICHOLAS. Much better inside than outside. The outside renewed from end to end, though the Dec windows in the chancel (except the E window) seem to represent the original design. So do most of the tower details, of the later C15, with angle buttresses and three-light bell-openings under segmental arches.* Inside, apart from harsh restoration of the roofs, the impression is almost entirely of *c*.1210 and surprisingly consistent, largely because the surviving details

---

* The main restorations were by *A. Blomfield* (1873: N transept extended; 1891: roofs renewed; 1894: tower restored) and by *E. Christian* (1874: chancel restored). The interior was redecorated in 1965.

form a coherent space in themselves.* Four-bay arcades and chancel arch, subtle and large-scale, clearly part of the advanced French-looking work of South-East England of c.1200, although a minor part. Clearly also connected with the Reigate arcades, because the only non-abstract capital has single upright trefoiled stiff-leaves of the same type as Reigate. The remainder have alternate circular and octagonal piers with matching capitals. The arches are two-order, the inner chamfered and the outer with a keeled roll-moulding. There are however differences between N and S. The N arcade is only three bays long, followed to the W by a C19 arch. Between the two parts is an old respond and the mark of the original W wall. The S arcade is of four bays, i.e. ran on regardless of the W wall. As there is no progress in style from N to S, the decision to pull down the old wall must have been taken while building went on. What then did the W end of the N side look like before the C19 arch was built? The chancel arch is a little later than the arcade – say mid-C13. It is complex and unchamfered with two distinct rolls and many smaller curves, all carved with a mixture of power and subtlety. The W tower is pronouncedly off-centre and off-axis. Bold four-centred tower arch of three orders on unusually shafted responds, not the normal Surrey style. The N transept is C19 now, but some chequerboard flint and stone masonry in the E and W walls (cf. Mickleham) shows that a Perp transept existed. – FONT. C15, octagonal, with quatrefoils. – CHEST. Under the tower, leather-bound with fancy patterns of studs, dated 1663. – STAINED GLASS. In the N aisle medieval fragments of all dates jumbled together to make queer Bosch-like compositions in their own right. Skilfully done in the 1940s by *Wall & Wall*. – PLATE. Large Cup 1661; Flagon 1704. – MONUMENTS. Richard Dalton † 1731. Sober black marble pyramid and sarcophagus. – Jacob Wishart † 1723 by *Stanton & Horsnaile*. Oblong tablet completely surrounded by a froth of military trophies with a relief of a man of war below; moderate quality.

(OUR LADY AND ST PETER (R.C.), Garlands Road. 1922–3 by *E. Goldie*. – SCULPTURE. Stations of the Cross by *Eric Gill* (carved by *J. Cribb*) in Caen stone. – STAINED GLASS by *P. Woodroffe*, 1936. DE, R. Hubbuck)

U.D.C. OFFICES. Arch Neo-Georgian with a very arch cupola

* It has, however, been suggested that the walls above the nave arcades may survive from a Late Saxon church.

by *C. H. Rose & H. R. Gardner*, 1935. There was a nice cedar tree in front, under which John Wesley is reputed to have preached his last sermon.*

(St John's School, Epsom Road. Extensive buildings of 1872–98 by *Ferrey and Good*. Later additions by *Leonard Martin* (swimming bath, 1925), *O. P. Milne* (classrooms, 1935), *H. M. Grellier & Son* (gymnasium block, laboratories, 1951–7), and *Seely & Paget* (chapel 1962–3, laboratory 1969).)

Bridge. 1782 by *Gwilt*. Fourteen arches, brick with corbelled-out refuges, widened on the s side in 1824. The same type as at Cobham, and the same low quality too.

The central crossroads has the fake-Tudor National Provincial Bank facing the fake-c17 plastered chemist's shop; both hideous. To the N there are a few cottages around Gravel Hill, to the E the High Street has absolutely nothing, to the W Bridge Street has a couple of very early c19 stock-brick buildings (Nos. 28–34, on the N side, and No. 43 opposite).‡ ⟨To the s, hidden away behind the bus station, Fire Station by the County Architect, *R. J. Ash*, 1967–9, in an especially attractive brown brick. The area around the bridge is a semi-industrial jungle. Elephantine Pumping Station dated 1935.§ More industry further N behind the station. In Randall's Road, opposite Ronsons, laboratories for the Printing and Packaging and Allied Trades Research Association, by *Michael Manser Associates*, 1963–4. Bold, clean-cut workshops with aluminium cladding. Then, off Cleeve Road on the r., Central Electricity Research Laboratories. The main building is by *Clifford, Tee & Gale*, 1958–61. It has a slightly curved curtain-walled façade of three storeys, and stands behind a large pool (which is used for cooling water). A windowless lecture theatre projects into the pool and is neatly linked to the main building by the entrance porch. In Kingston Road, Plannair by *Michael Manser Associates*, 1964, offices with ribbed aluminium cladding, white brick factory buildings behind. A little more in Church Street to the s, where the Crescent Cinema of 1939 has been replaced by the Thorndike Theatre by *Roderick Ham*, completed 1969.

---

* The tree died recently. When it was removed, the tree-rings showed it could only have been a sapling in Wesley's day.

‡ Also on the N side The Running Horse, a rambling timber-framed house, perhaps partly c15, with a block of *c*.1800 behind (MHLG).

§ Rodney Hubbuck's description.

The theatre is ingeniously fitted into a confined area behind new shops and offices in Church Street (these are by *Lovett Gill & Partners*). The auditorium is fan-shaped, with a projecting stage and no proscenium arch, and 562 seats in a single rising tier. One foyer is tucked beneath the seats; the upper foyers stand free of the auditorium walls, allowing vistas up and down despite the limited space.⟩ Then THE MANSION, a long front of *c.*1740, nine by two bays of brickwork, the garden side plain, the entrance side fitted out quite handsomely with classical window surrounds that look *c.*1830. Seven-bay centre, the end bays brought forward slightly and quoined. Beyond this No. 33, C16, with a blank three-by-two-bay front of *c.*1730, then WOOD DENE, wild classical of 1850 with pavilion roof. (E of Church Street, in Barnett Wood Lane, BARNETT WOOD FARM, mostly C17, with a steep tiled roof. There are a number of interesting timber-framed buildings around Leatherhead, e.g. ROWHURST, Oxshott Road, and PATSOMS COTTAGES, Woodlands Road, both C16 and C17. MHLG)

Further S again THORNCROFT, a small stock-brick house by *Sir Robert Taylor*, 1772, enlarged *c.*1800. Five by two bays, the main front plain except for a heavy porch and flight of steps. Nowhere near the standard of his best work. (In the grounds an ornamental flint footbridge, C18. MHLG)

To the SE, where suburban building stops abruptly, is HIGHLANDS FARM, a neat three-bay late C18 brick box with two weatherboarded bow windows on the ground floor, unfortunately now without its doorcase. Attached to it a good set of tarred-weatherboard barns and a granary on staddlestones. To the N at Leatherhead Common are a few early C19 weatherboarded cottages. (In Fortyfoot Road, GOLDEN GROVE, *Michael Manser*'s own house, a single-storey building with a central courtyard, 1961.)

FETCHAM. *See* p. 244.

LEIGH

2040

Trim village in trim flat Wealden landscape SW of Reigate. Completely tamed and park-like, like the country W of Windsor.

ST BARTHOLOMEW. Small unaisled Perp church in Reigate stone, with good simple details. Two- and three-light windows, some square-headed and some segment-headed. This pleasant design was spoilt in the usual Surrey way in 1856 by

Larmer (GS), and in 1890 by *F. C. Lees* – when the original timber belfry was replaced first by a stone tower, then by a bellcote and extended w end, and a lean-to porch added, all fussily picturesque with the wrong sort of stone dressings. The interior was killed off at the same time. – STAINED GLASS. E window by *Kempe*, 1890, with slightly more expression and a wider colour range than his normal selection of pious greens. – PLATE. Cup 1606; Paten 1773. – BRASS to John Arderne † 1449 and wife, with daughters below. Full face, civilian dress, main effigies 3 ft high.

LEIGH PLACE, N of the church. An old moated site, but the building on it is effectively an exasperatingly styleless Gothick rebuild of 1810. Inside a few C17 and C18 details.

MYNTHURST, 1 m. S. Big and very ugly Victorian Tudor. Symmetrical brick and stone with a W tower.

The village centre is a demure green with everything in its place. On the N side is the PLOUGH, a weatherboarded village pub, on the S side an asymmetrical Victorian village SCHOOL, and in the SE corner is the PRIESTS HOUSE, a very long range of medieval close-set half-timbering, with no overall pattern. Added to and renovated, but still quite impressive. Horsham slate roofs and big brick stacks.

SW of the village, in Shellwood Road, is PEVEREL, by *F. F. C. Curtis*, 1936, colour-washed and flat-roofed. Much less gauche than most thirties houses.

1040

LEITH HILL
4 m. SW of Dorking

The highest point in Surrey (and in South-East England) – 965 ft, now made up to exactly 1000 ft by the folly TOWER on top. This was built by *Richard Hull* of Bristol in 1766, heightened in 1788, and given battlements and an oversize stair-turret in 1864. Stone-built with brick dressings. If any of the detail goes back to 1766, or even to 1788, it is a remarkable design for the date, for it is in effect an accurate Wealden tower of *c.*1300, solidly proportioned and soberly detailed: only the multiple string courses seem out of place.

LEITH HILL PLACE. Originally a gabled house of *c.*1600, completely refaced *c.*1760 in a weak but delicate Palladian style. In a superb position on the S slope of Leith Hill. All stone-faced, the main front facing S with a five-bay two-storey centre and single-bay three-storey wings (the pedimented top floor apparently mid-c19). Inside, a sober staircase of Early Georgian type, but probably of the same date as the refronting.

LIMPSFIELD*

4050

On the Wealden ridge near the Kent border. One long village street with an overlay of expensive houses of c.1890. s of the ridge the parish includes the part of the Surrey Weald which is nearest to the Kentish pattern of yeoman building, with each farmhouse almost a small manor and almost all of them worth a look.

ST PETER. Above the street and approached by a C14 LYCH-GATE. A good, dour piece of Wealden building, enlarged too much for the interior to be impressive. The s side, however, with all the additions out of sight, is typically thick and gruff: blocky silhouette and Horsham slate roof sweeping down to low walls without clerestory or dormers. The oldest parts are the W wall (herringbone masonry) and the tower, of c.1180, unbuttressed, with a pyramid roof and a plain arch on the simplest imposts towards the chancel. Nave, chancel, N chancel chapel, and s aisle all C13, plain lancet work. The arcade has simple round piers with round abaci and arches with two slight chamfers.‡ In the chapel arcade the arches die against the responds. The same is the case in the chancel arch, which was raised in 1852. In the s window of the tower two-light plate tracery of c.1260, when the base of the tower was fitted up as a chapel. A similar window under a big relieving arch must have existed on the E side. It was removed to a new vestry in 1823 and destroyed in 1871. In the chancel E wall a recess with a flue, supposed to be an oven for baking communion bread. s aisle windows C15, s porch C16, N aisle 1852. The triple lancets of both chancel and chancel chapel are C19, filled with STAINED GLASS by *Clayton & Bell* (cf. Titsey), put in by *Pearson* in 1871. – FONT. C13. Plain square bowl on four renewed corner shafts and a complex-shaped central pillar, more or less octagonal, and presumably altered later. – MONUMENTS. Marmaduke Hilton † 1768, Palladian frame (s aisle). – Lord Elphinstone † 1860 by *Matthew Noble* (also

* We are grateful to Mrs K. Percy for much help in revising this entry.
‡ A kind of lowest common denominator of mid-c13 building. The church belonged to Battle Abbey and the style is very much like some of the uninspired C13 work in Battle church.

cf. Titsey), another competent recumbent effigy, in robes of
the Order of the Bath. His left hand lies on his heart. –
PLATE. Paten 1749; complete Set of 1764.

ST ANDREW, The Chart. 1895 by *Sir Reginald Blomfield*,
evidently not at home in Gothic. (Arts and Crafts REREDOS
by *H. Wilson.* R. Hubbuck) The adjoining Church Hall was
built in 1959 by *S. Senior.*

Limpsfield parish is full of vernacular buildings, many of them
now elaborately converted for commuting. It is easiest to
describe first the High Street from N to S, then the Weald
ridge, and then the farms in the Weald proper, beyond the
ridge.

At the extreme N end, near Titsey Park, is LIMPSFIELD
LODGE FARM, the outside of *c.*1700, tile-hung above and
local freestone below: attractive. Starting at the N end of the
High Street proper is the OLD COURT COTTAGE, Titsey
Road, altered, but incorporating the remarkable survival
of an early medieval timber-framed aisled hall, from which
two wooden carved capitals of *c.*1200 survive. The house belonged to the abbot of Battle, who held the manorial court
there. Then comes the RECTORY, on the W side, opposite
the church. Typical late C17 or very early C18 brick front
(before 1711, when it was struck by lightning), seven by two
crowded bays with an eaves cornice. Behind the church in its
own grounds is HOOKWOOD, a plain early C19 stock-brick
house (before 1809 – MHLG). Then High Street narrows,
starting with DETILLENS COTTAGES at the corner of
B2025, a picturesque row of six cottages, C16–18, timber-
framed and tile-hung. DETILLENS itself lies further S, with
an early C18 front to the road, seven by two bays, the doorcase with an ogee shape in the lintel (a typical mason's cliché
around London). This hides a C15 hall house with an impressive kingpost roof, now in the upper room. Opposite, on
the E side, is LILAC COTTAGE, pretty, early C18 brick and
tile-hanging. The W side further S then has an impressive long
terraced range of mixed building. JARRETT'S shop has one
big C16 gabled wing to the street and the remainder refronted in good rubbed brickwork; MILES'S shop is an
interesting building of four periods – early C16 jettied cross-
wing, two bays C17, one further bay and three jettied gables
to the E front of the later C17. The brickwork under the
jetties is pre-1825. The WHITE HOUSE is of *c.*1770, with a
mansard roof and a Palladian doorcase on the side elevation.

The E side then takes up the building line with restored tile-hung cottages and the OLD COURT HOUSE, now three dwellings and very restored, but originally one C15 hall-house. It retains a tie-beam and crown-post on the first floor in the solar cross-wing and remains of a fine open truss and king-post in the centre cottage. The W side finishes with ROSE-WELL COTTAGE, C18, timber-framed and tile-hung, and JESSAMINE COTTAGES, C19, a simple pair of brick and tile-hung cottages: Jessamine by the road-side and Rosewell behind them *en échelon*, the most picturesque group in the village. In the NW corner of the junction with A25, THE BOWER is again C17, with an early C18 brick front, this time with segmental windows, and again a rough mason's job. Beyond the main road is WOLFS ROW, a picturesque terrace in Weald sandstone, some timber and brick, starting C18 and stepping up via STONEWALLS, a battlemented front of 1903 by *George Wickham*, to Victorian semi-detacheds on the brow of the hill. Beyond again, ST MICHAEL'S SCHOOL by *John Norton*, 1886, ferocious utilitarian brick Gothic with a steep-roofed tower in the centre, visible for miles. Bad, but no worse than Butterfield at Chobham.

On the ridge, The Chart is a breezy hilltop common with a C17 MILL HOUSE (the windmill removed *c.*1925). TENCHLEYS PARK has an odd front of 1858 – an urbane ashlar façade with hood-moulds over all the windows. LANGSHAW seems to be the *Norman Shaw* house originally called PAINS HILL, 1872, long and tile-hung, not very attractive. N again, at MOORHOUSE BANK on the very edge of the county, the charmingly genuine and the remarkably olde face one another across A25. The olde is the GRASSHOPPER INN, over-timbered even in the context of Surrey road-houses. It has all been put together since 1950 by the owner, *W. M. Lawrence*, incorporating a lot of old materials: panelling and weather vane from Weald Park Essex, staircase from Buckhurst Park Sussex, and so on. This is a labour of love, a king of C20 follies. It is sad that the modern movement has not evolved a folly architecture, but has forced folly-builders into the past. The genuine is the group of cottages and barns around MOORHOUSE FARM on the S side of the road, all in Weald stone with brick dressings and tile roofs, a good example of the unconscious grouping of steep pitched roofs parallel with the slope of the hillside. To find a whole group like this without any false notes is a rare thing in Surrey now.

Back towards the village on the s side of A25 is THE GATE
HOUSE, built in 1924 by *Baillie Scott & Beresford,* all of old
bricks from a house in Bedford. The garden front is symmetrical and blowsy, but the entrance side is very picturesque, a
symmetrical mass with asymmetrical detail. Sober, nothing
overstated – Lutyens's style without Lutyens's affectations.
Inside, the billiard room still has its light fitting designed by
Baillie Scott, representing a 'walled eastern city with large and
small domes' floating sublimely above the baize. A surprisingly
fresh house considering its date.

The Weald plain s of the ridge contains several notable farms.
The road down from the ridge passes some picturesquely set
timber-framed cottages (PAINES HILL COTTAGES), originally all one C16 hall-house with later additions. At the
bottom of the hill is GRANT'S FARM, with a C16 frame, tile-
hung, with one big gable at the s end and a long tile-hung
range northwards up the hill: prototype-Voysey. STOCKEN-
DEN, ½ m. s, is a C15 house with a big wing of two periods,
late C16 and C17, making the house L-shaped, the whole
brick and tile-hung. Unrestored, with an impressive pair of
chimneystacks on the E side of the C17 range, three and two
shafts respectively, set diagonally. TENCHLEYS FARM (now
Tenchleys Manor), further E, is of *c.*1600, L-shaped and tile-
hung. TREVEREUX, almost on the Kent border, has a delightful early C18 front. Masons' work, but good quality, and well
above that of the other C18 houses in Limpsfield. L-shaped, in
red and grey brick with giant angle pilasters. Five bays with
Doric doorcase, plus one bay in the wing, and lower addition
to the w, Georgian, of *c.* 1900. 1 m. further s BATCHELORS
FARM is the typical Kentish hall-house (or Wealden house),
i.e. with a recessed centre containing the hall, and two overhanging wings. A further bay was added in the C17 at the E
end and there is a large addition of 1968 at the w end. BLACK
ROBINS FARM, ½ m. w of this, is outstandingly picturesque, a
C16 timber frame with a central chimneystack and a brick front
of *c.*1700, grouping with a black tile-and-weatherboard barn.

₃₀₄₀   LINGFIELD

A big village in the Weald, N of East Grinstead, Sussex. It has
picturesque corners but no coherent village centre, possibly
because the old village grew around a quadrilateral of lanes.
Suburbanized from the 1880s, when the railway came.

ST PETER AND ST PAUL. Surrey's only Perp church of any size [21] or pretensions (discounting Croydon as being a Victorian rebuilding). The tower, at the SW end of the nave, is C14. The rest was all rebuilt by Sir Reginald Cobham when he founded a college here in 1431. The result is sober but very satisfying, especially inside: it is architects' rather than wool-merchants' Perp, with very little display of any sort. Four-bay nave with N and S aisles, three-bay chancel with N and S chapels. No clerestory. Small by Gloucestershire or East Anglian standards. The S aisle has only two bays, and the S chancel chapel is smaller and later than the rest, so that the building reads spatially like a double-naved church,* with both chancel arch and an arch between N aisle and N chapel, an unusually coherent effect. The style could loosely be called Kentish; straightforward four- and five-light windows at the E and W ends and three-light windows under segmental hood-moulds all down the N side, which is broken only by the staircase turret for the rood, and is an impressive bit of understatement seen from outside. The arcade details are standard. Nave piers with four attached shafts and four hollows between them, chancel arch similar,‡ chapel arches with four shafts connected by deep undulations. The church could almost be a City church, and in fact St Olave Hart Street in the City of London has the same arcades and the same windows. Some Kentish churches have similar details (Woodchurch, e.g.), but nothing close enough to invite conjecture. This is clearly a deliberate design, so that parallels are worth looking for.

Fine set of late medieval FITTINGS. Lingfield is almost the only church in Surrey to have them. – ROYAL ARMS. Queen Anne (N wall of nave). – CHANDELIER. C18, brass, suspended by a wrought-iron pendant like a sword rest which is bigger than the chandelier itself. – FONT. Straightforward C15 design, octagonal bowl on octagonal base. Apparently contemporary ogee COVER. – LECTERN. In the N aisle, double-sided, wooden, and a puzzling piece. What date? – SCREENS. C15 screens between chancel and N and S chapels. Single-light ogee-headed panels with a crude beam above. Rough and poor work, which is surprising when compared with the STALLS.

* Was it in fact double-naved – one collegiate and one parochial? If so, this is a very rare case.

‡ Intersecting mouldings of a sort above the chancel arch capitals. They are very cackhanded and seem not so much attempted spatial ambiguity as simple confusion over the C15 equivalent of working details.

These have a fine set of MISERICORDS. Some of the carving is standard C15 (angels bearing shields, e.g.), but some of it is well above average, for example the first carved head on the N side, and the heads carved on the NW and SW corner posts.* – A very puzzling BENCH, fitted in on the N side of the chancel – the choir stalls were cut away to accommodate it – with Renaissance panels of medallion heads and the royal arms. This looks all of a piece, and hence must have been done in England; yet it is without a trace of provincial workmanship. The impressive tuft-bearded warrior in C16 armour is particularly good.‡ – PLATE. Cup and Cover 1572. – MONUMENTS. In the N chancel chapel: Reginald, first Lord Cobham, † 1361. Battlemented tomb-chest with stiff unappealing effigy in armour, but delightful if naïve English marginal comments at head and foot: the head rests on a Moor's-head helm supported by two gawky boyish angels, the feet rest on a rascally-looking Saracen who would be almost undatable out of his context, part of the perennial caricaturing impulse of folk art. – Unnamed tester altar tomb with thicker panelling (N wall of chapel). Said to be Sir Thomas Cobham † 1471. – In the chancel: Sir Reginald Cobham † 1446 and wife. The little vignettes at head and feet are vividly alive; the alabaster effigies have to be more conventional, but are still very good. At the head another Moor's-head helm and a pair of stiffly upright angels, at the feet a sea wolf and a wyvern, both wearing an evil grin. – On the S wall of the chancel, two fine Baroque cartouches, Francis Howard † 1695 and Mary his wife † 1718, nearly symmetrical designs wreathed round with luscious high relief foliage and cherub heads as though they were Grinling Gibbons altarpieces. Clearly by the same mason and in quite a distinctive style, out of the normal run of Baroque tablets. – BRASSES. The best set in Surrey. In the chancel two small half-length figures of priests, John Swetecote † 1469 and James Veldon † 1458, and a small brass of a girl without inscription; all minor. – In the N chapel: Reginald, second Lord Cobham, † 1403, full size on tomb-chest, and Eleanor, first wife of Sir Reginald, † 1420, three-quarter life size with canopy and marginal inscription. Both these are technically superb but a little mechanical. – Katherine Stoket † 1420, a small demi-

24

25

---

* i.e. whenever the carver could get away from conventional representation: exactly the same situation as in the big table-tombs.

‡ Mr Clifton-Taylor suggests that this piece of work comes from a chimneypiece.

figure with much more expression. – Brass without inscription
to a lady, probably Elizabeth, second wife of Sir Reginald. A
very good brass. Full-size figure with her head on a tasselled
pillow and a pet dog at her feet. Full face.* All the robes have
a delicate, just perceptible sway to one side. One of the rare
occasions when a c15 brass is a work of art in its own right,
and not a display of one more English virtuoso technique of
linear pattern-making. – An odd effigy on the N wall, transferred from the floor: incised figure under a canopy using a
brass technique but made up of encaustic tiles. Foreign, of
c.1530.

Of the college to which the church was attached nothing remains
except the OLD GUEST HOUSE to the N, now the County
Library, a c15 timber-framed hall-house in the Kentish
manner, i.e. with a recessed centre and curved braces
forming spandrels. Over-restored. On the site of the college
proper, W of the church, there is a splendid unrestored farmhouse, THE COLLEGE, one of the best in Surrey. Of c.1700,
brick below, semicircular-tile-hung above, with one central
dormer, Horsham slate roof, and – a rare survival which makes
a beautiful surface pattern with the tile-hanging – a complete
set of mullioned and transomed windows, thirty-six panes in
each.‡ The village centre, called Plaistow Street, is SW of this,
around a prettified duckpond and the CROSS and CAGE, a
tiny, queer composite building looking just like an early Irish
cell-church. The cage – built as the local lock-up – forms the
'cell', added in 1773. The cross, which is supposed to be c15,
is a stepped tower at one end. Actually the whole thing looks
c18, except for the base of a cross which is the finial to the
tower. There are some pleasant tile-hung cottages here on the
W side of the street, e.g. BILLHURST COTTAGES, formed
around a c15 core, and ROSE COTTAGES, partly weatherboarded.

The best corner of Lingfield is the S end of the churchyard,
where the road sweeps away to the E leaving a picturesque
funnel of buildings leading up to the church, focusing on the
S aisle, and forming a tiny square. The E side is a long range of
plain brickwork of c.1700, with segment-headed windows,
called STAR INN COTTAGES. The W side consists of the OLD
TOWN STORES at the churchyard end, c16, timber-framed
and tile-hung, and POLLARD COTTAGE at the S end, which

* The top half is c19 restoration, but authentically done.
‡ The tiles are c19, but the building may always have been tile-hung.

completes the enclosure. It is a C15 hall-house, again with recessed centre, and a projecting gabled C16 wing, close-timbered, and containing a very rare contemporary shop-front, now rather unhappily filled in. It was still used as a butcher's shop in the C20. E of the church is NEW PLACE, an attractive L-shaped Wealden stone house dated 1617. The details are familiar from the Cotswolds and Derbyshire, and used to good effect in Sackville College, e.g., just over the Sussex border at East Grinstead. Mullioned windows with hood-moulds, and an attractive pilastered Jacobean door-case – enclosing a four-centred door – now set diagonally in the angle of the L.

Finally to the S is the RACECOURSE, with pleasant buildings by *Walter Brierley*, 1924, more or less Georgian. BATNORS, opposite the main entrance to the course, has a mason's Baroque brick front dated 1718. Seven bays, with the wings brought forward slightly, plain angle pilasters, and panelled parapet.

(THE GARTH, Newchapel Road. Built in 1729 as the parish workhouse. Brick and tile-hung, converted first into six cottages and then into one house – in 1918, by *W. H. Godfrey*. Arthur Oswald)

(PUTTENDEN MANOR, E of Lingfield. Good timber-framed hall-house, early C16 with later alterations, built by the Sondes family. P. N. Reid)

LITTLE BOOKHAM

1050

Appropriately, a small edition of Great Bookham. The village street runs N-S on the spring line, with C20 suburbanization; church and manor house are by themselves further w.

CHURCH (dedication unknown). Now a single room, with a bell-cote. Basically C12: one original window in the W wall, one at the NW end of the nave, and a blocked S arcade of exactly the same type as the S arcade at Great Bookham. In the blocked arcade, moreover, is a C15 window and what looks like an authentic C13 lancet with deep splays and shafts inside. Was it moved back when the arcade was blocked?* The rest largely renewed (E window e.g.) so that there is little visual pleasure to be got from the building. – FONT. Big tub font bound with a complicated system of iron straps. Font and

---

* Excavations have revealed the foundations of the aisle wall.

ironwork look respectively C12 and C17, but any dating is a risky business. – MONUMENT. George Pollen † 1812. Grecian tablet with a boldly carved urn. Not bad (N side of chancel). To the S of the church is the MANOR HOUSE, with a double-bowed three-storeyed early C19 front. E of this, across the road, is the big TITHE BARN, probably C17, with weather-boarding and pantiles and double wagon entrances cut back into the deep roof. The village street has a few C17 cottages, and near the railway at the N end a good set of barns to MADDOX FARM, of standard tarred-weatherboard type, beautifully cared for. The different ridge heights make a delightful effect that was certainly unconscious.

LITTLE TANGLEY see BRAMLEY

LITTLETON

1½ m. SW of Guildford

9040

The estate village to Loseley. Mostly big unrestored Tudor yeomen's cottages with crude irregular timber-framing (particularly No. 20 on the E side and No. 13 on the W). Mission Church of ST FRANCIS in very picturesque former SCHOOLS of 1843, with small S tower with short shingled spire. Inside, a small piece of SCULPTURE, a Pietà; looks C15 Flemish.

LITTLETON*

0060

The first impression is the contrast between the vast bare embankment of the reservoir to the N and the vast bare sheds of the London Film Company to the W on the one hand, and the small group of church, rectory, manor farm, and manor house on the other. ⟨That was the situation in the 1950s. Now an ugly car park for the film studios encroaches on the view of the church, the old rectory has been replaced by a dull new house, and on the corner a new primary school is under construction (1969). The cohesion of the old group has gone completely.⟩

ST MARY MAGDALENE. The church is a study in brick, [22] although the C13 nave and chancel were originally ragstone and flint rubble. But the early C16 added a brick W tower, heightened early in the C18, a S porch, and a brick clerestory to the nave. There is also a N chapel, dated 1705, and, of c.1730, a further N extension of this. The C19 refaced the S aisle and

* Formerly in Middlesex.

its buttresses. Thus looking from NE all seems brick, dominated by the mauve of the old parts of the tower and the russet of the top. The clerestory is light red, the porch again mauve, the N chapel of 1705 has a chequerboard pattern with vitrified headers and a double-curved gable for the part of 1705 and a straight one for the later part. The interior is as delightful as the exterior, a very short nave of only two bays and a low chancel separated from it by a screen. The s pier is round and thick, c.1200, the N pier octagonal and later C13. The arches are double-chamfered, as is the chancel arch. The chancel has original deep-splayed N windows. Those in the s wall are copies. The walls of the chancel and the spandrels of the nave are rubble unplastered. An effective contrast in the nave is the brick clerestory. The church has a wealth of less usual furnishings: a late medieval LOCKER in the s aisle s wall; complete set of (restored) PEWS of about the same date; CHOIR STALLS (also restored) with cusped ogee arches and panelling in the spandrels, C15, said to come from Winchester; a very much and fancifully restored ROOD SCREEN of c.1500; ALTAR RAILS of sumptuous Flemish or French Baroque of c.1700; and an early C18 PULPIT with a curious narrow high window into the SE angle between nave and chancel to give it sufficient light. On the N and s wall at the w end of the nave an Italian Trecento PAINTING of six panels with six saints. – PLATE. Chalice and Paten, 1632; four Patens, 1677; Paten, 1680; Chalice, 1712; Flagon, 1726.

MANOR HOUSE. A picturesque group of buildings dating from the C15 to the C19. (The N front, of six bays and two storeys, is C18 or early C19; the garden front is earlier, a half-H with gabled wings. Inside is a large central hall and an early C18 staircase with armorial glass in the windows. MHLG)

The RECTORY, of five bays with hipped roof, c.1700, was demolished in 1966.

LITTLEWORTH CROSS see SEALE

LONG COPSE see EWHURST

LONG CROSS
2 m. N of Chobham

CHRISTCHURCH. Tiny spiky lancet chapel, disarming. By one *Willoughby*, 1847.

BARROW HILLS. Two (originally three) tree-covered but otherwise well preserved bowl BARROWS.

In a wood s of Long Cross another bowl BARROW with ditch
2–3 ft deep and prominently visible. The mound is 6–7 ft high
and 92 ft in diameter.

W of Flutters Hill remains of a huge bell BARROW, 105 ft in
diameter. There are several lesser mounds within the parish.

LONG DITTON

1060

ST MARY, Church Road. 1878–80 by *G. E. Street*. The church
replaces one built by *Sir Robert Taylor* in 1776 in the form of
a Greek cross. The floor and part of the walls of this church
survive in the churchyard. The new church is of buff stone,
with double bellcote between the nave and chancel. – SCULP-
TURE. Some capitals and bases at the w end come from the
church preceding the predecessor of the present one. – PLATE.
Cup 1659; Flagon 1715; Paten 1770. – BRASS. Robert
Castleton †1527 and wife (N aisle E wall), 13 in. figures.

The RECTORY, which was the only interesting house at Long
Ditton, has been pulled down.

LOSELEY

9040

1½ m. SW of Guildford

The best house of its date in the county. Built in 1561–9 by Sir
William More.* The building accounts have been preserved and
show that the chief mason for 1561–2 was named *Mabbanke*.
John Thorpe made a survey of the house soon after 1600,
which shows it as a half-H-shaped house with the open end
closed by a wall and gatehouse. What remains of the house is
the N wing, which always contained the main rooms. The w
wing was pulled down about 1835.‡ The E wing and gatehouse (which are only shown in outline in the survey) were

* Mr M. Binney has recently pointed out that it is likely that this house
incorporated an earlier house, which survived behind the new front. Thorpe's
plan shows only the latter, which, significantly, has no windows at the back
(*see Country Life* 2.10.69).

‡ 〈Although early C19 engravings show that the w wing was in almost the
same style as the surviving house (already conservative in 1560), it appears
to have been a later addition. Bray states that the w wing was built by Sir
George More, who succeeded in 1600, and Miss E. M. Dance has kindly
drawn our attention to a specification preserved in Guildford Muniments
Room, which refers to the gallery, which was in the w wing, being joined on
to the 'old house'.〉

12—S.

probably suggestions by Thorpe which were never carried out. Luckily the w wing did not overlap any part of the main front, but was only joined at the corners – an unusual effect – so that the design of the surviving block is complete in itself. A few alterations were made in the late C17, probably after *c.* 1689, when the house passed to Sir Thomas Molyneux, who married the Loseley heiress, in the course of which a handsome Baroque doorcase with scrolled broken pediment was let into the middle of the hall, replacing the original off-centre entrance, opening on to the screens passage, as shown in Thorpe. In the C19 this was re-opened and the doorcase moved there and replaced by a window. Also after 1689 the hall bay window was given a big double order of applied Doric pilasters, and a simple semicircular arch inside. The details of these have largely rubbed down, but are quite clear in early C19 drawings. The s front was always a utilitarian ramble of windows and gables, and now has a big loggia of 1812 and later C19 additions.

34   The N front, with its asymmetry and multiple gables, is at a quick look a good standard specimen of the picturesque Tudor manor house. In fact it is an ascetic and very carefully controlled essay in ornamental restraint and directed asymmetry. Each different gable-width and window shape represents some requirement of the plan – a narrow bay for the entrance, a three-bay hall plus tall bay window, a medium-size bay for the library, a bigger bay at the w end for the drawing room. The idea of this may be a Tudor commonplace, but the sobriety and freedom from fussiness is almost unique. A standard mullion width is used, grouped in either two, three, two paired or three paired bays according to the job each window has to do. Most of the windows have one transom, but the hall bay has two. The materials augment the austerity: Bargate stone rubble walling with whitewashed hard clunch dressings.* Ornamental detail is confined to the arched heads of the lights of the windows below the transom as well as at the top, and to simple hood-moulds. The whole design must have looked conservative to the 1560s, which had just discovered Flemish detail.

The inside is a medley. The entrance door leads to the screens passage, and then to the GREAT HALL, whose overall Elizabethan appearance is in fact a palimpsest, as most of it is

---

* Much of it came from Waverley Abbey.

due to the so-called Nonsuch fittings.* The fireplace consists of Kentian parts of *c.*1740 and an Elizabethan overmantel. It is in the centre bay on the N side, i.e. where the Baroque entrance doorway was originally, and the gallery above the screens passage has accomplished late C17 floral panels, probably put in *c.*1689. Some small unremarkable armorial glass panels in the big windows are original and are mentioned in the building accounts, and a window on the S side has good German glass dated 1664. The C16 fittings themselves comprise one set of *grottesche* painted on canvas, in the body of the hall, and one set with figures, partly displayed on the gallery. The former are mainly abstract, with HR for Henry VIII, H combined with KP for Henry and Katherine Parr, Dieu et mon droit, etc. Those on the gallery have ornamental motifs as fragile and attenuated as any Pompeian paintings. The style is amazingly up to date, even Europeanly speaking (cf. Cornelis Floris). Most of the woodwork on the W wall is also C16. Incidentally it makes an admirable composition with the big, Devis-like family group above by *Somers*, 1739, a subtle study in recessions and grey tones – outside the strict terms of reference of this book but obviously painted for this position and with a deliberate architectural effect in mind. The C16 panelling is crisply detailed with Ionic pilasters, French-looking, and includes (probably not as originally placed) superbly done *trompe l'œil* perspective carving, only half an inch deep, of elongated arches and passageways – an unearthly effect of Hawksmorean strangeness. If it were Italian it would be less exaggerated and gaunt. Next to it a clock dated 1537, the year before the start of Nonsuch.

The possibility that the fittings may have come from different sources may help to explain their varying quality: the *trompe l'œil* panels are first rate, the panelling is competent, the grottesche pitiful, and all from different Continental sources. The fireplace at Reigate Priory (*see* p. 427), if it is of the same date, has a different source again. Henry VIII's

---

* It used to be assumed that these fittings came to Loseley when Nonsuch was demolished in the late C17, but there is no evidence for this. Almost nothing is known about the interior decoration of Nonsuch (*see* p. 383). It is possible that the pieces were already at Loseley in the C16, through the connexions of Sir William More with Sir Thomas Cawarden. Although Cawarden was Keeper of Nonsuch, he was also Master of the Revels and Keeper of the Tents, and thereby responsible for miscellaneous stage properties and other equipment. He died in 1559, and More, who was his executor, may have inherited some of these pieces.

palaces – and Nonsuch *par excellence* – were a repository for most of the advanced ideas of the 1540s. Henry VIII imported the latest ideas from wherever he could get them; but whereas the School of Fontainebleau, which is the obvious parallel, developed slowly and along clearly defined Italian lines, Nonsuch was simply a mad scramble to put up a world-beater by a king as voracious for the biggest and most up-to-date as any American tycoon of the 1890s. The difference between Fontainebleau and Nonsuch is the same as that in our own day between the Stuttgart Weissenhof of 1927 (closely allied architects working together) and the Berlin Interbau of 1957 (architects invited from all over the world to make isolated contributions).

Beyond the Great Hall is the LIBRARY, mainly a C19 concoction in Jacobean style (is the queer fireplace original, with its four-centred rusticated opening?). The overmantel is made up from what is thought to be one of Queen Elizabeth's travelling cases, dated 1570. Beyond again is the DRAWING ROOM, mainly late C16, with a dainty ceiling on an equally dainty white and gold frieze of moorhens and cockatoos. Their ribs form close geometrical patterns and pendants. In contrast to this daintiness, the fireplace, illustrating better than most rooms in England the barbaric richness of which England was capable in the C16. It is enormous, and superficially looks Jacobean with some bizarre touches, but it could in fact be another Henrician quirk, an Anglo-Flemish hybrid of the late 1540s. Two-storeyed, with coupled columns below (with quite classical swags below that on the plinth) and coupled caryatids above. The fireplace surround rusticated partly with wild vermiculated rustication,* the panels above full of strapwork ornaments and caryatids, and all carved from one block of clunch with extraordinary technical skill. Finally, the thick central mullion in the N window ends in a huge paw,‡ a surrealist bit of detail which transports the visitor straight into the world of Giulio Romano. The staircase in the SW corner is simple and dignified late C17. The upper rooms have a few more Jacobean details, e.g. one more moorhen-and-cockatoo frieze and a crude fireplace.

LOWER KINGSWOOD *see* KINGSWOOD

* The same vermiculated rustication also appears on the arched back doorway in line with the front door.
‡ This also occurs, much reduced, in the upper storey of the fireplace.

LOWER VANN see HAMBLEDON

LOWFIELD HEATH
1½ m. sw of Horley

²⁰⁴⁰

A hamlet on the Sussex border, which modern transport is treating like a shuttlecock; first enlarged by the Brighton Road, and now sealed off again by the Gatwick runway extension.

St Michael. A delightful building by *William Burges*, 1867. Alone among Victorian architects, Burges visibly enjoyed himself, and his sense of fun got closer to the original childlike spirit of Early Gothic invention than did either piety or historical accuracy. Small, aisleless building with attached sw tower and pyramid spire, and lean-to w porch below a disarming and thickly detailed rose window, a first-rate bit of picturesque composition. The textures are very carefully chosen, e.g. the big Welsh slate louvres in the belfry. Inside, the most typical detail is the PULPIT, with painted naturalistic reliefs, and also the WEST DOOR, with stiff radial ironwork which is Art Nouveau in its attitude to decoration, but without an Art Nouveau vocabulary. – STAINED GLASS in the E end, a rose window above two lancets, very coherent, with brilliant reds and writhing backgrounds (also half Art Nouveau). It fits the building exactly, and in just the same way as the glass in Burges's completion of Waltham Abbey. Whose is it? ⁷⁴

LOWICKS
1 m. se of Frensham

⁸⁰⁴⁰

On the E side of Frensham Common, and hard to get at. A simple and very typical *Voysey* house, of 1894. Exactly like an enlarged lodge – single mass, battered corner buttresses, battered chimneys, slate roofs and roughcast walls. Inset dormers and just one half-timbered gable at the back. Delightful situation with pine woods all around and a tiny wild lake in front; the simple, low-toned house fits it like a glove. ^{See p. 598}

LOXHILL see HASCOMBE

LUKYNS see EWHURST

LULLENDEN see DORMANSLAND

LYTHE HILL see HASLEMERE

LYNE
2 m. w of Chertsey

A hamlet of Victorian artisan cottages and medium-size country houses.

HOLY TRINITY. 1849 by *Francis*. The perfect Gilbert Scott church almost before Scott had thought of it himself. Cruciform, rock-hard, First-to-Second Pointed, big spaces and utterly mechanical details. Memorable at a distance though for the way it is flanked by tall evergreens well planted to show off its compact proportions; Victorian landscaping at its best.

ALMNERS PRIORY. Demure roughcast elevations of *c.*1830 concealing a few late medieval fragments: the central kingpost of the roof and a pair of four-centred doorways. Formerly the house of the Almoner of Chertsey Abbey. (At the entrance a pair of early C19 lodges, and in the grounds a tall, square red brick dovecote with open cupola. MHLG)

(REDLANDS FARM, Lyne Lane. An attractive timber-framed house, C15–17.)

See p.
598 ST PETER'S HOSPITAL. *See* Chertsey.

MALDEN

ST JOHN, Church Road, Old Malden. The flintwork of the chancel is medieval. The rest is early C17, built apparently at the expense of John Goode † 1627, who, according to the inscription on the tablet commemorating him (chancel E wall), 'hanc ecclesiam penitus collapsam ab imis fundamentis restituit'. Brick, still laid in English bond, with very wide joints. W tower perfectly plain, with plain parapet. The windows here and in the body of the church are still Perp, with lights with depressed arches. In 1875 a new nave and chancel were built by *T. G. Jackson*, reducing the former to being a S aisle and S chapel (already restored by him in 1863).

(CHRIST CHURCH, New Malden. By *Freshwater & Brandon*, 1866. GS)

ST JOSEPH (R.C.), Kingston Road, New Malden. 1922–35 by *Osmund Bentley*, altered and completed by *Adrian Gilbert Scott*. Conventional Gothic, brick, no tower.

CHURCH ROAD is an oasis in this outer suburbia. Close to the church the MANOR HOUSE, *c.*1700 and earlier, of red brick, and to the NE of the church the MANOR FARM. To the NE a duck-pond, and the PLOUGH INN, which now looks entirely C20 but is in fact in its core of before the Reformation.

⟨By the station at New Malden, two anonymous, bulky sixteen-storey office blocks flanked by five-storey car parks. They are by *Martin Richmond* of *Planning & Development Ltd.*, 1963–8. Further s at the corner of Blagdon Road, some better shops and offices by *H. A. Halpern & Associates*, 1961–3.⟩

MARDEN PARK *see* WOLDINGHAM

MAYBURY *see* WOKING

MERRIST WOOD *see* WORPLESDON

MERROW

0050

The suburban NE extension of Guildford, with a few old houses left near the church. Very little character.

ST JOHN. Rebuilt by *R. C. Hussey*, 1842, N aisle by *Sir A. W. Blomfield*, 1881. The C20 has made the best of this by painting all the dressings white, giving it a spiky toy-church picturesqueness of its own – an example that could be followed in many other Surrey parishes. Left over in the rebuilding a few C12 fragments. The arch of the N door is of *c.*1150 with zigzag moulding. The s arcade, with round chamfered arches and plain circular capitals, is probably of *c.*1200. The arch at the E end of this aisle is also of *c.*1200, probably the original chancel arch re-set on new piers.

Two fragments of old Merrow are worth mentioning: opposite the church the HORSE AND GROOM, three-storeyed, three-gabled, and roughcast, dated 1615; to the N MERROW HOUSE, very blank brick of *c.*1800. To the W of these, towards Guildford, is LEVYLSDENE, a shapeless C17–18 house whose grounds were sold for building in 1955. The best houses on it were designed by *G. A. Jellicoe & Partners*, e.g. the two houses beside the main road, pleasantly crisp and free from whimsy, and HIGHFIELD, at the far end.

MERSTHAM

N of Redhill, on the Brighton Road, and unexpectedly pretty. The main road, curving and not yet broken open, sweeps round to the E leaving a delightful cul-de-sac continuation – Quality Street – running N to the gates of Merstham House. Famous for medieval stone (Westminster Abbey e.g.), and in the C19 for its limeworks, but, like many quarry villages, it has little evidence of architectural display itself. ⟨A prominent future landmark will be the very large multi-level junction of the M23 and the M25.⟩

ST KATHARINE, N of the village, on the slope of the Downs. The general impression is beetle-browed C13, largely due to the large stolid tower, dour and effective, of *c*.1220.* The bell-chamber has three simple grouped lancet lights, the central one blocked under a big shingled broach-spire. Also C13 are the proportions, the clerestory (renewed: quatrefoils and trefoils), the arcades, the s with circular and the N with octagonal piers and capitals, the standard Surrey C13 style. The chancel arch belongs to the same time, except that the foliage capitals appear a little earlier. They are in fact re-used, cf. the abaci, which are tripartite and do not fit the arch mouldings. Again of the principal C13 building period the fragmentarily preserved giant blank arcading in the chancel (cf. e.g. Merton). The most elaborate C13 piece is the w doorway, with jamb-shafts and an order of dog-tooth mouldings inside a continuous chamfered order, and with an inner trefoiled arch. It is a very handsome composition. The outer label with heads as label stops is probably Perp. The rest of the church is also Perp. Renewed N aisle (a fragment of one C13 lancet remains at the w end) and imitation s aisle. The N chapel has three-light windows with segmental heads, the s chapel two-light square-headed windows – both these ashlar firestone, whereas the C13 work was flint. The arcades of these two chapels are instructive, the N arcade a transcription of the C13 nave arches with all the chamfering hollow, the s arcade a gawky variant on the four-shaft-four-hollow type and four-centred arches. Perp also the five-light E window and the s porch, an admirable straightforward design, very like the porch at Oxted, and happily unrestored. The inside is still plastered, a rare thing in Surrey, though here not particularly pretty. – FONT. Big, square, C13, a poor example of a common type. Purbeck marble, shallow arcading round the bowl, four corner shafts. – SCULPTURE. Remains of a frieze with foliage and demi-figures of angels in the N chapel and at the w end of the aisle. Perhaps from the top of a stone parclose screen or a tomb recess. – STAINED GLASS. Interesting E and N chapel windows,

* Mrs Morris says that the centre of the tower arch is a bit of old London Bridge, brought back to the parish from which the stone was quarried.

the former of *c*.1877. They are influenced by William Morris
and could be by *Selwyn Image*. – PLATE. Silver Cup 1623;
Paten 1714; Flagon 1762. – MONUMENTS. Several brasses –
including a stiff figure of Lieutenant Woodhouse † 1916 (s
aisle). The only noteworthy example is John Elingbridge
† 1473, on a tomb-chest in the N chapel. The central figure has
gone, but the side figures of his two wives remain, about 15 in.
long, very elongated and not bad. – Early C15 effigy in the N
aisle, defaced to extinction, but resting on an ornate, better-
preserved slab. Not *in situ*. Carved with angels and a vine-
trail. – Lt George Jolliffe, R.N., † 1797 (on the *Bellerophon* at
the battle of the Nile). A pretty tablet, still Adamesque, and
hence probably a local job. As so often, the best part is the
spirited naval relief under the inscription.

(ST TERESA (R.C.), Weldon Way. 1959 by *J. H. Alleyn*. DE)

N of the church in the trees a circular FOLLY TOWER, probably
of *c*.1840. Opposite the church is the RECTORY, the *beau idéal*
of the comfortable C18 parson's home. Palladian, of about
1760, five by two bays of buff stucco.

The village lies further s and is easiest to describe from the s.
It starts with the join of the main road and School Hill, with
the OLD SADDLERY, pretty C18 brick. In the High Street
Nos. 23–31 on the w side, a simple collection of brick houses,
mainly C18, set back from the road which continues as
Quality Street while the main London road turns E.

QUALITY STREET is the perfect example of a particular kind of
well preserved Home Counties ensemble (the main street of
Denham, Bucks, is another), owing as much to 1900 as to
1700.* The original buildings, in firestone, brick, a little half-
timber, and a little tile-hanging, are tactfully welded together
by the trimmings and front gardens of the houses of *c*.1900,
making the whole more like a part of a garden city than the
Garden Cities ever were. Its effect is enhanced and not
weakened by the Brighton Road traffic roaring past the end,
and making it by contrast such an effective backwater. Of
individual houses the following are worth a look. On the w
side, HOME FARM, still a farm, with a big tarred and
tiled barn, in provincial brickwork of *c*.1760. THE BARN
HOUSE is the best of the insertions, by *H. Paxton Watson*,
1902. Roughcast like Voysey, but with a pretty bow window

* Ellaline Terriss and Seymour Hicks were living in the Old Forge at the
N end at the time that they were playing in Barrie's *Quality Street*; hence
the name.

with plaster reliefs as well. PRIORS MEAD, actually inside the park gates, is a bulky cottage of c.1700 with segmental windows, still keeping their wooden mullions and transoms. On the E side the OLD SCHOOLS, the oldest wing of 1847, in chequerboard brick with Perp windows. Behind it, humble ALMSHOUSES of 1816, and the OLD FORGE, with one C15 half-timbered gable, but so altered that the effect is really that of a *cottage orné.*

E of the High Street the STATION has a lot of harsh South Eastern woodwork of c.1870, a very familiar sight in Surrey, and also a simple Italianate house from the earlier station of the 1840s. The first (horse) railway from here to Croydon was actually laid down in 1805, to carry local stone and fuller's earth from the Nutfield quarries.

See p. 599

S of the High Street, School Hill has a long, irregular terrace of very humble tile-hung cottages, quite unrestored (Nos. 16–26). Beyond, E of the railway, is a bad LCC out-county ESTATE of c.1950; bad in its site in the Green Belt, and bad in its architecture. Anyone who thinks that LCC work in the fifties was always good should have a look here, especially at the shops.

Finally, NW of the village, on the Downs, ALDERSTEAD FARM is about the best vernacular farm on the Surrey Downs. C18 farmhouse of clunch, flint, and brick, and a complete range of farm buildings, including a tarred weatherboarded granary raised on dottles or staddlestones (i.e. mushroom-shaped stones to keep out rats).

2060

MERTON

Merton in the Middle Ages was known for its Augustinian Priory, founded in 1114. The Statute of Merton was enacted here in 1236, and Walter de Merton, founder of Merton College Oxford, came from here. Nothing of all the extensive buildings of the priory remains except for some walling on the S side of STATION ROAD, to the E of the factory of Messrs ALUMILITE, and behind some flats in WINDSOR AVENUE; and a gateway E of Abbey Wall Works in Station Road.* Tex-

* Excavations have, however, proved the church to have had a nave and aisles, transepts each with four straight-ended E chapels, and a larger straight-ended chancel, i.e. a Cistercian plan. In the C13 the E end was enlarged, the chancel received aisles, and a straight-ended Lady Chapel was added to the E of the big new chancel. The W end had a stepped porch. The cloister lay to the S, and the chapter house was apsed. The church lay just N of the railway, the chapter house and S transept across the lines. In the early C19 there was also

tiles had been printed in this area already in 1724. By the river Wandle stood William Morris's former workshops. 〈Almost opposite, on the s bank, an oasis in an industrial desert, there are still LIBERTY'S PRINT WORKS, mostly rebuilt since 1910, but the old colour-house, of brick, flint, and stone, dated 1742, survives. It is two-storeyed, with a pantile roof. Near by is the C18 wheel-house of brown brick, with pantile roof, and undershot iron water-wheel with four sets of spokes. The original tree-trunk wheel spindle has been replaced by an iron spindle.* N of HIGH PATH there is now HIGH PATH ESTATE by *A. J. Thomas, Clifford Culpin & Partners*, and *William Ryder & Associates*.〉

A little of the village of Merton survives further w, with the church in Church Lane and some later houses in the Kingston Road.

ST MARY. Norman nave, see a window in the N wall near the w end. Norman N doorway with zigzag, badly rebuilt. Early C13 chancel, cf. the blocked lancet windows on the N side. These have inside the fine tall blank arcading (four bays) often found in Surrey. Chamfered supports and slightly chamfered arches. The church has a pretty bell-turret in the shape of a broached timber spire sitting immediately on the roof. Excellent C15 timber porch, with openwork walls and gable. Traceried panels. Bargeboards. The chancel roof is a hammerbeam roof with the coving between wall and hammer ceiled. The s aisle dates from 1856 (by *F. Digweed*: GS), the N aisle from 1866. Excellent NORTH DOOR, Norman, with rude ironwork. – PLATE. Cup and Paten 1709; Flagon 1717. – MONUMENTS. Gregory Lovell † 1597 and wives. Good hanging wall-monument of alabaster, with kneeling figures. – Smith Family, erected to the family by the widow of Captain Cook. Grecian relief with kneeling figure. By *R. J. Wyatt*, signed Rome 1832. In the churchyard a sumptuous DOORWAY of c.1175, originally part of the priory precinct, has been re-erected. It had a number of elaborate boldly three-dimensional geometrical motifs.

---

still an outer chapel of c.1300 to the w of the priory, with a fine, characteristic six-light window. This is illustrated in Manning & Bray. A small part of the site, with some old stones, is visible behind some railings. After the priory was dissolved in 1538, stone was taken for the King's palace of Nonsuch (*see* p. 384n).

* Information kindly supplied by Miss E. M. Jowett.

(St James, Beaford Grove. By *Thomas Ford & Partners*, 1957. –
WALL PAINTING of the Resurrection by *Hans Feibusch*. –
STAINED GLASS. Shapland Memorial window, W window,
both by *John Hayward*.)

In KINGSTON ROAD are a few old houses: the MANOR HOUSE,
which looks Georgian outside, but is structurally earlier, with
timber-framing visible inside; and two Georgian houses,
DORSET HALL and LONG LODGE, the latter once the home
of the Pre-Raphaelite artist Frederic Shields.

In the area S of the Kingston Road, around the parish church, the
local squire John Innes developed the Merton Park Estate from
the 1870s. The estate architect was *H. G. Quartermain*. The
houses are of all shapes and sizes, the larger ones with plenty
of gables and bargeboards.*

The South Wimbledon UNDERGROUND STATION by *Charles
Holden*, 1926, belongs to the same standard set as others along
the S extension of the Northern Line. Massive and without
any period suggestions. Characteristic the two pillars on the
upper floor carrying balls (cf. Tooting Bec, Tooting Broadway,
etc., in *London*, vol. II, and Colliers Wood in this volume).

1050   MICKLEHAM
3 m. N of Dorking

In a famous part of the Mole valley, where the river runs between
wooded chalk hills. Now with a double character, for like so
much of Surrey it is full of C18 and C19 literary associations
and, more tangibly, of picturesque attempts to assist nature.
The Dorking gap is now a good fifty per cent man-made, and,
appropriately, Mickleham is by-passed with one of the best
pieces of C20 road landscaping in the country, the MICKLE-
HAM BY-PASS, cut in 1934 and designed by the County
Engineer, *W. P. Robinson*. Dual carriageways, completely separated, good use of the existing planting without false prettiness.
The village is unpretentious, with cottages staggered uphill
from a bend in the by-pass, plus one long walled street running
up to the church.

ST MICHAEL. Drastically restored, but at least the mutilations
are amusing and not merely dreary. The old parts are nearly
all Norman. Massive early C12 W tower with big later set-back
buttresses, now truncated with a perky broached spike on top.

* Information kindly supplied by Miss E. M. Jowett and Mr G. Wilson.

W doorway simple and effective, with shafts carrying two-scallop capitals and a very deeply cut roll-moulding.* The chancel arch was Norman too, but Late. Of it the outer order survives, with diamond and dog-tooth mouldings. The N and S sides of the chancel, with two windows on each side, belong to the chancel arch, though that can now hardly be recognized. Also genuine, but built-around, is the Late Perp NORBURY CHAPEL on the N side, with chequerboard flint and clunch walling, almost the only example in the county (but cf. Leatherhead). The fun started in 1823 with *P. F. Robinson*, who was surprisingly gentle, wrote a monograph on the church, and built neo-Norman at Leamington, and in earnest in 1871 with *Peacock*,‡ who added neo-Norman aisles, duffed up the chancel arch, and put in a very fancy E end and a round tower on the S side which parodies the W tower. The E end (three windows with a rose above in Barfreston style) is filled with STAINED GLASS in Flemish style and is quite effective. – FONT. C12, shallow blind arcading, the usual type. – PULPIT. Belgian, of *c.*1600, with ornately carved scenes on the panels and saints under crockets on the corners. Altered in restoration. – STAINED GLASS. E window, *see* above. – In the W window Flemish (?) glass of the early C16. – Oblong panel set in the woodwork of the W gallery. Probably again C17 Belgian. – MONUMENT and BRASS to William Widdowson † 1515 and wife, a big tomb-chest carved with quatrefoils in the usual way and an elegant but mechanical canopy carved into the wall behind. Four-centred recessed arch with vine-trail and cresting above. Inside the arch brasses of the pair, about 12 in. high. Lively and naïve carving. – PLATE. The church plate (Cup 1666; Flagons 1614 and 1702; Patens 1701 and 1702) was sold in 1968.

Mickleham is almost the only Surrey churchyard to have taken the trouble to preserve its GRAVE-BOARDS, which it was a local habit to erect. They are wooden tombstones, consisting of a long plank carried between two posts. Examples are dated 1813, 1875, etc.

Beside the by-pass nothing much – perhaps ROSE COTTAGE, with a crisp early C19 veranda. Up LONDON ROAD, starting from the N end, first the OLD HOUSE, Artisan brick dated

* The Rev. J. L. Connell says that the head of another arch is visible inside above the W doorway, and suggests that it is Saxon.

‡ Information from B. F. L. Clarke. *The Builder*, 1892, refers to work by *E. Christian* (GS).

1636. An impressive building, spoilt by insensitivity which is c18, for a change: sideways extension and wholesale window enlargement. The original part five-bay and E-shaped with good Dutch gables and a lot more Artisan detail – blind brickwork ovals and thick string courses, e.g. Even the gate from the street has Ionic pilasters. The garden front, equally altered, is oddly enough of better quality, with a Dutch gable at either end and a small broken pediment on a shaped gable in the middle above another oval brick panel – a rare and impressive detail which occurs only in a few other early c17 buildings.* Remains of pilasters and also of intermittent rustication above the windows.

At the s end of the street is JUNIPER HILL, a medium-size stock-brick house built c.1780 by *John Staff*, a local man. c19 extensions to the s. The original part of five bays and two and a half storeys with a central pediment, handsome and big-scale in the style of Henry Holland. Big arched ground-floor windows and big Ionic porch. Frontispiece effect above it with a moulded surround to the first-floor window, with balustraded panel below, and the second-floor window projecting into the split pediment above. This is still the same sort of composition as those of the early c18 Baroque houses in Surrey.

Beyond this is Juniper Hall (*see* p. 321). Beyond again, at the foot of Zig-Zag Hill, is FLINT COTTAGE, where George Meredith lived for twenty years. Pretty, symmetrical early c19 flint and brick.

NORBURY PARK. *See* p. 388.

9040

MILFORD
1½ m. sw of Godalming

Mostly Victorian and c20, beside the Portsmouth road, with a few restored old brick and tile-hung cottages (and one very pretty group by *Lutyens*, 1898, AFTON COTTAGE and its neighbours, of brown brick and tile-hanging – note the weathervane. NT).

ST JOHN. Bad c19, but STAINED GLASS in the N aisle by *Morris & Co.* (i.e. *Burne-Jones*), 1897 and 1907. Two windows with good gritty blue skies and rather weak figures. (In the churchyard big MAUSOLEUM *à la* Halicarnassus, covered in creeper, for the Webbs of Milford House. NT)

MILFORD HOUSE (now a hotel), Godalming Road. A striking, four-square house in the Queen Anne style (there is no better

* The panel is modern (J. Newman).

name for this specifically English version of Baroque), although
the house was built in 1730. Five bays, three storeys, plus an
attic in similar style but different bricks, probably later C18.
Entrance front with a stone pediment containing a lunette.
Aprons below the first-floor windows, banded stone rustication
at the corners, stone keystones to each window. Bold doorcase
with segmental head and intermittent rustication on the Ionic
columns. Garden front much plainer, with no pediment and a
big simple Doric porch and doorcase. Inside, a handsome
staircase beside the front door with fluted turned balusters;
the arches leading to the back of the house on both floors are
semicircular and divided into several panels with a rosette in
the middle of each. This is pure Early Wren, and an anachronism in a house of this date. As a whole the house is a little
gauche – though, as so often, the impression is strong enough
to carry a few weak details – and not outside the normal mason's
range. The style (and the hamfistedness) is a little like *John
James*.

Immediately N of Milford House, the REFECTORY is a former
barn ingeniously converted into something like a Lutyens
house by a Mr *Flenning* of Haslemere, 1937, with imported
details such as two-light Perp windows. In the grounds a
DOVECOTE in the same style as the Surrey barns: square,
tarred weatherboarding, on staddlestones, with the birds'
entrance as a cupola at the top.

W of A3 is AMBERLEY FARM, unrestored, of *c*.1700, brick and
stone with a tile-hung gabled wing and good barns. ½ m. SE
of the village, near the station, is RAKE MANOR, originally
built in 1602 and repeatedly restored: by *R. Nevill* in the 1880s,
by *Lutyens* in 1897 (new kitchen wing to the NW), and by
Baillie Scott (new drawing room, entrance lodge, etc., *c*.1910 *See
p.
599*
and *c*.1925). The original parts are at the E end, an L-shaped
house with tile-hung gable to the S, and timber-framing, close-
set on the ground floor and wider with herringbone (brick) infill
above. Inside, the staircase and the dining room are original.

MILLBRIDGE *see* FRENSHAM

MILLFIELD
½ m. S of Stoke d'Abernon

1050

Poor, prickly Tudor house, mostly of 1863, but incorporating an
earlier Tudor house – which is no better – by *P. F. Robinson*,
1814. Robinson could be bad in any style, an unusual attribute

for a Regency architect: Classical (Trelissick, Cornwall), Egyptian (Egyptian Hall Piccadilly), or Norman (Christ Church Leamington).

MILTON
1 m. w of Dorking

MILTON HEATH. Big red-brick house by *Hardwick*, c.1870. To the N of it is MILTON COURT, now a picturesque seven-bay house with shaped gables. Old photographs show a different story; it was in fact a typical small (five-bay) E-shaped house of c.1610 with straight gables and mullioned and transomed windows, the type of Pendell Court Bletchingley. Most of the work below the roof-line is still genuine, and a couple of the shaped gables at the back are original. The alterations date from 1864. Inside, a good, simple Jacobean staircase around a narrow well with bulbous newel posts carried up to support the flight above.

BURY HILL HOUSE. Originally built in 1753, burnt c.1950. The centre was then demolished, and the three bays at each end were repaired and converted into separate houses. They are crowded indifferent classical, stuccoed, with pedimented and pilastered end elevations. Part of the alterations are by *Decimus Burton*, 1831-3 (Colvin).

(On top of the hill to the N a small OBSERVATORY, by *Burton*, 1847-8. MHLG)

To the w, in MILTON'S LANE, a nice pair of cottages, of c.1840, picturesque but not spindly. Probably designed by *John Perry* of Godalming. ½ m. E is HOME FARM, also by *Perry* and illustrated in Loudon's *Encyclopedia*. Also in Milton Street pleasant tile-hung cottages (e.g. MALTHOUSE FARM), and on the corner of A25 a large, plain brick ORANGERY of c.1770 along one side of a big walled garden, originally serving Bury Hill House.

BOX HILL. Two BARROWS, of the bowl type, one in good condition. On Milton Heath, N of Westcott Road, also a fine bowl barrow, covered with trees, 66 ft in diameter and 6–7 ft high. There are Iron Age fields in the area.

MILTON PARK
1 m. s of Egham

SHELL TECHNICAL SERVICE LABORATORIES. 1955 by *P. A. Cranswick* of *Walker, Harwood & Cranswick*. A square modern block with a lake on the w side and a first-floor bay projecting over it on pilotis. The detailing is confused, especially in the vast variety of finishes – flint, concrete, two kinds of wood panels, and two kinds of brickwork. Very well landscaped by *Gordon Patteson*.

MITCHAM

2060

The epitome of London-over-the-border; an indescribable mess, yet with more Cockney life than inner London boroughs like Bermondsey, which have been sterilized by utilitarian rebuilding.

There are three Mitchams – the old village; the late c18 villas and the early c19 brick-box ribbon development down the road to Reigate that Cobbett disliked so much; and the final submersion by London sprawl in the 1920s. Upper Green is the shopping centre, the green having disappered under more items of street furniture than one could think possible even in outer London. Cricket Green is still a residential green, with Church Street on the w and Mitcham Common – which was big, flat, and desolate: Surrey's Wormwood Scrubs – on the E side as far as the Croydon boundary.*

The first Mitcham is represented by battered cottages in Church Street, by Eagle House (*see* below), by the Conservative H.Q. on Upper Green (early c18 brick with a transplanted bracketed doorcase), and by The Canons (*see* also below). The early c19 suburbanization left brick and weatherboard boxes all over the borough (now disappearing). The c20 has given Mitcham some of the worst council flats near London – mostly around six storeys, three sets of maisonettes with graceless access balconies, finished off by pitched and hipped tiled roofs; and, at the other extreme, MITCHAM GARDEN SUBURB, off Carshalton Road, a keyhole-shaped close with houses facing inwards, all different. This is the spirit of Blaise Hamlet a century late. Pleasant layout, poor half-timbered houses. 1929–32 by *Chart & Reading*.

ST PETER AND ST PAUL, Church Road, Cricket Green. 1819–21 by *George Smith*. Large and still of the Commissioners' type, stuccoed and with bald Perp detail. The only anomaly is the tower in a NW position, and this is medieval. Tall interior with very pretty tierceron- and lierne-vaults. – PLATE. Paten 1678; two Flagons 1729; Plates 1753 and 1803. – MONUMENTS. Sir

* It is to be landscaped and planted.

Ambrose Crowley † 1713 and Lady Crowley † 1727. Good, with profile portraits in a medallion. By *Rysbrack* (Gunnis). – Mrs Tate, 1821 by *Westmacott*. Woman holding a chalice. – Several late c18 tablets, e.g. Sophia Tate † 1780 by *C. Harris* (Gunnis).

ST BARNABAS, Gorringe Park Avenue. Big, thoughtful neo-Bodley, by *H. P. Burke-Downing*, 1914. A hall church with huge arcades, still lacking its N aisle. Quite sensitive.

(ST PETER AND ST PAUL (R.C.), Cranmer Road. 1889 by *F. A. Walters*. DE)

METHODIST CHURCH, Cricket Green. By *Edward Mills*, 1958. Big-boned, modern, honest, but unfortunately clumsily detailed. Zigzag timber roof, steel-framed, on Y-shaped columns, with the wall set back to form a loggia on the N side. The wall behind the altar made of rough-cut slabs of York stone. Very effective church hall on the N side.

The charm of Mitcham is the interlocking greens E of the church with the (ugly) VESTRY HALL of 1887 on an island site. Its architect was *R. M. Chart*. On LOWER GREEN the pretty SUNDAY SCHOOLS, founded in 1788, enlarged in 1812. Stock brick, nine bays, with a raised centre with tower. Off Upper Green, in WESTERN ROAD, the former ZION CHAPEL, now Leyens cardboard factory. Stock brick, three windows, central door.* Along CRICKET GREEN on the NE side the WHITE HOUSE, with a semicircular entrance bow with two Greek Doric columns. On the SW side the TATE ALMSHOUSES of 1829 (by *J. C. Buckler*). One-storeyed, of stock brick, with a central gable. At the SE corner of Cricket Green an OBELISK of 1822 with the inscription: 'In grateful recollection of the goodness of GOD through whose favour water has been provided for this neighbourhood.' Next to the obelisk in MADEIRA ROAD a good late c17 house, THE CANONS, two storeys, five by three bays, plus a two-bay addition on the l. Hipped roof. Stairs up to the entrance. Staircase inside with strong twisted balusters. In the grounds, square brick and stone DOVECOTE, c16. Madeira Road leads to the COMMON, where along Commonside West and Commonside East again minor Georgian houses.

The rest of interest is all along or near the London Road, except for one or two things further N. In WESTERN ROAD, in a dreary area by gasometers and factories, is some good new housing by the Borough Architect of Merton, *P. J. Whittle*. In

* Information kindly supplied by L. M. Montagu.

FOUNTAIN PLACE, two-storey terraces of white brick, all linked by a pedestrian system, 1966–9. Opposite, in BOND ROAD, old people's flats, arranged in five linked blocks of one and two storeys, 1966–8.* Further W, in PHIPPS BRIDGE ROAD, WANDLE VILLA is a five-bay house of stock brick, built in 1789. N of it No. 84, a FOLLY, a small tower of c.1875 said to have been made from stones from the Tower of London.

Now for LONDON ROAD. Starting a little N of Fair Green we have at once the finest house in Mitcham and one of the best of its date in the county: EAGLE HOUSE, built in 1705 for Fernandez Mendez, physician of Queen Catherine of Braganza. His initials are on the rainwater heads. In 1711 he leased it to Sir James Dolliffe, a director of the South Sea Company. The house is of yellow and red brick, five bays wide and two storeys high, with a three-bay projection and pediment, a hipped roof, dormers with segmental gables, and a balustrade and a cupola or belvedere on the roof. In spite of its noble and elegant composition it is a decidedly conservative house. If it were not for the slenderer windows one might mistake it for a building of 1650–60, of the school of Roger Pratt. The doorway is curiously humble – a plain apsidal hood on small carved brackets. It leads into a passage through to the back door, and in this rises the staircase, a staircase with a balustrade of three twisted balusters to each tread, and shaped but not carved tread-ends. Excellent wrought-iron GATES with Dolliffe's initials.

Immediately S of Eagle House the former BOARD OF GUARDIANS' SCHOOL of before 1855. Ten bays, two storeys, yellow brick. Arched ground floor, segment-headed upper windows.

At the corner of London Road and Cricket Green the KING'S HEAD, a good five-bay house of three storeys with a Tuscan porch, the back earlier. Opposite, the WHITE HART, C18, altered later. Further on was the MANOR HOUSE, now demolished. (It was an irregular composition, C18 and later, and had a nice staircase with two twisted and slim columnar balusters.) Yet further S, MITCHAM STATION. Three-bay house of c.1800, stock brick with three-bay pediment. Wide segmental entrance arch. Probably converted to a station after it

---

* A large new housing development by the London Borough of Merton is under construction at Pollards Hill, E of the centre; see below.

was built.* Opposite two pairs of big stock-brick houses, four-storeyed, also early C19. Beyond the railway, Nos. 421–445, Messrs LACTAGOL, using old stock-brick mill buildings. There was also a weatherboarded early C19 miller's house, now demolished. Oddly enough it was not at all like the weatherboarded villas, but big, rambling, and roughly executed: industrial vernacular. Finally, off the London Road, in RIVERSIDE DRIVE a handsome stock-brick house of *c.*1770–80. The ground-floor windows under blank arches. Parapet, intermittently balustraded. The MHLG ascribes the house to *Mylne* on account of its similarity to The Wick, Richmond. (In SOUTH LODGE AVENUE to the NE is the large POLLARDS HILL housing scheme by the Merton borough architect, *P. J. Whittle* (design team: *M. Kitchen, P. Bell,* and *R. MacCormac*), 1968–71. A locus classicus of the new school of 'high density, low rise' housing with a brilliantly concise layout of three-storey houses and some three-storey flats round courtyards. Everything may be Cartesian perfection on paper, but how can one justify in practice subjecting the inhabitants to being clad totally in shiny panels of white stove-enamelled steel? No doubt the landscape will mitigate this in time. NT)

MOLESEY *see* EAST MOLESEY *and* WEST MOLESEY

MOOR HAWES *see* DORMANSLAND

MOORHOUSE BANK *see* LIMPSFIELD

8040

MOOR PARK
1½ m. E of Farnham

The house is now effectively all late C18, but it encases a house of *c.*1630, one more example of the family of Dutch-inspired houses like Kew and West Horsley Place. Sir William Temple bought it in *c.*1680, called it Moor Park – after the Hertfordshire house, whose garden he admired – and simplified the ornate brick detail. This was the house where Swift was tutor to Stella and wrote *The Tale of a Tub.* All that survives of Temple's work – apart from the walls, altered and concealed

---

* There is no evidence to support the tradition that the station was built for the horse-drawn Croydon–Wandsworth Tramway, which was opened in 1803.

under stucco – is the loggia and doorway on the entrance side, in the most sober Wren style, with Temple's arms in the open pediment of the doorcase painted on a cast-iron cartouche, an unexpected reminder of the C17 Wealden iron industry. The late C18 added heavy stuccoed elevations which kept the proportions of the old house but changed its character completely, put in a big three-bay central bow window, and gave the remaining two-bay wings a grumpy Neo-Classical character by providing one window in a moulded brick semicircular arch above them. About the same time the top-lit stair-well was added in far from grumpy Neo-Classical; very tall and narrow, now beautifully decorated in blue and white, with a small central dome, apsed ends, and exquisite plasterwork in post-Chambers Classicism – delicate swags framing plaster roundels containing cherubs and musical instruments. This is basically the Rococo plasterwork of the 1750s, but refined and attenuated. By keeping all the detail at the top of the well the designer managed to overcome the extremely cramped proportions. The result, a little like an early Soane house – Letton Hall Norfolk, e.g. – is as successful as anything of its style in England.

The only name connected with the house is that of the elder *Cundy*, simply for 'alterations'; it is possible that he designed the stair-well, though this would date it *c.*1800–10, which is later than it looks. Later additions are quickly dealt with – w front to the stables, 1890, in competent neo-Tudor by *Paxton Watson*, and a startling green-tiled bathroom of the 1930s.

The gardens* are quite gone, though they could have been recovered – a wilderness of weeds and blocked-up lakes. Sir William Temple built them to exemplify the ideas set out in his essay *Of Gardens*, ideas which were really little removed from the current Anglo-Dutch formal practice. From surviving prints, it does not seem that he attempted anything like *sharawaggi*, the Chinese word for informal picturesque landscape which he brought into the language.

MORDEN

2060

St Lawrence. Brick church‡ of 1636 – an interesting and rare period in church building. Nave and chancel in one; s porch,

* In the kitchen-garden fragments of the bottom of a brick Baroque summer-house.

‡ Canon Livermore suggests that the brickwork was in fact piecemeal refacing of an existing stone church.

embattled w tower. Red brick with stone quoins. The brickwork in English bond with wide joints. Perp windows, more
probably of 1636 than re-used. Roof with tie-beams and kingposts, purely utilitarian. – PULPIT with original stair and
sounding-board; 1720. – COMMUNION RAIL. Three-sided,
with twisted balusters; also of 1720. – STAINED GLASS. E
window partly C17, partly of 1828. – PLATE. Silver-gilt Cup
and Paten 1633; two Flagons 1699; Paten 1711. – MONU-
MENTS. Sir P. Leheup † 1777. Bust before black triangle. – Mrs
Leheup † 1775. Good, large, simple, tablet. No figures.

Morden church lies on the periphery of the grounds of MORDEN
PARK, a good house of 1770. Five bays, two storeys, parapet.
Of yellow brick. The ground-floor windows are arched in
blank arched recesses. Venetian doorway with Tuscan demi-
columns and pediment. The window above with balustrade,
scrolls, and pediment. The door leads to an entrance hall
connected by a screen of two Ionic columns with a staircase
which starts in one arm, turns 180 degrees, and continues in
two arms. (In the park, swimming pool by *George Lowe &
Partners*, 1962–7.)

Near this part of Morden, in CENTRAL ROAD, the OLD SCHOOL
of 1731, a simple brick cottage with an inscription, and S of
this the EARL HAIG HOMES, Neo-Georgian, by *Grey Wornum*
and *Louis de Soissons*, 1931 and later. The original buildings are
on the NE side of Green Lane. The buildings on the SE side
are not part of the Earl Haig Homes. On the fringe another
addition. This is of after the Second World War. At the NE
end of Central Road, i.e. the corner of St Helier's Avenue, is
MORDEN GRANGE, externally Late Georgian, of five by five
bays with, at the corner, a bigger bow added.

Another centre of Morden, 1 m. NE, is MORDEN HALL in its
grounds. The house is of the late C17, with two long projecting
wings. It was altered about 1840, is stuccoed, and has lost
much of its attraction. The staircase with strong twisted
balusters is original. In the grounds to the S by the Wandle
the former SNUFF MILLS, with two wheels, now removed. The
two mill buildings are of brick; the C18 mill house, MORDEN
COTTAGE, has a handsome weatherboarded front. One part
is stuccoed and castellated.

A third centre is RAVENSBURY PARK, also by the Wandle. All
that remains is a fragment of the ruin of the MANOR HOUSE.

In LONDON ROAD is MORDEN UNDERGROUND STATION,
by *Charles Holden*, the southernmost of the stations built for

the extension of the Northern Line in 1925–6. Opposite is a
tall office building, CROWN HOUSE, by *A. Green*, 1959–61. It
consists of a curved slab of twelve storeys on a two-storeyed
platform, with shops on the ground floor.
⟨In EASTWAY, off Cannon Hill, old people's FLATS and DAY
CENTRE by the Borough Architect of Merton, *P. J. Whittle*,
under construction in 1969.⟩
For the ST HELIER ESTATE *see* p. 446.

MORTLAKE

Mortlake was once a handsome riverside village. By the church
one can still get the old flavour. But nowadays the most prominent
building from the river is the brewery.

ST MARY. Mostly by *Sir A. Blomfield*, chancel 1885, nave (by his
firm) 1905. What remains from an earlier time is the Perp w
tower of 1543, built by order of Henry VIII. The present
inscription is bogus. Top storey probably of 1694, and a pretty
open lantern and part of the N wall, brick with plain round-
arched windows, of 1815. Inside, a Perp w doorway instead of
a tower arch. Spandrels with blank tracery. The doorway is
probably a re-used piece. – FONT. Simple, Perp, octagonal. –
PLATE. Two Flagons *c.*1640; Cup and Cover 1660; Paten
*c.*1680; Almsdish 1686. – MONUMENTS. Francis Coventry
† 1699 by *William Kidwell*. Hanging wall-monument with
inscription plate flanked by two young standing figures carrying the scrolly entablature and an open pediment with an urn
in the middle. A fine, rich, luxuriant piece. – Nicholas Godschall
† 1748. Good, with a group of three cherubs' heads in the
'predella'. – Viscountess Sidmouth † 1811, by *Westmacott*.
Relief with the dying young woman on a couch held by an
allegorical figure. Faith stands on the l. The relief is flanked by
Greek Doric quarter-columns. – In the churchyard an ARCH
erected about 1865 out of the materials of the tower doorway,
when this was rebuilt. – Adjoining the church the pretty
VESTRY HOUSE of *c.*1660–70, brick with a doorway which has
a straight hood on carved brackets.

(ST MARY MAGDALEN (R.C.). By *G. R. Blount*, 1852.)

CEMETERY (R.C.), North Worple Way, s of the parish church.
In the cemetery the MONUMENT to Sir R. F. Burton † 1890,
the explorer and translator of the *Arabian Nights*, a life-size
stone tent with a crucifix above the place where the entrance
seems to be.

Near the church in the HIGH STREET to the W depressing
flats by *E. Colley*, to the E the best houses, especially No. 123.
Later Georgian façade with porch of four Tuscan columns.
Gatepiers and interior of *c.*1720. Good entrance hall and stair-
case. The house and garden were painted by Turner (Frick
Collection, New York, and National Gallery, Washington).
Other houses worth a look are Nos. 119 (L-shaped), 115, and
103–105, all Georgian.

Further W the following buildings deserve record. The BOOT
AND SHOE MAKERS' BENEVOLENT INSTITUTION, W of
the station between two blocks of flats. Built in 1836. Imitation
Tudor brick. In AYNSCOMBE LANE the GATEPIERS of the
former Cromwell House, rusticated with a niche in the street
fronts. The gate is C18 wrought iron. Another big house was
Tapestry House, now also demolished. Mortlake was the seat
of the English tapestry workshops which were founded in 1619
and flourished between that date and the Civil War. In
THAMES BANK an extremely pleasant group of houses facing
the river: especially THAMES COTTAGE, THAMES BANK
HOUSE, and LEYDEN HOUSE, all C18.

Thames Bank continues as a towpath to the NW under CHIS-
WICK BRIDGE (*see The Buildings of England: Middlesex*,
p. 37).

In WEST HALL ROAD lies WEST HALL, a good house of the
late C17, three by four bays, with a hipped roof on which a
tiny lantern is placed. Doorway with attached Tuscan columns.
S of the railway, in Fitzgerald Avenue, is the COACH HOUSE, an
engaging folly. It incorporates old fragments, including a big
Wren-type doorcase dated 1696 and several attached Ionic
columns.

₉₀₄₀

MUNSTEAD*
1 m. SE of Godalming

No village, simply an area of thickly wooded hills above Godalming. In the late C19 it became famous for the country houses
built there, largely by Lutyens and largely under the sponsorship
of Gertrude Jekyll. The houses have remained small enough and
convenient enough to adapt themselves without alteration to the
changed social climate of the mid C20, and the district still looks
much as it did in 1900; a Surrey invention worth a lot of study.

* This entry has been revised and expanded by Nicholas Taylor

The church for the area is St John Busbridge (*see* p. 124). Taking the houses in roughly chronological order, a perambulation should start ½ m. SE of the church, with MUNSTEAD HOUSE, in Munstead Heath Road. This was built for Gertrude Jekyll and her mother, on what was then an open heath, by *J. J. Stevenson*, 1877–8. The style, oddly in Surrey, is a kind of Scots vernacular; unfortunately the chimneys and the third floor have recently been removed. The single-storey wing to the r. of the entrance was *Miss Jekyll*'s workroom, with a witty Jacobean fireplace designed and made by her. The drawing room was remodelled by *Lutyens* in 1900 for Sir Herbert Jekyll, with round-arched windows for the extension. Also by Lutyens is the ORANGERY, rebuilt in 1969. *Sir Herbert Jekyll*, a sapper who had wanted to be an architect, carved the elaborate and convincing panelling of the dining room *à la* Grinling Gibbons. The hall fireplace was carved by Miss Jekyll.

Across the road to the N, in the woodland she planted, Miss Jekyll began her experiments in horticulture from 1881, with Lutyens visiting her constantly after 1890. At her recommendation *Lutyens* designed MUNSTEAD PLACE, 1891–2, built as Munstead Corner, further N, on the E side of Heath Lane. It is an immature work, starting, as late C19 architects so often did, from early Norman Shaw. Stone body under big and inadequately felt half-timbered gables. Sprightly interior, with spatially intricate classical staircase. Garden by *G. Jekyll*. The pyramid-roofed LODGE by *Lutyens* is of the same date, although it looks later.

In 1895 Mrs Jekyll died, and her son Sir Herbert took over Munstead House, so Miss Jekyll needed a home of her own. The result is MUNSTEAD WOOD, W of Heath Lane, 1896–7, a very different matter from The Hut, the picturesque cottage which *Lutyens* had previously built for her among the trees (*see* below). At Munstead Wood Lutyens's distinctive free Tudor style is already fully formed – though not fully worked out – in a kind of small-scale anticipation of the masterpieces of the next few years. The house is U-shaped with one arm of the U prolonged as a wall. This enabled Lutyens to contrive one of his *tour-de-force* entrances, a clever effect with wall and entrance arch balancing the taller house block on the right. The internal court or spatial kernel occurs here (*see also* Orchards, p. 378), in the well of the U, most successfully done, with Bargate stone sides and a completely unexpected half-timbered first-floor gallery across the middle. There is a second court for the kitchens, fully enclosed and entered through a timber arch between battered walls. The rest of the composition (the s and w fronts) is inadequate, by Lutyens's own later standards. The only interior of interest is the room behind the half-timbering, where Lutyens created a kind of long gallery with a barn roof only just above head level, a foretaste of later naughtiness. The house was doubtless originally intended to be integral with the gardens, the total effect that of a continuous give-and-take between landscape and architecture. Gertrude Jekyll revived or invented the image of the informal English cottage garden, and that is the effect here now; but her original planting scheme was rather different and much stranger than at present, with semi-wild trees growing to within a few feet of the s front. The detached group of potting sheds and storerooms, further down Heath Lane and mostly 1909, is now a separate house, THE QUADRANGLE. Further N again, at the corner where the garden wall turns away from the lane, stands the THUNDER HOUSE, a triangular belvedere dated 1895, with *Lutyens*'s typical battered walls, from which Miss Jekyll watched thunderstorms. Behind this, partly propped up on the boundary wall, is MUNSTEAD ORCHARD, the former gardener's cottage, a very pretty half-timbered and tile-hung job of 1898–9, best seen from the main road. Continuing back s along this road, one comes to THE HUT (now MUNSTEAD WOOD HUT), built by *Lutyens* in 1894–5 as a place where Miss Jekyll could entertain her friends. It is a self-conscious re-creation of the ideal Surrey cottage, cosily tile-hung. At one end is the living room, with an open timber roof and an ingle-nook. Down a lane on the other side of the road is LITTLE MUNSTEAD, an excellent small *Lutyens* house of c.1895, similar to Wood End, Witley (*see* p. 532). The service wing is tile-hung, but the main part has an oversailing upper floor of white plaster, anchored on the garden side by an enormous chimney. Next door are two *Lutyens* COTTAGES, grouping cleverly with Little Munstead's summer house; as well as the steep tile-hung gables there is even a tile-hung chimney. Next to these, the drive to NORTH MUNSTEAD, a C16 farmhouse virtually rebuilt by *Harold Falkner* c.1920. Garden front of Bargate stone with big Lutyens-style brick chimneys.

Back to Munstead House. ½ m. NE up Munstead Heath Road is ORCHARDS, 1897–1900, one of Lutyens's very best houses, part of the miraculous and short-lived flowering between immaturity and the fatal reversion to classicism. This period produced in Surrey Tigbourne Court and parts of Crooksbury and Fulbrook, elsewhere The Deanery, Sonning, Berks, and Little Thakeham, Sussex. In most of the houses Lutyens was obsessed or dominated by a spatial idea, as Soane was obsessed with top-lighting or, in another medium, Michelangelo with the Pietà. The idea is that of an immensely sophisticated entrance approach, deliberately calculated from the moment one turns into the drive, and an inner kernel of space, a court-yard or quadrangle, using the same motifs and sophisticated balance for the benefit of a static observer as the entrance does for a moving one. In Crooksbury and Munstead Wood the two experiences are separate, at Orchards they are linked. Orchards is a quadrangular courtyard (the spatial kernel) with one side prolonged to the w to form an L-shaped entrance, the 85 two linked by a big archway. The visitor sees first the gabled end of an almost windowless creeper-covered block with bat-tered buttresses. This is the prolongation of one of the sides of the courtyard, was originally partly open,* and leads the eye on to the entrance side of the quad and beyond, through the big barn-door arch running the whole height of the wall, to the simple gabled entrance porch. Characteristically, Lutyens has had fun here, putting in a dormer above the arch where it lights nothing but the roof beams, which are open to the ground anyway. The sensation of walking through to the quad, which lies beyond, is like entering a fairy palace with a union of buildings, exterior space, and landscape as miraculous in its way as anything the Baroque produced in uniting buildings, interior space, and painted decoration. The quad itself has a low arcaded wing on the r. and a tall blank wing on the l., with just one battered buttress to carry through the effect of the but-tresses outside. Straight ahead is the main part of the house, a central two-storeyed porch, and four chimneys high up on the roof to the l. balancing two lower down on the r., one of Lutyens's very best compositions. It is perhaps no wonder that after this the outside elevations of the house are an anticlimax, and the mind accepts this quite naturally, as it accepts the flaccid inner courtyards of Caserta after having experienced the terrific single-minded experience of the two-mile-long canal with the house towering up above the plain at the end of it: it is almost a psychological necessity. The E front is patently the back of the courtyard composition – almost like going to the

* Many minor alterations were carried out by Lutyens in 1909, and again in 1914.

back of a stage – and the elements do not balance. The gable is off-centre, and there is a long wing on one side and tile-hanging on the other. The N front, facing a formal garden, is a purposeless ramble, but the eye hardly bothers about it, swung w away from the house in a staggeringly unexpected view – for these closely wooded surroundings – across five miles of country to the North Downs. Inside only two things need special notice: the very pretty FIREPLACE in the Drawing Room, with blue and white tiles of cats and a plan of the house, all designed by the wife of the first owner, *Lady Chance* (née Julia Strachey) – a case of the amateur doing better than the professional of the time could; and the STAIRCASE, which is the normal small manor-house type with newel posts and a small well. It is C17 in style, but with two delightful touches: one, that the space between the supporting joists of the top treads is left open, so that the riser has gaps in it, tying the two levels together spatially; the other, that halfway up a small staircase of ten steps starts off waywardly at r. angles to its own landing and corridor.*

MUNSTEAD GRANGE, between Orchards and Munstead House, is by *E. W. Mountford*, 1902. *Jekyll* garden. STILEMANS, to the s on the Hascombe road, is of 1909 by *Nicholson & Corlette*; then MUNSTEAD OAKS, a tile-hung house of 1905 by *E. J. May*. For the houses further s, *see* Hascombe.

MYNTHURST see LEIGH

MYTCHETT see FRIMLEY

NETLEY HOUSE see SHERE

NEW ADDINGTON see ADDINGTON

0050

NEWARK PRIORY
½ m. s of Pyrford

A house of Austin Canons, founded 'de novo loco' in the late C12. A good deal of flint walling remains – s transept, and N and

---

* The other remarkable feature is the gigantic fireplace in the studio, a high open-roofed barn next to the entrance archway. It is in bright red brick, nearly 20 ft high, with niches inlaid with roofing tiles. The inside of the main house was much altered in 1939, when the dining room was stripped of panelling and thrown into one room with the drawing room (NT).

s walls of the presbytery to the height of the vault. It makes a very attractive ruin, in cornfields beside the Wey, but there is hardly a dressed stone left, and merely tantalizing imprecise holes to indicate window openings. Of the monastic buildings the only indication is the doorway in the s transept which led from the dormitory to the night-stairs into the church. Most of the remains are E.E., but a break in the direction between choir and presbytery, i.e. at the E end of the crossing, indicates the E wall of the C12 church, beyond which was added the E.E. chancel. The E.E. church had a straight E end and transept with E chapels. There is something highly irregular about these chapels. They were also straight-ended, but were not of equal length, and were separated by a very narrow passage; and although both had tunnel-vaults, the inner one was round, the outer one pointed. Round-headed also are the doorways from the inner chapels to the chancel. So perhaps the outer chapels were slightly later additions. Another strange feature of Newark Priory is that the transepts do not open out from a crossing strictly speaking, but from the two E bays of the C12 chancel. They appear two bays deep in the W–E direction. Moreover the canons' choir was closed to the N and s by solid walls 10 ft high, and these ran from the E wall of the 'crossing' to the E bay of the nave and at the W end of this returned with a (no longer existing) pulpitum. The chancel and the choir were vaulted. Evidence of this is the springers. The s transept, which is better preserved than the N transept, has lancet windows, but the windows in the chancel were placed high above very deep splays. The E wall is quite gone: if the window at Ockham (*see* p. 392) did in fact come from Newark, it must have been sited high above a big reredos. There is just enough detail to encourage speculation without satisfying it. The total architectural effect must certainly have been remarkable: today its satisfactions are purely picturesque.

NEWCHAPEL
1½ m. sw of Lingfield

Strange bedfellows beside the Eastbourne road: NEWCHAPEL HOUSE, an elaborate fake, half-timbered with a lot of tile-hanging, not too well done, by *Charles Bowles*, from 1908 onwards;* and the LONDON TEMPLE, the first European

* Built for the Pears of Pears Soap.

church of Latter-Day Saints (i.e. Mormons), 1958 by *Edward Anderson* of Salt Lake City, executive architects *T. P. Bennett & Son*. In the odd stripped Classical of say the Rome-University variety that one thought had died out by then, certainly in the United States. Tower and spire, attached to what appears to be a big church hall with long narrow windows but is actually divided into several floors. Only Mormons can get in.

NEWDIGATE

1040

A Weald village near the Sussex border; some pleasant tile-hung and timber-framed cottages, but no village group.

ST PETER. Much restored and renewed, as usual. Chancel c13, cf. the lancets on the N and S sides and also a two-light window of *c*.1260 (the E window dates from 1876–7, but may copy an original design). S aisle and arcade c14 with rough circular piers, octagonal capitals, and double-chamfered arches, the outer chamfer hollow. The aisle E window is two-light with ogee heads. Also a c14 PISCINA in the S wall. N aisle 1877. c15 timber belfry, the same type as Burstow, but heavily restored and without any of Burstow's vernacular charm. Three-sided weatherboarded base surrounding the four main posts, then a sloping shingled section, then the weatherboarded belfry and shingled spire. Inside, diagonal cross-bracing between the posts. – WOODWORK. The old W gallery front of 1627 set up under the tower. – STAINED GLASS. In the N aisle three jumbled ogee canopies, probably c14. – PLATE. Cup and Paten, 1699; Basin, c17.

Little in the village worth special notice. To the NE GATEROUNDS FARM has timber-framing in square panels which are regular but very closely spaced. Does this mean an early date? SE of this CUSWORTH MANOR is a c16 timber-framed moated house, very much altered. Further SE HOME FARM is a fragment of the original Newdigate Place, built as a timber-framed quadrangle in the c16. One unremarkable wing remains.

At PARKGATE, ½ m. NE, is an attractive c18 Wealden farmhouse, four by two bays, with the chimneys all but free-standing on a cross gable at either end. Paired lean-to wooden porches. Simple village detailing and no attempt at Palladianism, even though the house must be of *c*.1770.

S of this, just N of Hound House Farm, was an extraordinary survival for Surrey – a tiny half-timbered cottage, still lived in, of one storey and one room. If it is swept away it should at least be recognized for what it is, a representative of the primitive pre-yeoman housing. This example is probably of c.1600, but it is typical of what the C14 or C15 villagers actually lived in.*

IVYHOUSE FARM, 1½ m. SE, on the Sussex border. T-shaped timber framing, late (curved braces e.g.), but roughly done with completely random spacing of timbers.

NEWHAW

_0060_

1 m. N of Byfleet

A fearful example of C20 rock-bottom subtopia. The only thing worth notice is the VETERINARY RESEARCH LABORATORIES, 1956 by the Ministry of Works with _A. Swift_ in charge. One big humpbacked block between two long slabs of curtain-walled offices – a sort of architectural sandwich. Good routine modern building, the type of design which should be the average and not, as at present, the exception.

(LIBRARY, The Broadway. _By A. & A. Ballantyne_, 1969.)

NEW MALDEN see MALDEN

NONSUCH

_2060_

Nonsuch, that is _Nonpareil_, was Henry VIII's favourite building 30 enterprise during the last years of his life. The site of the palace lies in the present Nonsuch Park, next to Cherry Orchard Farm. What had been done in the way of unrestricted decoration for the ephemeral purpose of the building erected at Guisnes for the Field of the Cloth of Gold in 1520, was here given a permanent character. Nonsuch, of which alas scarcely anything has remained, but of which excavations in 1959–60 recovered the complete plan and many details of the decoration, was begun in 1538. By 1545 £23,000 had been spent on it. When Henry VIII died in 1547 it was not yet complete, though habitable. It was finished by the Earl of Arundel in 1556 and sold by his son-in-law, Lord Lumley, to Queen Elizabeth in 1592.

The palace was c.355 by c.170 ft in size and consisted of two courtyards, the inner and, to its N, the outer, and in addition an oblong kitchen court with a yard placed almost centrally on the E side. The arrangement of the two courts

* It has been swept away.

corresponded to Richmond and to Hampton Court, i.e. was in the Tudor tradition. The outer court was entered by a gatehouse with octagonal angle turrets just like those at Richmond and Hampton Court, and just as there a second, taller but smaller gatehouse led into the inner court. This second gatehouse had a tripartite oriel window of the same kind as Hengrave Hall in Suffolk, where the date is 1538. What distinguished Nonsuch from all other Henrician palaces was the decoration of all the inward-facing walls of the inner court, as well as the outer faces on the w, s, and E sides. The inner court building had a ground floor of stone, but the upper storey of timber-framed construction, and at the angles two big polygonal towers which, above the roof level, were corbelled out considerably for the height of one storey and after that receded again.* The timber-framed surfaces were given a fantastical, by no means restful or harmonious treatment. The timberwork itself was covered with carved and incised slate-hanging decorated in the French taste.‡ Evelyn tells us of this, and the excavations have shown that some such plaques have scratched-in notes in French.§ Some of the slate panels were gilded. The panels between the timber were filled with stucco-duro, a very hard plaster which was decorated in high relief. The style of the relief work was again French, not English. An illustration of the s front shows nearly life-size figures on the ground floor, emblems and cartouches above, and Roman Emperors (?) between the second-floor windows. That, as Sir John Summerson has rightly said, is reminiscent of the contemporary type of interior decoration at Fontainebleau. The only parallel for the decoration of the exterior of a building with stucco-duro is, as Mr Biddle has pointed out, at the Palazzo del Te at Mantua, where Primaticcio worked before he went to Fontainebleau. It can however also be pointed out that Holbein, on the pattern of what was usual in the early c16 in North Italian towns, had painted the façades of houses in Switzerland with, amongst other things, mythological figures and cartouches. On the garden front and perhaps the other fronts as well the stonework of the ground floor was decorated in the same manner as

* The stone was brought from Merton Priory. During excavations carved fragments were found in the foundations, including a large c14 boss, now in the London Museum.

‡ Mr Biddle, who excavated the site, is of the opinion that the octagon towers at least had the angle posts decorated with pilasters and entablatures of the freest kind – a motif of the French Loire School, as everyone knows.

§ The excavation finds are now in the London Museum.

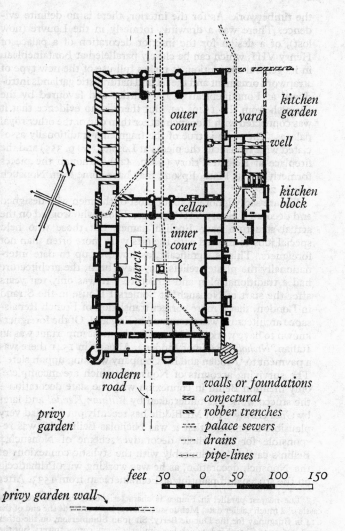

kitchen garden

yard

outer court

well

kitchen block

cellar

inner court

church

N

modern road

privy garden

	walls or foundations
	conjectural
	robber trenches
	palace sewers
	drains
	pipe-lines

feet 50 0 50 100 150

privy garden wall

Nonsuch Palace, begun 1538 (*Reproduced by courtesy of the Nonsuch Palace Excavation Committee*)

the timberwork. As for the interior, there is no definite evidence. There was a drawing, formerly in the Louvre (now lost), of a design for the interior decoration of a palace of Henry VIII, which can be closely paralleled at Fontainebleau in its general conception. It makes full use of the new type of strapwork ornament and the fat and naturalistic garlands introduced at Fontainebleau in the thirties and favoured by the Flemish from the 1540s on. But there is no evidence that it was connected with Nonsuch rather than one of the other royal palaces. The same is true of the fragments traditionally associated with Nonsuch: the pieces at Loseley (*see* p. 355) and the fireplace at Reigate Priory (*see* p. 427), although the pieces formerly at Pitt Place, Epsom, may have come from Nonsuch (*see* p. 218).

We are sadly ignorant about most of the men who designed and decorated Henry VIII's palace. Those who worked on the actual structure have English names, but those who held special jobs connected with the arts were more often than not foreigners. This is significant, as however up to date internationally the plaster reliefs may have been, the architecture had a traditional plan and structure.* It was only ten years after the start of Nonsuch, at Somerset House in the Strand in London, that a more correct translation of French Renaissance architecture was attempted in England. Of the foreigners known to have worked at Nonsuch, the most important was an Italian, *Nicholas Bellin* of Modena. Already in 1541 there was a payment to 'Moden and his Company working uppon slate'. The surviving accounts of Nonsuch (which are incomplete) only mention Bellin in connexion with the slate decoration – the stucco work was undertaken by *William Kendal* and later by *Giles Gering* – but Mr Biddle has recently put forward very plausible arguments that it was Nicholas Bellin who was responsible for the whole decorative scheme of Nonsuch.‡ Bellin's career fits admirably with the stylistic connexions of the Nonsuch decoration, as he was working with Primaticcio on the stucco and painting at Fontainebleau from 1533. After

* The nearest parallel in France is characteristically enough a country castle of a much earlier date, Mehun-sur-Yièvre, built towards the end of the c14 in Burgundy for the Duc de Berry. Sir John Summerson, on the other hand, refers to Chambord, which has similarly heavy corner towers, but the Renaissance details there are much purer.

‡ For further details *see* J. Dent: *The Quest for Nonsuch* (1962); M. Biddle, 'Nicholas Bellin of Modena', in *Journal of the Brit. Archaeol. Assoc.*, vol. 29 (1966).

1537 he was in England, and was employed by Henry VIII on various enterprises, including the decoration of Whitehall Palace (where he was working at the same time as Holbein). His work at Whitehall included a stucco fireplace. Previously, *Toto del Nunziata* of Florence (called by Vasari the architect of the 'principal palace' of Henry VIII) and the mysterious *John of Padua* who is called 'Devysor of H. Majesty's Buildings', but who did not enter the King's service until 1543, have been suggested as architects of Nonsuch, but there is no documentary evidence to support this. All the evidence suggests that it was the decoration rather than the architecture which was foreign, and that the direct links were with France and especially with Fontainebleau.

Nonsuch was one of the favourite residences of Queen Elizabeth I, but declined in favour in the C17. It was demolished between 1682 and 1688. What remains is to be seen near CHERRY ORCHARD FARM in the SW corner of the present park: the base of a chalk wall, flint with brick, 275 ft long, which probably was a garden wall, and the rectangular artificial platform on which the Banqueting House stood. This has bastion-like corners and slightly canted-forward sides. The Banqueting House itself was a two-storey timber-framed building, 44 by 38 ft, constructed on top of stone and brick cellars.*

The house which is called Nonsuch now has nothing in structure or siting in common with Henry VIII's palace. It was built in 1802–6 to the design of *Sir Jeffry Wyatville*. It is of two storeys with stuccoed walls and designed on the picturesque principle, i.e. asymmetrically. Its most prominent piece is a three-storeyed central tower with angle buttresses, battlements, and pinnacles. The kitchen wing belongs to a former C18 house.

NORBITON *see* KINGSTON UPON THAMES

NORBURY

3060

ST STEPHEN, Warwick Road. 1908 by *W. S. Weatherley*. Yellow and red brick in the Perp style. Nave and chancel in one. Nice, crisp interior with brick trim.

NORBURY HALL, Craignish Avenue. Early C19. Grey brick, of four bays, the outer bays projecting and connected by a pretty

* I am most grateful to Mr Martin Biddle for his suggestions concerning the text of this entry.

veranda of trellis woodwork with two columns with oddly
Moorish-looking capitals. The trellis is unusual because over-
scale. It recurs on a house at St Margarets, Twickenham.

LONDON ROAD, from Norbury to the centre of Croydon, has
taken part in Croydon's expansion of offices (*see* Croydon,
p. 179). The largest group is just s of Norbury station: ASTRAL
HOUSE is by *Ronald Ward & Partners*, 1962–5. (On the E
side, No. 2058 is an excellent nine-storey slab by *Riches &
Blythin*, 1966–7, in cool grey precast units, set back behind a
three-storey forebuilding. Set well forward by contrast is No.
2060, WATES, by *Fry, Drew & Partners*, 1962–3, a telling
example of the recent revival of palazzo forms for prestige
purposes (Maxwell Fry has moved far from the International
Style). Continuous bands of brown brick and of recessed
windows framed in purple tiling pulled together by a roof
canopy vaulted in concrete, the coving clad in bright red
mosaic. Attractive courtyard inside. After some indifferent
blocks (WINDSOR HOUSE by *Fuller, Hall & Foulsham*,
1963–4) comes RADNOR HOUSE, cleanly finished in ribbed
concrete panels, with a black steel entrance canopy, also by
Fuller, Hall & Foulsham, 1962–4. NT)

1500

NORBURY PARK
½ m. W of Mickleham

A plain, carefully detailed house begun by *Thomas Sandby*, 1774,
in something like Chambers's style for William Lane, the
connoisseur and amateur artist. Five bays and three storeys,
with detached pavilions l. and r., the three central bays
accented on the entrance side (N) with pedimented windows,
on the garden side by being made into a bow window. The N
front and pavilions stuccoed over, probably *c.*1840, the garden
front stock-brick. The magnificent thing about Norbury is its
situation – a belvedere site high above the Dorking gap, with a
s view directly down the valley and an oblique NE view as far
as the centre of London. If only modern planners would allow,
and modern architects justify, building on just a few such sites
today.

In the event Sandby justified it, not by the outside of the
house, but by the splendid PAINTED ROOM of 1783, taking in
the ground-floor bow window, with Augustan sunlit landscapes
framed by trees and trelliswork, painted by *George Barrett*,
who was paid £500 each for them (the ceiling by *Pastorini*, the

figures by *Cipriani*). They blend perfectly with the real land-scapes of exactly the same scale and mellowness framed by the windows. It would be difficult to find a better example any-where of the late C18 Englishman's delight in nature, in landscape rather than bricks and mortar. It is, if you like, an identification or rapture with Rousseau's ideas about natural man and the natural life equivalent to the rapture of the South German stucco workers in their representation of a happy Catholic Elysium. Everything in the room is directed towards trees and sky and light, just as everything in a Rococo church is directed towards expressing God's love for his creation. The other interiors are modest. The best is the ingenious Tuscan-Doric pillared entrance hall with plaster medallions and the staircase expertly fitted into a narrow well beside it.

NORMANDY

9050

CONGREGATIONAL CHAPEL. Dated 1825; a tiny domestic brick box.

(WESTWOOD HOUSE. An C18 three-storey façade, with a two-storey porch which may be earlier. To the r. an earlier wing. B. F. J. Pardoe)

(WESTWOOD FARM. C15 timber-framed hall-house with later inserted floor, and an C18 tile-hung and brick façade.)

NORTH HOLMWOOD *see* DORKING *and* HOLMWOOD

NORWOOD *see* SOUTH NORWOOD *and* UPPER NORWOOD

NORWOOD HILL *see* CHARLWOOD

NUTFIELD

3050

A Weald-ridge village E of Redhill, the street running E–W along the ridge as at Bletchingley and Oxted. Very prim and Victorian-ized, and no wonder, for there are more ferociously angular big houses of *c*.1860 at Nutfield than anywhere else in Surrey.

ST PETER AND ST PAUL. Renewed from end to end, and given a new s aisle in 1882. *W. O. Milne* did it. What is left is a kind of macedoine: C13 N arcade of standard type, C13 chancel s lancets (N lancet into the vestry), C13 blocked arch to a N chapel, chancel arch perhaps of *c.*1300, a couple of Perp windows, and a Perp tower with a patched-up brick top of 1786, now re-gothicized. Short splay-footed shingled spire. Quite an impressive tower arch, with continuous mouldings. – FONT. Octagonal C15 bowl put on a Gothic Survival stem dated 1665. – SCREEN. C14? Four-light bays with paired heads enclosing quatrefoils, the central bay with ornate trefoils in the spandrels. Very renewed. – STAINED GLASS. E window by *Burne-Jones*, i.e. *Morris & Co.*, † 1890, and a good example, especially the deep sultry blue in the tracery lights. – SE window of the S aisle († 1891) also by him. – PLATE. Cup of 1665, probably marking the same post-Restoration return to ceremonial as the replaced font. – BRASS. William Grafton and wife, stock C15 work (chancel S side). – MONUMENT. Probably to Thomas of Pulham, rector 1305–28, with indents for figures. The recess has slightly intersecting mouldings, typical of the early C14 (chancel S side).

NUTFIELD PRIORY. Formidable asymmetrical neo-Tudor built in 1872–4 for Joshua Fielden M.P. by *John Gibson*, the talented architect of many C19 bank buildings; alas, not much talent here. On a splendid hillside site, and impressive when seen from down in the Weald, but very dull and mechanical close to. Big tower at the back, plus what looks like the desperate afterthought of a flying buttress. Big Great Hall inside; carved texts all over the house.* COTTAGES and complete FARM QUAD-RANGLE to the SE, obviously also by *Gibson*.

Nothing to notice in the village on the ridge, but a genuine hamlet at Nutfield Marsh, ½ m. N, with a big rough green. On the E side is LEATHER BOTTLE COTTAGE, a good, unrestored C17 house. Brick and tile-hanging, Horsham slate roof, hipped ends with two tiny gables at the ridge, beautifully warm texture. Between Nutfield and Nutfield Marsh are PEYTON'S COTTAGES, which look to be two C18 terraces joined into one about 1870 (by whom?). Now one long uphill range. The way in which the stepped roof-line is managed is a first-rate piece of architectural subtlety.

S of the Weald ridge is HALE FARM, an attractive timber-framed house of *c.*1600, with wide variation in timber spacing on a fundamentally regular frame.

---

* The house replaced one to which additions had been made in 1858–9 by *John Norton* for Gurney, the Quaker banker. These included a conservatory, which was incorporated in the new building. Mr A. G. Sheppard Fidler kindly provided this information.

(EWELL HOUSE COUNTY HOTEL. A very small FOLLY TOWER in the grounds. B. Jones)

OAKWOOD

1030

No village; a collection of hamlets near Ockley, with the appearance of having grown up haphazardly in the middle of the Weald, here very thick. This impression is given even more strongly by the church, which is over-restored but has an unforgettable situation. It is completely surrounded by thick woods, with no other building near, approached only by a lane from the N and footpaths from the S. The churchyard is just a rough clearing, and looking out from it can still give the impression of frontier uneasiness, a refreshing thing to find in Surrey.

ST JOHN THE BAPTIST. The church was originally a chapel of ease to Wotton: one long single C13 room, with lancets in both N and S sides and simple Perp windows to E and W. Unhappily this was exactly doubled in 1879 by *Basil Champneys*, who added a N aisle the size of the original building and transferred the lancets to the new N wall. It is now too big and rather characterless. – FONT. Handsome restrained Victorian; black marble. – BRASS. Edward de la Hale † 1431. Figure in armour, 18 in. high. Normal rough C15 work.

Many humble C16 and C17 cottages, and many of them less restored than in most of Surrey because of the remote situation. Outstanding in this respect BOSWELL'S FARM, E of the church, near the main A29 road, doubtless because it is no longer lived in (it is used as kennels). It is an irregularly framed house with brick infilling and central projecting gable and porch and Horsham slate roof – an object lesson for the viewer who would like to know what such houses really looked like instead of as a C20 owner or architect fondly imagines them to have been. SW of this is RUCKMANS, an enlargement by *Lutyens* of 1894; as in many of his earliest houses, old and new are almost indistinguishable on the entrance side. (The three tall gables with strip windows running round corners on the garden side are characteristic of his earliest phase. The music room, added in 1902, is equally characteristic: Neo-Georgian, of local stone with brick dressing. Part of the *Jekyll* gardens survives. Lutyens also designed (*c.*1895) part of the courtyard of farm buildings, including a cottage, and also an isolated cottage with a big square chimney on the other side of the drive. NT)

0060

OATLANDS PARK
1 m. ENE of Weybridge

The medieval palace was rebuilt by Henry VIII from 1538 onwards. He was married here to Catherine Howard, and Elizabeth I, James I, and Charles I all stayed at Oatlands. The site of this is actually at Weybridge (*see* p. 517) and the present house was erected on the site of a hunting lodge. It was built for the Duke of York by *Henry Holland* in 1794. This was bought in 1827 by Edward Hughes Ball Hughes, a very rich man known as the Golden Ball, and he reconstructed it. In 1856 the mansion was purchased by a syndicate and converted by *T. H. Wyatt* into a hotel. The style of architecture looks more 1856 than 1827. Yellow brick and a big short angle tower with top loggia and Italian roof. Of Holland's time only the fine GATEPIERS. The celebrated GROTTO, built in 1747 by *Lane* of Tisbury at a cost of £40,000, was demolished in 1948 – an act of vandalism duly castigated by the *Architectural Review* and *Country Life*. It was a domed, two-storeyed structure of brick with vaulted chambers and dimly lit passages. Externally and internally the brick was hidden by rocks of porous lava with ammonites, coral, spar, quartz, etc.

0050

OCKHAM

No village group – largely model cottages of the 1860s in unspoilt country near Ripley. One of the older cottages has a wing dated 1770 which still keeps brick giant pilasters, another example of Surrey conservatism in the C18.

ALL SAINTS. Effectively a C13 framework (the plain tower arch without capitals might be either Norman or post-Reformation), with C13 chancel arch and N arcade of two bays with round capitals, round abaci, and double-chamfered arches; the standard type. The E window for which Ockham is famous is also C13 – seven lancets,* plain outside, but having marble shafts inside with first-rate stiffly carved foliage capitals like a set of musical variations. They are all different, yet all based on the same motif. Most of them are of the stiff-leaf kind, but they vary between early- and later-looking ones, and one is naturalistic. The arches have several roll-mouldings and one order of dog-tooth mouldings under a heavy label. The

---

* As elsewhere only at Blakeney in Norfolk (and Kilkenny Friary, Ireland, as the late R. N. Bloxan pointed out).

stepping up from sides to centre – quite a difficult aesthetic problem – is beautifully managed. The style is metropolitan, the date probably c.1260. Was it here originally? – it rests inside a c16-looking four-centred rere-arch, and is inserted above three single lancets which were probably c13* (the remains can be seen outside in the E wall). The outermost capitals and arches seem to have been altered to fit. Perhaps the earliest-looking capitals inside come from them, and perhaps the seven-light window came from near-by Newark Priory at the Dissolution. It is certainly the finest E.E. detail in Surrey. Also authentically medieval two good curvilinear windows in the nave S wall (three lights under two dagger shapes under a quatrefoil). Tower Perp, and probably post-Reformation, judging by the plainness. On the N side is the King Chapel, built c.1735. The outside is plain brickwork (headers only), with pointed arches with inserted c19 Gothic hoods to them, the inside a strictly detailed and vaulted bay with sober coffered entrance arch and niches, very much in Wren's St Paul's style. Not much feeling, in spite of the gravity, and unlikely to be by Hawksmoor, in spite of his connexion with Ockham Park.

The nave has a wagon roof above tie-beams, with original bosses and diamond-patterned panels datable c.1530. The same idea in the aisle roof, but this time using camber-beams, i.e. panels and tie-beams continuous. – NICHE (E end of N aisle). Elaborate and canopied, of the c14, mutilated, but of good workmanship. Possibly also an importation. – STAINED GLASS. S side of chancel, c15 figures in the tracery lights. – S side of nave, German c18 painted glass of various dates – 1710, 1746. Not very good. – E window designed by Sir T. G. Jackson and made by Powell's, 1875. Admirably fitted to the lancets – two tiers of figures against a background of slate-blue vertical vine trails. Weakly drawn, but a very good rhythmic pattern, which in this context is more important. – MONUMENTS. Brass to Walter Frilende † 1376 (N side of altar). The earliest priest's brass in Surrey. Demi-figure, 15 in. high. Good quality. – John Weston † 1483 and wife (S side of altar). Standard c15 figures, 20 in. high. – Peter, first Lord King, [63] † 1734, and wife. By Rysbrack. Big monument with the two figures sitting either side of a large urn, pyramidal background decorated in Rysbrack's typically rich and frothy Palladian style. The composition ordinary, the figures, as so often, very

* A triple Norman window starting so low in the wall is very unlikely.

good: the female figure a little stylized, Lord King himself a fine portrait, with his soberly modelled face contrasted with the rich dress and the tumbled symbols of office (he was Lord Chancellor). – Peter, seventh Lord King, † 1833. By *Westmacott Jun*. Simple design and refreshingly honest Byronic bust, well above the average of the time, and also of Westmacott Jun. – Ralph, second Earl of Lovelace, † 1906, and wife. Simple stone casket on a monolithic pedestal, not the usual Edwardian monument. It holds the ashes of Lord and Lady Lovelace. On the front of the casket two beautiful large heraldic enamel plaques. *Voysey* was the Lovelaces' favourite architect, and he could well have designed this memorial. (The lettering is by *Eric Gill*, 1907.)

OCKHAM PARK. Ockham Park was originally a Jacobean house built in the 1620s for Henry Weston. It was altered by *Hawksmoor* after 1724, when the front was refaced and the hall remodelled. This was Italianized about 1830, altered by *Voysey* in 1894–5, and burnt in 1948. Now all that remains of the house is one kitchen wing with an Italianate tower above plain brickwork which still keeps one unmistakable Hawksmorean touch – a tiny Venetian window in brick with the three parts split up and treated as separate units. Also remaining are the STABLES, U-shaped with a handsome central arch and moulded brickwork window above, and an ORANGERY, a brusque design of five deep windows under a pediment and enriched roof-line. The stables look like Hawksmoor, the orangery might be slightly later. Both at the time of writing are not in good condition; the orangery, at least, is certainly worth preserving.

The Earl Lovelace who enriched East Horsley Towers (*see* p. 204) in the 1860s also owned Ockham. Hence there are a series of estate buildings in Victorian polychrome brickwork, recently excellently restored, including an Italianate farm, now the ESTATE OFFICE, many cottages, the HAUTBOY HOTEL of 1864, and OCKHAM MILL on the other side of A3, dated 1862, a straightforward five-storey brick mill only mildly polychromed. UPTON COTTAGE (now CHIMNEYS), N of the church, is by *Voysey* (*see* above) – a simple, primitive design of 1903, without Voysey buttresses or ornament but with his typical capped chimneys.

1030   OCKLEY

Weald village on the main road to Bognor, under the slopes of Leith Hill, forming a long green which in its way is one of the most impressive in Southern England. The road runs along the E side, and this side is mostly built up or walled up. The W side has no road along it and forms an enchanting serpentine boundary of alternate cottages and fields, the green sometimes fifty yards wide and sometimes two hundred, sometimes bounded firmly by trees and cottages, sometimes penetrating into the countryside beyond by way of a cornfield or a meadow: i.e. the effect is paradoxically due not to the buildings but to the spaces between them. The road is slightly raised above the green, and westward views always have Leith Hill as a backcloth.

St Margaret, ½ m. NE of the village. Almost rebuilt in 1873, with a new aisle and larger chancel. Before then it was a simple unaisled sandstone building. The Dec tracery of the easternmost nave window on the S side approximates to what was there before. Visual pleasure can now only be got from the restored C15 wooden porch and the W tower, rebuilt in 1699, still in the Perp style, the lower stage with strongly battered angle buttresses, the upper stage unbuttressed with plain two-light windows in the bell-chamber – a simple, nicely proportioned, honest job. Inside, under the tower there are four roughly carved arches in the style of c.1200, as though this had originally been the central tower of a cruciform church, kept when the tower was rebuilt. This seems most unlikely, yet the mouldings are authentically rough and the stonework of 1699 is butted up against them in an authentic way too. They might on the other hand be of c.1750 (also an odd thing to do) or a later attempt at Gothic Revival. – Fittings. Nearly all of 1873, including a very bad Reredos made by Messrs *Powells* from a design by *Harry Burrow*.

Ockley Court, opposite the church. Plain, three-storeyed mid-C18 brick with two big bow windows; lumpish.

Broome Park, 1 m. N. Symmetrical stone Tudor-style house, with a nice eye for picturesque siting against the wooded S slopes of Leith Hill. Wearily detailed, close to.

Jayes Park, ½ m. W. Elegant classical stock-brick front which looks early C19 but is actually of 1913, very restrained and unusual for the date.

Many pleasant vernacular brick and tile-hung houses throughout the village. On the green the best houses are The Tuns, near the S end, with a formal C18 weatherboarded front, rare in this part of Surrey, then on the W side Carpoles Cottages, a very pretty brick and tile-hung pair, and Tanyard Cottages, outstandingly picturesque in a completely unplanned way – simply a pair of cottages with one house smaller than the other, each with small lean-to and porch at the end, each with C16 brick and timber-framing. Further N is the same thing, done consciously in ornate mid-C19 terms: Nos. 14–15 and No. 16, employing all manner of materials – timber-framing, brick, stone, and tile-hanging – the perfect definition of the *cottage orné*. Finally at the N end of the green is LIME TREE COTTAGES, a tile-hung pair with very odd single-storey additions at each end like small barns. They are roughcast with one pointed window.

OLD MALDEN see MALDEN

4040

OLD SURREY HALL
2 m. SE of Lingfield

On the Sussex border, and remote. The house was built *c.*1450, and the hall range survived as a farmhouse, divided up in the usual way. This was restored and metamorphosed into a moated quadrangle by *George Crawley* (cf. Crowhurst Place) in 1922. The result is indescribable, imitation carried to the point of genius. The architect must have been working quite cut off from reality, and his flair for detail carries the onlooker over into the fairy-tale world. It is an acquired taste, especially for anyone brought up in the Modern Movement, but the effort is worth making. Completely random use of brick, stone, and timbering. The entrance to the quad is under a low arch on the W side, opposite the hall. Further additions were made to the S side in a rather arch classical style in 1937 by *Walter Godfrey*. The total effect is like a rhapsody on Ightham Mote (and in fact oddly like the rhapsodies of early C20 British composers on Tudor and folksong themes).

The C15 part is in fact very impressive in itself: a big, close-timbered range with timber infilling and a very sophisticated
27   roof consisting of scissor rafters with four-centred* trusses and four enormous four-centred tie-beams below them at eaves level, two free-standing and one in each end wall. The coving outside and the oriel facing the quad (but not its gable) are genuine; the S oriel, the minstrels' gallery, the carved buttresses fitted into the timbers of the S front, the smoke aperture inside, and the elaborate finials to the beams are all due to Mr Crawley; yet the total impression is not at all false.

* These are literally four-centred – made up of four pieces of wood.

OLD WOKING   oo5o

The original centre of Woking, which was a market town in the
C17, though a little-known one. One old street, now gap-toothed.
The former centre, where A247 runs s towards Clandon, has
been sacrificed to traffic needs. The road has been widened and
the old houses on either side swept away.

ST PETER. Originally Norman. The N wall of the nave remains,
mostly puddingstone, with Perp windows. Chancel C13. Lancet
windows on the S side and a good renewed curvilinear E window
(cf. Worplesdon): three lights, with the centre light lower and
ogee-headed under a roundel which fills the head of the arch.
S arcade and aisle C15 with renewed windows. The piers are
octagonal, short and very fat, the arches have three chamfers.
Tower base C13, rubble with clasping buttresses; tower top
C15, of unbuttressed sarsens, not helped by C19 fancies like the
hood-mould over the clock. S porch Late Tudor (and Victorian)
brickwork, crow-stepped, the entrance hardly more than 6 ft
high. Inside over-restored as usual. The most interesting parts
of the church are under the tower: a simply carved, tall W
doorway which looks c.1100 or a little later (shallow-cut detail).
It still has the Romanesque DOOR in it, quite impressive. The
ironwork is chiefly three big horizontal iron bands penetrating
the neck of C-straps, just like the pattern of Saxon brooches. –
WEST GALLERY. 1622, rough Jacobean. – PULPIT, altered, in
similar style. – PEWS. A number of late medieval pews, a simple
pattern with two narrow buttresses at each end. – MONUMENTS.
Johannes Lloyd † 1663; crude. Artisan tablet, debased classical motifs piled up on one another (S wall of chancel). – John
Merest † 1752. In a sober frame, still Baroque (S aisle). – Rev.
Edward Emily † 1792. By the elder *Westmacott* and not bad: a
crisp classical frame enclosing an urn. No debased sentiment
(W wall of nave). – BRASSES. Joan Purdon, early C16, part of
a bigger family group now lost. – John Shadhet † 1527, plus
wife and children. Both in the S aisle, both about 15 in. high.

Old Woking consists of one long battered street running W–E.
The two most interesting houses face each other near the W
end. On the N side is the MANOR HOUSE, mid-C17, brick, with
one shaped gable at the W end and a bigger, slightly later addition at the E end with a mansard roof, a good deal like a simpler
edition of Brook Place (*see* Chobham). On the S side is a big
early C18 house now split into two: MAGNOLIA and THE
OLD BREW HOUSE (now Peartrees). Three-bay recessed

centre, bulky two-bay wings, bulky hipped roof – the type of Wrencote, Croydon, without any of the elaborate joinery details. Dated 1715 – old-fashioned by comparison with Willmer House in Farnham of 1718. Old Woking was evidently indeed 'out of the thorough-fare', to use Defoe's phrase.

Further E, a row of roughcast COTTAGES (Nos. 193–201) actually hides the framing of the original Market House of 1665, now quite unrecognizable. The MHLG despairingly says 'it is surmised that all that is left of the original building is now covered'. Opposite, CHURCH STREET runs S to the church, short, with nothing to notice except perhaps WEYLEA, by the churchyard, big, plain, three-storeyed C18 brick. Finally, where HIGH STREET turns N to become OLD WOKING ROAD another C18 front closes the vista, seven by two bays, the whole elevation rusticated, stucco on brick.

HOE PLACE, ½ m. N. Lumpish half-H-shaped house built by James Zouch († 1708). The exterior however is Regency in appearance, with a low portico joining the wings, and a bow window on the garden side. Inside, a handsome early C18 staircase in a stair-well, the painting of which is attributed to *Verrio*, but which is now thickly varnished over. Another room has a coved painted ceiling in rather better condition, said to be of the Peace of Ryswick, adapted from one of Verrio's now destroyed paintings at Windsor (E. Croft-Murray). The STABLES to the N appear to be C18. Attached to them is a C19 Gothic hall (now chapel) with a tower with skittish mid-C19 trimmings. Near them is a circular brick ICE HOUSE. The outbuildings on the S side may be C17.*

WOKING OLD HALL, ½ m. E. In an eldritch overgrown site by the Wey: commuters' Woking seems to be a hundred miles away. This was a favoured Tudor royal palace. *William Vertue* and *Henry Smyth* were responsible for alterations in 1515–16. Later *Lewis Stocket* and *John Symonds* added a large gallery for Elizabeth, in 1578. Then, in 1620, James I gave it to Sir Edward Zouch, who rebuilt at Hoe Place (*see* above; the present house there is another rebuilding) and let the old palace fall into decay. Now all that is left is a dank moated site and a few foundations. The long C16 BARN, clearly of Tudor brickwork, with a huge queenpost roof, plus a tiny square building like a pillbox attached to its S end, has recently been demolished.

---

* Mr G. G. Greenwood suggests that they may have formed part of the courtyard of the earlier Zouch house.

WOKING PARK FARM, near the site, is timber-framing of
*c.*1600 with additions. The building called THE OLD HOUSE,
on Old Woking Road where the track to the palace branches
off, is clearly connected with the site: early C17 brickwork,
L-shaped and gabled, gaunt and almost without windows.

ORCHARDS *see* MUNSTEAD

OTTERSHAW

Heaths and tiny brick houses between Chertsey and Woking, the
first countryside on the way out of London.

CHRISTCHURCH. 1864 by *Sir Gilbert Scott,* and in this case
surely done by one of his assistants. Tower built in 1885.
Polychrome brick and stone, broach-spire and apse; a few
tiles let into the outside walls. Quite ferocious, but no conviction behind it. The inside whitewashed, which has simply
made it dull.

(CHERTSEY UNION, Murray Road. 1836 by *Sampson Kemp-*
thorne. Two storeys, red brick, pedimented centre, pavilions
at either end. MHLG)

OTTERSHAW PARK. The house is of 1910, formidable and very
heavy-handed stone Palladian, by *Niven & Wigglesworth.* Two
earlier LODGES remain, now separated from the house, just w
of Ottershaw church. They are of *c.*1795, by *Wyatt* in his best
Neo-Classical style, with a weird plan. Each lodge consists of
two cubes joined at the corners to form a sort of figure-of-
eight. The cubes nearest the road have Greek Doric porticoes *in*
antis on three sides, and artificial stone plaques above the
windows. Behind the house there was a gimcrack stuccoed
DAIRY of *c.*1800, presumably also by *Wyatt,* in the form of a
cruciform church complete with central tower, apse, and mock
Perp tracery. It was demolished in 1962.

ANNINGSLEY PARK. Mock half-timbered Tudor – the careful
sort – by *Gerald Warren,* 1923. Of no artistic value, but a
period piece of a kind, as can be seen from the contemporary
Country Life description: '. . . the whole of the drawings were
prepared free hand with a view to inspiring the workmen with
a right feeling for the work, and as far as possible in the actual
building all plumb-bobs and levels were dispensed with'.

BOTLEYS. *See* p. 116.

OUTWOOD

Simple Weald hamlet s of Bletchingley. Unpretentious cottages
in scrubby heathland, caused by a tiny limestone cap, only a few
yards wide, on the surrounding clay.

ST JOHN THE BAPTIST. 1869 by *Burges*. Plain lancet style,
honest but not very good – nothing like his church at Lowfield
Heath. Simple brick interior which could easily be dated 1900.
Impressive w tower added in 1876, a big stuccoed saddleback
with almost no detail on it, about as far from the conventional
Gothic Revival as could be imagined. This is by *W. P.
Manning*, obviously an architect worth looking out for (e.g. St
Mary Primrose Hill, London).

Outwood is famous for its POST-MILL, dated 1665, with a brick
round-house base and a tarred weatherboarded top. In regular
use, a delightful sight – pre-industrial, demure and domestic,
without the scale of later mills, a point which was well enough
illustrated by the big, octagonal, all weatherboarded SMOCK-
MILL next to it, built in competition as late as *c.*1870. This,
sadly, collapsed in 1960.

Of old buildings only WASP GREEN FARMHOUSE is worth
notice. Wealden type, the outside late C17 with an overhanging tile-hung upper floor and hipped roofs with the ends
going up, not to a point, but to tiny triangular gables – a typical
local mannerism. The frame is in fact C15 and preserves an
original tie-beam hall roof.

OXENFORD *see* PEPER HAROW

OXSHOTT
2 m. s of Esher

Unaffected suburban (1880 onwards) among pine woods.

ST ANDREW. Poor free Late Gothic by *Caröe & Passmore*,
1912.

Of the original suburban houses perhaps ROBIN HILL (built as
WARREN MOUNT) is worth a mention: Voysey's style without
Voysey's talent, by *Walter Cave*.* Oxshott also contains a very
fine pair of modern houses by *Powell & Moya*, MILK WOOD
and HEADLONG HILL, in Stokes Heath Road, just w of the

---

* *Voysey* himself in 1898 published a design for a house at Oxshott, but
this never seems to have been built.

railway. 1955. Flat roofs, stock-brick walls, and deep white-painted eaves, a spare industrial style which only Powell & Moya in England at this date managed to humanize. The buildings are stepped downhill, facing NW across a big rough field. Single-storeyed, except for the two-storeyed downhill end of Headlong Hill, linked by screen walls and a separate unit containing two garages. The careful detailing and adjustment of the stepped roof-line to give a subtle composition of horizontal lines is very good indeed.

WILDWOOD. Nice modern house by *Kenneth Wood*, 1959. T-shaped, cedar boarding outside. Another good house in LEATHERHEAD ROAD by *Bartlett & Gray*, 1958.

(JESSOPS WELL, Prince's Coverts, Stoke Wood. Small brick C18 pump room with hipped roof. Originally a spa. MHLG)

OXTED*   ₃₀₅₀

Under the Downs near the Kent border, a mile w of Limpsfield and joined to it by new Oxted, which grew up around the station.

ST MARY. The usual Surrey story: a slow-growth medieval church over-restored. Short tower of the C12, in dark Bargate stone, unbuttressed, with renewed Dec detail on the bell-stage. Aisle and chancel effectively all Dec and with much of the tracery renewed and valueless (original the N aisle E window and those in the C19 organ chamber). The E window had all its tracery planed down in 1637 and now has some historic interest of its own because of it. Mid-C13 priest's doorway in the chancel. C14 chancel arch, raised after 1828, dying into its (C13 ?) imposts. Arcades and s porch C15, the only worth-while parts of the church. The arcades are identical with those of Lingfield nave – four shafts, four hollows, the w and E responds a single shaft inside a continuous moulding. This arcade replaces one of the C13, of which the E responds with graceful shafting remain, together with the E arch on the N side, much lower than the present arches. The line of the lower aisle roofs can easily be seen outside. The porch has a well detailed arch and hood-mould with the Cobham arms in the spandrels – another Lingfield connexion. Built of dark and light Bargate stone. The tops of the aisles are clunch and were clearly originally lean-to. One puzzle remains. To the w of the priest's doorway in the s wall of the chancel is a recess with a single-chamfered arch and a second one against the back wall of the

---

* Mrs K. Percy has kindly revised this entry.

recess. In this back wall in the C15 or early C16 a small two-light window was made. What was it for, and what had the recess been for? – CHEST. Iron, probably C15, with a very complex lock. – STAINED GLASS. Four evangelists in the tracery lights of the E window. Good colouring; probably C14. – The four aisle windows are by *Morris & Co.*, but after Morris's death. – PLATE. Chalice and Paten, 1634; large Dish with Nuremberg mark, 1760. – MONUMENTS. Brass to Johanne Haselden † 1480 (S wall of chancel). – John Aldersly and his wife † 1610 (N wall of chancel). The familiar Jacobean kneeler, but prettily carved. – William Finch † 1728 (S wall of chancel). A well carved Palladian tablet without trimmings.

ST JOHN, Hurst Green. By *J. O. Scott* (who lived at Oxted), 1912, an inept bit of flint Dec. Extended by one bay, with parish room and large porch area, in 1962, by *H. G. Nisbet*. – STAINED GLASS. Rose window in the baptistery by *J. & M. Kettlewell*, 1962.

(ALL SAINTS (R.C.). 1914–22 by *Leonard Williams*. Chancel ceiling by *Geoffrey Webb*.*)

(CHURCH OF THE PEACE OF GOD (Congregational). 1935 by *Frederic Lawrence*.*)

Old Oxted consists of one narrow, battered, and traffic-ridden High Street,‡ running uphill from E to W. At the E end, where the road forks to new Oxted, ELECTRIC HOUSE is a lush fake-oasthouse built as a road house (without an alcohol licence!) in 1936, probably by a Mr *Bing*. Travelling W, the S side has, above the road and over the 'Old Lock-up', a C16 timber-framed house fronting on to SHORTERS ROW, an informal early C19 terrace at r. angles to the High Street. Simple but genuine, almost the best thing in the street. A continuous terrace, still above the road, starts with STREETERS COTTAGE, C17, timber-framed, with a big gable to the road, some hard-bitten timber-framed cottages, and THE CROWN, sub-Norman-Shaw front but incorporating some C16 timber-framing on the W flank and rear. The N side has FORGE HOUSE and BEAM COTTAGES, all part of a late medieval hall-and-cross-wing house, with rough late C17 brick fronts. At the crossroads THE OLD BELL of *c*.1500, timber-framed with diagonal braces, an overhang on the front and the W side, and too much restoration. W of the crossroads is IVY COTTAGE, L-shaped and tile-hung. All this is barely worth a

* Information from Rodney Hubbuck.
‡ To be by-passed.

glance, and, coming between Godstone and Limpsfield, two *soigné* Wealden villages, Old Oxted is oddly grim; it could almost be a North Warwickshire industrial village.

New Oxted, by the church, is a station with a shopping parade on either side. Some of the terraces on the w side of the station are possibly the most outrageously over-timbered in the county, which is saying something* (there is plenty of the standard Shopping-Parade Tudor in the same street for comparison). Taken as far as this, it becomes interesting. The wildest block, opposite the G.P.O., seems to be by *Ivan Roberts*, 1933 – already the designers are becoming unknown.

The other buildings around Oxted are scattered and difficult to describe in a perambulation. N of new Oxted, below the Downs, there has been considerable development, some by Godstone R.D.C. and since 1962 some inappropriate building by Messrs Lawdons on the Court Farm fields. The character of the N half of the parish is now commuter belt. To the NW is BARROW GREEN COURT, with pleasant mellow brickwork. It is a half-H-shaped Jacobean brick house, the E front with three gables but all the ornamental detail altered, the s front inelegant double-bowed c18. Inside a Jacobean fireplace and an early c18 staircase. Just w of this is BARROW GREEN FARM, an attractive c16 Wealden farm with a timber porch and tile-hung overhanging upper storey. The MOUNT is a bowl-shaped mound, 200 ft in diameter and 30 ft high. It may well be natural, despite c18 references to 'Barrow'. This part of the manor was called the 'Burgh' from the c14 to the c17, which probably accounts for the name.

(BLUNT HOUSE, ¼ m. E of Barrow Green Court. Built by *J. Oldrid Scott* for himself. Neo-Georgian. Arthur Oswald)

(HOME PLACE, between Oxted and Limpsfield. By *Douglas & Fordham* of Chester, 1894. E. Hubbard)

s of the village is BROADHAM GREEN, whose cottages have more texture left to them than most of Oxted's old buildings, in particular MAYFLOWER COTTAGE, a hall-house of *c.*1400 with a remarkable roof with a very tall central post; also OLD COTTAGE opposite on the w side, with a Horsham slate roof, a c15 hall-house with a c16 extension. Further s is STOCKETS, a good yeoman farm, L-shaped, the front now c17 brick with a Horsham slate roof concealing (as so often) a c15 hall and its kingpost roof. The rearward wing was the solar, which also has

* This was part of a policy of deliberate control by the estate owners, which became too expensive in the 1930s after the depression (Arthur Oswald).

a kingpost roof inside. E of this again is COLTSFORD MILL, C18, weatherboarded, with a mansard roof, still milling until 1967 – now a restaurant.

PAINSHILL PARK
1 m. W of Cobham

The house was built c.1778, perhaps by *R. Jupp*. It lies nicely on a hill. It is white, with a porch of four Tuscan columns to the E and a bow to the W. Inside some good interiors, e.g. an oval drawing room and an oval staircase with wrought-iron balustrade. The E portico is also of the C18 but does not belong to the house.

But the fame of Painshill was its grounds, laid out picturesquely by the Hon. Charles Hamilton, son of the Earl of Abercorn, in the 1740s.* Mason and Horace Walpole praised them, Whately illustrated them. Now they are sadly neglected, and many of the ornamental structures are going or gone. Paths lead from the farm at the E end of the estate along a long LAKE towards an island. On the N side by the lake the GOTHIC ABBEY, of brick, with hexagonal angle turrets. On a hill a little further N the GOTHIC TEMPLE or TENT, an 'umbrello' with open sides.‡ On the island all kinds of tufa structures, an ARCH, perpendicular cliffs down into the water, and the two faces of a water tunnel. Mr Hamilton was consciously emulating 'savage Rosa' and 'noble Poussin' (to quote Thomson). Beyond the far (W) end of the lake the WATER WHEEL, for pumping water out of the river Mole into the lake. It is large, of cast iron, and probably belongs to the early C19.

At the extreme SW end of the grounds, beside the Portsmouth road, a tall FOLLY TOWER of c.1770, our storeys, brick, in good condition, with a big circular stair-turret and simple Gothick tracery in the windows. It resembles both the more lately demolished parts of The Oaks and Leith Hill Tower.

Just W of Painshill SILVERMERE, designed by *William Atkinson* for himself c.1820. The house is nothing special, but also lies above an artificial lake.

* He was very thoroughgoing in his improvements, being one of those few landowners who not only built a hermitage, now gone, but installed a hermit to go with it. Not unexpectedly, Hamilton went bankrupt as a result of his extravagance.

‡ Walpole was very critical of this. 'The Goths never built summer-houses or temples in a garden.'

PARKGATE see NEWDIGATE

PASTURE WOOD see HOLMBURY ST MARY

PEASLAKE
2 m. s of Shere

0040

A cosy stone and tile-hung hamlet on the N slopes of the Hurt-wood. Pretty, but too many fake buildings to have much character.

ST MARY. Simple big-scale stone chapel by *Ewan Christian*, 1889.

HAZEL HALL, ½ m. N. Very plain mid-C18 Palladian front, five bays and two storeys, with a Doric porch.

COTTERELL'S FARM, 1 m. NW. Copybook farmhouse elevation of the same type as Hazel Hall, with hipped roof and Doric doorcase, *c.*1750. No attempt at architectural pretensions. Good stone-and-weatherboard barns.

PENDELL
¾ m. NW of Bletchingley

3050

Not a village, but three separate houses of interest. The smallest, PENDELL MANOR HOUSE, is a plain five-by-two-bay brick house of *c.*1730, with a nice City-mason's Ionic doorcase.

PENDELL COURT. Stock Jacobean, brick, built in 1624. Very typical but not good. Five-bay W front, three-storeyed and gabled, conservative (still really the repertoire of Loseley, which was itself conservative), with simple mullioned windows and most of the detail renewed. The only post-Tudor orna-ment is a very simple central* porch and tiny square panels on the gables containing a single brick oval, worn almost like a brooch. The S side has two gables and a lot of C18 rebuilding; the N side has a billiard room in C19 Jacobean.

Inside, the SW room has simple plasterwork and a fireplace of *c.*1760. There is a cramped newel-post staircase, and the hall (entered off-centre) has odd panelling with Jacobean proportions but dainty arabesque detail in French Renaissance style. Is this possibly C16 and removed from Bletchingley Place? E of the house a garden wall with the same swooping

---

* Central with respect to the gables but not in the middle of the front; the gables are a standard size but the brickwork between varies in length, a typical piece of heedless design, if one can call it that. Presumably no asymmetry was intended.

pattern as that to Pendell House (*see* below), and a small GARDEN HOUSE, which must be later C17: it has giant angle pilasters framing the same type of two-light mullioned windows as used in the house.

43 PENDELL HOUSE. Built only twelve years later – dated 1636 – but a complete change in style; a compact symmetrical brick box with hipped roof. It is in fact one of the most puzzling of the houses traditionally connected with *Inigo Jones*, and in its progressive features comparable with Chevening of 1638, within 10 m. of Bletchingley. But much at Pendell is not progressive. The outside detail is all restrained 'Artisan Mannerist', i.e. the City of London style which used 'regular' design but not academic detail, a parallel to Nicholas Stone's sculpture. Yet the house is formidably symmetrical with a narrow central hall – barely a corridor – running through to the staircase at the back of the house, and symmetrical rooms on either side, all raised on a symmetrical and well constructed system of vaulted cellars. This interior arrangement is however not beyond suspicion. The wall to the l. of the corridor is thinner than the others, and it is not unlikely that there was originally no wall there. Thus a 'hall' would have been entered in the traditional direction from the porch and stretched out to the l., whereas a wall might have existed between the corridor and the staircase. This staircase is similar to the smaller staircase in the Queen's House at Greenwich and is undoubtedly original. To sum up: is this a case where Inigo Jones really did give a 'platt' – i.e. a plan and some rough guidance – and left the elevations to be worked up by the mason? If so, the mason worked them up very competently, compared with such better-known 'Artisan' buildings as Cromwell House in Highgate. The main front faces s. Five by two bays, all brick (still English bond), with eaves cornice. Big rectangular windows in moulded surrounds. The centre bay is brought forward and pedimented, and its ground floor is rusticated, with big vertical and diagonal rustication of the lintel, again a precocious motif. Odd surrounds to the windows on the ground floor – segmental top standing on slightly convex pieces. But the oddest thing is a complete set of recessed single-storey brickwork panels – pilasters in reverse, as it were, even to having a sort of recessed capital in fancy brickwork. They occur in precisely the same position and shape as the pilasters themselves would have been. I know of no parallel for this anywhere in the country. The w (garden) side has similar details. On the E side a motif

as surprising as any if it is original – two sash-windows fifty years before they are supposed to exist, but made probable by the fact that they are blind (one has recently been opened) and are supposed always to have been blind.* In 1747 the house was bought by *Andrews Jelfe*, the architect of Rye Town Hall and mason-contractor for Westminster Bridge, who added the elegant semicircular courtyard walls with a big scallop pattern, the crests capped by balls. This sets off the house perfectly, and shows an extreme and rather unexpected sympathy for the C17 on the part of a successful mid-C18 business man.

PEPER HAROW

9040

1½ m. W of Godalming

A small estate village on a cul-de-sac leading to the house. Completely rural.

ST NICHOLAS. The S nave wall is old – unbuttressed, and presumably Norman. The S doorway is plain Norman, and there is one ogee-headed Dec lancet in this wall. Once again all the rest is effectively C19: W tower 1826, simple good Gothick, and the N aisle, mortuary chapel, tower arch, and ^{See} chancel windows, all by *Pugin*, 1844. The aisle is made to look ^{p.}₅₉₉ E.E., the chancel violently Dec, the chancel arch (a far cry from the 'True Principles') accurate and ornate Late Norman. Neo-Norman is almost unique in Pugin's work and must here be explained by the fact that traces of the original Norman chancel arch still existed. Evidence of this can still be seen at the back. The shallow recesses to the l. and r., as usual for nave altars, are also said to be partly original. The inside in fact has quite some character; for nothing Pugin did is completely dull. The contrast between the Norman chancel arch, the Dec chancel, the violent E.E. arcade, in the style of Walsoken, using Irish marble, and the excitable STAINED GLASS is highly effective. Pugin must have been trying to imitate a slow-growth medieval church. – PLATE. Paten 1717; Chalice and Paten of uncertain date, Danzig-made. – MONU-MENTS. Brass to Joan Adderley, dated 1487. Small kneeling figure, about 14 in. high, under an ogee niche (N side of chancel). She is unexpectedly commemorated on the chancel floor also, with a brass cross and inscription. – Sir Thomas

---

* There is no denying the fact that all evidence so far published points to a date in the 1680s for the introduction of sash-windows (NP).

49 Broderick † 1641 and his wife † 1678. The most worth-while thing in the church. Attributed to *Bushnell*,* and could well be by him. Sombre big inscription tablet in black marble, with two magnificent busts resting on the base. Sir Thomas, particularly in the treatment of hair and clothes, is as good as Bernini: the best thing of its date in the county. Brought from All Saints Wandsworth in 1900. – Viscount Midleton † 1836 by *Weekes*. Placid semi-reclining figure (a Georgian type) against a background of Perp tracery: Victorian portraiture fully arrived.

PEPER HAROW HOUSE. An unprepossessing example of *Sir William Chambers*'s careful academism. Built in 1765–8, a simple stock-brick cube of five by seven bays, compromised by later additions – a porch on the entrance side by *C. R. Cockerell*, 1843, and a N extension and a third storey above the cornice, added in 1913 (together, presumably, with the upper part of the porch, an ill-advised bit of neo-Baroque). This third storey confuses the effect irretrievably, and the house now looks both dull and muddled. Entrance (E) and W sides identical, the original parts of two storeys and five bays, with quoined three-bay centre slightly projecting, and Venetian windows on the ground floor of the other two bays: exasperatingly dumb. The S side of seven bays and completely plain. Inside, a small precise entrance hall, pilastered, with a characteristic frieze of rams'-heads and swags, statues of the Graces, and plaster casts. Beyond, an elegant simple iron staircase in a narrow well, top-lit by lunettes, with an iron tie like an arch on the landing. Two decorated rooms with plaster ceilings in the SE and SW corners of the house (former dining and drawing rooms). Both have elegant chimneypieces designed by *Chambers* and carved by *Wilton*. In the drawing room the main ceiling motif is a big central oval consisting of Greek key ornament with roses twined in and out of it; the dining-room ceiling has a lot of naturalistic painting, said to have been added by *Pugin* c.1840.

Complete set of outbuildings also by *Chambers*, 1762: also FARNHAM LODGE to the N with lunettes, EASHING LODGE to the SE with a pediment; octagonal DOVECOT near the house, with rusticated quoins and tiny lunette openings for the doves; and big three-sided STABLES, in many ways the most impressive of the C18 buildings here, the quadrangle closed by convex screen walls. The centre has a three-bay pediment

* On the basis of similarity to one of the Bushnell monuments at Chirk.

with single-bay sides. All quoined and all apparently stock-brick – in fact parts are Bargate stone cut to the size of bricks and matching the colour exactly (they also occur on Eashing Lodge). This ultimate, and probably extremely costly, snobbish elegance must have pleased Chambers a good deal.

The park was laid out by *Capability Brown* in 1762–3.* In the park a lumpish three-arch BRIDGE with iron balustrade, built in 1813. Beyond to the SW is OXENFORD, and a strange collection of buildings. Oxenford was first a medieval dependency of Waverley and then the original site of Peper Harow House. Walling of two dates remains, made into an attractive ruin but without any detail except a very bogus-looking Dec window, of accurate style but in suspiciously good condition. Three lights with a cusped roundel above. In addition there is OXENFORD LODGE, presumably by *Chambers*, another building with imitation stock bricks, a big C17 brick farmhouse, OXENFORD GRANGE, and two farm buildings designed by *Pugin* in 1843, a BARN and a GATEHOUSE, which are among his best buildings, a proof that for him, at least some of the time, medieval architecture was not simply an -ism but a complete method of design.

The barn is six bays long, of angular uncompromising Gothic, like a tithe barn, the central gabled entrance using the simplest form of arch without capitals, and no Revival trimmings at all. The gatehouse has a big gable, with two windows side by side in it, a pyramidal turret and a bellcote, and more of these angular arches. The connexion with the C19 structural Gothicists is clear (particularly with Butterfield's first masterpiece, the lychgate of 1844 at Coalpit Heath), and show Pugin as a much more profound architect than such things, however brilliant, as his décor for the Houses of Parliament. The connexion with Nash, or at least with Picturesque theory, is also clear, for the whole group is now a picturesque set-piece with weeping willows and a pond. Did the duality by any chance go far enough to make Pugin arrange the ruin mentioned above in what he would castigate in others as the worst kind of C18 superficiality? It has been attributed to him, but there is no documentary evidence. (½ m. NE, BONVILLE SPRING HOUSE, a charming 'holy well' by *Pugin*, inside a polygonal chamber. In poor condition at the time of writing. NT)

* Brown was also consulted over the house, but his designs were not accepted (J. Harris).

PEPER HAROW FARM. Simple, pretty C17 farmhouse, L-shaped, tile-hung above a stone ground floor. Attached to it the best collection of FARM BUILDINGS in the county. SE of the farm is a medium-size tiled barn, and further E a complete quadrangle of buildings the size of a college quad. In the NW corner of this is a very good tiled and tarred weatherboarded barn, with half-hipped roof ends, probably the best of a common Surrey type. Along the N side a complete terrace of cottages in Bargate stone, on the E and S sides single-storey terraced stables and pig-sties, with a square mid-C18 red brick dovecote W of the farmyard
7 entrance. In the middle of the quad a GRANARY, probably of c.1600, the style and dimensions of a good-size market hall. Tile-hung above, with few windows, and open below, resting on twenty-five wooden pillars, four bays on each side. One of the best vernacular buildings in the South of England.

PETERSHAM

ST PETER. A church of uncommon charm, lying along a path off the main road. Chancel of the late C13 with one N window, a cusped lancet. Nave and W tower of red brick, probably C17. The tower has battlements and a pretty octagonal lantern. A N transept was added in the C18, a long S transept in 1840 by one *Meakin*. They are of brick with arched windows. The
62 interior is well preserved in its pre-Victorian state. – FONT on baluster stem, C18. (It is signed '*John Long* fecit 1797'. M. R. Airs) – BOX PEWS, GALLERIES in the transept. – Two-decker PULPIT, C18, with iron handrail to the steps. – READING DESK, raised and corresponding to the pulpit. – PLATE. Silver-gilt Cup 1562; Cup and Paten 1570; two silver-gilt Patens 1663, 1696; Flagon 1740; Paten 1760. – MONUMENT. George Cole and his wife and their grandson George Cole, 1624. Stiffly reclining effigies. Recess flanked by columns, its shallow arch coffered. In the 'predella' the small kneeling figure of the grandson. – (In the churchyard, gravestone of Albert Henry Scott † 1864 by his father *Sir G. G. Scott*. NT)

ALL SAINTS, Bute Avenue. 1907–8 by *John Kelly*. The gift of Mrs Lionel Warde. A large, very red church, brick and red terracotta. The mixture is Waterhousish, the style emphatically Italian Early Christian or Romanesque. Round-arched windows etc. and a tall S campanile. Faced and decorated with various marbles inside. Also an octagonal baptistery with ambulatory, a separate church hall, and an institute.

Petersham, for its small size, is exceptionally rich in fine houses of the late C17 and C18. They lie close together at a sharp bend of the main road, and traffic makes it almost impossible to see them. When the houses were built, the main road did not run here. ⟨On the s side, much recent private housing, mostly mediocre, has been allowed, but nothing has been done about the traffic.⟩ Coming from Richmond or from the church one finds them as follows. Immediately after the path to the church PETERSHAM HOUSE, late C17 front with a charming semi-circular domed early C19 porch with Ionic columns. Of the same time the addition of the top storey. Excellent staircase with strong twisted balusters and mythological wall paintings of c.1710 by *Laguerre*. Three excellent fireplaces of c.1775. Excellent wrought-iron gates and railings. Opposite RESTON LODGE of the early C19. Five bays, two and a half storeys, stuccoed, with a porch of two pairs of Tuscan columns. Cast-iron gates with thick ornament. Then MONTROSE HOUSE, early C18. This is of yellow and red brick, the original centre five bays wide. Brick quoins. Segment-headed, slender windows. Aprons below the first-floor windows. Two-storeyed attachments. Roman Doric porch.

Opposite Montrose House RUTLAND LODGE. Built in 1666 for a Lord Mayor of London and altered and heightened c.1720, an exquisite example of the style of its time. Seven bays and two storeys plus an attic storey above the cornice. The windows are slender and vertically laced together. Beautiful doorway, broad, with a segmental pediment on Roman Doric pilasters placed in front of a rusticated background. The railings of the front garden form a semicircle. Fine gates. The house was gutted by fire in 1967, and the interior completely destroyed. It is now being converted into flats. Inside was a staircase with coved ceiling and noble plasterwork of c.1740. Slender balusters, three to the tread, and carved tread-ends. The drawing room had a glorious big Rococo cartouche above the fireplace.

Rutland Lodge is at the corner of RIVER LANE, which bends down to the river. Set back from the road, two modern houses by *L. Manasseh*, 1964–7. The smaller one, COURTYARDS, has an internal court; the larger, DRUM HOUSE, is of one and two storeys, L-shaped, with roof terraces. Large semicircular projection at one end (containing a swimming pool). Further on a few more worthwhile houses, especially PETERSHAM LODGE of c.1740, irregular, but with a fine pediment with Rococo decoration towards the garden. In the garden a ROTUNDA. The house was built by the Duchess of Queensberry. *Soane* was responsible for repairs and decorations in 1781. Another good house in River Lane is the MANOR HOUSE. Early C18. Five bays, two storeys, segment-headed windows. Fine doorway with attached Ionic columns, a carved frieze, and a segmental pediment. This is a later introduction.

Further on in PETERSHAM ROAD yet two more houses, before Ham is reached. They are Gort House and Douglas House. GORT HOUSE is of the early C18, seven bays wide and of two storeys. Its side turns into SUDBROOK LANE and is now called GORT LODGE. The doorway here has a charming frieze curving up in the middle. In the same lane one or two more good if less spectacular houses, particularly HARRINGTON LODGE of *c.*1700 with a segmental pediment. At the end of Sudbrook Lane the entrance to the Golf Club, whose enviable club house is *James Gibbs's* SUDBROOK PARK, built in 1726 for the Duke of Argyll and Greenwich. Nine bays, brick and stone dressings. Basement, main and upper storey. Slender segment-headed windows with aprons. Brick quoins, parapet. The main accent on the garden as well as the entrance side a giant portico of Corinthian columns with frieze and raised balustrade. This projects only slightly in front of the façade, so that the space behind the columns is actually a loggia. On the entrance side the effect has been spoiled by an extension forward of the portico. On the garden side splendid open stair towards the entrance, starting in two flights parallel with the façade and then joining up into one. The plan is curious. The centre is a cube room which runs through from front to back portico. The other rooms open out from it, and on the upper floor have to be reached from the small staircases. The cube room is luxuriously decorated. Giant coupled pilasters, coved ceiling, marble fireplace, doorways with very finely designed heads and pediment – Gibbs at his most Baroque.

Back into Petersham Road. (In Hazel Lane, THE OLD HOUSE (Whornes Place), a timber-framed house built in 1487 at Cuxton, Kent, for Sir William Whornes, Lord Mayor of London, and re-erected here in 1925.*) Then, to end with, DOUGLAS HOUSE, which lies by the E drive to Ham House, overlooking it. Built *c.*1700, yellow and red brick, five bays and two storeys, with hipped roof and one-bay pediment. The doorway frieze curving up in the middle and a segmental

* Mr N. G. W. Marsh kindly drew our attention to this.

pediment on brackets. Big stable block on the r., with projecting wings, a hipped roof, and a pedimented one-bay centre.

PICKHURST see CHIDDINGFOLD

PIERREPONT

8040

½ m. NE of Frensham

Formidable medium-size house by *Norman Shaw*, on top of a
sandy bluff. Built in 1876, one of a chain of houses in which he
moved from the standard mid-Victorian product to his own
personal and picturesque style of the 1880s. Here the main
block is still half-timbered – none of it structural – on a stone
ground floor, but the service quarters are intricate and tile-
hung. It is hard to believe they were designed at the same time
by the same man. Five-gabled entrance front to the N, slightly
V-shaped for effect. The s side is quite asymmetrical, with the
great hall prominent at one end and a big oriel on the returned
side just as at Merrist Wood (*see* p. 540). The inside planned on
a huge scale but insensitively detailed. Most rooms and the
staircase open off one spine corridor. The biggest room is the
great hall, with tall collar-braced roof and central louvre. Some
of the original decoration of leather panels survives – in a small
room at the s end of the corridor, for example – and a couple of
fireplaces. One of them, in a room to the r. of the entrance, is
very fine, a deep angle recess like a small room in itself, leather
panels above and tiles below, all dark green, dark blue, and
gold – as rich and effective as the William Morris room in the
Victoria and Albert Museum.

PIRBRIGHT

9050

A scattered village near Woking. It only developed in the C19,
around a huge green which is really a wedge of the surrounding
heathland.

ST MICHAEL. Rebuilt in 1784. Very pretty Georgian, minuscule
detailing. Red and grey brick nave with rubbed heads to the
big windows, and a tower of sarsens, round-headed windows,
battlements, and a spike, with the stone all galletted (i.e. tiny
dark pebbles inserted in the mortar between the dressed stones)
to make the effect even prettier. The chancel was like this,
too, but was alas gothicized for the worse in the C19: it would
be an act of charity to make it classical again. Inside, one

Doric post-and-lintel arcade and a big L-shaped gallery fitting round it, all very domestic – again ruined by the chancel. – PLATE. Chalice 1654.

PIRBRIGHT LODGE. Stuccoed and veranda'd three-bay Regency house with very suave rounded ends. Who did it?

CATTLE TESTING STATION, Bullswater Common. Straightforward modern blocks, including a boiler house with a parabolic shell concrete vault, by *Bryan Westwood*, 1955–6.

PIRBRIGHT CAMP. The Guards' training depot, mostly self-effacing early C20 blocks among a lot of trees: an object lesson to later military buildings in neatness and landscaping.

Three EARTH CIRCLES, E of Baker's Gate Farm, Bullswater Common, may be Late Bronze Age hut circles (but *see* Chilworth).

PITCH PLACE *see* WORPLESDON

PIXHAM *see* DORKING

1050   POLESDEN LACEY
1 m. S of Great Bookham

The original house was medieval. The second house, built in 1631, was bought by Sheridan, the playwright. He called it 'the nicest place, within a prudent distance of town, in England'. That is still fair comment; there are unspoilt grounds all round and a fine view S across a valley to the crest of the North Downs. This house was replaced by a simple Grecian villa built by *Joseph Bonsor* under the supervision of *Thomas Cubitt* in 1824, and extended and entirely refitted inside by *Ambrose Poynter* in 1906. Its character is now entirely Edwardian, and, be it said, some of the most attractive Edwardian in the country. Cubitt's building consisted of six bays in the centre of the present S front, with an octastyle Ionic colonnade in front – an attractive, impressionistic style far more concerned with atmosphere than accuracy. Poynter extended this one bay to the W and three bays to the E, and converted the house into a quadrangle with a symmetrical E-shaped entrance front* facing E, with a cupola behind, an asymmetrical W front, and a simple open internal courtyard with an apsidal end. All the

---

* The Doric columns from the original entrance portico were set up in the garden at the E end of the Long Terrace. There is now also an ENTRANCE ARCH by *Sir Hugh Casson*, 1958.

elevations are two-storeyed, buff-stuccoed, and unpretentious, with the join of old and new work invisible, and the result is as comfortable and as natural as a Voysey house. The interiors are eclectic and of varying quality. The HALL and STAIRCASE are poor mock-Jacobean, but incorporate the former REREDOS from Wren's St Matthew Friday Street, in the City, demolished in 1881. It fills one wall and serves as an overmantel: big and big-scale, the centre with a segmental pediment, the sides with straight tops and swags over modern doors. Very big-boned carving, not Gibbons's style, with a fine sweep to it – the central cherub's head, e.g. – and the best Wren-style woodwork in the county. Very skilfully fitted in. The fireplace it encloses has a little C17 woodwork remaining from the pre-Cubitt house. The two main rooms face S: the DRAWING ROOM behind the Cubitt colonnade, and the LIBRARY adjoining to the E. Both are successful, but of wildly differing character. The Drawing Room is a sumptuous mock-Louis-Quatorze confection in white, gold, and red with wall mirrors, ornate pilasters, and imported French Rococo fireplaces and Italian ceiling paintings. It is a double revival – for this is exactly the style of the Apsley House and Windsor Castle interiors of the 1820s – done with superb skill and taste. For us, the style is now valid in its own right as an expression of the last few years before the Great War. The Library is much cooler, with a rhythm of coupled Ionic pilasters with alternate lunettes and deep square recesses between. Again expertly done, with the recesses acting as spatial joists, as it were, fixing and defining the spatial character. Painted white, with a fine orange carpet, here obviously a deliberate architectural effect.

POYLE*

2 m. N of Staines

Along the straggling main street of the village a few cottages, half-timbered or of brick, for example THE HOLLIES, and a house 60 yds further N.

(CONGREGATIONAL CHAPEL. 1823. Brick, with small turrets.)

(POYLE MANOR HOUSE. C18, incorporating earlier work. Brick, of two storeys. Inside, staircase and panelling of c.1700, probably not all *in situ*.)

(POYLE COUNTY INFANTS' SCHOOL, Rodney Way, N of Bath Road. 1969–70. One of two prototype schemes in the MACE

* Formerly in Middlesex.

constructional method, designed by the County Architect's
Department in association with the MACE development
group.)

Bath Road leads to COLNBROOK END, on the Buckinghamshire
border. Here is KING JOHN'S HOUSE, c.1600, with plastered
front and a tall carriageway. TAN HOUSE FARM, E of the
bridge, is a pretty whitewashed brick group by the mill stream.
For the rest of Colnbrook see The Buildings of England:
Buckinghamshire.

POYLE, near Tongham, see TONGHAM

PRIOR'S FIELD see PUTTENHAM

PURLEY

1½ m. s of Croydon

3060

See (ST JOHN THE BAPTIST (R.C.), Dale Road. Nave 1939 by E. J.
p.   Walters, N and S chapels 1958 by Walters & Kerr Bate. DE)
599
(KENLEY STATION, Godstone Road, dates from the building of
the Caterham line in 1856.)

WATERWORKS, Brighton Road. Sober, round-arched design.
Dated 1901, but looks fifty years earlier.

RUSSELL HILL SCHOOLS. See Croydon, p. 184.

WOODCOTE. See p. 537.

PUTTENDEN MANOR see LINGFIELD

PUTTENHAM

9040

One long village street in a pretty situation just s of the Hog's
Back. It lies on the exact dividing line between chalk and sandstone, so the cottages use both, with a lot of demure C18 brickwork also.

ST JOHN BAPTIST. Medieval details merged into a thorough
restoration of 1861 by Woodyer, who at least provided some
new character in exchange for the old – naughty triangular
dormers on the N side, e.g. The inside still keeps plastered
walls and a pleasant village appearance. C12 features of various
dates, including one very renewed window on the S side, and
the four-bay N arcade, c.1160, of the same handsome, large-
scale type as Compton or Great Bookham. Round piers, square

scalloped capitals, unchamfered arches with crimped plaster-work surrounds (cf. Compton and Worplesdon). The oddest thing about the arcade is that the bases rise from bay to bay as if the floor had originally been kept as an incline. S doorway a little later, perhaps c.1170, still with scalloped capitals but with a curious, unusual decoration of the scallops, and still with a round-headed arch. The arch mouldings however are complex, deeply cut, and include keeling – the same type as Ash but a little earlier. Chancel arch a little later still, c.1200, with simple imposts and a pointed arch with a chamfered inner order with unmoulded soffit and outer order of complex section. The two-bay N chancel arcade takes the story into the early C13. Simple unmoulded arches, the responds square but the central pier bearing a crude edition of the familiar Surrey circular capital. The chancel has mainly Perp windows, badly renewed, the westernmost of three lights with one lower than the other two to form a low-side window. C15 tower, patched with brick, the same type as Worplesdon but terribly restored. N chancel chapel partly rebuilt in brick in 1770. – PULPIT, LECTERN, etc. All eclectic Comper-style, part Classical and part Gothic, by *Randoll Blacking*, 1936. – (STAINED GLASS. E window of the N chapel by *Hardman*. – W window 1874, de-signed by the Rev. *Charles Kerry*, curate of Puttenham (R. Hubbuck). – PLATE. Cup, 1686; Paten, 1674; brass Almsdish, German, (?) C16.) – BRASS (chancel floor). Edward Cranford, rector, c.1430. In priest's vestments; 20 in. high.

PUTTENHAM PRIORY, S of the church. A handsome pattern-book builder's house of 1762. The main front faces W. Five bays and two and a half storeys, faced with golden stucco in a very good imitation of stone. Bold central three-bay pediment on Adamesque capitals, i.e. capitals fluted with vestigal leaves at the bottom (very up-to-date for 1762), Ionic doorcase, the attic storey above with ball finials. There are not many of these provincial Palladian houses in Surrey, and this would be a good example for any county. Inside, handsome simple staircase with iron balustrade in a narrow well returning to a landing, which forms a gallery above the entrance. Doric columns below supporting the landing, Ionic columns on the landing itself, a little very simple plasterwork on the ceiling – a nice indication of the range of a local mason.

Opposite the W end of the church is GREYS HOME FARM, vernacular C18 with good weatherboarded barns. Immediately to the W again another set of barns, L-shaped, and including a long tarred weatherboarded range ending in four oasthouses, a rarity in the county. GREYS, further N, by *Forsyth & Maule*, 1912. E of the church first the RECTORY, picturesque Tudor by *John Perry* of Godalming, and then HURLANDS of 1898, the last country house of *Philip Webb*. A disappointment – an almost styleless jumble of brick and tile-hanging without any of the forceful rhythm of his late work such as Standen, Sussex. ½ m. SE of this, and nearer Compton village than Puttenham, is PRIOR'S FIELD, formerly Prior's Garth.* This was built in 1900 by *Voysey* and was a simple rectangular block with a plain hipped roof. Soon afterwards it was turned into an experimental school by Mrs Leonard Huxley, and was altered by *T. Muntzer*, Voysey's pupil, who added the big three-and-a-half-storey central gable and nearly symmetrical side gables to the garden front, and was responsible for most of the buildings round the courtyard. The insipid laboratory building on the road frontage was added after Muntzer's death. Additional classrooms were built to the N by *Brandon-Jones & Ashton* in 1964. *Gertrude Jekyll* was consulted on the planning of the garden, unfortunately spoilt recently by a new bungalow.

(LASCOMBE, ½ m. SW, is an inexpensive *Lutyens* house of 1894–6, of rough plaster on a brick plinth. Attractive forecourt with the porch coming forward at a diagonal next to a projecting gable and a massive chimney. Well-preserved interior, particularly the staircase, with a 'landing-room' diagonally over the porch. All internal details already classical. Pretty lodge. Originally a *Jekyll* garden. NT)

SHOELANDS, 1 m. W. Very restored, but keeps one central two-storey gable and porch of brick, dated 1616 or 1618. Contemporary staircase inside.

GREYFRIARS. See p. 267.

FROWSBURY. The bowl BARROW on the golf course has not been improved by the erection of a flagstaff and stone commemorating Queen Victoria's visit in 1857.

PYRFORD

1½ m. E of Woking

A genuine village – not even a preserved one – in watery fields near the Wey, equidistant from Woking and Byfleet. Barely a village centre, just a few honest brick cottages loosely grouped

* Mr J. Brandon Jones kindly helped to revise this account.

near the church. Pyrford Common to the N is pleasant and un-affected heathland suburbia. ⟨This part is increasingly being developed as a commuter area.⟩

ST NICHOLAS. As unexpected as the village: a humble, un-altered Norman church, built of puddingstone with dressings of clunch, stuccoed over.* Later shingled bell-turret with broach-spire. Norman windows in the N side of the chancel and, at the odd W end, which has one big central buttress, a Norman window on either side of it, close in. Apparently all original. The buttress must be Perp, but the two windows call for a buttress, and so it may replace a flat Norman one. Norman also the plain S doorway and the more elaborate N doorway. Big in scale, and abstract – jamb-shafts, simple capitals (one scalloped, one with plain leaves), and one order of zigzag. The E window is C14, the N porch simple C16 half-timbered work. The inside is as demure as the outside. Plain, low, one-step Norman chancel arch, simple bell-turret framing, simple fittings. Attractive, though possibly the Surrey traveller over-rates it because of its rarity. The C19 architect to whose charity we owe this should be recorded: *Sir T. G. Jackson*, who restored the church in 1869. – PULPIT. Dated 1628. Geometrical patterns on the sides (as in the very battered example at Byfleet), Jacobean detail only on the tester. –⟨ WALL PAINT-ING, S wall of nave. Simple outline drawings, identified as the Flagellation and another scene from the Passion, *c.*1200. Beneath these, some of them only revealed in 1967, earlier paintings in solid colour, of horsemen, perhaps a Psychoma-chia, and a mysterious procession of men carrying staves. – STAINED GLASS, E window. Quatrefoil with Trinity, C14.⟩ – PLATE. Cup 1570; Paten and Flagon C17.

⟨CHURCH OF THE GOOD SHEPHERD. By *David Nye*, 1963–4. T-shaped plan, with steeply pitched roof. – STAINED GLASS, S transept by *M. Traherne* (cf. Salfords).⟩

All the buildings at Pyrford are scattered. ½ m. E of the church, by the river, is Pyrford Green, with PYRFORD PLACE, a nonde-script house with a heavy, square late C17 SUMMER HOUSE in the garden. N of this is first the WAIFS AND STRAYS HOME, now Rowley Bristow Orthopaedic Hospital, built in 1907 by *E. J. May*.‡ Half-Lutyens, half-Voysey, and half as attractive as its Academy elevations. N again is THE OLD HOUSE, a typical early C18 Surrey façade with the proportions unusually good.

* Now partly worn away.
‡ Damaged by fire, 1970.

Five by three bays, with string courses between storeys and recessed panels above. Authentic details (small-paned window e.g.), and in good condition. Comparison with the same thing done without care (e.g. at 25 London Street Chertsey) is instructive. ⟨The façade, however, is a casing of an earlier building. Inside are two fireplaces with four-centred arches, one dated 1604. One of the chimneys has diagonally set stacks in the Tudor tradition. Upstairs there is a priest's hole between two chimneystacks. The back wing is probably at least partly C17.⟩ To the w of this, on Pyrford Common, *Voysey* built a house called VODIN, now Little Court, fronting Old Woking Road. Dated 1902 with stable buildings of 1904, forming a courtyard which, although quite informal, is crisp and positive because of Voysey's architectural integrity and respect for mass and solidity. That none of his imitators had this can be seen well enough from the other houses around. The house itself is a single long block with a steep roof (tile instead of Voysey's favourite slates), the entrance door in an arched recess balanced by a gable, the corners with sloping buttresses, the garden side without any accent.

87

Between Pyrford Common and the church, PYRFORD COURT is very expensive Neo-Georgian, done in both house and stables with a good deal of panache. The original house by *Clyde Young*, c.1910, the additions between the wars designed by the former owner, *Lord Iveagh*.

Finally, s of Pyrford, by the river, is the ruin of Newark Priory (*see* p. 380), and beyond it was NEWARK MILL or PYRFORD MILL, the best of the Surrey weatherboarded buildings, early C19, T-shaped with a huge gambrel or mansard roof and a hoist at one end. It was burnt to the ground in 1966, one of the most regrettable recent losses in the county. Near by, the MILL HOUSE survives, a plain early C19 house, with, inside, an unexpected and delightful staircase curving up to an oval landing lit by a small circular roof-light towards the far end.

8

RAMSNEST COMMON *see* CHIDDINGFOLD

1050

RANMORE COMMON
1 m. NW of Dorking

On top of the Downs, and still remote in bad weather, though not on a summer Sunday. A 'long green' of the same type as those high up in the Chilterns, with few houses around it. First-rate views s, with the same headlong foreground that makes Box Hill so impressive.

ST BARTHOLOMEW. *Sir George Gilbert Scott* or one of his assistants at his best. Built in 1859 for Thomas Cubitt's son. The church is hard and competent, and makes no attempt to achieve anything but a C19 effect. Cruciform, with octagonal central tower, hard firm masses, and hard C13-derived detail. It is faced entirely with cobbles, i.e. round flints, not cemented over. The central tower and spire are particularly successful, especially the dormers above the belfry. They are not at all pretty or graceful, but neither were the Early Gothic originals. Scott's knobbly detail could define volume but not space; hence the heavy interior, a period piece, becomes merely a collection of applied details. However, these are often superb – 'a certain horrid splendour' says the MHLG – especially under the vaulted crossing, with multiple marble shafts and big well-carved naturalistic capitals, not held together by an inner tension as C13 capitals are but spilling over in a vegetable riot: the cornucopia of Progress. All the fittings are to match. The best is the FONT, in maroon and black marble, C13 in style but wholly C19 in inspiration. A dark, grand, moving piece. (There are also a PULPIT of variegated alabaster on fluted white marble columns, a rich REREDOS, and much STAINED GLASS by *Clayton & Bell*. P. F. Anson)

Immediately NE of the church SCHOOLS and former RECTORY, also presumably by *Scott*, the schools quite a clever piece of asymmetry, the Rectory just dull. Of DENBIES, the swagger Italianate house which the famous builder *Thomas Cubitt* designed and built for himself in 1849, only the stables remain; the rest was demolished in 1954. It stood looking s on the very top of the ridge, probably in an attempt to out-face Deepdene, which was clearly visible to the SE beyond Dorking town.

REDHILL

Reigate's plebeian twin, which developed when first the Brighton road (1807) and then the Brighton railway (1841) ran side by side through what had previously been open country. It now has over 20,000 people, and is a perfect repository for common or garden architecture of the last hundred years, in all styles.

ST JOHN, s of the town centre, on a breezy common. Flint aisles by *Ford & Hesketh*, 1867, re-used by *Pearson* in 1889–95, when he built a new nave and chancel and a towering mock-Midlands s w tower, a stock-brick paraphrase of Grantham. Inside, vaulted chancel with big eclectic iron screen in front, also by *Pearson*. The nave is formidable, with a giant order embracing the earlier arcade and the added clerestory, roofed with transverse stone bows combined with a kingpost roof. The effect much bolder than the usual late Pearson church. – (FONT. 1882 by *J. Whitehead*. A gross angel with scallop shell. NT)

ST MATTHEW, Station Road. 1866, apparently by one *Hähn*. A very spiky performance. Firestone body with gabled dormers and a free-standing Bargate stone broached spire, the contrast in texture and colour quite exciting. However, all hopes are dashed by the thin interior.

(ST JOSEPH (R.C.), High Street. 1898 by *A. E. Purdie*. DE)

ROYAL EARLSWOOD HOSPITAL. The old building 1853 by *W. B. Moffatt*, the partner of Sir George Gilbert Scott. Immense Jacobean with a central tower. Not nice. ⟨The first phase of redevelopment, the STAFF RECREATION CENTRE, a long low brick building with triangular roof lights, by *Richard Mellor* of the *South West Metropolitan Region Hospital Board*, was built in 1962–3 and extended in 1967–8. This was followed by low-density villas and a school, 1965–8.⟩

A lot of Redhill is surprisingly early – pre-1850 – such as the big classical houses in LINKFIELD LANE, NW of the centre, and one stock-brick terrace – Nos. 1–10 LADBROKE ROAD, near the station – which is still Georgian-derived and looks like a straight import from Brixton or Camberwell. The main buildings are around the Brighton Road–A25 crossroads. None are of architectural value, all are very typical. One is still effectively Georgian, the STRICT BAPTIST CHAPEL in Station Road, 1858, a plain classical front with good lettering. No foundation plate – a revealing touch; Nonconformity was still humble. Then comes the MARKET HALL, at the NE corner of the crossroads. Of 1860, architect unknown. Standard commercial Jacobean. Diagonally across from it, the WHEATSHEAF is sub-Norman Shaw of 1900. The c20 is represented by the ODEON, beside the railway, 1938 by *Andrew Mather*, all glazed tiles, white above and black below, with sweeping rounded ends; and modern architecture by the CROWN OFFICE, London Road, by *E. H. Banks*, 1958.

Apart from St John's church the only building worth a special visit in Redhill is on the Brighton Road, ½ m. s of the centre.

This is THE FIRS, a suave Regency-style house with two bow
windows, built probably as late as 1830. In 1936 *Basil Ward* of
Connell, Ward & Lucas added an uncompromising modern
wing approximately the size of the older house; a very early
and very brave case of not 'keeping in keeping' and one which
was ahead of most continental practice at the time. Two
horizontal bands of windows, a vertical glazed stair-well with a
typical roof garden and canopy above, and a pattern of cantilevered larders to each flat. Perfect counterpoint between old
and new, for example in the very careful but not servile relation
of roof-lines, and the graded recession from the old to the new
via the stair-well. Restored in 1960, when the larders were
given little pitched roofs, an extraordinary thing to do.

Round the corner in Mill Street is No. 4, roguishly called THE
FIRKIN, a complete *Connell, Ward & Lucas* house. This was
a bloody-minded white cube – concrete plus a white brick
chimney – with big first-floor balcony and chunky stair-wells,
reacting from the polished simplicity of houses like Corbusier's
Villa Stein at Garches. ⟨It has recently been given a skin of
yellow brick and weatherboarding, and all its bloody-mindedness has gone.⟩

REIGATE

2050

A characterless little town in the middle of the county, with the
typical Surrey mixture of poor original buildings, and alternate
vandalism and gentility in rebuilding (cf. Dorking, Epsom,
Leatherhead). The main street runs W–E with the former
market place, the only accent the Old Town Hall of 1728,
free-standing at one end in almost the same position as in the
better known high street of Amersham, Bucks. Immediately E
of this is the main cross roads, and on the London road to the N
is Reigate's one notable townscape feature – a tunnel cut in
1824 under the mound on which the castle stands, which
pitchforked the southbound traveller suddenly into the middle
of the town, the effect achieved so dramatically at Salzburg.
Now, ironically, one-way working ensures that only the north-
ward traveller out of Reigate uses the tunnel, and it loses most
of its effectiveness. This could be re-arranged, and ought to be. *See p. 599*
Otherwise it is fair comment to say that Redhill, despite its
modernity and complete lack of architectural value, has more
to offer in the way of honest character than Reigate's conglo-
meration of old and olde.

ST MARY, SE of the town centre, on a slight hill, the same

relative position as at Godstone. Big, the standard type of South-East England town church – nave without clerestory and wide, separately roofed aisles. A bad job outside. The detail is nearly all new, mostly by *Woodyer* in 1845, but also *George Gilbert Scott Jun.* in 1877–81. From the outside effectively all Perp – tower, aisles, chancel chapels early C15, two-storeyed NE vestry built as a vestry *c.*1513 (a brass plate in the chancel commemorates a benefaction in this year). The s aisle windows are three-light Perp with panel tracery. The s chapel is Dec (cf. the PISCINA and a recess with ogee arches inside), the windows renewed. The tower was refaced in Bath stone by *Scott* and wears an untrustworthy Cotswold look, but in fact most of the detail represents original work.

All this gives no indication of the chief interest of the church, the unexpectedly noble arcades of *c.*1200, still intact in a typically restored and thumbed-over interior. They were in fact rebuilt stone for stone by *Scott*. They were begun at the s w end directly under the influence of the new-built choir of Canterbury of 1175–80 and the Canterbury school,[*] and continued in a more normally English stiff-leaf way. Their details are always large-scale and assured. The piers are octagonal, round, and in one case quatrefoil, as if meant for Purbeck shafts (cf. again Canterbury), a very suave shape. The capitals show every variety of foliage, just beginning to lose Romanesque rigidity; not yet even that first angular striving which is called stiff-leaf, simply a disciplined regular movement, a windblown ripple round the capital, with the impression of growing radially out of the stone. Still also close-patterned and curly. The carving is good rather than great, but certainly worth a special visit in a lean county. One very strange thing about the arcades is that the piers are nowhere exactly in line across the nave. The reason may be that the new aisles were built around the walls of the Norman nave, which was not demolished until they were complete. The s arcade has two hollow chamfers with a keeled roll-moulding set into one and again ornamented with leaves. The N arcade, slightly later, has the simplest pattern of two chamfered orders. To the E this arcade of the early C13 was continued in the C14. The break is clearly visible in the foliage of the easternmost s pier, of which the w half was the old respond whereas the E half belongs to the new style. On the N side the two easternmost arches and the easternmost pier are C14. The arches of both

* One of the capitals has a twin at New Shoreham.

arcades die into their new E responds. The S chancel chapel is also C14 – see the PISCINA and the SEDILIA recess with ogee arches. The rest is Perp, except for the late C13 N aisle W window (two lights with bar tracery; spherical triangle in the head). Perp tower arch, three orders with shafts. Perp chancel arcades, the standard four-shaft-four-hollow pattern. – SCREEN. Straightforward Perp, with long, thin bays (six-bays-plus-door to the N chapel, eight-bays-plus-door to the chancel and S chapel). Terribly restored. – The REREDOS was C14, restored to destruction in 1845. – PISCINA and SEDILIA. Thin C14 with ogee canopies, hardened and then gilded to look purely C19. – (SCULPTURE. Anglo-Saxon fragment with interlace.) – STAINED GLASS. E window by *L. Lobe* of Tours, 1851. – PLATE. Spoon Strainer 1710, 'being originally intended for removing obstructions from the mouth of a teapot'. – MONUMENTS. Several Rococo cartouches skied in the tower. – A dismembered and reassembled collection of Jacobean monuments, nothing out of the ordinary run. Sir Thomas Bludden † 1618 and wife, N chapel, under canopy. – Richard Elyot † 1608 and son, recumbent, originally under an elaborate canopy (a figure now on the E wall of the S chapel was connected with this). – Kathleen Elyot † 1623, in the sedilia of the S chapel. Straightforward, competent figure, with the rest of the monument gone. – Finally, and a great relief after so much low quality and such mangled remains, Richard Ladbroke † 1730 in the N transept, signed by *Joseph Rose the Elder*. A towering, three-part composition with Justice and Truth flanking the reclining figure in Roman dress, all in a rich but restrained surround of polychrome marble. The centre is a huge broken and split Corinthian pediment. Very much in the style of Green of Camberwell, even to the flecks of gold heightening the solidity of the figures. Very high quality, especially the humane, unaffected face of Ladbroke; not in the least academic, and completely overcoming the disadvantage of the Roman dress (compare especially with the average Scheemakers monument). These high-quality Baroque designs suddenly produced by dozens of native sculptors are one of the most unexpected high-water marks of English art. Typically, as with Crutcher at Bletchingley, Rose is almost unknown and we have record of only one other monument of his. He became bankrupt in 1735. Historically, it belongs to the generation after Bletchingley, with the handling more assured, especially in the architectural frame, but the emotional level lower.

In the CHURCHYARD, two revealing studies of C19 senti-ment. NE of the church, the Masseres Tomb, dated 1825 and signed by *James Colecom* of Reigate. 10-ft obelisk with dull Grecian scenes round the base, and sickly carving which has just ceased to be crisp in the Wedgwood way. – S of this is Rebecca Waterlow † 1869 by *Samuel Ruddock** of Pimlico: the more demonstrative grief of the mid C19, and actually in this case more acceptable too. Two angels guard a sarcophagus on an enormous Egyptian base. The extraordinary thing is that there are four splendidly detailed copper urns at the corners, still in what one could also call the Wedgwood tradition of industrial design, i.e. crisp, and respecting the material.

ST MARK. *See* p. 431.

ST PETER, Dover's Green. On the edge of a depressing council estate S of the town. 1955 by *E. F. Starling*, a good idea spoilt in the details. Elliptical, and divided into church and hall, each approximately semicircular, by movable screens. The tops of the screens are made of glass, so that in either half one is spatially aware of the other, and also, via the curved walls, of the shape of the church as a whole.‡ Functionally, however, this kind of plan has its drawbacks. The elliptical drum is faced with flint, the clerestory above is brick, the details terribly fussy – e.g. random brick panels set into the flint outside, and the conflict of brick, concrete mullions, and acoustic panels inside. – (STAINED GLASS by *P. Fourmaintreaux*.)

REIGATE CASTLE. Immediately N of the High Street, forming a strange oasis in the middle of the town, for the top of the motte is on a level with the roof tops of the houses below. It is in an intense public rose-garden, and this creates a strange effect of out-of-place luxuriance that is both surreal and Pre-Raphaelite. No original masonry remains, simply a large C11 motte and bailey, and a sham gatehouse made up in 1777 from what stones remained: a poor little ivy-covered affair.

REIGATE PRIORY. Opposite the castle, on the other side of the High Street. Founded in 1235 for Augustinian Canons, granted in 1541 to Lord Howard of Effingham by Henry VIII, and converted into a Tudor house. Of this there is only the re-mains of a big mullioned and transomed window – of five lights at least – with depressed arches at the heads of the lights as well as below the transom. This is on the first floor, at r. angles to

* Information from E. J. Skevington.
‡ The same effect is achieved in a much more sophisticated way by Gsaenger's Matthäuskirche in Munich, 1953.

the main axis of the building. To the Tudor house also belongs some corbelled-out wall jutting into the dining room. From the outside everything now looks late C18; for the whole building was disguised under weak Late Palladian stucco elevations in 1779 – and embellished with terracotta figures and the arms of Elizabeth I in 1835.* The former stables to the N were joined to the house in 1895 and are simple late Artisan work, perhaps of c.1670 – brick, hipped roof, and coved eaves, with simple patterns in the brickwork.

None of this suggests the interest of the interior, which is primarily the superb so-called Holbein fireplace in the HALL. 36 This consists of two parts, the modest stone fireplace itself, with a frieze of naked figures, a jester, a trumpet-blower, etc., in Early Renaissance style, and the huge wooden surround and overmantel, much too big to belong to its present site. It was seen in 1655 by John Evelyn, who called it the Holbein fireplace and said it came from Katherine Parr's house at Bletchingley – not a big house. The house later belonged to the Howards, and the Howard arms are on the stone fireplace. But the Howards came too late to Bletchingley Place to fit the style of the stone fireplace, and so this may well be *in situ* in the Howard house of Reigate Priory. About 1540 is a good date for it. The wooden surround is much more worth-while and much more puzzling. It has the royal arms and plenty of Tudor roses. So it must come from a royal house. Nonsuch has been suggested, without documentary confirmation. Bletchingley Place is possible. But what is its date? The style has nothing to do with Holbein, whose own surviving design for a fireplace is much more restrained, even if it has some strapwork motifs. Strapwork only came in, in Flanders, about 1540, and in the Reigate fireplace it is used outrageously. A date before 1550–60 appears therefore very improbable, though admittedly Nonsuch was a house in which novel motifs seem to have been introduced with gusto. But Nonsuch was still in good order when John Evelyn saw the Reigate fireplace at Reigate. Mr Sears has suggested Bridewell Palace in London instead. The framework of the surround and overmantel is two pairs of tall correct Corinthian columns, resting on corbels ending in vast paws (cf. Loseley) and supporting a huge entablature.‡ The

* The late C18 work may be attributed to *Michael Searles* (J. Harris), that of 1895 was by *J. H. Pollen* (GS).

‡ Beneath the entablature, a pair of cherubs support a crown, but these are probably C17 work and are not in their present place in early illustrations of the fireplace.

centre of the overmantel is a cartouche with a strapwork frame, itself part of a larger oblong frame, with strapwork and roses intertwined. Between each pair of columns is a seat with a curved strapwork back panel surmounted by a towering canopy in three stages, like a crazy Serliesque font-cover. The first stage is set diagonally, i.e. comes forward to a point. Each of the two visible sides has a pediment, and above and behind this a miniature tripartite triumphal arch. The second stage consists of two arches of equal size intersecting at r. angles. At the top is a very slender rotunda or tempietto with a dome. The whole of this is not English, nor is it connected with the fussy if picturesque later Flemish style which became so familiar in imitation in later C16 England (represented here at Reigate by two moderate Jacobean fireplaces in the dining room, brought from Eastnor in the C19). The hall in which the fireplace is forms the centre of the house. It faces s. A second row of rooms is behind to the N. This has two gables and looks across a N courtyard to the stables. To the s the house has two projecting wings, originally large, and shortened after the fire of the 1770s. To the w of the hall Sir John Parsons, who had purchased the estate in 1703, installed a painted STAIRCASE, which is certainly the best of its date in Surrey, and, in its combination of painting and architecture into a homogeneous and satisfying space, one of the best in England. Everything is 'returned': all the spatial loose ends are tied up as the visitor travels up the staircase. The stair-well is one continuous room,* and its proportions are credible from any point on the journey. The paintings, attributed to *Verrio*, have classical scenes – Hercules between Virtue and Vice, Pluto and Proserpine, an Assembly of Gods on the ceiling (all paintings on plaster (staircase and ceiling of upper landing) or wood (walls of upper landing), not canvas). The decoration in itself is only adequate, but the spatial composition is admirable. The staircase rises round three sides of the well with the landing on the fourth side. The second flight is against the outside wall and has three arched windows above, the landing has Corinthian columns with allegorical figures (the four Arts). The staircase balusters have the familiar pattern of elegant and close-set

* Literally of course a truism: but to go up the main staircase at e.g. Hatfield is to experience a stair-well which is discontinuous, to the mind if not to the measuring-tape. Even Neumann's staircases at Brühl and Würzburg do not turn the visitor around as deftly as this one (there is, of course, no comparison with Neumann on other grounds).

small columns, three to a step – twisted, fluted, twisted – and daintily carved tread-ends.

The remaining interior features are modest. One of the first-floor rooms has an unexpected Hawksmorean alcove in it – a quadripartite vault behind a segmental arch and columns (cf. Carshalton). A few late c 18 additions, notably the pretty LIBRARY, on the E side of the house, now headmaster's study, with original Late Palladian bookcases and panelling and a ceiling probably of c.1910.

Finally, the N courtyard is closed to the W by iron GATES, formerly the entrance gates to Bell Street.* They are of c.1710 and very fine indeed, approaching the standard of the miraculous Davies brothers of Wrexham. Fine, very delicate patterns, partly naturalistic, partly openwork. Corinthian columns, a little battered, between two pairs of rusticated piers. Clearly Surrey c 18 ironwork was as good as any in the country (cf. Durdans, Epsom): much of it has now gone.

MUNICIPAL OFFICES, Castlefield Road. Built in 1901 in Aston Webb style, by *H. Macintosh*. Town Hall and Magistrates' Court in a symmetrical composition on a sloping site, with the Fire Station and its tower at one end. Bad but very typical.

OLD TOWN HALL, High Street. A free-standing, forthright building of 1728, the only building in the centre of Reigate to rise above mediocrity. Open arcaded ground floor, a plain first-floor room reached by an apsed staircase at the W end (added later ? – it looks oddly suave for 1728). The first-floor elevation just as though it were one storey of a Baroque house: segmental windows, no decoration, rubbed brick cornice above. Well proportioned but pedestrian. Oddly enough, the most Baroque feature was only added in the c 19, the four staccato chimneypots at the corners, two of them dummies.

Most of Reigate's domestic building is not worth anything more than a glance. The main crossroads is just E of the Old Town Hall. N is the tunnel, E is Church Street, completely contemptible, widened and then rebuilt in flabby Neo-Georgian. But at the E end of it is THE BARONS, dated 1721, a very typical mason's-Baroque house. Pedestrian front, five by two bays, the centre brought forward slightly with a thick Corinthian doorcase, which is probably of c.1750, and deep aprons under the first-floor windows. The back is more attractive, with less attempt at display, simply a deep window for the stair-well and

* Moved in the late c 19 by a teetotal owner because the entrance was opposite a pub.

the decorative pattern of red and grey bricks. The w wall
facing the town is made into a composition: two chimneystacks
in the centre with the parapet swept up to them from front and
back.

BELL STREET runs s from the crossroads, cottagey and nondescript. Nos. 37–39, with a double porch, date from c.1760.
No. 15 has a C14 tie-beam roof inside that was originally part
of ST LAURENCE'S CHAPEL. The HIGH STREET runs w
and has little more to offer than the other streets; there is far
too much of what J. M. Richards* has called 'keeping-in-
keeping'. On the s side the CONGREGATIONAL CHURCH is
an awful bit of 1869 Romanesque, followed immediately by the
METHODIST CHURCH, an awful bit of 1884 Free Gothic by
one *Frederick Boreham*. Further w the street becomes more
domestic, e.g. No. 65, with a late C18 porch. On the N side No.
48 is modestly tile-hung and gabled.

From the w end of the High Street four streets fan out: this was
probably the original town centre. PARK LANE to the s is
straightaway cottages and a nice Victorian butcher's front,
BELLINGHAM'S, porticoed and marbled. To the NW is
SLIPSHOE STREET, obviously once much more picturesque.
No. 6 on the corner is C16, timber-framed with an overhang,
now tile-hung. The street leads to UPPER WEST STREET,
where No. 20 is the simplest possible late C18 house, three by
two bays, plain brick, with a clipped pattern-book doorcase.

The main road continues w as WEST STREET, probably once
very cosy, but spoilt by the effects of piecemeal clearance and
road widening. No. 31, a cottage on the s side, has ogee windows of c.1800. Opposite is No. 22, or BROWNE'S LODGE,
dated 1786, the best house in Reigate, and the type of unaffected late C18 house common in most country towns but
comparatively rare in Surrey. A wedge-shaped site is used in an
unorthodox way to give two façades. To the street is the 'entrance front', which is actually the side of the house, with a
handsome porch which seems to be lacking some of its details.
Cornice above and the side of the chimneystacks above that.
The main front faces w down a tapering garden (between West
Street and Upper West Street) and makes a very handsome
entry into the town from this side. Four by two bays, the
ground-floor windows arched, central pediment with a swag,

* Who incidentally produced a very perceptive and pessimistic study of
Reigate in the *Architectural Review* in 1938. It has been fulfilled almost to the
letter.

and a pretty *Coade* stone plaque. The style is more or less Mylne's. Beyond this again is OLD WEST STREET HOUSE of *c.*1720, five by two bays with dormers, with a later doorcase and concave-sided pediment.

The main Brighton line by-passed Reigate, and the railway came only in 1849 with a branch line (Redhill to Reading) running N of the castle. The land N of this was developed immediately as an estate of big, detached, clunch-built houses, mostly in bulgy Gothic, with a bulgy church, ST MARK, to go with them. This was built in 1860, in a thin, high-pitched Middle Pointed style, by *Field & Hilton* (who probably did the whole estate). Many leases fell in in the late 1950s, and the result is one of the few places in Surrey where a whole neighbourhood has developed with modern houses, however demure. The best-detailed is probably No. 7 ALMA ROAD, opposite the E end of St Mark's, by *Gooday & Noble*, 1953 (assistant *Donald Pierce*). A familiar type, but nicely detailed and landscaped. Pitched slate roof, one band of vertical cedar bonding on the front, and the open treads of the staircase seen behind a window beside the door – a cliché as effective as the C18 house with its central Venetian window at the back to light the half-landing. There are several more in ALDERS ROAD, e.g. JUNEBERRY, 1955 by *J. R. Stammers*, with the whole upper storey weatherboarded and drainpipes canted inwards from big eaves, and also in RAGLAN ROAD, e.g. HIGH BROOMS by *C. E. Hanscomb* of Epsom, 1957.

To the E of this is WRAY COMMON, a lush and effective open space surrounded by big houses in gardens, and a model of good open suburban landscape. Plain grass, clumps of big trees, simple seats. On the E side is a WINDMILL of 1824, a brick tower-mill, with sweeps and fantail complete, and the sail blades recently restored. The pattern is the same as the standard Late East Anglian tower mill – at Haddenham Cambridgeshire, e.g. – but more self-conscious, as befits the Home Counties: pointed windows and a Palladian doorcase.

A few oddments W and S of the town. First PAVILION COTTAGES, off Colley Lane, N of the Dorking Road. 1937 by *Sir Edwin & Robert Lutyens*, in pretty weatherboarded Colonial style, with a cottage at either end and the cricket pavilion in the middle. They have a spontaneity normally hard to find in late Lutyens. Then further W is Reigate Heath with another WINDMILL, this time a post-mill, 1765, with brick round-house (used as a chapel since 1880) and tarred weather-

boarded top, in exactly the same vernacular as the local tarred
barns. Beyond this in Trumpets Hill Road is JUNE FARM,
half-timbered and so heavily converted as to look like a
Lutyens house. Long, low, and comfortable, now a courtyard
house. The attached timber-framed barn has been converted
into a cottage. S of this is SANTON FARM, an unrestored tile-
hung and brick building, probably C17. (It has a secret room
between two chimneys.)

1 m. W of the town, on the heath, seven BARROWS in groups of
four and three. Four were opened in 1809. The largest included
a cremation pit, and a second had a cremation and urn. The
three may not necessarily be of Bronze Age date.

On the main road S of the town is THE ANGEL, Woodhatch, a
very queer half-timbered building, almost like a folly. Very tall
and thin – three deep storeys and a gable, with two lean-tos
giving the effect of a clerestory. Regular timbering, possibly of
c.1650. Oddly deliberate and formal, especially for South-East
England.

½ m. SE of this, and – for the moment – still in the country, is
HARTSWOOD MANOR, mostly plain three-storey Georgian
but incorporating parts of a gabled and plastered house dated
1615. The gable pargetted, in a simple way, a rarity S of the
Thames.

RICHMOND*

CHURCHES

ST MARY MAGDALENE. Perp W tower of flint and stone. The
body of the church of 1750. Yellow and red brick. Five bays,
arched windows. On the S side pediment over the three middle
windows, a cross-accent, not in harmony with medieval
principles. It was originally balanced by a projecting porch in
the centre of the N side, removed in 1824. Higher chancel of
flint and stone, designed in 1904 by *G. F. Bodley*. Arcades of
five bays with slender Tuscan columns, a straight entablature,
a clerestory, and an ill-fitting open timber roof of 1866 (by
A. W. Blomfield: GS). The tower arch is genuine work of
c.1500. – FONT. C18. It consists of a fluted bowl on a new

* Since 1963, the London Borough of Richmond upon Thames has in-
cluded Barnes to the E, and Twickenham, N of the river in Middlesex. For
Twickenham *see The Buildings of England: Middlesex*, for Barnes *see* p. 103.
The following places in the borough also have separate entries in this volume:
East Sheen, p. 206; Ham, p. 295; Kew, p. 322; Mortlake, p. 375; Petersham,
p. 410.

stem. – PULPIT. A nice C18 piece. – STAINED GLASS. In the windows of the E parts designed by *Bodley*. – PLATE. Silver-gilt Cups 1630 and 1663; silver-gilt Basin and pairs of Flagons 1660; silver-gilt Paten 1700; Salver 1711; Spoon 1805; Salver 1818. – MONUMENTS. Several C17 monuments with kneeling figures and without figures. – Robert Cotton † 1591. Brass plate with kneeling figures. – John Bentley † 1660, with three busts in a thin architectural frame. – Randolph Greenway † 1754. Very fine hanging monument; Rococo decoration in the Kent style. – William Rowan † 1767. Bust before obelisk. – Major Bean † 1815, by *John Bacon Jun*. With a kneeling desperate woman by an urn on a pedestal. – Barbara Lowther † 1806, by *Flaxman*. Exactly the same ingredients, but handled with much greater restraint, indeed just a little coldly. – Edmund Kean, 1839 by *Loft* (Kelly). Draperies with attached profile medallion. – Mrs Hofland † 1844, by *E. W. Wyon*. Again a weeping female by an urn. The urn bears just the one word, 'Hofland'. – In the churchyard monument to Sir Matthew Decker, 1759 by *Scheemakers*. Sarcophagus and obelisk.

CHRIST CHURCH, Kew Road. By *Sir A. Blomfield*, 1893.

ST ELIZABETH (R.C.), Vineyard. 1824. Chancel and Presbytery by *F. A. Walters*, 1903. Yellow and red brick, with a W tower carrying a Baroque cap.

ST JOHN THE DIVINE, Kew Road. 1831–6 by *L. Vulliamy*. A Commissioners' church. It cost £5,633. Chancel added 1905 by *A. Grove*. A horrible façade of grey brick with the craziest W spire and senseless flying buttresses from the W porches up to the nave. No aisles; flat ceiling. Pretty W balconies above the W gallery, with their parapets projecting on a ribbed coving. (The chancel is externally a fine composition in free Gothic, with a Crucifixion over the gable. Various carvings and lettering by *Eric Gill*, 1905–7; paintings by his brother *MacDonald Gill*. PARISH HALL also by *Grove*, 1910–11. NT)

ST MATTHIAS, Friars' Stile Road. 1858 by *Sir G. G. Scott*. The grandest church in Richmond. NW tower with tall spire. Nave and aisles, chancel and apse. Tall interior with lancet clerestory. Other windows with Geometrical tracery.

OUR LADY OF PEACE (R.C.), Sheen Road. By *Goodhart-Rendel*, *Broadbent & Curtis*, 1953–4. See p. 599

HOLY TRINITY, Townshend Road. 1870 by *R. Brandon*. (Additions by *Luck*, 1880. GS)

BETHLEHEM CHAPEL, Church Terrace. 1797. Nice stuccoed

façade. Three bays with blank arcading. To the l. and r. one-bay, one-storeyed entrance attachments.

CONGREGATIONAL CHURCH, Vineyard. 1831 by *Vulliamy*. Grey brick, Norman. Porch with a remarkably elaborate tympanum. All the ornamental work is of brick.

PUBLIC BUILDINGS

TOWN HALL, Hill Street. 1893 by *W. J. Ancell*. Mixed Renaissance.

PUBLIC LIBRARY, The Green. 1880 by *F. S. Brunton*. Gothic.

THEATRE, The Green. 1899 by *Frank Matcham*. A remarkably self-assured contribution to The Green, designed in total neglect of any Georgian responsibilities. Red brick and brown terracotta. Plenty of ornament. Two symmetrical turrets with copper-covered cupolas.

RICHMOND COLLEGE (University of London). Built as the Wesleyan Theological Institution. 1841–3 by *A. Trimen*. Large and prosperous neo-Tudor building. Long symmetrical front of fine ashlar stone with projecting wings. Four-storeyed, but in the recessed centre the two lower storeys taken as one. In the middle the familiar gatehouse motif. STATUE of Wesley by *S. Manning Jun.*, 1849. A corridor leads to the LIBRARY, added by *Sir E. Maufe* in 1931. (In the chapel, PULPIT from The Foundry, in Moorfields, from which Wesley preached on many occasions.)

OBSERVATORY, Old Deer Park. By *Sir W. Chambers*. Complete at the time of the transit of Venus in 1769. Now a block of five by three bays. Originally a central block with basement and two upper storeys flanked by one-storey wings. The wings were raised in the C19. The observatory proper on the roof, like a cupola or belvedere. The long sides have a central canted bay. Inside, an octagonal room corresponds to each of them. The two octagons have one side in common – an ingenious plan. Nice, somewhat Chippendale-Chinese woodwork inside, especially the gallery in one of the octagons.★ Close to the Observatory three OBELISKS, a reminder of the time when the observatory measured London's official time. They were paid for in 1778, and are by *Edward Anderson*.

STAR AND GARTER HOME, Richmond Hill. 1921–4 by *Sir Edwin Cooper*. Built for invalid and incurable servicemen. A large Neo-Georgian-Imperial building of brick with ample

★ The woodwork is by *James Arrow* (J. Harris).

stone trim. The chief accents are pairs of recessed giant
columns. Large hipped roof. The style and the position, with
its view across the plain, like those of a Swiss or American
luxury hotel of fifty years ago. Memorial Hall of marble with
Ionic columns.

⟨ROYAL HOSPITAL, Kew Foot Road. The core is a house of
c.1750 (ROSEDALE HOUSE). Inside, a stately staircase.
Additions of 1896 by *Smith & Brewer*.⟩

KINGSMEAD, Grove Road. Formerly the workhouse, now an
old people's home. The core is a nice plain brick building
with projecting wings and a cupola. This is dated 1786. Many
additions. In the former chapel a FONT with fluted bowl,
formerly in the parish church.

⟨RICHMOND BATHS, Old Deer Park. By *Leslie Gooday*, 1966.
Good, straightforward buildings of dark brick. The main
block with the pool has a large window facing the park, with
strongly projecting mullions. Lower flanking ranges and long
brick walls successfully tie the group into its surroundings.⟩

RICHMOND BRIDGE. 1774–7 by *Kenton Couse* and *James
Paine*. Widened in 1937, and the curve of the roadway flattened. Beautiful design of five arches.

TWICKENHAM BRIDGE. Opened 1933. Concrete. By *Maxwell
Ayrton*. Very similar in design to Waterloo Bridge, but all the
detail clumsy.

RAILWAY BRIDGE. 1848 by *Joseph Locke*, the engineer who
built much of the London and South Western Railway.

PERAMBULATION

The main traffic which nowadays runs through Richmond and
crowds its busiest streets happily notices nothing of the
extraordinary wealth of fine architecture, chiefly of the
Georgian age. Of pre-Georgian, or at least pre-Charles II,
Richmond very little remains. Yet Sheen Palace was one of
the most favoured royal palaces, first under Edward III, who
died here, then under Henry V, who rebuilt it, then under
Henry VII, who rebuilt it again after a disastrous fire in 1499
and called it RICHMOND PALACE after his own title, and
then on through the C16 and into the C17. Queen Elizabeth I
died at Richmond Palace, and Henry Prince of Wales as well
as Charles I as Prince of Wales lived in it. The appearance of
the palace is superficially known from Wyngaerde's drawings
at the Bodleian Library of 1562, Hollar's engraving of 1638, 29

and other illustrations. Soon after Hollar's time it became ruinous. Wren was asked by James II to restore it, but nothing came of that idea, and at the beginning of the C18 it had definitely ceased to be a palace. The palace consisted of ranges round an inner and an outer courtyard. Round the inner courtyard lay the river range, three-storeyed with a big tower at the N end and fourteen quite irregularly placed turrets, then on the N side the hall, on the S side the chapel, and on the E side the range with the gateway. Hall and chapel seem to have been treated more or less symmetrically, and the same seems to have been true of the E front of the W range. The outer courtyard was 200 by 200 ft in size and surrounded by two-storeyed brick buildings. It is of these that more will be said later. The Old Deer Park to the N was the garden and park of the palace, the green the jousting place. Of the architectural details of the palace we know near to nothing, but it is perhaps worth bearing in mind that John Aubrey compared them with Henry VII's Chapel at Westminster Abbey. This may well be a telling comparison, if we remember such contemporary work as that at Thornbury.

The following perambulation starts on THE GREEN and takes everything in one long walk, except for the appendices. Richmond Green is one of the most beautiful urban greens surviving anywhere in England. After the first shock of the theatre all is quiet happiness: Nos. 1 and 2 with Roman Doric porches, No. 3 Gothick, stuccoed and embattled, No. 6 with a blank-arched ground floor and a recessed Roman Doric doorway, Nos. 8–9 of eight bays, with a pedimented four-bay centre, No. 10 a fine three-bay early C18 house of three storeys, No. 11 of the same time with an outstandingly good carved doorcase and good wrought-iron work outside, No. 12, again of the same time, with a carved doorcase, and so on to Nos. 21–22 with doorways with Roman Doric pilasters and friezes, where the S corner is reached. The Green extends here to the S and forms a square. On its E side OLD PALACE TERRACE, a group of six identical early C18 houses, with identical doorways (straight hoods on carved brackets). In the middle pair the doorways adjoin. Doorways also towards The Green and King Street.* Behind this square and the E side of The Green towards George Street several lanes, e.g. PAVED COURT with an excellent early C19 shop-front. Along the SW

* In No. 1 a CHEMIST'S SHOP, founded in 1826 and with complete original furniture and fittings.

side of the square three noteworthy houses. First OAK HOUSE, of three bays with a broad Tuscan porch. Inside, the principal room on the first floor has a sumptuous classical plaster ceiling of shortly after 1760. The second house is OLD PALACE PLACE of *c*.1700. This is seven bays wide. Pedimented doorcase with curved brackets.* Thirdly OLD FRIARS, dated 1687 on a rainwater head. This house is part of the site of the house of Franciscan Observant Friars founded by Henry VII about 1500. Cellars of that period survive. The house is of two and a half storeys. The first windows on the l. on all floors extremely slender, a motif typical of *c*.1700–10. Excellent wrought-iron gate. Attached to the house on the r. and a little recessed an addition of *c*.1735–40 which was probably used as a private theatre or assembly room. It has a rusticated Venetian window to the back and to the front that anomaly, a Venetian window which is quadripartite, not tripartite, by having the arched middle part doubled.

Then follows the SW side of The Green with MAIDS OF HONOUR ROW, built in 1724 for the maids of honour of the 54 Princess of Wales, who lived at Richmond Lodge (cf. Kew Gardens). Terrace of three-storeyed five-bay houses. Brick aprons to the windows. Doorcases with Roman pilasters and metope friezes. There are fine wrought-iron gates and railings. No. 4 in 1744–9 belonged to J. J. Heidegger, manager of the King's Theatre in the Haymarket. For him, probably in 1745, his scene painter *Antonio Jolli* decorated the entrance hall. The panels are topographical landscapes taken from Zeiler's *Topographia Helvetiae* (Heidegger was Swiss), Merian's *Topographia Italiae*, and, for the more exotic subjects, Fischer von Erlach's *Historische Architektur*. Above the door leading to the staircase a painted music book open at the beginning of an aria from an opera performed at the Haymarket in February 1745.

At the end of this terrace of houses a recessed brick structure, and attached to it the GATEWAY to Richmond Palace. It is a simple gateway of Henry VII's time – his arms are above the archway towards The Green – and led into the outer courtyard of the palace, now Old Palace Yard (*see* below). The house attached on the l. to the gateway, called OLD PALACE, is a symmetrical castellated brick house with two bay windows and a middle porch. It is partly made up of Tudor material, but is in its appearance essentially C18 Gothic. In it a Jacobean

* Remains of Tudor WALL PAINTINGS have been discovered.

staircase with flat cut-out balusters. After the gateway there follows only the OLD COURT HOUSE, again early C18. The NW side is mostly Italianate villas, semi-detached and otherwise. These were built after the demolition of Pembroke House, later Fitzwilliam House, about 1854. CEDAR GROVE dates from 1813 and has giant pilasters on the garden façade. Little Green is another extension of The Green – to the NE. But there are no old houses here.

OLD PALACE YARD is the name which has remained for the secluded square which represents the base court of the palace. On the l. THE WARDROBE, early C18, but with much of the Tudor brickwork (with blue diapering) surviving. The building is now a terrace of houses. One has a good iron gate. Along the s side THE TRUMPETERS' HOUSE,* where the middle gate of the palace stood. This is datable c.1701, and an outstanding building, very close in style to *Wren*. Its main façade is towards the river. Eleven bays, giant portico of two pairs of Tuscan columns with pediment. The end bays have separate pediments and beneath them tripartite lunette windows and Venetian windows. The centre towards Old Palace Yard has a curious gabled motif with angle turrets which looks early C19 but existed already in the early C18. It may connect back to the palace. In one room a delightful Rococo ceiling with profile busts of Milton and Pope.‡ To the r. lying back TRUMPETERS' INN, a skilful Georgian pastiche of 1954–6 by *C. Bernard Brown*. Portico and lantern are both his.

From here to OLD PALACE LANE. Nice terrace of humble early C19 cottages on the NW side. In the SE corner, facing the river, ASGILL HOUSE by *Sir Robert Taylor*, 1760–70. Built for a 67 Lord Mayor of London. Stone. River front of three wide bays. The centre a broad canted bay.§ The middle window on the ground floor with a rusticated surround. On the side elevations also canted bays. Exceptionally deep, boldly detailed eaves. Interior ingeniously arranged so that an octagonal room lies behind the front bay, two rectangular rooms with apsed ends behind it, one of them containing the staircase, and two

---

* The name comes from stone figures of trumpeters which formerly stood on either side of the portico.

‡ In the garden a copper beech planted in 1813 and also, close to the river, a castellated SUMMER HOUSE.

§ But C18 drawings show the side bays lower, with a half-pediment on either side flanking the canted bay. The house is being rehabilitated, and it is proposed to restore it to the original design.

large rectangular rooms l. and r., enlarged by the side bays. Good interiors, notably the octagonal room on the upper floor with wall paintings by *A. Casali*, the upper staircase landing with Ionic columns l. and r. carrying orders, and the principal bedroom with an alcove connected with the room by a 'Venetian' arch. Exceedingly fine fireplaces, Rococo as well as classical.

Now along the Thames. In RIVERSIDE, high above a terrace with vaults under a number of houses of *c.*1815–20, lie ST HELENA HOUSE, and then ST HELENA TERRACE, both recording Napoleon's banishment. This is followed by the WHITE CROSS HOTEL, with a Greek Doric porch.

Up Water Lane into HILL STREET, where for the first time the shops and the bustle of present-day Richmond are met. Next to the Town Hall the dignified façade of *c.*1836 of the former ASSEMBLY ROOM of the Castle Hotel. Blank upper floor with two tall Ionic columns. Off Hill Street a tucked-away house at the end of HERON COURT, the somewhat altered PALM COURT HOTEL, of the early C18. Near by was HOTHAM HOUSE, of eight bays, early C18, demolished in 1960. At the corner of BRIDGE STREET and Hill Rise the KING'S HEAD HOTEL, red brick, Late Georgian, and on the other side of Bridge Street, by the river, TOWER HOUSE, with its Italian-Villa tower (*c.*1840–50).

Off Hill Rise first to the NE up ORMOND ROAD into the neighbourhood of the parish church. Ormond Road has a string of good early C18 houses on its S side. First LISSOY, with a doorcase towards Hill Rise with exceedingly fine carved brackets. Then Nos. 1–7 and Ormond House. Another fine door-hood on No. 6. On, past the church, to HALFORD ROAD, where No. 27 consists of two parts, the l. one earlier than the other. Then down The Vineyard with QUEEN ELIZABETH'S ALMSHOUSES, dated 1767, but in their present stucco-Tudor appearance clearly Early Victorian, then BISHOP DUPPA'S ALMSHOUSES, founded 1661, Victorian-Jacobean by *Thomas Little*, 1850, but with an original archway into the front garden, an original tablet over the entrance, and probably a little more of original work round the entrance. The garden archway is classical. The surround of the entrance contains elements more likely to be Early Georgian than either C17 or C19. On the other side of the street NEWARK HOUSE of *c.*1750, with a doorway with Gibbs surround and a broken pediment on carved brackets. Close to this MICHEL'S ALMSHOUSES, a modest range of 1811 with a three-bay pediment and another range at r. angles which is dated 1858.

So back to Hill Rise and up this to RICHMOND HILL. First a few nice houses on the l., then a stretch without interest, then a plain Early Victorian terrace with a first-floor veranda, then the OLD VICARAGE SCHOOL, a symmetrical castellated and turreted, stuccoed building. Then on the other side CARDI-GAN HOUSE, of seven bays and two and a half storeys, grey brick. Towards the street Venetian window in the middle with oval window over and a relief of two crossed cornucopias below the raised pediment. To the river central canted bay window. Greek Doric lodge. The house was the pump room of Richmond Wells, popular in the C18. Again on the other side of Richmond Hill, in CARDIGAN ROAD, block of flats by *Eric Lyons*, 1953–4, a good, lively composition, if perhaps a little too varied in its surfacing materials (including tile-hanging, and yellow and blue corrugated perspex). Round the corner in FRIARS STILE ROAD Nos. 19–23 is another smaller job by the same architect, with shops on the ground floor. Back in Richmond Hill, TERRACE GARDENS opposite, sloping down the hill. They were laid out in 1887. Here, in the lower part, at the opposite corner of the lawn by the Petersham Road entrance, STATUE of Father Thames by *Bacon*, of *Coade* stone (cf. Ham House). In the upper part Aphrodite, a sturdy girl in a pond, by *Allan Howes*, 1952. On the E side a long four-storeyed mid-C19 terrace, then two nice C18 houses, Nos. 116 and 124–6, both yellow brick, Late Georgian and somewhat altered. After that No. 3 The Terrace, a fine, ambitious, three-bay house of a mid-Georgian date (perhaps by *Sir Robert Taylor*; cf. Ely House, Dover Street, London of 1772). Rusticated ground floor, frieze above it. First floor with only two windows, half-storey over, pediment. Inside plaster ceilings, fireplaces, and a staircase with wrought-iron balustrade. Then two houses on the opposite side, the pair standing on their own in this enviable position. First THE WICK, by *Robert Mylne*, 1775. A delicately decorated front with a charming porch and a broad bow to the river. Fine interiors, especially the oval drawing room with its decoration by widely spaced stucco garlands. In front of the house good arched iron lamp-holder. In the garden SUMMER HOUSE with Tuscan columns. The neighbour is WICK HOUSE, built in 1772 for Sir Joshua Reynolds by *Sir William Chambers*. The exterior not now specially attractive.

The view over the river Thames at its bend is famous. It even inspired Reynolds to paint it; no wonder – he had, as we have seen, a proprietary interest in it. For the last hundred years the view has suffered a little from the STAR AND GARTER HOTEL (formerly Nightingale Hall), an unrepentant High Victorian crudity. It is of 1874 by *C. J. Phipps*, replacing an earlier building by E. M. Barry (GS). The end of Richmond Hill to the s is a delightful long late C18 to early C19 group on the E side, lying back from the road. All different heights and sizes, with balconies and verandas, bows and bays. The end is punctuated by ANCASTER HOUSE, at the corner of Queen's Road and the park gate. Built in 1772, yellow brick with later additions. Elegant porch to the street. Front to the park, where there is a similar porch.* Between it and the STAR AND GARTER HOME (by *Sir E. Cooper*, 1924) a FOUNTAIN of red granite. This is a memorial to the Duchess of Teck and was made in 1901 by *Williamson* of Esher. There is another FOUNTAIN at the top of Queen's Road, with an iron cage or arbour. This was designed by *T. E. Collcutt* in 1891 (R. C. Gill).

This is really the end of the perambulation, and Richmond Park ought now to be explored. But a subsidiary drive is recommended to pick up some minor items N of The Green. They are, first in PARKSHOT, N of Little Green, a nice minor early C18 terrace with doorways with rusticated surrounds. The centre is spoilt by a later insertion. Then in SHEEN ROAD, No. 36, MARSHGATE HOUSE of 1699, red brick with good interiors, and HICKEY'S ALMSHOUSES, the earlier parts 1834 by *Vulliamy*, grey brick, big, neo-Tudor. Next to them a mid-C19 range of houses in polychrome brick. ⟨s of Sheen Road, in PARADISE ROAD, THAMES HOUSE by *R. Seifert & Partners*, 1963–4. Large, with neat white and grey details. Better and simpler than some of this firm's more recent work.⟩ In LOWER MORTLAKE ROAD, at the corner of Crofton Terrace, the laboratories for Electronic Instruments Ltd, by *Llewellyn Smith & Waters*, 1954–5, a tall, good modern block, visible from afar. ⟨In MANOR ROAD, offices and restaurant for North Thames Gas by *Tripe & Wakeham*, 1968–9.⟩ Finally w of KEW ROAD, in KEW FOOT ROAD, an odd, equally prominent CAMPANILE, noticeable especially from Kew Gardens. This belonged to the MODEL LAUNDRY, built by *Cubitt* to Prince Albert's design to serve the royal

* The house is mostly by *Adam* (J. Harris).

palaces. Off Kew Foot Road the GRANDSTAND of the Richmond Athletic Association. This is by *Manning & Clamp*.

In conclusion, if the journey is continued from Richmond to Petersham and Ham, one will walk along the PETERSHAM ROAD and take in a number of C18 houses on the W side, starting with BELLE VUE HOUSE, No. 39, which has in its pediment a medallion with a figure playing a lyre, then Nos. 43 etc., early C18, and BINGHAM HOUSE HOTEL, with a handsome late C18 porch.

RICHMOND PARK

Richmond Park is more than 2000 acres in size. It was first enclosed by Charles I. The building of the tall wall was complete in 1637. The park was stocked with deer and remained a favourite hunting ground right into the C18. White Lodge was built as a hunting lodge proper for George II. Private shooting ceased only in 1904.

LODGES. At HAM GATE a plain brick cottage of 1742. At RICHMOND GATE the gate and stuccoed lodges are of 1798.

WHITE LODGE. The centre was begun by George I and built *c.*1727–9. The architect was the *Earl of Pembroke*, assisted probably by *Roger Morris*. The house is a very early monument to the Palladian Revival, much influenced by Lord Burlington. Fine ashlar stone. Five bays, one and a half storeys towards the entrance, basement plus one and a half storeys towards the garden. Towards the garden rustication below, then a four-column attached portico of Tuscan three-quarter columns and a pediment. The centre window is of the Venetian type. A large open staircase leads up to the portico, starting in one flight and then opening into two.[*] Towards the entrance a corridor and porte-cochère were added in 1801 by *James Wyatt*. The quadrant wings were added earlier, by *Thomas Wright*. They were begun in the 1750s, but their appearance and that of the angle pavilions is of the early C19. Inside excellent staircase with wrought-iron balustrade, not belonging to the house.[‡]

PEMBROKE LODGE. Irregular C18 house with a porch of two pairs of Tuscan columns. Some good fireplaces inside.

THATCHED HOUSE LODGE. Built originally by Sir Robert

---

[*] This is a C20 addition.

[‡] According to *Repton*'s 'Fragments' of 1816, he was concerned with the layout of the grounds.

Walpole *c*.1727. The core is of white brick, three windows wide, with a canted bay in the middle. The w wing is of 1872. In the garden the THATCHED HOUSE, a delightful little summer house with thatched roof and a balcony towards the valley. The two principal rooms inside painted probably by *Angelica Kauffmann c*.1780.

RICKETTSWOOD
¾ m. N of Charlwood

By *Halsey Ricardo*, 1885, but in no way out of the run of the Norman-Shaw-style houses so common in Surrey. In fact, below the average: shapeless and not very sensitive.

RIPLEY

Originally a coaching village on the Portsmouth Road between Guildford and Cobham. Cheerful curved High Street. An odd plan, for beside the street on the w side is a long wedge-shaped green on which the village has turned its back completely.

ST MARY. Late Norman puddingstone chancel with some impressive details – clasping buttress and two windows on the N side, and, internally, enriched string course and piers for an intended rib-vault. The string course has a diamond ornament enclosing stiff flower-like shapes. Single shafts in each corner and complex attached piers at the mid-sides consisting of a square core, two attached shafts, and one bigger attached demi-shaft. The capitals are an intricate variation on the standard scallop type. All this looks late (*c*.1150–60 ?) and does not correspond to any other C12 work in Surrey. The E end now has three C13 lancets, the s side another two, the easternmost with a continuous order around the splay with circular mouldings at the base but no capitals (cf. Pamber, Hants). The two Norman N windows are nook-shafted internally. All the rest is Victorian – lancet nave by *Ferrey*, 1846, aisle 1869 by *Jackson*. Particularly sad the spindly chancel roof.

Nothing outstanding in the High Street, though many minor attractions. From the N, first RIDE HOUSE (w side), delicate three-bay late C18, then opposite a small house of *c*.1700 (original casement windows without reveals) and the TALBOT HOTEL, a big mid-C18 front with the coach arch the most important motif. Then nothing until the crossroads. To the l. down the road to Ockham is RIPLEY COURT, with a five-by-two-bay front of *c*.1730 in a rough imitation of Hawksmoor or

Vanbrugh, and complex glazing bars to all the windows. To the r. down the road to Pyrford the LODGE to Dunsborough Park, a strange Tudor pastiche of 1939 by *W. Braxton Sinclair*. Polygonal outer wall with four angle turrets forming a quad through which the drive runs. Back in the High Street the CLOCKE HOUSE (W side) is early C18 with an eaves cornice, the ANCHOR HOTEL (E side) is a long, pretty, half-timbered range like a row of cottages, mainly single-storeyed with multiple gables. Opposite this is the MANOR HOUSE, the most interesting building in Ripley. E-shaped, dated 1650, with three shaped gables, one more example in the Surrey series of C17 ornamental brickwork. The analogies here seem to be as much with the Low Countries as with the City of London, especially in the window lintels, which have curved shoulders, a distinctly Dutch trick which also occurs at Shalford Manor House and Godalming. Finally, beside the church are simple stone and flint SCHOOLS by *Woodyer*, very much spoilt.

NEWARK PRIORY, *see* p. 380; NEWARK MILL, *see* Pyrford.

ROUNDSHAW *see* BEDDINGTON

9070   ROYAL HOLLOWAY COLLEGE
½ m. W of Egham

78 The most ebullient Victorian building in the Home Counties; its enormous front is a source of amazement to westbound travellers on the A30. It was built by *W. H. Crossland* in 1879–87 for Thomas Holloway, as one of the first women's colleges (Girton 1869), a twin building to the Holloway Sanatorium at Virginia Water. Crossland was an interesting man. He was a pupil of Sir George Gilbert Scott and the architect of Akroydon, at Halifax, one of the earliest planned working-class estates in England. Holloway had built up great riches by hard day-to-day work and an uncommon knack for advertising. The source of his income was Holloway's Pills. Their sale was world-wide. Holloway was however as interested in the spending of his money for deserving causes as in the making of it. The college and the sanatorium were the two major enterprises, but there were others such as *Holloway's Almanac and Family Friend*. For the college Holloway chose Chambord as his model, and Crossland and his assistant

Taylor spent two years detailing the elevations and revisiting the Loire. The result is a stupendous paraphrase of the French C16 Renaissance style which perhaps only Crossland could have brought off, combining a brilliant decorative sense with utter self-confidence. Rectangular plan of 550 ft by 376 ft enclosing two courts. The E and W wings of six storeys with a forest of *tourelles*, containing all the accommodation (each student had two separate rooms, now converted to bed-sitters), the joining blocks two- and three-storey, containing the principal rooms of the college. Each wing is surmounted by cupolas, Chambord-derived, as rollicking and decorative as the Zwinger. Much of the detail is mechanical close to, but the total effect is magnificent, especially the distant skyline and especially when seen from the E or SE in conjunction with the Continental Gothic of Holloway Sanatorium. It has no connexion whatsoever with the average public building of the 1880s, whether Gothic or Classical. Crossland, like William Burges, was a freak architect, and the nearest comparison is in fact Burges's Cardiff Castle. After this, the interiors are generally disappointing. The LIBRARY is a set of very tall tunnel-vaulted rooms. The ART GALLERY and apsed CHAPEL in the entrance (N) front are imposing but dead, perhaps partly the fault of the prototypes selected. No grand staircase, and no triumphant exposition of surface gilding like the hall-staircase sequence at the sanatorium. On the other hand, a number of collegiate staircases which are very interesting and somewhat bewildering. The detail is not period-tied at all, and with its strange chamferings reminiscent of the (later) work of Berlage in Holland rather than of anyone in the 1880s in England. The best parts are the unabashedly Victorian BOARD ROOM and DIRECTOR'S OFFICE in the NW corner, with dark green and gold embossed wallpaper and formidable furniture. (The HALL is in the central block, with an extraordinary polygonal vestibule under the cupola. NT)

All SCULPTURE by *Fucigna* (who had worked with George Gilbert Scott), including the large figures against the chapel ceiling. The rest of the chapel decoration by *Clayton & Bell*. Queen Victoria in the N quadrangle and Mr and Mrs Holloway in the S quadrangle are by *Count Gleichen*. The picture gallery is a period piece of great historic value in so far as most of the paintings were bought in the course of two years, between 1881 and 1883. They thus represent what at that moment was recognized as best in contemporary art. They include *E. Long*'s 'Marriage Market', *Luke Fildes*'s 'Applicants for Admission to a Casual Ward', and works by *Landseer* and *Frank Holl*.

RUNNYMEDE see ENGLEFIELD GREEN

RYDINGHURST see CRANLEIGH

ST ANN'S HILL see CHERTSEY

ST GEORGE'S HILL see WALTON-ON-THAMES and WEYBRIDGE

2060

ST HELIER ESTATE
s and e of Morden

An LCC estate, designed in its extensive original parts by the County Architect, *G. Topham Forrest*, in 1935.

On the estate ST PETER, Middleton Road, a disappointing church of 1932 by *Sir C. Nicholson* (GR), and BISHOP ANDREWES'S CHURCH, Wigmore Road, 1933 by *Geddes Hyslop*, rather modernistic, small, with a big, broad, short crossing tower and roofs over the other parts reaching very low down. Several tricks of brick ornamentation. (ST TERESA (R.C.), Bishopsford Road, is of 1930 by *W. C. Mangan*. DE)

ST HELIER HOSPITAL. Big, tall and broad, symmetrical composition, in a utilitarian modern idiom. 1938 by *Saxon Snell & Phillips*.

ST JOHN'S see WOKING

2040

SALFORDS
2 m. s of Redhill

A rootless affair on the Brighton Road.

⟨CHRIST THE KING. Designed by *David Nye* and built by local voluntary labour, 1958–67. Steeply pitched roof of laminated timbers. – STAINED GLASS. w window by *M. Traherne*.⟩

MULLARDS RESEARCH LABORATORIES. Straightforward concrete-framed buildings with brick infilling in the four-storey offices and patent glazing elsewhere. Sadly lacking in any *joie de vivre*. By *Norman & Dawbarn*, 1955 (assistant in charge *Peter Clarke*).

See
p.
599

SANDERSTEAD

The centre of Sanderstead, a pleasant open space with a pond, is, alas, about to be sacrificed to road widening.

ALL SAINTS. Flint. With a bell-turret with spike. All windows renewed. Low arcade with octagonal piers and double-chamfered arches. C13, built from E to W and cut into by the C14 tower. The chancel is C14 too, but excessively restored in 1832. The tower is very curious, decidedly oblong below, but by means of two W–E arches reduced to a square shape above. – PAINTINGS. L. and r. of the E window, King Edmund and an Archbishop, two very elongated figures; C14. – ROYAL ARMS. Of Charles I. Very large, painted, on the chancel arch. – PLATE. Flagon 1654; Plate 1713. – MONUMENTS. Brass to John Atwodde † 1525 and wife. The figures are 18 in. long. – John Ownstead † 1600. Small hanging monument with kneeling figure. – Mrs Mary Audley † 1655. Black and white marble. Sarcophagus and on it recumbent effigy bundled up in a shroud, but the face visible. – Tablet at the w end of the N aisle. This is of *c.*1730 but carries no name or date, only a poem. Bust with wig under arch in an architectural surround with open segmental pediment. The monument is supposed to be to the son of Mr Henry Mellish. The poem reads as follows:

> Here lies a youth who virtue's race had run
> When scarce his yeares of manhood were begun:
> So swift a progress call'd for early rest,
> And plac'd his soul betimes among the blest.
> Another such our age despairs to find
> Of charming person and accomplish'd mind:
> Where manly sense and sweetest temper join'd.
> Bur fame's large volume would be fill'd to tell
> Those qualities in which he did excell:
> Then reader, drop a tear and only say
> Death saw the virtuous youth prepar'd to pay
> Great nature's debt – and call'd before its day.

ST MARY, Sanderstead Hill. 1926 by *Greenaway & Newberry* (GR).

SANDERSTEAD COURT. Bombed in 1944 and now almost completely demolished and replaced by two-storey terrace houses. The grounds survive, with some splendid cedars. The house was an impressive building of 1676, but the external features clearly early C18. Recessed centre and far-projecting wings. Segment-headed windows. In the centre, however, a spectacular doorway (pushed forward by a later porch) with Corinthian columns. Above it coat of arms in an aedicule with segmental pediment. The windows to the l. and r. of this motif very tall and arched. The three bays together framed by giant pilasters and in addition emphasized by a raising of the parapet. The end of the N wing survives, much altered, as SELSDON PARK GOLF CLUB. It has a small polygonal room at the far end. N of this, the stables, of red and yellow brick, with a central cupola. Good iron gates.

In LIMPSFIELD ROAD, THE WHITE HOUSE, timber-framed, L-shaped, of two storeys, with later windows, and later additions at the back.

¾ m. SE of Sanderstead church lies a much eroded EARTHWORK, D-shaped in plan, with an entrance at its 'apex'. This enclosed a cobbled area containing two huts. Excavation revealed C1 and C2 A.D. pottery and a number of extremely crude flint implements. It was possibly the site of a small farming community.

For the SELSDON PARK HOTEL *see* Selsdon, p. 450.

SANDHILLS *see* WITLEY

8040

SEALE
3 m. E of Farnham

A pleasant village in a beautiful situation in a valley S of the Hog's Back. The best view is the one most people see, in plan from the ridge above, with houses scattered around the churchyard like the spokes of a wheel.

CHURCH. Almost all new, rebuilt by *J. Croft* in 1861–73. Heavy picturesque style, with a big central tower and pyramidal spire, a kind of transcription of the old one. Good proportions and effective polychrome: the church clunch, the tower green Bargate stone. A few medieval fragments are built in, e.g. the C14 or C15 wooden S porch. The inside heavy but not picturesque. Altogether an interesting byway of C19 church-building. – PAINTING. Altarpiece attributed to *Cima*. – PLATE. Chalice, two Patens, and Flagon, all with London hall-marks of 1760–80. – MONUMENTS. Edward Noel Long † 1809 in a naval accident, shown in an attractive relief under the inscription; the rest dull. By *Bedford*. – Anne Woodroffe † 1762. Good small Rococo tablet. Familiar Palladian frame wreathed round with Rococo plasterwork, cartouche and urns above. By *J. Nutcher* of Swaythling (Southampton), as good as London firms would have done at that date.

The best cottage is EAST END FARM, to the E. c16 timber-framing on a clunch base. An odd plan: two blocks *en échelon*, both with chimneystacks.

(LITTLEWORTH CROSS, 1 m. s, is an interesting foretaste of Norman Shaw's half-timbered Pierrepont manner, dated 1873 on the door, and quite possibly by *Shaw* himself. Big open-roofed drawing room added in 1886. Pretty garden gate and walled kitchen garden of 1896, probably by *Lutyens*, who had certainly in 1890 designed the cottage on the road to the w, now called SQUIRREL HILL. Its half-timbered gables with an unbelievably tall chimney survive at one end of a house of *c.* 1920. The Victorian owner was Harry Mangles, famous as a rhododendron grower (there is a jungle of these in the surrounding woods); and it was there that Lutyens first met Gertrude Jekyll. NT)

SELSDON
3 m. SE of Croydon

3060

ST JOHN. 1935–6 by *Newberry & Fowler*. A satisfying design, once one accepts lancet windows etc. as fitting for 1935. Red brick, square and simple NE tower. Narrow aisles with straight-headed seven-light windows. Nicely plain interior of cream-coloured brick.

(ST COLUMBA (R.C.), Queenhill Road. 1962 by *Tomei & Maxwell*. DE)

⟨CROYDON HIGH SCHOOL FOR GIRLS, Old Farleigh Road. Very large, by *Greenwood & Abercrombie*, 1964–6. The buildings, well sited in spacious grounds, are quite hard in style, of red brick with exposed concrete floors, some concrete roof lights, and a considerable variety of window types.⟩

⟨JOHN NEWNHAM SCHOOL, Selsdon Park Road. Long ranges of dark red brick. By *C. F. Blythin & L. C. Holbrook*, 1951–3. Also in Selsdon Park Road, FARLEIGH VIEW, old people's homes by the *Borough of Croydon's Architect's Department* (*R. C. Crippen & A. F. M. Murray*), 1965, a long four-storey building with an excessive number of contrasting surfaces and colours. Opposite is one of the most deplorable recent housing developments in the area. Further s, off Featherbed Lane, and much better, is FORESTDALE, a *Wates* estate begun in 1966

15—S.

(chief architect *J. Bridges*). Terrace housing on a hilly site, with garages in the slopes below, as at Coulsdon.)

SELSDON PARK HOTEL. Of a medieval core nothing can be seen. The visible core of the present buildings seems early C19 and was illustrated by Neale in 1819. It was of eleven bays, symmetrical and castellated then, and Neale says it was chiefly designed by the owner, *George Smith* M.P. To the same time belong apparently the outbuildings, including the castellated tower with the higher turret. The roof of the early C19 building was raised and the little lantern put on some time early in the C20. Then, from 1925, the building was converted into a hotel and for the purpose spectacularly enlarged by *Hugh Macintosh*. All the new parts are neo-Jacobean.

0050

SEND

A sad, characterless village overrun with sprawl from Woking. The group of church and Send Grove away from all this is still unspoilt and attractive.

ST MARY, Studgrove, ¾ m. NE of Sutton Place. C13 chancel with lancets on the N and S sides and blocked lancets in the E end, replaced by a Geometrical window of 1819. Perp nave with simple square-headed three-light windows (the masonry is older). Perp tower with three-light 'Lingfield' W window, two-light bell-openings, probably Late Georgian, and tower arch without capitals. Simple C15 timber S porch. The inside equally direct. Wide, aisleless nave and now no chancel arch, simply an arrangement of trussed beams. – WEST GALLERY. Rustic late C17. – SCREEN. Simple Perp, but terribly restored: the mullions cut off, new battlemented cresting, etc. – PLATE. Paten 1711; Cup and Flagon 1844. – MONUMENT. Brass to Laurence Slyffeld † 1521 and wife. Small effigies (13 in. high) and rough engraving.

SEND GROVE HOUSE, beside the church. Plain late C18 house, seven-bay centre and two bow windows. Stables behind in C18 vernacular with two rusticated entrance arches.

SEND COURT FARM, NE of the church. A good C17 timber-framed building, L-shaped, with regular timbers and warm red brick infilling. Beyond it to the N is SENDHOLME, a medium-sized house by *Devey*. Nearly symmetrical Tudor. *See p. 599* Nothing out of the ordinary, but restrained and competently done. The back an asymmetrical tangle of chimneys and gables worthy of Norman Shaw.

SEND MANOR HOUSE, Sendmarsh. Sober C17 brick, three
storeys, three plain gables, five bays. No ornamental detail.
This type, which was almost national, obviously went up
concurrently in Surrey with the more ornate pilastered and
Dutch-gabled designs.

SHABDEN

½ m. SW of Chipstead

2050

Very Victorian. Uncompromising symmetrical French Renaissance plus an elephantine timber porch. Of c.1870 by *E. M.
Barry*, who was nearly as heartless as Waterhouse.

SHACKLEFORD

9040

In unspoilt sandstone country W of Godalming. One street of
already picturesque sandstone and brick houses, given a piecemeal overlay of careful early C20 planting and walling, especially
at the N end, so that the whole village reads like a serial unfold-
ing of a good Lutyens house, especially e.g. the sudden paved
and covered pathway from the street to Aldro School via the
garden. There is nothing else quite like this anywhere in the
county. It is not in the least affected, and probably not done
deliberately at all – the reverse of the model village.

ST MARY. By *Sir George Gilbert Scott*, 1865. Above his average.
It has everything in its favour except convincing detail. Central
tower and lower stair-turret, clerestoried nave, big apse. All
E.E., and all Bargate sandstone. Proportions admirable,
especially the build-up of masses around the tower. The simple
detail and the stone keep it amenable to the *genius loci*.* Inside,
perhaps inevitably, grim but mechanical.

In the street itself no house worth special notice, though almost
every house pretty – except ALDRO SCHOOL (built as Hall
Place), keeping plain stables of 1743, a big, rather harsh house
of 1906. (The architect was *Henry Tanner Jun.* – to the chagrin
of Lutyens, who had designed Sir Edgar Horne's previous
house, Tigbourne Court. NT) Assorted C16 and C17 detail and
one enormous plastered gable almost in E. S. Prior's style.
Opposite, behind THE OLD COTTAGE, is a famous C18
'crinkle-crankle' wall, i.e. brick in a continuous series of bows.
It is possible to build walls thinner like this (because they are

* And has now become the *genius loci*; this is the epitome of the picturesque
C19 Surrey church surrounded by pine trees.

self-stiffening in the way a Gothic arch is self-stiffening), but the reason here was probably to get as much wall area as possible facing S and W, for ripening fruit trees. N of the village, LYDLING FARM is of *c*.1700, bulky in plan, Wren-style, with coved eaves and a very narrow centre deeply recessed, a little like Wrencote, Croydon: an unusual style for a Surrey farm. NW of the church, with a typical LODGE, is NORNEY, a house by *Voysey*, 1897, with stables and additions 1903. Big but oddly unsympathetic. Voysey is here almost making clichés out of his own style, particularly in the entrance front with the ugly doorway and asymmetrically battered gabled wings. The garden front is better and simpler, the main part two-gabled and symmetrical, with three smaller gables to the N. Typical long, low proportions, and typical low-key materials (slate, roughcast, and violent yellow limestone – this last an unhappy mistake for Surrey). The house also has Voysey's disconcerting quality of appearing more solid the longer the viewer looks at it.

SHALFORD

0040

The first village out of Guildford on the Horsham road. A winding, cottagey street widening to the S into a big, formless green largely lined with C19 workers' houses.

ST MARY. 1846 by *Benjamin Ferrey*, replacing a classical church of 1790. Mostly lancet. Clerestory, attached NW tower; high-pitched literally and metaphorically. Typical spindly interior of the 1840s. – STAINED GLASS. In the E window commemorative glass by *W. R. Eginton* and *Samuel Rowe*, probably signed by *Robert Morrow* (TK). Also typical 1840s: bright colours on grisaille background, still decorative rather than moral. – MONUMENTS. Several C18 tablets from the old church. Robert Austen Sen. † 1759, by *James Moorhouse* of Greenwich, Palladian, and Robert Austen Jun. † 1797, by *Bacon*, Grecian. Both crisp and typical, an interesting comparison.

(CHURCH OF ENGLAND SCHOOL. One of *Woodyer*'s best schools. 1866, enlarged in 1883. NT)

SHALFORD PARK, W of the church, was demolished in 1968. It was effectively all heavy stuccoed Classical of 1797. The main (N) front of nine by three bays had an elegant porch of four Ionic columns shielding a big Adamesque fanlight, up to the best Dublin standard.

Not a lot in the village. Opposite the church a long row of old

cottages given some form of roughcast uniformity in the early
C19, picturesque but without much character. Further s THE
COTTAGE is an early C19 box with ogee windows, one of
several between Guildford and Bramley. Further s again is a
short lane leading E to SHALFORD MILL, in another variety
of Surrey vernacular, this time with tile-hanging, and very
pretty. Three storeys, with a second-floor extension overhanging the path and supported by big posts containing mill
hoists. Beside it is THE OLD HOUSE, originally Mill House,
with another C17 Artisan elevation, this time very confused
and altered. It would make sense as two-thirds of a larger
house: it is now three-storeyed, stone with brick dressings,
two Dutch gables with a shaped gable between them. The l.-
hand Dutch gable contains a window with shouldered lintel
(cf. Ripley), the r.-hand gable has a simple surround to the
second-floor window and a huge architectural frame of Ionic
pilasters to the first-floor window below, very gauche and
bulgy. (Inside an interesting contemporary staircase with
rusticated newel posts and pierced oblong banister panels, like
that at Slyfield Manor.)

SHALFORD HAMLET see CHILWORTH

SHAMLEY GREEN
2½ m. NW of Cranleigh

A good village w of the Surrey hills, with a complex green formed
out of unequal triangles on either side of a main road. Being
spoilt, very slowly, by too great a separateness and fussy
picturesqueness in the buildings, something which started at
least a century ago with over-dressed Victorian cottages. The
true spirit is more that of the very simple brick and tile-hung
cottages of c.1800 N of the Red Lion. Many picturesque cottages, but none worth special mention; the minor felicities of
half-timber and tile-hanging are easily found. More minor
cottages around the green at Lordshill Common to the w.
(These were built by a local Nonconformist sect, the Cokelers;
hence the name Lordshill.)

CHRISTCHURCH. Stone chapel of 1864 by *C. H. Howell*, in
decent Dec style.

SHEEN see EAST SHEEN and also RICHMOND,
pp. 206, 435

SHEPPERTON*

The view of the little square at Shepperton towards the SE, if one places oneself so that the filling station is concealed, is one of the most perfect village pictures this area has to offer.

ST NICHOLAS. Its most characteristic feature is its oblong brick W tower of 1710, crowned by five battlements on the W and E, and only four on the N and S. The church behind is of flint rubble and dates from 1614. Evidently much old material was used in the reconstruction. The plan is unusual, with substantial transepts, so that to the length of about 65 ft corresponds a width of about 48. The church is aisleless, but has a wooden gallery of early C19 date across its W end and another, on thin iron columns, across the W side of the N transept, of rude and homely workmanship. The BOX PEWS in the nave, also early C19, are completely preserved. The roof is ceiled and whitewashed. No monuments of importance. – PLATE. Of 1822, 1848, and 1869.

RECTORY to the N of the church lying back too far to play its part in contributing to the village square. An exquisite front of c.1700, seven bays and two one-bay slightly projecting wings, coved cornice, and hipped roof. The material is not brick but mathematical tiles. The exterior does not reveal the fact that inside is a spacious hall of c.1500 with moulded beams (the hall of Grocyn's rectory when he held the living of Shepperton from 1504 to 1513). ⟨Recently a clumsy Neo-Georgian garage has been built in the front garden. Surely it could have been more discreet.⟩

The village square has a delightful row of C18 houses opposite the church on the S side, chiefly the KING'S HEAD and WARREN LODGE, both of two storeys and three bays. CHURCH ROAD leading to the N out of the square is also at the beginning uncommonly complete in its cottages. It ends with IVY COTTAGES on the l., L-shaped, of timber-framing and brick, basically C16, but recently so 'completely renovated' that the result looks entirely bogus. On the r. some unfortunate recent building, then the wall of the MANOR HOUSE. This can be seen only from the river, a friendly stuccoed five-bay front of c.1830 with veranda.

At the end of Church Road, HIGH STREET leads N to the station, with much recent undistinguished building. RUSSELL ROAD runs by the river towards Lower Halliford, with several

* Formerly in Middlesex.

worthwhile houses: THAMESFIELD, a large house of yellow brick, C18 with later alterations, of three storeys and five bays, then CLONSKEAGH, early C18, and WILLOW HOUSE and WILLOW BANK, a pleasant C19 group. HALLIFORD SCHOOL is another large C18 house, of brown brick, with a five-bay front with pedimented centre. At the bend of the river, facing the green at the beginning of WALTON LANE, PEACOCK HOUSE, early C19, a weatherboarded cottage opposite, then DUNALLY HOUSE, C18 with later alterations. On the other side of Walton Lane are some surprisingly rural farm buildings. On the N side of the green first some barrack-like Neo-Georgian terraces, then BATTLECREASE, an C18 house of three bays and three storeys. Further E, behind trees, HALLIFORD MANOR HOUSE, with an early C18 façade, now stuccoed.

EARLY SAXON CEMETERIES have been found near Walton Bridge (VCH). For the BRIDGE *see* Walton-on-Thames, p. 497.

SHERE

Between Downs and Surrey Hills, in the Tillingbourne valley, E of Guildford. A pretty but overrated village. The trouble is that although there are occasional pretty corners, they never form a coherent village pattern. Many of the houses in fact are surprisingly hard-bitten C19. A complex plan, with one long street, Upper Street, forming A25 and another running S from it to Church Square. To the E of this is the church, and to the W Lower Street runs uphill. Between Upper and Lower Streets a stream flows from E to W, but it is not brought into the village pattern. The best vignettes are the views out of Church Square, N along High Street, with a pattern of timber gables like a tiny edition of a German village, and E towards the church, which is seen at the end of a funnel of cottages. Church Square itself would be very much improved if the horribly mutilated tree in the centre could be replaced. It will now never grow to a proper shape, and it blights every view it appears in. The village has mercifully been given a good simple by-pass (1960).

ST JAMES. A complex building history, though the overall effect is beetle-browed heavy C13, the type of Merstham. Central tower Norman, probably early, with severe unmoulded details, e.g. the two-light window on the N side (with renewed dividing shaft) and the tall, noble single bell-openings. Big shingled broach-spire. Part of the arch to the S transept remains above the present arch, and a w window high up in the s transept; so that also is Norman,* and the N nave wall is doubtless Norman too. The s doorway has a Norman arch with two orders of zigzag, but this was apparently re-used c.1200 when the s doorway was built, together with the s aisle and s chapel. These two parts are connected by a beautiful arch with shafts of Petworth marble‡ carrying crocket capitals. Petworth marble is also used in the s doorway and the w doorway. Possibly of the same date the one blocked bay of the N arcade and the s arcade, at an unknown date converted into something unbelievably gross, with fat octagonal piers and a crude type of square capital. About 1300 the s chapel was lengthened. The tracery of the windows, especially the E window, is eminently characteristic (large circle with four quatrefoils in two tiers). Again one generation later the chancel was lengthened too, and its E window is a very interesting improved edition of the chapel E window – identical but for one prominent ogee arch. A little later the N window of the shortened N transept. The comparison between this and the stiffer forms of the E window is well worth making. The curvilinear window is undoubtedly a better pattern, filling each part of the window head with a convincing shape, yet never losing itself in over-elaboration. The dates of the crossing arches differ, but remain doubtful. The N arch and the arch from the chancel into the s chapel may be of c.1330. In the N wall of the chancel, quatrefoil window and squint; C14. Two Perp windows in two styles. One in the s aisle, of Lingfield type, can be dated approximately by a brass inscription to the donor, who died in 1512. Subtly detailed vestry of 1895 by S. *Weatherley*, who was responsible for the sensitive restoration of the church. Old roofs throughout, mostly of scissors-truss type. – FONT. Of c.1200, not first-rate, but the best in the county. Big central stem and four corner shafts with stiff-leaf capitals supporting a bowl with three scallops on each side. – CHEST. Big, early C13. Probably a 'Crusader chest', i.e. one of the series put in churches by order of Innocent III to collect money for the Crusades. – STAINED GLASS. Medieval fragments in several windows, and splendid fragments, apparently C14, in the aisle E window – e.g. the richly coloured eagle. – (The chancel fittings have been

* According to the VCH there is evidence that the transept originally had an apse. That indicates a Norman pattern of three staggered apses as at St Mary Guildford.

‡ i.e. polished limestone, not true marble.

renewed since 1956 by *Louis Osman*. CROSS and CANDLE-STICKS with bronze reliefs on wrought iron; ALTAR RAIL of stainless steel; bronze AUMBRY. – FRONTALS. Two by *Osman* and *Geoffrey Clarke*, one by *Osman* and *Frank Avray Wilson*. – STATUE of St James by *John Cobbett*. NT) – BRASSES. Robert Scarcliff, Rector of Shere, † 1412. 12 in. high; standard work. – John Lord Audley † 1491. Figure in armour, 20 in. high. Very delicate linear design, with a Late Gothic complexity rare in English brasses. (But only the top half of the figure and part of the inscription are original. The rest was added by *J. S. M. Ward*, who restored the brass in 1911.* LYCHGATE by *Lutyens*, 1901.)

SHERE MANOR HOUSE. Gloomy mid-C19 Tudor style, in stone. *Basevi* worked here, but the depressing elevations cannot be his. The LODGE on the main road to the SE is a very different thing – very free, high-spirited massing of 1894, with a big bold chimney, by *Lutyens*. (He also designed a pair of COTTAGES a few yards to the W, grouping cleverly with their genuine ancestors. NT)

NETLEY HOUSE, ½ m. NE. As heavy and gloomy Classical as the manor house was Tudor. Big porte-cochère. Built in 1851.

A walk around Shere is pleasant, but there is not much to excite special notice. The following walk will take in most of it. Starting N from Church Square, turn to the l. into LOWER STREET. Here immediately on the l. is a brick house dated 1705, unremarkable in itself but showing just how the Artisan patterns in brickwork gradually died away. Beyond, ASH COTTAGE is of *c*.1600, with a half-timbered overhanging first floor at both ends. Beyond again, the OLD PRISON HOUSE, the most picturesque house in Shere, is derelict. C17 half-timbering with a variety of fillings, including flint. Quite a rarity. A path goes N from here to the W end of UPPER STREET, where there is another half-timber and flint cottage (KNAPPS COTTAGE) and further E the gate lodge of the manor house (*see* above). Finally HIGH STREET runs s back to Church Square, with the most demonstratively half-timbered houses almost opposite one another at the N end: the POST OFFICE on the E and BODRYN on the W, both of *c*.1600 with big-scale timbered gables, and quite impressive. Next to Bodryn is a WELL HEAD, a simple arched stone recess with 84 seats under, dated 1886. It has an extraordinary pair of iron guard rails, approximately in the form of growing irises – i.e.

* Mr N. E. W. Marsh kindly pointed this out.

purely Art Nouveau, and very well done. Who, at that date, could have done them? (Further down the street on the w a half-timbered shop by *Lutyens*, 1892, with an oversailing plaster upper floor and a little tiled seat in the timber porch. NT)

SHIRLEY

3060

ST JOHN. By *Sir G. G. Scott*, 1856. Flint and stone and deliberately villagey, although not small. Bell-turret with spike. Inside, this rests on two mighty round piers with crocket capitals. – In the churchyard (SE corner) MONUMENT to Ruskin's parents. Small Greek Doric temple and sarcophagus.

Two good SCHOOLS of the fifties in the neighbourhood, one the ST JOHN'S CHURCH OF ENGLAND SCHOOL, in Shirley Church Road, by *C. T. Ayerst*, the other the JOHN RUSKIN GRAMMAR SCHOOL, Upper Shirley Road, by *A. G. Gavin* (*Paul Mauger & Partners*). ⟨Now also the TRINITY SCHOOL of John Whitgift, Shirley Park, moved from Croydon. The new buildings are by *George Lowe & Partners*, 1962–5.⟩

Immediately behind the John Ruskin School rises the Shirley WINDMILL, a tarred brick tower-mill with a boat-shaped weatherboarded cap, probably early C19. Repaired in 1936. (Now the changing room of the school.)

In COOMBE ROAD, about ¾ m. SW of the church, is COOMBE HOUSE, now St Margaret's School. This is a good early C18 house of red brick, eight bays, two storeys, with a three-bay pediment. Doorway with Tuscan columns and broken pediment. (The best room inside is the library, early C19, and somewhat Soanish, with a shallow coffered vault and segmental apses. MHLG)

(On both sides of ORCHARD WAY, ½ m. NE, good housing by *G. E. A. Huyton*, 1968–71, with a lively rhythm of butterfly roofs and an ingenious layout of houses in echelon round courtyards, set back behind three-storey flat blocks over garages. NT)

SHOTTERMILL *see* HASLEMERE

SIDLOW BRIDGE
2040
2 m. s of Reigate

EMMANUEL. A small flint church by *Clutton*, 1861. Not attractive, but carefully thought out. Nave, chancel, and bellcote.

SILVERLANDS
Between Chertsey and Lyne, near Botleys

The E front is an example of just how sober and restrained
Victorian classicism could be. Five-by-three-bay centre, two-
storey wings, all stock brick with pure Palladian detail. It looks
c.1845; who did it? The back is more typical of the date, with
its asymmetrical elevations and a Barry-like Italianate tower.

SLYFIELD GREEN see GUILDFORD, p. 287

SLYFIELD MANOR*
½ m. s of Stoke d'Abernon

Puzzling fragments of a larger house of c.1625–40, all belonging
to the mass of mid-C17 Artisan brickwork in Surrey. Luckily,
enough remains here, and of good enough quality, to be of
artistic as well as historical importance. This C17 house, which
incorporates a late medieval timber-framed building, was originally a square courtyard house. In 1743 the NE and SW parts
were demolished, including the great hall in the S range. What
is left is part of the principal range (originally the private apartments), with a seven-bay centre to the S, articulated by very
bulgy giant brick pilasters with again very bulgy Ionic volutes.
The pilasters have badges half way up (cf. the College of
Heralds in London somewhat later). To the l. of this a broad,
taller bay with a big Dutch gable. To the r. there is a garden
wall coming forward with apparently original archways. The
details of the S front are odd, as so much is in the mid-C17
Artisan style. The Dutch gable is carried on two superimposed orders of coupled pilasters, framing a square-headed
window on the ground floor and a big segment-headed window
on the first floor, breaking through the cornice (but presumably original, as it fits the curve of the vault inside).

To the W of the gable are the bottom few feet of a wall
showing the feet of small-scale pilasters (not like the giant
pilasters to the E). The back of the main range has friezes of
brick with dentils, and two gables. The E wing is an extension
of c.1650–65.

To the N of the main range, but not in line with it, is
SLYFIELD FARM, orginally part of the service wing of the C17

---

* This account has been revised from information kindly supplied by Mr
John Harvey.

house, with similar thick brick cornices linking heavily-moulded Tudor windows. But at its E end is just one pair of coupled pilasters (very like Old House at Shalford e.g.), of not nearly as good quality as the gable elevation. This could have formed the r. side of the surround of a gateway. A low wall further to the E seems to continue this N range. The style of Slyfield Manor is that of the most advanced City of London work of c.1640 – copies of Inigo Jones's Covent Garden piazzas and particularly of *Peter Mills*'s houses in Great Queen Street of 1637, which also use a giant order and the same sort of cornice. Cf. also Old Westmoor Cottage, Effingham (p. 208) and Old House, Mickleham (p. 365).

Inside, there is more of this mixture of styles. Behind the Dutch gable there is a panelled room with a segmental tunnel-vault (as they occur sometimes in Devon, but very rarely in South-East England) and plasterwork with naïve swags, birds, cherubs, and strapwork curves made into a ceaselessly writhing folk-art composition. A remarkable performance, which could well be of c.1625. Underneath this and in two first-floor rooms there are on the other hand simple geometrical ceilings of ovals inside oblongs, roughly executed but clearly Jones-derived, which go with the external work. The staircase at the E end of the hall is typical of c.1640 in that it has openwork panels instead of balusters, but is still decorated with strap-like distorted circles, etc. The newel posts are rusticated. So are (very thinly) the door surrounds of the staircase. Pretty dog-gate (as at Hatfield but at very few other English houses). One more remarkable piece of Mannerism occurs in several of the doorcases – violently rusticated half-pilasters inset in the door-jambs, giving an over-wrought look to the doors.

SMALLFIELD PLACE
1 m. N of Burstow

The best example in Surrey of the stone-built manor house, more common over the Sussex border. Built c.1600 and altered in 1665. Parts of it were demolished in the C18. Dour, and very unlike Surrey; it could easily be in Derbyshire or Lancashire, the repertoire of C16–17 stone building was so similar. It is very difficult to guess how far this similarity was accidental. Long, two-storeyed front, all ashlar Wealden stone, ornament kept to a minimum and that thickly carved. Central gabled porch with simple finials and four-centred door; on one side

two big battlemented bow windows, on the other side one and
a big flush bay. Simple mullioned and transomed windows with
straight labels above, to a considerable scale: five and six lights
in the bow, six and seven lights in the flush bay. The back
asymmetrical with one polygonal bow window set on a corner,
also battlemented. (The inside is now divided into two, but
keeps a Jacobean screen, a newel-post staircase dated 1610,
and several stone fireplaces.)

SNOWDENHAM HALL *see* BRAMLEY

SOUTH HOLMWOOD *see* HOLMWOOD

SOUTH NORWOOD

3060

HOLY INNOCENTS, Selhurst Road. 1894–5 by *Bodley*. Along
the road, with nave and chancel in one and no tower. Stone.
Tall interior with slim Perp piers and no clerestory. – STAINED
GLASS. E window by *Kempe*.
ST ALBAN, Grange Road. *See* Thornton Heath.
(ST CHAD (R.C.), Whitworth Road. 1932 by *G. Drysdale*.)
METHODIST CHURCH, South Norwood Hill. 1873 by *Lander*.
Gothic, with tower and spire.
CLOCK TOWER, corner of Station Road and High Street. 1907,
of cast iron. It looks as though it could have come from the
1851 Exhibition. ⟨Near by, the STANLEY HALLS, a pictur-
esque Edwardian composition, completed in 1903. They were
designed and built by the benefactor, *W. F. Stanley*.⟩
⟨BRANCH LIBRARY, Selhurst Road. By *Hugh Lea*, Borough
Architect of Croydon, 1966–8. Boldly detailed, windows with
thick mullions above dark brick. The upper floor on one side
is a windowless area of ribbed concrete, with 'Library' in
aggressively large letters.⟩
⟨SWIMMING BATHS, Portland Road. Also by the Borough
Architect, *Hugh Lea*, 1967–8. Well composed. The baths have
one tall wall of green glass, a plain brick end wall, and a lower
entrance wing on one side.⟩

SPREAKLEY *see* FRENSHAM

STAINES*

0070

The development of the last fifty years has raised the population
* Formerly in Middlesex.

of Staines from 6,000 in 1901, to 21,000 in 1931, 39,000 in 1949, and 56,190 in 1968. Until recently this by-passed the church and its neighbourhood, and this area still preserves some of its character of a hundred years ago.

ST MARY. The pleasant peace of the neighbourhood makes up for the few attractions of the parish church. Its w tower is its most interesting feature: brick, and in its two lower storeys dating from *c.*1631. These have plain buttresses and segment-headed windows on the upper storey. The top storey, also brick, belongs to 1828, when the rest of the church was re-constructed by *J. B. Watson*, a poor job, though spacious, with yellow stock-brick walls and lancet windows, and inside a gallery with leafy iron balustrade on three sides. The E apse and chancel roof date from 1885. – PLATE. Paten of 1798 and Set of 1842. – No MONUMENTS of importance.

ST PETER, Laleham Road. A prosperous brick building with entrance and tower at the side, facing the Thames, 1893–4 by *G. H. Fellowes Prynne*. Impressive interior: nave of four bays, of polychrome brick on stone columns and arches. – Enormous stone tracery SCREEN the whole height of the chancel arch, with low iron grilles. – Delicate brass and iron PULPIT on a marble and stone base. – Carved wooden ALTAR. – All the windows have their original STAINED GLASS, designed by *Fellowes Prynne*, 1901–32.

(CHRIST CHURCH, Kingston Road and Warwick Avenue. By *H. Norman Haines*, 1961–2. Square, with a central lantern above the altar, and a very thin reinforced concrete spire on top. The aisle roofs slope upwards to each corner, with clerestory lighting on two sides.)

The CONGREGATIONAL CHURCH in Thames Street, *c.*1830, stuccoed with Ionic w loggia, has been demolished.

DUMCROFT (now an Approved School), to the NE of the church, is of 1631, but so much altered and added to that little original material survives. Are the three curved and scrolled gables genuine? The interior possesses one room with old panelling and a fine fireplace with marquetry landscapes.

LONDON STONE, w of the church, in the recreation ground by the river. It is a poorly preserved stone, probably post-medieval, on a pedestal of 1781, marking the former w limit of the jurisdiction of the City of London over the Thames.

CHURCH STREET leads from the church into the town, still with some Georgian houses towards its w end. The HIGH STREET has no common character any longer except that of 1920 onwards. Of the old houses the best are the BLUE ANCHOR, quite a stately inn of *c*.1700 with red and vitrified bricks in a chequerboard pattern, and Nos. 32–36, also of *c*.1700. Off the High Street is the TOWN HALL, 1871–80, Italianate, white brick and stone. Two storeys, five bays, with a central clock-turret. Well sited at the end of a small market place. The architect was *J. P. Hearson*.*

CLARENCE STREET, between High Street and the bridge, is a good example of a market town development of the latest Georgian phase, datable by its name to the time of George IV. It leads to the BRIDGE, of three noble stone arches, 1829–32, by the great *Rennie* of Waterloo Bridge fame.

LONDON TRANSPORT GARAGE, 49 London Road. By *C. H. C. Kirby*, 1934. A good, early example of the Modern Movement in English architecture.

(YEOVENEY LODGE, Moor Lane. A C19 Gothic villa, of three bays and two storeys, with lower wings. Gothic porch with Tuscan columns. MHLG)

(BELL-WEIR BRIDGE, ½ m. N on the bypass. Designed by *Lutyens* in 1937, executed in 1959–60. NT)

STANWELL‡

ST MARY. Its chief attraction is its tower as it appears from the green: first stage C13 flint rubble like the rest of the church, second stage flint and chequer, C14, third stage smaller flint, late C14, spire shingled. The short nave has a C13 S arcade with piers alternating between circular and octagonal. The chamfered arches have hood-moulds. The E window of the S aisle and the N and S windows of the chancel are early C14, the chancel E window is early C19 Perp. The clerestory and roof are of the C15; the chancel roof of trussed-rafter type may even belong to the same date as the elaborate blank wall arcading on the N and S sides of the chancel, and the SEDILIA in which every curve is ogee. The old roof of the C14 S aisle has gone, but the figured corbels (a queen, two kings, a bishop, a knight, a man, a woman, a pilgrim) remain. The N aisle is 1863 by *Teulon*. – PILLAR PISCINA, C12, and PISCINA with credence and aumbry discovered in 1951. – (PAINTING.

* Information kindly supplied by Mr W. P. J. Critcher, Staines and Sunbury Librarian.

‡ Formerly in Middlesex.

Virgin and Child, said to be by *Murillo*.) – PLATE. Flagon
1688; Chalice 1799; Almsdish 1800; Paten 1806; Communion
Plate 1817. – MONUMENTS. Brass in the chancel to Richard de
Thorp † 1408, demi-figure praying, of the same type as Robert
Lance at Hayes. – Lord and Lady Knyvett † 1622, by *Nicholas
Stone*. Standing wall-monument with more than life-size white
marble figures kneeling opposite each other; flanking black
columns with crumpled alabaster curtains tied to them, broken
segmental pediment with achievement. On the base inscription
and thick hanging garlands.

LORD KNYVETT'S FREE SCHOOL. 1624. Unattractively
situated, but of architectural importance. As against the original
Harrow School and the Enfield Grammar School, the school-
house proper and the masters' lodgings are here combined into
one composition of two three-bay halves. Each half has a
central door with a heavy flat plastered surround and a pediment and two windows. On the school side they are tall and
renewed, on the living-house side they are in two storeys with
unmoulded surrounds and original. The building is of brick
with a pitched roof. It is now two houses.

(STANWELL SECONDARY SCHOOL. Large new buildings by
Sir John Burnet, Tait & Partners in association with the
County Architect, *Raymond Ash*.)

The village centre is a triangular green with at its S end the
church, on the SE a few mellow Georgian houses (chiefly one
of the early C18 with seven bays and two storeys). Towards
Stanwell Moor lies STANWELL PLACE in its grounds, a plain,
cement-rendered Late Georgian house. At Stanwell Moor
THE CROFT, with a C17 core and an unadorned Georgian
brick front.

4040   STARBOROUGH CASTLE
                      1½ m. E of Lingfield

The original castle was built by Reginald de Cobham, who was
given licence to crenellate in 1341. It had four towers and a
gate, some traces of whose stumps survive on the edge of the
moat.* Otherwise, nothing remains but a moated jungle which
now contains a battlemented Gothick SUMMER HOUSE of
1754. The house itself is thick-set Victorian classical of *c.*1880
with a tower at the NW end, almost a Fitzjohn's-Avenue house

* The same type as Bodiam. It stayed intact until the Civil War, and was
drawn by Hollar.

in the country. The STABLES are older, consisting of a very pretty late C18 cottage centre (apparently original, not a conversion) and single-storey wings which are the stables proper.

STOKE *see* GUILDFORD, pp. 272 and 287

STOKE D'ABERNON

1050

Mostly untidy suburbanization, continuous with Cobham. No recognizable village centre: church and manor house are by themselves beyond the southern end of the mess, near the river Mole.

ST MARY. Possibly the classic example of bad restoration, the worst even in Surrey. First, the original work. Attributed to an early Anglo-Saxon date the bit of an apse now exposed inside the N chapel and a doorway high up in the S wall which, if the attribution is correct, led no doubt into a wooden W gallery such as has been established for Wing and other Saxon buildings. The S wall incorporates a lot of Roman bricks. Of *c.*1190 the two easternmost bays of the N aisle, of a type which is not common in Surrey, though it is in Hants: slightly chamfered pointed arches on simple, square, many-scalloped capitals and round piers. The two-bay chancel with quadripartite rib-vaulting is of *c.*1250. Very good work, keeping two original window splays on the S side, exactly adjusted to the size of the vaulting bays (renewed outside; the E window is completely new). Elegantly moulded ribs and transverse arch. No ornament except one band of dog-tooth between two rolls of the transverse arch, a good example of the care taken with the design. The Norbury Chapel, N of the chancel, is of *c.*1490,[*] in sloppy Late Perp (e.g. the weak arch shapes of the windows on the N side). It includes a fireplace, a very rare thing in a private chapel before the Reformation. All the rest is mid-Victorian misplaced piety at its silliest, due to *Ford & Hesketh*, 1866.[‡] New chancel arch replacing a Saxon one,[§] to the l. of which was a C13 altar recess of which the PISCINA remains. New W end of nave replacing C11 details, extra W bay to the arcade, new thin NW tower, new transept, complete set of new roofs. Full of fittings. – PULPIT. Given by Sir Francis Vincent

* Perhaps as a thank-offering for Bosworth Field.
‡ There was a *Butterfield* restoration in 1853 (P. Thompson).
§ This, according to Mr C. Ralegh Radford, is C7; the abaci were re-used slabs of Roman cornice.

Stoke d'Abernon, brass to Sir John d'Abernon † 1277

Stoke d'Abernon, brass to Sir John d'Abernon † 1327

in 1620, the most violently Jacobean pulpit in Surrey. Heptagonal body with sounding-board (suspended by elaborate wrought-iron ties) standing on a single column and seven wooden volutes leading to seven gross monsters (male head, animal paws, single female breast). The rest of the ornament in character. Very typical, inventive but not really imaginative. Beside it C17 HOURGLASS in an elaborate wrought-iron holder. – LECTERN. English eagle on Late Baroque barley-sugar stem. – COMMUNION RAIL. Simple C17, perhaps c.1630. – AUMBRY, in the sanctuary. Violent Baroque design, perhaps German. – (Fine C13 oak CHEST. – REREDOS. The Annunciation, mid-C15, Flemish.) – PAINTINGS in the chancel. C13 fragments of an Adoration of the Lamb (E wall) and floral patterns (surround of westernmost lancet on S side). – STAINED GLASS. E window with C15 scenes from Costessey Hall Norfolk (cf. Great Bookham) in the central light, and a pair of bigger panels from Cassiobury in the outer lancets, recently attributed to the Cologne School. – All down the S side fragments made up into patterns in lancet windows. In the chancel note the top scenes in each lancet, good C15 English work. In the nave, from E to W (among others), a huge roundel of the Virgin, French, c.1510 (first lancet), and a similar roundel (second lancet), also of the Virgin, and an interesting comparison. Above it a C15 English king with first-rate colouring. The third nave lancet is filled with C15 English glass in the style that Kempe unwisely tried to copy. More C15 and C16 glass in the baptistery and the N transept. – In the Norbury Chapel, C16 Flemish roundels. – The W window is by *Westlake*. – (PLATE. Almsdishes, C17 Flemish and 1756 by *Paul Crespin*.) – BRASSES. Sir John d'Abernon † 1277, the oldest English brass, 6 ft 6 in. long and monumental, with the same superiority in quality over the average C15 brass as the best C13 tombs have over C15 shop-work. Knight in armour, full face, carrying a lance, with outstretched feet inimitably turned around rather than resting on a lion. Everything completely realized in terms of a single plane and an etcher's line. Shield still coloured blue; it was enamelled on copper and inserted separately. – Sir John, his son, † 1327, next to him. Already a decline, the figure smaller (although still 5 ft long) and fussier, under an ogee canopy. The lion has become a joke, instead of being a ferocious heraldic beast. – The others are much smaller: Anne Norbury † 1464 on the arch between chancel and Norbury Chapel, good C15 figure, 15 in. high, with eight children among robes at foot. – Ellen Bray † 1516, in swaddling clothes. – Finally a priest (s side of sanctuary), a replica of that to John Prowd † 1497, now lost. – MONUMENTS. Francis Lyfelde † 1592. Small tablet incorporating a naturalistic Elizabethan brass. – Lady Sarah Vincent † 1608 (E wall of Norbury Chapel) and Sir Thomas Vincent † 1613 and his wife (N wall of chapel). Both with life-size effigies, lying on their sides and backs under crested semicircular canopies. Stiff routine work, acceptable standard. – Sir John Norbury (the founder of the chapel), erected in 1633 in place of his old monument, 'being by injury of time demolisht'. A naïve and attractive small kneeler in Carolean armour. – Below this Viscount d'Abernon † 1941, incorporating a small Roman ciborium from the Catacombs.

MANOR HOUSE. Immediately E of the church, a very pretty situation beside a bend in the river Mole. Fragments of a C16 house remain inside, but it is effectively all of 1757, in a plain and rather dispirited brick mason's style, still with Baroque intentions but without any ornamental detail. The entrance front L-shaped, quite plain except for a two-storey Baroque-style porch, by *Sir Aston Webb*, 1911. The s front facing the river is of five bays with brick pilasters and three-bay central pediment. Any effect it might have had is spoilt by Webb's loggia of 1903, which cuts the whole front in two. The interiors have almost a pot-pourri of C18 detail in various styles, none remarkable: the STAIRCASE still of the Baroque type, with twisted balusters, a big Palladian SALOON in the middle of the river front, and a demure Adam-style room at the W end. Also brick STABLES of the same Artisan character (plain pilastered doorway etc.) as so much else in Surrey. Probably of c.1630.

Nothing in the village itself, but to the E along the road to Leatherhead first WOODLANDS PARK, elephantine Late Victorian Tudor by *Rowland Plumbe*, with a fearsome quadrangle of farm buildings on the opposite side of the road (mentioned in *The Builder*, 1886: GS). Then PACHESHAM, with two unspoilt cottages, one tile-hung with a lean-to, the other of c.1600 with exposed timber frame and brick infilling. Examples as authentic as this are rare in this part of Surrey.

To the s are SLYFIELD MANOR (*see* p. 459) and MILLFIELD HOUSE (*see* p. 367). For ASHFORD FARM HOUSE, *see* Cobham.

STREET COBHAM see COBHAM

SUNBURY*

Up to Hampton the Thamesside has for centuries been a
villeggiatura of London. W of Hampton it is less closely attached
to the town. River villages such as Sunbury still have a number
of bigger houses, but nothing like the continuous Georgian or
pre-Georgian row of well-to-do houses on the river front of
Chiswick, Twickenham, or Hampton.

ST MARY. Of the modest church designed by one *Wright*, Clerk
of the Works at Hampton Court, and built in 1752, only the
walls of W tower and nave remain, without distinguishing
features. In 1856 *Teulon* descended upon this guileless building and recast it vigorously. The effects of his steamroller sensitivity are here particularly revolting: a heavy chancel with
round-headed windows, multi-coloured brick decoration
everywhere, even, to add 'interest', to the tower. A gloomy,
depressing interior with iron-ornamented gallery (the E part of
this was removed in 1953). – SCREENS and PULPIT of stone
and marble inlaid with glass mosaic. – SGRAFFITO MURALS
in the chancel, of 1892. – PLATE. Chalice of 1662, Flagons of
1670 and 1746, Pie Dish of 1752. – The church is now disused
(1969) and its future is uncertain. The stone and glass mosaic
REREDOS is in the temporary church in Green Street.

See
p.
599

See
p.
599

ST SAVIOUR, Upper Sunbury. 1911–13 by *J. S. Alder*. – PLATE.
Chalice acquired from a private collection and attributed to the
German C14.

SUNBURY COURT (Salvation Army Youth Centre) is the only
surviving large mansion of Sunbury, now cut off from the
Thames by a road and small houses. It was originally of seven
bays with straight passages leading to outer pavilions. The
centre survives, the passages are altered. The centre has Ionic
pilasters and a pediment (a glaring red brick with stone
dressings is used). The date is *c.*1770. In the Saloon Arcadian
wall paintings by *Elias Martin*, the Swedish painter who lived
in England from 1768 to 1780.

Between Sunbury Court and the church a few more good houses.
DARBY HOUSE is Late Georgian, of two storeys, with a central semicircular projection with three windows. The windows
are arched. In FRENCH STREET, WILMARY HOUSE, C18,
two storeys, five bays, the central window with curved brick
surround. IVY HOUSE, further N, is early C18 with later
additions, and a similar central window. Opposite, Nos. 179–

* Formerly in Middlesex.

183, C18, much altered, the central part of four storeys. Back in Thames Street more villagey cottages; also RIVERMEAD HOUSE, late C18, with two tall bow windows, now very dilapidated, and MONKSBRIDGE on the other side, a large attractive C18 house at r. angles to the street, with pedimented centre and windows in giant blank arches. Then a one-storey BANK, brick with Doric pilasters, dated 1888, now painted bright blue. On the same side ORCHARD HOUSE, c.1700, three storeys, five bays, with a good iron gate. In CHURCH STREET and GREEN STREET, the OLD VICARAGE and VICARAGE COTTAGE, mostly C18, and HOLLY COTTAGE, C18, of three bays and two storeys. Further N, HAWKE HOUSE, C18 with later alterations. (Good staircase and other interior features. MHLG) More C18 houses W of the church: Nos. 2–4 Green Street, and WEST LODGE in Thames Street (now a nursing home), C18, three storeys, five bays, surrounded by badly sited recent buildings.

The modern centre of Sunbury is to the N around the station, at the junction of Green Street and Staines Road West.* Near the station there are still some modest mid-C19 houses. At the corner, a large complex of shops, offices, and flats, PYRENE HOUSE, by *R. Seifert & Partners*, 1966–9. Two thirteen-storey blocks at r. angles to the road and one six-storey one set at an angle, on top of shops fronting a fancy curved pedestrian walk, with a well designed car park behind. In the middle the old CLOCK TOWER, incongruously placed in a small sunk area. On the N side of Staines Road, BRANCH LIBRARY by *B. L. Adams* and the Surrey County Architect, *R. J. Ash*, 1964–7, a simple façade faced with nice mottled bricks, gable facing the street, split-pitched roof. To the N, off Beechwood Avenue, council housing by *Basil Spence & Partners*, 1950–1, much praised at the time. Well laid out terraces of one, two, and three storeys, in brick painted in pale pastel colours, now a little worn. Extended in 1953 by *Braddell, Deane & Bird*. (Further W, in Cadbury Road and Chertsey Road, BRITISH PETROLEUM RESEARCH CENTRE. Extensive buildings from 1928 onwards by *Wilson, Mason & Partners*.)

Charlton, 1½ m. W, by the Queen Mary Reservoir (opened 1925), was originally a small hamlet, but is now much built up. There is still THE HARROW, a small thatched C16 inn, and MANOR

---

* The area has developed rapidly. The population of Sunbury Urban District was in 1968 39,000, an expansion of 70% since 1951.

FARMHOUSE, a nice C18 red brick house of two storeys and four bays.

The whole neighbourhood of Sunbury, also E and N of Kempton Park, stands under the sign of the METROPOLITAN WATER BOARD. The large buildings were originally put up by five different companies after the Metropolis Water Act of 1852, and before the MWB was founded in 1902. They range from the typical official Italianate of 1853–5, with towers and chimneys, to sound, plain modern brick and a monstrous big affair on the Hanworth–Sunbury Common road (1927–9), which with its pompous symmetry and its lack of windows looks like an expensive war memorial.*

SURBITON

1060

ST ANDREW, Maple Road. By *Sir A. Blomfield*, 1871, i.e. early, and therefore more vigorous than he usually is. Yellow and red brick. With an almost separate N tower continuing the porch. W front with apsed baptistery and two small doorways. Very wide nave with clerestory. Narrow aisles. Transeptal chancel chapels wide open to the chancel. Straight E end. – STAINED GLASS. By *Lavers & Westlake*. – The surrounding houses are in the same style.

CHRIST CHURCH, King Charles' Road. 1862–3 by *C. L. Luck*. Lengthened 1866, N chancel aisle 1864, S chancel aisle 1871. Brick and stone dressings. No tower. W front elaborate and rather 'chapelly' (GR). – STAINED GLASS. E window by *Clayton & Bell*, 1866. The rest mostly by *Lavers & Westlake*.

ST MARK, St Mark's Hill. 1845, but completely remodelled by *P. C. Hardwick*, 1855. Destroyed in the Second World War, except for the tower, and rebuilt in a deplorable style by *Milner & Craze*, 1960.

ST MATTHEW, St Matthew's Avenue and Ewell Road. 1874–5 by *C. L. Luck*. The stateliest church in Surbiton. Big and prosperous, with SW tower with tall stone spire. Lancets and bartraceried windows. Transepts, apse.

ST RAPHAEL (R.C.), Portsmouth Road. *See* Kingston upon Thames, p. 332.

CONGREGATIONAL CHURCH, Maple Road. 1865 by *A. Phelps*. Gothic with tower and spire. Its predecessor, by *James Wilson*

* Mr W. S. Chevalier of the MWB tells us that this building was designed to filter forty-eight million gallons of water a day, and contains rapid gravity filters, which avoided the construction of some thirteen acres of filter beds.

of Bath, 1854, is close by, and with its stumpy twin towers wider and less churchy.

WATER WORKS, Portsmouth Road (technically Long Ditton). With two Norman towers close together, as castellated as they are unexpected. 1852 by *James Simpson*.

STATION. 1937 by *J. R. Scott*. One of the first in England to acknowledge the existence of a modern style. Beside it WIN-THROP HOUSE, a ten-storey office block in a simple modern style, 1959–60 by *Fitzroy Robinson & Partners*.

Surbiton was formerly Kingston New Town, or Kingston-on-Railway as it was starting to be called in 1840, when the railway had arrived (*see Companion to the Almanac*, 1840). The present railway station is good enough to justify such a name.

SOUTHBOROUGH HOUSE, Ashcombe Avenue. By *John Nash*, 1808. L-shaped plan with a pretty octagonal domed porch in the angle. Garden front of seven bays, the middle one a canted, only one-storeyed bay window. Stuccoed. Upper windows arched. Pediment over the centre. Two-storeyed SUMMER HOUSE in the garden.

Opposite, No. 9, an attractive house by *Ronald J. Robson*.

WOODBURY, Kingsdowne Road. A good example of Norman Shaw's tile-hung style.

⟨By the river, at the corner of Portsmouth Road and Grove Road, ANGLERS REACH, good new flats by *Fitzroy Robinson & Partners*, 1963–4.⟩

SUTTON

Sutton, i.e. since 1965 the London Borough of Sutton, has 166,430 inhabitants (1969). In 1961 there was little to see at Sutton. The situation has now changed dramatically. The centre is the crossing of Carshalton, Cheam, and High Streets. Here was THE COCK. It had a pretty façade of 1897: round angle bay and two shallow minor bays, all three with scrolly ornament, but was demolished in 1961, and its successor is sadly characterless, a waste of a focal point. The old inn sign has been preserved above the signpost at the cross-roads. Behind this modern centre lay the old centre with the parish church. However, hardly anything reminds one of the past here either.

ST NICHOLAS. Rebuilt by *Edwin Nash* in 1862–4. Flint, with broach-spire, not attractive. – In the churchyard MAUSOLEUM of 1777, with pyramid roof, rusticated quoins, and a rusticated door surround. It is to the Gibson family of London.

Just s of St Nicholas in CHEAM ROAD two more remarkable
churches. One is the TRINITY METHODIST CHURCH, 1907
by *Gordon & Gunton*, with a bold tower carrying a 'crown'
like Newcastle and Edinburgh Cathedrals. Polygonal apse.
Church Hall attached to the 'E' end. The other is the
BAPTIST CHURCH, 1934 by *Cachemaille-Day*. Red brick with
'moderne' details; the secular parts well grouped.

ALL SAINTS, Benhilton. By *S. S. Teulon*, 1863–6. Large and
very prominently placed. Big broad w tower. Dec details.
Broad nave, cruciform piers with chamfered corners. Circular
clerestory windows. None of the more obtrusive mannerisms
of Teulon. – (STAINED GLASS. 1965, outstandingly good. E
window by *J. & M. Kettlewell*, s aisle windows by *John Hayward*. A. Clifton-Taylor)

ST BARNABAS, St Barnabas Road. 1884–91 by *Carpenter &
Ingelow*. Red brick.

CHRIST CHURCH, Christchurch Park. 1888 by *Newman &
Jacques*. Red brick, with polygonal apse. No tower. Lancet
windows. The w end with the quite separate porch with
doorways in three directions and the baptistery between two
low bays is of *c.*1910–12 (by *J. D. Round*). Inside, spectacular
ROODSCREEN with the rood supported on an openwork crown.

ST JOHN BAPTIST, Belmont. 1915 by *Greenaway & Newberry*
(GR).

OUR LADY OF THE ROSARY (R.C.), St Barnabas Road. Converted from a school into a church by *E. Ingress Bell* in 1887
(GR). His is the tall polygonal roof over the chancel, which has
a domical vault inside.

(ST EDWARD (R.C.), Sutton Park. 1876 by *C. A. Buckler*. DE)

ROYAL MARSDEN HOSPITAL, Sutton Downs. Big new blocks
by *Lanchester & Lodge* 1960–2.

In the HIGH STREET, a few modern buildings of 1957–8:
LILLEY & SKINNER by *M. Egan*, and, much better detailed,
WILLERBY'S by *C. J. Epril*. ⟨These now seem small fry in
comparison with what has been built since. Apart from Croydon, Sutton has more recent tall buildings than any other town
centre in this book. Their contrasting styles are an instructive
illustration of the shift from the use of glass curtain-walling in
the Miesian tradition to the more expressionistic use of reinforced concrete that has been gaining ground in the sixties.
But apart from Eagle Star House at the N end, which closes
the vista downhill (*see* below), the tall blocks are set back from
the High Street, so that the old scale of the centre has been

preserved.* The most prominent new building in the High Street itself will be BOOTS and SAINSBURY'S, opposite Willerby's, now building (1969), architect *Basil Whiting*. It has a large blind upper wall. Further up the hill on the E side is W. H. SMITH, with a good plain new front of concrete and glass bands, in scale with the older shops. Hiding behind this, but very prominent from a distance, are the CIVIC OFFICES, 98 a nine-storey block on stilts, with the entrance in Throwley Road. The whole complex is by the *Owen Luder Partnership*, 1961–4. The tall block is a forceful, boldly profiled rectangular building with canted corners. There is a staircase tower at either end, the one nearer the High Street projecting well above the main building. The towers have continuous vertical bands of rough concrete, the office block has chamfered horizontal bands, projecting forward from the window plane. In ST NICHOLAS ROAD, off the other side of the High Street, is the most interesting new shop-front in Sutton, the extension to AMOS REYNOLDS, by *Michael Manser Associates*, 1965–6. Brilliantly simple. A plain wall faced with narrow white un-bonded tiles, laid vertically, cut through by two tiers of canti-levered steel-framed glass boxes which act as miniature rooms for furniture display. At the end, simple warehouse door, grey, with white monogram. Opposite, ST NICHOLAS HOUSE, by *Lane Bridges*, 1965. Four-storey block, grey curtain-walling above shops, interlocking with an eight-storey block above. w of the churchyard in ROBIN HOOD LANE, a new HEALTH CENTRE, building 1969, by the *London Borough of Sutton*. Two storeys, white brick. Back to the High Street. Past the crossroads in SUTTON COURT ROAD is the tallest building of all, VIGILANT HOUSE by *Robert J. Wood & Partners*, 1961–6. Seventeen storeys of impressive sheer glass curtain-walling. The structure is of reinforced concrete, cantilevered out on two sides, so that, as one approaches, the building seems to float above a void (in fact a sunken car park). Spandrel panels are in a neutral pale green; the top floor is finished off neatly by a broad black band. The companion building, SENTINEL HOUSE, is of four storeys, with the same details, but on stilts. The two are linked by an ingenious T-shaped entrance bridge over the car park. Beyond the railway, in BRIGHTON ROAD, SUTHERLAND HOUSE, shops and offices, also by *Robert J. Wood & Partners*, 1961–6. Eleven storeys with horizontal

* The development plan for Sutton intends the High Street eventually to become a pedestrian area.

bands of white mosaic cladding. Further s, the Victorian villas along the Brighton Road are being replaced by flats.

Finally the N end of the town. At the bend at the end of the High Street, EAGLE STAR HOUSE, another composition in concrete by the *Owen Luder Partnership*, 1963–7 (still largely unoccupied at the time of writing). A nine-storey office block above two projecting storeys with shops. The line of shops follows the curve of the road, then turns back along two sides of a little precinct. In front of this is a free-standing building with glazed upper floor on concrete stilts. Wilfully complicated stairs link this and the main block to a car park behind. The tall block has horizontal bands of concrete with a rough surface, and round-ended lift-shafts and stairs of concrete with the shuttering marks exposed. The group looks best from the N, making an emphatic statement at the entrance to the High Street, but closer up there are too many tricky details (e.g. the low concrete lintels of the shop doorways). Further N, HELENA HOUSE, by *Morgan & Branch*, 1962; curtain-walling with green spandrel panels. To the w, off COLLINGWOOD ROAD, CHAUCER HOUSE, depressing fifteen-storey flats by the *London Borough of Sutton*, 1965.

(E of Belmont Rise, 1½ m. SE, some red brick walling, part of a C17 HARE WARREN, survives as the front garden walls of houses in Warren Avenue and High View.*)

SUTTON near Abinger *see* ABINGER

SUTTON PLACE

Sutton Place is, side by side with Layer Marney, the most important English house of the years following immediately after Hampton Court. It has in common with Layer Marney and a group of buildings in Suffolk, near Old Shrubland Park, the use of terracotta for the ornamentation of windows and the use of small-scale Renaissance forms in the terracotta pieces. The material was indeed something suggested by the itinerant Italians, and had first been used in England, glazed, i.e. as faience or maiolica, at Hampton Court in 1521. Layer Marney was begun by Lord Marney before 1523. Sir Richard Weston was granted the Sutton estate in 1521. When he started building there is no knowing, nor when the house was completed. Henry VIII was his guest at Sutton in 1533. The

* Information from Mr N. H. Nail.

style of the details points to the early 1520s, but there are features at Sutton Place which make such a date appear prodigiously early.

Sir Richard Weston was a protégé of Henry VIII. He was a Knight of the Bath, a Gentleman of the Privy Chamber, and later Under-Treasurer of England. In 1520 he accompanied the King to the Field of the Cloth of Gold. In the 1530s his only son was involved in the scandals created round Anne Boleyn and was beheaded in 1536. The father however remained in favour until he died in 1542.

Sutton Place was built as a nearly square house, c.140 by c.130 ft, round a courtyard. The N side was demolished in 1786 (*Gent. Mag.*), so that the house now appears to have far-projecting wings like Barrington Court in Somerset, which was begun shortly after 1514 and is supposed to be the earliest house in England with an E-plan. We shall have to revert to it presently. Sutton Place is of brick and two storeys in height. It was (and is) approached from the N, where the entrance range is now missing. This had a four-storeyed gatehouse with yet higher polygonal turrets – the motif familiar from before the time of Henry VIII, and also from Hampton Court, St James's Palace, etc. – and stepped gables at the ends of the E and W wings. These remain. They are a motif which already the C15 had taken over from the Netherlands.

The surprising thing is the composition in the courtyard. 33 The HALL range is the one opposite the entrance. It is perfectly symmetrical, with the doorway in the middle and two exactly identical projections in the angles to the W and E ranges, which are also nearly symmetrical. Barrington Court had had a central porch and projections in the angles to the wings too; but there had been slight irregularities in the fenestration. At Sutton Place it is all large windows of two, three, or four lights, all of identical height, and all of identical detail. The detail is largely of terracotta. The windows have a transom and still – a medieval survival – cusped arches at the tops of the lights and below the transom. The symmetry in the wings includes a small doorway close to their S ends and a canted bay window not quite midway between the S and the former N range. How dear symmetry – that Italian virtue – was to the heart of the designer of the house is best seen by the fact that the l. angle projection of the S range represents the bay window of the hall, but the r. one represents nothing. The S side incidentally is quite irregular, with a broad projection at the E end, then the other hall bay, opposite that to the N, then attached to this the projection of the hall fireplace, then the back doorway of the hall, in line with the N doorway, and further W another projection, judging by the blocked original windows formerly containing the principal staircase. To the W lies an office court whose E range forms part of the house of the 1520s to 1530s, but whose other ranges are mid-C17. Yet further W an isolated C18 stable range, and W of that a walled garden with an octagonal SUMMER HOUSE of the same date as the house.

In detail the most interesting part of the elevations is the Italian terracotta motifs, culminating in panels with naked amorini of which there are twenty in the parapet over the centre of the hall range, twelve, in two tiers of six, above the curiously insignificant N doorway to the hall, and one tier of six above the S doorway. The details of the parapet however (and the thin polygonal turrets which flank the centre parapet) – blank cusped arches, quatrefoils, etc. – are Perp, and so are the details of the door surrounds, especially the spandrels. That applies also to the doorways of the W and E ranges. On the other hand the curious panels with the initials of Richard Weston and a tun which appear in the quoins etc. ought to be called Renaissance of a sort, as are the lozenge panels in the parapets.

But more Renaissance, or rather more Elizabethan, than these individual elements is the general tenor of the façades of the courtyard, the large size, the regularity, and the even character of the windows. Even more Elizabethan, or indeed Jacobean, is one further motif, if it must be accepted as original, as has so far been done in the literature: the fact that the hall is entered not close to one end but somewhere near its middle. However, it is more likely that this was not so. In the SW corner lay the original kitchen. The partition walls in this part of the house are all thin and later. Should it not therefore be assumed that the hall of the 1520s ended just W, or just possibly one bay W, of the doorways, that there was a proper wall there with the customary entrances to kitchen and offices and also one in this case to the staircase to the S, and that a wooden screen ran E of the doorways? It would make the planning of the S range much more natural and remove a baffling anachronism from English architectural history.

Another problem is the height of the hall. Its present coved plasterwork ceiling cannot be original. Original roof beams are supposed to be beneath, and in addition the fenestration and the height in relation to width make it likely that the hall as built by Weston occupied only the ground floor. Of the other interiors not much need be said. The spectacular LONG GALLERY in the E range dates in its present form only from 1878. The wing had been gutted by fire in the C18. Yet Kirby Hall of 1570 had a long gallery in exactly this position, and long galleries existed at the time of Henry VIII (e.g. at Richmond). The present STAIRCASES date from the C17. They are in the two projections of the S front and nothing very special. There are also several Elizabethan or Jacobean overmantels and a large number of very impressive TAPESTRIES not originally belonging to the house. The most noteworthy of the fitments however is the heraldic STAINED GLASS in the hall. The earliest group certainly belongs to the time of Henry VIII and is close in style to the glass in King's College Chapel Cambridge. The details are in the new Renaissance style, though different from those of the terracotta. The second group is of c.1640, the third of varying dates down to 1844.

TADWORTH
2¼ m. SW of Banstead

2050

TADWORTH COURT. A splendid house of some time between 1694 and 1704, built for Leonard Wessels. Eleven bays wide and two storeys over a basement. Hipped roof, with dormers. Yellow brick, in the five-bay centre with ample stone dressings. The centre is emphasized moreover by quoins, a doorway with big Corinthian columns, a carved lintel, an open scrolly pediment, a staircase with carved balustrading leading up to the doorway, an upper window with decorated side-scrolls, and a pediment. In the pediment oval with garlands. Two-storeyed hall with high panelling and gay Rococo plasterwork above, including trophies and medallions with men in armour. This work is of c.1750. The ceiling on the other hand is clearly of the time when the house was built. Division into panels, the centre being oval with a wreath. At the back of the hall gallery with the strong twisted balusters fashionable about 1700.

HOUSING. An estate of 532 houses and 150 flats was built in 1953–6 by *Clifford Culpin & Partners* for three different councils, joining forces for this job. The estate consists of two- and three-storeyed units. In it the medieval manor of PRESTON HAWE. This has been under excavation by the Ministry of Public Building and Works.

3050

TANDRIDGE

ST PETER. The interest of the church is its timber-work. Bell-turret with shingled spire resting internally on big timbers with cross-braces not uniformly arranged. Trussed rafter roofs in the nave and chancel assigned to *c.*1300. One tie-beam E of the timbers supporting the turret. In the chancel Norman slit-window and simple Norman N doorway. They are probably of before 1100. The aisles are both C19: S 1844, N 1874 by *Sir G. G. Scott*, who lived at Rooksnest, now Ouborough (*see* Godstone, p. 261). – REREDOS. By *Scott*.

In the churchyard a yew tree with a trunk over 30 ft in diameter. Also MONUMENT to Lady Scott † 1872 (opposite the Garden of Remembrance). Richly sculptured marble tomb-chest.

TANDRIDGE COURT, S of the church. Mostly of 1926 by *Arnold Mitchell*. Core of the early C19, and older traces.

TANDRIDGE BROOK FARM, 1 m. S. Handsome early C18 brick farm, five by two bays, with a string course between storeys and an eaves cornice.

4050

TATSFIELD

A curiosity. High up on the Downs, part of the shack colony of Biggin Hill, over the Kent border. This grew up about 1920 with tiny houses almost lost in foliage, which ironically makes just as effective a suburban landscape as the most contrived planting at Welwyn or Hampstead Garden Suburb. The estate was originally advertised in London as 'Come to London Alps'. The old village green is at the S end of this.

ST MARY. Further S again, by itself right on the crest of the Downs (790 ft), with a magnificent view S over the Weald. Nave walls all Norman, in dark sandstone with light sandstone quoins. The N side, with only two tiny windows in it, is impressive. The S side has one window of *c.*1300 and one Perp window. C13 chancel arch dying against the imposts. The E window is like the S window of *c.*1300. The tower, standing inside the nave, is a pinchbeck Gothic affair of 1838. The oddest things in the church are two lancet windows, one on each side of the chancel. Outside they are quite plain; inside the N lancet is decked out with mouldings almost on a cathedral scale, and the S lancet clearly had similar detail, now gone. The main order has a complex keel-shaped section, resting on shafts with circular abaci, and a continuous inner order. The date is *c.*1230. Pleasant village interior. – PAINTING. Crucifixion (N wall). A Rubens copy. – PLATE. Cup 1569. – MONUMENT. John Corbett † 1711 (s side of nave). Simple architectural frame, but painted wood, not marble.

THAMES DITTON

1060

ST NICHOLAS. Flint and stone. Low, broad, early C13 W tower with a pretty weatherboarded top stage and a spike. Early C13 chancel, cf. the N window, now inside, with a round-headed rere-arch, but a lancet-shaped opening. The N chapel opens towards the chancel by a low four-centred brick arch below the early C13 lancet. This looks early C16. The arcade between nave and N aisle is Latest Perp: octagonal piers, depressed rounded arches. The outer N wall is brick of 1826 by *W. McIntosh Brooks.* The S arcade, S aisle, and S chapel are by *Ferrey,* 1864. The E view of the church, with four gables, is handsome. Most of the window details are renewed. – FONT. Norman, in the shape of a block capital, with the four lunettes carrying small motifs in medallions, e.g. the Lamb and the Cross and an ibex falling on to its horns. Small heads at the corners. – EASTER SEPULCHRE. A most unusual Perp stone structure in the form of a six-poster. Heavy attic with crenellation. – PLATE. Chalice and Cover 1637; Paten 1715; Flagon and Almsdish 1724; Strainer 1807. – MONUMENTS. A number of brasses, e.g. Robert Smythe † 1539 and his wife † 1549 and children; kneeling figures. Also a plate with an arched top that would fit into the Easter Sepulchre. This commemorates Erasmus Forde † 1533 and his wife † 1559 and children. – Sidney Godolphin † 1732. Hanging wall-monument with bust standing above the inscription plate.

(OUR LADY OF LOURDES (R.C.), Hampton Court Way. 1965 by *D. A. Reid* of *F. G. Broadbent & Partners.* Circular, with central altar and segmented shell concrete dome. – SCULPTURE. Crucifix by *D. McFall.* – STAINED GLASS by *P. Fourmaintreaux.* DE)

The part of Thames Ditton where the church stands still offers a relatively unspoilt picture of a riverside village. The big house, now the HOME OF COMPASSION, is the former BOYLE FARM. Probably Georgian, though altered in the C20, of red brick, seven bays and two and a half storeys. The centre towards the river with a big bow, towards the entrance with a

16—S.

three-bay pediment. Brick quoins. Entrance hall with a screen of two Ionic columns and an upper gallery. Early C19 stables of yellow brick with a lantern. Also a brick chapel, 1925 by *Christopher Wright*. Opposite a handsome modern house by *Michael Lyell*. Two-storeyed with a low-pitched roof and a one-storey attachment containing the living and dining rooms. By the river a nice group of whitewashed houses and a pretty suspension bridge (completed in 1914) on to a small island. A little s of Boyle Farm at a crossing PICTON HOUSE, tall, three bays, with Ionic porch. Further s, in STATION ROAD, by the s end of High Street, a terrace of three early C18 brick houses with giant brick pilasters separating them. Door hoods on carved brackets. Next to these OLD MANOR HOUSE of the same date. The doorcase with Roman Doric pilasters and a triglyph frieze is unaltered. MANOR VANE, with central pediment and weathervane dated 1766, was the former stables. Further w ALMSHOUSES built in 1720. Two-storey block of six dwellings. Upper windows segment-headed. Brick.

Less than ½ m. SE GIGGSHILL GREEN. Here on one side ST LEONARD'S COTTAGES, nine bays, two storeys, with a pediment. On the opposite side (sw) the building of the MILK MARKETING BOARD, large, Neo-Georgian, by *H. S. Layton*, completed 1940.

HINCHLEY WOOD see Claygate.

WESTON GREEN. *See* p. 515.

WATER WORKS. *See* Surbiton, p. 473.

THORNCOMBE STREET *see* HASCOMBE

3060

THORNTON HEATH

(ST ALBAN, Grange Road, South Norwood. By *Bucknall & Comper*, nave 1889, chancel 1894 – in fact *Sir Ninian Comper*'s first church. Red-brick Perp, with a high E end over a crypt, the s chapel window being corbelled out as an oriel. Six-bay nave and three-bay chancel, with clerestory and hammerbeam roof throughout. The influence is clearly G. G. Scott Jun., with plain square piers and arches dying straight into them, transversely over the aisles as well as the main arcades – an austere effect, even a little papery, as Comper's glorious furnishings were never executed (except for the STAINED GLASS in the s chapel E window, 1903). NT)

MINISTRY OF WORKS, No. 72 High Street. Quite a good
  modern building. By *E. H. Banks*, 1954.
⟨Several more recent office blocks in LONDON ROAD, including
  CITY HOUSE, a large fourteen-storey slab by *David Stern &*
  Partners, designed in 1963.⟩

THORPE   *0060*

Like a Middlesex village, with curving walled streets screening
medium-sized houses in small parks; the only example in the
county. Enlarged since 1945, but all the walls kept, hence the
village has stayed intact. This was clearly a deliberate and praiseworthy effort on the part of the planning authorities.

ST MARY. Authentic C17 brick tower, very like a simple Essex
  tower. Two-light brick bell-stage, diagonal buttresses on the
  W side only, plain tower arch without capitals, a rarity in
  Surrey. The rest has medieval walling but is effectively all
  renewed outside, though a little Dec detail remains on the S
  side. The C13 arcades (with the familiar circular capitals and
  circular abaci) were pulled down at some time and rebuilt in
  the C19. The chancel arch is C12, of two orders, completely
  plain, with two-light C15 squints on either side giving a clear
  view from aisles to altar. In the chancel authentic Dec windows
  on the N side (now blocked by the organ chamber), probably
  representing Chertsey Abbey work, especially the single-light
  window with ornate head consisting of a trefoil under a
  quatrefoil and two dagger-shapes. Also in the chancel PISCINAE
  and SEDILIA, a strange, circumstantial C14 piece. Four bays,
  two unequal sedilia flanked by identical piscinae, all ogee-
  headed, all under a hood-mould. The nave roof is very tall and
  has tie-beams with kingposts and four-way struts. – FONT.
  Early mock-Perp, possibly C18. – COMMUNION RAIL with
  twisted balusters. – STAINED GLASS. Several windows of
  *c.*1847. – PLATE. Good Cup, Copenhagen, 1704; Flagon 1738;
  Paten late C17. – MONUMENT. Elizabeth Townsend † 1754.
  Praying cherub, with a big head, in niche above inscription;
  quite clever asymmetry but not much feeling. Style something
  like Cheere's, and in fact done by Cheere's pupil *Sir Robert*
  Taylor before he turned architect. These big-headed, almost
  Mongol, cherubs are a Taylor trade-mark (cf. Richard
  Emmott at Colne, Lancs.).
CHURCH APPROACH is pretty in a typical Home Counties way:

short lane with old brick cottages – and also, alas, a new Neo-Georgian vicarage – blocked by the church. To the w in Coldharbour Lane is SPELTHORNE ST MARY, big, featureless late C18 stock brick with a C17 half-timbered barn and good early C18 gates brought from Feltham Middlesex. w from here a long stretch of curving walls, with behind them on the N side THORPE HOUSE, an attractive provincial C18 front, five by two bays, extended later by one bay to the E; an odd design with the bays at either end accented with giant pilasters. Stock brick with red brick trimmings. The house as a whole looks *c*.1735 (cf. e.g. Sherman's at Dedham Essex for a grander example), but some of the details, such as the delicate string course dividing the storeys, seem fifty years later. Heavy Doric porch.

To the E of Church Approach the VILLAGE HALL, converted from an unusual brick C17 barn. Pilastered, with three tiny lancet windows per bay, the type of a medieval tithe barn. Beyond this again, MANOR HOUSE FARM is a simple, big, early C18 brick farmhouse, and ½ m. further E is EASTLY END COTTAGE, a good unrestored C17 building, part brick and part half-timber, still with its casements.

THURSLEY

2 m. N of Hindhead

On the N slopes of Hindhead, cared for but not suburbanized. At the N end an open green faces N with a wide view to the Hog's Back. From it the village street leads s to the church.

ST MICHAEL. Effectively all new, except for the belfry. One more example of appalling restoration, by *Ferrey* in 1860 (N aisle) and far more by *J. W. Penfold* in 1883–6. The style now is hard E.E., but in fact the original church was largely Saxon, and two tiny windows came to light in 1927 in the N side of the chancel: double-splayed, still with a crude (Norman) red pattern of ashlaring and rosettes in the splays, and with their original mid-wall windowboards still in place. A Norman window remains above the N arcade. There are also two lancets in the s wall of the chancel, and the chancel arch is probably of *c*.1270. It has no capitals, and springs from squinched jambs – a queer effect. In the late C15 a new central belfry was added and an enormous timber cage was planted in the middle of the nave to support it, an extraordinary thing to do in a small

church. It consists of four immense corner posts (tree trunks
2 ft 6 in. thick), two against the N, two against the S wall of the
nave, just clear of it. They support tie-beams on arched braces.
Longitudinally (from W to E) they are joined by four-centred
arches. The arches carry beams, and on these stand two more
strut posts on each side supporting two more tie-beams on
arched braces – a construction so elaborate as to be worthy of
Essex. The difference between Thursley and Essex is that the
Essex system is to build up homogeneous constructions of
framing and belfry, whereas at Thursley the timberwork simply
supports a vast platform. A nice refinement is that the beams
and braces are carefully designed to keep the E views unblocked. The whole construction has an almost Vanbrughian
air of overstatement, for what it supports is not a particularly
big bell-turret. – ROYAL ARMS. Of 1783, in good condition. –
FONT. Certainly pre-1100, possibly Saxon. One protean
tapered bowl 3 ft high, with a ring-moulding halfway up. No
other ornament, except a crude band of chevrons round the
top. – CHEST. Excellent vernacular; 1622. – STAINED GLASS.
In the N aisle, saint and donor, C15, Flemish, from Costessey,
Norfolk. – PLATE. Cup 1662. – MONUMENTS. Katharine
Woods † 1793. The provincial tradition of polychrome marble
(four types are used) carried over to the Grecian tablet with urn
and sarcophagus. The result is a bit crude, but lively. Unsigned.
– CHURCHYARD TOMBS. A group of table tombs of c.1800,
opposite the W end. Lumpish, as the C18 generally was in
Surrey. (But the most famous gravestone at Thursley is that
which portrays a sailor being 'barbarously murdered' on Hindhead, 1786, unusual in that it is signed *R. M. Paye del.* and *J.
Eads sc.*. but their efforts are crude. The white cross to
Lutyens's mother † 1906 is plain, but that to his nephew Derek
† 1918 has a characteristic splayed base and bronze reliefs. The
bombastic American equivalent to Lutyens can be seen in the
family grave of the New York skyscraper architect turned
English Conservative politician, *Alfred Bossom*, 1931. NT)
The plan of Thursley is a rough green with a wide view to the N,
a through-road running E–W, and two cul-de-sac roads leading
off to the S end of the green: The Lane going SW and The
Street going S past the church to end on the N slopes of Hindhead. No coherent village views, but some of the best individual cottages in the county. (THE CORNER is a row of
cottages converted by *Lutyens* (in 1888–90, when he was only
nineteen) into a single house with a big tile-hung wing at the

back. Further additions *c*.1895. Lutyens grew up at Thursley at THE COTTAGE (now Lutyens House) in The Street. NT)

Down The Lane first OLDE HALL, on the S side. C16, black and white timber-framing at either end and a rubble stone centre. Opposite this ROSE COTTAGE and PAX COTTAGE, a very pretty tile-hung pair (with timber-framing underneath, as usual). Beyond, at the end of the lane, is BADGERS, plain, rustic C18 brick with a very pretty monopitch-roofed small house in the garden. 1952, by *Russell Brockbank* (of *Punch*), nicely painted.

The Street has most of its notable buildings on the W side, starting with WHEELER'S FARM, straightforward C16 timber-framing. Then, after a gap, WHEELER'S COTTAGE, a copybook unrestored Surrey cottage, the N end C18 brick, the S end a long tile-hung first-floor overhang on a rubble base, all with half-hipped tile roof. The contrasting textures are delightful. This is set back from the road: close to it comes first THE LODGE, demure C18, then BOXALLS and VINE COTTAGE, both timber-framed and both with very pretty fronts of quite unselfconscious C19 red and grey brickwork – perhaps *c*.1840. A beautiful group beautifully kept. (Opposite, *Lutyens*'s Village Institute of 1900, now PROSPECT COTTAGE. NT) The road then bends round towards the church, passing the OLD PARSONAGE, which looks as though it might be a hall-house inside, the centre half-timbered C16 with diagonal braces. Finally, beside the church is HILL FARM, a rustic symmetrical brick front of *c*.1700 added to a big older farmhouse. Four-bay centre and shallow wings of two bays apiece.

See p. 599

TIGBOURNE COURT
1¼ m. S of Witley

9030

86 *Lutyens*'s gayest and most elegant building, and probably his best. It was built in 1899–1901 for Sir Edgar Horne, and stands right beside the main road from Milford to Petworth, its superb geometry a startling shock in these leafy but sedate surroundings. Here the free Tudor style of Munstead Wood and Orchards is stiffened with a dash of C17 vernacular classicism, a style Lutyens rarely used; for once he was really and unselfconsciously gay, witty instead of facetious. The crispness and panache is like nothing else he built. It could only have been done by a young man – Lutyens was thirty – and perhaps it

could only have been done once in a lifetime. The entrance front is U-shaped, with the single-storey wings brought forward and ending in immense coupled chimneys flanked by big curved screen walls. This sets up the liveliest kind of counterpoint to the main block in the centre, which consists of three gables close together above three incredibly thin and elegant pedimented windows. The ground floor is a simple Doric loggia *in antis*. The texture is the most intricate and carefully worked out of all Lutyens's buildings and gives Tigbourne an extraordinarily feminine – not effeminate – appearance: Bargate stone, galletted throughout, with brick quoins and thin horizontal bands of tiles running across the whole house. There is hardly a better building in England to give an idea of the effect of architectural geometry pure and simple. The prodigious accentuation of the wings has the odd side-effect that, although the front is completely symmetrical, it never seems so because the eye is led away completely by the play of chimneys and screen walls. The back and sides have relatively little to offer after this:* the gardens are good, original (by *Gertrude Jekyll*) and largely intact, and there is a good cottage by Lutyens to the s, overlooking a green.

The inside planning is as unforcedly happy as the entrance front. The loggia opens into the middle of a long narrow hall running from side to side across the house. In front of the visitor a glazed roundel in a plain wall hints at the stair-well beyond, reached from one end of the hall. The stair-well fills the centre of the house, the visitor mounting between walls a few steps at a time, an easy irresistible flow which makes the ninety-degree turns at the top perfectly natural. The idea is an adaptation of Norman Shaw's 180 Queen's Gate, Kensington. One of the wings contains the kitchen, the other waywardly contains the drawing room, with a charming little columned sub-room at one end around the fireplace. All the detail is classical, but never obtrusively so. Tigbourne leaves the visitor uncertain whether simply to be profoundly thankful for what is there, or to regret that Lutyens never afterwards came up to this level.‡

* Billiard room added *c.*1910 by *Horace Farquharson* (NT).

‡ (Lutyens himself had cause to regret Tigbourne Court, as his then technical partner *E. B. Badcock* allowed numerous constructional errors, and the influential Horne (M.P. for Guildford and Chairman of the Pru.) did not employ Lutyens again (*see* Shackleford, p. 451). Badcock incidentally was a building contractor by trade, and had no part in the design. NT)

TILFORD
2 m. SE of Farnham

A delightful village, with just enough houses leading from one part to the next to give continuity to a charming plan. Triangular green sloping downhill to the river Wey and the medieval bridge, with the road climbing beyond through scattered cottages on the other side to tile roof and weatherboarded barns of the C16 UPPER STREET FARM. Not yet suburbanized.

ALL SAINTS. Honest small job in the style of c.1260 by *Ewan Christian*, 1867, in dark Bargate stone. Inside empty, but with a good selection of Late Victorian STAINED GLASS of various styles: E window like *Powell*, most of nave and aisle windows like *Kempe*. (By *Lutyens* Mrs Chapman's GRAVE, 1908. NT)

BRIDGES. Both medieval, and very similar, one at the N end on the way to Farnham, another at the bottom of the green to the E. Dark Bargate stone, the cutwaters pointed upstream and rounded downstream. Probably built by Waverley Abbey (cf. also Elstead and Eashing); they have something of the unaffected functionalism that one might expect of a Cistercian bridge.

(INSTITUTE, by the village green. By *Lutyens*, 1893. On a slope, with a long seat below and an outside stair on the r. Half-timbering above. NT)

TILFORD HOUSE, N of the village. A splendid small early C18 house connected with the Farnham masons. This one looks c.1740, when the Baroque spirit was still alive in the provinces but Baroque details were beginning to be replaced. Its nearest relation is Sandford House in West Street at Farnham. S front of five by two bays with a similar extension on the W side. All windows segment-headed, all details very simple. Tiny split pediment over the central bay, Doric doorcase with a sundial between lintel and hood. Most of these houses manage one memorable effect (and much of their success is that they do not attempt anything more tricky): here it is the way that the doorcase and sundial echo the upward shift of the central pediment. Coeval front walls with wooden half-Chinese gates, and a simple brick outbuilding E of the stables built as a PRESBYTERIAN CHAPEL in 1776.

(SHEEPHATCH HOUSE (formerly Heathy Field), ¾ m. N, is a villa of c.1840 with a delicate shell-hooded doorway by *Lutyens*, 1890. TANCREDSFORD, further E, large and hand-

some Neo-Georgian, is by *Falkner*, *c.*1920, GREYFRIARS by
E. Turner Powell, *c.*1910. NT)
CROOKSBURY HOUSE. See p. 175.

TITSEY

4050

Small, little more than estate cottages under the Downs on the
Kent border.

ST JAMES. 1861 by *Pearson*. If Pearson had died in 1867, when
he was fifty, he would have been remembered not as a gentle
Late Victorian architect, but as a violent Mid-Victorian one.
This church lacks the ferocity of buildings like Daylesford in
Gloucestershire or Scorborough in the East Riding, but it is
crisp and hard in the Butterfieldian sense. Attached s tower
and shingled broach-spire, and a few bloody-minded details
like the vestry door on the N side, set diagonally behind a
knobbly free-standing column. The inside is rock-hard and
almost without feeling, just the opposite of the qualities of a
late Pearson church. The E end stays in the memory because of
the good STAINED GLASS by *Clayton & Bell*, exactly fitting
the mood of the church, with gritty blues and maroons. –
MONUMENTS. Sir John Gresham † 1643, erected 1660. A
pedestrian aedicule (N wall of nave).* – In the N chapel, two
Victorian effigies: Granville Leveson-Gower † 1895, adequate,
figure by *Thomas Brock*, canopy designed by *Pearson*, and
Emily Leveson-Gower † 1872, competent (i.e. just a little
better), by *Matthew Noble* (cf. Limpsfield). – The most moving
monument is almost fortuitous, the first-war battlefield cross
of Lt R. C. Leveson-Gower, laid on top of a foliated C13
cross-slab. – BRASS. Wm. Gresham † 1579 with his wife and
children. The main figures 10 in. high. – PLATE. Chalice and
Cover 1569; Flagon 1678.

TITSEY PLACE. Built in 1775, but the outward appearance all
now indifferent 1832. Two-storeyed stucco Gothick s front
with slightly higher tower behind. There are hundreds of
country houses like it. *George Devey* is known to have added a
lodge *c.*1855; this must be the picturesque half-timber and
stone lodge on the way to Limpsfield.

Titsey is just too far N to have any really picturesque Wealden
cottages. The best are CHURCH COTTAGES, opposite the
church, a C16 timber-framed range with a later wing at r.
angles in brick and flint dated 1673.

* This is a C19 copy with the original inscription tablet (R. Gunnis).

In Church Field, near Pilgrims Lodge Field, a ROMANO-
CELTIC TEMPLE was excavated in 1879. It is near the line of
the old London–Brighton road, and is actually visible in
Tatsfield parish. The *cella*, *c.*30 ft square, was within a *temenos*
whose wall was 100 ft square. Occupation material of both the
C3 A.D. and, strangely, the medieval period was found; it was
thus in use later than the temple on Farley Heath (*see* Albury).

ROMAN VILLA. The Romano-British villa in Titsey Park was
excavated in 1864. It was of corridor type, with two corridors
running along most of the length of the N and S fronts, and
measured 130 by 55 ft. Seven of its nine rooms were concentrated at the W end, and one was of apsidal construction
with decorations in red stucco. The W end originally had a
hypocaust. The original occupation (166–80, on the coin
evidence) was followed *c.*320–40 by conversion into a fulling
works – or so it is suggested, judging by considerable alterations to the heating system. Small finds include *terra sigillata*
and Castor ware from Northamptonshire, from the earlier
occupation. A bronze mask of Neptune was also found.
Within 1 m. other Roman buildings have been deduced from
remains near the temple, one of plain unbonded flint and with
fragments of stucco and a stamped tile perhaps from Ashtead.

TOLWORTH
1 m. S of Surbiton

1060

On and around the Kingston by-pass, and looks it. Improvement
has come from an unexpected direction, in additions to two
churches, by *Kenneth Wood*, 1957–9. Both are poor wee things
of the 1930s: ST GEORGE has a handsomely detailed flat-
roofed church hall attached to it, and EMMANUEL has been
given a false W front which might seem anathema to puritan
interpreters of modern architecture. In fact the idea is very
successful and could be extended to very many more similar
buildings around London. ⟨But the two most prominent
features of Tolworth are now the underpass, completed in
1970, and the recent shopping and office development by
R. Seifert & Partners, 1962–4, with a twenty-two-storey tower
– now one of the most obtrusive landmarks in this part of
Surrey. The most noticeable feature, though not one that is
pleasing aesthetically, is the splaying of the stilts on which the
tower rests, with the end ones tapering up to the top.⟩

⟨TOLWORTH HOSPITAL, Red Lion Road. Geriatric ward blocks

and Day Hospital by the *South West Metropolitan Region Hospital Board* (*Richard Mellor & B. W. East*), 1966–8.)

TONGHAM

A few old timber-framed cottages – some with quite complicated curved braces. The rest C19 and C20 sprawl from Aldershot.

St Paul. 1865 by *Ewan Christian*. Apsed chapel with very high-pitched roof. At the back was a very slender detached timber belfry of 1898, kept up with iron tie-rods and containing a peal of tubular bells – 'a disastrous and happily rarely used invention', said J. C. Cox. About 1950 it was replaced by a detached brick tower with a C17 Scots cap.

Poyle, now demolished, was a C16 house. Inside, it had a complete room with pine chimneypiece and panelling in the most violent Artisan style of *c*.1650 (cf. Thomas Carter's work at Ham House).[*] Around 1880 the owner embellished the estate with brickwork in which every fourth course is made up of diamond-shaped studs. It occurs in fragments of the park wall, in Poyle Farm, dated 1883, and particularly in a big pair of cottages on the corner of Poyle Road, where it is used over the whole building, making it look like an armadillo.

TUESLEY

1 m. s of Godalming

A few picturesque cottages in a steep valley. The best is Crowts, an authentic mixture of tile-hanging, half-timber, and stone, with a big tile roof carried down over the lean-to ends, Sussex fashion. To the N is Tuesley Court, by *Sir Guy Dawber*, *c*.1911.

UNSTEAD MANOR HOUSE *see* BRAMLEY

UNSTEAD PARK

1 m. E of Godalming

Built *c*.1780 and then called Farley Hill. A carefully detailed late C18 stock-brick house of five by three bays with central pediment. Ground-floor Venetian windows under round-headed arches, as at Waverley. A simple but effective juggling with the limited motifs in the Late Palladian repertoire.

[*] The chimneypiece is now in the London Museum.

UPPER NORWOOD

3070

ALL SAINTS, Beulah Hill. A Commissioners' church, built in 1827–9, by *James Savage*; chancel by *Edwin Nash*, 1861, w baptistery of 1952–4. Stock-brick with Y-tracery and cusped lancet windows, w tower with pinnacles and recessed spire and flying buttresses against it starting from the pinnacles. – (The former SCHOOL next to the church is no doubt by *Savage* too. NT)

ST JOHN EVANGELIST, Sylvan Road. 1878–87 by *Pearson*. Very similar to St Michael Croydon, and as noble. E.E. Plain red brick exterior. Façade with grouped lancets and two typically Pearsonian turrets. Transepts and straight E end. Very tall clerestory, taller than it would have been in the Middle Ages. Lofty stock-brick interior with an arcade not high in comparison with the clerestory, a wall passage at clerestory level, and brick rib-vaults throughout. The E chancel bay has six ribs. Aisles and outer aisles, and at the E end to the S of the chancel aisle an outer chapel with an apse. The S transept was meant to carry a tower, and is therefore detailed differently from the N transept. The spire was to be 208 ft high. – Canted stone WEST GALLERY. – Stone ROOD SCREEN of large open arches, echoing the twin sets of five lights at the E end. Well restored after war damage by *Caröe & Partners*, 1946–51.

ST PAUL, Hamlet Road. *See The Buildings of England: West Kent and the Weald*, Anerley.

WINDERMERE HOUSE (Rehabilitation Centre), Westow Street. Built by *Sir M. D. Wyatt* as a private house, called The Mount, and converted and enlarged by *John Norton* in 1873–6 into the Royal Normal College and Academy of Music for the Blind. Stuccoed and rather dreary. Gabled centre, symmetrical sides, with the upper windows tall and reaching up into the roof. (The LODGE is by *Sextus Dyball*, 1880. GS)

VIRGO FIDELIS CONVENT (R.C.), Central Hill. Stock brick, Gothic. Several ranges of various dates. The earliest buildings, quite extensive, are by *Wardell*, 1857. Their centre is a slightly asymmetrically placed tower against which rises a canted, steeply roofed bay, and in this the entrance is placed. Windows in two tiers and steep dormer windows in the roof. A steeply roofed little turret at the l. end, where a range adjoins at r. angles which was added by *George Goldie* in 1862 (St Joseph's Wing). This wing was lengthened c.1880 by *E. Goldie* (Bishop Grant Memorial Hall). Adjoining this, again at r. angles, i.e.

opposite Wardell's wing, the convent (*E. Goldie*, 1881). The polygonal apse of the chapel projects near its r. end. More extensions of 1904 and 1928 (opposite St Joseph's Wing and adjoining the r. end of Wardell's wing).

ST JOSEPH'S COLLEGE (R.C.), Beulah Hill. The college consists of a Grecian villa of 1839 (Beulah Hill Road), enlarged in 1883 by *G. Highton*, a s wing of 1910–11, the N wing with chapel and senior dormitories of 1913–28 (these two by *B. McAdam*), and additions of 1948. The style is Edwardian Classical to Neo-Georgian.

CRYSTAL PALACE. *See The Buildings of England: West Kent and the Weald.*

NORWOOD GROVE, Gibsons Hill. Early C19, stuccoed, with a bow in the middle of the façade.

SYLVAN HILL. Good housing, taking advantage of the trees existing on the site. By *Riches & Blythin*, completed 1956.

VALLEY END *see* WINDLESHAM

VIRGINIA WATER

0060

1½ m. S of Egham

High-class suburban. For the lake and ruins *see* Windsor Great Park in the Berkshire volume of *The Buildings of England*.

CHRIST CHURCH. 1839 by *W. F. Pocock*. Hard, pinched lancet Gothic. No attempt at accurate detail, but perhaps an attempt to reproduce Gothic structural hardness. Cruciform, with a spiky W tower and spire. Crow-stepped gables to the transepts. All stock brick. (The SCHOOL opposite is also by *Pocock*.)

HOLLOWAY SANATORIUM. *See* p. 314.

WENTWORTH ESTATE. Wentworth is a battered, roughcast Gothick house whose grounds were cut up for housing estates and a golf course early in this century. All the natural pinewood landscape was preserved, the houses sited with the utmost care, and the trim kept quite informal – largely gravel roads, no kerbs, rhododendrons everywhere. The result is the best expensive suburb in Surrey, well worth a visit in itself. Most of the houses are sub-Voysey and sub-Lutyens. One, by *Colin Lucas* of *Connell, Ward & Lucas*, is very good International Modern (in Portnall Drive, best seen from Wentworth Drive; built in 1937). First floor with large rooms oversailing the ground floor, roof terrace on top, 'total design' as opposed to a few modern ideas applied to the basic English house. The latter can in fact be seen in two other houses on the Wentworth estate, though both are themselves above average: HOLTHANGER, in Portnall Drive, by *Oliver Hill*, 1936, modern clichés nicely applied to a long low brick house, and RIDGE END, 1931 by *Maxwell Fry*, and really pre-Maxwell-Fry as one knows him, in the plainest possible Neo-Georgian but using sun-trap angled wings or car ports with the main entrance between them. The post-war houses on the estate have been very mild. The best is a house in CHARTERS ROAD by *James Crabtree*, 1955. Pitched roof, stock brick, with one big rendered panel on the first floor.

WADDON *see* CROYDON pp. 181, 185, 191

2060

WALLINGTON*

HOLY TRINITY, Manor Road. 1867 by *Habershon & Brock* (GR). Flint and stone, with a w tower and spire, and a broad, low apse.

(PRESBYTERIAN CHURCH, Stafford Road. By *J. Wills*, 1887. Red brick. GS)

(METHODIST CHURCH, Beddington Gardens. By *Frank Windsor*, c.1908.)‡

(CONGREGATIONAL CHURCH, Stanley Park Road. By *P. W. Meredith*, 1928.)‡

TOWN HALL, Woodcote Road. 1935 by *Robert Atkinson*. A decidedly pretty design, though, if compared say with Dudok's work at Hilversum, very minor and still very traditional. Still, this is not Georgian, as all other municipal buildings of those years were in England. Brick and stone. Nine bays, the middle ones more widely spaced. Central turret. Much fluting of the stone verticals. ⟨Behind the Town Hall, COURT HOUSE, by *Robert Atkinson & Partners*, 1962; LIBRARY, 1936, altered in 1962–3 by *Robert Atkinson & Partners*; and CLINIC, by the *Surrey County Architect's Department*, 1964 – not progressive for their dates.⟩

⟨On the other side of Woodcote Road, a well designed and well functioning shopping centre, WALLINGTON SQUARE, by

---

* Wallington is now part of the London Borough of Sutton.

‡ Information from Mr H. V. Molesworth-Roberts.

Robert J. Wood & Partners, 1962–5. The street façade has two
storeys of curtain-walling above shops, neatly taking in the
slope of the road. The centre shops step back toward a passage
leading to an open precinct with more shops, a pub, and at the
far end, a thirteen-storey block of flats in dark brick with exposed concrete floors. Further s, Woodcote Road is fringed
by many recent flats, like so many of the main roads in this area
(cf. Sutton).⟩ To the N, a few nice houses in LONDON ROAD,
by the river Wandle. WANDLE BANK is on the s bank,
BRIDGE HOUSE, with arched ground-floor windows and an
Adamish porch, on the N side. A little further N on the r. THE
GRANGE RESTAURANT, 1967 by the *London Borough of
Sutton*, replaces THE GRANGE, a rich house of 1879–80, picturesquely grouped, with gables and much tile-hanging, which
was destroyed by fire in 1960. Opposite two blocks of flats
placed at r. angles with a fully glazed connecting link. This
composition was designed under the supervision of the Borough
Engineer, *A. W. Poynor*. Various good estates of flats in the
borough designed in the fifties by *Pite Son & Fairweather*, e.g.
the group ½ m. N at the corner of London Road and MILL
GREEN ROAD.

For South Beddington, *see* Beddington.

Near Wallington County Grammar School, on a sandy spit near
the Wandle, was the bank of a miniature Iron Age FORTIFI-
CATION. Roman and medieval sherds suggest some subsequent settlement.

WALTON-ON-THAMES

ST MARY. Flint and stone dressings. The buttresses of the w
tower repaired and strengthened probably early in the C19,
when the set-offs were straightened out and replaced by a
steep slope: a curious thing to do. Brick parapet. The oldest
part of the church is the N arcade. This is Late Norman. Four
bays, circular piers with circular many-scalloped capitals.
Then much work in the early C14. First the chancel – cf. the
SEDILIA and PISCINA and the details of the chancel arch.*
The same details in the s arcade and the arches of the N arcade.
Compare also the w wall of the N aisle. The masonry here
incorporates that of the Norman period. The N windows are
straight-headed and Perp and may date from the same time as

* The windows are C19.

the brick clerestory. The upper part of the N aisle and the nave roof date from c.1630. – ORGAN CASE. A fine piece of c.1700. – PLATE. Patens 1713 and c.1728; Cup and Flagons 1757. –
64   MONUMENTS. *Roubiliac*'s monument to Richard Boyle, Viscount Shannon, † 1740 deserves a visit all to itself. This monument, of a size to emulate the largest of Roubiliac's works in Westminster Abbey, was erected in 1755 by the Viscount's daughter, 'justly sensible of the inexpressible loss of her respectable parents'. The Viscount was a great general and died a marshal. He is represented standing, or comfortably leaning, against a gun. Behind him a flag boldly draped and a large square tent. There is a big pedestal on which the tent stands and a narrower one on which the general is placed. To the l. of the latter a gun on a gun-carriage, to the r. a tree with a drum and a flag and the seated figure of the Viscount's daughter, exquisitely rendered and carved. One of her arms hangs over an urn. – Other monuments. Brass to John Selwyn, Keeper of Oatlands Park, † 1587, with a man riding a stag, a commemoration of his exploit in leaping on to a stag, guiding it towards Elizabeth I, and stabbing it dead at her feet. – Henry Skrine † 1813, by *J. Bacon Jun*. Hanging wall-monument with a pretty oval relief of divers trees. – Mr and Mrs Christopher D'Oyly, 1821 by *Chantrey*. Relief with seated lady bent disconsolately over the monument of her husband. – Lady Williams † 1824. By *Joseph Gott*. Relief with seated woman crying and figure of Faith on the l. – CURIOSA. Model of a SCOLD'S BRIDLE dated 1633. The original was stolen in 1964.

In CHURCH STREET, a little SW of the church, a house (Nos. 13–17) of the mid C17. Dutch shaped gable and broad framed windows. The door seems original too. Opposite the church, MANOR ROAD leads to the one important house left in Walton, the OLD MANOR HOUSE, a fine timber-framed house of about 1500 with a central hall and projecting two-storeyed wings. The hall originally had an open timber roof with tie-beams and kingposts. Good brick chimneybreasts and stacks. The hall still has its screen and gallery.

Nearer the river was MOUNT FELIX, the former WALTON HOUSE, demolished in 1967. It was built about 1740 and grandly remodelled by *Sir Charles Barry* in 1837–40 for the fifth Earl of Tankerville. Of the earlier building the splendid staircase survived with a large Venetian window facing the river. The staircase started in one arm and returned on itself in two. Barry gave the house a dominating Italian villa tower above a big porte-cochère. He also altered the façades and roofed the house with pantiles (their first use in England, according to Professor Hitchcock). The renewed building was illustrated in *The Companion to the Almanac* in 1840.

From the sw end of Church Street BRIDGE STREET turns w towards the BRIDGE (iron, of 1863–4 by *E. T. Murray*).* ⟨Opposite Church Street, a completely new road has been made, HEPWORTH WAY, on the site of Nettlefold Film Studios. On the r. WELLINGTON CLOSE, flats, including three ten-storey blocks with pale blue spandrel panels; on the l., THE CENTRE, with shops, offices, and a multistorey car park all by *R. Seifert & Partners*, 1963–5. This starts with a good, long, curving two-storey range with shops, leading from the crossroads to the pedestrian area, but then come a distracting number of fussy angles and garish colours. The car park has white and yellow ceramic cladding (wearing badly). The Centre ends in NEW ZEALAND AVENUE with a range with sky-blue panels, on tapering stilts. Opposite, WALTON TOWN HALL by *Sir John Brown, Henson & Partners*, 1963–6. Y-shaped plan, with three continuous three-storey curving façades. Porches project from two of them. Concrete construction, cast-stone cladding with ponderous coffered pattern. Next to The Centre two refreshingly plain office blocks: WELLINGTON HOUSE, red brick, 1960, and H.M. INSPECTOR OF TAXES, part of The Centre redevelopment, and much better than the shops, with neat, dignified curtain-walling: upper storey with dark panels, projecting on columns over a ground floor in orange and white.

The E end of New Zealand Avenue leads to HERSHAM ROAD, which runs s. Off KINGS ROAD to the l. is the most satisfactory recent building in Walton (and one of the best in Surrey), the new SWIMMING POOL by *Arup Associates*, 1962–5. This 95 is an ingenious and impressive building which makes excellent sense functionally. The pool is entered from the first floor, with changing rooms cantilevered out on either side. The exterior walls are of concrete slabs faced with dark chippings. The pitched roof is made of folded concrete beams which taper toward the top, and the V-shaped spaces between these are

---

* This replaced a bridge by *Paine* of 1780, which in turn had replaced a wooden 'geometrical' bridge of 1748–50 with all the structural members tangential to a circle. It was claimed that any member could be removed without disturbing the timbers adjacent.

glazed, so that the effect inside is extraordinarily light and airy. In addition the w wall is all of glass, looking out over the park. In the s of Walton were expensive houses of *c.*1900. These are now disappearing (the best was WILLINGDON HOUSE by *Niven and Wigglesworth*, 1899, in Station Avenue, with four Dutch gables and three bow windows with pretty swags and plasterwork), and their gardens are being filled with flats and terrace houses. In STOMPOND LANE opposite Kings Road, a small scheme, more attractive than most, by *B. & N. Westwood, Piet & Partners*, 1963–5; two small staggered cottagey terraces, in dark brick.

Finally, in STATION AVENUE, offices of BIRDS EYE FOODS, by *Sir John Burnet, Tait & Partners*, 1960–1. One of the first prestige offices to be built for a firm moving out of London. It is a large oblong building of three storeys, symmetrical in plan, with two internal courtyards and elegantly proportioned, even façades. An extension has been added (1967–8) at r. angles, linked to the main building by a transparent corridor on three floors. The details of the façades are of the somewhat broken, not quite rigidly horizontal and vertical kind introduced into London by Saarinen's American Embassy. The two upper floors have a rapid flickering rhythm created by bands of sharply defined projecting hexagons of aluminium set against dark blue panels. The entrance is at the back. In front of the main range is a long pool. At one end, semi-abstract sculpture of flying birds by *John McCarthy*. The internal courts also have pools, with live birds.⟩

ST GEORGE'S HILL. An Iron Age HILL-FORT, partly covered by the housing estate. It is roughly rectangular, and covers 13–14 acres. To the NW the fortifications are double with an entrance, while an outer NE earthwork may be a later addition for a cattle pound. Occupation seems to have been from the C3 B.C. to the period of Caesar's landings.

WALTON-ON-THE-HILL

2050

On the Downs s of Epsom. Pleasant, mainly Victorian village with older houses in three different materials – flint, tile-hanging, and weatherboarding. The flint is perennial, but the other two really represent successive vernacular fashions, the tile-hanging of *c.*1700 overflowing N from the Weald, the weatherboarding of *c.*1800 spreading s from the Thames valley.

ST PETER. All flint. Chancel C15, terribly renewed, nave and

base of tower poor Gothic of 1818 by *Daniel Alexander Junior*,
the son of the famous warehouse designer. N aisle 1870, tower
top 1895. The tower top of 1818 was octagonal and flanked by
oversize turrets. The Perp work is impressive even after
restoration: simple, assured, and big in scale. Outside there
remain only two windows on the N side (the similar ones on
the S side are completely but correctly renewed). Inside there
is a big chancel arch with attached demi-shafts and a continuous moulding around, the size and scale of a biggish tower
arch. Also PISCINA and SEDILIA, admirably direct and
neither over-designed nor mechanical, the usual faults of English Late Gothic shop-work. The piscina has a simple ogee
arch, and the triple sedilia have mouldings like the chancel
arch and simple spandrels. The vaulted base of the tower of
1818, in almost the same basic style, would have been a copybook example for Pugin's *Contrasts*: shafts seven-eighths
detached and moulded arches above to go with them. – FONT.
Small but remarkable, C12 work, a lead bowl with frieze of 13
foliage at top and bottom and eight seated figures in high relief
under round-headed arches. The figures are extremely delicately moulded, yet have the authentic large-scale power of the
best Late Romanesque sculpture (cf. the S porch at Malmes-
bury, for example), as if the material had been forced into
shape by some immense natural catastrophe rather than
modelled. Dated *c.*1150–60 by Dr Zarnecki, and probably the
oldest surviving lead font in Britain. It was made in one long
strip and consisted of the same pattern of four arches im-
pressed probably three times to make twelve figures (i.e. the
Apostles). This has now been cut down to make eight and a
half arches. The style is derived from manuscripts like the Bury
Bible of shortly before 1148. The nearest parallel is the
slightly later font at Dorchester, Oxon; the group of lead fonts
from the Mendips is crude by comparison. – GLASS. A lot of
etched and painted glass fragments made up into the SE window
of the nave. Tiny in scale, mostly C17 Dutch or Flemish. –
PLATE. Cup 1568.

WALTON MANOR. Medium-size house of 1891 in a typical tile-
hung Norman Shaw style. Embedded in one end of this,
however, are the walls of a stone-built C14 manor house,
consisting of a two-storeyed hall and a chapel projecting
forward at the E end. Floors and partitions were added in the
C16 and copious additions were made in 1891 when the house
was built at the back; the result is now almost impossible to

decipher, let alone appreciate. At the w end there is certainly one C14 doorway and possibly the remains of two windows. Nothing else remains on the ground floor. On the first floor there is a delicate C14 door with daggers in the spandrels between hall and chapel, and another C14 door on the outside of the E wall of the hall, presumably the end of an outside staircase leading to a gallery in the hall and then to a gallery in the chapel. Also on the first floor of the chapel is quite an ornate small recess or window, with small moulded jamb-shafts and circular capitals, which looks *c.*1270 rather than C14. This would suggest a chapel on the upper floor only; yet the top of a window existing on the N side of the chapel was clearly two-storeyed, tall and narrow perhaps with two-light tracery and also looking *c.*1270. Traces of the original E window of the chapel also exist in an attic. This is the only house of its type in Surrey, and it is a pity that more was not investigated before the alterations of 1891;* what remains is good work.

In the grounds a MOTTE, and also PHANTASSIE by *Colin & Jennifer Jones*, 1956, a bungalow with thoughtful pitched roof-lines and relation of parts, rather Swiss.

SE of the church an area of expensive villas of *c.*1910, including two sadly pedestrian Classical houses by *Lutyens*, CHUSSEX, 1908, and THE DORMY HOUSE, 1906, now derelict. All his mastery of carefully built-up masses disappeared with the change in style. (Well preserved *Jekyll* garden at Chussex. THE ISLAND (formerly Frog's Island) is a villa of *c.*1905, with a *Lutyens* wing and formal garden of 1913. NT)

ROMAN VILLA. A Romano-British villa at SANDILANDS ROAD, N of Walton and close to Tadworth, was systematically excavated in 1948–9. The villa measured approximately 110 by 60 ft and was of corridor type. It contained thirteen rooms, including a bath block. An unusual feature was a strange, isolated, circular structure containing a polygonal-sided internal room. The use of the structure is unknown. The villa was built in the C1 A.D., was deserted for half a century, and was then renovated and continued in use until its destruction *c.*400. The foundations are still visible. A group of fields lies in the region of the villa.

WANBOROUGH

9040

On the N slope of the Hog's Back, w of Guildford, and unlike any

---

* The account in the VCH does not altogether correspond with what has turned up subsequently.

other West Surrey village – small, hard-bitten brick and flint, huddled around a circular concrete silo. Really just one big farmyard, looking up bare slopes to the top of the ridge; a beautiful group from the main road above. Remarkable geological fidelity here: within five miles, N to S, Worplesdon on sand and clay is comfortable brick; Wanborough on chalk is as compact and hard as a North Hampshire hill-village; and Puttenham a mile S beyond the Hog's Back is on sandstone and consequently drawn out and Wealden.

ST BARTHOLOMEW. Tiny single-roomed C13 flint chapel, disused in the C17 and gently restored in 1862. One Dec window and a three-light square-headed Perp E window. The remainder C13 lancets. Inside, elegant roof (partly C19), with braces, collars, and a well-moulded longitudinal beam joining the collars. – SCREEN. Straightforward square-headed panels, framing old, tracery new.

WANBOROUGH MANOR. 'Dated' 1527, but in fact a ham C17 Artisan front. Three-gabled, with prodigiously rustic brick cornice which at one point turns 90 degrees and carries on again 3 ft above its former level.

TITHE BARN. Honest and undemonstrative, like a normal Surrey barn but bigger. 95 ft by 30 ft, weatherboarded and brick sides, tiled roof (taking in 'nave' and 'aisles' inside in one sweep), timber-framed ends. Complicated roof with arcades and tie-beams supporting kingposts which go up not, as is usual, to the ridge, but to a collar a couple of feet below it.

FLEXFORD, N of the village, near Normandy. C17 Artisan brick, whitewashed, with a central shaped gable and two-order pilasters. Rough and graceless, the detail a crude edition of West Horsley Place.

WARLINGHAM

3050

The extreme SE end of continuous London building, on the downs E of Caterham. A sad place, its village green a roundabout and a public garden, its cottages replaced piecemeal by shopping arcades.

ALL SAINTS. Flint. Aisleless nave and chancel C13, restored in 1857 by *Scott* and 1887 by *P. M. Johnston*. New S aisle 1893, effectively removing the village character. Old and renewed lancets on the N side, one two-light Perp window on both N and S sides, E window mid-C14, renewed by *J. O. Scott*. Inside, restored single space without chancel arch. – FONT. Octagonal,

C15. – PISCINAE and SEDILIA. Two sets on the s side plus another piscina opposite on the N side. Two of these evidently served the rood. – WALL PAINTING. Big, rough figure of St Christopher carrying Christ, C15. – PLATE. Cup and Cover 1568; Flagon 1690.

ST CHRISTOPHER. *See* Chelsham.

A few old cottages. In Leas Road, s of the green, are the ATWOOD ALMSHOUSES, or THE COLLEGE, of 1663, a miniature, humble, but very companionable group. Half-H-shape, a two-storeyed cottage in the centre and single-storey cottages on the sides, without any ornament at all. Near this, in Westhall Road, the VICARAGE, also of 1663, brick, one more Surrey compromise between Artisan details and the post-Restoration style. Five by two bays with deep sash windows, but keeping a double order of pilasters. Ground floor plain, first floor Doric. On the green itself the old part of the WHITE LION is attractive, a flint and brick C18 cottage with a tile-hung wing.

To the NW is HAMSEY GREEN (where there was another house of c.1700, HAMSEY GREEN FARMHOUSE, again five by two bays, with eaves cornice and hipped roof, flint with brick dressings, modestly elegant). N of this, off the road to Sanderstead, is CHERRY TREE GREEN, a council estate, 1948 by *A. W. Kenyon*. Simple pantiled houses around a big green, a model of what can be done by giving extreme care to a few details, e.g. verges, linking walls between houses, and careful design of the house units themselves.

8040

WAVERLEY ABBEY

The first Cistercian monastery in England, founded in 1128 by the Bishop of Winchester with monks from Aumône in Normandy. The FIRST CHURCH was complete by c.1160 and rebuilt in the C13. The only things now that are more than heaps of masonry are part of one transept and most of the cellarium and one end of the monks' dorter. The complete ground plan has been recovered by excavation, including the plan of the first church, but this only makes the loss the more tantalizing. Waverley must have been in any case the central power-house for a great deal of English architecture, and the plan of the first church has been established as a long aisleless nave with short square-ended presbytery and flanking chapels forming squat transepts. This is almost the quintessential English plan – elongated, square-cut spaces added together. It

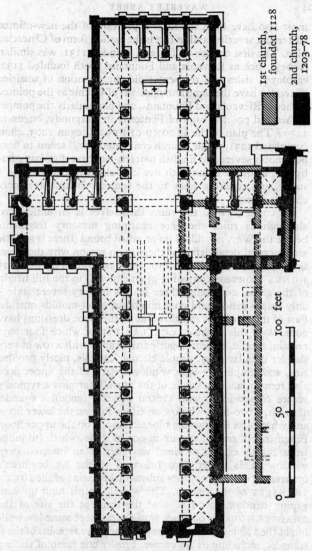

1st church, founded 1128

2nd church, 1203–78

100 feet

Waverley Abbey, plan of the first and second churches (*Redrawn by Sheila Gibson from plans in the Victoria County History by courtesy of the editor and publishers*)

must also have been the ideal expression of the new-minted Cistercian severity, and in fact is the earliest form of Cistercian plan. The first church at Tintern, founded 1131, was similar. Abbeys such as Rievaulx and Fountains (both founded 1132) employed aisles and transepts; did the elevation of unaisled Waverley have the same anticipations of Gothic as the pointed arches at Rievaulx and Fountains, and particularly the pointed arches and pointed vault of Fontenay in Burgundy, begun in 1139? The plan of the SECOND CHURCH (begun 1203, choir completed 1231, whole church completed 1278) seems to have been nobly severe and English too: ten-bay nave, five-bay presbytery, a square E end with five chapels in it, like stalls in a stable, and square E walls to the transepts with three more chapels apiece.

To come back to the ruins themselves is an anticlimax, although as ruins they are charming masonry fragments beside the Wey, not tidied up or railed round (there is so little architectural detail left that there is no reason why they ever should be). Near the E end of the site is one end of the mid-C13 MONKS' DORTER, consisting of an end wall to the full height of the gable, containing three lancets in very severe style – only splays inside, and only minimum hood-moulds outside. Part of the side walls remains, but all the stone dressings have gone. W of this is the C13 CELLARIUM, of which four bays remain, simple, elegant quadripartite vaults with a row of very slender circular piers, simple circular capitals, nicely profiled ribs, and simple two-light windows. Parts of the upper floor also remain, and the whole of the W wall, forming a typically severe composition, with central buttress (gone), a roundel above it, a two-light window on either side on the lower floor, and what looks like two big blocked lancets on the upper floor. Fragments of tracery remain in one of these, which (to judge from Buck's early C18 view) was part of an inserted Perp window. This upper floor belonged to the lay brethren's quarters. N of the dormitory substantial remains of the SOUTH TRANSEPT of the church. The W wall stands high up with gaping window openings. S of the transept the site of the CHAPTER HOUSE is obvious, W of the transept some low walling of the S aisle, N of the transept the scantier remains of the N transept, including its NE corner. Finally one lump of walling of the INFIRMARY CHAPEL E of the S transept. Most of the walling is dark Bargate stone, with clunch or firestone dressings, making quite a subtle polychrome. Ironically, next door to the site is a tangle of concrete blocks, a relic of the desperate invasion defence lines of 1940.

WAVERLEY ABBEY HOUSE

8040

A puzzling house, almost unknown. *Colen Campbell* built a house here *c.*1725 for Aislabie, the Chancellor of the Exchequer who was disgraced by the South Sea Bubble. This is shown in mid-C18 engravings as a blunt building of five bays with a three-bay pedimented centre. To this wings were undoubtedly added before 1754.* A new house was built by Thomas Orby Hunter († 1770), to which wings were added by 1786. The existing house would fit these dates, although it is said that the whole was completely renewed after a fire in 1833. The present design consists of a three-bay centre linked to single-storey wings, consisting of one long room each (the E side with an early C19 attic storey), and then curving on the E side via a quadrant wall to a pedimented two-storeyed stable block. The w side is truncated, and this wing is now returned with an inept arcade of 1880. The detail is very bold and a little rough. The centre has big Ionic pilasters and a huge tripartite square-headed window; the wings are three-sided with equally big Venetian windows under brick arches, flanked by oval paterae and plaster panels carrying swags.‡ An ornamental frieze of rosettes drives straight through from end to end of the façade, forming both a cornice for the wings and the string course between the storeys of the centre.

The N (entrance) front is just as forthright: five by two bays with the centre composed of another square-headed tripartite window and a lunette above (with fancy oval tracery in it), all swept together under a giant arch. The whole house is built of the typical late C18 green stock brick (another reason for it not being simply Campbell's house re-used).

Inside again the planning of the rooms is ruthless (and functional in the C20 sense; it can almost be worked out from the outside elevation, a very rare thing in C18 houses). The entrance hall is simply a space in front of the staircase, which has two arms going up to a landing with a pair of columns which becomes the spine corridor for the whole suite of first-floor rooms. And these are utterly commonsense: dining room in the E wing, drawing room in the w wing, simple withdrawing

* i.e. on Pococke's authority.

‡ The same type as on Adam's Home House, Portman Square, London.

rooms in the centre between them, with a connecting sequence of doors running the whole length of the suite. The dining room is simple Late Palladian with columned recesses (and was reconstructed in 1833 after the fire). The drawing room is in an elegant simple Adam style, with a very distinctive frieze of alternate arabesques and fans. The other rooms are almost plain. Clearly some very individual designer was at work who cared more for convenience and functional expression than for ornamental delicacy. Who was he? The detail is Adam-derived, but used in an utterly un-Adam way. It is in fact the same type of sweeping adaptation of other men's motifs as Boodle's Club of 1775, which also crowds together the paterae, the big Venetian window under an arch, and the tripartite square-headed window (this time on a curve). So perhaps *John Crunden* was the architect; and just as Boodle's is a very decorative street inflection, but a roughly composed design, so Waverley is admirable in its landscape (viewed from near the abbey, e.g.), but slapdash when seen close to.

WENTWORTH see VIRGINIA WATER

WEST BYFLEET see BYFLEET

WEST CLANDON

One long, straggling street running N–S for over a mile between Guildford and Leatherhead, with the buildings never close enough to give any group or individuality.

St Peter and St Paul. The detail nearly all new or renewed. Attached N tower of 1879 by *J. C. Boys*, with wooden spire, rebuilt in 1913 by *Jackson*. Old walls apparently of a wide C13 nave and chancel, with indications of lancets in the E wall. The present E window Dec on the old pattern. The inside of no interest. PILLAR PISCINA of *c*.1200, the head in the form of a capital (nave SE corner). Good scratch sundial built into the S side of the chancel. – STAINED GLASS. C17 medallions reset among early C19 glass, the colouring light and bright. – PEWS. Onslow Pew at the W end. Handsome; one pew with tall back and three more plus one front. The arm-rests carved with cherubs' heads. Probably Italian and probably late C17. – PAINTING. Three figures on board (S side of chancel). Probably from the old rood screen. – CARVING. One very good panel of a dragon and a reptile fighting, attached to the s porch. Where from? – PLATE. Cup 1569; Paten 1712.

A little in the village. Starting from the s (all on the E side), GARDNERS COTTAGES is half-timbered with flint infilling (cf. Shere). CLANDON REGIS is a spirited neo-Renaissance house by *Basil Champneys*, c.1890, not much detail but what there is well used. s front with steep pediments at either end. Beyond, SUMMERS (originally Summer Farm), c 17, cosily tile-hung. Multiple additions nicely done without obvious mannerisms: a tall brick music room of 1902 by *Lutyens* (but the interior is not his) and a tile-hung service wing of c.1920 probably by *Troup*. *Lutyens* garden with a timber cloister cleverly created out of the framework of an old cow byre; the cottage is also his (NT). *See p. 600*

CLANDON PARK. The old Clandon was in what might be called the official Jacobean style, a big, half-H-shaped house with a multitude of shaped gables – the type of Holland House Kensington, and the style of Abbot's Hospital at Guildford. The new was completely rebuilt for Thomas Onslow by *Giacomo Leoni* in 1713–29 and has not been substantially altered since: an interior of copybook Palladian symmetry and elegance clothed with four oddly gauche, oddly dissimilar, and oddly un-Palladian brick elevations.

Leoni was a Venetian who had worked as an architect in Germany. We do not yet know when he came to England, but in 1715 he published the first English edition of Palladio, quite independent of Lord Burlington, and in collaboration with Nicholas Dubois.* The first mention of plans for Clandon is in fact in 1713 and the house was largely complete by 1729. In between these dates Leoni had made the acquaintance of Lord Burlington, and this perhaps explains the disparity between inside and outside: he may have designed the elevations first, without much regard for strictness (his work at Lyme Park in Cheshire is simply a German Baroque palace front), much in the way that Gibbs's early houses were, and the interiors later, when some sort of rigorous standard had been laid down. But perhaps it is easier to suggest – and this certainly would account for the poor quality of the outside – that Leoni was only called in after the walls were erected.‡

* Connected with the pre-Burlington and still partly Baroque early houses of Colen Campbell and the even earlier Palladianism of William Benson, Wren's successor as Surveyor-General.

‡ A third possibility, suggested by John Harris, is that so much was altered in 1876 that the outside bears little relation to the original.

The house is a simple rectangle, brick with sparse stone dressings, with each front different in character and even in style. The entrance front (w) has nine bays, the three centre bays stone-faced and pedimented, more or less Palladian, with a shocking mock-Baroque porch and porte-cochère added in 1876. The N front has five bays of plain brickwork, the centre three bays projecting slightly. The s front, facing the grotto, is very much like a fragment of Wren's Hampton Court. Five bays and two and a half storeys, with very heavy central stone pilasters and cornice, overscale for the rest of the front, and swags above the first floor of the other bays. Finally, the E front has eleven bays with much thinner first-floor stone trim to the central three bays, with swags this time between the pilasters – and this time underscale for the rest of the front, and rather French – above heavy, coupled, round-arched windows that could be by Vanbrugh. The confusion of details here is rather amusing. All the corners have brick quoins, and all windows have plain brick aprons beneath, both ornamental tricks of the English Baroque school.

The inside is a different story. In a true Palladian way, the whole house depends on a vast two-storeyed entrance hall, easily the biggest room in the house, and one of the grandest early Palladian rooms in England. It is crisp, imposing, and a little cold. Everything is proud and taut, resilient with newly discovered authority. Two superimposed Corinthian orders, the upper one smaller to give a false perspective effect. On the first floor aedicules – blind on three sides, framing a sort of gallery on the fourth, actually part of the main first-floor corridor. From the ground floor doors lead to all parts of the house – to the two cramped stair-wells and to the saloon. The effect is of knowing the extent of the whole house as soon as one enters the front door, exactly as at the Queen's House at Greenwich. Two superb fireplaces and overmantels by *Rysbrack*, technically among the best things he ever did. Grey and white veined marble with reliefs on the overmantels – of the Sacrifice to Bacchus and the Sacrifice to Diana – whose resilience and crispness completely overcome the classical frigidity of the subjects. (Restoration now in progress (1969) has revealed the original colour scheme of the hall, which has been restored. The former dead white decoration has been replaced by marbling of the columns and skirting.) On the wall opposite the door two panels of a cassowary and an ostrich by *Francis Barlow* (although they fit perfectly in this position they in fact come from a house at Pyrford). They are very good examples of Barlow's eerie intensity. Finally the plasterwork of the ceiling is still effectively Baroque, though subordinated in an un-Baroque way. Central circle with a relief of seated figures and a complex symmetrical pattern around it with shells and cartouche shapes in the corners. It employs a typical Baroque trick of having fully modelled limbs overflowing – spilling over the cornice from high relief figures on the ceiling itself. The sculptor is said to be *Artari*; in fact the ceilings fall into two groups, the differences small but perceptible. One group includes the hall, and the saloon, with Baroque curves in the corners and a lot of projecting limbs; the other consists of the Palladio Room and the Red Drawing Room, with geometrical patterns in the corners and exquisite carving in the central feature, in low relief but with more sparkle, as though the plaster were buoyant.

The remainder of the house has nothing on the scale of the hall. The noteworthy ceilings are mentioned above. On the l. of the hall is a plain C18 staircase with iron handrail; on the r. now a wooden C19 staircase of late C17 type with competent carving. The completely subordinate position of both is very typical of this particular phase of C18 architecture (cf. Chiswick and Mereworth). Beyond is a suite of rooms altered *c.*1770: the Morning Room, plain Late Palladian, the Palladio Room with C18 fireplace and quite exceptional late C18 flock wallpaper, and the Hunting Room. Beyond again, working round to the back of the hall, is the Green Drawing Room. The original C18 wallpaper was discovered during restoration. The room has another big fireplace, of *c.*1730 but probably not by Rysbrack, this time of wood with complete architectural frame with scrolled pediment surrounding a classical landscape – a very good match.* Beyond again is the Saloon. (Here the interesting early C18 colour scheme of the plasterwork has been discovered and restored. The ceiling has a pale blue ground, with biscuit-coloured medallions and details in white; the frieze has biscuit and stone details on a darker blue ground. The state bed has been moved into the original State Bedroom adjoining the Saloon, with a fireplace brought from upstairs, probably originally in this room. Above the saloon the former Great Dining Room has been reconstituted. In the late C18 it was a billiard room, and in the C19 it was

---

* The overmantel may be a slightly later addition, as the wallpaper was found to extend behind it.

divided up into bedrooms. Two large *Barlows* also from Pyrford hang in this room. The kitchen in the basement is also being restored.) Finally in the NW corner of the house the Speaker's Parlour, with an original ceiling, but otherwise largely redecorated in the lush mock-Louis-Quatorze style of the early C19.

The grounds were landscaped by *Capability Brown* c.1770. From this the general lines of the park remain, and also the STABLES W of the house, heavy and routine Late Palladian, and the pair of LODGES further W again, almost in Merrow village. Between them good early C18 gates, moved to their present site in 1776, presumably from the forecourt of the pre-Palladian house. Also of this date the simple rockwork GROTTO of flint and brick with statues of the Three Graces inside, immediately S of the house. ½ m. to the N is a small circular Ionic TEMPLE by *W. & H. W. Inwood*, 1838, unexpectedly late and chaste, and to the E is the improbable sight of a MAORI HOUSE, making a garden ornament of the most startling sort. It was brought back by a Lord Onslow who was governor of New Zealand, after it had been buried in the eruption of Waitoa in the late C19. It is probably C18. Brightly and prettily painted in red and grey.

₄₀₀₁
WESTCOTT

A main-road village between Dorking and Shere, mostly Victorian and suburban around a small triangular green. Well kept.

HOLY TRINITY. 1852 by *Sir George Gilbert Scott*. Prettily sited on a hill above the green. In the Surrey style with a shingled bell-turret, but the details mechanical. Still, it respects the *genius loci*.

Westcott is at the point where the chalk North Downs and the sandstone Surrey Hills are within a few yards of one another, and hence has cottages in several different vernacular styles. To the S are pretty cottages in both half-timber (LOGMORE FARM) and sandstone, and also LOGMORE, a small, dull Neo-Georgian house by *Ernest Newton*, 1912. Down a lane running N from the village green is THE BARRACKS, a gabled brick and sandstone C17 house with a few simple Artisan details, e.g. brick string courses raised to become hood-moulds round segment-headed windows. To the W was THE ROOKERY, stuccoed and battlemented, now demolished.* On the main road, at the corner of Balchin's Lane is the very pretty small CHURTGATE HOUSE, T-shaped, one arm stone-built and gabled C16, with a lean-to built on to it containing quite a big early C17 brick doorcase with Doric pilasters in the Artisan style. The other arm of the T also brick and probably a little later.

WEST END see CHOBHAM

WEST HORSLEY

ooso

One long, rambling street between the Guildford-Leatherhead road and the railway. No station; hence the suburbanization has been gentler than in East Horsley or the Bookhams. Quite an acceptable leafy blend of old and new. Church and West Horsley Place are by themselves to the E.

ST MARY. Slow-growth medieval, basically C13. Unbuttressed flint W tower with shingled cap. All the details are now C13, but the tower is possibly older, judging by its shape of three slightly recessed stages. No tower arch, but a W doorway of *c.*1200 with pointed head and a lancet above. Chancel arch in the same style, reset S door just a little later (keeled instead of chamfered jambs), N arcade later again, of *c.*1210, with well moulded circular piers, capitals, and abaci, and arches with unmoulded soffits with roll-mouldings at the edges and hood-mould over. The chancel (renewed) is in yet another E.E. style, this time with the familiar mid-C13 shafted E triplet of lancets and single N and S lancets. None of this has much visual value. One good curvilinear window in the chancel, connected compositionally with the Berners monument underneath (*see* below), and a big and simple Late Perp S aisle with a rough arcade (octagonal piers and capitals). N aisle widened in 1869. One feature remains mysterious: the blocked half-arch to the l. of the chancel arch. What remains recognizable of its details looks later than the chancel arch. Was it built as a squint then, or as an entrance to the rood-stair, or for both purposes? Pleasant outside texture of whitewash and plaster, which has minimized the effects of restoration. – WALL PAINTINGS (W

* It was gothicized *c.*1760 for Daniel Malthus, the father of T. R. Malthus, who was born there in 1766. (Sir Alexander Carr Saunders kindly provided this information.) Nothing remains of Malthus's picturesque garden with temples and grottoes.

wall). Early; now almost gone. – SCREEN. Partly old (C15 or C16). Very simple; narrow bays with straight-headed tops. – CARVING. Small C14 alabaster Nativity, probably Nottingham work (S side of the chancel). – STAINED GLASS. Good small C13 medallions in the N and central lancets of the E end (the S lancet medallion is C19); also Sir James Berners † 1388, represented kneeling (N side of chancel).–CHEST. Big, oblong, iron-bound, probably C13. – PLATE. Cup and Paten 1634; Flagon and Paten 1666. – MONUMENTS. C14 monument to a priest, probably Ralph de Berners. Recumbent figure under crocketed ogee arch, the face stiff, the folds with just a little of that classic quality of arrested movement of the best C13 sculpture. – Sir Edward Nicholas † 1669 (behind the organ). Big tomb without figures, in the newly arrived City of London style. Architectural frame with barley-sugar columns, open pediment above. Insensitive, particularly in the careless way details of widely different scale and degree of delicacy are put next to one another. Said to be by *Grinling Gibbons*, and would fit in well with his pedestrian stone sculpture (as distinct from wood-carving). – Sir John Nicholas † 1704 (also behind the organ). Much better; architectural frame around a delicate marble urn, cherubs and obelisks at the sides. Lively square-cut composition. – John Kendal † 1750, aged twenty-three, by *Nicholas Read* 'Inv^t. E^t. Sculp^{t}' (S aisle). Better still; a very subtle composition of marble urn and asymmetrically draped cloth, with below it a charming relief of a rose-tree with one blossom fallen. No attempt to toe any stylistic line, and very much the better for it. Read was a Roubiliac pupil.

Immediately W of the church is CHURCH HOUSE, C16, half-timbered, with an overhanging upper floor. In the village street there are many more timber houses, all in the comfortable vernacular of NW Surrey; the OLD SCHOOL HOUSE is typical and one of the prettiest. Also here, W of the road, is the OLD RECTORY, a smooth stucco Regency house, dated 1819, with a five-bay veranda. Behind it is a medieval flint BARN. N of the railway is LOLLESWORTH FARM, part half-timber, part C18 brick with a big crow-stepped chimney on the N side. To the W is WIX FARM, a very picturesque collection of tile roofs, farm and barns, part C17 brick and part C16 half-timber – the yeoman's equivalent of West Horsley Place.

WEST HORSLEY PLACE. From the road the house looks entirely C17 and C18. In fact this is a facing of a big medieval house, itself altered in the C16. The back and sides show this clearly in a ramble of brick, plaster, and half-timbering; the rear (N) elevation has four plastered gables and a medieval stone chimneystack in the NW angle. The medieval building must have been big if not spectacular, because the whole of the W wing has big kingposts in the attic with four-way struts, probably of the C15. It was perhaps L-shaped, with the hall in the angle, converted to an H-plan in the C16. But the architectural interest is entirely in the handsome and very comfortably English brick S front of c.1630, clearly in the Artisan style of 42 the Dutch House at Kew and equally clearly not by the same designer, for none of the details correspond. Nor do they correspond with the parts of Slyfield which date from c.1640–50. Single-bay wings, ten-bay centre, the first floor throughout with bold brick pilasters and cornice, the bases carrying a diamond motif, the capitals with a Composite order simplified into plain projections echoed in the entablature above to give an almost Borrominesque effect. Originally each wing projected by three bays, but the projection of the E wing was reduced to one bay in the C18 and given a straight-sided gable. The central lunette, and probably the parapet and Dutch gable, are C18 too. The shaped gable on the W wing is probably original, although the lunette and Venetian window below it are not. Big central brick doorcase with Doric pilasters, and inside it a smaller Gothick doorcase with brick hood-mould, very much in Kent's style and very early, certainly before 1750. Windows all sashes but probably keeping the C17 window openings. The atmosphere of happy domesticity, one of the most important achievements of British architecture, is very strong here. This is partly due to the accident of warm materials, but far more to the comfortable proportions and irregular roof-line; Versailles is a very long way away. Inside, the hall was divided into two in the mid C16, and part of a ceiling dated 1547 survives in an upper room, now called the Geraldine Room, an unprepossessing affair of badges and spindly ribs. There is one small late C16 staircase in the E part of the house, but the main staircase is plain late C17, and most of the interiors are very plain C18, e.g. the hall, the lower part of the medieval hall, with a screen of Doric columns at the W end. The STABLES to the E are simple late C17.

WOODCOTE LODGE, 1 m. S. Plain, gabled Victorian house of flint and brick. *Voysey* made simple additions in 1899, whiteharled and easy to distinguish: the gable at the E end and extensions at the back,

17—S.

WEST HUMBLE

CHAPEL. Ruined, with only parts of the E end and W walls re-
    maining. A small rectangle, all flint, and possibly late C12 (cf.
    the round hole in the W wall). No architectural details left at all.
Opposite, CHAPEL CROFT has a good set of barns, both ver-
    nacular (flint and weatherboarding) and C20 industrial (con-
    crete Dutch barns and circular aluminium silos).
BOXHILL STATION. A delightful, rather ecclesiastical little
    building. Porch at the side, with elaborate Gothic capitals;
    turret with weathervane.
½ m. E, beside Boxhill station and the Mickleham by-pass, is
    CAMILLA LACEY, another of the Surrey high-class suburbs
    (built on the site of Fanny Burney's house). It is entered
    through a mock-Perp arch dated 1923. Small but superbly
    kept with hedges, grass verges, and grass roundabouts. At the
    W end a simple modern house, CEDARWOOD, by *A. W. Cleeve
    Barr* of the LCC, 1955. Two storeys, pitched roof, flint on the
    See ground floor and weatherboarded above, between brick end
    p. walls. Nicely detailed.
    600

WEST MOLESEY

CHURCH. Perp W tower of ragstone with higher stair-turret. The
    rest of the church of yellow brick, 1843. – FONT. Perp, octa-
    gonal, with quatrefoils. – PULPIT. Jacobean, a good piece,
    complete with back panel and sounding board. – PLATE.
    Porringer given in 1686; Paten of about the same date; Flagon
    1782; Cup 1800.
(ST BARNABAS (R.C.), Vine Road. 1931 by *W. C. Mangan*. DE)
⟨HURST PARK. The racecourse has been built over with a large
    estate by *Wates* (*K. G. Bland*), 1962 onwards. Quite nicely
    grouped houses, with the familiar tile-hanging and weather-
    boarding, and a few monopitch roofs as a concession to the
    sixties. By the main road, a rather mean shopping centre, a pub
    (by *Mayall Hart & Partners*), and, near by, OLD PEOPLE'S
    HOMES by *R. J. Ash*, the County Architect, 1967–9. Further
    W, Hurst Park PRIMARY SCHOOL, one of the best recent
    schools by the County Architect's Department (1965–7). The
    school is set back from the road, by the river. Neat single-storey
    blocks around a taller square hall with a folded roof decreasing
    in height towards the centre of each side. On the entrance side
    the hall is lit by clerestory windows with thick white mullions;
    on the river side the hall windows run to the ground, facing a

little courtyard designed for outdoor teaching. Further s, in
West Molesey High Street, HOMES FOR PHYSICALLY
HANDICAPPED, by *Leonard J. Multon & Partners* and
Raymond Ash, the County Architect, 1967–9. One and two
storeys, grey and buff brick with dark grey spandrels.⟩

WESTON GREEN
½ to 1 m. sw of Thames Ditton

1060

ALL SAINTS. 1939 by *Sir E. Maufe*. Whitewashed, with a NE
campanile. Very tall, slender arched windows, the w window
more fanciful. Impressive interior with plain piers without
capitals and round arches.

The church lies on the N side of the green, with a pond immediately to the s. Close to it the RED HOUSE, a nice C18
group. The green is large. At its sw end, by the Orleans Arms,
a MILESTONE of 1767, circular with ball finial and good
writing of places and distances. At the NE corner of the green
THE ELMS, a very handsome early C18 brick house of five
bays and two storeys with parapet. Doorcase with Roman
Doric pilasters and a triglyph frieze. From that corner WESTON
GREEN ROAD leads into Thames Ditton. Here soon NEW-
LANDS (St Agnes House), late C17, of five bays and two and a
half storeys. Doorcase with garlands down the thin pilasters.
Inside a swagger plaster ceiling of the same date. Very
luxuriant, richly moulded frieze. Contemporary also the stair-
case, with sturdy twisted balusters. Good wrought-iron gates
and railings. (In WESTON PARK, ROSEWOOD HOUSE and
BRAMHAM COTTAGE, C17 with an C18 façade. Wooden cornice; one original door with carved brackets. MHLG) WESTON
GRANGE, further on, has a nice C18 doorcase. At the extreme
E end is an early estate by *Eric Lyons*, 1952, with too many
clichés (monopitch roofs, leaning chimneys) to be impressive.
Another estate at the extreme w end of the green is much
simpler and very much better: WOODEND, by *G. B. Imrie*,
1948–9, just short brick terraces of houses and bungalows,
each group linked with walls and trees – like a New Town
neighbourhood but more carefully and lovingly done than
most things in the New Towns.

WEYBOURNE
¾ m. NE of Farnham

8040

Aldershot-over-the-border, with one superb local Baroque house,

THE OLD HOUSE. Rainwater heads dated 1724. Five by two bays, all windows with segmental heads, first floor with aprons. Rubbed brick cornice and entire central bay, which is made up vertically into a splendid frontispiece. Tuscan Doric doorcase, segment-headed window on the first floor, and a blind pilastered aedicule in the parapet above the cornice. The garden elevation has random windows but a similar centre-piece; the side elevation is composed with a big central chimney. The first-floor central window is identical with Willmer House Farnham of 1718: clearly the same local 'little master' at work.

0060   WEYBRIDGE

Four layers of suburbia cancelling one another out: C18 Thames-side, railway lower middle class of c.1850, high class of c.1890 (mainly to the s), and standard Outer London expansion from 1930 onwards. ⟨There is now a fifth layer – exclusive small estates built recently in older gardens, the best by *Eric Lyons* of Span – *see* below.⟩ Pleasant, with a lot of trees, but very little positive character of any sort.

ST JAMES. By *J. L. Pearson*, 1848 (extra aisle 1864), his first medium-size church after his early buildings in the East Riding. Adequately accurate but not inspiring. Broach-spire, Dec detail. Everything thin and wiry and rather heartless. This is Pearson's 'early' style, completely different from both Titsey of the 1860s and St Michael Croydon of the 1880s. The inside is better because of the good proportions and the rich chan-cel decoration of polychrome marble mosaic (altogether over twenty types of marble are used). The PISCINA and SEDILIA are particularly intricate, with some brilliant touches – red marble for the sedilia seats, e.g. – MONUMENTS. The brasses to John Woulde † 1598 and his two wives with children below are standard Elizabethan, but on the other side of the tower are two brasses which are far from standard. First, Thomas Inwood the elder † 1586 and his three wives, all made up into a small-scale, spirited, intricate composition which exploits the linear qualities of the brass perfectly. Everyone kneeling. Well above average. The other brass consists of three grisly, primitive, but very striking skeletons, 2 ft high, with texts between. It shows far more understanding of metal technique than many more accomplished brasses. This is apparently C15, and does not refer to the three children represented on the plate above as dying c.1600. The skeletons are datable by the lettering of the texts and are similar to brasses at Margate and St Laurence Norwich (SAC 33). – Skied under the tower several C18 and early C19 tablets, and Frederica, Duchess of York, † 1820 (the wife of Frederick of the Duke of York's column; she lived at Oatlands) by *Chantrey*, dated 1825. Kneeling figure with crown beside her feet, an opportunity for one of Chantrey's favourite moving young women. Good, but too high up the wall to judge properly.

⟨St James Church Hall. By *B. & N. Westwood, Piet & Partners*, 1965–6. An inviting but discreet building of yellow brick on a small site N of the church. Hexagonal hall with floor-to-roof concrete mullions on two sides.⟩

St Michael. By *Butterfield*, 1874. Polychrome brick with bellcote, clerestory, and lean-to aisles. Cheap (not necessarily a drawback), but in this case clearly over the border from genuine protest to careless harshness.

(St Charles Borromeo (R.C.). Attached to the church is a small domed and castellated mausoleum of King Louis Philippe † 1850. F. Burgess)

Congregational Church. 1864 by *Tarring*. Ferocious.

⟨Library and Museum, Church Street. By the County Architect, *R. J. Ash*, 1965–7.⟩

Weybridge contains nothing old that is really worthwhile, but a lot of intriguing snippets. The High Street is completely undistinguished. At the E end is Monument Green with the monument, set up in 1822, and using the pedestal and columns from the original Seven Dials, designed by *Edward Pierce* in 1694. Tuscan Doric and oddly thin and skimped – doubtless better seen simply as a townscape inflection. From Monument Green Thames Street goes down to the river, passing first on the r. the Tudor brick walling of Oatlands Palace (no detail remains, except one blocked four-centred arch).* This now encloses Palace Gardens, part of a pleasant council estate by *Lanchester & Lodge, Louis de Soissons*, and *A. W. Kenyon*. Next on the W side comes the former entrance to Portmore Park, a pair of thick gate-piers with trophies. They look like mid-C19 military display, but in fact are C17 and probably by *Talman*, who designed the

* Excavations by the Ministry of Public Building and Works are now in progress. They have revealed numerous carved fragments of medieval masonry, brought as building material from various Surrey abbeys. For Oatlands Park, *see* p. 392.

house, long demolished. They are a smaller edition of some of
the Hampton Court gates.* Beyond on the opposite side is the
C18 core of ST MAUR'S CONVENT, c.1750, five bays with
pedimented centre and Gibbs-rusticated doorcase; much
altered. Opposite it is No. 49, an early C19 stock-brick house
with a big primitive bracketed Doric doorcase. Now up Monument Hill, E of the monument. The date of ARLINGTON
LODGE flats may be wanted by the future historian (it is unlikely to be wanted by anyone else): a huge, half-timbered,
multi-gabled, open-ended courtyard. That date is 1957, and
the architect responsible was *R. C. Parrott*. In Oatlands Drive
is FINNART HOUSE, lumpish mid-C19. *George Walton* undoubtedly made alterations here c.1905 in his advanced Art
Nouveau style, e.g. by adding an 'eating room'. These seem
to have disappeared, and the present furnishings are part C20
Baroque and part C18, but the gate lodge to the E looks very
like *Walton*. Roughcast, Voysey style, but tense, not restful.
Buttresses concave, a queer effect.

Much new housing N and E of Weybridge, including four estates
by *Eric Lyons*. In OATLANDS DRIVE to the N, TEMPLE-
MERE, 1962–4. An outstanding estate with short two-storey
terraces carefully sited among very large trees. Some houses
in straight blocks, others, of polygonal plan, in a fan around
back gardens and garages. Beautifully detailed high garden
walls of dark brick. CASTLE GREEN opposite, at the end of
Victoria Road, of 1963–5 is quite different: straight terraces
loosely grouped in an F-shape around an open space. The
terraces are of yellow brick, with split-pitched roofs, and have
projecting porches with doors set at an angle. The other
estates are to the S. First BRACKLEYS, N of Queens Road,
1963–5, excellent and ungimmicky. Two-storey blocks, dark
brick, butterfly roofs with broad white fascia. The entrance
sides are nearly all glass, broken by projecting porches and
white slatted fences. HOLME CHASE, of 1964–6, off St
George's Avenue, has cottagey terraces, again of yellow brick,
with much stepping back, and monopitch and butterfly roofs
of different heights. The effect is slightly tricky and comes off
best with the houses on a slope.

Eric Lyons was a pioneer in the imaginative layout of housing
estates in the fifties, and these all continue this tradition,
though compared with his earlier houses (e.g. Parkleys, Ham,

* Information from Mr John Harris.

see p. 300) there is less interest in surface textures and colours, more in the play of projecting shapes, sharp angles, and plain brick walls.⟩

To the w of the High Street there is first a pretty three-arched iron BRIDGE of 1865, with stone piers and openwork spandrels in Westminster Bridge style, and beyond in Addlestone Road, now by-passed, the ROUND HOUSE, a circular stuccoed building of *c.*1800, attached to a later cottage, and probably connected with the Wey Navigation. To the s HEATH ROAD runs off from the w end of Church Street, with a couple of plain c18 houses and a TELEPHONE EXCHANGE of 1954. It is by *W. S. Frost* of the Ministry of Works, the architect of the Caterham Exchange (*see* p. 138), and just like Caterham it has standard motifs handled very sensitively and carefully with good landscaping, a rare combination in British architecture of the fifties. Simple reinforced concrete frame with brick infilling to the offices on the street, rubble stone end wall to the building behind – clichés in the best sense of the word.

⟨s of the station, off St George's Avenue, the NATIONAL COLLEGE OF FOOD TECHNOLOGY (University of Reading). Plain additions in yellow and red brick by the *Building Design Partnership* (1960–6) to Firfields, a late-c19 house.⟩ w of Heath Road is BROOKLANDS, now a technical college, originally built *c.*1860 without an architect but completely altered by *Sir Reginald Blomfield* in 1891 after the roof slipped. One of Blomfield's earliest buildings, in free Queen Anne that had not yet become dogmatic. Bright, with spirited gabled roof-line as with Norman Shaw. It was a pity that Blomfield turned Neo-Georgian: his work is always alive, however heavy. ⟨On the r., dull additions. Behind, and much better, a new brick and glass building of one and two storeys for the Catering Department, by the County Architect, *R. J. Ash*, 1966–7. Near Brooklands is HEATHSIDE SECONDARY SCHOOL, by the former County Architect, *J. Harrison*, 1964–7; pale brick, shallow pitched roof, pale green spandrel panels and typical fifties porch.⟩ Further s again is the ST GEORGE'S HILL ESTATE, another example of the Surrey speciality, the high-income suburban estate where houses are completely lost in landscape, like Wentworth and Camberley. The tone is set immediately at the w entrance with LONG BARN, very sophisticated mock Tudor. Of the other houses two of the best are CONEY WARREN and HAMSTONE HOUSE, representing two successive generations of suburban building. The first is by *Imrie & Angell*, 1914, comfortably tile-hung, the second by *Ian Forbes*, 1938, Neo-Classical with a big gatehouse and sun-trap plan, all – as the name implies – in Ham Hill stone from Somerset. In 1958 modern architecture crept in too with SERENITY, by *Leslie Gooday*, with a butterfly roof. (In Golf Club Road is LONGWALL, *Leslie Gooday*'s own house, 1964–6, an ingenious design on a sloping site, with a double-height living room cantilevered out over a long retaining wall.)

0060

WHITELEY VILLAGE
2 m. NW of Cobham

William Whiteley of Whiteley's Stores who died in 1907 left a million pounds for a village for thrifty old people. The area finally purchased in 1911 for its erection is 225 acres in size. The plan chosen, after a competition limited to six architects, is by *Frank Atkinson*, the architectural execution was by a number of selected architects, including Atkinson. The style adopted by all of them is broadly speaking that of the Hampstead Garden Suburb begun in 1907, both in its Parker & Unwin and in its Lutyens aspects. But whereas Sir Raymond Unwin's layout is informal and picturesque, the layout of Whiteley Village is as formal and symmetrical as that of an ideal Renaissance town. There is a circle of turf in the centre with a monument to Whiteley (by *Sir G. Frampton*). Buildings stand around this, and the building plots border at the back on to an outer octagon road with buildings on both sides. There are four radial roads from the centre, the main ones for traffic to the N and W, and there are diagonal cuttings as well, wide and turfed. The houses are one- and two-storeyed. The only accent is that along the N–S avenue the centres of the distance between circle and octagon have houses l. and r. with cupolas. The houses in North Avenue are by *Sir Reginald Blomfield*, those in South Avenue by *Sir Mervyn Macartney*, West Avenue *Frank Atkinson*, East Avenue *Ernest Newton*, The Green *Sir Aston Webb*, Chestnut Walk (with stores, post office and communal kitchen) *Walter Cave*, Hornbeam Walk and Heather Walk *Sir Ernest George*. The entrances and lodges are by *Atkinson*. The group of village hall, club, and assistant warden's House is by *Sir Aston Webb & Son*. The church of St Mark, by *Sir Walter Tapper*, is in the style of 1300. It is the only Gothic effort in a composition otherwise keeping away from medieval precedent. Mr Whiteley must have preferred the grander classical mode himself. To obtain it he went to architects of distinction – Webb of Buckingham Palace, Blomfield of the Quadrant, and Macartney, author of a monumental book on Georgian architecture. The village was built from 1914 to 1921. Later buildings are by *Maurice Webb*, son of Sir Aston: the chapel (known as the Sanctuary) of 1925–6, Cheshunt Crescent of 1929, and the office of 1937. The chapel is of the Wren type, of square plan with inscribed Greek cross, i.e. a square centre on four big (Roman Doric) columns.

WHYTELEAFE *see* CATERHAM

WILLINGHURST *see* CRANLEIGH

WIMBLEDON

2070

The centre of Wimbledon is the parish church and the area to the High Street on the SW and to Wimbledon Park on the N. It was there that WIMBLEDON HOUSE stood, the manor house built in 1588 for Sir Thomas Cecil, first Earl of Exeter, son of Lord Burghley. By a splendid piece of detective work, the late Mr C. S. S. Higham showed that it stood approximately astride Home Park Road, facing N downhill. It was altered in the 1640s for Queen Henrietta Maria, by *Inigo Jones* and *Nicholas Stone*, and demolished in the early C18. Sarah, Duchess of Marlborough, built a house in 1732, designed by *Henry Herbert* and *Roger Morris*, which lay to the SW, the Tudor house being cleared away to provide a northern vista. This house was burnt down in 1785, and replaced by Wimbledon Park House, built by *Henry Holland* for Earl Spencer in 1799–1802. The Spencer house was built on the foundations of the Marlborough house stables. It survived, in Arthur Road, until 1949, when it was demolished. Parts of the extensive park survives as golf course, public park, and the All England Tennis Club. Now that the house has disappeared Wimbledon has little left that dates back to a time earlier than 1800, and its present character is that of a wealthy C19 and C20 suburb. The population of Wimbledon was 2,700 in 1851, and 42,000 in 1901; in 1966 it was 55,000. All shades of architecture, from the Late Classical villa with drive and shrubbery to the best of up-to-date housing estates with point blocks, can be found. The latter, it is true, appear mostly in that part of Wimbledon which lies within the County of London, but as they did not exist yet when the second volume of *The Buildings of England* was published, they are, for the time being, included here, and for this purpose the boundary runs along Wimbledon Parkside and from the crossing of this at its N end with West Hill to the SE to Wimbledon Park.

CHURCHES

ST MARY. Chancel masonry of the later Middle Ages. The rest first rebuilt by *John Johnson* of Leicester in 1788, then again in 1843 by *G. G. Scott & Moffatt*. The chancel largely rebuilt by *Scott* in 1860. Flint with stone dressings. W tower with spire. Perp details. Interior with three galleries. To the S of the chancel the Cecil Chapel, built in 1626–36 and containing the simple black marble MONUMENT to Sir Edward Cecil, Viscount Wimbledon, † 1638. No figures, nor any figural relief. The chapel is of brick with small windows below the roof and a simple rib-vault. – ARMOUR. In the Cecil Chapel. – STAINED GLASS. Handsome figure of St George; C14. – Heraldic glass of the C17 (both in the Cecil Chapel). – In one S window three figures by *Henry Holiday*, 1919–20. – PLATE. Silver-gilt Cup and Cover 1562; silver-gilt Cup and Cover 1665; silver-gilt Flagon 1714; two silver-gilt Plates 1727. – MONUMENTS. James Perry † 1821, erected by the Fox Club. Seated figure below a bust of Charles James Fox. – (John Miland † 1877, bust by *W. Calder Marshall*. – Sir Joseph Bazalgette † 1891 by *Gaffin*. NT) – In the churchyard Gerard de Visme † 1797. Pyramid of blocks of vermiculated rustication with corner acroteria to the base.

ALL SAINTS, All Saints Road, South Wimbledon. By *Micklethwaite & Somers Clarke*, 1891–3. Brick with big bellcote over the W end. Nave and wide N aisle. The S aisle not yet built. Octagonal piers with arches dying into them.

CHRIST CHURCH, Copse Hill. By *S. S. Teulon*, 1859–60; enlarged 1881. Stone, with tower over the chancel. The tower with a pyramid roof and circular stair-turret. Dec detail.

VICARAGE, Copse Hill, by *David Rock & Robert Smart*, 1964–6. Dark brick, monopitch roof, with garage and parish room projecting in front.

ST JOHN, Spencer Hill. 1875 by *T. G. Jackson*. Red brick, without a tower. Dec detail. Between nave and chancel, odd bellcote on a buttress with many set-offs.

⟨ST MARK, St Mark's Place, Worple Road. By *Humphrys & Hurst*, 1968–9. Ingenious pentagonal plan with the altar in front of a straight side, and seats on three sides, but placed across the angles. Good indirect lighting behind the altar, and above, by means of a raised section of the roof. The effect is surprisingly spacious, despite some fussy detailing.⟩

(ST MATTHEW, Wimbledon Park. Of *c*.1910 by *E. C. Shearman*, rebuilt after the war by *J. S. Comper*. NT)

(CHRIST THE KING (R.C.), The Crescent. 1928 by *A. G. Scott*. DE)

(OUR LADY QUEEN OF HEAVEN (R.C.), Victoria Drive. A 1930s house converted by *Tomei & Maxwell*, 1962. DE)

(ST WINEFRIDE (R.C.), Latimer Road. 1905 by *F. A. Walters*. DE)

STE MARIE REPARATRICE (R.C.). Old buildings of 1867. Chapel of 1957 by *John Osburn*, light brick with small NE tower.

ST PAUL,* Augustus Road. 1877 by *Micklethwaite & Somers Clarke*. Brick, with a flèche and Dec tracery. Lozenge-shaped piers with chamfered angles. Wagon roof. – STAINED GLASS. By *Kempe*, 1893–1901. – REREDOS by Kempe's partner and successor *Tower*.

SACRED HEART (R.C.), Edge Hill. 1886–1901 by *F. A. Walters*. Large, tall, and long, without any special vertical accent. Flint and stone. Nave and aisles and polygonal apse. Dec, with pinnacles on the buttresses. Flying buttresses for the apse. Interior with much figural stone decoration.

PUBLIC BUILDINGS

TOWN HALL, Wimbledon Hill Road and Broadway. Stone-faced, symmetrical, and dull. By *A. J. Hope* (*Bradshaw, Gass & Hope*), 1931.

WIMBLEDON COLLEGE, Edge Hill. The long NW range facing towards Ridgway Gardens is of 1898. Behind it the original building of 1860 by *S. S. Teulon* (J. M. Crook) and the CHAPEL by *F. A. Walters* (1910). At the N angle a big extension of 1951 by *Hudson & Hammond*. The C19 buildings are of brick, and Gothic.

KING'S COLLEGE SCHOOL, South Side Common. Transferred from Somerset House to Wimbledon in 1897. A plain rendered Georgian house (Cooke: 1750), with a Tuscan porch and, attached to it, the broad chapel-like brick front of a neo-Perp range by *Sir B. Fletcher*, 1899. More buildings of the C19 and C20.

* In fact in the County of London, Borough of Wandsworth.

SOUTHLANDS COLLEGE, Wimbledon Park Side and Queensmere Road. The original house (Belmont) dates from *c.*1850–60. New buildings by *Yorke, Rosenberg & Mardall*. Completed in 1957 the hall and gymnasium at the SW end. Exterior with Yorkshire slabs, brick, and ornamental tiles by *Peggy Angus*. Block with lecture rooms E of the old buildings. This has sunbreaks over the S windows and a bold exposed outer staircase against the end wall. Another block with lecture rooms and gymnasium 1959–62. Moreover, across Queensmere Road, a range of 197 study-bedrooms, dining hall, etc. This was begun in 1961.

QUEEN ALEXANDRA'S COURT (Royal Homes for Widows and Daughters of Naval and Military Officers), St Mary's Road. 1904–5, 1908, 1912, by *Sir Ernest George, Yates & Parkinson*. Group of large brick and stone blocks in the Neo-Georgian style.

TELEPHONE MANAGER'S OFFICE, Worple Road. By *W. S. Frost* of the *Ministry of Public Building and Works*, 1958–62.

TENNIS CLUB, Church Road. Covered tennis court by *C. J. Pell & Partners* (engineers). A shell-concrete vault of 175 by 175 ft covers two existing courts. The vault is only 3 in. thick. Shallow segmental lunettes on all four sides. Centre with a 14-ft dome of glass-fibre laminate. In addition two hundred 21-in. glass domes for daylighting and a system of tubes for artificial lighting.

SOUTH WIMBLEDON UNDERGROUND STATION. *See* Merton.

PERAMBULATION

Immediately to the N of the church is the OLD RECTORY, a house of *c.*1500 with considerable additions, especially of 1846. Original one range with specially thick walls, two stair-turrets, and some interior features, including a pointed arch in the former chapel. Also good panelling of *c.*1600, probably brought in. To the NE of the church in ARTHUR ROAD a WELL HOUSE which was built by Earl Spencer in 1798 in order to raise water for his house. Octagonal with a dome. The well is 563 ft deep. In LEOPOLD ROAD, RICARDS LODGE SCHOOL, a large C19 Gothic house, with good new buildings behind. To the SW of the church, a few minutes away, is the HIGH STREET, running W towards the common. It starts with the WESTMINSTER BANK of 1895 by *Cheston & Perkin*. Further on is EAGLE HOUSE, the most important house in Wimbledon. This was built in

1613 and has a façade of three widely spaced bays with three big shaped gables. Brick, now mostly rendered. Three canted bay windows, central entrance. The entrance leads into the middle of one short side of the hall, which runs at r. angles to the front through to the back of the house, still an unusual arrangement at that time (but cf. e.g. Hardwick). Three original plaster ceilings on the first floor and one on the ground floor, the hall overmantel on the ground floor, and the panelling of the former dining room (1730) are preserved. The house was bought by the architect *Sir T. G. Jackson* and restored, 1887. Nos. 44–45 is a nice simple L-shaped late C17 brick house with Georgian alterations.

SOUTH SIDE COMMON faces the Common and was built essentially in the Late Georgian and Early Victorian years, though many of the houses were later altered or replaced. No. 4, 1900 by *E. J. May*, e.g., is Neo-Georgian with hipped roof. Off South Side in LAURISTON ROAD No. 15 (CUMNOR) is of 1891 by *Ransome*, with irregular gables. Back in South Side SOUTH LODGE has its original front of 1840.

South Side faces WIMBLEDON COMMON. In it the famous WINDMILL, a hollow post-mill built in 1817–18 and rebuilt in 1893 (repaired 1956). By its S end, S of Robin Hood Road, CAESAR'S CAMP, a circular Iron Age HILL-FORT with a straight section on the N side. It has a single ditch and bank; the W entrance may be original. It was reduced in the C19 by a speculative builder who, for once in Surrey, didn't succeed. Excavations in more recent times have shown that the bank behind the ditch was faced with timber on both sides and stood before a 10-ft-wide berm. Pottery suggests a first occupation in the C3 B.C. Near Tibbett's Corner, to the E of the block of flats called Wildcroft Manor, an OBELISK erected in 1776 to commemorate David Hartley's Fire-Proof House, which was built with thin layers of iron and copper encased in plaster and placed between floor and ceiling. The King and Queen took a repast in the house while fires were being lit in the room underneath.

From the SW end of South Side one can continue to the N along WEST SIDE COMMON. Here also Georgian houses, mostly altered, e.g. WEST SIDE HOUSE (two storeys, five bays, hipped roof). Then CANNIZARO HOUSE, rebuilt (or repaired?) after a fire of 1900 in a lavish, rather Baroque Neo-Georgian. Thirteen bays wide, the centre with two orders of columns and a big pediment. Then STAMFORD HOUSE, dated by Cooke

1720. Three storeys, five bays. Finally THE KEIR, stuccoed, with a Grecian porch with closed sides. The continuation of West Side is WEST PLACE, a nice, humble, unified early C19 street, also overlooking the common.

Back to the S end of South Side and down WOODHAYES ROAD. Nos. 2 and 4 are a pair of C18 five-bay houses, each with a slightly projecting, pedimented three-bay centre. Brick and rubbed brick. Tuscan doorways. No. 4 has its original glazing bars. No. 6 is called GOTHIC LODGE. It is indeed in a Gothick style, with pretty ogee-arched and crocketed heads to the upper windows. The date 1763 on a lead pump-head. Original staircase and some chimneypieces. The house was much enlarged c.1880–90.

S and W of this is RIDGWAY. No. 70, in a drive N of the road, is violent polychrome brick by *Roumieu*, 1866; No. 54 is by *Sir T. G. Jackson*, 1908. A little further E, END HOUSE, No. 13 BERKELEY PLACE, is a nice, freely detailed building by *James Ransome*, 1894, with a big shaped gable.

See p. 600

The character to the N of the W end of the High Street is very different. The stretch to the N end of PARKSIDE and the area to its E to PRINCE'S WAY and beyond consisted of villas from the Late Classical to Voysey, Lutyens, and beyond. The part over the London border was gradually converted into a model estate of the LCC. Examples of the various phases are as follows. FAIRLAWN, Late Classical, stuccoed. – GAYTON, grand symmetrical Tudor with ornate decoration, brick with stone dressings. – GORDON DENE, No. 15 Prince's Way. 1899 by *Voysey*, with a large double-gabled r. addition. Typical of Voysey's free neo-Tudor, with its roughcast and stone window surrounds. The interior is much altered. – CARDIFF HOUSE, Parkside. Handsome mock-Wren of 1903 by *George Hubbard* and *A. W. Moore*. – (LINDEN LODGE SCHOOL (formerly NORTH HOUSE), large late *Lutyens*, 1934–5, but a curious reversion to the all-brick Tudor manner of New Place, Shedfield, Hants of 1906. The LODGE is also by *Lutyens*. NT) – No. 55 VICTORIA DRIVE, corner of Augustus Road, by *Kaufmann & Benjamin*, 1935, a typical, good modern house of its date. – No. 21 QUEENSMERE ROAD, by *Maxwell Fry*, also of 1935, is only of interest because of the name of its architect.

Then the work of the LCC (architects at the time first *Robert Matthew*, then *Sir Leslie Martin*). This is chiefly the Ackroyden Estate and the Argyle Estate. In one sense, the Surrey volume does not deserve them, because at the time they were built nothing so modern would have been allowed inside the county. The northernmost is the ACKROYDEN ESTATE, the first and in some ways the best of the LCC estates to mix up low and high housing. There are not too many tower blocks, and there are plenty of humane details at ground-floor level. Two-, three-, four-, five-, eight-, and eleven-storey blocks were used. The low buildings are decent and unremarkable (but note the ingenious way of turning the corner at the junction of Parkside and Inner Park Road), and the eight- and eleven-storey blocks of identical design are admirable, and as good as any subsequent LCC point blocks. T-shaped, the end walls brick and the sides cement-rendered, with a simple pattern provided by generous balconies. No fussiness, no applied pattern-making. Good roof shape enclosing the top of the lift shaft. The architect in charge was *H. G. Gillett*. The estate includes shops, club room, and a good PRIMARY SCHOOL, faced with roughcast concrete slabs on an 8-ft-3-in. grid. In Inner Park Road is ROUNDACRE, a quadrant of houses and a three-storey block of flats by *Kenneth Capon* of *Architects' Co-Partnership*, 1960. The ARGYLE ESTATE, further S, is much less interesting, except for WINTERFOLD CLOSE, a group of flats and maisonettes off Albert Drive. Built by the LCC in 1956; it seems to be impossible to find the names of the actual designers. ⟨In SOMERSET ROAD N of the Tennis Club, at first plenty of examples of the depressingly popular Neo-Georgian terraces of the sixties; then, refreshingly, CEDAR COURT and OAKFIELD; plain staggered terraces in dark brick, and two eleven-storey towers of flats and some linked three-storey blocks, all by the *Building Design Partnership*, 1966. The architectural details are excellent, but the layout is poor, with far too many internal roads.⟩

WINDLESHAM

9060

On the Berkshire border, half heath and half meadows. Big C19 houses and a busy nest of Victorian brick boxes on the former; sleek old farms on the latter, which is almost the first true countryside on this bearing coming out of London.

ST JOHN BAPTIST. Rebuilt in 1680 after a fire, in quoined brick. Almost submerged since, first by grafting stucco and Gothic detail on to the tower in 1838* (a poor effort by *Robert Ebbels*, who did so well with the tower of Ewhurst church in the same

* Now removed.

year), and second by adding a chancel and an enormous new nave and N aisle in raw polychrome brick in 1874 (by *Ewan Christian*, and not too bad inside, but hopelessly out of place). The S side has a bit of C17 brickwork, a C17 porch, and what look like three windows reset from the medieval church: two-light Dec and one three-light square-headed Perp. – PLATE. Silver-gilt Set 1841. – MONUMENT (E wall of old chancel). Reserved Palladian tablet to Lt. Col. Robert Hemington † 1757. – (In the far NW corner of the churchyard two TOMBS for Australian millionaires showing the best and worst of *Lutyens*'s monumental classicism. – Mrs Clark † 1934 has a sublime altar of travertine with exquisite abstract curves. – William Baillieu † 1936 has a confused mixture of columns and a flattened vase. NT)

The church forms a pleasant group with THE CEDARS, a rough early C18 brick house.

ST SAVIOUR, Valley End. 1867 by *Bodley*. The standard chapel of ease, but done sensitively. Brick with a shingled belfry and well-managed W hipped gable. Honest interior with exposed bricks and big iron tie-rods. A real attempt to re-interpret Surrey traditions in C19 terms; a great pity that it had to have Gothic detail.

POUND COTTAGE, Pound Lane. Pure Hampshire C17: timber-framed, brick infilling, with a thick thatched roof coming down in hips to the ground-floor ceiling. In beautiful condition, without being at all dolled up.

(WINDLESHAM MOOR. A big house of 1915 by *Percy Newton* in the style of Lutyens (fine roof and chimneys) and Baker (round-arched loggias). NT)

(At Valley End, VICARAGE by *Bodley*, dated 1868 (P. Thompson); PEMBROKE PLACE by *Scott, Brownrigg & Turner*, 1961.)

HEATHSIDE, Ridgemont Road, Sunningdale. A Middle Bronze Age BARROW was excavated here in 1901, revealing a Late Bronze Age cremation cemetery inserted in its SW side. There were twenty-five burials in twenty-two urns in separate stone settings.

WINDSOR GREAT PARK

OBELISK. *See The Buildings of England: Berkshire.*

WISLEY

Like Farleigh, a remarkable survival of a tiny hamlet very much as it was in the C12: church, farm, and a couple of cottages beside the Wey. Yet it is only three quarters of a mile from Byfleet. The church makes a pretty and completely genuine group with CHURCH FARM, big and L-shaped, partly C16 half-timber and partly C18 brick.

CHURCH. Also like Farleigh, the original simple Norman pattern unaltered. Nave, chancel, and bellcote, all carstone (cf. Byfleet) mostly stuccoed over, with windows either C12 (N and S sides of chancel) or C17 Gothic Survival (two two-light windows in the nave and the E window, dated 1627). Also a little bad neo-Norman of 1872 – two windows in the W wall and the N door. Unsophisticated interior with barn-like queen-post roofs. Plain Norman chancel arch of one order without any ornament, with later pointed recesses (C13 ?) on either side cutting into the jambs. – PLATE. Cup 1713; Paten 1714.

ROYAL HORTICULTURAL SOCIETY. The main buildings are in a weakened and sweetened version of Lutyens Tudor, by *Imrie & Angell*, 1914, with some surface picturesqueness. See p. 600

BARROWS. There are two on Cockcrow Hill and one to the N, near Foxwarren Park. On the Common is a fine bell barrow, 144 ft in diameter and 10 ft high. It contained a secondary cremation high in the mound, but there is no record of the main burial.

WITLEY   *9030*

Probably the most typical Surrey village in the proportion of tile-hanging, half-timber, and brick, though not in any distinct local style. It is in fact a softer and more intimate edition of the Weald villages of Sussex. Strung out for more than a mile along the Milford to Petworth road, with picturesque groups every few yards but never for long enough to form a coherent village.

ALL SAINTS. Rambling building of Weald stone with a complex building history. Moderately restored. Attractive more for the picturesque group it makes with cottages and churchyard than for any architectural qualities. Nave originally big, tall, and Saxon – cf. one double-splayed window on the S side and another high up in the W gable. S doorway C11, Norman, big-boned and roughly carved, like a simpler edition of the Ewhurst door. Jamb-shafts with block capitals supporting abaci with a chip-carved star pattern. The E end of the Saxon-Norman nave can still be seen on the S side, now incorporated in the crossing tower. This, with the S transept and the

chancel,* was added *c.*1180–1220 in an Early Gothic style familiar in Hampshire. The tower arches are single-chamfered,‡
some of them with tiny squinches above and below the capitals.
Windows simple lancets with squat splays, now seen only in
the s transept. The s lancet in the chancel is later c13, as was
the N chapel originally – cf. the N lancets, the aumbry, and the
arch to its w. The main arch between chapel and chancel
however seems to be early c14, a double-chamfered arch on
responds in continuous mouldings. Then the customary quota
of piecemeal insertions and additions. One nave window late
c13: two lights, but not the familiar Y-shape. Instead, the
subsidiary lights come away from the outer arch and have
apexes of their own, as at Albury; a queer, unresolved effect.
E window three-light curvilinear (i.e. mid-c14), of the same
elegant character as the similar windows at Woking and
Worplesdon. The tower pinnacles, and possibly the whole bell-
chamber, are c17. N aisle and transept partly 1844, and partly
1890 by *Aston Webb.* The s porch is a good bit of patchwork
done in the c19. The bargeboarding is apparently genuine,
from a cottage in the village, and the outer arch, c13 in style,
is supposedly genuine too. The chancel inside has more than
its fair share of bad Late Victorian veined marble and stencilling, but includes a queer chunky c13 PISCINA with square
aumbry above. – FONT. c13, and a little more elaborate than
usual. Octagonal bowl with octagonal stem and eight shafts all
merging into one large capital. The bowl is presumably cut
down. – WALL PAINTINGS (s side of nave). Indistinct, but
clearly c12. Stilted figures under round-headed arches. The
subjects come from the life of the Virgin. Professor Tristram
dated them *c.*1120, one of a group done from Lewes Priory
which includes Hardham and Clayton in Sussex. – (PLATE.
Paten, 1889 by *G. Jekyll.*) – BRASS. Thomas Jonys, one of
Henry VIII's court officials, and his wife, *c.*1530. Civil dress,
figures about 15 in. high. The usual rough c16 quality.

See
p.
600

Few of the cottages need special mention; the picturesque parts
are easily seen by the main-road traveller. The best known is
undoubtedly STEP COTTAGE, tile-hung and timber-framed,
forming a delightful group with the church spire and the

---

* The chancel has the wall-plates of the roof exposed outside, a very odd
feature. Was there a lean-to chapel here?
‡ The w arch is narrower than the others, a fact probably connected with
the former E wall of the Early Norman nave, which would have had only a
small chancel.

churchyard at the corner of Church Lane, the epitome of small-scale Surrey prettiness. s of this are picturesque cottages of both the C16 and the C19. N of it is another group, where the road narrows and the timber-framed SUN INN faces a high brick wall. Then, further N in Wheeler Street, the OLD MANOR, C16 with an C18 wing with segment-headed windows.

1 m. SW is SANDHILLS, a hamlet with a few more picturesque cottages on a steep hillside site looking s across the Weald, and two late C19 houses: BANACLE EDGE by *Champneys*, 1893, an ordinary essay in the usual tile-hung Norman Shaw style with pargetted gables, and KINGWOOD, built as Sandhouse by *F. W. Troup* about 1902, a good, plain neo-Tudor house, refreshingly free from coy mannerisms. Symmetrical and gabled, little ornament apart from diaper brickwork and the rhythm of segmental windows – almost Philip Webb's style. It looks much better in the flesh than it does in photographs.

WITLEY PARK, 1¼ m. w. Originally Lea House. A big neo-Tudor house, built for Whitaker Wright, the financier,* c.1890, by *H. Paxton Watson*, gutted in 1952, and now completely demolished. There remain a quadrangle of STABLES and complete set of LODGES dated 1896, all in clever free-Tudor style. The best is BROOK LODGE at the NE corner of the park, L-shaped, with one arm forming an arch over the drive and a picturesque copper-roofed dovecote in the angle of the L. (*Lutyens* also worked for Wright, in 1897: the BATHING PAVILION beside the upper lake is his, and the elegant BOAT-HOUSE overlooking the lower lake. The latter has an open colonnade of white-painted timber on a massive stone base with round arches at each end. NT) *See p. 600*

Wright was an amateur landscape gardener in the true English tradition and built, among other things, an extra-ordinary room beneath the lower lake in the grounds. (It is approached by spiral concrete steps, then a concrete corridor with a curious pointed roof, which leads into the central circular chamber. The point of the glazed dome supports the giant STATUE of Neptune which appears to walk on the surface of the lake. Also in the lake is the stone octagonal pavilion of the pumping system which regulates the water. NT)

(In the park there is now a new, very lavish, house by *Patrick Gwynne*, 1960–1. Two wings based on hexagons (cf.

* He promoted a vast number of mining companies in the 1890s and committed suicide in 1904 after having been sentenced to seven years' imprisonment for fraud.

the same architect's theatre restaurant at York), meeting at an obtuse angle. The main rooms are on the first floor, with large corner windows allowing for views in all directions. The ground floor is of reinforced concrete faced with stone.)

(WITLEY COURT (formerly The Hill), further s, built for the painter *Birket Foster* to his own design, in freely composed half-timbering, remarkably progressive for its date (1861), has been replaced by a recent villa except for some outbuildings.* Opposite, on the way down to Tigbourne Court (*see* p. 486), WOOD END, an attractive small house by *Lutyens*, 1897. Excellently composed, on a corner, the oversailing upper storey of white plaster, on a base of Bargate stone with brick dressings, being anchored by a giant chimneystack, into which a miniature porch fits snugly. Green-painted timber windows are clipped on to corners. The interior is split-level, a big living room opening off the staircase halfway up. *Jekyll* garden. NT)

KING EDWARD'S SCHOOL, Wormley, near Witley station, 1 m. s of the village. 1867 by *Sydney Smirke*, a rather sad example of the sort of compromise forced on classically minded architects by the mid C19. Fifteen bays, the centre with a big two-storey entrance arch and windowless tower above, quite well composed and nearer Vanbrugh's style than anything else. The effect is spoilt by insensitive handling and carving and by the neo-Jacobean touches Smirke felt compelled to add: shaped gables at the ends and diaper brickwork everywhere. Additions by *G. D. Sykes*.

WOKING

A period piece, though not a very creditable one. The railway came in 1838, bringing a station in open heathland 2 m. from the original village (*see* Old Woking). A Victorian gridiron mushroomed around it, and the present population is 77,220 (1968). The Urban District of Woking is now the largest town in Surrey. With all the income that travels daily up to London, the town has so far retained its mean and joyless public buildings, offices, and chapels of the 1860s and 1870s – one consequence of using a town simply as a place to eat and sleep in. A town of this size founded in 1738 would have looked very different by the 1860s. ⟨But in a few years much will have changed. Immediately N of

* *Burne-Jones's* STAINED GLASS of St Cecilia of *c.*1873 and tiled overmantel of scenes from 'Beauty and the Beast' (1862) are now in the William Morris Museum, Walthamstow.

the station there is already ALBION HOUSE, a slab on a podium filling an irregular plot between the High Street and Commercial Road. The side of the podium which faces CHURCH PATH, with a pub and shops, has effectively varied levels and surfaces (dark brick, broad bands of concrete). At the corner of Commercial Road and Percy Street, MAPLES, a crisp six-storey block with dark grey spandrel panels and thin mullions. The area N of Commercial Road, now full of car parks and vacant lots, is to be comprehensively redeveloped. There is to be a pedestrian area around Christ Church, a new Civic Centre (by *Gollins, Melvin, Ward & Partners*), Police Station and Magistrates' Courts (by the *County Architect's Department*), and a tall office block, car park, and shops (by *Scott, Brownrigg & Turner*). (Earlier buildings in the centre are the CONSERVATIVE CLUB of 1898 by *H. A. Whitburn*, and CO-OPERATIVE HOUSE, Church Street, Dudok-modern by *L. G. Ekins, c.* 1935. NT)

Woking S of the station is nearly all residential, with many terraces and flats of the sixties between Guildford Road and White Rose Road. In Coley Avenue, OLD PEOPLE'S HOMES by the County Architect, *R. J. Ash*, 1968.⟩

CHRIST CHURCH. 1889 by *W. F. Unsworth*. Big in scale, honest lancet brick. Inside, a big kingpost roof above a big apsed space with tiny ambulatory-aisles. It makes an instructive comparison with the same architect's frigid and expensive church at Woodham; as with many Late Victorian architects, the cheaper the building, the better the design.

⟨METHODIST CHURCH, Brewery Road. By *E. D. Mills & Partners*, 1966. Excellently planned. The church is octagonal in plan, but with a pitched roof with a lantern at an apex above the pulpit and communion table at the E end. Simple white window mullions, reaching to the ground at the sides. – Good bold STAINED GLASS above the W door by *G. Rees Thomas*. – Adjoining at the back, compact brick block containing halls and offices.⟩

SHAH JEHAN MOSQUE, Oriental Road. Of 1889, by *W. I. Chambers* for Dr Gottlieb Leitner, who took over the existing buildings of the Royal Dramatic College (built 1865, architect *T. R. Smith*; poor Tudor) and founded a centre for oriental studies which is now also the centre for Muslims in England. An extraordinarily dignified little building, especially by comparison with other mock-Oriental buildings of the same date, such as the Greek Orthodox Church in Bayswater. In an Indian rather than Arabic style: onion dome on delicate rubble walls, with a decorative three-part frontispiece in blue and gold, as pretty as the Brighton Pavilion. The inside is a well-thought-out square with a dome on squinches, three ogee niches in each wall, and a sober panelled apse and preaching box.*

ST MARY OF BETHANY, York Road. 1907 by *Caröe*. Only interesting in that the w front shows how Caröe had taken over Lutyens's whole domestic repertoire: careful brickwork, cosy details, voussoirs all made up of thin tiles.

ST JOHN, at St John's, ¾ m. w of the town centre. Built in 1842 as an aisleless chapel by *George Gilbert Scott* and repeatedly enlarged. Not in Scott's own list of his early 'ignoble' churches. It ought to be.

ST PETER'S CONVENT, Maybury. Free Perp, by *J. L. Pearson*, begun 1897, and built in 1898–1908 by *F. L. Pearson*, after his father's death. Vermilion brick and stone, asymmetrical and friendly, as Pearson's work became towards the end of his life. (The interior is vaulted, and has a complex E end with three apsidal lobes rising to the full height of the building from the crypt. This Byzantine effect is increased by the mosaic decoration of the crypt, presumably designed by F. L. Pearson.)‡

See p. 600 Very many expensive private houses were built near Hook Heath and Smarts Heath, s of the railway. The land was originally to have been part of Brookwood Cemetery, and was sold off in 1891. One is by *Lutyens*, FISHERS HILL of 1900–1, neo-Tudor brick already beginning to go heavy and lose spontaneity. (The interesting part is the s end, where the garden drops a whole storey (with a complicated arrangement of pergola and steps) and tall bay windows are carried up in a foretaste of blocks of flats a generation later. *Jekyll* garden. NT) FISHERS HILL COTTAGE, also by *Lutyens*, 1907, is smaller, simpler, and better.

HORSELL *see* p. 320.

KNAPHILL *see* Bisley, p. 111.

WOODHAM *see* p. 538.

---

* The orientation towards Mecca is exactly right: 'a captain of a P & O boat kindly went to Woking and took the bearings' (*Building News*, 2 August 1889). The courtyard and some decoration are not by the architect; there was evidently some dispute between him and the client, fought out in the *Building News* ('We wish the Mosque at Woking had been built at Jericho or some place distant enough never to have troubled us.' Editor, *Building News*, 22 November 1889).

‡ Mr A. Quiney kindly provided this information.

WOLDINGHAM   3050

This tiny downland hamlet SE of Caterham has gradually become
a very leafy suburb. The parish is full of steep-sided valleys and
the houses are hidden away in these, usually drowned in trees –
an object lesson to the the brutally expanded Warlingham, next
door.

ST AGATHA, up on the Downs. The meanest little village church
  in Surrey. A tiny chapel, rebuilt in flint in 1832. Only one room
  and no fittings. Now replaced by

ST PAUL, ½ m. N, among the new houses. 1933 by *Sir Herbert
  Baker* for Lord Craigmyle of the P. & O., an arch neo-Perp
  building in flint, more or less East Anglian. The W tower has
  'Praise Him/and Magnify Him/Forever' in flushwork on three
  sides. The inside is suavely eclectic. It has a kingpost roof, but
  also an apse, quite impressive, and a sort of Romanesque baptistery. The apse has more flushwork: 'Glory to God in the
  Highest . . .', set in agates. 'The Nizam of Hyderabad has
  kindly sent us some 300 of them', said Baker, a sentence which
  somehow sums up his whole epoch. All in all, a creditable job.
  – STAINED GLASS in the apse by *Douglas Strachan*: acceptable
  Expressionism. – PLATE. Paten 1686.

Most of Woldingham is high-class, but one area, called the Gar- *See
  p.
  600*
  den Village, E of the station, consists of tiny working-class
  houses built during the First World War, with road names like
  Hill 60. It has the best site in the village.* Here also a couple
  of flat-roofed timber HOUSES, nicely set on a hillbrow, by
  Elie Mayorcas, 1937. In Lunghurst Road, CARIAD and NEW
  ENGLAND, two houses by *Derek Lovejoy*, 1960. New England,
  the architect's own house, terraced out of the hill, has a main
  room with two impressive glass walls. In Slynes Oak Road,
  NETHERN COURT, C16 with later additions. FLINTHOUSE
  FARM, I m. SE, on the crest of the Downs, has a walled garden
  in the style of the C17 and a 1650-looking gazebo, all in old
  brick and flint, but all in fact C20 – another example of the C20
  Surrey habit of cultivating the appearance of antiquity at all
  costs.

MARDEN PARK, ½ m. W, in a charming valley. (Formerly Roe-
  hampton Park.) A ferocious Victorian house of 1880 by *Arthur
  Cawston* in polychrome brick. Tudor. The late C18 stables

---

* Mr A. C. Silverthorne tells us that the garden village was built as an
army camp.

remain, though altered, with a bulky and impressive octagonal cupola.

WONERSH

SE of Guildford: one dignified, sinuous street of brick, Bargate stone, tile-hanging, and half-timber. Now a little suburbanized, but still a good place to look at minor varieties of Surrey architecture.

ST JOHN THE BAPTIST. Mostly pulled-about C18, keeping earlier fragments. The old parts of the N wall of the nave are apparently pre-Conquest (on the strength of details found in the restoration but not kept). Tower to the N of this, the base late C12, unbuttressed carstone, with a crude pointed arch opening into the nave. The top simple classical of 1751. Chancel originally C13 (blocked lancets in the N and S walls), arch to the S of c.1300, arch to the N Perp. The S side of the nave and the S transept were rebuilt in 1793 (after a fire) in a simple brick village Classical, almost without ornament. Typically, the mason took in the whole width of the former S aisle, thus leaving the chancel arch off-centre inside. Finally, this character was partly removed by *Sir Charles Nicholson* when he rebuilt the E end in 1901 and also did the SCREEN and FONT COVER. – CHANDELIERS. Several, C18 pattern, but mostly modern Belgian copies. They give the interior some character. – STAINED GLASS. Good armorial glass, strong reds and blacks, on the S side of the nave. The E window is the first work of *A. K. Nicholson* (Sir Charles Nicholson's brother), dated 1914. Kempe-style, but predominantly blues and reds, without Kempe's overall green tinge. Quite effective. – ROYAL ARMS. Painted; of George III. Also several hatchments. – MONUMENTS. C14 table tomb (N chancel chapel), with wiry side panels as on the tomb at Godalming. – At the W end of the nave, small fragments of the architectural frame of an Elizabethan tablet, roughly carved, but the details themselves surprisingly accurate Italian Renaissance. – Brass to Thomas Elyot † 1467 and wife, bad 18 in. effigies – Henry Elyot † 1503, his wife, and twenty-three children. Also 18 in. effigies and also badly done, but with a little naïve vitality in the expressions.

WONERSH PARK. A C17 and C18 house, demolished in 1935. The entrance GATEWAY remains on the road E of the church, pretty though ham-fisted C18 brick Gothick, with battlements and also quoins in reverse – i.e. inset instead of being raised. A quadrangle of plain C18 STABLES also survives, now converted and called Wonersh Court.

Very little worth special mention in the village. Opposite the churchyard entrance, GREEN PLACE has quite a big C16 half-timbered rearward wing. The GRANTLEY ARMS in the centre is also C16 half-timber, and DOWER HOUSE further E has a simple five-bay front of 1710 with a big segment-headed fanlight and doorway added c.1790.

CHINTHURST HILL, ¼ m. NW. Bargate stone house in the Tudor style, by *Lutyens*, 1893–5, before he had found his feet, architecturally speaking. Fine hillside site above the river valley, inadequately served by a limp assembly of gables and bow windows. (Inside there is a fine central hall with a heavy timber roof, in a free Gothic style derived from Leonard Stokes. The staircase is rather blatantly half-timbered, but the upstairs corridor has cool white arches, plastered, which prophesy a later Lutyens. Terraced garden planted by *Gertrude Jekyll*. Nice LODGE at the foot of the hill. NT)

ST JOHN'S SEMINARY, ½ m. SE. Long brick range in mixed Jacobean–Georgian with a chapel at one end in the same style; one of the less fortunate consequences of Norman Shaw. All by *F. A. Walters*, 1895.

DERRY'S HILL, 1 m. SE. By *J. F. Bentley*, c.1890, and oddly enough also mixed Jacobean–Georgian, with multiple later additions. The entrance porch and window above in an odd style which looks like one more attempt to break through to a personal language similar to Art Nouveau.

THE HALLAMS. *See* p. 295.

WOODCOTE *see* EPSOM

WOODCOTE VILLAGE   *2060*
1 m. S of Wallington

High-class garden suburb, the houses mostly half-timbered. Very *See* leafy, expensive and handsome. Winding roads, and an *p.* incredibly trim triangular green at the centre with nine of the *600* houses fronting on to it. No shops built and none intended. It was laid out and partly designed in 1901–20 by *William Webb*, a Deal business man and horticulturalist, who called it the 'Garden First' system: 'the name Garden First means that the garden shall not only have prominence but that partial garden construction shall be carried out before any buildings are erected . . . the house is but the complement of the garden in a general survey of the estate'.*

Despite the fact that the C16 antiquary William Camden 'was very sanguine upon Woodcote' as a Roman settlement, and more particularly as the site of Noviomagus of the Antonine Itinerary, little definite is known except that the remains of a VILLA and BATH BUILDING of the C2–4 A.D. were found at Park Farm, Beddington, 3 m. N of Woodcote, in 1871.

WOODHAM
1 m. NE of Woking

Expensive houses in pinewoods, plus the LCC post-war SHEER-WATER ESTATE, a poor effort, with interminable vistas of cottage units and most of the original trees grubbed up, except in one higher-income neighbourhood. In this, the effect of trees on commonplace elevations and layouts is startling.

ALL SAINTS. 1893 by *W. F. Unsworth* (cf. Woking). Competent but joyless Old-Surrey style. Tile-hung crossing, and even a mock-Norman S door, to give the impression of slow growth. The inside lavish, well detailed, and stone dead.

WOODHAMBURY, Woodham Lane. Good house of 1889, built by *W. F. Unsworth* for himself,‡ taking up the Norman Shaw style at its prettiest. Long roof-line with a big tile-hung gable, all the detail made even prettier than the Kate Greenaway house at Hampstead: tiny windows with tiny panes, done quite simply without affectation or coyness.

WOODHATCH *see* REIGATE

WOODMANSTERNE

ST PETER. 1876–7 by *Joseph Clarke*. Flint with bell-turret. N aisle 1960–1 by *E. F. Starling*. In the NW corner of the church one small lancet window from the medieval church. – PLATE. Chalice and Paten 1711.

WOODSIDE
2¼ m. NE of Croydon

ST LUKE. 1870 by *W. V. Arnold* (GS), with additions by *W. D. Caröe*. E end largely rebuilt in 1949. Brick with lancet windows

---

* From Webb's 'Garden First in Land Development'. All this information is due to Mr T. E. Callander, former Chief Librarian of Croydon.

‡ Information from D. Lloyd.

and no tower. The interior is made impressive by the pointed diaphragm arches across the nave.

WOOLPIT see EWHURST

WORCESTER PARK

2060

The name derives from one of the two parks of Nonsuch Palace (*see* p. 383). Worcester Park was of 911 acres.

ST MARY, The Avenue, Cuddington. 1895 by *A. Thomas* (*Whitfield & Thomas*). Flint and not brick, with a polygonal apse and a flèche. – (STAINED GLASS. w window by *L. Lee*, 1959.)

(ST MATTHIAS (R.C.), Brinkley Road. 1906 by *B. Williamson*. DE)

MALDEN GREEN FARM, immediately N of the station. The district was traditionally called Maldengreen.

WORMLEY see WITLEY

WORPLESDON

9050

Between Woking and Guildford, on the edge of the heaths, and still genuinely rural, although Guildford gets nearer every year. Mellow brick houses and a shaggy triangular green on a hill.

ST MARY. Above the village, and shows itself off as few old Surrey churches do. C13 N chapel, badly restored in 1866. Genuine curvilinear chancel E window, like Old Woking. C15 nave, clerestory, lean-to aisles, and w tower, all in sarsens. The tower is probably the best Perp tower in Surrey, magnificently compact, making the very best of its dour material and straightforward details. A re-interpretation with a distinctive local flavour of the Kent–Sussex Wealden spirit. Stairturret, diagonal buttresses, four-centred belfry lights, big no-nonsense five-light w window (like the E window at Stoke-next-Guildford) above well carved door, big-scale tower arch inside. Inscription on inner face reading 'Richard Exfold. made XIV fote of yis touor'; his will was proved in 1487, and another dated 1480 left money for building it. Cupola on top transferred from the rectory stables in 1766. The body of the church has tiny Wealden clerestory windows, one- and two-light with trefoil heads, C15, and big oblong aisle windows divided simply by one mullion, presumably C17. The arcades between nave and aisles are of the late C13, with round piers, round capitals, and double-hollow-chamfered arches. The capitals are typically later in their mouldings than that of the pier in the N chancel arcade. Crimped plaster around the nave arcade arches and the aisle window recesses. – FONT. Late C17, metropolitan standard. From Eton College. Fluted bulgy top on a fluted bulgy stem. – PULPIT. Cut down, late C17; also from Eton College. – STAINED GLASS. In the easternmost window of the N aisle, two figures under ogee canopies, almost complete, with rich greens and reds; C14. – E window by *Clayton & Bell*, 1887. – PLATE. Cup 1572; Flagon 1598; Salver 1612. – MONUMENTS. Two empty ogee-headed C14 canopies in the N chapel.

MERRIST WOOD. Not well known, but in fact one of *Norman Shaw*'s most likeable houses. Built in 1877 on a beautiful site looking S to the Hog's Back, showing Shaw as the pattern for Voysey. A big advance on Pierrepont (*see* p. 413), built the year before; in fact the first example of what is the traditional image of the 'Norman Shaw' house. Moderate size and no false monumentality, combining tile-hanging, half-timber, and Bargate stone in happy, carefully balanced asymmetry. Dominated, like Pierrepont, by the half-timbered projecting gable of the hall at the W end, with a big and very pretty two-storey window on the returned side. Melts into the landscape both at a distance and close to. The entrance side, with its big porch and chimney-stack, is the prototype for Lutyens. The interiors are altered and were in any case mechanically detailed – again like Pierrepont. The hall is now divided into two storeys.

A lot of old houses, mostly genuine in Worplesdon itself, mostly done up in Jacobswell, which is in the parish but too near Guildford for comfort. On the green, one cottage has a mason's brick front of *c.*1700 (three by two bays, two gables in exactly the same style as Littlefield Manor, *see* below) clapped inconsequentially on to a timber frame. Also two farms which achieve unconsciously the union with landscape that Merrist Wood has created so artfully. NORTON FARM, N of the village, has typical West-Surrey–Berkshire–Hampshire C17 timber-framing, comfortable proportions, brick infilling, and widely spaced timbers. COBBETTS, at Pitch Place, on the Guildford Road, is a five-bay mid-C17 house, half-H-shaped, with two Dutch (i.e. pedimented) gables. The detail is late and deft, in the spirit of Brook Place at Chobham.

SW of the village is LITTLEFIELD MANOR, with a handsome

brick front, still Artisan-derived. It must thus be of *c*.1700, the latest in the county (cf. the doorcase and the brickwork). Seven bays, two wings of two bays each with straight-sided gables with shoulders, originally a Flemish idea, and a three-bay centre with a central shaped gable. All the windows still casements.

WHITMOOR COMMON. There are two small barrows here, of intermediary bell/disc form, with Late Bronze Age urns. Originally there were also six Saxon mounds.

BROADSTREET COMMON. In 1829 a Roman villa was excavated, probably the earliest in the county to be scientifically examined. It was of simple corridor type, and measured 62 by 25 ft. It was paved, and had a black and white tiled border. A coin of Carausius gives a date of A.D. 286–93. A mosaic floor was removed to Clandon Park.

WOTTON

1040

In heavily picturesque, hilly country w of Dorking. No village, just a line of C19 estate cottages s w of the house.

ST JOHN. Bargate stone with Horsham slate roof. Quite pictures-que, especially from the N, in a lovely situation facing the North Downs on the answering slopes of the Surrey hills. Early Norman the tower, which was originally centrally placed in a building without transepts, cf. the blocked arch on the w side. This is identical with the present tower arch to the E. Both have the simplest imposts and unmoulded arches. The tower has a two-stage pyramid roof, oddly like towers in Monmouth-shire or Shropshire. The parts to the w of the tower were probably removed in the course of the C13 and a chancel built (the present detail is all C19) with a N chapel with genuine groups of three lancets to the E and a N aisle of one bay. Also C13 the odd s doorway with fine C13 arch mouldings but crude C12-looking jamb shafts with a heavy shaft-ring around their middle. The innermost chamfer of the arch bears altogether eight tiny, well-carved busts, only 3 in. high, an extraordinary detail. The two bottom busts are modern restorations, the remainder are original. Plain brick Evelyn Mausoleum to the N of the N chapel, C17, but unlikely to be by *John Evelyn*, who asked to be buried 'in the chapel where his ancestors lay but by no means in the new vault lately joining to it'. The interior is pleasant but overborne by the marble shafts of the fake E end. – FONTS. One C19, a free variation on C13 themes. Quite original.

The other, old font is in the N chapel. Classical C17 with simple ogee cover. – SCREEN. Between N aisle and N chapel. Simple post-Jacobean. – PLATE. Several pieces, C17 and C18. – MONUMENTS. In the N chapel. Many minor mural tablets. George Evelyn † 1603 and two wives. Tripartite, small-scale, three kneelers, innumerable children below. Standard rough Jacobean. – Richard Evelyn † 1634, next to it. The same roughness but a slightly different vocabulary, this time debased Nicholas Stone. Facing kneeling figures under a heavy pediment, figures at the sides holding back drapes. – Elisabeth Darcy † 1634, opposite. Here a similar vocabulary, better organized but still roughly carved. Bust; the head leaning on a hand, in an architectural frame, a baby in swaddling clothes below. A lot of rich, basically Michelangelesque detail in the way of heavy swags and fragments of pediments. – John Evelyn himself † 1706 and his wife † 1709, a complete contrast. Two coffin-shaped stone slabs and no ornament whatsoever. – Sir John Evelyn, erected by his son in 1778, a crisp classical tablet by *Robert Chambers*. – George Evelyn † 1829 by *Westmacott*, with an inscription by Dr Arnold which is oddly like a retrospective school report: 'His early years gave a beautiful promise of vigour of understanding, kindness of heart and Christian nobleness of purpose.' Fag end of the Greek Revival. – In the churchyard another late C18 Evelyn monument of a marble slab supported on two iron Doric columns and two iron Evelyn griffins, an odd effect.

WOTTON HOUSE. The Evelyn family seat, now leased to the Home Office as the Fire Service College. John Evelyn was born here in 1620 and eventually came into possession when his brother died in 1699. The house itself is now a medley of fragments, largely C19: the chief interest has always been in the landscaped gardens, designed and laid out by *Evelyn* for his brother from 1643 onwards. Most of them remain.

The house in 1640 was a complicated multi-gabled Tudor jumble to the S and a U-shaped courtyard to the N. The S front has remained a jumble, with seven or eight piecemeal C18 and C19 additions, and two C17 brick gables on the return side of a projection which corresponds to one of the Tudor wings. The N side was first given a dour Georgian centre; then the W wing was rebuilt with fancy C17 detail – the broad brick window surrounds are very curious – in 1828, probably by *Francis Edwards*.* Finally the E wing was rebuilt and the centre refaced

* The door seems original Jacobean work.

in hard Tudor style by *Woodyer* in 1864. Inside there are
several fanciful Jacobean doors and doorcases, some with strapwork spandrels and fierce diamond-rusticated pilasters, a big
flat Tuscan Doric doorcase in the present entrance hall that
could well be by Evelyn, of *c.*1650, and a plain late C17 staircase. The C18 contributed the ORANGERY, now the dining
room, extended to the s by 3 ft along its whole length in 1877
and given a front with much terracotta decoration. The interior
is intact, with a plaster ceiling in the Inigo Jones style and
elegant niches in three-part surrounds at either end (that on
the E end was formerly a fireplace). This is by *Kent*, who certainly worked here (drawings are preserved in Christ Church
Library Oxford). It is good but not great. Simple plasterwork
panels on the walls were later decorated with oil paintings in
Chinese style by the Belgian *Jean Deneux*. One is dated 1775.
There are two rooms of *c.*1770 in a pretty Chambers style.
First the OLD LIBRARY (now College Museum), with an apse
at each end and swags in the spandrels above. Surprisingly
elegant, even though it is now merely a connecting link – it
seems to have been altered from a room by *Hawksmoor*.* Also
in the same style the ANTEROOM, on the axis of Evelyn's
temple, which is close to the house, with an entrance from the
garden. Columns in pairs l. and r. of the way from the entrance
through the room and an apsed E end, apparently concealing
C16 work behind. Of the C19 interiors *Woodyer*'s extraordinary
LIBRARY in the E wing deserves notice, a dashing essay like a
hall-church. Seven bays. Painted blue and buff and with care-
free Burges-like fireplaces full of texts. A room with a good
deal of character.

Of *John Evelyn*'s GARDEN alterations, his artificial terraced
hill and temple remain intact, probably the first attempt to
build a genuine Italian garden in Britain, and a very successful
one. What seems to have happened – and Evelyn's diaries are
not very easy to unravel on this point – is that he started in a
small way in 1643 and continued in 1651–2, and that the
general lines of the planting are his. But the temple was
definitely designed by a relation, *George Evelyn*, whilst John
was abroad, apparently before 1649: Evelyn refers to him as an
architect and says rather sadly in one place that 'he over-built
everything', and in another complains of 'great faults in the

---

* 'Hawksmoor came in ye evening . . . and took the dimensions for the
house and offices in order to draw a plan for some new rooms.' Evelyn Journal,
15 August 1713.

colonade' of the temple. The layout is done in a thoroughly
typical spirit of amateur innovation, the spirit of Burlington
and of Payne Knight in the next century. Evelyn made one
steep artificial hill and terraced the upper half, punctuating it
with statues of the Four Seasons and recessing the temple into
the bottom so that the whole hillside becomes one elevation in
a romantic and effective way. The temple was simply a dumpy
Roman Doric portico of three bays with a room behind containing niches with surrounds in vermiculated rustication, and
a ham-handed statue of Venus. The ceiling is a remarkable
affair of three shallow tunnel-vaults covered with a very busy
small-scale honeycomb pattern. The most effective part of the
layout is the extremely steep slope of the terrace and the extremely short distance between temple and house, which seems
to be quite dominated by it – a romantic, anti-French Salvator
Rosa effect.*

Miscellaneous other buildings in the park. w of the temple is
the very puzzling TORTOISE HOUSE, a building with a tall
Ionic portico of four bays on the ground floor and an open upper
floor above it with Corinthian pilasters, from which visitors
apparently took tea and watched terrapins in a deep pool to the
N. The detail is all delicate, the idea reminiscent of a Chinese
Teahouse, the date perhaps 1820 or 1830: no parallel building
comes to mind. It is now, alas, a near ruin.

To the w, outside the park is an early C19 pedimented stone
MAUSOLEUM built into a hillside. Immediately to the E of the
house is a GROTTO above ground where, in the late C19, the
reigning Evelyn used to retire and sulk when displeased. To
the N is HILL COTTAGE, probably by *Woodyer*, with a picturesque timber bell-tower which was used when this same
Evelyn wanted to call his retainers together.

BARROW. A fine bell-disc barrow of Bronze Age date exists in
Deerleap Wood. It has an overall diameter of 180 ft and a height
of 6–7 ft. The berm measures 20 ft across.

WRAY COMMON see REIGATE

8040

WRECCLESHAM
1 m. s of Farnham

A village with a few very battered cottages and a bad CHURCH

---

* Beautifully maintained by the college at the time of writing. Good-
conduct prisoners from Wandsworth Gaol are brought daily to tend it.

(St Peter) by *James Harding*, 1840, enlarged in 1862 and 1877 by *C. H. Howell*.

WYKE *see* ASH

WYPHURST *see* CRANLEIGH

YOCKLEY *see* FRIMLEY

YORK TOWN *see* CAMBERLEY

GLOSSARY

ABACUS: flat slab on the top of a capital (q.v.).

ABUTMENT: solid masonry placed to resist the lateral pressure of a vault.

ACANTHUS: plant with thick fleshy and scalloped leaves used as part of the decoration of a Corinthian capital (q.v.) and in some types of leaf carving.

ACHIEVEMENT OF ARMS: in heraldry, a complete display of armorial bearings.

ACROTERION: foliage-carved block on the end or top of a classical pediment.

ADDORSED: two human figures, animals, or birds, etc., placed symmetrically so that they turn their backs to each other.

AEDICULE, AEDICULA: framing of a window or door by columns and a pediment (q.v.).

AFFRONTED: two human figures, animals, or birds, etc., placed symmetrically so that they face each other.

AGGER: Latin term for the built-up foundations of Roman roads; also sometimes applied to the banks of hill-forts or other earthworks.

AMBULATORY: semi circular or polygonal aisle enclosing an apse (q.v.).

ANNULET: see Shaft-ring.

ANSE DE PANIER: see Arch, Basket.

ANTEPENDIUM: covering of the front of an altar, usually by textiles or metalwork.

ANTIS, IN: see Portico.

APSE: vaulted semicircular or polygonal end of a chancel or a chapel.

ARABESQUE: light and fanciful surface decoration using combinations of flowing lines, tendrils, etc., interspersed with vases, animals, etc.

ARCADE: range of arches supported on piers or columns, free-standing: or, BLIND ARCADE, the same attached to a wall.

ARCH: round-headed, i.e. semicircular; pointed, i.e. consisting of two curves, each drawn from one centre, and meeting in a point at the top; segmental, i.e. in the form of a segment;

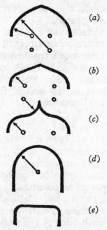

Fig. 1

pointed; four-centred (a Late Medieval form), see Fig. 1(a); Tudor (also a Late Medieval form), *see* Fig. 1(*b*); Ogee (introduced *c.* 1300 and specially popular in the C14), *see* Fig. 1(*c*); Stilted, *see* Fig. 1(*d*); Basket, with lintel connected to the jambs by concave quadrant curves, *see* Fig. 1(*e*) for one example; Diaphragm, a transverse arch with solid spandrels carrying not a vault but a principal beam of a timber roof.

ARCHITRAVE: lowest of the three main parts of the entablature (q.v.) of an order (q.v.) (*see* Fig. 12).

ARCHIVOLT: under-surface of an arch (also called Soffit).

ARRIS: sharp edge at the meeting of two surfaces.

ASHLAR: masonry of large blocks wrought to even faces and square edges.

ATLANTES: male counterparts of caryatids (q.v.).

ATRIUM: inner court of a Roman house, also open court in front of a church.

ATTACHED: *see* Engaged.

ATTIC: topmost storey of a house, if distance from floor to ceiling is less than in the others.

AUMBRY: recess or cupboard to hold sacred vessels for Mass and Communion.

BAILEY: open space or court of a stone-built castle; *see* also Motte-and-Bailey.

BALDACCHINO: canopy supported on columns.

BALLFLOWER: globular flower of three petals enclosing a small ball. A decoration used in the first quarter of the C14.

BALUSTER: small pillar or column of fanciful outline.

BALUSTRADE: series of balusters supporting a handrail or coping (q.v.).

BARBICAN: outwork defending the entrance to a castle.

BARGEBOARDS: projecting decorated boards placed against the incline of the gable of a building and hiding the horizontal roof timbers.

BARROW: *see* Bell, Bowl, Disc, Long, *and* Pond Barrow.

BASILICA: in medieval architecture an aisled church with a clerestory.

BASKET ARCH: *see* Arch (Fig. 1*e*).

BASTION: projection at the angle of a fortification.

BATTER: inclined face of a wall.

BATTLEMENT: parapet with a series of indentations or embrasures with raised portions or merlons between (also called Crenellation).

BAYS: internal compartments of a building; each divided from the other not by solid walls but by divisions only marked in the side walls (columns, pilasters, etc.) or the ceiling (beams, etc.). Also external divisions of a building by fenestration.

BAY-WINDOW: angular or curved projection of a house front with ample fenestration. If curved, also called bow-window: if on an upper floor only, also called oriel or oriel window.

BEAKER FOLK: Late New Stone Age warrior invaders from the Continent who buried their dead in round barrows and introduced the first metal tools and weapons to Britain.

BEAKHEAD: Norman ornamental motif consisting of a row of bird or beast heads with beaks biting usually into a roll moulding.

BELFRY: turret on a roof to hang bells in.

BELGAE: Aristocratic warrior bands who settled in Britain in two main waves in the C1 B.C. In Britain their culture is termed Iron Age C.

BELL BARROW: Early Bronze Age round barrow in which the mound is separated from its encircling ditch by a flat platform or berm (q.v.).

BELLCOTE: framework on a roof to hang bells from.

BERM: level area separating ditch from bank on a hill-fort or barrow.

BILLET FRIEZE: Norman ornamental motif made up of short raised rectangles placed at regular intervals.

BIVALLATE: Of a hill-fort: defended by two concentric banks and ditches.

BLOCK CAPITAL: Romanesque capital cut from a cube by hav-

Fig. 2

ing the lower angles rounded off to the circular shaft below (also called Cushion Capital) (Fig. 2).

BOND, ENGLISH or FLEMISH: see Brickwork.

BOSS: knob or projection usually placed to cover the intersection of ribs in a vault.

BOWL BARROW: round barrow surrounded by a quarry ditch. Introduced in Late Neolithic

times, the form continued until the Saxon period.

BOW-WINDOW: see Bay-Window.

BOX: A small country house, e.g. a shooting box. A convenient term to describe a compact minor dwelling, e.g. a rectory.

BOX PEW: pew with a high wooden enclosure.

BRACES: see Roof.

BRACKET: small supporting piece of stone, etc., to carry a projecting horizontal.

BRESSUMER: beam in a timber-framed building to support the, usually projecting, superstructure.

BRICKWORK: *Header:* brick laid so that the end only appears on the face of the wall. *Stretcher:* brick laid so that the side only appears on the face of the wall. *English Bond:* method of laying bricks so that alternate courses or layers on the face of the wall are composed of headers or stretchers only (Fig. 3*a*). *Flemish Bond:* method of laying

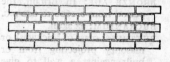

(a)

(b)

Fig. 3

bricks so that alternate headers and stretchers appear in each course on the face of the wall (Fig. 3*b*).

BROACH: see Spire.

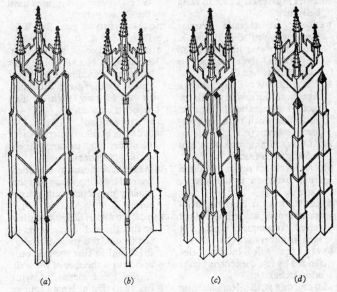

(a)　　　　　(b)　　　　　(c)　　　　　(d)

Fig. 4

BROKEN PEDIMENT: *see* Pediment.

BRONZE AGE: In Britain, the period from *c.*1600 to 600 B.C.

BUCRANIUM: ox skull.

BUTTRESS: mass of brickwork or masonry projecting from or built against a wall to give additional strength. *Angle Buttresses:* two meeting at an angle of 90° at the angle of a building (Fig. 4*a*). *Clasping Buttress:* one which encases the angle (Fig. 4*d*). *Diagonal Buttress:* one placed against the right angle formed by two walls, and more or less equiangular with both (Fig. 4*b*). *Flying Buttress:* arch or half arch transmitting the thrust of a vault or roof from the upper part of a wall to an outer support or buttress. *Setback Buttress:* angle buttress set slightly back from the angle (Fig. 4*c*).

CABLE MOULDING: Norman moulding imitating a twisted cord.

CAIRN: a mound of stones usually covering a burial.

CAMBER: slight rise or upward curve of an otherwise horizontal structure.

CAMPANILE: isolated bell tower.

CANOPY: projection or hood over an altar, pulpit, niche, statue, etc.

CAP: in a windmill the crowning feature.

CAPITAL: head or top part of a column.

CARTOUCHE: tablet with an ornate frame, usually enclosing an inscription.

CARYATID: whole female figure supporting an entablature or other similar member. *Termini Caryatids:* female busts or demi-figures or three-quarter figures supporting an entablature or other similar member and placed at the top of termini pilasters (q.v.). Cf. Atlantes.

CASTELLATED: decorated with battlements.

CELURE: panelled and adorned part of a wagon-roof above the rood or the altar.

CENSER: vessel for the burning of incense.

CENTERING: wooden framework used in arch and vault construction and removed when the mortar has set.

CHALICE: cup used in the Communion service or at Mass. *See also* Recusant Chalice.

CHAMBERED TOMB: burial mound of the New Stone Age having a stone-built chamber and entrance passage covered by an earthen barrow or stone cairn. The form was introduced to Britain from the Mediterranean.

CHAMFER: surface made by cutting across the square angle of a stone block, piece of wood, etc., usually at an angle of 45° to the other two surfaces.

CHANCEL: that part of the E end of a church in which the altar is placed, usually applied to the whole continuation of the nave E of the crossing.

CHANCEL ARCH: arch at the W end of the chancel.

CHANTRY CHAPEL: chapel attached to, or inside, a church, endowed for the saying of Masses for the soul of the founder or some other individual.

CHEVET: French term for the E end of a church (chancel, ambulatory, and radiating chapels).

CHEVRON: Norman moulding forming a zigzag.

CHOIR: that part of the church where divine service is sung.

CIBORIUM: a baldacchino.

CINQUEFOIL: *see* Foil.

CIST: stone-lined or slab-built grave. First appears in Late Neolithic times. It continued to be used in the Early Christian period.

CLAPPER BRIDGE: bridge made of large slabs of stone, some built up to make rough piers and other longer ones laid on top to make the roadway.

CLASSIC: here used to mean the moment of highest achievement of a style.

CLASSICAL: here used as the term for Greek and Roman architecture and any subsequent styles inspired by it.

CLERESTORY: upper storey of the nave walls of a church, pierced by windows.

COADE STONE: artificial (cast) stone made in the late C18 and the early C19 by Coade and Sealy in London.

COB: walling material made of mixed clay and straw.

COFFERING: decorating a ceiling with sunk square or polygonal ornamental panels.

COLLAR-BEAM: *see* Roof.

COLONNADE: range of columns.

COLONNETTE: small column.

COLUMNA ROSTRATA: column decorated with carved prows of ships to celebrate a naval victory.

COMPOSITE: see Order.

CONSOLE: bracket (q.v.) with a compound curved outline.

COPING: capping or covering to a wall.

CORBEL: block of stone projecting from a wall, supporting some feature on its horizontal top surface.

CORBEL TABLE: series of corbels, occurring just below the roof eaves externally or internally, often seen in Norman buildings.

CORINTHIAN: see Order.

CORNICE: in classical architecture the top section of the entablature (q.v.). Also for a projecting decorative feature along the top of a wall, arch, etc.

CORRIDOR VILLA: see Villa.

COUNTERSCARP BANK: small bank on the down-hill or outer side of a hill-fort ditch.

COURTYARD VILLA: see Villa.

COVE, COVING: concave undersurface in the nature of a hollow moulding but on a larger scale.

COVER PATEN: cover to a Communion cup, suitable for use as a paten or plate for the consecrated bread.

CRADLE ROOF: see Wagon roof.

CRENELLATION: see Battlement.

CREST, CRESTING: ornamental finish along the top of a screen, etc.

CRINKLE-CRANKLE WALL: undulating wall.

CROCKET, CROCKETING: decorative features placed on the sloping sides of spires, pinnacles, gables, etc., in Gothic architecture, carved in various leaf shapes and placed at regular intervals.

CROCKET CAPITAL: see Fig. 5. An Early Gothic form.

CROMLECH: word of Celtic origin still occasionally used of single free-standing stones ascribed to the Neolithic or Bronze Age periods.

Fig. 5

CROSSING: space at the intersection of nave, chancel, and transepts.

CROSS-WINDOWS: windows with one mullion and one transom.

CRUCK: big curved beam supporting both walls and roof of a cottage.

CRYPT: underground room usually below the E end of a church.

CUPOLA: small polygonal or circular domed turret crowning a roof.

CURTAIN WALL: connecting wall between the towers of a castle.

CUSHION CAPITAL: see Block Capital.

CUSP: projecting point between the foils in a foiled Gothic arch.

DADO: decorative covering of the lower part of a wall.

DAGGER: tracery motif of the Dec style. It is a lancet shape rounded or pointed at the head, pointed at the foot, and cusped inside (see Fig. 6).

Fig. 6

DAIS: raised platform at one end of a room.

DEC ('DECORATED'): historical division of English Gothic architecture covering the period from *c.*1290 to *c.*1350.

DEMI-COLUMNS: columns half sunk into a wall.

DIAPER WORK: surface decoration composed of square or lozenge shapes.

DIAPHRAGM ARCH: *see* Arch.

DISC BARROW: Bronze Age round barrow with inconspicuous central mound surrounded by bank and ditch.

DOGTOOTH: typical E.E. ornament consisting of a series of four-cornered stars placed diagonally and raised pyramidally (Fig. 7).

Fig. 7

DOMICAL VAULT: *see* Vault.

DONJON: *see* Keep.

DORIC: *see* Order.

DORMER (WINDOW): window placed vertically in the sloping plane of a roof.

DRIPSTONE: *see* Hood-mould.

DRUM: circular or polygonal vertical wall of a dome or cupola.

E.E. ('EARLY ENGLISH'): historical division of English Gothic architecture roughly covering the C13.

EASTER SEPULCHRE: recess with tomb-chest usually in the wall of a chancel, the tomb-chest to receive an effigy of Christ for Easter celebrations.

EAVES: underpart of a sloping roof overhanging a wall.

EAVES CORNICE: cornice below the eaves of a roof.

ECHINUS: Convex or projecting moulding supporting the abacus of a Greek Doric capital, sometimes bearing an egg and dart pattern.

EMBATTLED: *see* Battlement.

EMBRASURE: small opening in the wall or parapet of a fortified building, usually splayed on the inside.

ENCAUSTIC TILES: earthenware glazed and decorated tiles used for paving.

ENGAGED COLUMNS: columns attached to, or partly sunk into, a wall.

ENGLISH BOND: *see* Brickwork.

ENTABLATURE: in classical architecture the whole of the horizontal members above a column (that is architrave, frieze, and cornice) (*see* Fig. 12).

ENTASIS: very slight convex deviation from a straight line; used on Greek columns and sometimes on spires to prevent an optical illusion of concavity.

ENTRESOL: *see* Mezzanine.

EPITAPH: hanging wall monument.

ESCUTCHEON: shield for armorial bearings.

EXEDRA: the apsidal end of a room. *See* Apse.

FAN-VAULT: *see* Vault.

FERETORY: place behind the

high altar where the chief shrine of a church is kept.

FESTOON: carved garland of flowers and fruit suspended at both ends.

FILLET: narrow flat band running down a shaft or along a roll moulding.

FINIAL: top of a canopy, gable, pinnacle.

FLAGON: vessel for the wine used in the Communion service.

FLAMBOYANT: properly the latest phase of French Gothic architecture where the window tracery takes on wavy undulating lines.

FLÈCHE: slender wooden spire on the centre of a roof (also called Spirelet).

FLEMISH BOND: see Brickwork.

FLEURON: decorative carved flower or leaf.

FLUSHWORK: decorative use of flint in conjunction with dressed stone so as to form patterns: tracery, initials, etc.

FLUTING: vertical channelling in the shaft of a column.

FLYING BUTTRESS: see Buttress.

FOIL: lobe formed by the cusping (q.v.) of a circle or an arch. Trefoil, quatrefoil, cinquefoil, multifoil, express the number of leaf shapes to be seen.

FOLIATED: carved with leaf shapes.

FOSSE: ditch.

FOUR-CENTRED ARCH: see Arch.

FRATER: refectory or dining hall of a monastery.

FRESCO: wall painting on wet plaster.

FRIEZE: middle division of a classical entablature (q.v.) (see Fig. 12).

FRONTAL: covering for the front of an altar.

GABLE: Dutch gable: A gable with curved sides crowned by a pediment, characteristic of c.1630–50 (Fig. 8a). Shaped gable: A gable with multi-curved sides characteristic of c.1600–50 (Fig. 8b).

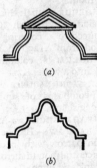

(a)

(b)

Fig. 8

GADROONED: enriched with a series of convex ridges, the opposite of fluting.

GALILEE: chapel or vestibule usually at the w end of a church enclosing the porch. Also called Narthex (q.v.).

GALLERY: in church architecture upper storey above an aisle, opened in arches to the nave. Also called Tribune and often erroneously Triforium (q.v.).

GALLERY GRAVE: chambered tomb (q.v.) in which there is little or no differentiation between the entrance passage and the actual burial chamber(s).

GARDEROBE: lavatory or privy in a medieval building.

GARGOYLE: water spout projecting from the parapet of a wall or tower; carved into a human or animal shape.

GAZEBO: lookout tower or raised

summer house in a picturesque garden.

'GEOMETRICAL': *see* Tracery.

'GIBBS SURROUND': of a doorway or window. An C18 motif consisting of a surround with alternating larger and smaller blocks of stone, quoin-wise, or intermittent large blocks, sometimes with a narrow raised band connecting them up the verticals and along the face of the arch (Fig. 9).

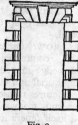

Fig. 9

GROIN: sharp edge at the meeting of two cells of a cross-vault.

GROIN-VAULT: *see* Vault.

GROTESQUE: fanciful ornamental decoration: *see* also Arabesque.

Hagioscope: *see* Squint.

HALF-TIMBERING: *see* Timber-Framing.

HALL CHURCH: church in which nave and aisles are of equal height or approximately so.

HAMMERBEAM: *see* Roof.

HANAP: large metal cup, generally made for domestic use, standing on an elaborate base and stem; with a very ornate cover frequently crowned with a little steeple.

HEADERS: *see* Brickwork.

HERRINGBONE WORK: brick, stone, or tile construction where the component blocks are laid diagonally instead of flat. Alternate courses lie in opposing directions to make a zigzag pattern up the face of the wall.

HEXASTYLE: having six detached columns.

HILL-FORT: Iron Age earthwork enclosed by a ditch and bank system; in the later part of the period the defences multiplied in size and complexity. They vary from about an acre to over 30 acres in area, and are usually built with careful regard to natural elevations or promontories.

HIPPED ROOF: *see* Roof.

HOOD-MOULD: projecting moulding above an arch or a lintel to throw off water (also called Dripstone or Label).

Iconography: the science of the subject matter of works of the visual arts.

IMPOST: bracket in a wall, usually formed of mouldings, on which the ends of an arch rest.

INDENT: shape chiselled out in a stone slab to receive a brass.

INGLENOOK: bench or seat built in beside a fireplace, sometimes covered by the chimneybreast, occasionally lit by small windows on each side of the fire.

INTERCOLUMNIATION: the space between columns.

IONIC: *see* Order (Fig. 12).

IRON AGE: in Britain the period from *c.*600 B.C. to the coming of the Romans. The term is also used for those un-Romanized native communities which survived until the Saxon incursions.

JAMB: straight side of an archway, doorway, or window.

KEEL MOULDING: moulding whose outline is in section like that of the keel of a ship.

KEEP: massive tower of a Norman castle.

KEYSTONE: middle stone in an arch or a rib-vault.

KING-POST: see Roof (Fig. 14).

KNOP: a knob-like thickening in the stem of a chalice.

LABEL: see Hood-mould.

LABEL STOP: ornamental boss at the end of a hood-mould (q.v.).

LACED WINDOWS: windows pulled visually together by strips, usually in brick of a different colour, which continue vertically the lines of the vertical parts of the window surrounds. The motif is typical of c. 1720.

LANCET WINDOW: slender pointed-arched window.

LANTERN: in architecture, a small circular or polygonal turret with windows all round crowning a roof (see Cupola) or a dome.

LANTERN CROSS: churchyard cross with lantern-shaped top usually with sculptured representations on the sides of the top.

LEAN-TO ROOF: roof with one slope only, built against a higher wall.

LESENE or PILASTER STRIP: pilaster without base or capital.

LIERNE: see Vault (Fig. 21).

LINENFOLD: Tudor panelling ornamented with a conventional representation of a piece of linen laid in vertical folds. The piece is repeated in each panel.

LINTEL: horizontal beam or stone bridging an opening.

LOGGIA: recessed colonnade (q.v.).

LONG AND SHORT WORK: Saxon quoins (q.v.) consisting of stones placed with the long sides alternately upright and horizontal.

LONG BARROW: unchambered Neolithic communal burial mound, wedge-shaped in plan, with the burial and occasional other structures massed at the broader end, from which the mound itself tapers in height; quarry ditches flank the mound.

LOUVRE: opening, often with lantern (q.v.) over, in the roof of a room to let the smoke from a central hearth escape.

LOWER PALAEOLITHIC: see Palaeolithic.

LOZENGE: diamond shape.

LUCARNE: small opening to let light in

LUNETTE: tympanum (q.v.) or semicircular opening.

LYCH GATE: wooden gate structure with a roof and open sides placed at the entrance to a churchyard to provide space for the reception of a coffin. The word *lych* is Saxon and means a corpse.

LYNCHET: long terraced strip of soil accumulating on the downward side of prehistoric and medieval fields due to soil creep from continuous ploughing along the contours.

MACHICOLATION: projecting gallery on brackets constructed on the outside of castle towers or walls. The gallery has holes in the floor to drop missiles through

MAJOLICA: ornamented glazed earthenware.

MANSARD: *see* Roof.

MATHEMATICAL TILES: Small facing tiles the size of brick headers, applied to timber-framed walls to make them appear brick-built.

MEGALITHIC TOMB: stone-built burial chamber of the New Stone Age covered by an earth or stone mound. The form was introduced to Britain from the Mediterranean area.

MERLON: *see* Battlement.

MESOLITHIC: 'Middle Stone' Age; the post-glacial period of hunting and fishing communities dating in Britain from c. 8000 B.C. to the arrival of Neolithic communities, with which they must have considerably overlapped.

METOPE: in classical architecture of the Doric order (q.v.) the space in the frieze between the triglyphs (Fig. 12).

MEZZANINE: low storey placed between two higher ones.

MISERERE: *see* Misericord.

MISERICORD: bracket placed on the underside of a hinged choir stall seat which, when turned up, provided the occupant of the seat with a support during long periods of standing (also called Miserere).

MODILLION: small bracket of which large numbers (modillion frieze) are often placed below a cornice (q.v.) in classical architecture.

MOTTE: steep mound forming the main feature of C11 and C12 castles.

MOTTE-AND-BAILEY: post-Roman and Norman defence system consisting of an earthen mound (the motte) topped with a wooden tower eccentrically placed within a bailey (q.v.), with enclosure ditch and palisade, and with the rare addition of an internal bank.

MOUCHETTE: tracery motif in curvilinear tracery, a curved dagger (q.v.), specially popular in the early C14 (Fig. 10).

Fig. 10

MULLIONS: vertical posts or uprights dividing a window into 'lights'.

MULTIVALLATE: Of a hill-fort: defended by three or more concentric banks and ditches.

MUNTIN: post as a rule moulded and part of a screen.

NAIL-HEAD: E.E. ornamental motif, consisting of small pyramids regularly repeated (Fig. 11).

Fig. 11

NARTHEX: enclosed vestibule or covered porch at the main

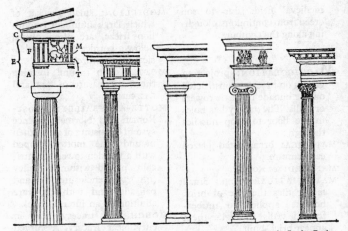

Fig. 12. Orders of Columns (Greek Doric, Roman Doric, Tuscan Doric, Ionic, Corinthian) E, Entablature; C, Cornice; F, Frieze; A, Architrave; M, Metope; T, Triglyph.

entrance to a church (*see* Galilee).

NEOLITHIC: 'New Stone' Age, dating in Britain from the appearance from the Continent of the first settled farming communities *c.* 3500 B.C. until the introduction of the Bronze Age.

NEWEL: central post in a circular or winding staircase; also the principal post when a flight of stairs meets a landing.

NOOK-SHAFT: shaft set in the angle of a pier or respond or wall, or the angle of the jamb of a window or doorway.

NUTMEG MOULDING: consisting of a chain of tiny triangles placed obliquely.

OBELISK: lofty pillar of square section tapering at the top and ending pyramidally.

OGEE: *see* Arch (Fig. 1c).

ORATORY: small private chapel in a house.

ORDER: (1) *of a doorway or window:* series of concentric steps receding towards the opening; (2) *in classical architecture:* column with base, shaft, capital, and entablature (q.v.) according to one of the following styles: Greek Doric, Roman Doric, Tuscan Doric, Ionic, Corinthian, Composite. The established details are very elaborate, and some specialist architectural work should be consulted for further guidance (*see* Fig. 12).

ORIEL: *see* Bay-Window.

OVERHANG: projection of the upper storey of a house.

OVERSAILING COURSES: series of stone or brick courses, each one projecting beyond the one below it.

PALAEOLITHIC: 'Old Stone' Age; the first period of human culture, commencing in the

Ice Age and immediately prior to the Mesolithic; the Lower Palaeolithic is the older phase, the Upper Palaeolithic the later.

PALIMPSEST: (1) *of a brass:* where a metal plate has been re-used by turning over and engraving on the back; (2) *of a wall painting:* where one overlaps and partly obscures an earlier one.

PALLADIAN: architecture following the ideas and principles of Andrea Palladio, 1518–80.

PANTILE: tile of curved S-shaped section.

PARAPET: low wall placed to protect any spot where there is a sudden drop, for example on a bridge, quay, hillside, housetop, etc.

PARGETTING: plaster work with patterns and ornaments either in relief or engraved on it.

PARVIS: term wrongly applied to a room over a church porch. These rooms were often used as a schoolroom or as a store room.

PATEN: plate to hold the bread at Communion or Mass.

PATERA: small flat circular or oval ornament in classical architecture.

PEDIMENT: low-pitched gable used in classical, Renaissance, and neo-classical architecture above a portico and above doors, windows, etc. It may be straight-sided or curved segmentally. *Broken Pediment:* one where the centre portion of the base is left open. *Open Pediment:* one where the centre portion of the sloping sides is left out.

PENDANT: boss (q.v.) elongated so that it seems to hang down.

PENDENTIF: concave triangular spandrel used to lead from the angle of two walls to the base of a circular dome. It is constructed as part of the hemisphere over a diameter the size of the diagonal of the basic square (Fig. 13).

PERP (PERPENDICULAR): historical division of English Gothic architecture covering

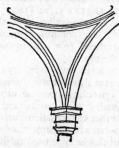

Fig. 13

the period from c.1335–50 to c.1530.

PIANO NOBILE: principal storey of a house with the reception rooms; usually the first floor.

PIAZZA: open space surrounded by buildings; in C17 and C18 England sometimes used to mean a long colonnade or loggia.

PIER: strong, solid support, frequently square in section or of composite section (compound pier).

PIETRA DURA: ornamental or scenic inlay by means of thin slabs of stone.

PILASTER: shallow pier attached to a wall. *Termini Pilasters:* pilasters with sides tapering downwards.

PILLAR PISCINA: free-standing piscina on a pillar.

PINNACLE: ornamental form crowning a spire, tower, buttress, etc., usually of steep pyramidal, conical, or some similar shape.

PISCINA: basin for washing the Communion or Mass vessels, provided with a drain. Generally set in or against the wall of the S of an altar.

PLAISANCE: summer-house, pleasure house near a mansion.

PLATE TRACERY: see Tracery.

PLINTH: projecting base of a wall or column, generally chamfered (q.v.) or moulded at the top.

POND BARROW: rare type of Bronze Age barrow consisting of a circular depression, usually paved, and containing a number of cremation burials.

POPPYHEAD: ornament of leaf and flower type used to decorate the tops of bench- or stall-ends.

PORTCULLIS: gate constructed to rise and fall in vertical grooves; used in gateways of castles.

PORTE COCHÈRE: porch large enough to admit wheeled vehicles.

PORTICO: centre-piece of a house or a church with classical detached or attached columns and a pediment. A portico is called *prostyle* or *in antis* according to whether it projects from or recedes into a building. In a portico *in antis* the columns range with the side walls.

POSTERN: small gateway at the back of a building.

PREDELLA: in an altarpiece the horizontal strip below the main representation, often used for a number of subsidiary representations in a row.

PRESBYTERY: the part of the church lying E of the choir. It is the part where the altar is placed.

PRINCIPAL: see Roof (Fig. 14).

PRIORY: monastic house whose head is a prior or prioress, not an abbot or abbess.

PROSTYLE: with free-standing columns in a row.

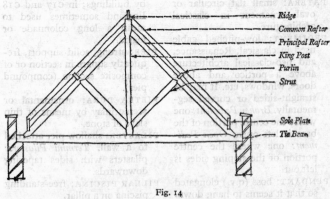

Ridge
Common Rafter
Principal Rafter
King Post
Purlin
Strut
Sole Plate
Tie Beam

Fig. 14

PULPITUM: stone screen in a major church provided to shut off the choir from the nave and also as a backing for the return choir stalls.

PULVINATED FRIEZE: frieze with a bold convex moulding.

PURLIN: see Roof (Figs. 14, 15).

PUTHOLE or PUTLOCK HOLE: putlocks are the short horizontal timbers on which during construction the boards of scaffolding rest. Putholes or putlock holes are the holes in the wall for putlocks, which often are not filled in after construction is complete.

PUTTO: small naked boy.

QUADRANGLE: inner courtyard in a large building.

QUARRY: in stained-glass work, a small diamond- or square-shaped piece of glass set diagonally.

QUATREFOIL: see Foil.

QUEEN-POSTS: see Roof (Fig. 15).

QUOINS: dressed stones at the angles of a building. Sometimes all the stones are of the same size; more often they are alternately large and small.

RADIATING CHAPELS: chapels projecting radially from an ambulatory or an apse.

RAFTER: see Roof.

RAMPART: stone wall or wall of earth surrounding a castle, fortress, or fortified city.

RAMPART-WALK: path along the inner face of a rampart.

REBATE: continuous rectangular notch cut on an edge.

REBUS: pun, a play on words. The literal translation and illustration of a name for artistic and heraldic purposes (Belton = bell, tun).

RECUSANT CHALICE: chalice made after the Reformation and before Catholic Emancipation for Roman Catholic use.

REEDING: decoration with parallel convex mouldings touching one another.

REFECTORY: dining hall; see Frater.

RENDERING: plastering of an outer wall.

REPOUSSÉ: decoration of metal work by relief designs, formed by beating the metal from the back.

REREDOS: structure behind and above an altar.

RESPOND: half-pier bonded into a wall and carrying one end of an arch.

RETABLE: altarpiece, a picture or piece of carving, standing behind and attached to an altar.

RETICULATION: see Tracery (Fig. 20e).

REVEAL: that part of a jamb (q.v.) which lies between the glass or door and the outer surface of the wall.

RIB-VAULT: see Vault.

ROCOCO: latest phase of the Baroque style, current in most Continental countries between c. 1720 and c. 1760.

ROLL MOULDING: moulding of semicircular or more than semicircular section.

ROMANESQUE: that style in architecture which was current in the C11 and C12 and preceded the Gothic style (in England often called Norman). (Some scholars extend the use of the term Romanesque back to the C10 or C9.)

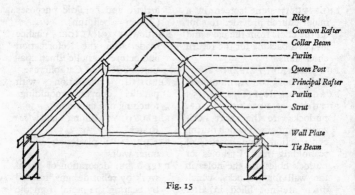

Fig. 15

ROMANO-BRITISH: A somewhat vague term applied to the period and cultural features of Britain affected by the Roman occupation of the C1–5 A.D.

ROOD: cross or crucifix.

ROOD LOFT: singing gallery on the top of the rood screen, often supported by a coving.

ROOD SCREEN: *see* Screen.

ROOD STAIRS: stairs to give access to the rood loft.

ROOF: *Single-framed:* if consisting entirely of transverse members (such as rafters with or without braces, collars, tie-beams, king-posts or queen-posts, etc.) not tied together longitudinally. *Double-framed:* if longitudinal members (such as a ridge beam and purlins) are employed. As a rule in such cases the rafters are divided into stronger principals and weaker subsidiary rafters. *Hipped:* roof with sloped instead of vertical ends. *Mansard:* roof with a double slope, the

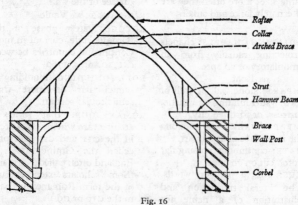

Fig. 16

lower slope being larger and steeper than the upper. *Saddle-back:* tower roof shaped like an ordinary gabled timber roof. The following members have special names: *Rafter:* roof-timber sloping up from the wall plate to the ridge. *Principal:* principal rafter, usually corresponding to the main bay divisions of the nave or chancel below. *Wall Plate:* timber laid longitudinally on the top of a wall. *Purlin:* longitudinal member laid parallel with wall plate and ridge beam some way up the slope of the roof. *Tie-beam:* beam connecting the two slopes of a roof across at its foot, usually at the height of the wall plate, to prevent the roof from spreading. *Collar-beam:* tie-beam applied higher up the slope of the roof. *Strut:* upright timber connecting the tie-beam with the rafter above it. *King-post:* upright timber connecting a tie-beam and collar-beam with the ridge beam. *Queen-posts:* two struts placed symmetrically on a tie-beam or collar-beam. *Braces:* inclined timbers inserted to strengthen others. Usually braces connect a collar-beam with the rafters below or a tie-beam with the wall below. Braces can be straight or curved (also called arched). *Hammer-beam:* beam projecting at right angles, usually from the top of a wall, to carry arched braces or struts and arched braces. (*See* Figs. 14, 15, 16.)

ROSE WINDOW (or WHEEL WINDOW): circular window with patterned tracery arranged to radiate from the centre.

ROTUNDA: building circular in plan.

RUBBLE: building stones, not square or hewn, nor laid in regular courses.

RUSTICATION: *rock-faced* if the surfaces of large blocks of ashlar stone are left rough like rock; *smooth* if the ashlar blocks are smooth and separated by V-joints; *banded* if the separation by V-joints applies only to the horizontals.

Sₐddleback: *see* Roof.

SALTIRE CROSS: equal-limbed cross placed diagonally.

SANCTUARY: (1) area around the main altar of a church (*see* Presbytery); (2) sacred site consisting of wood or stone uprights enclosed by a circular bank and ditch. Beginning in the Neolithic, they were elaborated in the succeeding Bronze Age. The best known examples are Stonehenge and Avebury.

SARCOPHAGUS: elaborately carved coffin.

SCAGLIOLA: material composed of cement and colouring matter to imitate marble.

SCALLOPED CAPITAL: development of the block capital (q.v.) in which the single semi-circular surface is elaborated into a series of truncated cones (Fig. 17).

Fig. 17

SCARP: artificial cutting away of the ground to form a steep slope.

SCREEN: *Parclose screen:* screen separating a chapel from the rest of a church. *Rood screen:* screen below the rood (q.v.), usually at the W end of a chancel.

SCREENS PASSAGE: passage between the entrances to kitchen, buttery, etc., and the screen behind which lies the hall of a medieval house.

SEDILIA: seats for the priests (usually three) on the S side of the chancel of a church.

SEGMENTAL ARCH: see Arch.

SET-OFF: see Weathering.

SEXPARTITE: see Vault.

SGRAFFITO: pattern incised into plaster so as to expose a dark surface underneath.

SHAFT-RING: motif of the C12 and C13 consisting of a ring round a circular pier or a shaft attached to a pier.

SHEILA-NA-GIG: fertility figure, usually with legs wide open.

SILL: lower horizontal part of the frame of a window.

SLATEHANGING: the covering of walls by overlapping rows of slates, on a timber substructure.

SOFFIT: underside of an arch, lintel, etc.

SOLAR: upper living-room of a medieval house.

SOPRAPORTE: painting above the door of a room, usual in the C17 and C18.

SOUNDING BOARD: horizontal board or canopy over a pulpit. Also called Tester.

SPANDREL: triangular surface between one side of an arch, the horizontal drawn from its

apex, and the vertical drawn from its springer; also the surface between two arches.

SPERE-TRUSS: roof truss on two free-standing posts to mask the division between screens passage and hall. The screen itself, where a spere-truss exists, was originally movable.

SPIRE: tall pyramidal or conical pointed erection often built on top of a tower, turret, etc. *Broach Spire:* a broach is a sloping half-pyramid of masonry or wood introduced at the base of each of the four oblique faces of a tapering octagonal spire with the object of effecting the transition from the square to the octagon. The *splayed foot spire* is a variation of the broach form found principally in the south-eastern counties. In this form the four cardinal faces are splayed out near their base, to cover the corners, while the oblique (or intermediate) faces taper away to a point. *Needle Spire:* thin spire rising from the centre of a tower roof, well inside the parapet.

SPIRELET: see Flèche.

SPLAY: chamfer, usually of the jamb of a window.

SPRINGING: level at which an arch rises from its supports.

SQUINCH: arch or system of concentric arches thrown across the angle between two walls to support a superstructure, for example a dome (Fig. 18).

SQUINT: a hole cut in a wall or through a pier to allow a view of the main altar of a church from places whence it could not otherwise be seen (also called Hagioscope).

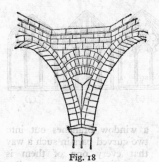

Fig. 18

STALL: carved seat, one of a row, made of wood or stone.

STAUNCHION: upright iron or steel member.

STEEPLE: the tower of a church together with a spire, cupola, etc.

STIFF-LEAF: E.E. type of foliage of many-lobed shapes (Fig. 19).

Fig. 19

STILTED: see Arch.

STOREY-POSTS: the principal posts of a timber-framed wall.

STOUP: vessel for the reception of holy water, usually placed near a door.

STRAINER ARCH: arch inserted across a room to prevent the walls from leaning.

STRAPWORK: C16 decoration consisting of interlaced bands, and forms similar to fretwork or cut and bent leather.

STRETCHER: see Brickwork.

STRING COURSE: projecting horizontal band or moulding set in the surface of a wall.

STRUT: see Roof.

STUCCO: plaster work.

STUDS: the subsidiary vertical timber members of a timber-framed wall.

SWAG: festoon formed by a carved piece of cloth suspended from both ends.

TABERNACLE: richly ornamented niche or free-standing canopy. Usually contains the Holy Sacrament.

TARSIA: inlay in various woods.

TAZZA: shallow bowl on a foot.

TERMINAL FIGURES (TERMS, TERMINI): upper part of a human figure growing out of a pier, pilaster, etc., which tapers towards the base. See also Caryatid, Pilaster.

TERRACOTTA: burnt clay, unglazed.

TESSELLATED PAVEMENT: mosaic flooring, particularly Roman, consisting of small 'tesserae' or cubes of glass, stone, or brick.

TESSERAE: see Tessellated Pavement.

TESTER: see Sounding Board.

TETRASTYLE: having four detached columns.

THREE-DECKER PULPIT: pulpit with Clerk's Stall below and Reading Desk below the Clerk's Stall.

TIE-BEAM: see Roof (Figs. 14, 15).

TIERCERON: see Vault (Fig. 21).

TILEHANGING: see Slatehanging.

TIMBER-FRAMING: method of construction where walls are built of timber framework with the spaces filled in by plaster

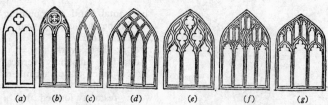

(a)   (b)   (c)   (d)   (e)   (f)   (g)

Fig. 20

or brickwork. Sometimes the timber is covered over with plaster or boarding laid horizontally.

TOMB-CHEST: chest-shaped stone coffin, the most usual medieval form of funeral monument.

TOUCH: soft black marble quarried near Tournai.

TOURELLE: turret corbelled out from the wall.

TRACERY: intersecting ribwork in the upper part of a window, or used decoratively in blank arches, on vaults, etc. *Plate tracery: see* Fig. 20(a). Early form of tracery where decoratively shaped openings are cut through the solid stone infilling in a window head. *Bar tracery:* a form introduced into England *c.*1250. Intersecting ribwork made up of slender shafts, continuing the lines of the mullions of windows up to a decorative mesh in the head of the window. *Geometrical tracery: see* Fig. 20(b). Tracery characteristic of *c.* 1250–1310 consisting chiefly of circles or foiled circles. *Y-tracery: see* Fig. 20(c). Tracery consisting of a mullion which branches into two forming a Y shape; typical of *c.* 1300. *Intersecting tracery: see* Fig. 20(d). Tracery in which each mullion of

a window branches out into two curved bars in such a way that every one of them is drawn with the same radius from a different centre. The result is that every light of the window is a lancet and every two, three, four, etc., lights together form a pointed arch. This treatment also is typical of *c.* 1300. *Reticulated tracery: see* Fig. 20(e). Tracery typical of the early C14 consisting entirely of circles drawn at top and bottom into ogee shapes so that a net-like appearance results. *Panel tracery: see* Fig. 20(f) and (g). Perp tracery, which is formed of upright straight-sided panels above lights of a window.

TRANSEPT: transverse portion of a cross-shaped church.

TRANSOM: horizontal bar across the openings of a window.

TRANSVERSE ARCH: *see* Vault.

TRIBUNE: *see* Gallery.

TRICIPUT, SIGNUM TRICIPUT: sign of the Trinity expressed by three faces belonging to one head.

TRIFORIUM: arcaded wall passage or blank arcading facing the nave at the height of the aisle roof and below the clerestory (q.v.) windows. (*See* Gallery.)

TRIGLYPHS: blocks with vertical

grooves separating the metopes (q.v.) in the Doric frieze (Fig. 12).

TROPHY: sculptured group of arms or armour, used as a memorial of victory.

TRUMEAU: stone mullion (q.v.) supporting the tympanum (q.v.) of a wide doorway.

TUMULUS: *see* Barrow.

TURRET: very small tower, round or polygonal in plan.

TUSCAN: *see* Order.

TYMPANUM: space between the lintel of a doorway and the arch above it.

UNDERCROFT: vaulted room, sometimes underground, below a church or chapel.

UNIVALLATE: of a hill-fort: defended by a single bank and ditch.

UPPER PALAEOLITHIC: *see* Palaeolithic

VAULT: *Barrel-vault: see* Tunnel-vault. *Cross-vault: see* Groin-vault. *Domical vault:* square or polygonal dome rising direct on a square or polygonal bay, the curved surfaces separated by groins (q.v.). *Fan-vault:* Late Medieval vault where all ribs springing from one springer are of the same length, the same distance from the next, and the same curvature. *Groin-vault* or *Cross-vault:* vault of two tunnel-vaults of identical shape intersecting each other at r. angles. Chiefly Norman and Renaissance. *Lierne:* tertiary rib, that is, rib which does not spring either from one of the main springers or from the central boss. Introduced in the C14, continues to the C16. *Quadripartite vault:* one wherein one bay of vaulting is divided into four parts. *Rib-vault:* vault with diagonal ribs projecting along the groins. *Ridge-rib:* rib along the longitudinal or transverse ridge of a vault. Introduced in the early C13. *Sexpartite vault:* one wherein one bay of quadripartite vaulting is divided into two parts transversely so that each bay of vaulting has six parts. *Tierceron:* secondary rib, that is, rib which issues from one of the main springers or the central boss and leads to a place on a ridge-rib. Introduced in the early C13. *Transverse arch:* arch separating one bay of a vault from the next. *Tunnel-vault* or *Barrel-vault:* vault of semicircular or pointed section. Chiefly Norman and Renaissance. (*See* Fig. 21.)

VAULTING SHAFT: vertical member leading to the springer of a vault.

VENETIAN WINDOW: window with three openings, the central one arched and wider than the outside ones. Current in England chiefly in the C17–18.

VERANDA: open gallery or balcony with a roof on light, usually metal, supports.

VESICA: oval with pointed head and foot.

VESTIBULE: anteroom or entrance hall.

VILLA: (1) according to Gwilt (1842) 'a country house for the residence of opulent persons'; (2) Romano-British country houses cum farms, to which the description given in (1)

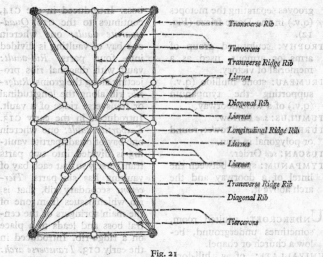

Transverse Rib

Tiercerons
Transverse Ridge Rib
Liernes

Diagonal Rib
Liernes
Longitudinal Ridge Rib
Liernes

Liernes

Transverse Ridge Rib
Diagonal Rib

Tiercerons

Fig. 21

more or less applies. They developed with the growth of urbanization. The basic type is the simple corridor pattern with rooms opening off a single passage; the next stage is the addition of wings. The courtyard villa fills a square plan with subsidiary buildings and an enclosure wall with a gate facing the main corridor block.

VITRIFIED: made similar to glass.

VITRUVIAN OPENING: A door or window which diminishes towards the top, as advocated by Vitruvius, bk. IV, chapter VI.

VOLUTE: spiral scroll, one of the component parts of an Ionic column (see Order).

VOUSSOIR: wedge-shaped stone used in arch construction.

WAGON ROOF: roof in which by closely set rafters with arched braces the appearance of the inside of a canvas tilt over a wagon is achieved. Wagon roofs can be panelled or plastered (ceiled) or left uncovered.

WAINSCOT: timber lining to walls.

WALL PLATE: see Roof.

WATERLEAF: leaf shape used in later C12 capitals. The waterleaf is a broad, unribbed, tapering leaf curving up towards the angle of the abacus and turned in at the top (Fig. 22).

Fig. 22

WEALDEN HOUSE: timber-framed house with the hall in the centre and wings projecting only slightly and only on the jutting upper floor. The roof, however, runs through without a break between wings and hall, and the eaves of the hall part are therefore exceptionally deep. They are supported by diagonal, usually curved, braces starting from the short inner sides of the overhanging wings and rising parallel with the front wall of the hall towards the centre of the eaves.

WEATHERBOARDING: overlapping horizontal boards, covering a timber-framed wall.

WEATHERING: sloped horizontal surface on sills, buttresses, etc., to throw off water.

WEEPERS: small figures placed in niches along the sides of some medieval tombs (also called Mourners).

WHEEL WINDOW: *see* Rose Window.

LIST OF PLATES

INDEX OF ARTISTS

INDEX OF PLACES

ADDENDA
(SEPTEMBER 1970)

The addenda (except where otherwise stated) are due to the further researches of Mr Nicholas Taylor, to whom we are most grateful.

p. 63 [Introduction.] *Butterfield* also built St Matthew, Ashford (formerly Middlesex) in 1858–65.

p. 67 [Introduction.] Further on Foxwarren Park, *see* addendum for p. 246.

p. 94 [Albury.] At Newlands Corner, 1¼ m. NW, is HARROW-HILL COPSE, designed for his father-in-law St Loe Strachey by *Clough Williams-Ellis*, *c.* 1914. Thatched, with a semicircular bay over the classical porch. Also various experimental cheap COTTAGES by *Williams-Ellis*, *Arnold Mitchell*, and *Strachey* himself.

p. 103 [Banstead.] BANSTEAD HALL. C19 Italianate house of brick altered by *Newton*, 1891–4 and 1905. Typical Newton COTTAGE, 1902, to the NE, at the corner of the B280 and B2219

p. 119 [Bramley.] In SNOWDENHAM LINKS ROAD are two houses by *Imrie & Angell*, *c.* 1935, and Sir Hubert *Bennett*'s own house, *c.* 1965.

p. 130 [Camberley.] Between High Street and Park Street a large TOWN CENTRE was begun in 1969. Promising design by *Leonard Vincent, Raymond Gorbing & Partners* with *Turner, Lansdown, Holt & Partners*. HARVEY'S store in Park Street, 1965, is by *R. J. Cole.*

p. 135 [Carshalton.] The weatherboarded houses in POUND STREET and CARSHALTON ROAD have been demolished (H. V. Molesworth-Roberts).

p. 144 [Charterhouse School.] The Art School has recently been spoilt by infilling under the projecting upper storey (B. Watkin).

p. 145 [Cheam.] ST ALBAN, Elmbrook Road, 1929–33 by *Edward A. Swan*, an ingenious re-use of the C17 barns of Cheam Court.

p. 163 [Claremont.] On the other side of Portsmouth Road from The Homewood is UPPER COURT, a surprisingly strict Italianate villa of *c.* 1845, with a Palladian colonnade and a lunette in the pediment.

p. 176 [Crooksbury House.] CROOKSBURY FARM, close to *Lutyens*'s wrought-iron GATES, was rebuilt by him (since much extended). Behind it a large walled garden has a delicious GAZEBO, with sloping buttresses.

p. 180 [Croydon.] ST GEORGE, Waddon. 1932 by *W. Curtis Green*. A sound brick church with big gables. White-washed diaphragm arches inside, and complicated timber roof between them.

p. 187 [Croydon.] Close to the Atelier 5 housing is RED LODGE, Stanhope Road, a good crisp Lutyens-style house, tile-hung, by *W. Curtis Green, 1910*.

p. 203 [East Clandon.] SNELGATE COTTAGES, on the main road, are a nice symmetrical group by *Goodhart-Rendel, c. 1920*.

p. 205 [East Horsley.] COTHELSTONE, Forest Road, is a C20 villa imaginatively remodelled in 1965 by *Team 4*.

p. 206 [East Sheen, Percy Lodge.] The house owes a lot to the careful restoration of *Robert Atkinson*, whose home it was.

p. 213 [Englefield Green.] Opposite Park Close is PARKWOOD, a bad house of 1902–3 with a LIBRARY of *c.* 1935 by *Lutyens*. Near Ridgemead House is THE WHITE HOUSE, *c.* 1905 by *Nicholson & Corlette*, with red pantiles on white walls. Pretty LODGE.

p. 214 [Englefield Green.] SHOREDITCH TRAINING COL-LEGE, Coopers Hill. The big white brick semi-Gothic house was by *F. & H. Francis, c.* 1865 for that bad character, 'Baron' Albert Grant. After his bankruptcy it became in 1871 the Royal Indian Engineering College and *Sir Matthew Digby Wyatt* added the big bald s wing (redeemed only by the neat plate tracery CHAPEL). For the training college the *LCC Architect's Department* (*Sir Hubert Bennett*) added in 1961–3 a forecourt of yellow brick residences with a zigzag roof-line, some quieter teaching blocks, and a hyperbolic-paraboloid-roofed assembly hall.

p. 246 and p. 67 [Foxwarren Park.] The true story of the design seems much more complicated, to judge by a book, *Notes of Thought*, by the then owner, *Charles Buxton*, which was kindly lent by Mr D. A. J. Buxton of Caister. To quote from the introduction:

Having spent four summers in hired houses near Wey-bridge, he had succeeded in purchasing, at the end of 1855, a piece of land overlooking Wisley Common, upon which he determined to build a house of his own. The opportunity applied the torch to his latent architectural ambition, and he resolved to be his own architect, and to build a house in a style which he had learned to like in Norfolk. Architecture became now a study of the most absorbing interest to him. Not only did he work eagerly at all the details of his own house, but he had the enterprise to send in designs for the Government Offices, for which competition had been invited in 1856. For these, as for the building of his own house, he had the assistance of a professional architect in the working out of the drawings; but the designs were substantially his; and it was no small triumph for him when it was announced that he was placed by the judges sixth on the list of competitors, and was to receive a prize of £100. This success encouraged him in a continued devotion to the art. Thenceforward he made the study of architecture one of his chief pleasures. He arranged parties and expeditions for inspecting churches and old buildings both in London and in the country; he became one of the public advocates of the Gothic style for modern buildings; he caught at every opportunity of designing a lodge or a farmhouse or any other building.

The variety of style to which he especially devoted himself was Gothic with brick mouldings. Brick ornamentation, which is now not uncommon, had scarcely been employed in recent architecture when he built Fox Warren; and he made it an object to encourage this feature as widely as he could. 'Feb. 1856. I wonder whether our house will turn out as beautiful and picturesque as we intend. I think our plan of having brick mullions, mouldings, etc., which sounds common enough, is, in fact, very rare. I have never seen any house done so except the one at Harrow; the effect is surprisingly good, especially in sunshine, which gives it a rich warm effect, pleasant to the eye in our climate.' 'April 1856. Mr B. C. much excited by the idea of our moulded brick ornamentation; the fact is, I find we are striking out a new line, and that the world does not even know what one means by moulded brick. I hope we shall stimulate that style of building, and also set an example of the use of the pointed arch in house-building; I think our house will be singularly pretty and *original*. Lord E told me he thought our site the most beautiful spot in England.' One of his best known works is the fountain near Westminster Abbey, which he built in 1863 as a memorial of his father's anti-slavery labours. It was his fine ambition to add to the objects of beauty by which the common taste may be educated and

delighted. He thus notes his occupation on a solitary journey, – 'Enjoying my thoughts, chiefly on architecture. That
is what I turn to for enjoyment – *planning picturesqueness.*'
Apparently, therefore, he was also the designer of the
Buxton Memorial Fountain, which was executed by
S. S. Teulon. *See The Buildings of England: London,*
vol. 1, p. 546.

p. 248 [Frimley, Frimley Park.] In the grounds a large new
HOSPITAL has been started (1970) by the Ministry of
Health and Social Security (chief architect *W. E.
Tatton Brown*) in association with *Hospital Design
Partnership.* It is an experimental design, developing
from the Ministry's first prototype hospital at Green-
wich.

p. 249 [Frimley, Yockley.] Wing to r. of entrance added *c.* 1910.
Good formal garden on the principles of *Blomfield*'s
book.

p. 307 [Haslemere, Lythe Hill.] Elaborate interiors by *George
Aitchison*, 1888–9.

p. 312 [Headley.] HEATH LODGE is capable neo-Georgian,
c. 1914, by *Sir Guy Dawber*, with polygonal bay windows. BELASIS, 1¼ m. SW, was remodelled *c.* 1920 by
Philip Tilden for Viscountess Ridley.

p. 312 [Hersham.] The Nonconformist chapel and Rookwood
have been demolished (J. C. M. Blatch).

p. 314 [Hindhead.] In the same road (Hazel Grove) is HIND-
HEAD COURT, very competent half-timber, of *c.* 1910.
Close to the centre of Hindhead is UNDERSHAW
(now a hotel), 1897 by *J. H. Ball* for Sir Arthur Conan
Doyle. ST EDMUND'S SCHOOL, *c.* 1895, is by *Dudley
Newman.*

p. 335 [Kingston, Coombe.] The development of Coombe Hill
was begun by John Galsworthy, father of the novelist
(who set Soames Forsyte's house here). He built three
large spec. mansions in rogue-Gothic *c.* 1867–70,
probably by *Archer & Green*; COOMBE LEIGH (now
Coombe Ridge and a convent) and COOMBE RIDGE
(now a school) survive in George Road. THE PAVIL-
ION, Warren Road, is a Louis XV lollipop by *Oliver
Hill*, *c.* 1960.

p. 357 [Lowicks.] Alterations and additions, all by *Voysey*, in
1898, 1904, 1907, and 1911.

p. 358 [Lyne.] LYNE GROVE, a villa of *c.* 1820 and *c.* 1850, was extended by *Arthur Bolton*, *c.* 1912, in the clever neo-classicism one would expect from an authority on Soane.

p. 362 [Merstham.] There are specimen iron plates and stone sleepers of the IRON RAILWAY just s of the Joliffe Arms (B. Watkin).

p. 367 [Milford, Rake Manor.] *Baillie Scott* in fact worked three times at the house, the middle phase (*c.* 1914) producing the fine brick ballroom wing to the r. of the entrance.

p. 407 [Peper Harow, St Nicholas.] But some of the C19 work is due not to Pugin but to *T. G. Jackson* (1876–7).

p. 416 [Purley.] CHRIST CHURCH, Brighton Road, the parish church of Purley. By *James Fowler* of Louth, 1878–9, in his usual competent but uninspired Dec.

p. 423 [Reigate.] In 1970 the tunnel was closed to traffic, which now circulates clockwise round the larger block, and its effect can be gained only on foot. As too much traffic now flows through the main shopping streets there would be much to be said for opening the tunnel to southbound traffic (B. Watkin).

p. 433 [Richmond.] ST PHILIP, North Sheen. 1928–9 by *Edward A. Swan*, insignificant outside, but with a genuine C16 timber interior – bodily removed from Woodhall Farm, Oxted.

p. 446 [Salfords, Mullards' Research Laboratories.] There is now a much larger complex of laboratories to the s, by *Norman & Dawbarn* again, 1960–1 and 1965–6. Much crisper elevations, curtain-walled with spandrels of white glass, but still rather soulless. – SCULPTURE. 'Polar Theme' by *Keith Godwin*, 1963.

p. 450 [Send.] Further E is the former RECTORY of 1863–4, *Sir T. G. Jackson*'s first job, designed in 1861 when he was still in Scott's office. An excellent brick Gothic house of the Philip Webb kind, with segment-headed windows. Jackson began his career vigorously like Bodley.

p. 470 [Sunbury, St Mary.] The nave is to be greatly enlarged and given a new chancel; the old one will be retained as a chapel (B. Watkin).

p. 470 [Sunbury, St Mary.] The SGRAFFITO is by *Heywood Sumner*.

p. 486 [Thursley.] WARREN MERE (built as Warren Lodge),

¾ m. NE, was rebuilt by *Lutyens* in 1896–7. Typical entrance front with three tile-hung gables. *Jekyll* garden. C17 hearth re-used inside; dining room already classical. Long guest and service wing added in 1909 by *Lutyens* for Lord Stamfordham.

p. 507 [West Clandon.] Opposite Summers are ONSLOW ESTATE COTTAGES, half-timbered, by *George & Peto*, 1884.

p. 514 [West Humble.] BURFORD BRIDGE HOTEL was greatly extended in 1935 by *Harry Redfern*, using a C17 barn from Abinger Manor, with a good queen-post roof. Murals by *E. M. Dinkel*.

p. 526 [Wimbledon.] No. 15 BERKELEY PLACE, down a drive, was *F. C. Penrose*'s own house, 1860. A grey brick Italianate villa, classically composed but inlaid with polychromatic Italian-medieval ornament. *Penrose* also designed in Ridgway THE FIRS, a remarkable semi-detached pair with a 'common room', built in 1857 for the Christian Socialists J. M. Ludlow and Thomas Hughes (of *Tom Brown's Schooldays*) and alas demolished in 1967.

p. 529 [Wisley, Royal Horticultural Society.] The Society's GARDENS were originally laid out for himself by *G. F. Wilson*, a friend of Gertrude Jekyll, whose influence is everywhere apparent. The new formal garden next to the buildings is by *Geoffrey Jellicoe*, 1970.

p. 530 [Witley, All Saints.] Mrs Barbara Webb †1897, bronze tablet designed by her protégé, *Lutyens*.

p. 531 [Witley, Witley Park.] ORMISTON LODGE is later and chaster, by *E. P. Warren*, c. 1910.

p. 534 [Woking, Hook Heath.] SOUTH HILL was *Horace Field*'s own house, c. 1905, cosily thatched. He designed a number of other houses in the Hook Heath area, including HOOKEREL, tile-hung with a Georgian centrepiece.

p. 535 [Woldingham.] The best of the Edwardian villas is naturally *Leonard Stokes*'s own, LITTLESHAW, on a steep hillside. The polygonal bay window of the dining room and the veranda of the hall are supported on a bold cliff-like terrace wall. Built in 1901–2.

p. 537 [Woodcote Village.] ST MARK, Peaks Hill. 1909–10 by *G. Fellowes Prynne*, a typically opulent example of Edwardian Gothic.